Reform
and
Authority

Reform and Authority in the Medieval and Reformation Church

Editor

Guy Fitch Lytle

Contributors

Uta-Renate Blumenthal
Elizabeth T. Kennan
Thomas E. Morrissey
Hermann Schuessler

Guy Fitch Lytle
Richard J. Schoeck
Nelson H. Minnich
Robert Trisco

The Catholic University of America Press
Washington, D.C.

Library of Congress Cataloging in Publication Data
Main entry under title:

Reform and authority in the medieval and
reformation church.

Includes bibliographical references.
1. Catholic Church—History—Middle Ages,
600-1500—Addresses, essays, lectures.
2. Church history—Middle Ages, 600-1500—
Addresses, essays, lectures. 3. Reformation—
Addresses, essays, lectures. I. Blumenthal,
Uta-Renate, 1935-   II. Lytle, Guy Fitch,
1944-
BX965.R43   282'.09'02   79-17380
ISBN 0-8132-0544-1

To the Memory of

HERMANN SCHÜSSLER
(1929-1975)

in gratitude for
his friendship and inspiration
and in acknowledgment
of a responsibility to
Reformation scholarship
demanded by those feelings

Table of Contents

Introduction
  Guy Fitch Lytle

1. The Beginnings of the Gregorian Reform:
   Some New Manuscript Evidence
     Uta-Renate Blumenthal   1

2. Innocent III, Gregory IX, and Political Crusades:
   A Study in the Disintegration of Papal Power
     Elizabeth T. Kennan   15

3. Franciscus Zabarella (1360-1417):
   Papacy, Community, and Limitations upon Authority
     Thomas E. Morrissey   37

4. Sacred Doctrine and the Authority of Scripture
   in Canonistic Thought on the Eve of the Reformation
     Hermann Schuessler   55

5. Universities as Religious Authorities in the
   Later Middle Ages and Reformation
     Guy Fitch Lytle   69

6. The Fifth Lateran Council:
   Its Partial Successes and its Larger Failures
     Richard J. Schoeck   99

7. *Incipiat Iudicium a Domo Domini:*
   The Fifth Lateran Council and the Reform of Rome
     Nelson H. Minnich   127

8. Reforming the Roman Curia: Emperor Ferdinand I
   and the Council of Trent
     Robert Trisco   143

Introduction

Guy Fitch Lytle

Despite the conflicts and upheavals of the later Middle Ages and the Reformation, there was a strong continuity of concerns and attitudes. Few would deny that the hierarchical society and the corresponding mentality of pre-modern Europe was consistent with a respect for, or at least an acceptance of, authority. Still it would be very wrong to think that authority was never open to challenge. Abuses, injustice, arbitrary repression—each of these occurred, and they were often resisted by those most affected. But authority could also be challenged in less immediate and less personal ways. In part due to a variety of social and political changes which transformed much of Europe between the twelfth and sixteenth centuries, but perhaps in even larger part due to numerous philosophical, theological, legal, and educational changes, the institutional and intellectual foundations of the papacy experienced a particularly severe shock. Rome emerged partly victorious, partly defeated, considerably transformed, yet clinging to claims to eternal truths. The sources, agencies, and limitations of authority became matters for speculation, debate, and at time violent action. New authorities (nation states, vernacular Bibles, human reason) made new or renewed claims to powers of judgment, validation, or protection in matters of faith. New authorities emerged to challenge, reform, or replace traditional modes of ecclesiastical administration and discipline. Reform, as concept and demand, underwent similar vissisitudes. In the seventeenth century these tensions would explode much of the unity and continuity that Europe had earlier known, even throughout the first few decades of that last and most powerful medieval religious reform movement, the Reformation.

All of the studies in this volume share a concern with the complex motives and ambiguous consequences of these two vitally important forces in the history of western Christianity: *reform* and *authority*. The authors focus their attention on popes and emperors, councils and religious intellectuals, ecclesiastical institutions and Holy Scripture, overt actions and theoretical speculations; but they share the insight that reform and authority are almost invariably interrelated. It has been common for writers in all ages, many of

ix

whom have felt instinctive attraction or repulsion toward one or the other of these forces, to emphasize the antipathy between them and to concentrate on their often spectacular confrontations. Indeed historians of reform, heresy, authority, and repression have been far more prone than most to Whiggish or Troyish biases. The duties of political or religious hagiography have led those who knew the Truth to extol martyrdoms, to reiterate condemnations, and to identify both saintly ancestors of their own persuasion and demonic forebears of their enemies. But while recent historiography has, for a number of reasons, corrected old excesses and either muted or eliminated ideological hostilities,[1] the essential dialectic of reform and authority remains to many minds more a basic dichotomy than a variegated relationship which could produce by turns a delicate or stormy tension or a formidable alliance.

Of course, conflicts occurred between advocates of reform and those of authority, but the two must not be viewed as always standing in necessary opposition as the embodiments of the dynamic and conservative aspects of the Christian tradition. Reformers sometimes cajoled or negotiated with the authorities, and, at other times, they felt called upon to rail against some intolerable condition. The establishment often absorbed demands for reform and modified accordingly some feature of the structure or doctrine of the church. On occasion the authorities moved, most frequently with the full support of both the secular power and popular opinion, to silence the troublesome voice of a self-proclaimed reformer or innovator. The forceful and cruel inquisitor to some observers' eyes could be the educator, corrector, or necessary preserver of Truth to others. In its most positive guise, authority maintained continuity and upheld tradition. It proclaimed and elaborated the vitality of the past and embodied history's constant connection with and judgment of the present. In the same spirit, when society agreed that some reform was necessary, its advocates almost always sought its legitimation in a recovery or reinterpretation of the past. In order to understand medieval and early modern mentalities more fully, we must look beyond the dramatic encounters of articulate reformers and repressive authorities, as important as these often were, to see that it was also possible for reformers and the authorities to coexist and even to function as allies.

This suggested revision of much previous historical writing on reform and authority does not imply a rejection of all other interpretations (some of which have provided the starting point for various essays in this collection)[2] nor a defense of either authority *per se* or a descending theory of government during this period.

---

[1] The authors include scholars with Roman Catholic, Anglican, and Luthern commitments, as well as a variety of political, philosophical, and methodological opinions. Perhaps it should be noted that the editor is an Anglican layman.

[2] On *reform,* see the excellent bibliographical notes in Louis B. Pascoe, S.J., "Jean Gerson: the 'ecclesia primitiva' and reform," *Traditio,* 30 (1974), esp. p. 379, note 1;

Much emphasis will be placed on the mistakes and intransigence of some ecclesiastical authorities, on the opposition to authority in the name of freedom of conscience or some similar argument, and on the alternative authorities which were proposed or established in important situations to replace other authorities which some people came to view as erroneous or incompetent. Frequent references will be made to conceptions of a "higher law" or an ultimate authority which could either support or be used as a norm to corect lesser authorities, and which can lead in many cases simply to the replacement of one authority or orthodoxy by another. The authors examine the nature of authority, the institutional bases of authority, and the relationships of individuals to authority both as theory and reality. Finally, several of the studies explore the tension between the dual roles of the Church as an active reforming authority on the one hand and a passive (or obstructionist) authority being reformed on the other.

Neither this book as a whole nor, certainly, the introduction intends to offer a narrative account or a full analysis of all these issues between the eleventh and the sixteenth centuries. Since much research remains to be done before such a history would become possible, the following chapters should be regarded instead as independent statements on major topics as the investiture controversy, the papal "monarchy," conciliarism, the authority respectively of Holy Scriptures and Church traditions, and the relationship between reform and authority in a number of important ecclesiastical settings and institutions. Most of these papers were discussed in the monthly Medieval Studies Faculty Seminar at The Catholic University of America during the mid-1970s, but no synthesis or common approach was attempted. The Folger Shakespeare Library's Institute for Renaissance and Eighteenth Century Studies and conferences of the American Catholic Historical Association provided further opportunities for exchanging, revis-

---

also, G. Ladner, *The Idea of Reform* (Cambridge, Mass., 1959) and G.R. Elton, *Reform and Renewal* (Cambridge, 1973). On *authority*, in addition to the various writings of Walter Ullmann (and his critics) and George Tavard, see Karl F. Morrison, *Tradition and Authority in the Western Church, 300-1140* (Princeton, 1969); R. Bainton, "The Problem of Authority in the Age of the Reformation," in *Luther, Erasmus and the Reformation* (ed. J.Olin, *et al.;* New York, 1969), 14-25; B. Lohse, "Conscience and Authority in Luther," in *Luther and the Dawn of the Modern Era* (ed. H. Oberman; Leiden, 1974), 158-183; and two unduly neglected volumes: John M. Todd (ed.), *Problems of Authority* (Baltimore/London, 1962), the papers of an Anglo-French symposium at the Abbey of Notre-Dame du Bec; and R.R. Williams (ed.), *Authority and the Church* (London, 1965). The historical, philosophical, and social science literature on both topics is far too vast to cite here; but for *authority*, a beginning can be made with L. Krieger, "The Idea of Authority in the West," *A.H.R.,* 82 (1977), 249 - 270; R. Sennett, *Authority* (New York, 1980); and the essays and bibliography in R.B. Harris (ed.), *Authority: a philosophical analysis* (University, Alabama, 1976).

ing, and augmenting our ideas.[3] But each of the papers retains its distinctive voice. They vary widely in length, documentation, and intention. Some have been substantially revised and expanded, while others stand essentially as delivered. As editor, I have not tried to homogenize these differences.

While the essays speak for themselves, it may be worthwhile to suggest some more specific questions and themes that recur from essay to essay. The papacy is the direct or indirect subject of every article: the authors concern themselves with popes as reformers and crusaders, with popes and councils, the infallibility of popes and the papacy's role in the preservation of orthodoxy. In addition to the analyses of papal authority, various questions are posed about relations between Rome and other powerful interests both within the Church itself and among the laity, about papal mistakes in administration and in doctrine, and schism. The authors deal with the inability of popes to control some of their agents or certain institutions when sacred authority had been delegated or usurped, or when local leaders turned papal policies to their own profit. From harsh experience, the papacy learned the importance of keeping the initiative for reform, and thus its control, in its own hands.

If the personal and institutional role of the papacy is the central theme, most of the essays also deal with contributions made to the theory and implementation of reform and authority by religious intellectuals, especially theologians and canon lawyers. In no case were these men merely academic theorists: that role was both an impossible luxury and an undesired isolation in an age filled with profound threats and with a deep need for fundamental redefinitions. Several of the authors are also concerned with the institutions which served as the vehicles, or at time the battlegounds, for the advancement or containment of reform or authority. No historian can allow himself to forget that these theological speculations, legal decisions, and institutional proclamations were not pursued or

[3]All of us who are or were teaching at the Catholic University of America acknowledge the significant impact of our colleagues in the Medieval Seminar in the early and middle 1970s on our thinking and writing. The collegiality of that group, under the superb leadership of Elizabeth Kennan and Fr. John Wippel, would be very hard to duplicate. Much the same can be said of the spirit of the Colloquium of the Renaissance Institute of the Folger Shakespeare Library, under the direction, first, of Richard Schoeck, and now of John Andrews.

As editor, I wish to thank the contributors to this volume for their efforts and forbearance through both the usual delays that plague any collective project and the unusual ones none of us anticipated. I would like to express particular gratitude to David McGonagle of the Catholic University for his support and patience, to Fr. Robert Trisco, also of the Catholic University, for his unstinting help (of the kind only fellow editors can appreciate) and his unfailing friendship through a long project (and, of course, for his *major* contribution to this book); and to J.M. Winter of Pembroke College, Cambridge, for his critical insights and comments concerning this introduction. I would also like to thank my wife, Maria Rasco Lytle, for her considerable help, especially for reading proofs.

rendered in a void; practical consequences gave meaning to the theories and, a times, a painful relevance to some apparently arcane intellectual debates.

Finally, these eight contributions toward a better understanding of some very complex issues constitute just that—contributions, not exhaustive studies. Several of the authors intend to return to their topics on future occasions. Other matters need to be explored and different approaches employed. Perhaps the most regrettable omission from the present volume is some consideration of the changes and continuities in the iconographical representations of authority. Much more empirical and conceptual work remains to be done on the composition, processes, and results of reform movements. More sophisticated psychological analyses of the distinctive and shared personality traits of innovators and conservatives, of reformers and authoritarians (or authoritarian reformers) and their respective followings, is surely called for. These, and countless others, are studies that will or should be written.

The basic value of any collection of essays lies in the quality of the research and insights of the individual authors. But as important as these are, the worth of this volume will be enhanced if we have both forced and helped others to begin to reconsider all of the ramifications of the web of relationships linking reform and authority during the Middle Ages, the Reformation, and beyond.

The Beginnings of the Gregorian Reform:
some new manuscript evidence

by Uta-Renate Blumenthal
The Catholic University
of America

Under Pope Leo IX (1049-1054) the varied movements for reform of the church crystallized into a reform led by the papacy.[1] Rome became the driving force for the liberty of the church and asserted the primacy of the papacy. The renewed consciousness of the sanctity of the ecclesiastical *ordo* and its place in the world would, when carried to its logical conclusion, lead to the well-known claims of Gregory VII and his successors.[2] The origins of this movement for reform are still debated, and there is even disagreement about its characteristics among historians, some of whom prefer to describe the eleventh- and early twelfth-century changes in the relationship between the *regnum* and the *sacerdotium* as a revolution.[3] Nobody, however, would deny the impact of the pontificate of Leo IX.

---

[1]For Leo IX see the bibliographies given by B. Sutter in *Lexikon für Theologie und Kirche* (2nd ed.) 6 (1961) 949-50 and in the *Handbook of Church History*, ed. H. Jedin and J. Dolan (tr. A. Biggs) 3: *The Church in the Age of Feudalism* (New York, 1969) esp. 351-57 and 539. Also important although partly outdated is the bibiliography given by C.J. von Hefele and J. Leclercq *et al.*, *Histoire des conciles* 4/2 (Paris, 1911) 995-7. Recent bibiliography will be cited in the course of the article.

[2]Classical interpretations of the various movements of the Gregorian reform are E. Sackur, *Die Cluniacenzer in ihrer kirchlichen und allgemeingeschichtlichen Wirksamkeit bis zur Mitte des ll. Jahrhunderts*, 2 vols. (Halle, 1892-94); K. Hallinger, *Gorze-Kluny, Studien zu den monastischen Lebensformen und Gegensätzen im Hochmittelalter*, 2 vols. (Studia Anselmiana, fasc. 22-23 and 24-25; Rome 1950 and 1951); A. Fliche, La Réforme grégorienne, 3vols. (Louvain and Paris 1924, 1926 and 1937); G. Tellenbach, *Church, State and Christian Society at the Time of the Investiture Contest*, tr. R.F. Bennett (London, 1959); R.L. Benson, *The Bishop-Elect* (Princeton, 1968), esp. chapter 2; cf. also G. Ladner, *The Idea of Reform: Its Impact on Christian Thought and Action in the Age of the Fathers* (Cambridge, 1959). Most historians agree that the *Dictatus papae* is a significant expression of the reform under Pope Gregory VII. See *Das Register Gregors VII.*, ed. E. Caspar, MGH Epistolae Selectae 2, fasc. 1 and 2 (Berlin 1920-23) 201-08 (II, 55a). CF. the recent article by H. Mordek, 'Proprie auctoritates apostolice sedis. Ein zweiter Dictatus papae Gregors VII?' *Deutsches Archiv*, 28 (1972), 105-32 with earlier literature.

[3]e.g., Tellenbach, *Church, State and Christian Society*, 111.

Not a small part of Leo's fame as reformer rests on his travels to the north of the Alps[4] and the councils held by him in October 1049 at Reims [5] and a little later at Mainz.[6] The first synod, especially, is often treated as the beginning of the Gregorian reform. Leo himself was fully aware of the significance of the Reims legislation, and he decreed that it should be added to the canons of the church: "After the consecration of the church we celebrated a synod there in order to confirm with our decrees what is necessary and of use to the Christian religion with the advice of our co-bishops as well as the assent and the approval of the clergy and the people who had come in large numbers with great devotion to the celebration; we commanded that all of these things which were formulated as decrees should be added to the canons. We afterwards took care to confirm them in all of the synods which we held."[7]

This paper presents some new evidence for one of Leo's councils which came to light among addenda in an eleventh-century codex of the Biblioteca Apostolica Vaticana, MS Reginensis lat. 711/II.[8] The new text illuminates aspects of Leonine legislation which were hitherto at best dimly perceived and which explain perhaps in part the wide appeal of the great pontiff. It is likely that the text can be attributed to the synod of Reims,[9] but the manuscript attribution is—as so often in the case of conciliar canons—not very precise. The analysis of the most prominent features of the new text is, therefore, here preceded by a brief discussion of the provenance of the codex, of the inscription accompanying the canons, and a comparison of

---

[4]A. Hauck, *Kirchengeschichte Deutschlands,* 3 (Leipzig, 1896), 601-607.

[5]See J.D. Mansi, *Sacrorum conciliorum nova et amplissima collectio* 19 (Venice, 1774), (cited 'Mansi' below) 727-750. The text found in Mansi depends indirectly on the edition of the text by C. Baronius, *Annales ecclesiasticae* 11 (Rome, 1605) 166-67 and 806-818; a recent account of the synod is the summary of S. Giet, 'Le concile de Reims de 1049,' *Mémoires de la Société d'agriculture, commerce, sciences et arts du département de la Marne,* 85 (1960) 31-36; see also O. Capitani, *Immunità vescovili ed ecclesiologia in età 'pregregoriana' e 'gregoriana,' L'avvio alla 'restaurazione,'* Biblioteca degli '*Studi Medievali*' 3 (Spoleto, 1966), chapter 6.

[6]Very little is known about the synod of Mainz; see Mansi 19.749; Hauck, *Kirchengeschichte* 3, 601, esp. n.2 and Fliche, *Réforme* 1, 155-146; *MGH Const.* 1 (1893), no. 51, 97-100.

[7]JL 4185: Post consecrationem ecclesiae in eadem synodum celebrantes, ad utilitatem Christianae religionis necessaria, consilio coepiscoporum nostrorum, assensu etiam et laude cleri, et populi quorum innumera multitudo ad tantae devotionis celebritatem confluxerat, statuendo confirmavimus, quae omni capitulis digesta inter canones haberi precipimus et postea in omnibus synodis quas habuimus, idipsum confirmare curavimus.

[8]The codex was described together with MS Reg. lat. 711/I by Montfaucon under MS no. 173. See *Les manuscrits de la Reine de Suède au Vatican, Réédition du Catalogue de Montfaucon et côtes actuelles,* Studi e Testi 238 (Vatican City, 1964) 14.

[9]U.-R. Blumenthal, 'Ein neuer Text Für das Reimser Konzil Leo IX. (1049)?' *Deutsches Archiv,* 32 (1976), 23-48.

the discovered decrees with familiar material from other synods of Pope Leo IX.

The Vatican manuscript Reginensis lat. 711/II consists of fragments of what were originally eight different codices of mostly French provenance.[10] Of interest here are folios 63-66 from the Benedictine abbey of Saint-Magloire in Paris. The abbey was founded between 963 and 970 by Hugh Capet,[11] but its rise to eminence as well as disappearance in the early seventeenth century are both scantily documented.[12] Nothing is known about the fate of the abbey's library.[13] Apart from some cartularies[14] only two of its manuscripts are known to have survived; both are now at least partially at the Bibliothèque Nationale.[15] One of them, the famous Nithard codex, BN lat. 9768, was once in the possession of Paul Petau.[16] Queen Christina of Sweden acquired it[17] when she obtained the collections of Paul Petau (1568-1614) and of his son Alexander (1610-1647).[18] From the Swedish queen it passed into the Fondo Reginensis of the Vatican.[19] The reference to the Nithard codex is pertinent here because MS Reg. lat. 711/II has very probably shared its fate. The manuscript shows notes in the hand of Paul Petau on fols. 1r and 61r. Unfortunately, it is not known how he ob-

---

[10]The Institut de Recherche et d'Histoire de Texte, Paris, has assembled detailed information on the codex. The author would like to thank the Institut for their kind assistance and permission to use their material.

[11]R. Merlet, 'Les origines du monastère de Saint-Magloire.' BECH, 56 (1895), 237-73; H. Cottineau, Répertoire topo-bibliographique des abbayes et prieurés 2 (Macon, 1939), col.2214.

[12]Charters and documents of Saint-Magloire for the years 1280-1330 are edited by A. Terroine and L. Fossier. Chartes et documents de l'Abbaye de Saint-Magloire, vol. 2: 1280-1330, (Paris, 1966). The editors did not discuss their plans with regard to the first volumes.

[13]Franklin, Les Anciennes Bibliothèques de Paris, Histoire Générale de Paris, 3 vols. 2 (Paris, 1870) 365-68, discussed only the library of the Seminary of Saint-Magloire. The Seminary took the place of the abbey in 1618.

[14]H. Stein, Bibliographie générale des cartulaires français ou relatifs à l'histoire de France (Paris, 1907) 395-96, nos. 2883-2886. The great cartulary (Paris, BN lat. 5413) once belonged to Paul Petau. It was compiled between 1331 and 1440, containing documents from the tenth century to the latter date.

[15]See L. Delisle, Cabinet des Manuscrits 2 (Paris, 1874) 258 n.1 and 407. The manuscripts are Paris, BN lat. 13701 and Paris, BN lat. 9768.

[16]This is indicated by Petau's note on fol. 1r. For another Saint-Magloire codex that was obtained by Petau see n.14 above.

[17]Nithard was bound together with what is now MS Reg. lat. 1964. Se A.A. de Meyier, Paul en Alexandre Petau en de geschiedenis van hun Handschriften. Dissertationes inaugurales Batavae ad res antiquas pertinentes, 5 (1947), 5-6 and n.21.

[18]See J. Bignami Odier, Le Fonds de la Reine à la Bibliothèque Vaticane. Collectanea Vaticana in honorem Anselmi M. Card. Albareda, Studi e Test, 219 (Vatican City, 1962), 163. Vossius bought the collections for the queen in 1650 for 40,000 1. from the Petau heirs.

[19]For the history of the collection see Bignami Odier, Le Fonds de la Reine, 159ff.

tained the volume, but its provenance from Saint-Magloire is certain. An ex-libris on fol 63r and especially the texts which are found there lend proof. Several of the latter refer directly to Saint-Magloire. They were published by L. Auvray.[20] Not directly pertaining to the affairs of the Benedictine abbey are two columns found on fol.65v. which Auvray did not publish or identify.[21] The text, written in a late eleventh- or early twelfth-century hand, is introduced by: *Hec est sanctorum patrum auctoritas a Leone papa corroborata.* It seems certain that the 'Pope Leo' to whom the inscription in MS Reg. lat. 711/II refers is indeed Leo IX.[22] *Auctoritas*[23] *sanctorum patrum* is a solemn term which is here equivalent to *sententiae patrum*, or in other words refers to the canons and writings of the Church Fathers which were transmitted through canonical collections. [24] On several occasions Pope Leo IX stressed the renewal of the *decreta patrum* at his own synods,[25] and as seen earlier the pontiff expressly commanded that the decrees from the synod of Reims were to be added to the corpus of canon law. The inscription of fol.65v of MS Reg. lat. 711/II, therefore, can readily be interpreted as introducing conciliar canons promulgated by Pope Leo IX.

Unfortunately, it is rather more difficult to establish where the decrees were promulgated. Official synodal protocols usually preserved the name of the location, the date, and at least a general reference to the participants. But none of this information is found in the Reginensis codex which seems to preserve unofficial notes taken by a participant at one of Leo's synods, for the phrasing of the

---

[20]L. Auvray, *Documents Parisiens tirés de la Bibliothèque du Vatican (VIIe-XIIIe sièle)*, Extrait des Mémoires de la Société de l'Histoire de Paris et de l'Ile-de-France, 19 (1892), 17-35; the codex is described *ibid.*17, n.1. It should be noted that Auvray erroneously speaks of MS 711 A instead of MS 711/II.

[21]*Ibid.*,33.

[22]See Blumenthal, 'Ein neuer Text,' 37-38.

[23]For the use of *auctoritas* meaning conciliar canon, see *Mittellateinisches Wörterbuch* 1, 1181.

[24]As an introduction to pre-Gratian collections see P. Fournier and G. Le Bras *Histoire des Collections Canoniques en Occident.* 2 vols. (Paris, 19031-32). A good example for the use of the expression *sententiae patrum* is the *Collection in Seventy-Four Titles* which was known to contemporaries mainly under the title *Diversorum patrum sententie.* The collection was recently edited by J.T. Gilchrist, Monumenta Iuris Canonici, Series B: Corpus Collectionum 1 (Vatican City, 1973).

[25]See, for example, the *Vita Leonis* (ed. W. Watterich, *Pontificum romanorum*...vitae 1, Leipzig, 1862), 154, for the council of Rome (1049): 'Quantam autem solertiam in catholica lege conservanda adhibuerit in primo Romano concilio...demonstravit, ubi statuta quatuor synodorum principalium viva voce corroboravit, decretaque omnium antecessorum suorum pontificum tenenda confirmavit.' The *Historia dedicationis ecclesiae S. Remigii apud Remos*, ed. J. Mabillon, Acta Sanctorum O.S.B. 6,1 (1701) 711-727, refers on several occasions to Leo's emphasis on the *decreta patrum* at the council of Reims in 1049, e.g.: ...quod in canonibus de sacrorum ordinum venditoribus sit decretum, iussit tantum modo recitari...(p.723); lectae sunt sententiae super huiuscemodi re promulgatae ab orthodoxis patribus...(*ibid.*).

text is rather awkward and occasionally French vernacular terms are found among the Latin.[26] The only means, therefore, to identify the council of Pope Leo IX to which the Reginensis text refers is a careful textual comparison of the Reginensis notes with other sources documenting the legislation of his synods. Leo IX celebrated at least twelve synods, but about a majority of them little more is known than that they were held.[27] There is some evidence that the councils of Mainz (1049) and Rome (1050) issued decrees against simony and/or nicholaitism, but the material is too scanty for textual comparisons.[28] Such a comparison is only possible for two of Leo's synods: the council held in Rome in the spring of 1049 before the pontiff's departure to France and Germany, and the council of Reims of October 1049. Especially helpful for the Roman 1049 synod are the *Vita Leonis*[29], the writings of Peter Damian,[30] and of Bonizo of Sutri.[31] Still better documented is

---

[26]See Blumenthal, 'Ein neuer Text,' 29-36.

[27]Mansi's *Sacrorum conciliorum amplissima collectio* has to be used with great caution, but offers nonetheless still the most accessible collection of conciliar materials for the synods of Pope Leo IX. For the Roman synod of April 1049 see Mansi 19,721-26; for Pavia (June 1049), *ibid.* 725-26; for Reims, *ibid.* 727-50; for Mainz (October 1049), *ibid.* 749-50; for Rome (April 1050), *ibid.* 759-72; for Vercelli (1050), *ibid.* 773-782; for Rome (spring 1051), *ibid.* 795-98; for Mantua (spring 1052 or 1053), *ibid.* 799-800; for Rome (spring 1053), *ibid.* 809-812. To these synods three have to be added which probably took place during 1050 in southern Italy (cf. Jaffé, *Regesta* before JL 4212).

[28]For the synod of Mainz see particularly JL 4188 *(MGH Const.* 1, p.97 n.51) and Adam of Bremen, *Gesta Hammaburgensis Ecclesiae Pontificum* 3, 30 (ed. B. Schmeidler, MGH, SS Germ. 2, 3rd, ed. 1917, p.172): 'Praeterea multa ibidem sanctita sunt ad utilitatem ecclesiae, pre quibus symoniaca heresis et nefanda sacerdotum coniugia olographa synodi manu perpetuo dampnata sunt. For Rome (1050) cf. Bonizo, *Liber ad amicum*, MGH Libelli de lite 1, p. 589: 'Sequenti vero anno prefatus pontifex sinodum congregavit, in qua omnibus tam clericis quam laicis auctoritate sancti Petri et romane ecclesiae preceptum est, ut abstinerent se a fornicatorum sacerdotum et levitarum communione.'

[29]*Vita Leonis*, p.154-55. The *Vita Leonis* (see above n.25) was written shortly after the death of Pope Leo IX (1054), possibly by a cleric from Toul, but the question of authorship is still debated; cf. H. Tritz, 'Die hagiographischen Quellen' zur Geschichte Papst Leos IX.,' *Studi Gregoriani* 4 (1952) 191-353; H. Hoffmann, 'Von Cluny zum Investiturstreit,' *Archiv für Kulturgeschichte*, 45 (1963), Exkurs pp. 203-209; H. Hoesch, *Die kanonischen Quellen im Werk von Humbert von Moyenmoutier*, Forschungen zur kirchlichen Rechtsgeschichte und zum Kirchenrecht, 10 (1970).

[30]Opusc. 18: Contra clericorum intemperantiam (PL 145, 411 B): 'In plenaria plane synodo sanctae memoriae Leo papa constituit, ut quaecunque damnabiles feminae intra Romana moenia reperirentur presbyteris prostitutae, extunc et deinceps Lateranensis palatio adjudicarentur ancillae.' See J.J. Ryan, *Saint Peter Damiani and His Canonical Sources,* Studies and Texts 2 (Toronto, 1956) no.197.

[31]*Liber ad amicum*, p.588: '...synodum mox congregavit...in qua etiam sub anathemate interdictum est non licere alicui episcopo archidiaconatus et preposituras vel abbacias seu beneficia aecclesiarum vel prebendas vel ecclesiarum vel altarium commendationes vendere, et ut sacerdotes et levitae et subdiaconi cum uxoribus non coeant...' See also W. Berschin, *Bonizo von Sutri: Leben und Werk* Beiträge zur Geschichte und Quellenkunde des Mittelalters, 2 (Berlin/New York, 1972) p.43 n.221.

the assembly at Reims. Leo IX, the former Bishop Bruno of Toul, had been invited to come to Reims by Abbot Hérimar of Saint-Rémi to dedicate the abbey's new basilica.[32] The pontiff used the occasion to hold a synod. Despite some obstruction on the part of King Henry I of France (1031-1060), who at first had promised to be present but then decided to go on a campaign instead in the company of lay nobles and a good part of the clergy,[33] the council became a great success.[34] Lest the events be forgotten, Abbot Hérimar eventually asked one of his monks to write the *Historia dedicationis S. Remigii*.[35] The author of the Historia is usually identified as one Anselm on the basis of a passage in Sigebert of Gembloux's *Liber de scriptoribus ecclesiasticis*,[36] but the identification is very tenuous. Sigebert might have referred to an account entitled *Itinerarium* as Baronious suspected.[37] The *Itinerarium*, however—if it existed at one time—has to be considered lost, and the *Historia dedicationis* was hitherto the most explicit source for the canons of the Reims synod.

---

[32]*Historia dedicationis ecclesiae S. Remigii apud Remos* (see n.25 above), cap.5, p.714.

[33]*Ibid.*, cap. 9, p.716. The *Historia* contains no evidence that Henry I and his advisors considered Leo as an ally of Emperor Henry III and that his visit was rejected for this reason. Cf. J.F. Lemarignier, *Le gouvernement royal aux premiers temps capétiens. 987-1108* (Paris, 1965)99; J. Dhondt, 'Quelques aspects du règne d'Henri Ier roi de France.' *Mélanges d'histoire du Moyen Age Louis Halphen* (Paris, 1951) 199-208, esp. 206-207 and Capitani, *Immunità*, 149-50.

[34]The *Historia dedicationis* although certainly not written by an impartial observer is convincing; see esp. cap. 11, p.717. See also Leo's letter JL 4185 quoted above, n.7.

[35]C. Baronius, *Annales Ecclesiastici*, 11 (Rome, 1605), 806-818, was the first to edit extensive excerpts from the *Historia dedicationis*. For subsequent editions see *Repertorium Fontium Historiae Medii Aevi* under *Anselmus monachus S. Remigii Remensis*. The only complete edition, cited in this article, is that by J. Mabillon (see above n.25).

[36]On Sigebert in general see Wattenbach/Holtzmann, *Deutschlands Geschichtsquellen im Mittelalter*, 1/4 (1948), 727-737; *Liber Sigeberti Gemblacensis monachi de Scriptoribus ecclesiasticis*, ed. J.A. Fabricius in: *Bibliotheca Ecclesiastica* (Hamburg, 1718), 93-116, cap. 152, p. 111: Anselmus Remensis monachus scripsit Itinerarium noni Leonis Papae a Roma in Gallias; ob hoc maxime ut notificaret quanta auctoritate Remis, vel in aliis urbibus Synodum celebrarit; quanta subtilitate et justitia examinarit causas ecclesiasticas; qua discretione peccantes correxerit; quomodo ei virtus Dei cooperata sit. Quod satis patuit in una causa Remensis Synodi ubi dum Episcopus Frisingensis contumaciter ageret contra Apostolicam auctoritatem, repente in oculis omnium obmutuit.' It should be noted that the bishop of Freising at that time, Nitger (1039-1052), is not known to have come to Reims and that the *Historia* does not refer to him. It also has to be pointed out that Sigebert's note does not mention the dedication of the church, the main subject of the *Historia*.

[37]See *Annales ecclesiastici una cum critica...*, ed. A. Pagi, 17 (Lucca, 1745) under the date 1049. Pagi's note was included by Mansi 19, 727-730n.

The *Historia* emphasizes the dedication of the basilica of Saint Rémi. This is well indicated not only by the title, but also by the prologue.[38] The description of the synod is almost an afterthought. But despite this emphasis, the monk of Saint-Rémi who began to write at the earliest in late 1055,[39] preserved much valuable and some very detailed[40] information about the synod. Among the items reported is a short summary of twelve or thirteen[41] canons which the council promulgated. The narrative also contains additional references to the legislation.[42] Some historians, in particular Augustin Fliche, have warned that the canons transmitted in the *Historia dedicationis* should not be overvalued, pointing out that the *Historia* was written several years after the synod assembled.[43] Another French scholar, S. Giet, remarked recently once again that the decrees of the *Historia* constitute at best fragments from a fuller account.[44] This much is readily apparent to an attentive reader, but it is more difficult to accept the reasoning of O. Capitani who describes the *cosidetti canones,* as he calls them, as a creation of the monk of Saint-Rémi modelled on the *sanctorum patrum decreta*[45] and the agenda of the council which had been read by the Roman deacon Peter during the first meeting.[46] The similarity between the promulgated decrees and the agenda, however, is only what is to be

---

[38]*Historia dedicationis,* 713:'...quapropter ex imperio domini abbatis Herimari seriem Dedicationis huius sanctissimi Patris ecclesiae silentio non patiar oblitterari. Sed quoniam a beatae recordationis Papa nono Leone, Deo auctore, facta est, eo magis dignam litteris tradam pro modulo ingenioli mei. Unde in primis paucis praelibabo, quorum industria constructa fuerit anterior ecclesia, et ex cuius causa iam prae vetustate ruinam minitantis, haec quae nunc, Deo propitiante, subsistit, sumsitque exordia. Additur etiam, ut quia ex huius dedicationis occasione a ministris diaboli multa excitata sunt scandala, et postea ex Synodo ab eodem Papa ibidem celebrata multa provenerunt utilia.' The author began with the dedication of the ancient church by Archbishop Hincmar (845-882) in 852 and outlined the construction of the new basilica, begun under Abbot Airard in 1005, until its completion under Hérimar. Cf. especially L. Demaison, 'L'Eglise de Saint Rémi, Histoire abrégée de sa construction.' *Travaux de l'Académie Nationale de Reims,* 111 (1901-1902), 273-285.

[39]Fliche, *Réforme grégorienne,* 1, 140.

[40]e.g., the careful description of the seating arrangements at the synod which Leo had introduced in order to avoid a flaring up of the quarrel between the archbishops of Reims and Trier about the primacy of Belgica Secunda. See the diagram given by Hefele-Leclerq. *Histoire* 6/2, 1018.

[41]G. Marlot, *Metropolis Remensis Historia a Frodoardo primum arctius digesta,* 2 (Reims, 1679) 101-102, divided the canon usually numbered 2 (ed. Mabillon p. 724 and Baronius, *Annales,* 11, p. 816) into two parts.

[42]They follow immediately upon the canons, but are part of the general narrative. *Historia,* 724.

[43]Fliche, *Réforme grégorienne,* 1,140.

[44]Giet, 'Le concile de Reims,' 36, n.23.

[45]The context of this phrase in the *Historia* shows that it was the pontiff himself who chose the sentences of the Fathers as his model. (*Historia,* 724.)

[46]Capitani, Immunità, 164-166.

expected. It was customary to propose synodal legislation in the form of a draft or by an official speaker.[47] In the case of the council of Reims, this speaker was the deacon Peter.[48] It ought to be kept in mind that the *Historia* canons are summarized excerpts from the Reims legislation, but there is no need to doubt their authenticity with regard to content.

As the preceding discussion has shown there are two councils with sufficient information on respective legislation to permit a comparison with the text found in MS Reginensis lat. 711/II, the synods of 1049 held in Rome and at Reims. According to the *Vita Leonis*[49] the discussions in Rome did not differ greatly from those held north of the Alps. Simony, the sale of altars, and consanguinical marriage were condemned in Rome as they were in the autumn at Reims.[50] Another important subject in Rome was the regulation of tithes which "had fallen into oblivion in Apulia but which all Christians owed to their church."[51] At this point the first difference between the Roman and the Reims legislation can be noticed, for if the wording of the *Vita Leonis* faithfully reflects the original content of the canon, then Leo legislated in Rome not only against the lay possession of tithes as was the case at Reims,[52] but also regarding the division of the tithes between bishops and parish priests.

The Roman legislation must have covered several other issues. The *Vita Leonis* states that many other canons were 'renewed' but does not mention them. One of these 'other' canons dealt according to Bonizo of Sutri with the prohibition of clerical marriage.[53] Since simony and nicholaitism formed an important part of Leo's program,[54] it has been vehemently argued that Leo prohibited clerical

---

[47]See R. Somerville, *The Councils of Urban II*, 1: *Decreta Claromontensia*, Annuarium Historiae Concilorum, Supplementum Nr.1 (Amsterdam, 1972), chapter 2, esp. 20-25.

[48]*Historia dedicationis,* 721.

[49]*Vita Leonis,* 154-155.

[50]For Rome see *ibid.,* For Reims *Historia dedicationis,* p. 724, c.3 and c.11.

[51]*Vita Leonis,* 155. On the division of tithes in the eleventh century see H. E. Feine, *Kirchliche Rechtsgeschichte: Die katholische Kirche,* 4th ed. (Berlin/Graz, 1964), 195. The division of tithes into three parts was customary in Spain and southern Gaul (U. Stutz, *Geschichte des kirchlichen Benefizialwesens* 1,1 Berlin 1895, 241.) On Leo IX and the lay possession of tithes cf. in general G. Constable, *Monastic Tithes* (Cambridge, 1964) esp. 85.

[52]*Historia dedicationis* c.3: Ne quis laicorum ecclesiasticum ministerium vel altaria teneret nec episcoporum quilibet consentirent. MS Reg. lat. 711/II c.4: Laici altaria et queque ad altaria pertinent dimittant: hoc est, tertiam partem annonae, oblationes, sepulturam, atrium et censum, nec ullam consuetudinem in atrio accipiant propter hoc quod diffinitum est.

[53]See above, n.31.

[54]J. Haller, *Das Papsttum: Idee und Wirklichkeit* 2, 2nd ed. (Esslingen, 1962)291; J. Drehmann, *Papst Leo IX. und die Simonie: ein Beitrag zur Untersuchung der Vorgeschichte des Investiturstreites,* Beiträge zur Kulturgeschichte des Mittelalters und der Renaissance 2 (Leipzig/Berlin, 1908) esp. 1-21; N.-N. Huyghebaert,

marriage not only at the Italian councils but also at Reims as three twelfth-century sources[55] and (in this interpretation) c.8 of the *Historia dedicationis (Ne quis monachus vel clericus a suo gradu apostataret)*[56] and the fifth item on the agenda of the Deacon (*de monachis et clericis a sancto proposito recedentibus)*[57] have sometimes been thought to indicate. Opponents of this theory, in particular W. Bröcking, have pointed out that it is very arbitrary indeed to assume that *a suo gradu apostataret* and a *sancto proposito recedentibus* in the two versions of c.8 refer to nicholaitism.[58] Bröcking's position receives confirmation from the Saint-Magloire text: *Ut clerici ad clericatum et monachi ad monachicam vitam redeant.* Pope Leo IX was usually very outspoken in his condemnation of clerical marriage as we know through Peter Damian.[59] Since not a trace of such controversial legislation has been reported from Reims, it must be assumed that he did not include it among his French canons. Nicholaitism, therefore, appears to be a second criterion that can be used to distinguish the legislation of Rome from that of Reims. Since both with regard to the regulation of tithes and to nicholaitism MS Reg. lat.711/II appears in line with the text of the *Historia dedicationis* rather than the sources for the Roman council of 1049, it seems permissible to attribute the Reginensis canons to the council of Reims, at least until further evidence comes to light.

The similarities between the *Historia dedicationis* decrees and the notes in MS Reg. lat. 711/II are striking, but there are also considerable differences. All canons of the *Historia* as well as the agenda read by the Deacon Peter are reflected in the Vatican codex, but the new text also contains numerous additional decrees. The chief

---

'Saint Léon IX et la lutte contre la simonie dans le diocèse de Verdun,' *Studi Gregoriani 1 (1947) 417-432*, esp. *426; A. Michel, 'Die folgenschweren Ideen des Kardinals Humbert und ihr Einfluss auf Gregor VII.,' ibid.,* 79ff; G. Miccoli, 'Il problema delle ordinazioni simoniache e le sinodi Lateranensi del 1060 e 1061; *ibid.,* 5 (1956), 47 n.27.

[55]See P.-P. Brucker, *L'Alsace et l'Eglise au temps du pape Saint Léon IX* (Strasbourg, 1889),2, p. 20ff. He relied on the Vita of Hugh of Cluny by Hildebert of Lavardin (see PL 159, 857ff, esp. 866, and cf. Wattenbach/Holtzmann, 1/4, 794-98) and the dependent vita of Hugh by Rainald (see PL 159, 893ff. esp. 903 and cf. Wattenbach/Holtzmann, 1/4,795) as well as the *Ecclesiastical History of Orderic Vitalis* (book 5, ch. 12) ed. M. Chibnall, 3 (Oxford 1972), 120: presbiteris arma ferre et coniuges habere omnino prohibuit. The sources are unreliable and imprecise. This author has drawn the same conclusions as C.N.L. Brooke, 'Gregorian reform in action,' *Cambridge Historical Journal,* 12 (1956), 2 n.3.

[56]*Historia dedicationis,* 724.

[57]*Ibid.,* 721.

[58]W. Bröcking, *Die französische Politik Papst Leos IX.* (Stuttgart 1891) 21 and esp. idem, *Deutsche Zeitschrift für Geschichtswissenschaft,* 9 (1893), 290-95, esp. 290-291.

[59]See above n.30.

distinction between the *Historia* and the Reginensis canons arises from a series of regulations concerning the behavior of the laity where Leo IX takes into his own hand some of the *negotia saecularia* in order to assure stability, peace and well-being for the ordinary Christian. Certain decrees immediately recall the precedents of the Pax and Treuga Dei legislation of the tenth and eleventh century in France and northern Spain. H. Hoffmann concluded on the basis of the Anselm material alone that Leo was indeed the first pontiff who actively supported these institutions, although in a far from revolutionary form.[60] The Saint-Magloire decrees confirm this argument. Conceivably, Leo intended to fill at Reims the void that existed in France because of King Henry I's inactivity with regard to the Treuga movement,[61] perhaps by substituting universally binding legislation[62] for arrangements that were geographically limited in their application. This concept would lend boldness to the pontiff's decrees even although some of them at least were certainly conservative, as for example the canons for the protection of *pauperes* (including merchants) and clergy: *Clericum nec monachum nec monacham nec laicam feminam seu eos qui cum eis erunt non accipiant*[63] *nec ea que sua sunt tollant*[64] and *Mercatores et peregrinos non assalliant nec suum habere eis tollant.*[65] Leo's prohibition of the blood feud (*Pax de homicidiis patrum, filiorum, nepotum vel consanguineorum omnino fiat),* however, is not ordinarily found among the decrees of the Pax,[66] but an interesting precedent does exist.

Around 1035, the blood feud was to be outlawed in a Pax proposed among the northern French episcopate. The bishops required that *arma quisquam non ferret; direpta non repeteret; sui sanguinis vel cuiuslibet proximi ultor minime existens percussoribus cogeretur indulgere.* Also demanded were strict fasts and an oath to be sworn by all who did not wish to be excluded from the community of Christians.[67] Bishop Gerhard I of Cambrai (1013-1048) was urged to join the movement, but refused at first, ostensibly because the demands of the proposed formula would not only upset the right

---

[60]H. Hoffmann, *Gottesfriede und Treuga Dei,* MGH Schriften 20 (Stuttgart 1964), 217-18.

[61]*Ibid.,* 66-67 and G. Duby, 'Les Laîcs et la paix de Dieu,' *Hommes et structures du moyen âge* (Paris, 1973), 227-240, 229, and 231.

[62]The partially conservative character of Leo's legislation may also derive from a conscious attempt to promulgate only canons that would be equally welcome in the different parts of Latin Christendom, particularly both in France and Germany.

[63]For *accipere* see Niermeyer, *Mediae Latinitatis Lexicon minus: prendre, saisir, s'emparer de qqch.*

[64]The canon reads as follows in the *Historia dedicationis:* Ne quis pauperes homines rapinis vel captionibus vexaret. (c.10).

[65]*Historia dedicationis* c.9: Ne quis cum aliquibus sacri ordinis iter agentibus violentiam ullam inferre audeat.

[66]Cf. Hoffmann, *Gottesfriede,* 21 and n.45, as well as *ibid.,* 62-63.

[67]*Gesta Pontificum Cameracensium,* ed. L. Bethmann, *MGH,* SS 7, (1846)485-86.

order of the world, divided into three classes of *oratores, pugnatores* and *agricultores,* but also lead to perjury.[68] H. Hoffmann interpreted this proposed Pax as possibly similar to the amnesties later proclaimed by Emperor Henry III in 1043, 1044, and 1047.[69] The argument of mutual influence carries even greater weight with regard to the canon of Leo IX who frequently cooperated with the Emperor. It should be noted, however, that Leo's demands are much more modest than those of the French bishops. The pontiff prohibited only clergy from carrying arms (*Clerici arma non ferant)*[70] and legislated only against feud among relatives.

A particularly good example of the connection between Leo's Reims decrees and the Pax legislation is c.14 of the Vatican codex: *Terras sanctuarii laicus invadere non praesumat nec novas consuetudines adcrescat.* The protection of ecclesiastical property that is stipulated here was one of the main springs of the movement, and *mala consuetudines* had been condemned together with the physical invasion of ecclesiastical lands as early as 936 by the association for the defense of the church of Brioude.[71] C.12 in MS Reg. lat. 711/II extends a similar protection if not to lay lands then at least to lay possessions: *Praedam penitus non faciant; qui vero fecerint et non resipuerint a communione totius christianitatis in vita et morte alieni fiant.* The canon echoes a decision of the Pax council of Le Puy, held in 994: *Praedam in istis comitatibus neque in istis episcopatibus homo non faciat.*[72] Examples could be multiplied, but one more reference to a particularly interesting canon may suffice here to prove Leo's reliance on French Pax legislation. In c.16 of the Reginensis text the pontiff demanded judicial settlement of disagreements before bishop or archbishop:

Si aliqua querimonia inter homines exhorta (sic) fuerit ante episcopum veniant et capitale si fuerit aut fundum terre reddant. Sin autem ante archiepiscopum. Quod si noluerint totidem sicut alii ab omni christianitate priventur, et episcopi litteras suas pape mittant.

According to Hoffmann, adjudication had frequently been imposed in connection with the Pax during the first third of the eleventh century, but tended to disappear when the Treuga gradually replaced the Pax.[73] Interestingly enough the one exception mentioned by

---

[68]The incident was discussed in detail by Hoffman, *Gottesfriede,* 57-64.

[69]*Ibid.,* 63 and n.59. G. Ladner, *Theologie und Politik vor dem Investiturstreit* (Darmstadt, 1968) 70-74, also discusses the peace politics of Henry III and contrasts them to some extent with the Pax and Treuga Dei.

[70]*Historia dedicationis,* c.6: Ne quis clericorum arma gestaret aut mundanae militiae deserviret.

[71]On the association see Hoffman, *Gottesfriede,* 15-16.

[72]Mansi 19,272.

[73]Hoffmann, *Gottesfriede,* 70. For examples of adjudication decrees in older peace statutes see the index under *Besitzstreitigkeiten,* and esp.*ibid.* 31-2.

H. Hoffmann dates from 1054, that is five years after the synod of Reims.[74] The *capitula de treuga et de pace* concluded in 1054 at Narbonne also urged arbitration of quarrels, but with one considerable difference: judges are to be both bishop and prince.[75] Leo in contrast left no doubt that the *querimonie* may only be judged by bishop or archbishop. Moreover, the text of the canon does not clearly identify the litigation: *si aliqua querimonia* could possibly apply to any kind of suit betwen two men (presumably in connection with the Pax), not necessarily qualified by *et capitale si fuerit aut fundum terre reddant*. The use of *aliqua* is a little disturbing. Royal justice in France was at its nadir in the mid-eleventh century;[76] secular lords,too independent and powerful to be subject to a chatellany,[77] could not be brought to justice by anyone.[78] It is possibly this class of noble litigant the canon had in mind, suggesting as it does that a bishop might not be competent enough to act as judge in a law suit that might arise. In this light it is also understandable that the pontiff was to be informed of an excommunication if it should become necessary. This speculative interpretation of the decree, however, faces the serious objection that in this case the canon intentionally challenged secular jurisdiction. This seems unlikely. Since the Reginensis text in the fragment from Saint-Magloire consists of unofficial notes it seems more reasonable to interpret the canon as referring to loan and mortgage litigation alone as was the case in the Narbonne legislation referred to earlier.[80]

MS Reg. lat. 711/II itself provides some evidence for this interpretation of Leo's intentions. The two canons following upon the decree dealing with litigation deal with usury whose early history was examined by Franz Schaub.[81] Schaub, familiar with the *Historia dedicationis,* pointed out that Leo began at Reims a series of legislative decrees that was to culminate with the canons of Pope

[74]*Ibid., 94-98.*
[75]Mansi 19,830-31.
[76]Lemarignier, *Gouvernement,* 163-64.
[77]G. Duby, 'Recherches sur l'évolution des institutions judiciaires pendant le Xe et le XIe siècle dans le Sud de la Bourgogne,' *Hommes et Structures,* 7-60, 30
[78]*Ibid.,* 31: A la fin du XIE siècle, il n'existe plus d'institution judiciaire qui soit capable de maintenir la paix à l'intérieur de la classe chévaleresque.' It should be noted that Duby's study is based on southern Burgundy. He himself points to Flanders as an exception (*ibid.* 44) and Normandy can be added.
[79]Blumenthal, 'Ein neuer Text.' 29-36.
[80]Mansi 19,830-831, c.18: Statuimus autem, inter vos de contentionibus terrarum, et de debitoribus et fidejussoribus, Dei authoritate, et nostra ut nemo ex eis vindictam sumat donec ante proprii sui episcopi, et potestatis cuius ditionis fuerit, praesentiam veniens, causam suam exponat, ut alicuius eorum judicio terminetur, atque definiatur. Episcopus autem et princeps regionis ipsius, quibus eadem res pertinuerit ad distringendum, noceat resistenti, et adjuvet obedientem.
[81]F. Schaub, *Der Kampf gegen den Zinswucher, ungerechten Preis und unlauteren Handel im Mittelalter* (Freiburg, 1905,), esp. 27-28 with n.4. Schaub's findings were accepted by J.T. Noonan, Jr., *The Scholastic Analysis of Usury* (Cambridge, 1957).

Alexander III.[82] He was unaware of the Reginensis canon[83] and was thus led to believe that Leo rested content with a simple prohibition. In the light of the new text the differences between the usury legislation of Leo IX and Alexander III appear much less significant than they were thought to be earlier.

The new evidence uncovered in the Reginensis manuscript shows conclusively that the pontiff endowed several features of the Pax and Treuga Dei with universality and added precision in certain areas. Moreover, Leo IX also took steps to prevent abuses to which this institution might lead. The Pax had placed new emphasis on the ancient asylum.[85] The accumulation of treasures in churches, however, had often been an incentive to the infraction of this right,[86] and had at least once been dealt with earlier in connection with the Pax and Treuga Dei.[87] According to MS Reg.lat. 711/II Leo deprived thieves and robbers from the immunity ordinarily accorded sanctuaries.[88] In short, the canons in the French manuscript show Leo IX active in secular as well as ecclesiastical affairs, addressing himself to a surprising extent to the laity. It is conceivable that this appropriation by the papacy of a type of legislation that had won broad and enthusiastic support by the French and Spanish population provides another partial answer to the puzzling question why certain ecclesiastical demands that were vainly repeated for centuries[89] should suddenly become effective in what is known as the Gregorian reform.

---

[82] Schaub, *Zinswucher*, esp. 126-132.

[83] Usuram nemo clericus vel laicus accipiat (c.17) and Qui vuadimonia tenent tam diu teneant quousque capitalia habeant et capitalibus acceptis vuadimonia dimittant et amplius non accipiant. Si autem ex hoc neglegens aliquis extiterit in excommunicatione erit. (c.18) Cf. *Historia dedicationis*, 724, c.7.

[84] Schaub, *Zinswucher*, 126.

[85] For asylum in general see *DHGE*, 4, (1930), 1035-1047 (G. Le Bras) and P. Timbal Duclaux de Martin, *Le Droit d'Asile* (Paris, 1939). See also Hoffman *Gottesfriede*, 55 and 151 as well as further references listed in the index.

[86] *DHGE*, 4, co.1083 and esp. Hoffmann, *Gottesfriede*, 151, for an example from Arras, dated ca. 1100.

[87] *Ibid.* 260-62.

[88] MS Reg. lat. 711/II c.12: Praedam penitus non faciant; qui vero fecerint et non resipuerint a communione totius christianitatis in vita et morte alieni fiant. C.13 *ibid.*: Si autem praedator ad ecclesiam confugerit ubi consecutus fuerit presbiter si adfuerit eum cum praeda reddat. Si vero abfuerit presbiter ipse consecutor eum et quod secum habuerit accipiat. See Blumenthal, 'Ein neuer Text,' 32.

[89] An example for ecclesiastical legislation that used to fall largely on deaf ears is the Sermo synodalis, now published in a critical edition by R. Amiet, 'Une "Admonitio synodalis" de l'époque carolingienne: Étude critique et édition,' *Mediaeval Studies*, 26 (1964), 12-82.

Innocent III, Gregory IX, and Political Crusades:

a study in the disintegration of papal power

by Elizabeth T. Kennan
Mount Holyoke College

Political crusading in Europe, that is conquest of territories or forceful assertion of power in the name of conversion and under the strictures of canon law, had a multifarious history in the twelfth and thirteenth centuries. We are all aware of the ambivalent motives of armies which conquered the lower Elbe and penetrated the Iberian peninsula, recruited and reinforced by plenary indulgences. There is no confusion about the human mingling of zeal and ambition which produced them. What is at issue is the reaction of two thirteenth century popes to this state of affairs which both inherited, and the effect which their actions had on the course of papal history.

Innocent III and Gregory IX, two of the shrewdest lawyers produced by the medieval church, two of its most tenacious politicians, men related to one another and to the powerful Conti family of Campagna, these are the popes traditionally held responsible for diverting the great crusade into the narrow channels of European political warfare. On the whole, no one has jibbed at this attribution. Attempts have been made, particularly on Innocent's behalf, to justify the pope's motives and to palliate accusations of personal ambition. But no one has doubted that political crusades resulted from individual papal decisions. Papal theocracy, powerful and impatient, is accused of taking up the crusade to assert its own dominion in Europe.[1]

The crusading issue is complex, for it involves at least two levels of papal intervention. In the first, the pope unambiguously calls a crusade as a preliminary to military action against an identifiable

---

[1] See for example, Joseph R. Strayer, 'The Political Crusades of the Thirteenth Century,' *The Later Crusades 1189-1311 (A History of the Crusades*, ed. Kenneth M. Setton II; Philadelphia, 1962) 343-78, or Steven Runciman, *The Sicilian Vespers* (Cambridge, 1958), 17.

political enemy: Markward of Anweiler or Frederick II. In the second, the pope may only encourage or simply tolerate crusades such as those in the Baltic, the Rhineland or the south of France, which bring tangible advantage to a third party.

Of the two, crusades against Italian rivals are easier by far to penetrate. Quite simply, there were no such crusades until 1240. It is quite true that Innocent III offered an indulgence in 1199 when, responsible for the protection of the infant Frederick II and for the maintenance of his claims to the kingdom of the two Sicilies, the pope failed to contain an invasion of German adventurers bent on the destruction of the boy and his regency. In November, when that army had conquered all of Apulia and was poised to sail to Palermo where the boy was undefended, Innocent proclaimed a phantom crusade against it. He first promised indulgences to any who would fight the Germans and then, almost as an afterthought, harried the Sicilian Moslems to his cause by threatening a crusade against them. But, once having asserted his position unequivacably, he dropped all further references to crusading and proceeded conventionally to assemble a ramshackle army and to play politics and time against the Germans.[2]

It is possible that Innocent's momentary crusade in 1199 was inspired by the actions of his legate to the invaders, Cardinal Hugolino. In a dramatic confrontation at the monastery of Casimari that summer, Hugolino had by sheer intransigence faced down an attempt to bully the legation into ceding Frederick's rights to the insurgent Germans. Surrounded by a mob of German soldiers demanding political concessions from the papal emissaries, Hugolino alone among the cardinals coolly produced his instructions and refused to capitulate. His bravado won the day. Markward of Anweiler was frustrated in his attempt to falsify the papal position in Sicily and the legation was released. Hugolino's heroics at Casimari seem to have made a deep impression on the curia. The *Gesta Innocenti*, the official record of Innocent's pontificate, lionizes him for fortitude:

(The cardinals) were desperately confused and did not know what to do. But Hugolino, Cardinal Deacon of S. Eustachio, having taken up the spirit of fortitude, brought out the bull of the Lord Pope...and he said, 'Behold the mandate of the Lord Pope. We cannot make it otherwise.[3]

---

[2]For a discussion of this crusade see Elizabeth T. Kennan, 'Innocent III and the First Political Crusade: A Comment on the Limitations of Papal Power,' *Traditio*, 27 (1971), 232-249.

[3]"Vehementer ergo confusi, quid facerent ignorabant. Sed praefatus Hugolinus, sancti Eustachii diaconis cardinalis, resumpto spiritu fortitudinis, coram omnibus...protulit scriptum bulla domini papae...et ait: "Ecce mandatum domini papae. Nos aliud facere non valemus"'; *Inn. Gesta* 23 (PL 214.xliv).

The lessen in the *Gesta* is clear: against hopeless odds, intransigence alone is a defense.
This is the lesson which Innocent seems to have been following in November. Faced with almost certain defeat and, temporarily, lacking resources for a counter offensive, he signified his intransigence with the promise of a plenary indulgence.[4] The crusade went no further than that, nor, apparently, did he intend it to.

In fact, Innocent seems already to have developed a distrust of crusades which involved territorial conquest in Europe. In the same year a German missionary party from the archdiocese of Bremen applied to Rome to undertake a crusade to Livland in the eastern Baltic where they proposed to establish a bishopric. Expeditions of this sort were, of course, nothing new in the Baltic: from Charlemagne to the Second Crusade German hegemony in this area marched with conversion.

By 1180, however, German influence in the Baltic had been largely replaced by Danish. As early as 1171 the Danes obtained an indulgence from Rome to encourage them and their allies from Sweden and Norway in an attack on the heathen in Estland.[5] This first offensive slipped by degrees into a Baltic war with commerical overtones. New Danish expeditions were sent in the 1180's and 90's and Estland was still subject to combined Danish-Sweden raids as late as 1226.[6]

So strong was the spiritual hegemony of Denmark in the Baltic by the end of the twelfth century that when the Breman expedition formed in 1199 its leaders sought Danish permission before setting out to Livonia. Once that permission was granted, the newly minted Bishop of Livland, the German Albert of Bremen, signed 500 men with the cross. *Then* he travelled to Rome apparently confident that the enabling indulgence was a matter of form.[7]

He must have been somewhat chagrined by Innocent's response. Instead of *carte blanche* to conquer Livland for the faith, Innocent granted a carefully restricted commission.[8] German crusaders were empowered to protect Livonian neophytes from heathen neighbors resentful of their conversion. That is all. They were permitted only to fight a holding action, more suitable to a garrison than an army. It could hardly have been an appealing charge to northern German adventurers and in 1202 the crusading army in Riga was replaced by a new military order, the Brethern of the Sword, especially

---

[4]*Inn. Reg.* 2.22L (PL 214.781).
[5]Friedrich Benninghoven, *Der Orden der Schwertbrüder; fratres milicie Christi de Livonia* (Koln-Graz 1955) 17-18. See also P. Johansen, *Nordische Mission, Revals Grundug und die Schwedensiedlung in Estland* (Stockholm, 1951).
[6]Benninghoven, *op. cit.,* 264.
[7]*Ibid.,* 37.
[8]*Ibid.,* 38; Potthast 849; *Inn. Reg.* 2.191 (PL 214.739).

created by Albert for his garrison.[9] Behind their stockade, the Christian mission to Livonia entered a period of prosperity.

Innocent's intentions for the Baltic were further clarified in 1206-07. In the earlier year the Cistercian abbot of Lekno had travelled to Prussia, then in the hand of indigenous Pruthenians who were heathen, to seek release of some brethren held captive there. Perhaps it was his surprise at a mild welcome which made him travel next to Rome and volunteer to evangelize the Pruthenians. Innocent welcomed the suggestion, commissioned him, and provided for other Cistercians to accompany him.[10] Throughout the rest of his pontificate, Innocent nurtured that mission, deputizing the Archbishop of Gniezno to regulate it,[11] preventing the Cistercian General Chapter from recalling it,[12] and, finally, creating a Cistercian bishop of Prussia from amongst its ranks to maintain it.[13]

In fact, the only thing which Innocent did *not* do for the Pruthenian mission was to create an army to advance it. By contrast, he pressed hard for peaceful conversion using the least forceful of agents, contemplative monks. In contrast to earlier treatment of Baltic peoples he spoke of the Pruthenians in the mildest of terms, as recipients ripe for the Gospel.[14]

And, to some extent, he seems to have been right. By 1215 the Cistercian, bishop of Prussia, whose name was Christian, could claim startling success. Not only had a number of Pruthenian nobles converted, they had furthered the mission by a significant grant of land.[15] In 1216 Christian travelled to Rome for a confirmation of that grant. But in his absence, a heathen reaction swept away most of his congregation. The issue of force was now raised.

Christian appealed to Rome for a crusade. The new pope, Honorius III, responded with crusading bulls for service in 1217, 1218 and 1219.[16] In part his formula was an old one: crusaders from Poland and later from Germany already pledged to defend Jerusalem could convert their vows to service in Prussia. But beyond this formulaic beginning, Honorius, like Innocent III in 1199, severely limited the crusading commission. Crusaders were to

---

[9]Benninghoven, *op. cit.*, 39.

[10]*Ibid.*, 259. Albert Hauch, *Kirchengeschichte Deutschlands* IV (Berlin, 1958), p.671ff; F. Winter, *Die Zisterziener des nordöstlichen Deutschlands*, I (1871) gives a general history of this mission. See also, A. Philippi, *Preussiches Urkundenbuch,* I, 1 (Königsberg, 1882) 4, pp. 2-3.

[11]*Preuss. UB* I, 1, 5, p.4.

[12]*Ibid.*, 6, p.5.

[13]*Ibid.*, p.7, n.1.

[14]*Preuss. UB* I, 1 7 p.6, warns off the dukes of Poland and Pomerania from military intervention in Prussia, leaving the entire responsibility for conversion to the monks and the Archbishop of Gniezno.

[15]*Ibid.,* 10, p.7.

[16]*Ibid.*, 16, pp. 11-12 (1217), 26, pp. 18-19 (1218), 31, p.22 (1219).

be responsible exclusively to Bishop Christian. They were to do nothing to detract from potential (peaceful) conversions among those still heathen, and they were not so much as to set foot on land held by the newly baptized.[17] Throughout, Honorius' intention was to make the crusaders the instruments of the mission not its successors.

Whether because of these strictures or because the fluctuating host of a crusading army is not an efficient defense, the first Pruthenian crusade failed. Repeated calls for recruits had to go out and in 1224 Christian, like Bishop Albert Livonia, abandoned the crusade for a garrison of knights, this time drawn from the military order of Calatrava dependent on the Cistercians.[18]

Although 1224, unfortunately, did not mark a permanent end to crusading in Prussia, still it does clearly mark the end to an important phase of the mission effort in the area. Innocent III in 1199 and again in 1207 created a new Baltic policy based on restricted use of force, and, in Pruthenia, no force at all. When hostility from the unconverted made war necessary, it was a stockade war which both Innocent and Honorius prescribed. Crusaders were not to win territory but only to protect lives. Within the limits of the possible, these crusades were apolitical.

In the light of their Baltic policy, therefore, it is ironic in the extreme that Innocent and Honorius should be held responsible for the most political all European crusades, that against the Cathars in the territories of Toulouse and Trencavel. In the 1220s, Guilhem Figueira poet and longtime imperial propagandist made the case against Rome:

Rome, truely,
I know without doubt
That under a false pardon
You deliver the nobles of France
To the torture of hell...
Rome, may God give me no part

---

[17]Benninghoven, op. cit., 261; Preuss UB I, 1, 16 p.12, 26, pp. 18-19. 'Quod circa universitatem vestram monendam duximus et hortandam, per apostolica scripta mandantes, quatinus non que vestra sunt, sed que Christi, querentes, ad convertendum ad dominum, non ad subiugandum vestre servituti paganos intendere studeatis...Nos enim eidem episcopo [Christiano] nostris dedimus literis in mandatis, ut, si qui contra voluntatem eius terram baptizatorum vel baptizantdorum totius Pruscie intrare, vel in ea disponere quicquam presumpserint, per quod possit paganorum conversio prepediri, vel deteriorari conditio conversorum, eos presumptione huismodi monitione premissa per censuras ecclesiasticas appellatione remota compescat.' This prohibition is repeated in 1219. See Preuss UB I, 1, 31 p. 22.
[18]Benninghoven, op. cit., 263.

Of the indulgences
Nor of the pilgrimage
That you make to Avignon...[19]

The poet was writing after Louis VIII's invasion of the Midi in
1226, in the name of crusade against the Cathar heretics. But it is in
Rome, not in Paris, that he lays the blame. That he should do so is
witness to the miscarriage of Innocent III's policies in the Albigensian war.

Military action against the Cathar heretics in Toulouse certainly
presented opportunities for political exploitation. And it is true that
Innocent repeatedly proposed the use of force against these stubborn enemies. But he did not, initially, envision a crusade. From the
promulgation of the canon *De haereticis* in 1184, civil authorities
had been bound to join the church in suppressing heretics and were
liable to both civil and ecclesiastical penalties in case of failure.[20] It
was under this canon that Innocent first attempted to generate
military action in the south. In June 1204, he invoked the aid of
Philip II in enforcing confiscation and exile on barons who collaborated with heretics.[21] This was to be less a war than a police action. In a letter of the following winter, the pope explained that
royal intervention was necessitated by the failure of his Cistercian

---

[19]Guilhem Figueira, 'Sirventès contre Rome':

Roma, veramen — sai eu senes doptanssa
C'ab galïamen — de falsa personanssa
Líuretz a turmen — lo barnatge de Franssa,
Lonh de paradis...

Ja Dieus part no-m don,
Roma, del perdon - ni del pelegrinatge
Que fetz d'Avinhon.
(st. 6-7)
Les Troubadours. II. Le Tresor Poetique de l'Occitane, Texte et trad. Rene Nelli et
Rene Lavaud (Paris, Deslcee de Brouwer; Bibliotheque Europeenne, 1966), 806-08.

[20](1. V. tit. VII c.9, De haereticis); C. J. Hefele and H. Leclercq, *Histoire des Conciles* 5, pp.1119-1127.

[21]'Monemus igitur serenitatem regiam et exhortamur in Domino, et in remissionem injungimus peccatorum, quatenus vel per te ipsum, si fieri poterit, vel per
charissimum in Christo filium nostrum, L. natum tuum, aut alium virum prudentem,
perversitati eorum potenter occurens, quantum ecclesiasticam diligens unitatem,
patenter ostendas, et tam comites quam barones, ut eorum bona confiscent et per-
sonas proscribant, tradita tibi coelitus potestate compellas (Caeterum, quia non
caret scrupulo societatis occultae, qui manifesto facinori desinit obviare, ut fa-
cientes et consentitentes par poena constringat, si qui comitum, baronum, vel
civium eos de terra sua eliminare noluerint, aut eos receptare praesumpserint, aut
ausi fuerint confovere, ipsorum bona confisces, et totam terram eorum domanio
regio non differas applicare.' *Inn. Reg.* 7.79 (PL 215.361-62).

mission to win even the attention of the heretics. The cutting edge of the spiritual sword, he argued, must be honed by application of the temporal one, and the powers who protected heretics admonished by the loss of their gods.[22] But, because of the great merit of such disciplinary action, the letter concluded, for his efforts the king deserved pardon of sins equal to that won by fighting in the Holy Land.[23]

Technically, then, Innocent appears to have offered Philip a crusade to Toulouse in 1205. But the pardon was to be for the king alone. Innocent assumed that the Cistercian mission would continue and would still bear the burden of extirpating heresy. Philip's role was to restrain those who hindered the missionaries, and did not, in fact, exceed the duties envisioned by *De haereticis*.

In November, 1207, however, Innocent spoke with a different tone. By this time, attempts to reform the local clergy had stalled in the mechanism of jucidial appeals and in the general lethargy of local councils.[24] The elaborate mission of Cistercians and Spaniards mounted to convert the Cathars was bankrupt and close to despair.[25] In the face of their heroic attempts at evangelization, the numbers of the faithful actually declined, while the Cathars became more defiant and more violent.[26] In the frustraion of this deteriorating situation, Innocent proposed a full crusade. He wrote to the French king not of disciplining magnates but of suppressing monsters.[27] There was no mention now of conversion or of support

[22]'Nos igitur, affectu paterno compatientes eisdem, et ad lucem ipsos volentes a tenebris, prout ad nostrum officium pertinet, revocare, dilectos filios...Cisterc. abbatam, P. et R. monachos Fontisfrigidi, apostolicae sedis legatos, ad illos in sermone Domini duximus destinandos, ut, instantes opportune, importune, arguerent, obsecrarent, et increparent eosdem in omni patientia et doctrina. Verum, sicut dicti legati per suas nobis litteras intimarunt, iidem sanam doctrinam nequaquam recipiunt, sed, ad sua desideria coacervantes sibi magistros auribus prurientes, a veritate auditum avertunt, in ovile Chirsti tanto licentius debacchantes, quantio sibi amputari dexteram auriculam non formidant, eo quod gladium quem Petrus per seipsum exercet, non metuunt, qui sunt extra ovile Domini constituti. Quia igitur hi... quasi aspides, aures suas, ne voces sapienter audiant incantantum expedit ut saecularis gladius potestatis, qui ad malefactorum vindicandam evaginetur injuriam Salvatoris... (et igitur gladium, quem Dominus tibi tradidit, non videaris sine causa portare... oportet ut, apprehensis armis et scuto, causam Dei alleges gladiis apud eos, qui, habentes causas quasi vulpeculae colligatas, messes in regno Francorum compurere incoeperunt...' *Inn. Reg.* 7.212 (PL 215.526-528).

[23]'ut praeter hoc, quod ex tam commendabile opere apud homines consequeris gloriam et honorem, eam obtinere peccatorum veniam merearis, quam euntibus in terrae sanctae subsidium duximus indulgendam.' *Inn. Reg.* 7.212. *loc. cit.*

[24]A. Fliche, C. Thouzellier, Y. Azais, *La Chrétienté Romaine* (A. Fliche and V. Martin, *Histoire de l'Église*, 10 (Paris, n.d.) 120-1125.

[25]Christine Thouzellier, *Catharisme et Valdeisme en Languedoc a la fin du XIIe et au debut du XIIIe siecle* (2nd ed.) (Louvain/Paris 1969), 204-205.

[26]*Ibid.*, 205.

[27]'Inveterata pravatis haereticae corruptela, quae succrescit assidue in partibus Tolosanis, fetus non desinit parere monstruosos, per quos in alios corruptione propriae vesaniae derivata, reviviscit instanter et pullulat destestabilis successu damnorum...' *Inn. Reg.* 10.149 (PL 215.1246-47).

for a missionary effort. The heretics were no longer conceived even as capable of salvation. Instead, they were to be prostrated by war and subjected to truth.[28] The king who fought them was to receive an indulgence and his realm was to be taken under papal protection for the duration of the war.[29]

The murder of Peter of Castelnau, papal legate to the south of France in the ensuing months, of course, crystallized the pope's determination to bring this crusade against the Albigensians. In the series of letters of 1208 resulting from that murder, Innocent bitterly denounced the violence and depravity of the heretics and their protector, Raymond of Toulouse, whom he accused personally.[30] The church's loss was now public and the crusade general.

But even in the fury of 1208 and 1209 when Innocent was fulminating against Raymond of Toulouse, he still took precautions to insure that this crusade would be fought for the aims of the church and not for those of its soldiers. He carefully avoided accepting the leadership of Peter of Aragon who had considerable interests in the area.[31] Instead, he insisted on an army from the north which, at the outset, would have no policital interests to pursue. To lead it, he concurred in the choice of Simon de Montfort, a satisfyingly minor baron who could be bullied by papal legates—and who was.[32]

As the war progressed, Innocent struggled to contain the political ambitions of the crusaders. The bulk of the army presented few difficulties; they were highly transient, spinning out a bare forty days in the Midi to qualify their indulgences. But Simon de Montfort learned to ally himself with the local hierarchy and even with the papal legates against the pope. Innocent could do nothing when Peter of Aragon enfeoffed him with the country of Carcassone after

---

[28]'Licet autem ad corrigendum hoc pessimum genus hominum in tuo regno degentium...nec terrentur comminationibus, nec possunt blanditiis deliniri. Ideoque...serenitatem regiam monetes attentius et exhortantes in Domino, in remissionem tibi peccaminum injugentes, quatenus ad exstirpandos tam degeneres palmites, qui missis radicibus in profundum labruscos generant et non uvas, ad eliminandam quoque spuricitiam tam nocivam accingaris viriliter et potenter, ut et fidei tuae puritas, quam tanquam princeps cahtolicus servas in mente, strenuis actibus in opere declaretur, et haereticae perfidiae sectatores potentiae tuae virtute contriti ad veritatis notitiam saltem inter afflictiones bellicas reducantur.'*Ibid.*
[29]*Inn. Reg.* 10.149 (PL 215.1247).
[30]*Inn. Reg.* 11.17 (PL 215. 1354-1358).
[31]Pierre Belperron, *La Croisade contre les Albigeois et l'union du Languedoc a la France,* 1209-1249 (Paris, n.d.), 139.
Peter II of Aragon married Marie du Montpellier, sole heiress to William VIII of Montpellier and by 1204 had asserted his rights to the city. The Trencavel family, vicounts of Carcassonne and Béziers, were his vassals. A crusade under his leadership would have allowed extension of Aragonese power across the Pyrenees to Montpellier and north as far as Toulouse.
[32]At Moret the legates refused Simon permission to engage in battle. In 1213 at Toulouse the pope effectively ordered Simon to stop harassment of the city. See, *Inn. Reg.* 16.172 (PL 216.959).

the fall of that city.[33] But when the Council of Montpellier attempted to bestow on him the full territories and jurisdiction of the count of Toulouse, the pope refused to contenance it. In the face of heavy pressure from his own legates and from the bishops of southern France, he insisted that Simon could be no more than custodian of the Toulouse possessions. Permanent rights would have to rest on the outcome of Raymond's trial, to be held in conjunction with the Fourth Lateran Council.[34]

In the event, Raymond of Toulouse was found guilty of heresy at the Council and a substantial portion of his lands transferred to de Montfort.[35] But Innocent had succeeded in insuring that the transfer occurred through the offices of a disinterested ecclesiastical court, and not through conquest of gerrymandering. And, he had set a precedent in maintaining the integrity of a European crusade. As pope he called the crusade; through his legates he supervised the fighting; by a general ecclesiastical council he regulated the division of spoils. Insofar as possible, local political interests were kept under heavy restraint.

By the time Guilhem Figueira was writing his vilification of Rome, all these precedents had been overthrown. On the death of Philip Augustus in 1224, the new king, Louis VIII, moved to intervene in the Midi. The crusade he envisioned, however, was to be royal and not papal. In a remarkable letter he requested Pope Honorius III to resign the Albigensian crusade into his hands. The pope was to issue letters patent without further adjudication, stripping the heir to the house of Toulouse of all his possessions and consigning them unconditionally to the monarch. To direct the spiritual aspect of the crusade, Honorius was to create for the French Archbishop of Bourges a special legatine mission empowered to preach the crusade and to adjudicate all matters related to it. From his decisions there was to be no appeal allowed to Rome. But, lest the pope be entirely excluded from the crusade, Louis asked him for 60,000 livres a year to finance it![36]

---

[33]J.D. Mansi, *Sacrorum Conciliorum Nova, et amplissima Collectio*. 53 vols., 22 (Venice, 1778), 935, 939.

[34]"Cum igitur totam terram, quam comes tenuit Tolosanus, cum aliis terris a cruce signatis obtentis, quae a dilecto filio nostro Petro S. Mariae in Aquito diacono cardinali apostolicae sedis legato tenentur per obsides vel custodes, usque ad tempus concilii generalis, in quo de ipsis consilio praelatorum plenius possium ut salubriter ordinare, prudentiae tuae duximus committendas, ut eas conserves, custodias et defendas...' *Ibid.*, 938.

[35] Mansi 22.1069-70. See also, Hefele-Leclercq, 5. pt. 2, 1396 and note 1.

[36]"Item petit quod habeat litteras domini pape potentes de adjudicatione comitatus Tholose cum omnibus pertinentiis suis, ab utroque Raimundo, scilicet patre et filio et eorum heredibus in perpetuum, et totius tere de qua dictus Raimundus pater et Raimundus filius fuerunt tenentes, que est in regno domini Regis, et totius vicecomitatus Biterrensis, et Carcassonensis cum omnibus perturentiis in regno domini Regis, et omnium terrarum — in eodem regno existentium eorum qui guer-

In 1224 Honorius III was not willing to sell out. He opened negotiations with the young Raymond VII of Toulouse and allowed his discussion with Louis to drift.[37] But in 1225 he began to relent. The legate he sent to France in that year, Romano Frangipani, cardinal deacon of St. Angelo, cooperated with the French king in staging a series of local councils designed to give an aura of plausibility to the royal plans for a crusade. Councils at Paris, Melun and Bourges took up the Albigensian business and presumed to adjudicate the conflicting claims of Amaury de Montfort and Raymond VII of Toulouse.[38] In January, 1226, a council at Paris, with the legate presiding, signed Louis with the cross, bestowed an indulgence on him and his army for a war against the heretics, and gratuitously promulgated excommunication against any magnate who might oppose him.[39]

It was nothing short of a French coup d'etat. The crusade which Innocent had struggled to preserve from dynastic ambition had become the cover for the royal conquest of the Midi. Amaury de Montfort was forced to resign all his father's possessions into Louis' hand. Raymond's rights were held confiscated by the French council.[40] And, in all this, the pope weakly concurred. The crusade which followed was a parade of confiscation.

In abdicating control over the second phase of the Albigensian cursade, Honorius III set a dangerous precedent. It was now clear not only that European crusades could admirably suit political

---

raverunt aperte cum eis vel pro eis. Et petit dominus Rex, quod omnes terre predicte sibi et heredibus suis in perpetuum confirmentur et illis quibus eas dabit, si eas dare volueret, retento sibi et heredibus suis hommagio tamquam domino principali. Item petit sibi dare archiepiscopum Biturricensem legatum, qui inter cetera habeat potestatem reconciliandi omnes illos qui ad debitam Ecclesie satisfactionem venerint. Omnia supradicta fiant, appellatione remota. Item petit dominus Rex, quod cum expense sint infinite et inestimabiles, ecclesia Romana provideat ei in LXm. lib. paris. singulis annis usque ad X annos, que convertentur in usus illius terre." J. Vaissete, *Histoire Générale de Languedoc*, 16 vols. (Toulouse, 1872-92) vol. 8, 236, col. 792-794.

[37]*Ibid.*, #239, Col. 804-807; Potthast, 7212, 7299.
[38]Mansi 22, col. 1113-1114; 1211, 1212, 1213 ff.
[39] Vaissete, *Hist. Lang.* 8 #243, col. 816, 817; #244 col. 817; cites a letter from Romanus, cardinal deacon of St. Angelo and the bishops present at the Council of Paris, notifying the pope, " quod cum dominus noster Ludovicus, rex Francorum...negotium Crucis assumpserit contra Albigenses hereticos et pravitatem hereticam expugnandam, nos ipsium regem, familiam suam et regnum suum et omnes, qui cum eo in hoc negotio ibunt et laborabunt, in ecclesie protectione suscepimus, quamdiu fuerint in servico Jesu Christi et concessimus eidem autoritate Dei omnipotentis et beatorum apostolorum Petri at Pauli et nostra indulgentiam quam habent crucesignati de terra Jerosolimitana, sicut etiam continetur in Lateranensi concilio." The last phrase refers to canon 3 of the Fourth Latern Council which authorizes "Catholici vero, qui crucis assumpto charactere ad haereticorum exterminium se accinxerint, illa gaudeant indulgentia illoque sancto privilegio sint muniti, quod accedentibus in Terrae Sanctae subsidium conceditur." Hefele-Leclercq. 5, pt. 2, p.1331.
[40]Mansi, *Sacr. Council.* 23 (Venice, 1779) col. 9.

ends, but that the papacy might be willing to allow them to do so. And, as Guilhem Figueira's broadside on this very phase of the crusade demonstrated, Rome would harvest the blame for local profiteering.

Local interests were quick to see a lesson in the crusading successes of the Capetian house. Within a year both the Archbishop of Bremen and the Bishop of Utrecht were experimenting with crusading indulgences to solve the military problems of their own jurisdictions.

In Bremen, the Stedinger, a cohesive group of peasants living along the lower Weser, had long resisted episcopal taxes and protested unfavorable leases. In the 1220's, they violently rejected all attempts to collect ecclesiastical dues. Archbishop Gerhard II, hardly a man to allow his rights to wither by default, responded with military force. In the winter of 1229 he sent his brother, Hermann von Lippe, with an army of knights down the Weser to break Stedinger independence. Instead, the archbishop's army was crushed and his brother killed. Gerhard determined not only on victory but on revenge. In March 1230, he convoked a synod at Bremen which condemned the Stedinger as heretics and placed them under ban on excommunication.[41] Six months later he travelled to Rome to seek Gregory IX's permission to preach a crusade against them.[42]

Gregory's reaction was guarded. He first requested the provost of Munster to attest the legality of the excommunication and the validity of charges of heresy against the Stedinger.[43] Once satisfied on these points, he wrote to the Bishop of Luebeck and two prominent Dominicans in the archdiocese of Bremen, asking them to intervene and recall the Stedinger from their errors.[44] When nothing came of his peaceful initiative, he requested the Bishops of Luebeck, Ratzeburg and Minden to investigate the charges of 1230 once again.[45] Not until October 29, 1232, two years after the original request had been made, did Gregory authorize a crusade.[46] He empowered only the three bishops who had investigated the case to preach the crusade, and authorized only a partial crusading in-

---

[41] For the Stedinger affair, see C. Krollmann, "Der Deutsche Orden und die Stedinger." *Alt Preussiche Forschungen* (Histoire Kommission für ost-und-westpreussiche landesforschung) Königsberg, 14 (1937), 1-13 and Carl Woebcken, "Die Schlacht bei Altenesch am 27. Mai 1234 und ihre Vorgeschichte." *Oldenburger Jahrbuch* (Verein für landesgeschichte und altertumskunde), 37 (1933), 5-35, and Schumacher, *Die Stedinger, Beitrag zur Geschichte der Wesermarchen* (Bremen, 1865).

[42]Krollmann, *op, cit.*, 4.

[43]*Ibid.*, 5.

[44]Potthast, 8773; Ehmck, *Bremisches UB* I, 196 n.66.

[45]Krollmann, *op. cit.*, 5.

[46]*Ibid.*

dulgence. In January 1233, he extended permission to preach the crusade to five more bishops in northern Germany.[47] Not until June did he issue a general license to preach the Stedinger crusade and grant a full indulgence, equal to that won by fighting in the Holy Land.[48]

Even authorizing it, Gregory seemed to have reservations about the crusade in Bremen. In March 1234, while the crusade was very much in progress, he approached his legate, William of Modena, asking him to settle the discord in the archdiocese.[49] In August 1235, he cancelled the crusade.[50] But by that time, the Stedinger army had been massacred and the survivors forced to capitulate to the archbishop.[51] The political ends of the war had already been served before the pope intervened to stop it.

In Utrecht there had been civil war since 1225. Although alliances were diverse, the principal antagonists were Egbert, prefect of Groenigen and Rudolf, leader of the tribe of Drenther who lived to the south and west of Groenigen. Egbert was supported by the bishop, Otto II. When the Drenther beseiged Groenigen in 1227, the bishop himself came to the city's relief. In July he led his forces out to meet Rudolf, having first granted them an indulgence for fighting.[52] Perhaps he had some intimation of the outcome, for his troops were massacred and he himself martyred with peculiar brutality.[53]

When the lords and clergy of Utrecht met to assess losses after the battle, they decided to seek an experienced warlord as the next bishop. The man they chose, Wilbrand, bishop of Paderborn, recommended himself to them for his service in the war of Lombardy and Sicily.[54] Gregory IX must have approved their choice and their

---

[47]Potthast, 9076.
[48]Potthast, 9236.
[49]Potthast, 9420. Ehmck, *Bremisches UB* I, 215 n.179.
[50]Potthast, 9992.
[51]May 27, 1234. See Krollmann, *op. cit.,*7.
[52]'Qui tandem in die Pantaleonis de consilio prudentum, sed non prudentes, se ipsum armat, totum exercitium convocat....Hartatur eos per indulgenciam, in suum et ecclesie allegat et, data benedictione, ipse cum omnibus illis ad paludem progreditur.' *Gesta Episcoporum Traiectensium* (ed. L. Weiland) *MGH.*SS 23.414.
[53]'Et ne aliquid desit eorum crudelitati, ipsum episcopum quem ceperunt, expoliantes, coronam suam gladio cum tota carne abradunt, guttur suum cultellis incidunt, et diversis plagis mactant et conficiunt." *Ibid.*
[54]'De quo (Wilbrando) nostra sperabat ecclesia, ut ac vindictam tantorum malorum competencior esset, tum propter dictorum comitum et aliorum cognatorum potenciam quia nobilis fuit,...tum propter plurimam guerram et temporalium rerum exercicium et experienciam. Aliquot enim annus laboravit in Langobardia, in Apulia, Calabria et Sicilia circa negocia imperialia domne Frederici imperatores huius nomines secundi.' *Ibid.* 415-416.

reasoning, for he translated Wilbrand from Paderborn to Utrecht.[55] The new bishop committed himself as his constituency expected, to the defeat of Rudolf and the Drenther.[56] As much as the lords of Utrecht expected victory from their bishop, they did not provide him with an army. Support from the surrounding nobility though occasionally brilliant, was still occasional, and Wilbrand found himself forced to recruit troops among the old allies of Groenigen, the Frisians. In 1228, he enticed a group of them into service by exhortation and by "an indulgence of the lord pope."[57] Their campaign, part of a complicated six-pronged attack, was successful, and by the feast of St. Martin, the Drenther were forced to sue for peace, while the armies disbanded.

Peace was not to last, however, and by August of the following year, Rudolf had retaken the strategic castle of Corvodia and the bishop was obliged to renew the fighting. After a year of inconclusive campaigning, perhaps pushed by a council of war at the cathedral in 1230, Wilbrand mounted a major effort to gather new forces for a decisive confrontation. He went personally, and apparently on his own authority, into Frisia, proclaiming an indulgence and preaching a crusade against the Drenther.[58] The Frisians responded with a religious fervor which, considering their previous service for the bishops of Utrecht, could only have been naive. Not only did free men fall in to fight "as true pilgrims" and "most special defenders" of their church,[59] the people sent them off amidst an outburst of intercessions and processions.[60]

In preparing so great a display for his crusading troops and raising such expectations, Wilbrand may have overspent his spiritual

---

[55]*Ibid.*, 416.

[56]The Utrecht chronicler gives the following description of the festivities accompanying Wilbrand's enthronement: "Igitur celebratis missarum solempniss et prandio in palacio cum expensis debitis splendide consummato, ministeriales surgunt gladios nudant, cum quibus miserabiliter contra Covordenses et Trentones proclamant, vindictam a novo suo domino cum multis lacrimis deposcunt.' *Ibid.* 417.

[57] 'Secundo loco et in alia parte terre accesserunt quidam Frisones de Westergo, per indulgenciam domni pape et exhortacionem domni espicopi evocati.' *Ibid.*

[58]'Igitur episcopus ad recuperationem perditorum et ad vindictam sui antecessoris totis viribus semper intentus, ecclesiam suam convocat, super dando consilio eam ut decuit sollicitat. Et tandem post multum tractatum ab omnibus in eo convenitur, ut episcopus personaliter ad Frisones discurrat, indulgentiam clamet et predicet et eis iter contra Prentos et Covordenses in quandam certam remissionem peccatorum suorum iniungat.'*Ibid.* 421.

[59]'Et post pauca dies belli contra Drentones indicitur, ad quam nostri Frisones tanquam veri peregrini et sue ecclesie Traiectensis specialissimi defensores, non ex iure, cum sint homines liberi et ab omni iugo servitutis et cuius libet pertinentis dominii exuti, ex mera et pia compassione et propter indulgentiam predicatam...'*Ibid.*

[60]'Et pro omnibus istis exercitibus indesinenter fiebant a popula ieiunia et elemosine et processiones, a monachis et monialibus, conversis et inclusis, clericis et canonicis orationes et devote supplicationes per omnes angulos episcopatus et ecclesias illi adiacentes.' *Ibid.* 422.

28   REFORM AND AUTHORITY

capital. The army was promptly defeated and that defeat struck not only at the military posture of the bishop, but at the spirituality of his see. All of Frisia was aroused over the issue of the bishop and his indulgence and there was some question whether he could make it back to Utrecht in safety.[61] The scars of that disillusionment must have been deep, for when the Dominicans came to preach the crusade against the Stedinger in the hinterland beyond Groenigen in 1234, they were stoned.[62]

The crusade against the Drenther was ominous in the extreme. It is impossible to know from the extant records whether the papacy had even been informed of these indulgences. Although the first two are described as "papal" in the Utrecht chronicles, this adscription may have been formulaic—or simply convenient. The indulgence of 1230 seems to have been initiated entirely by the bishop, though he certainly had no legal right to do so. He may have claimed authority from canon sixty-two of the Fourth Lateran Council, which recognizes the power of bishops to grant indulgences, but, in fact, that canon has only the most limited application: short-term remission of penance on the occasion of jubilees or consecration of new churches.[63] There is nothing here which would justify an episcopal indulgence, especially a plenary indulgence, for military service. Canon three of that same council does provide that those who take part in a crusade against heretics are eligible for plenary indulgences.[64] But, in Utrecht, there was seemingly no effort to establish that the Drenther were heretics. The *Gesta* of the bishops of Utrecht simply treats them as political enemies, though uniquely savage ones.

---

[61]'Tota Frisia clamat et querulatur: quidam pro episcopo et indulgentia, quidam contra ipsum. Groninge in nimia ponitur desperatione. Et ab omnibus dubitatum est, an etiam episcopus aliqua via vel per terram vel per mare secure recedere permittatur, cum ipse tamen predicanto indulgentiam et penitentias in iunctas relaxando vel minuendo, penitentes et eliminatos reconciliando, ob ecclesie sue deliberationem nichil demeruit.' *Ibid.*

[62]P. Fredericq, *Corpus documentorum Inquisitiones Neerlandicae* (5 vols.) 1, (1889) 102-3.

[63]'Ad haec quia per indiscretas et superfluas indulgentias, quas quidam ecclesiarum praelati facere non verentur, et claves ecclesiae contemnuntur et poenitentialis satisfactio enervatur, decernimus ut cum dedicatur basilica, non extendatur indulgentia ultra annum, sive ab uno solo sive a pluribus episcopis dedicetur, ac deinde in anniversario dedicationis tempore quadraginta dies de iniunctis poenitentiis indulta remissio non excedat; hunc quoque dierum numerum, indulgentiarum literas praecipimus moderari, quae pro quibuslibet causis aliquoties conceduntur, cum Romanus pontifex, qui plenitudinem obtinet potestatis, hoc in talibus moderamen consueverit observare.' J. Alberigo, P. Joannou, C. Leonardi and P. Prodi, *Conciliorum Oecumenicorum Decreta* (1962) 239-240. C. 14 X. V 38 (Fr 2, 888-889); and H. C. Lea, *A History of Auricular Confession...* III (Philadelphia 1896), 14, 163-165, 286, 552; A. Gottlob, *Kreuzablass und Almosenablass. Eine Studie über die Frühzeit des Ablasswesens* (Stuttgart, 1906), 250-252.

[64]'Catholici vero qui, crucis assumpto charactere, ad haereticorum exterminium se accinxerint, illa gaudeant indulgentia, illoque sancto privilegio sint muniti, quod accedentibus in Terrae Sanctae subsidium conceditur.' J. Alberigo *et. al., op. cit.*, 210.

The Utrecht indulgences, then, represent another *coup* of papal prerogatives. The crusade which, until this time, had been initiated solely by the pope, was now usurped by no grander a figure than the bellicose bishop of Utrecht. In 1230 he called a crusade without any consideration of the legality, to say nothing of the righteousness, of his action. The Drenther were charged with no heresy. No papal legate supervised the fighting. No disinterested ecclesiastical court pondered the denouement. Wilbrand's indulgence was a gimmick. It worked a total, perhaps, of three times. But the third time it brought him into bitter disrepute with his own people.

As in the Low Countries, so in the Baltic, crusading in the 1230's became a tool of political aggrandizement. But here the breakdown of Innocent III's original policy was sharper and more poignant.

Within a year of the failure of the Pruthenian crusades, the Teutonic Knights, looking for a base of operations, approached the Polish Duke Conrad of Masovia for territorial concessions in Prussia including the lands around Chelmno on the Vistula.[65] From Frederick II they subsequently received rights to whatever else in Prussia they could conquer.[66]

In an attempt to forestall an invasion by the Knights with its explicit territorial ambition and its disregard of conversion, Bishop Christian seized the moment when the Teutonic Knights were in Jerusalem with Frederick II to form his own military order, the Knights of Dobrin, to take over from Calatrava.[67] In 1228 and 1229 this tiny force (a total of about 15 men) began to establish themselves in southern Prussia. But time ran out. In 1230 Gregory IX made peace with Frederick II and began receiving reports on the Baltic from his new legate, William of Modena, close associate of Hermann von Salza. The Knights used the moment to press their claims to Prussia. In an astonishing coup, Hermann von Salza persuaded the pope to abandon Innocent III's first principle in managing a European crusade: Gregory confirmed the territorial claims of the Teutonic Order at the same moment he authorized them to undertake a crusade in the lands affected. In his letter of January 18, 1230, the pope acknowledged:

Recently, our esteemed son, Hermann, Master of the Teutonic Order of St. Mary, proposed in our presence,

[65] The terms of this grant and the motives of the grantor are a source of controversy. For an introduction to the bibliography, see Karol Gorski, "The Teutonic Order in Prussia," *Mediaevalia et Humanistia* 17 (1966), 24.

[66] "auctoritatem eidem magistro (Herman von Salza) concessimus terram Pruscie cum viribus domus et totis conatibus invadendi, concedentes et confirmantes eidem magistro, successoribus eius et domui sue in perpetuum tam predictam terram, quam a prescripto dure recipiet, ut promisit, et quamcumque aliam dabit, necnon totam terram, quam in partibus Pruscie, deo faciente, conquiret." From the Golden Bull of Rimini, 1226. *Preuss. Urkund.* I, 1. 53, pp. 41-43.

[67] Benninghoven, *op. cit.*, 265.

that the noble Conrad duke of Poland had conceded the castle at Chelmno with its appurtenances and certain other castles in the terrritory of the Pruthenians to your Order in pious liberality, adding whatever of their lands you and your assistors could take. We accept that agreement with no little satisfaction, in the hopes that the faithful living near those boundaries who are daily exposed to the danger of death might receive timely aid from you. Wherefore...we urge you in the Lord to seize that land from the hands of the Pruthenians and we prescribe this for you and those who help you for the remission of sin...[68]

For the remainder of the year 1230, the Knights worked to buttress their claims to Prussia. Further concessions were garnered from Conrad and even from Bishop Christian, and these, in turn, confirmed by Gregory.[69] On September 12, Gregory repeated the terms of his January concession; five days later he issued an order to the Dominicans in Northern Germany, Poland and Pomerania, to preach a crusade against the Pruthenians.[70]

It is impossible to know wether conditions had changed in Prussia over the course of 1229 and 1230. Was there new hostility between the heathen and the converted Pruthenians which would give substance to claims that the baptized suddenly needed military protection? Bishop Christian, as he made grants of land to the Order in 1230, did allow that their presence would be a useful shield.[71] Beyond this, there is little indication of new Pruthenian warfare. More important than the military posture of these Baltic tribes, however, is the fact that Gregory himself made no attempt to investigate local conditions before he proclaimed the crusade. He was, perhaps, lulled into this laxity by the confidence of his papal legate in the Knights. More likely, however, his willingness to acquiesce in the extraordinary demands made on him by Hermann von Salza is a mark of his extreme anxiety to patch matters up with the imperial party in the wake of the treaty of San Germano. However that may

---

[68]*Preuss. UB* I, 1. 72 pp. 52-53. Nuper siquidem del. fil. Hermannus magister dom. S. M. Th., in nostra proposuit presentia constitutus, quod nobilis vir C., dux Polonie, castrum Colme cum pertinentiis suis et quedam alia castra in Prutenorum confinio domui vestre pia liberalitate concessit, adiciens, quidquid de terra illorum per vos et coadiutores vestros poteritis obtinere: quod utique gratum non modicum gerimus et acceptum, seperantes, quod fideles existentes iuxta fines terre predicte cotidie periculo mortis expositi, per vos recipere debeant subsidium oportunum. Quia...monemus et hortamur in domino, vobis et omnibus adiutoribus vestris in remissionem peccaminum iniungentes, quatinus ad eripiendum de Prutenorum manibus terram ipsam...
[69]*Preuss. UB* I, 1. 79 11.60-61.
[70] *Ibid.,* 81. pp. 61-62.
[71]*Ibid.,* 73, pp. 53-54.

be, his new found relationship with the Teutonic Knights cost him the reversal of twenty five years of papal policy in the Baltic. The bull which authorized the Knight's crusade stigmatized a people who had long been considered ripe for the mildest possible evanglization with ferocious and uncontainable barbarity. It then authorized their extermination.

Once the crusade was initiated, Gregory continued an active interest in it though he never investigated its local ramifications. His role was limited to recruiting on behalf of the Knights. For several years he issued a stream of bulls empowering and urging Dominicans to preach the crusade.[72] But for reports on affairs in the fields, he relied solely on his legate, William of Modena, who continued to work closely and collaboratively with the Knights. Gregory had virtually no contact with Bishop Christian after 1231 and, indeed, when the bishop was captured in 1234, he may have believed him dead.

The crusade was devastatingly effective. In 1234 at Sirgune a combined army of Poles, Germans and Pomeranians crushed Pruthenian resistance. The Knights were free to follow up their territorial claims. Dominicans, assigned to the crusade as its official preachers, moved in with them to replace the Cistercian mission. From 1234 to 1240, there was no mention from Rome of Bishop Christian. But, the bitterness of Gregory's last years must have been increased by a violent indictment of the Teutonic Knights and their Prussian crusade brought in 1240 by that bishop, now discovered to be merely captive and not deceased. Gregory reported Christian's comments in a letter to the Bishop of Meissen:

We hear from our venerable brother, the Bishop of Prussia, that the...(Teutonic Knights) remaining in Prussia will not permit the Pruthenian catechumens who wish to be admitted to the grace of baptism to be signed with the Christian symbol....They have not been afraid to afflict those neophytes who have been baptized and who were bound by a vow of fidelity to the same bishop with a variety of tortures unless they obeyed them. Because of fear of tortures many others were forced to return to the errors of unbelief....Beyond that, when the bishop was in captivity (from which the Knights did not take opportunity to release him), the same brothers with (other) newcomers invaded the episcopal church and the entire land of the see, and the city and castle of Sanctir in a hostile manner, and they despoiled them of all the chattels found there; they detained the episcopal rights, the

---

[72]Potthast, 8861, 8862, 8864, 8865, 8867, 8868, 8877, 9501, 10094, 10101.

tithes and purveyance and other rights pertaining to the episcopal table by violence; they abused whatever they could usurp for themselves against law and permission in the parochial churches and chapels...and in the institutions of priests and clerics, for the dereliction of that episcopal office.[73]

It is a measure of Gregory's abdication of responsiblity for this crusade that he had no way of knowing whether Christian's accusations were true or false. His letter to the Bishop of Meissen asked him to do justice in the case, but it also asked him to ascertain the facts. The possibility must now have appeared to Gregory himself that he had allowed an unregulated crusade to wreak havoc on the legitimate mission of the Church in Europe.

From the vantage of the ruined Prussian crusade, we can finally consider what might be called Gregory's personal crusading adventure. And in this the first salient feature is his hesitation to employ a crusade, *per se*, against his enemies in Italy. In 1227 and 1228 provocation must have seemed great. Frederick had not only broken his own pledge to crusade in 1227 and jeopardized the fate of the other crusaders by lingering at Brindisi, but when he did sail for the Holy Land he left sealed orders creating Rainald of Urslingen imperial vicar for Ancona and the Mathildine lands, and stripping the pope of all rights in these sectors of the patrimony.[74] In the late autumn, 1228, Rainald launched a two-pronged attack on Ancona and Spoleto, thereby opening a second front in Frederick's challenge to the papacy. Frederick, excommunicated since October 1227, threatened the pope's leadership of the church as well as his special relationship with the Latin Kingdom when he sailed for Jerusalem in defiance of Gregory's orders. Simultaneously, his agents moved to shatter that territorial base which Innocent had so carefully constructed for the papacy in central Italy. Yet Gregory resisted

---

[73]*Preuss. UB* I, 1. 134 pp. 100-101. "Ven. fr. nostro...episcopo Pruscie accepimus conquerente, quod fratres hosp. S. Marie Teuton. Jeresol. in Pruscia morantes Prutenos catechumenos, qui ad gratiam baptismi pervenire cupierunt insigniri christiani caractere nominis non permittunt....Baptizatos vero neophytos, et eidem episcopo iuramento fidelitatis astrictos, qui servare illud cupiunt, nisi eis obediant, diversis cruciatibus affligere non verentur propter quod quamplures alii horum timore cruciatuum ad infidelitatis errores sunt redire compulsi....Insuper in dicta captivitate eodem episcopo existente, ecclesiam episcopalem ac totam terram episcopatus, civitatem et castrum Sanctir, iidem fratres cum neophitis hostiliter invadentes, ipsos omnibus mobilibus ibidem inventis nequiter spoliarunt; iura episcopalia, decimas ac proventus alios ad mensam episcopi pertinentes per violentiam detinent occupata; in ecclesiis parrochialibus et capellis ipsarum dicti episcopatus, in institutionibus sacerdotum et clericorum ac destitutionibus eorundem episcopali officio, quod sibi contra fas usurpant ac licitum, abutentas.
[74]Daniel Waley, *The Papal State in the Thirteenth Century* (London, 1961), 134-35; H. Huillard-Breholles, *Historia diplomatica Federici Secundi* 3, 165-68.

Frederick's challenge by traditional means: a massive propaganda campaign was mounted against the emperor's person,[75] and mercenaries were sent into the Regno to offset Rainald's invasion of the patrimony.[76]

Gregory IX just barely waged a conventional war against Frederick and his lieutenants in 1228 and 1229. He considered the emperor, in his defiance of papal tutelage and his outright attacks on papal independence, an enemy of Christendom. And he certainly made the most of excommunication in his own counter attack. Not only was the anathema to provide a theatrical setting for stating his case against Frederick,[77] it was also the occasion for releasing the emperor's subjects from their obligations to him.[78] More daring still, Gregory encroached on the great crusade in 1228 by diverting funds from the clerical tenths designed to support it to pay for his campaigns in Apulia[79] Yet, despite these confusions of spiritual and secular means, Gregory never actually granted an indulgence for his war in Sicily. With a crusade already in progress in the East and Frederick himself in possession of Jerusalem, such a stroke must have seemed a monstrosity, and perhaps especially so to the man trained in Innocent's curia.

Defeat of the papal army in 1229 and a new conciliatory mood in the imperial camp made it possible in 1230 to negotiate a peace between Gregory and Frederick which lasted the strains of nine years of Italian politics. In 1239, however, under the pressure of an escalating campaign for Sicilian hegemony in northern Italy, that peace finally snapped. When it did, the pope once again attacked his imperial adversary with an intense onslaught of propoganda. Frederick was excommunicated as a signal for the papal engagement against him and agents were sent from Rome throughout the West to announce and re-enact the anathema.[80] At the same time, Gregory made tentative overtures to secure the election of a new emperor.[81] In quick succession, all of the imperial party in Germany

---

[75]Potthast 8044: Huillard-Breholles, *Hist. dipl.* 3 24; J. F. Böhmer, *Regesta Imperii V: 1198-1272* ed. Ficker and Winkelmann (Innsbruck, 1881-1901), 9, p. 33.

[76]For an account of the papal invasion, see D. Waley, *loc. cit.* and Peter Partner, *The Lands of St. Peter, the Papal State in the Middle Ages and the Early Renaissance* (Berkeley/L.A. 1972) 246.

[77]It is interesting that Gregory IX orchestrated his propaganda campaign against Frederick in 1228 along the patterns set by Innocent III in his war against Markward of Anweiler and the German invaders of Sicily in 1199. After officially excommunicating Frederick on Maundy Thrusday, 1228, he circulated that excommunication with a letter of justification to all the bishops in Apulia, ordering that they publish the sentence 'every Sunday and every feast day.' See Potthast 8162; Huillard-Breholles, *Hist. dipl.* 3, 52.

[78]Potthast 8254, August 30, 1228; Potthast 8431; *Raynaldi Ann. ad a. 1229* 23-28 "Inter alia flagitis."

[79]Peter Partner, *op. cit.,* 247.

[80]Potthast 10721,10724,10725,10756,10766,10798, 10799.

[81]Potthast 10806. Daniel, *Hist. de France* 4. 326.

was excommunicated and placed under interdict.[82] But it was not until Frederick had invaded the papal patrimony and marched within striking distance of Rome itself that Gregory initiated a crusade against him.

Accompanied by a barrage of political mythmaking, Frederick moved into Ancona and Spoleto late in 1239, taking papal strongholds in his stride. Pausing at Viterbo, the pope's traditional sanctuary, he flaunted his control over the last of Gregory's sanctuaries and published his intention to stop next at Rome. With insulting flamboyance, he challenged the Romans to open their city to him and join him in making it, once again, the imperial capital of the world.[83]

His challenge to Gregory could not have been more pointed. He held the papal patrimony and was on the verge of destroying papal rule in Rome. The pope, who had heard reports of Frederick's excesses in the north, might well have feared for his life. He certainly despaired for the independence of his office. Yet he was virtually a prisoner in Rome; German possession of his strongholds meant that there was nowhere to flee. He had no army; his allies in Lombardy were cut off; many of the cardinals seemed about to desert him; the Romans were on the point of defection.[84]

Gregory responded with a gesture that was resonant of the event in 1199. In an event made famous to our generation by the prose of Ernst Kantorowicz, he rallied the Roman people to the relics of Sts. Peter and Paul and declared a crusade against the Hohenstaufen. The antidote to helplessness was once again intransigence.

Political crusades in the pontifacates of Innocent III and Gregory IX, then, were invariably signs of papal weakness. When such crusades were fought at a distance from Rome they were almost impossible to control. Innocent III spent a great deal of ingenuity and even more determination to counter the centrifugal forces of the first Albigensian crusade and bring it home to the Fourth Lateran Council for judgment. Gregory IX, with similar misgivings but considerably less forcefulness, tried to regulate the Stedinger Crusade, but failed. In managing a crusade from Rome, papal legates were more often a hindrance than a help. The legates at Albi in 1210 tried to give the whole of Toulouse away to de Montfort. It was the papal legate Romano Frangipani, who bestowed the second Albigensian crusade on Louis VIII. William of Modena covered for the Teutonic

---

[82]Potthast 10811.

[83]'Restat igitur ut favente nobis universo populo Romano nostroque sicut cepit adventui acclamante, Urbem feliciter ingredi disponamus ut antiquos imperii fastos et triumphales lauros victricibus aquilis debitas reformemus.' Frederick II, Ep. Feb. 1240, Huillard-Bréholles, *Hist. Dipl.* 5 pt. 2 762f. See also Ernst Kantorowicz, *Frederick the Second 1194-1250* (English version by E. O. Lorimer) (New York, 1931), 511-516.

[84]The best account of this confrontation is still to be found in Kantorowicz, *loc. cit.*

Knights in Prussia so consistently that Gregory IX never heard of Bishop Christian's appeals for ransom.

Worse than the legates were the bishops who had their own political goals to pursue in crusading. The Bishop of Utrecht's utter disregard for Rome, of course, is an extreme case. But the Archbishops of Narbonne and of Bremen pursued their own ends under the guise of hierarchical obedience. In the light of their undeflected self interest, the doctrine of *plenitudo potestatis* loses much of its sheen.

In the end the European crusades brought bitterness indeed. They were worst of all, of course, for the victims: the heathen of the lower Vistula, the peasants of the Weser, the converts, real and potential, of the Pruthenian mission. But not all the victims were direct targets of the crusaders: Raymond of Toulouse was disinherited as was, ironically, Amaury de Montfort whose father's spoils from the first Albigensian Crusade did not last even a generation. For Christian, Bishop of Pruthenia, held from 1234 to 1240 at a ransom which the Teutonic Knights neglected to pay, the Prussian crusade must have been Kafkesque.

But the ebb of the European crusading movement was bitter, too, for the papacy. It left exposed in its wake the outlines of a pervasive contempt for the power of Rome. Louis VIII manufactured his crusade to annex Toulouse and then informed the pope. The Archbishop of Bremen requested a papal crusade but conducted his war against the Stedinger without regard for papal misgivings. The Bishop of Utrecht seems to have acted as if the plenary powers of the papacy did not exist. And the Teutonic Knights manipulated the pope with nice calculation to the abandonment both of his training and of his principles. By 1240 the double-bladed sword of the crusading movement had been repeatedly lifted out of the pope's hands by others grasping for place and profit. The question now was whether it might not prove as dangerous to its maker as to its victims.

Franciscus Zabarella (1360-1417):

papacy, community and limitations upon authority

by Thomas E. Morrissey
State University of New York, Fredonia

Unlike the extremist critics of papal authority in the late middle ages, a canonist such as Zabarella[1] at all times had to maintain a balance between the papal prerogatives and the rights of the Chris-

*This paper was presented at the Regional Conference of the American Catholic Historical Association held at Villanova University in April, 1973, and I am grateful for the comments and suggestions for improvement that I received there.

[1]For biographical information on Zabarella and on his general contribution to the canonistic tradition one could consult: August Kneer, *Kardinal Zabarella (Franciscus de Zabarellis, Cardinalis Florentinus) 1360-1417. Ein Beitrag zur Geschichte des grossen abendländischen Schismas.* Erster Teil; Dissertation, Münster, 1891. Friedrich Merzbacher, "Die ekklesiologische Konzeption des Kardinals Francesco Zabarella (1360-1417)," in *Festschrift Karl Pivec* (Innsbrucker Beiträge zur Kulturwissenschaft, Bd.12), hrsg. v. Anton Haidachers und Hans Eberhard Mayer (Innsbruck, 1966), p. 279-287; Pietro Pinton, *Appunti biografici intorno al grande giurista et umanista card. Zabarella* (Potenza, 1895); Brian Tierney, *Foundations of the Conciliar Theory* (Cambridge, 1955), Part III, ch. IV: "Franciscus Zabarella," p. 220-237; Walter Ullmann, *Origins of the Great Schism* (London, 1948), Appendix: "Cardinal Zabarella and his Position in the Conciliar Movement," p. 191-231; Giuseppe Vedova, *Memorie intorno alla vita ed alle opera del cardinale Francesco Zabarella Padovano* (Padua, 1829); Antonio Zardo, "Francesco Zabarella a Firenze (il Cardinale Fiorentino)," *Archivio Storico Italiano*, Series 5, Vol. 22 (1898), 1-22; Gasparo Zonta, *Francesco Zabarella* (1360-1417) (Padua, 1915).

Under the direction of Professor Tierney I undertook a re-evaluation of Zabarella's life and thought since the research in medieval canon law for the past twenty years has altered the whole outlook on conciliarism and its leading figures. My research resulted in a Ph.D. dissertation at Cornell University (January, 1973) entitled: *Franciscus de Zabarellis (1360-1417) and the Conciliarist Traditions.* In the intervening years, I have published four articles on Zabarella and his era in addition to the present study: "The Art of Teaching Law: The Manuscripts of a Tract by Franciscus Zabarella (1360-1417)," *Bulletin of the Institute of Medieval Canon Law,* N.S. 4 (1974), 78-79; "Cardinal Zabarella on Papal and Episcopal Authority," *Proceedings of the First Patristic, Medieval and Renaissance Conference* at Villanova University 1 (1976), 39-52; "The Decree 'Haec Sancta' and Cardinal Zabarella, His Role in its Formulation and Interpretation," *Annuarium Historiae Conciliorum* 10 (1978), 145-176; "After Six Hundred Years: The Great Western Schism, Conciliarism and Constance," *Theological Studies* 40 (1979), 495-509.

37

tian community, for this polarity was found within the canonical tradition. In the twelfth century one canonist had simply stated that no one else could impose a law upon the pope since the pope was freed from the laws and could change them.[2] In the view of Zabarella and most canonists, this text did not grant to the papacy a *carte blanche* right to do what it pleased. Zabarella did assert in a variety of ways the rights, privileges and powers of the pope,[3] but our main concern is what Zabarella wrote on the limits upon this authority. What were the constitutional restrictions upon papal authority; what recourse did the Christian community have against the abuse of authority by a pope, or in the situation where the person occupying the papal office was clearly seen to be incompetent or unworthy?

In the area of limits on papal authority the great canonist of the twelfth century, Huguccio, had written that the pope could modify the laws of the Church provided he did not do anything contrary to the faith and did not interfere with those matters which pertained to salvation.[4] Huguccio then had imposed a strict constructionist interpretation upon these words and severely limited the cases in which papal authority could be questioned or challenged. By the late middle ages this interpretation had become inadequate. The expression of another canonist of the thirteen century, Ricardus Anglicus, that the pope could not issue a law that infringed the Old and New Testaments or the well-being of the Church,[5] was much closer to the mind of the canonists in the era of the Great Western schism.

This expression: the general well-being of the Church (or the *status ecclesie*) can be seen as one of the keys to understanding Franciscus Zabarella and the approach he took to resolving the schism. As mentioned, it was by no means a new phrase but part of the common tradition of the canonists.[6] Further in 1392 a question had arisen at the court of the Avignon pope, Clement VII, whether the pope had the authority to grant a dispensation in an area that

---

[2] Alanus, *Apparatus Ius naturale*, "Set nunquid alius pape posset legem imponere cum papa canonibus sit solutus et possit eos mutare," as quoted in B. Tierney, "Pope and Council: Some New Decretist Texts," *Medieval Studies*, 19 (1957), 197-218, at p. 218

[3] A full treatment of Zabarella's views on papal authority can be found in chapter four: "The Papacy in the Church," of my doctoral dissertation at Cornell: *Franciscus de Zabarellis (1360-1417) and the Concliarist Traditions.*

[4] Huguccio,*Summa,*in Tierney, "Pope and Council," p. 211: "Dummodo contra fidem non faciat uel nonobuiet his que pertinent ad salutem." For the origin and early history of this exception clause, cf. James M. Moynihan, *Papal Immunity and Liability in the Writings of the Medieval Canonists* (Rome, 1961), p. 27ff.

[5] Ricardus Anglicus, *Summa Breuis,* in Tierney, "Pope and Council," p. 211: "Potestatem habere ut ius commune statuat omni ecclesie dummodo non ledat nouum uel uetus testamentum uel statum uniuersalis ecclesie."

[6] Cf. Tierney, "Pope and Council," *Summa Et est sciendum,* p. 211: "que spectant ad...statum ecclesie."; Ricardus Anglicus, *Summa Breuis,* p. 211: "Statum uniuer-

would change the general state of the Church. The case in point had to do with a dispensation for a marriage. The response of the canonist who handled this case, Giles Bellemere, was that even the pope could not grant such a dispensation on the *de iure* level, and further in the time of schism, even if *de iure* he could act so, the pope should not on the *de facto* level make such a decision which might further upset the state of the Church.[7]

Papal dispensations then were a complex question with an immediate bearing on the state of the Church.[8] Zabarella's opinions granted extensive power to the pope in individual cases but not for the pope to set a general law for the whole Church. The ultimate parameters which bound papal authority remained: whenever a council was acting or deciding on a matter of faith or when the papal action would affect the state of the Church. [9] That these two limits are closely tied is immediately evident, for the faith of the whole community and orthodoxy of the pope could not for long go their own separate ways. Over and again Zabarella came back to these questions.[10] In November, 1394, he lectured on this problem at

---

salis ecclesie,"; Alanus, *Apparatus Ius naturale,* p. 212: "ecclesie statum generalem."; *Glossa Palatina,* p. 212: "dominus papa non potest contra generalem statum ecclesie." For some of the difficulties that sometimes appear in the phraseology here, cf. Gaines Post, "Copyists' Errors and the Problem of Papal Dispensations *Contra Statutum Generale Ecclesiae* or *Contra Statum Generalem Ecclesiae* According to the Decretists and Decretalists ca. 1150-1234," *Studia Gratiana,* 9 (1966), 357-405. This confusion also appears at a much later period, as in the commentaries of Zabarella, cf. *Comm. ad X,* 1,30.4., fol. 317ra-b; "Dic quod papa omnes non potest deponere quia hoc esset mutare generale statutum ecclesie.", where it is clear the readind should be "generalem statum."

[7]Cf. Henri Gille, "Gilles Bellemere et le tribunal de la Rote à la fin du XIVe siècle," *Mélanges d' archéologie et d'historie,* 67 (1955), p. 281-319, at p. 301-302

[8]Two of the principal modern views on the papal powers of dispensation are most clearly represented respectively by (a) Walter Ullmann (that there was practically no limit upon papal power according to the canonists), cf. his *Principles of Government and Politics in the Middle Ages* 2nd ed. (London, 1966), esp. p. 35, 48, 50; and his *Medieval Papalism* (London, 1949), p. 47,50-52, 65ff. and (b) by Stephan Kuttner (that the canonists treated very carefully the relationship of papal power of dispensation to the divine and Archbishop of Palermo," in *Medieval Studies Presented to Aubrey Gwynn* p. 409-454, where Professor Kuttner shows how gingerly the canonists dealt with the question whether the pope could allow someone to be ordained after being twice married since this seemed to be contrary to a supposed command of St. Paul.

[9]Zabarella, *Comm. ad X,* III.30.24., fol. 168ra: "Nam cum Papa fungatur vice Dei, debet distinguere ius divinum quod facit aliquando ampliando illud ..., aliquando interpretando vel alio modo, secus autem si ex toto tolleret, quia per hoc videretur immutare statum ecclesie, quod non potest: sed debet potius conservare." Cf. also Paul Ourliac, "Les sources du droit canonique au XVe siele: le solstice de 1440," de 1440," in *Edutes d'historie du droit canonique dédiées à Gabriel LeBras* (Paris, 1965), I:293-305, at p. 296-297.

[10]*Comm. ad X,* I.6.4. (Venice, 1502), fol. 114ra: "Cum tamen non possit immutare universale [sic] statum ecclesie."; *ibid.,* I.4.4., fol. 88vb: "Quo ad ea que spectant ad articulos fidei."; an entire list of the passages in which Zabarella discussed or mentioned this limiting clause would cover a couple of pages.

Padua and by this time the schism was some sixteen years in existence and two new popes (Benedict XIII and Boniface IX) occupied the respective papal thrones of Avignon and Rome. In his lecture Zabarella came back to his fundamental position that at no time could the pope ever infringe upon the state of the Church, upon the well-being of the whole community.[11]

For Zabarella this expression *status ecclesie* was not any vague idea but denoted a definite reality with certain constitutive elements. There were rights, institutions and privileges that belonged to the constitution of the Church and which any and every authority in the Church must respect. One of these elements, for example, was canonical election. The reform of papacy of Gregory VII had demanded respect for and adherence to the principles of canonical election in the eleventh century. Later medieval popes had often paid little attention to this and in fact did much to undermine its validity. Zabarella asserted that this was an abuse. Following Innocent IV he had pointed out that if in a church the canons of the chapter or those duly authorized had elected one man to be their bishop and the pope had chosen another candidate, the pope should not press his candidate but drop him and let the will of the electors prevail lest the pope act against canonical election which was something that could not be allowed.[12] Zabarella's opinion in this legal brief had a concrete application a few years later in this own life when in fact he was chosen by his fellow canons to be bishop of Padua but Gregory XII voided this election out of hostility to Zabarella for his attempts to reform and unite the Church. Gregory was also anxious to take care of a member of his own family.[13]

---

[11]*Comm. ad X*, V. 39.23., fol. 129vb-137rb, at 130va: "et ratio est quam dixi: quia non potest immutare universalem statum ecclesiae, cum debeat potius conservare."

[12]The text is found in *Consilium* No. 142, Fol. 72ra (Milan, 1515 edition): "Hinc dicit Innocentius, de electione, *Innotuit*, quod si canonici eligunt aliquem in episcopum et papa ad quem spectat de plenitudine potestatis alium postea elegit, debet papa cassare suam electionem alias esse valde absonum quod electionem canonicam cessaret (cassaret?) quod fieri non debet."

[13]In the year 1409 the bishop of Padua, Albano Michieli, had died and the chapter elected their own native son and fellow member of the chapter, Franciscus Zabarella. But Pope Gregory XII rejected this election and appointed his own nominee, Pietro Marcello (a friend of Zabarella), to be bishop of Padua, transferring him from the see of Ceneda. The characters of the two men (Gregory XII and Zabarella) are revealed in this episode. For Gregory used the opportunity to promote one of his nephews, Antonio Correr, to the vacancy created at Ceneda, which showed that even in that time of crisis for the Church and while the Council of Pisa was in session and afterwards, his own family ranked first for "good Pope Gregory." Zabarella on the other hand supposedly lost this appointment because Gregory considered him a person of "doubtful faith" (*dubbia fede*) because of the principles he had espoused in his treatise *De scismate* and in his defense of the Council of Pisa. For the account of these events, cf. Luigi Zanutto, "Pier Paolo Vergerio Seniore e le sue aspirazioni al decanato Cividalese," *Nuovo archivio Veneto* N.S. 21 (1911), 101-127, esp. at p. 112 and notes 1 and 2.

In his treatise *On the Schism (De scismate)* written in three parts between 1403 and 1408 Zabarella repeated his assertions that the pope could not change the state of the Church nor block what had been established to protect and to promote this.[14] If the pope tried to grant a dispensation by which the state of the Church would be adversely affected, by this very act he would be found to be erring. Zabarella then attacked certain aspects of the late medieval papacy: overcentralization, attribution of all authority to itself, dimunition of the rights and status of lower prelates, and as he observed, those flatterers around the popes who kept telling them that they were all powerful and could do as they pleased, rather than telling them what they should do.[15] It was from these circles: the papacy and the Roman Curia that Zabarella saw all the evils of his time arising. As an example Zabarella said that the present papal claimants could not absolve themselves from their promises to do all that was necessary to end the schism even by resigning if this were the only viable solution. He added that if the popes tried to ignore or to renege on their promises, they were to be considered as acting against the state of the Church and so were not to be obeyed.[16]

That the pope should act for the good of the Church and not for his own interests was spelled out in Zabarella's treatment of the question on papal resignations. He stated that the director or one in charge of a body could resign if he found that he lacked the knowledge to handle his position. This assertion applied equally to the papacy as to any other rank. Furthermore, it was not just a question of resignation, for if the head were unwilling, he could be removed from his position.[17] It is to be noted that papal resignations had received extensive treatment in medieval canonistic writings because of the example of Celestine V in the thirteenth century.[18]

---

[14] *De scismate*, (Venice, 1502), fol. 119vb: "Nec in hoc potest papa per suas constitutiones vel alio modo resistere quia hoc esset subvertere ecclesiam."

[15] *Ibid., loc. cit.,* "Nam neque potest papa dispensare in eo per quod decoloratur status universalis ecclesiea ... nam ex hoc committeretur errare, dicto capitulo *sunt quidam* in fine que iura sunt notanda, quia male considerata sunt per multos assentatores qui volentes placere pontificibus per multa retro tempora usque ad hodierna suaserunt eis ut omnia poterant et sic quod facerent quidquid liberet, quasi omnia possent etiam illicita et sic plus quam Deus. Ex hoc enim infiniti secuti sunt inferiores prelati sunt pro nihilo et nisi Deus succurrat status ecclesie universalis periclitatur."

[16] *De scismate*, fol. 120rb: "Non possunt contendentes se absolvere quia ex hoc turbaretur status universalis ecclesie in quo pape non est obediendum.

[17] *Comm. ad X*, I.9.10., fol. 218rb: "Nota quod propter defectum scientie potest presul cedere. Et dicitur presul etiam papa: eo titulo, c. 1, *Liber Sextus*. Et quod dixi quod cedere, dic quod etiam deiicitur invitus."

[18] Cf. Martin Bertram, "Die Abdankung Celestins V. (1294) und die Kanonisten, " *Zeitschrift der Savigny-Stiftung für Rechtsgeschichte. Kanonistische Abteilung*, 56

Another institution (besides canonical election) that the pope had to respect was the episcopate. In dealing with the other bishops the pope was to be wary of violating their rights and status. Thus while it was accepted that the pope could unite an episcopal see without consulting anyone, as normal practice this unification was only to be carried out with the consultation of the college of cardinals.[19] The pope ought always bear in mind that the power which Christ had granted was not given to Peter alone but to the whole college of apostles. [20] A keen dispute of the medieval centuries had been whether the bishops depended upon the pope both for the exercise of their authority and for the authority itself. The extreme papalists asserted both.[21] Zabarella and others said that bishops depended upon the pope only for the exercise of their authority and not for the authority itself.[22] On this basis then it is not surprising that Zabarella took a dim view of the practice of some popes of removing or depriving bishops of their sees. For Zabarella this would be a rare event. He noted that Clement IV had deposed eleven bishops at one time and Urban VI supposedly even more. He asked whether this was just or not and did not give a direct answer but left no doubt of his opinion, for he commented that Urban was now answering to God for his action.[23]

(1970), 1-101. This volume has also a complementary article by Horst Herrmann, "Fragen zu einem päpstlichen Amtsverzicht,"p. 102-123. The study by Edward M. Peters, "Rex Inutilis: Sancho II of Portugal and Thirteenth Century Deposition-Theory," *Studia Gratiana,*14 (1967), 253-305 is also useful, especially p. 294ff. on the deposition of a bishop.

[19]*Comm. ad X,* V. 31.8., fol. 99vb: "Dico tamen, quod licet dixerim Papem posse unire episcopatum sine consensu vel consilio alicuius, hoc non procedit de potestate ordinata, sed de absoluta.... In talibus enim arduis collegium Cardinalium est in possessione, ut requirantur consilia Cardinalium."

[20]*Comm. ad X,* I.1.1., fol. 12rb: "Septimo nota quod claves promissas Christus concessit apostolis et eorum successoribus et ex eo quod dicit de apostolis infertur quod non soli Petro."

[21]Cf. Ulrich Horst, "Papa und Konzil nach Raphael de Pornaxio O.P.," *Freiburger Zeitschrift für Philosophie und Theologie,* 15 (1968), 367-402 and *idem,* "Papst, Bischöfe und Konzil nach Antonin von Florenz," *Recherches de théologie ancienne et médiévale,* 32 (1965), 76-116; J.G. Sikes, "John de Pouilli and Peter de la Palu," *English Historical Review,* 49 (1934) 219-240; and several studies by Yves Congar, "Aspects ecclésiologiques de la querelle entre médiants et séculiers dan la seconde moitié du XIIIe siècle et le debut de XIVe,"*Archives d'historie doctrinale et littéraire du moyen age,* 36 (1961), 35-151; "Apostolicité de ministère et apostolicité de doctrine. Réaction protestante et Tradition catholique," in *Volk Gottes. Festgabe furJosef Hofer.* hrsg. v. Remigius Bäumer und Heimo Dolch (Freiburg, 1967), p. 84-111; "Un temoinage des desaccords entre canonistes et théologiens," en *Etudes d'historie du droit canonique dédiées à Gabriel LeBras* (Paris, 1965),II:861-884. The most ardent proponent of this descending thesis on the derivation of all authority in the Church, at least among modern scholars, is Walter Ullmann who has proposed his ideas in any number of books and articles.

[22]*Comm. ad X,* I.6.4., Fol. 113va: "Sexto nota ibi 'fratribus,' quod episcopi sunt fratres pape."

[23]*Comm. ad X,*V.1.8., fol. 35rb: "Nota casum in quo episcopus removetur ab episcopatu.... Ex qua nota quod rara accidebat tempus horum iurium ut privaretur

There was no doubt that a pope (it was always presumed for a good reason) could remove any one bishop but he could not abolish or degrade the entire episcopate.[24] There was no mathematical answer to the question how many bishops had to be removed before it seemed that the pope was disrupting the state of the Church. But to remove even one bishop without a good reason gave the presumption that the pope was acting from evil intention.[25] The bishops were not the pope's agents but his co-workers,[26] and as such they existed as a reality with their own authority derived from Christ independently of the pope since the fullness of power resided not in Peter alone.[27]

Another group to whom Zabarella attributed extensive rights and authority as a check against the abuse of papal authority was the college of cardinals. This was natural because of the role the cardinals played in the medieval Church.[28] In some ways the cardinals

---

episcopus. Refert tamen Speculator, de accusatore, No. 2, quod Clemens quartus deposuit simul undecim episcopos, qui adhaeserant Manfredo in occupatione Siciliae et interfuerant eius coronationi. Sed multo plures deposuit Urbanus sextus, maxime in regno Apuliae propter adhaerentiam antipape, et alias causas. Et an iuste, coram iusto iudice nunc rationem reddet."

[24]*Comm. Ad X,* I.2.7., fol 20va-b: "Pro hoc quod notat glossa singulariter, 9 q.3 *per principalem,* in eo quod dicit quod papa potest deponere episcopum, sed non omnes episcopos quia sic universalem ecclesiam turbaret."

[25]*Ibid., loc. cit.,* "Illa tamen glossa non dicit quod facit sine causa et dic quod sine causa facere non debet ne presumatur motus mala intentione."

[26]*Comm. ad X.,* V. 6.17., fol. 61vb-62ra: "Et ob hoc redemptor noster potestatem tanquam capiti dedit Petro, et caeteris apostolis tanquam coadiutoribus...." A prominent modern theologian has expressed similar ideas that the episcopate is not the pope's civil service and at his disposal, cf. Karl Rahner, *Studied in Modern Theology* (London, 1964), 308-309

[27]*De scismate,* fol. 119va: "Et in hoc...etiam apparet quod licet Petrus fuerit princeps apostolorum tamen plenitudo potestatis non fuit in eo solo."

[28]This subject has been studied by Karl A. Fink, "An Historical Note on the Constitution of the Church," *Concilium* 58 (1970), 13-25; Giuseppe Alberigo, *Cardinalato e Collegialità. Studi sull' ecclesiologia tra 1' XI e XIV secolo* (Florence, 1969); *idem,* "La collégialité épiscopale selon quelques théologiens de la papauté," in *La collégialité épiscopale. Historie et théologie* (Unam Sanctam 52; Paris, 1965). In this same volume cf. also, Yves Congar, "Notes sur le destin de l'idée de collégialité épiscopale en occident au moyen age (viie—xvie siècles),"; the Alberigo article is on p. 183-221, the Congar article on p. 99-129. Other important studies are: Stephan Kuttner, "Cardinalis: The History of a Canonical Concept," *Traditio,* 3 (1945), 129-214; Walter Ullmann, "Cardinal Humbert and the Ecclesia Romana,"*Studi Gregoriani,* 4 (Rome, 1952), 111-127, *idem,* "The Legal Validity of Papal Electoral Pacts," *Ephemerides Iuris Canonici,* 12 (1956), 246-278; Jean Lulves, "Päpstliche Wahlkapitulation. Ein Beitrag zur Entwicklungsgeschichte des Kardinalats," *Quellen und Forschungen aus italienischen Archiven und Bibliotheken,* 12 (1909), 211-235; *idem* "Die Entstehung der angeblichen Profession fidei Papst Bonifaz' VIII.," *M.I.Ö.G.,* 31 (1910), 375-391; *idem.* "Die Machtbestrebungen des Kardinalskollegium gegenüber dem Papsttum," *M.I.Ö.G.,*35 (1914), 455-483; P.M. Baumgarten,*Untersuchungen und Urkunden über die Camera Collegii Cardinalium* (Leipzig,1898); Martin Souchon, *Die Papstwahlen in der Zeit des grossen Schismas*

had even begun to supplant the episcopate in their authority,[29] mainly because the cardinals were a body permanently in session and existing at the heart of the Church whereas the bishops were scattered throughout the dioceses of Europe. Some even claimed that the college of cardinals could judge the pope.[30]

For some critics Zabarella's defense of the rights of the cardinals was feathering of his own nest, since his name has come down in history as Cardinal Zabarella. The fact is, however, that when he wrote his legal commentaries and tracts on the rights of the cardinals vis-a-vis the pope, he was still only a secular master at the University of Padua.[31] He gave a clear but restricted power to the college of cardinals: they elected the pope and in doing so they acted in the name of the whole Christian community.[32] Zabarella rejected any claim by the cardinals to judge the pope. Only a general council could do this. [33] He avoided the questions whether the cardinalate was an institution of divine origin as some medieval writers claimed or whether the cardinals shared in the apostolic succession.[34]

It was of some importance that Zabarella followed the tradition which asserted that in all serious matters the pope should act only with the advice and consent of the college of cardinals.[35] He added that if a pope should go on with a serious matter without consulting them, it

1378-1417. 2 vols. (Braunschweig, 1898-1899); Guillaume Mollat, "Contribution à l'histoire du sacré collège de Clément V à Eugène IV," *Revue d'histoire ecclésiastique*, 46 (1951), 22-122, 566-594.

[29]Lulves, "Die Machtbestrebungen," p. 456, 462-463
[30]Lulves, "Die Machtbestrebungen," p. 456.
[31]Zabarella only became a cardinal under Pope John XXIII in 1411 and all of his major legal commentaries as well as his treatise *De scismate* were written long before this date and at a time when he had no way of knowing that he would himself someday be a member of the college of cardinals. He would be named bishop of Florence in 1410 by the same Pope John XXIII but never was consecrated as bishop since he resigned the position on being nominated as a cardinal six months later. As a matter of fact Zabarella seems never to have received any of the major orders despite his intense involvement in ecclesiastical affairs and his career as a prominent churchman.
[32]*De scismate,* fol. 118vb: "Ubi considerandum quod in hiis que concernunt electionem pape collegium cardinalium representat universalem ecclesiam et eius vice fungiture."
[33]*Ibid.,* fol. 120va:
"Sed quia receptum est de pape dispositione solum concilium iudicet; ideo collegium licet possit eligere non tamen deponere."
[34]As Walter Ullmann has pointed out "(The Legal Validity of Papal Electoral Pacts," p. 271, n. 69), Zabarella in talking of the cardinals' rights and prerogatives often followed Johannes Monachus and the latter spoke neither of the apostolic succession nor of the divine institution of the cardinalate, and so neither topic was really treated by Zabarella.
[35]Zabarella made this demand throughout his legal writings: e.g., *Comm. ad X,* I.6.54, fol. 195rb; *ibid.,* I.41.5., fol. 393rb; ibid.,II.13.19., fol. 27vb, and many other places.

would be presumed that he was acting in bad faith and so his action should be revoked by his successor.[36] John Watt has attempted to show that this opinion was not part of the mainstream of the canonistic tradition. For Watt Hostiensis represented the mainstream of canonistic thought and Hostiensis did not hold this position. Watt's interpretation does not, however, appear to bear up under scrutiny.[37] The cardinals were not, as Watt would have it, merely an advisory body but rather their advice and consent were to be sought.[38] This was especially so when the matter at hand affected the state of the Church,[39] and so they represented a real check on papal authority.

In presenting Zabarella's theory up to this point, then, it is clear that Zabarella, following the tradition of medieval canon law, upheld certain constitutional and institutional checks upon papal authority. First of all the pope could not act against the state of the Church; he had to respect the rights of the episcopate and of canonical election. He was to consult with the cardinals on any major decisions. In each of these instances if the pope did not act according to the traditional structure of the Church, he was presumed to be in error and action could be taken against him. This latter point was the crux of the question for the medieval canonist. For Zabarella it was in reality two questions: one theoretical—what could be done against a pope who acted against the state of the Church, i.e., who had in fact become a heretic? And on the immediate practical level for that era the question was: what could the

---

[36]. *Comm. ad X*, III.4.2., fol. 18 va: "Si papa in maximis procederet sine consilio fratrum, praesumeretur non ex bona conscientia facere, et per successorem deberet revocari."

[37]Cf. John A. Watt, "The Constitutional Law of the College of Cardinals: Hostiensis to Johanne Andreae, "*Medieval Studies,33* (1971), 127-157, especially at p. 131-132.

[38]*Ibid.*, p. 134-136. Watt's thesis is based on distinguishing between *consilium* and *consensus* and between *decet* and *debet*. "Advice" and "it is fitting" were applied to the papal position vis-a-vis the cardinals; "consent" and "obligation" to the relationship of prelates to chapters and other collegiate bodies. He claims that this is how Hostiensis thought. Zabarella, however, did not always distinguish between these words and definitely intended more than an advisory role. Thus, he wrote: *Comm. ad X.*, V. 31.8., fol. 99vb: "Dico tamen quod licet dixerim Papam posse unire episcopatum sine consensu vel consilio alicuius, hoc non procedit de potentia ordinata sed de absoluta....In talibus enim arduis collegium cardinalium est in possessione ut requirantur consilia cardinalium." Also, *Comm. ad X.*, V.33.23., fol. 113ra: "Ex his arguit Hostiensis quod parvum vel nihil debet Papa facere sine consilio fratrum"; Walter Ullmann, in his book, *The Origins of the Great Schism* (London, 1949), p. 207 says that none of the later canonists ever referred to Hostiensis' opinion on this point. Zabarella would seem to be the exception then. In his *De scismate*, fol. 118rb and fol. 118va Zabarella spoke of both the consultation with the cardinals and of the consent of the cardinals.

[39]*De scismate*, fol. 119rb: "Unde ut dicunt Laurentius et Archidiaconus 25 q. 1 *sunt quidam*, papa sine cardinalibus non potest condere legem generalem universali statu ecclesie quod est notandum."

Christian community do to resolve the Great Western Schism since the popes would not do anything other than hurl threats and excommunications at each other and in other ways concerned themselves solely with their own vested interests.

First on the theoretical level, every medieval canonist admitted the possibility that the pope could become heretic.[40] Where they disagreed was what that implied and what could then be done about the situation. This dispute centered on the right and power to depose the pope: who had this right and when could it be exercised? Everyone knew that popes had been deposed.[41] The medieval canonists agreed that while sacred orders and jurisdiction were common to only some members of the Church (i.e., the clergy and the hierarchy), the faith was held and shared by all in the Church. Since heresy, particularly heresy in the pope, was a threat to all, then all, the whole Christian community, was involved in the heresy of a pope and so could act for its own self-preservation.[42] The principle behind this reasoning was that what affected all was to be decided by all.[43] Against the need of the whole Church, against the *status ecclesie* in other words, no one could claim papal immunity or prerogatives.[44] How this problem was to be solved in the practical order was a question that found no unanimity in the canonistic tradition and the variety of opinions expressed covered the whole

---

[40]Cf. G. Tierney, "Ockham, the Conciliar Theory and the Canonists," *Journal of the History of Ideas*, 15 (1954), 40-70, at p. 50: "On the other hand another text of the *Decretum* implied quite clearly that a Pope could be brought to trial and deposed if he erred in faith. 'Papa a nemine est iudicandus, *nisi deprehenditur a fide devius.* '"Cf. also, James L. Moynihan, *Papal Immunity and Liability in the Writings of the Medieval Canonists (Analecta Gregoriana* vol. 120; Rome, 1961), p. 46ff. Cf. also, A.M. Koeniger, "Prima sedes a nemine iudicatur," in *Festgabe A. Ehrhard. Beiträge zur Geschichte* and Leipzig, 1922), p. 273-300. There are two studies on one pope who in the medieval canonistic writings was believed to have been guilty of heresy, cf. A. Amore, "Il preteso 'Lapsus' di Papa Marcellino," *Antonianum*, 32 (1957), 411-426 and W. Schwarz, "Marcellus I," *Zeitschrift für Kirchengeschichte*, 73 (1962), 327-334.

[41]Cf. Tierney, "Pope and Council," *Summa Prima Primi*, p. 218: "Quia causa fidei omnibus communis est...et eo inuito potest ecclesia decidere questionem fidei.";
Alanus, *Apparatus Ius Naturale*, p. 218: "Nisi de crimine hereseos in quo propter criminis enormitatem et commune periculum ecclesie..."; behind these texts and implicit in their argument there was the basic principle that what affects all must be decided by all (*Quod omnes tangit ab omnibus approbatur*), for a discussion of this principle, cf. Gaines Post, "A Romano-Canonical Maxim, 'Quod Omnes Tangit,' in Bracton, *"Tradition*, 4 (1946), 197-251

[43]Cf. the general study of this maxim by Yves Congar, "Quod omnes tangit, ab omnibus tractari et approbari debet," *Revue historique de droit français et étranger*, Series 4. vol. 36 (1958), 210-259.

[44]Cf. Tierney, "Pope and Council," *Summa Inperatorie Maiestti*, p. 214: "In causa autem fidei sedes apostolica iudicari potest."; Simon de Bisignano, *Summa*, p. 214: "Pro heresi potest sumus pontifex a subditis iudicari."

gamut of possibilities. Some simply said that if a pope became a heretic he automatically ceased to be pope.[45] Needless to say this solution created more problems than it solved since it left open the question how the Church was to know and decide that the pope was a heretic especially if he denied the charge.

For Zabarella the pope was to be obeyed and his decisions accepted unless he became a heretic or acted contrary to faith.[46] In the latter situations not only was he not to be obeyed but he was also liable to judgment and condemnation.[47] Zabarella never doubted that a pope could become a heretic;[48] further he stated that this had occurred on occasion.[49] The judgment of the pope was to be rendered in this situation by a general council.[50] Now Zabarella saw the schism of his day as a matter that affected the *status ecclesie* and so involved the faith. On this basis the general council was empowered to intervene in this question, to act to preserve the faith and to protect the state of the Church.[51] The council was not to be called as a matter of mere expediency as some had urged at the outbreak of the schism. Cardinal Peter Flandrin had written in this vein in 1380. It was of the very nature of the situation that it required a council to solve it.[52]

Within the canonistic writings on the powers of a general council in relation to the pope there was an inherent ambiguity since in

---

[45]*Ibid., Summa Duacensis*, p. 217: "Simul enim et papa et hereticus esse non potest."; Alanus, *Apparatus Ius naturale*, p. 218: "uidetur enim quod si hereticus est caput ecclesie non est."

[46]*Comm. ad X*, I.4.4., fol. 89ra: "Tunc enim in omnibus spiritualibus obediendum est et in his que ad animam spectant nisi sunt contra fidem vel ei specialiter sint prohibita."

[47]*Comm. ad X*, I.6.4., fol. 114 ra: "Et ex notis in premissis locis colligitur quod standum est pape quam [read praeterquam] in his que concernunt fidem in qua si erraret posset accusari."; *ibid.*, I.33.16., fol. 350ra: "Solutio ibi...ratione heresis papa fit minor ideo ligari protest."

[48]*Comm. ad X*, III.42.3., fol. 258va: "Stat ergo quod Papa singulariter consideratus posset esse haereticus."

[49]*De Scismate*, Fol. 117vb: "Finge enim sicut aliquando accidit quod papa esset hereticus."

[50]*Ibid.*, fol. 117rb: "Cum papa accusatur de heresi competens iudex est concilium."

[51]*Comm. ad X*, III.37.3., fol. 219 va: "Dic etiam quod Papa non posset derogare concilio ubi ageretur de fide, quae ex facto Papae periclitaretur."

[52] Cf. Hermann Heimpel, "Studien zur Kirchen- und Reichsreform des 15. Jahrhunderts I. Eine unbekannte Schrift Dietrichs von Niem über die Berufung der Generalkonzilien (1413-1414)," in *Sitzungsberichte der Heidelberger Akademie der Wissenschaften. Philosophisch-historische Klasse*. Abhandlung 1 (1929-30), 1-64, at p. 22, n. 2, the text of Zabarella said: "quia congregatio concilii de sui natura fit ubi agitur de his que spectant ad fidem Catholicam," whereas Cardinal Peter Flandrin in February, 1380 had written that a council should be called, "non quod sit iuris, sed pro tunc videbatur esse de expedienti," cf. Franz Bliemetzrieder, *Literarische Polemik zy Beginn des grossen abendländischen Schismas* (Wien-Leipzig, 1909), p. 89.

general the assumption was that a general council usually included
the pope or somehow involved him in its activities.[53]Moreover there
were claims that the power of a general council was derived from the
pope, and echoes of this claim are found in Zabarella.[54] Even in these
assertions, however, Zabarella made allowance for the case where it
was a question touching upon faith in which case the council was to
take precedence over the pope.[55]

Zabarella was well aware that the question of the authority of
councils, their make-up, structure and membership and the derivation of their authority could not be divorced from the question on
the right of summoning a general council.[56] Throughout his comments he addressed himself to various aspects of the problem and so
a variety of opinions could be found in a diligent search of his legal
tomes. It is much more important, however, to start with his initial
indirect definition of a general council and work towards his final
and full definition of a council, its constitutive elements and its
authority in order to see his complete thought in this question.

First of all for Zabarella a general council was one through which
and in which the authority of the whole Church was excerised.[57] He
was perfectly willing to admit that a general council was normally
summoned by the pope,[58] and that the bishops should take part in it,
i.e., that they were obliged to attend.[59] But at no point did Zabarella
make the leap which some modern writers have made when they
deduced that for the medieval canonistic tradition a general council
was simply an assembly of the bishops together with the pope and
which had been called by the pope.[60] Rather, for Zabarella a general

---

[53]Cf. in Zabarella's commentaries, *Comm. ad X*, V.33.23., fol. 112vb: "Nota quod in
generali concilio Papa disponit concilio approbante."

[54]*Comm. ad X*, III.37.4., fol. 219 va: "Et dicitur generale, quia a Papa emanavit
generalem potestatem habente."

[55]*Comm. ad X*, I.6.4., fol. 114ra' "Standum est pape praeter quam in his que concernunt fidem in qua si erraret posset accusari."; and *ibid*, I.6.6., fol. 116va: "dic
quod imo quia concilium habet iudicare."

[56]*Comm. ad X*, I.30.4., fol. 317ra-b: "Secundo quero in eo quod glossa dicit quod
congregatio generalis concilii reservatur pape. An hoc sit indistincte verum. Dic ut
dico de electione *licet.*" The reference here significantly was to the decretal on which
Zabarella wrote his treatise *De scismate.*

[57]*Comm. ad X*, II.1.1., fol. 2ra: "unde dic verius quod bene possit recusari concilium provinciale sed general non: quia tota ecclesia non potest errare." For
Zabarella's general opinion in this area, cf. also Friedrich Merzbacher, "Die Ekklesiologische Konzeption des Kardinals Francesco Zabarella (1360-1417)," in
Festschrift Kark Pivec (Innsbruck, 1966), p. 279-287.

[58]*Comm. ad X*, III.5.28., fol. 44rb: "Sed semper est generale quando generaliter
congregatur per Papam."; *In Clem.*, "Prohemium" (Rome, 1477), fol. 3va: "Papa
celebrat generale concilium."

[59]*Comm. ad X*, II.24.4., fol. 61ra: "Item ibi 'vocatus ad sinodum etc.,' quod non ac-
cedens ad consilium et non perpeditus est periurus."

[60]Cf. Joseph Gill, "The Representation of the *Universitas Fidelium* in the Councils
of the Conciliar Period," *Studies in Church History*, 7 (1971), 177-195, at p. 194-195;

council had authority because it was the representative of the whole Church.[61] If a council took authority away from the pope, this would not be a merely human action but it would be God acting through the council which removed the authority.[62] As a consequence Zabarella saw no contradiction in saying that the pope ruled by divine right and had his authority directly from Christ and at the same time could have this authority taken away from him by the community, the congregation of believers, who would be acting in the name of God and so with divine authority.

In the original draft of his treatise *On the Schism (De scismate)* Zabarella had argued that the universal Church was represented by and made present by the general council,[63] and that once the council was assembled its authority resided in its more important part. This latter argument was a basic tenet of the corporation theory of the middle ages and so Zabarella said that he did not need to elaborate on this point since it was commonly accepted. In his final draft of the treatise in the months just prior to the Council of Pisa, and therefore in November, 1408, Zabarella raised the question of how the general council could be truly representative of the divided Christendom, and he gave a number of possible solutions. Once again he applied medieval canonistic theories on corporate bodies, how they were structured and how they functioned. Thus Zabarella followed Pope Innocent IV's doctrine that for corporations only the directors and the more fitting part need be present. Thus a general council need not require the presence of every member of the Church.[64] Here Zabarella explicitly opposed the ideas of William of Ockham who would not grant that any representative body could ever truly represent the whole community and so would allow ultimate authority only to the entire community acting unanimously. In this opinion Ockham rejected the entire conciliarist tradition

---

and Hubert Jedin, *Bischöfliches Konzil oder Kirchenparlament?* (2nd ed. Basel, 1965), p. 9ff. John B. Morrall has shown to be sure that this was the view of a council that Jean Gerson held, but that did not make it the view of the canonists; on Gerson, cf. John B. Morrall, *Gerson and the Great Schism* (Manchester, 1960), esp. p. 82.

[61]*De scismate*, fol. 117rb: "Regimen universalis ecclesie vacante papatu penes ipsam ecclesiam universalem que representatur per concilium general."

[62]*De scismate*, fol. 120 va: "Respondeo quod quando concilium privat papam potestas non dicitur sibi auferri ab homine sed a deo cum dispositione concilii sit divina."

[63]Hubert Jedin, *Bischöfliches Konzil oder Kirchenparlament?* (2nd ed. Basel, 1965), p. 8 sugests "make present" as a better translation than "represent"; he used the two German words: *gegenwärtigsetzen* as opposed to *vertreten*. Whereas Jedin would distinguish between the two words and apply only the former to the council, to Zabarella both terms would apply equally well to the council. In fact he would see them as reciprocal: the council because it "represents" the whole Church makes the whole Church present and vice versa.

[64]*De scismate*, fol. 117rb: "Pro hoc quia ut eleganter dicit Innocentius de maioritate et obedientia *solite*, c. fin., quod in rebus et negociis universitatum requiruntur rectores vel pars idoneior."

and the common teaching on corporations that were at the heart of canonistic thought.[65]

In the crisis of his age Zabarella responded with a series of measured proposals to the call on what grounds could one act and what could anyone do to save the state of the Church. To be sure it took him five years between the first and last version of his tract to explicate his ideas. The schism was now at the end of its third decade and something had to be done; therefore something could be done. A general council must assemble since it alone could give a definitive answer and represent in its decision the mind of the whole Church. There were a number of possible ways this council could be assembled: at the call of the pope in possession or by a joint invitation of both claimants; failing in that, the cardinals could summon a council since it was their duty to take those steps before and after the election of a pope to ensure its acceptance. If these two sources failed then the emperor should act in the name of the Christian people to summon a council. Further if all these previous means failed, then if in any way two-thirds of those who should be present at a council could somehow come together, they could invite the remaining third to join them and in default of a response from the latter, they could go on to act as a legitimate body. Since this latter possibility (of two-thirds of the members seemingly by accident assembling) appeared remote, Zabarella concretized this method. He said that in the case of the negligence of the above leaders, then the greater prelates, whether one alone or several, could convoke a general council.[66] Furthermore, if in any of these instances, the popes tried to forbid the prelates from attending, this would be strong evidence to presume that the popes were acting against the state of the Church and so should not be obeyed.[67] Once the council were assembled it could judge the validity of the papal claims,[68] and if necessary compel the popes to do whatever would be necessary and best for the good of the Church, including resignation or deposition if this were the only way. The council could judge in this case because to impede the unity of the Church, to promote or foster

---

[65]On Ockham's views, cf. John B. Morrall, "Ockham and Ecclesiology," in *Medieval Studies Presented by Aubrey Gwynn, S.J.*, ed. by J.A. Watt and F. X. Martin, O.S.A. (Dublin 1961). p. 481-491; B. Tierney, "Ockham, the Conciliar Theory and the Canonists," *Journal of the History of Ideas*, 15 (1954), 40-70; Silbernagl, "Ockhams Anischten über Kirche und Staat," *Historisches Jahrbuch* 7 (1886), 423-433; Georges DeLagarde, "L'idée de représentation dans les oeuvres de Guillaume d'Ockham," *Bulletin of the International Committee of Historical Sciences* t. IX, fasc. IV, no. 37 (1937), No. 3, p. 425-451.

[66]*De scismate*, fol. 118ra: "Poterunt prelati maiores unus vel plures facere convocationem concilii."

[67]*Ibid.*, fol. 118ra-b: "Pracepto pape non est obediendum quando ex hoc vehementer praesumitur statum ecclesie perturbari vel alia mala esse ventura."

[68]*Ibid.*, fol. 118rb: "Sed debeant prius facere hoc discuti per concilium."

schism, was to become guilty of heresy.[69] The popes who continued to insist on their own rights and continued to ignore the needs of the whole Church furthered the schism and so were falling into heresy and thus the whole community could act against them through the council.

Here Zabarella had been able to leap over the petty squabbling over the mechanisms of convocation to the key issue: how could the Church protect itself in a time of schism and of disputed authority? Once again he employed corporation theory to the Church at large and to a general council. It was of little importance how it was that the greater part came to a decision on an issue, just as it mattered little by whom or in what way the council with the greater part of the Church represented in it came to be assembled. So long as it was assembled, that was what counted. If a truly general council assembled, it was valid because it was truly general and so was representative. This then defined a general council for Zabarella: a council that had the authority of the whole Church because it represented the whole Church, regardless of how it came to be assembled.

Zabarella then spelled out some of the implications of his ideas. He asked how his ideas could be reconciled with the canonistic texts that said that the pope was above the council and that the councils were constituted through the authority of the Roman Church and received their authority from this source. Zabarella explained that the terms: Roman Church and Apostolic See did not exclusively refer to the papacy. Here he was unmistakably clear: "He was not talking about the Roman Church but about the pope"; or again the Apostolic See was one thing, the pope another! He showed that the terms Roman Church and Apostolic See could be understood to mean the whole Church, the congregation of the faithful, and so shared in the latter's authority and inability to err. It is significant that Zabarella did not allow the pope to stand for the whole Church or have its authority. This was why he could and had to say that in matters of faith the council (which represented and embodied the authority of the whole Church) was greater than the pope.[71] He went on to stipulate what precautions a council should take lest a pope so

---

[69]*Ibid.*, fol. 118va: "Respondeo quod concilium,...quia quando isti pontifices persistant et nolint cedere et sic pro sua voluntate impediant unitatem ecclesie et hoc censebuntur esse in notorio crimine scismatis....Scisma vero inducit heresim quia scismaticus intendit sibi constituere ecclesiam et universalem impugnare...de heresi autem pape iudicat concilium."

[70]*Ibid.,*fol. 119ra: "Qui cum effectu non tollunt scisma sed potius fovent heretici sunt, ab hereticis autem et scismaticis et ab universitate ecclesie precisis debemus recedere nec eis communicare."

[71]*Ibid.*, fol. 119rb: "Opponitur ad hoc quia pape auctoritas videtur esse super concilium....Sed concilia per ecclesie Romane auctoritatem facta sunt et robur acceperunt....Solutio hoc non disputatur de ecclesia Romana sed de papa. Aliud autem papa, aliud sedes apostolica,...nam sedes errare non potest, ...papa sic,...quod tamen

disposed should try to undo the work of the council after it closed its
sessions.[72] The council should mandate that its decisions could only
be changed by a subsequent council.[73]

The general council which was to act for the common good had to
represent the whole community and so Zabarella gave some ways in
which this could be realized. The council was not just an assembly of
bishops, although as major figures in the Church he expected and
demanded that the bishops fulfill their obligation to come; the same
was true of other major prelates in charge of large areas.[74] Their
absence would weaken the council's representative nature but
Zabarella added that others should also be present: the significant
people, the emperor. He did not say whether other rulers should also
be at the council,e.g., rulers who had imperial or regalian rights over
their own lands, nor did Zabarella say whether representatives of
cities, universities or other corporations should be present; yet in so
far as he based the authority of the council on the fact that it
represented the whole Church, it would seem that his logic would
lead him in this direction. At any rate his list of those who should
take part in the council did include: the cardinals, bishops and
prelates, clerics, judges, those trained in law and theology, and in
the end he gave reasons why the laity should be present and take
part, especially when matters affecting faith or concernng marriage
were to be discussed, for what touched all was to be decided by all.[75]

From this framework of authority in the Church Zabarella drew
definite conclusions on the nature of papal authority and how it was
related to the whole Church and its authority. He said that there
was a papal fullness of power but also a fullness of power that
belonged to the body politic and its representative, the council. The
papal fullness of power did not belong to the pope by himself but as
head of the corporation, so that the power was in the corporation *in*

---

dicitur sedem apostolicam errare non posse videtur intelligendum accipiendo sedem
pro tota ecclesia, id est congregatione fidelium....Cum autem agitur de fide sinodus
maior est quam papa."

[72]*Comm. ad X*, I.33.6., fol. 42va-b: "Et inter cetera vellet statui per concilium quod
tales constitutiones non possent revocari interpretari nisi per aliud concilium."

[73]The problem of a pope undoing the work of a council has been well discussed by
Karl A. Fink, "Papsttum und Kirchenreform nach dem grossen Schisma," *Tübinger
theologische Quartalschrift*, 126 (1946), 110-122.

[74]*De scismate*, fol. 117rb: "Puta episcopi et alii prelati ecclesiastici qui presunt
magnis locis ut magni abbates habentes quasi episcopalem."

[75]*Ibid.*, fol. 119rb-va: "Dic quod opus congregari ecclesiam id est totam congregationem catholicorum id est principales ministros fidei, scilicet prelatos qui tantam
congregationem representant. Videtur tamen quod ad concilium sint vocandi etiam
alii..., ubi colligitur quod vocandi sunt episcope et clerici et iudices....Debent ibi esse
iuris periti...et tres casus in quibus etiam laici debent interesse conciliis
notantur,....scilicet quando specialiter mutantur vel tractantur causa fidei vel
matrimonii quia tales cause eos ligant et per illam glossam videretur quod ubicum-
que in concilio tractantur cause que eos tangunt debeant interesse quia quod omnes
tangit ab omnibus approbatur,... et hec congregatio appellatur concilium."

principle and in the pope as its agent or minister, the one through whom usually this power was exercised.[76] He explained then that Jesus had entrusted the salvation of the whole body to all the apostles. but in a special way had committed this task to Peter as the leader or head (*principaliter*).[77] He repeated and explicated this latter statement and its meaning: the authority was not totally (*totaliter*) in Peter (nor in the pope his successor consequently) to the exclusion of all others, but was in Peter chiefly or principally (*principaliter*). Thus the fullness of authority was in the corporation formed by all and was exercised by individuals. To be sure it was exercised chiefly by Peter, since he was the head, but not in such a way that if Peter should err, he would have to be supported and agreed with.[78]

Zabarella referred to the tradition with the famous scene of Saint Paul correcting Saint Peter and drew the inevitable conclusion once again that the fullness of power was in the pope so long as he did not err, but if he did err, the duty of the council was to correct him. The pope could not resist this correction since this would be to subvert the Church and the pope could not change the state of the Church.[79]

Zabarella's view then of the respective roles of the papacy, episcopate, cardinalate and general council have been set forth. They were naturally very closely bound together. Each of the last three played a particular role in its function of a limiting agent upon papal power. Each was supportive and yet limiting upon others. Thus the cardinals in default of papal action were to summon a council, the bishops were to be among the principal agents in any such council. But the council once it was assembled was superior to the college of cardinals and it was not to be seen as just an assembly of bishops. On the other hand, the power of the council, like that of the pope, was a ministerial authority; it was not free to do as it pleased but as it should. It was not free to do everything, but had to respect the state of the universal Church, just as the papal authority had to, and among the elements which in Zabarella's scheme constituted this state of the Church were precisely: the papacy, the

---

[76]*Ibid.*, fol. 119va: "Et ex hoc apparet ad id quod dicitur quod papa habet plenitudinem potestatis debet intelligi non solus sed tanquam caput universtitatis ita quod ipsa potestas est in ipsa universitate tanquam in fundamento sed in ipso tanquam ministro per quem hec potestas explicatur."

[77] *Ibid., loc. cit.*, "Dicitur quod Iesus comisit salutem universitatis omnibus apostolis ita tamen quod in Petro principaliter collocavit."

[78]*Ibid.*, fol. 119va-b: "Nota quod non dicit totaliter ut alii excludantur sed dicit principaliter ut sic plenitudo potestatis sit in universitate ipsorum et per singulos exercetur, sed principaliter per Petrum. Non tamen ita per Petrum ut ei errante standum sit."

[79]*Ibid., loc. cit.*, "Ex his infert quod potestatis plenitudo est in papa ita tantum quod non erret. Sed cum errat hec habet corrigere concilim apud quod ut predixi est plenitudo potestatis tanquam in fundamento nec in hoc potest papa per suas constitutiones vel alio mod resistere quia hoc esset subertere ecclesiam....papa non potest immutare statum ecclesie."

episcopate and the cardinalate. And so while the council was superior to each of these, in its turn it had to respect the rights of each of these institutions which also in some way shared in the fullness of power of the whole Church, although in a different and more limited way than did the council. Perhaps the clearest way to describe Zabarella's system is to say that no matter what body was called to act, whether the pope, the bishops, cardinals or a council, it had to act with the authority given to it according to the divine plan. It had to act with a structured and rational authority (*potestas ordinata*) and so any notion of absolute power (*potestas absoluta*) was denied to every human person or institution and even the very claim or mere appearance of a claim to any such absolute power had to be avoided.[80] In the end Zabarella's scheme was that of a jurist or lawyer who thought in terms of a corporation, that is of groups of people bound together by inescapable ties and relationships. These very ties embodied duties and obligations that had to be respected, for if this ordered system could be disregarded by any member or combination of members, then the whole system was endangered and this would be subversion of the state of the Church which was never to be allowed.

---

[80]Cf. the discussion of this terminology by Francis Oakley, "Jacobean Political Theology: the Absolute and Ordinary Powers of the King." *Journal of the History of Ideas,* 29 (1968), 323-346.

Sacred Doctrine and the Authority of Scripture

in Canonistic Thought on the Eve of the Reformation

by Hermann Schuessler
University of Maryland

In 1519 Luther denied the inerrancy of general councils and claimed that on this point he was in agreement with "all teachers of Scripture and *law*."[1] After 1528 he also disputed papal magisterial authority and began to appeal to the overriding norm of the Bible. In this connection, too, he invoked canonistic precedent, repeatedly[2] citing a famous late medieval canonist, Nicholas de Tudeschis (d. 1445 as archbishop of Palermo and who thus was known as "Panormitanus"), who had stated: "In matters of faith anyone armed with better reasons and authorities of the New and Old Testament is to be preferred even to the pope."[3] A student of Luther will hasten to

---

[*] *Revised version of a paper originally presented at the American Historical Association Convention (Boston, 1970). Since then two studies of especial relevancy have been published: Remigius Bäumer, *Nachwirkungen des konziliaren Gedankens in der Theologie und Kanonistik des frühen 16. Jahrhunderts* (Münster, 1971), and Brian Tierney, *Origins of Papal Infallibility 1150-1350. A Study on the Concepts of Infallibility: Sovereignty and Tradition in the Middle Ages* (Leiden, 1972). These important publications, while not affecting the substance of this paper, have brought more light to certain aspects of the subject. The following article is based on more comprehensive research on the same theme. Acquaintance with the general literature on conciliarism and papalism is assumed throughout. (The editor, who has revised this article at the late author's request, wishes to thank Fr. John Lynch, of the Catholic University of America, for reading the final version. G.F.L.)

[1] WA Br I, p. 472, 257.
[2] Cf., R.H. Bainton, "Probleme der Lutherbiographie," *Lutherforschung Heute,* (ed. V. Vajta; Berlin, 1958), 27. See also C. Tecklenburg-Johns, *Luthers Konsilsidee in ihrer historischen Bedingtheit und ihrem reformatorischen Neuansatz* (Berlin, 1966), 130-135; R. Bäumer, "Luthers Ansichten über die Irrtumsfähigkeit des Konzils und ihre theologiegeschichtlichen Grundlagen," *Wahrheit und Verkündigung. Michael Schmaus zum 70. Geburtstag* (Paderborn, 1967), 987-1003, esp. pp. 997-999; *Martin Luther und der Papst,* (2nd ed.; Münster, 1970), 24-25, 28, 31, 52.
[3] The full wording is found in Panormitanus' (or "abbas' ") commentary on c. 4 (*significasti*) X. I. 6 and is accessible in K. W. Noerr, *Kirche und Konzil bei Nicolaus*

add that the reformer's concept of scriptural authority was certainly not derived from the canon lawyers. Nevertheless, it remains a
noteworthy fact, not fully explored as yet, that Luther felt his appeal to the overriding authority of the Bible was supported by a
canonistic tradition. Was his assumption correct? The following
observations will attempt to shed a little more light on a particular
aspect of this question, namely, how the teaching to which Luther
referred was interpreted in the period immediately preceding the
Reformation. Accordingly, first we must indicate briefly the
original context of the canonistic statement in question. The major
portion of this article will then be devoted to an analysis of a
selected number of reactions to this teaching in the fifteenth and
early sixteenth centuries. We shall conclude with a suggestion that
at least one aspect of Ockhamist thought had a significant impact in
the early Reformation.

The canonistic idea of the Scriptures as a corrective norm of doctrine ultimately goes back to Gratian's *Decretum.* It presupposes,
of course, the concept of the Scriptures as a fundamental authority
for, and a constitutive norm of, church doctrine. Professor Tierney
has shown that there is abundant evidence for "sola scriptura" in
medieval canon law.[4] Gratian in distinctions 1, 5, 6, 8-11, 19, 20 and
elsewhere, as well as the subsequent interpretive tradition, make it
clear that the canonical scriptures were regarded as the source and
norm of faith by which even the highest ecclesiastical authority was
bound.[5] Leaving aside the complex question of whether the sufficiency of the Bible as the source of faith was unambiguously upheld
by the canonists down to the Reformation period, we will note that
from the *Decretum* there also derived a tradition which insisted on
the corrective function of the biblical norm. In D. 20, for example,
Gratian discussed the relative weight of pontifical decisions and

---

de Tudeschis (Panormitanus) (Köln/Graz, 1964), 104-106. The crucial portion: "papa
potest...de haeresi iudicari...puto tamen quod si papa moveretur melioribus rationibus et authoritatibus quam concilium, quod standum esset sententiae suae,
nam et concilium potest errare, sicut alias erravit" (reference to the matrimonial
case discussed in C. 36 q. 2, cc. 8, 11 and referred to in the Glossa Ordinaria, c.1 D.
20). "Nam in concernentibus fidem, etiam dictum unius privati esset praeferendum
dicto papae, si ille moveretur melioribus rationibus et authoritatibus novi et veteris
testamenti quam papa." Later on: "dico, quod licet concilium generale repraesentet
totam ecclesiam universalem, tamen in veritate ibi non est vere universalis ecclesia,
sed repraesentative"..."unde possibile est, quod fides non deficit in ecclesia, sicut
ius universitatis potest residere in uno solo aliis peccantibus....Hoc patuit post pas-
sionem Christi, nam fides remansit dumtaxat in Beata Virgine...." The commentary
was begun in 1421 (p. 5).'
[4] "'Sola Scriptura' and the Canonists," *Studia Gratiana,* 11 (1967), 345-366;
Origins of Papal Infallibility, 15-31.
[5] "'Sola Scriptura,'" 352-262.

biblical expositions of the learned exegetes (i.e., the Church Fathers). In judicial matters, he stated, the pope should be preferred to the exegete, since the pope has been given the "key of power," while in matters of scriptural interpretation, however, the Fathers should be preferred to the pope.[6] The Decretists elaborated certain implications. For example, what if a particular exegesis and a papal decision touching the same matter proved to be in conflict? In an influential passage, the *Glossa Ordinaria* argued that in judicial cases the legislator is to be followed unless the respective Patristic authority is supported by biblical evidence.[7] However, Decretists and Decretalists tended to ascribe to official (conciliar or papal) decisions a higher authority *in matters of faith.*[8]

By the early fifteenth century papal plenitude of power had for well-known reasons been rendered doubtful both in theory and fact; even conciliar inerrancy was being disputed, and the whole question of supreme doctrinal authority in the church had been reopened. In this situation Nicholas de Tudeschis offered what he himself once described as a rather novel theory ("*magis novum*") in which he made use of the aforementioned dictum of the Glossa Ordinaria. The pope, he conceded, can be tried for heresy, according to c. 6 (*si papa*) D. 40. However, he suggested that in the case of a disagreement between pope and council, the pope ought to be preferred to a council if he (the pope) was armed with better reasons and biblical authorities, all the more so since a council, too, was liable to err in a matter of faith.[9] Thus his famous dictum had a conservative rather than a revolutionary meaning. He was really thinking of the pope when he formulated the maxim that anyone (presumably a doctor) armed

---

[6] *Dictum ante* c. 1 D. 20. For an interpretation see B. Tierney, " '*Sola Scriptura*' " 356, and "Ockham, the Conciliar Theory, and the Canonists," *J. Hist. of Ideas* 15 (1954), 40-70, esp. pp. 47-48. Cf. also C. Mounier, *Les sources patristiques du droit de l'église du VIIIe au XIIIe siècle* (Mulhouse, 1957), 183-204.

[7] *Decretum Gratiani...una cum glossis* (Lyons, 1613), col. 89, on c.1 D. 20 ad v. illorum: "His videtur, quod potius iudicandum sit secundum illum, qui innititur auctoritati Hieron. vel Aug. quod verum est nisi Augustin iuvetur auctoritate no. vel vet. Test. vel etiam aliquo canone" etc., referring to the precedent c. 8, c.11 36 q. 2

[8] See Tierney, " '*Sola Scriptura*' " 357-358.

[9] Mansi, *Sacrorum conciliorum nova et amplissima collectio*, t. 30 (Venice, 1792), col. 1186-1188 (Panormitanus, Consilium "Episcopus") at col. 1187: "Dico etiam unum, quod videbitur magis novum, quod si papa etiam in facto fidei moveretur melioribus rationibus et authoritatibus, quam concilium, standum esset diffinitioni papae." The 'novelty' may also refer to the Ockhamist tradition in which all individual components of his teaching were already present. However, the theory seems to owe its precise canonistic formulation to Tudeschis' combinatory gift. The author of this article has been unable to find it elsewhere in the considerable body of contemporary canonistic literature. Cf. above note 3. For a detailed interpretation see K.D. Noerr, op. cit., 104-133. Cf. also my "Scripture and Church in the Later Middle Ages: The Canonist 'Panormitanus' and the Problem of Scriptural Authority," *Concordia Theological Monthly*, 38 (1967), pp. 234-241.

with better reasons, and authorities of the New and Old Testament, had to be given pride of place. Yet Panormitanus himself opened the door to a more radical interpretation by formulating this theory in quite general terms and, moreover, by combining it with the idea of the remnant church which he adopted apparently under Ockhamist influence.[10] According to the Ockhamist version of this ancient idea, which was also subscribed to by Panormitanus, the true faith may be preserved in one sole individual, as was the case at the time of Christ's passion when only the blessed Virgin remained faithful. This consideration would have led ultimately to a complete separation of the realm of faith from the realm of jurisdiction.[11] However, neither Panormitanus nor any of his canonistic followers even remotely thought of denying the hierarchical order or the doctrinal tradition of the Catholic church. Moreover, at the Council of Basel, Panormitanus later reversed his position on doctrinal infallibility and affirmed conciliar inerrancy in matters of faith.[12]

A full discussion of the ecclesiology of Nicholas de Tudeschis would transcend the scope of this contribution. Suffice it to say that his theory concerning the overriding force of better scriptural insight proved to be a provocative teaching. It attracted the attention of canonists and theologians and was frequently discussed or alluded to in subsequent debates, often without regard to its original context and author.

First, let us consider a few reactions from the period of the Council of Basel. Juan de Segovia (D. after 1456), the prominent spokesman of the rump council, could be expected to disagree with the earlier opinions of his colleague and fellow cardinal at Basel, Nicholas de Tudeschis. He consistently identified the powers of the general council with those residing in the church universal. Accordingly he insisted on the infallibility of a general council (irrespec-

---

[10]Cf. Ockham, *Dialogus* I, 5, c. 32, in M. Goldast, *Monarchia S. R. Imperii* (Frankfurt/M., 1614), p. 503. Simlarly Conrad of Gelnhausen, Noerr, op. cit., p. 132 n. 57) or Pierre d'Ailly. Cf. P.E. Sigmund, *Nicholas of Cusa and Medieval Political Thought* (Cambridge, Mass., 1963), 103. On the theme of Mary's fidelity under the cross - the archetype of the remnant church - see Y.M.-J. Congar, "Incidence ecclésiologique d'un thème de dévotion marial", *Mélanges de science religieuse*, 8 (1951), 277-292.

[11]Noerr, op. cit., 133: "Der Glaube zerreisst die Fesseln des Institutionalismus." The voice of the layman "ist ausserhalb des gewaltigen Gebaeudes kirchlicher popestas zu horen," 176.

[12]*Deutsche Reichstagsakten* t. 16, 2. Haelfte, (ed. H. Herre, and L. Quidde (1957), p. 491, 15 (1442). See also Noerr, op. cit., p. 132. M. Watanabe, "Authority and Consent in Government: Panormitanus, Aeneas Sylvius, Cusanus," *J. Hist. Ideas*, 217-236, esp. p. 227, states that Panormitanus' "ideas concerning church government are ambiguous and flexible," in contrast to Noerr's more persuasive interpretation of his theories as basically consistent. Both authors tend to ascribe his change of views to political exigencies. Tudeschis was then a representative of Alfons V of Aragon, a supporter of the rump council. But does this fact explain entirely a modification of doctrine in so important a point?

tive of papal approval). He angrily dismissed as absurd the arguments against conciliar inerrancy inasmuch as these were based on the idea that the church-at-large or even the remnant church was the sole subject of the continuity of faith. Without an unerring tribunal, the faith and indeed everything in the church would be rendered utterly uncertain, a familiar argument of in-fallibilism of whatever shading. His solution instead lay in a combination, or re-combination, of *fides* and *potestas* within the framework of his conciliarist constitutional concept. Not surprisingly, this led him to reaffirm the theological doctrine, widely held,[13] that it was only through the church (i.e., for Segovia, the council) that one can gain absolute certainty concerning the extent and content of the canonical scriptures. There is no room here for an overriding claim that *anyone*, even if he be the pope, can be armed with a special or better insight into scriptures.[14]

It was not so easy for the theoreticians in the camp of Eugenius IV to come to grips with the issue raised by Panormitanus. On the one hand they naturally tended to reduce conciliar authority; on the other hand the lessons of the past and, of couse, the weight of c.6 (*si papa*), D. 40, on the heretical pope made many Eugenists hesitate to ascribe to the pope infallible doctrinal authority. The following examples may serve to illustrate the varieties of solutions attempted in the matter of "Bible and Magisterium" by supporters of a papalist position.

An early manifestation of the papalist dilemma can be found in the anonymous treatise *de potestate papae et concilii* composed in 1434.[15] In summary, its author tended to locate supreme doctrinal authority in the pope. General councils have erred in the past. The pope (as pope) is more likely to enjoy preservation from error as long as he does not bolt his heart against divine grace. However, it cannot be taken for granted that a pope will persevere in the *fides formata*. An erring pope needs to be corrected (not judged) by a successor or a council. Thus the church ought to recognize a process of mutual correction of popes and councils. (This idea was advocated

[13]Cf. H.A. Oberman, *The Harvest of Medieval Theology* (Cambridge, Mass., 1963), ch. 11 *passim*.
[14]For the observations above see *Monumenta Conciliorum Saeculi XV, Concilium Basileense*, vol. III part 3 (Vienna, 1895), *Historia Gestorum Generalis Synodi Basileensis*, (ed. E. Birk and R. Beer) t. 2, book 17. Although Panormitanus is not mentioned by name, certain allusions betray familiarity with his theories.
[15]Edited as a work of Torquemada by J. Friedrich (Innsbruck, 1871). Ascribed to Raphael de Pornaxio, O.P., by R. Creytens in *Archivum Fratrum Predicatorum*, 13 (1943), 108 ff., disputed by L. Robles, "El Catalan Juan de Casanova," *Studium*, 6 (1966), 309 ff.; cf. R. Bäumer, *Annuarium Historiae Conciliorum*, (1969), 288, n. 108, and *Nachwirkungen*, 184, n. 143. An analysis of the treatise is found in U. Horst, "Papst und Konzil nach Raphael de Pornaxio, O. P.," *Frieburger Ztschr. f. Philosophie und Theologie*, 15 (1968), 367-402.

by other writers of this period also, as will be remembered, e.g., by
Pierre d'Ailly and, it seems, by Nicholas of Cusa at a certain point of
his career.)[16] In this connection the scriptural norm was introduced
as the ultimate criterion of truth and error. Suppose, our author
says, an opposition occurs between two councils equal in number of
members and in weight. In this case we would have to follow the one
whose desicions accord better with the Bible.[17] Indeed, in matters of
faith conciliar decisions can claim our obedience only inasmuch as
they do not conflict with the Scriptures.[18] Moreover, the author ad-
duces the Panormitan's consideration that the dictum of even one
sole doctor corroborated by scriptural testimony overrides a conciliar sentence.[19] Yet, he believes that it is impossible for successive
councils and popes to err indefinitely. Nevertheless, it is striking
that one strand in his thought points in the direction of a coex-
istence of a papalist consitutional theory and some sort of naive
"Scripture principle."

A similiar tension can be detected in the discussion of our problem
by Antoninus of Florence (d. 1459). In fact, the dilemma leads here
to an outright inconsistency.[20] On the one hand, Antoninus ascribes
to the pope the power to define doctrine: freedom from error is to be
presumed if the pope acts with the counsel and advice of the universal church (a formulation taken from Herveus Natalis[21]). On the
other hand, when he discusses the relation between pope and council, he cites verbatim the respective passages of Panormitanus
regarding conciliar and papal fallibility and the overriding force of
better scriptural argument advanced by *anyone*.[22] No attempt is
made to reconcile the two lines of thought.

A more consistent solution to the problem was elaborated by
Juan de Torquemada, the influential papalist theologian and

---

[16]Cf. Friedrich (ed.) op.cit., especially pp. 45-46, 66-67, 86. Bäumer,
Nachwirkungen, 184-187, notes frequent agreement with Panornitanus. Concerning
d'Ailly, cf. G. de Lagarde, *La naissance de l'esprit laique au déclin du moyen âge*
(Louvain/Paris, 1963), v. 331. Regarding Nicholas of Cusa, cf. Segovia, op. cit., 698,
"Invicem corrigere se posse ac debere" (1441).

[17] Friedrich (ed.), 93. This judgment would have to be made by a third council.

[18]Loc. cit. He adds the *decreta praecedentium conciliorum* as a subsidiary norm
which, however, according to the context can claim only relative validity.

[19] Op. cit., 118, without naming Panormitanus. He refers to the Glossa Ord. on c.1
D. 20.

[20] This is the persuasive suggestion of H. Horst, "Papst, Bischofe und Konzil nach
Antonion von Florenz," *Recherches de théologie ancienne et médiévale*, 32 (1965),
107.

[21]*Summa Theologica Moralis*, para. III (Verona, 1740), col. 1277. On Antoninus'
dependence on Herveus Natalis, see Horst, "Papst," pp. 88, 112-113.

[22]*Summa* III, pp. 1269-1270, cf. above note 3. Horst, "Papst," pp. 102-103 failed to
recognize the verbatim quotation from Panormitanus. Perhaps Antoninus inserted
this excerpt simply as a canonistic opinion a critical discussion of which he omitted
for some technical reason. In that case his papalist position would be more consistent.

SACRED DOCTRINE AND THE AUTHORITY OF SCRIPTURE   **61**

canonist (d. 1468). Torquemada, perhaps somewhat surprisingly, must be numbered among those late medieval authors who paid the highest tribute to the pre-eminence of Holy Writ in the church.[23] His view of the relation between scriptural and magisterial authority is expressive of the high esteem in which he held the Bible: Holy Scripture is the light and rule by which all doctrines must be examined; indeed, nothing taught, even by a Church Father, can claim validity unless corroborated by the authority of the Sacred Scripture or manifest reason.[24] Holy Scripture is the fullest and sufficient source of faith and morals (occasionally he qualifies this sufficienty, however).[25] Later explications of the faith were necessary in order to safeguard the "consonancy" of church doctrine with Scripture.[26] Accordingly, the teachings of councils and theologians are to be strictly subordinated to Holy Writ. This principle is also applied to the case of a conflict between exegetical and conciliar authority. A theologian supported by the norms of the New or Old Testament is to be preferred to a council which lacks support.[27] As for the pope, he, too, has to yield to a council or to *anyone* armed with better insight. In this connection Torquemada, like Panormitanus, mentions the instance of the fidelity of Mary who alone preserved the Catholic faith during Christ's passion.[28] These familiar considerations, however, are subject to one decisive limitation: in matters of faith the final decisions of the supreme magisterium are infallible. Torquemada locates this supreme magisterium in the Apostolic See and the "plenary" council where pope and council act in conjunction.[29] A final doctrinal

---

[23] Cf. K. Binder, "Zum Schriftbeweis in der Kirchentheologie des Kardinals Juan de Torquemada, O. P.," *Wahrheit und Verkündigung* (1967), 511-550.

[24]*In Gratiani decretorum primam commentarii* (Lyons, 1555), 40 v. (c.3 D.9): "scriptura sacra est lumen et regula: ad quam et secundum quam omnes doctrine doctorum ecclesie veniunt dirigende et examinande"..."nulli doctori creditur: nisi quatenus dictum eorum aut scripture sancte auctoritas aut manifesta ratio roborat," cf. Thomas Aquinas, *ST* I q.1 a.8 ad 2.

[25]Op. cit., Proemium a 3 r (quicquid credendum plenissime contineatur etc.), v (sufficienter tradatur disciplina morum). Elsewhere T. qualifies the sufficiency of Scripture, see *Summa de ecclesia* (infra n. 28), book IV, part II, ch.9. His treatment there of extrabiblical traditions is rather unspecific, however, if compared with other late medieval discussions of this problem.

[26] Op. cit., a 3v.

[27]Op., cit., 81 r.

[28]*Summa de ecclesia* (Venice, 1560), book III, ch. 64, 353 r, papa "etiam unicuique qui melius sentiret deberet credere" etc. The nature and order of the arguments strongly suggest dependence on the unmentioned Panormitanus.

[29]Op. cit., ch. 58, 334r-345 v, ch. 60, 347. The pope ceases to be pope if he falls into heresy, and is not to be followed if he contradicts a unanimous council, cf. P. Massi, *Magistero infallibile del papa nella teologia di Giovanni da Torquemada* (Torino, 1957), 100-101, 120-121. On this inconsistency in Torquemada's papalism see also P. de Vooght, "Esquisse d'une enquête sur le môt 'infaillibilité' durant la période scolastique," *L'Infailibilité de l'eglise,* (ed. O. Rousseau, *et al.,* Chevetogne, 1961), 139.

decision terminates the corrective process of the deliberative phase. Thus, Torquemada's answer to our question consists in a clear re-institutionalization of the canonistic 'sola scriptura.'

This solution, however, was by no means universally accepted, not even among papalists, during the half century before the Reformation. Opinions continued to differ on this matter, if indeed clear opinions were expressed at all. When we turn to the relevant sources of the last few decades before the Reformation, the first superficial impression we gain is that a "lack of clarity"[30] persists. However, we may ask whether, upon closer inspection, we cannot at least discern certain tendencies in the debate of our subject? These tendencies are not likely to coincide automatically with the divisions indicated by the rather too general terms "Papalism" and "Conciliarism." The canonists and theologians of the pre-Reformation period committed themselves often only by degrees to a particular conception of ecclesiastical polity. Moreover, in both "camps" there is to be found a variety of theories concerning infallibility. Leading spokesmen of the *conciliarist* tradition such as Jacques Almain (d. 1515) or Filippo Decio (d. 1519) were not of one opinion in this matter. A'lmain asserted conciliar inerrancy,[31] Decio questioned it,[32] thus confirming Almain's impression that the canonists, following Panormitanus, tended to deny this prerogative of a general council.[33] For different reasons *papalists* such as Cajetan joined in this denial. On the other hand, not all papalists subscribed to the pre-Vatican I version of papal infallibility which Cajetan advocated.[34] It is well known that the doctrine of papal infallibility was then only a minority opinion anyway. It was not accepted by many prominent contemporaries, including such a conspicuous figure as Adrian of Utrecht, later pope Adrian VI[35] More detailed research currently in progress will certainly give us a more

---

[30] This is the term used by Joseph Lortz in his description of the theological situation of the later Middle Ages. See especially his *The Reformation in Germany*, i., book 1.

[31] Cf. F. Oakley, "Almain and Major: Concilia Theory on the Eve of the Reformation," *AHR* 70 (1965), 679.

[32] *Super decretalibus* (Lyons, 1564), p. 90 r a (C. 4 X I 6), discussing Tudeschis' arguments.

[33] "Panormitanus in cap. Significasti de electione...dicit, et *plerique iuristae* cum eo quod falsum est, quod consilium non possit errare" etc., *Expositio de suprema potestate ecclesiastica et laica* (1512), in Goldast I, pp. 621-622. Those jurists also included the influential Piero da Monte (d. 1457), who relied on Panormitanus and Pseudo-Turrecremata, see Bäumer, *Nachwirkungen*, 190, n. 188.

[34] On Cajetan's position see O. de la Brosse, *Le pape et le concile: la comparaison de leurs pouvoirs à la veille de la Réforme* (Paris, 1965), 189-191, 328-330; G. Hennig, *Cajetan und Luther: Ein historischer Beitrag zur Begegnung von Thomismus und Reformation* (Stuttgart, 1966), 24-29.

[35] *Hadriani VI Pont. Max. quaestiones de sacramentis in IV. sententiarum lib.* (Rome, 1522?) f. 26 v a/b.

complete picture of the varieties of opinions touching this matter.[36] Naturally, the further discussion of the relationship of "Bible and Magisterium" and specifically the corrective function of the biblical norm, did not remain unaffected by the ecclesiological divergencies. The state of the respective debate on the very eve of the Reformation may be summarized in two observations. First, the idea that the Bible as the principal, if not only,[37] source of revelation provides a corrective for the church magisterium, wherever located, was generally upheld by the canon laywers. Any deviation from scriptural truth in matters of doctrine cannot be tolerated and must be corrected in one way or another. Furthermore, there was a widespread willingness to admit (theoretically at least) that an insight based on better scriptural authority must be given due weight in deciding doctrinal, as well as other, matters. At the same time the corrective function of the scriptural norm was subject to specification or limitation according to the different theories concerning magisterial authority. The more clearly a particular concept regarding the locus and scope of unerring teaching authority was elaborated, the more the potentially revolutionary implications were eliminated from the canonistic "Scripture principle." It appears, however, that the process of clarification in this respect was more advanced in the theological than in the canonistic contributions to the discussion of our problem in the phase immediately preceding the Reformation. The following examples can serve to illustrate this situation.

Two canonistic opinions from the end of the fifteenth century are indicative of the respective problem in canon law: Felinus Sandaeus (d. 1503, as bishop of Lucca) gained fame as the author of a commentary on the Decretals. His frequent reliance on Nicholas de Tudeschis notwithstanding, he betrays an inclination toward a

---

[36] Cf. the various publications by R. Bäumer, U. Horst, P. de Booght, *et al.* The volume edited by E. Castelli, *L'infaillabilité: son aspect philosphique et théologique* (Paris, 1970), contains only scattered articles on the history of the concept. But in the last three years interest in that history has intensified thanks to the "infallibility debate" provoked by H. Küng's well-known 'inquiry' and the numerous reactions to it. Aside from the study by Tierney which was undertaken independently of Küng's inquiry, no comprehensive history of either the origins or the development of the concept has as yet emerged.

[37] The problem of a "second source of revelation," which in recent debates has been given in my opinion an undeserved prominence is not a subject of this article. While there are indications that the fifteenth century canonists did not discard such a source altogether, it appears that theology had taken the lead in the elaboration of this problem. The acceptance of extrabiblical revealed truths did not necessarily imply that the magisterium enjoyed discretionary power to authenticate such truths ad libitum. This point has not always been considered adequately in recent studies dealing with the problem of *tradition* in the later middle ages. Besides, most of these publications cannot be said to have done justice to the canonists. Tierney, in his "'Sola Scriptura,'" provided salutary corrective.

"papalist" position.[38] Nevertheless, he felt compelled to admit that in matters of faith the pope is liable to err, and he seemed to think that this must be said not only of a pope as a private person but also of a pope acting in his official capacity.[39] Normally, however, the pope enjoyed supreme doctrinal authority. Therefore, papal decisions would override Patristic expositions (generalizing, one can say any theological interpretations). Felinus added the familiar exception: If a dictum of the sacred doctors is grounded in biblical authority, it must prevail, according to the *Glossa Ordinaria* on the *Decretum* and Panormitanus. "For if (the pope's decision) contradicts the New and Old Testament, it is clear that he is in error." Moreover, as a general rule the Patristic authority has precedence over papal decisions in matters of scriptural interpretation (cf. Gratian, c. (*de libelis*), D. 20). Yet, this rule was qualified in turn: If scriptural interpretations touch upon things necessary for salvation, the pope is to be preferred to the exegete, and if the pope errs in such matters, he is to be corrected only by a council.[40] Thus Felinus was able to preserve the corrective Scripture principle, although in a mitigated form. His discussion was restricted to the classical case of conflicting Patristic and papal statements; and the ultimate authority of the Magisterium in matters of faith was upheld, in accordance with the classical Decretalist tradition. The dangers of a more radical interpretation of the *Glossa Ordinaria* and Panormitanus were forestalled. The still cautious attitude toward the latter's dictum was unmistakable.

By contrast, cardinal Sangiorgio (d. 1509) was quite unreserved in his affirmation of the supremacy of Scripture. This we would perhaps not expect in a canonist who was elevated to the purple by Alexander VI. Indeed, Sangiorgio is generally regarded as a papalist.[41] But, then, again "papalism" does not necessarily mean a commitment to one particular position in the matter of Scripture and Magisterium. According to Sangiorgio, the highest doctrinal authority is exercised by pope and council. In case a pope deviates from previous conciliar pronouncements, he can be proceeded against by a general council. This would indicate a certain superiority of the general council. With Tudeschis, however, Sangiorgio considered the possibility that in a matter of faith a pope could be moved by better reasons and authorities; in that case, *he* would have to be followed.[42] For councils, too, may err, inerrancy being an

[38]See H. Jedin, *Geschichte des Konzils von Trient*, i. (2nd ed.; Freiburg, 1951), 76.
[39]*Commentaria*, pars I (Basel, 1568), col. 30 (c. 1 X I 1 ad v. una, with reference to Dominicus de S. Geminiano).
[40]Op. cit., col. 84 (c.5 X I 2).
[41]See Jedin, op. cit., 76-77.
[42]*Commentaria super decretorum volumina* (Pavia, 1497), f. k 6 v a (c. 9 D. 19).

attribute only of the universal ("Roman") church-at-large. Accordingly, Sangiorgio envisaged a system of mutual correction of ecclesiastical authorities. A pope deviating from faith would be subject to conciliar correction; an erring council may in turn be corrected by a pope armed with better insight and in general by exegetic authority based on the *jus divinum*. On the other hand, Sangiorgio stated that councils can claim the obedience of faith, just as Holy Writ does, inasmuch as both have received the sanction of the church. Nonetheless, the gospels are of infinitely higher dignity: more reverence is due to the words of a king than to those of his messengers.[44] In this sense Sangiorgio taught a rigorous subordination of all ecclesiastical authority to Holy Writ: all authority that deviates from Sacred Scripture is to be rejected.[45] He does not develop the implications of these considerations which certainly contain elements of a "Scripture principle." But an apparent tension remained between these elements and his rather conservative conception of ecclesiastical jurisdiction. We seem to have returned to the original dilemma.

The lack of clarity and agreement on this issue is reflected also in the penitential "Summae,'" i.e., the heavily canonistical handbooks or dictionaries for the clergy, of the late fifteenth and early sixteenth centuries. The *Summs Angelica*, the *Summa Baptistiniana*, and the *Summa Tabiena*, for example, all refer to the dictum of Panormitanus when discussing our problem. While the *Summa Angelica* and the *Summa Baptistiniana* on the whole accepted his view that even the highest magisterial authority (pope with council) was subject to correction by better scriptural argument, the *Summa Tabiena*, which was dedicated to cardinal Cajetan, strongly disagreed with Nicholas de Tudeschis and supported Cajetan's doctrine of papal infallibility.[46] (The *Summa Sylvestrina* will be discussed in the next section because of the rank of Prierias as a theologian).

Because of their importance, the ideas of Panormitanus eventually had to be disputed and critically discussed by a number of *theologians* during the years immediately preceding the Reformation controversies. Cajetan, for example, found occasion to com-

---

[43]Loc. cit.: "Nam concilium errare potest" etc. "Et contra si papa in fide erraret posset corripi a concilio," and if persistent in his error, even tried and punished (in contrast to the statement to which Jedin refers, op. cit., p. 77).

[44]Op. cit., f. h 7 r b (c. 2 D. 15), where he refers to Augustine's famous statement in the version "evangelio non crederem nisi ecclesia illud reciperet."

[45]Op. cit., f. d r a (c. 3 D. 9): "nam cum auctoritas sacre scripture sit potior inter omnes scripturas...quecunque auctoritas deviaret ab ista esset reicienda." (d. 1495)

[46]Angelo Carleto di Chivasso, *Summa de casibus conscientiae* (Strassburg, 1512), ff. 73 v a, 218 r b; Baptista de Salis Trovamala (d. 1494), *Summa casuum conscientiae* (Novi, 1484), ff. u 6 v b/7 r a; Johannes de Tabia, *Summa casuum conscientiae* (Bologna, 1517), ff. 94v-95r.

plain about the fact that many authors thought it legitimate to prefer individual teachers to the pope, even in matters of faith. Yet he himself made use of a different version of the Panormitan argument in his controversy with Almain when he stated that if a single Patristic authority based on Holy Scripture could prevail against a conciliar decision, how much more must the cloud of witnesses against the Councils of Constance and Basel weigh?[47] As far as papal decisions were concerned, there could of course never be a ultimate conflict between scriptural truth and doctrinal definitions.

Similarly, Sylvester Prierias (d. 1523) made a timely attempt to check the influence of Nicholas de Tudeschis. In his *Summa Summarum* (1514; 2nd ed. 1518), he took issue with the same statement to which Luther appealed in 1518 and later. If church doctrine is an infallible rule of faith according to Thomas Aquinas, he argues then inerrancy must be conceded to the supreme magisterium. This magisterium is exercised by the council and by the pope (acting together with, or even without, a council).[48] Councils do err sometimes, he conceded; yet they do not perservere in their errors. At this point he felt he should do justice to the corrective norm of the Scriptures. Like Torquemada, he admitted that in the preparatory stage of a doctrinal decision the sentence of a council may be corrected through *any learned man's better scriptural insight* inspired by the Holy Spirit.[49] Naturally, such corrective process reaches the terminal point when the final pronouncement is made. Consequently, an authoritative papal interpretation would *always* override the dictum of an exegete, unless the pope taught something manifestly contradicting Holy Writ.[50] Only in this sense was Prierias willing to retain a residual Scripture principle.

The theological revision received a forceful canonistic support in the monumental work on conciliar authority which cardinal Domenico Jacobazzi (d. 1528) composed in the period of the Fifth Lateran Council.[51] Jacobazzi shared the opinion that general councils, if considered in themselves, did not enjoy the privilege of inerrancy. Moreover, he agreed with Nicholas de Tudeschis that any

---

[47]De la Brosse, op. cit., 295 *(De comparatione auctoritatis papae et concilii,* 11, 172, in the Edition by V.M.J. Pollet (Rome, 1936).
[48]On Prierias' view of doctrinal authority see H. A. Oberman, "Wittenbergs Zweifrontenkrieg gegen Prierias und Eck: Hintergrund und Entscheidungen des Jahres 1518," *Zeitschrift für Kirchengeschichte,* 80 (1969), 331-358, esp. pp. 336-337.
[49]*Summa summarum que Zylvestrina dicitum* (2nd ed.; Strassburg, 1518), f. 202 v a, cf. the conclusions contra Panormitanum, f. 73 r a.
[50]Op. cit., f. 348 v b (against Panormitanus and the Glossa Ordinaria on the Decretum).
[51]*Tractatus de concilio,* published with certain additions in 1538 and included in Mansi's *Collectio,* Introductio, 1-580. Cf. Jedin, op. cit., 77, 494, n. 71. On Jacobazzi, see J. Klotzner, *Kardinal Domenico Jacobazzi und sein Konzilswerk* (Rome, 1948). Jacobazzi's work proved influential down to 1870.

person armed with better reasons and biblical authorities was to be given preference even in questions touching faith.[52] And, indeed, why should the pope not be this person? By a characteristic turn, however, he argued, correcting Panormitanus, that the pope enjoyed overriding authority of necessity, since it is incumbent upon the head of the church and the vicar of Christ to pronounce final judgment in matters of faith *de plenitudine potestatis*. And in this case the assistance of the Holy Spirit was to be presumed.[53] It was not only possible, but necessary, that official teaching and correct scriptural interpretation should coincide.

However, such renewed attempts at clarification, whatever their merits, certainly came too late to prevent a different reading and use of the canonistic tradition in question by the writers of the early Reformation. But a few tentative conclusions may be drawn from this inevitably selective survey of pre-Reformation opinions on one complex aspect of doctrinal and ecclesiastical authority.

First, the canonistic theory concerning the overriding normative force of better scriptural insight, as enunciated by Panormitanus, underwent a variety of interpretations and modifications during the later fifteenth and sixteenth centuries. In the light of this inconclusive debate it would seem that Luther's appeal to the original teaching of Nicholas de Tudeschis was by no means wholly unacceptable by contemporary orthodox canonistic standards. Clearly no consensus had as yet been reached on this question, any more than on the related matters of doctrinal authority and inerrancy. Even Luther's tendency to separate the sphere of faith from the realm of hierarchical jurisdiction appears to have been nothing entirely novel in the light of canonistic thought. However, this tendency contrasted obviously with the ecclesiological presuppositions of the more influential representatives of the conciliarist or papalist traditions. The question also remains whether there was more than a superficial connection between the respective strand in the canonistic heritage of the later middle ages and Luther's incipient ideas regarding these problems (or, for that matter, Karlstadt's ideas which may have directed Luther's attention to the relevant passage in Panormitanus).

Secondly, and incidental to the preceding observation, Luther's remark that "all" teachers of theology and *law* denied conciliar inerrancy, although hyperbolic, is much better supported by the evidence found in fifteenth century sources than has often been sup-

---

[52]Mansi, pp. 242 b A, cf. pp. 239 b A/B, 240 a D, and elsewhere.

[53]"Si ergo hoc contingere potest in una privata persona, quanto magis in papa? Qui est caput ecclesiae," etc., op. cit., 239 b B/C (reference to Nicholas de Tudeschis (abbas); cf. 242 b D. There are, however, cases in which the pope is subject to conciliar correction and action, see the detailed discussion of Jacobazzi's rather involved position in Klotzner, op. cit., 160-163.

posed.[54] Needless to add, Luther's early opposition to the concept of *papal* infallibility was nothing unusual at all by contemporary canonistic and theological standards.

Finally, the teaching of Nicholas de Tudeschis to which Luther referred clearly showed the influence of certain ideas of William of Ockham. In the tradition of fifteenth century canonistic thought, therefore, an Ockhamist element was present[55] which the reformer made use of in the early controversies, especially with regard to the questions of the continuity of faith and supremacy of Holy Writ. In view of this fact we may again have to re-assess the significance for the the Protestant Reformation of the multivalent heritage of Ockham, and the channels of its transmission, in the matter of Scripture and Tradition.

---

[54]The motives for disputing conciliar inerrancy varied considerably, as we have seen. Cf. also Bäumer, "Luthers Ansichten," 997-1003.

[55]The indications above make it clear that the Ockhamist element was by no means confined to the teachings of Nicholas de Tudeschis, as C. Tecklenburg-Johns seems to suggest, op. cit., 131-132. For a brief discussion of the influence of Ockham's ecclesiological ideas in 15th century canonists thought see G. de Lagarde, op. cit., 323-337.

5 Universities as Religious Authorities in the later Middle Ages and Reformation

by Guy Fitch Lytle
University of Texas, Austin

Almost from their earliest days of incorporation, universities had been assigned, or had assumed, the power to proclaim and explain orthodox religious beliefs and to proscribe heterodox opinions. It could even be argued that such a role was an essential cause of their creation. Of course universities did much else in late medieval society. Primarily they educated future members of the ecclesiastical hierarchy, church administration, and royal bureacracies, as well as parish priests, monks and friars, schoolmasters, and an increasing number of laymen, both gentlemen and bourgeois. They made themselves available to be consulted on legal, political, diplomatic, and medical matters, as well as on questions of doctrine. They formed *national* educated elites which would interact with, but also transcend, regional interests and popular cultures. Neither the medieval nation-state nor the Roman Catholic church, as they developed, were really conceivable without the universities.[1] But in an age of high spiritual

[1]On medieval universities, while H. Rashdall, *The Universities of Europe in the Middle Ages* (Oxford, rev. ed. 1936), 3 vols., remains an essential reference work, now see also J. Verger, *Les universités au Moyen Age* (Paris, 1973) and A.B. Cobban, *The Medieval Universities* (London, 1975) and the works cited in their bibliographies. Although nothing similar yet exists for the Renaissance or Reformation periods, see J. Paquet and J. IJsewijn (eds.), *Les universités à la fin du Moyen Age* (Louvain, 1978). A very interesting, though seldom cited, approach to medieval and Reformation universities is G.H. Williams, *Wilderness and Paradise in Christian Thought* (New York, 1962), esp. Part Two: "The Theological Idea of the University," esp. 158 ff. For the most recent research, see the annual bibliographies, *The History of European Universities: Work in Progress and Publications* (ed. J.M. Fletcher; Birmingham, Eng., 1977-), and the new annual periodical, *History of Universities* (ed. C. Schmitt, *et al.*), which will commence in 1981. Also still very useful for the topics discussed in this paper are the bibliographical notes in E. Delaruelle, *et al., L'Église au temps du Grand Schisme et de la crise conciliare (1378-1449)* (Paris, 1962-4), ii. 459 ff. For the specific points made in this paragraph, as they affected one country, see my book, *University Scholars and English Society, 1300-1550,* which should appear next year.

aspirations, with a genuine taste and ability for precise, formal intellectual definitions and a confidence in the accessibility of *truth,* we can understand how universities could legitimately come to be viewed, and to view themselves, as essential bodies of theological experts who could serve as religious authorities for all of Christendom.

Such a role was not always easy. Universities were almost as often the wet-nurses of heretics as the nurturers of inquisitors. It is perhaps a telling point about the nature of universities that virtually no major intellectual figure from Abelard, Aquinas, and Ockham through Wyclif, Erasmus, and Luther to Descartes, Pascal, and Hobbes escaped the censure of one academic body or another. (It is also important that most of these philosophers and theologians spent considerable time and effort trying to avoid, refute, or appeal the condemnations and prohibitions cast against them.) Universities themselves often had difficulty reaching a collective decision. Rival philosophical *viae* or the sibling competitions of seculars vs. regulars, Dominicans vs. Franciscans, or some such conflict, made concensus elusive. External conditions—the hostility of prelates, royal interventions, the pride of charismatic intellectuals under attack—and the lack of effective enforcement procedures also limited the practical impact of university decisions. Yet, with rare exceptions, universities (even Oxford after Wyclif and Prague after Hus) remained constantly aware of their religious function and steadfast in their opposition to all heresy. This role as intellectual arbitors and theological censors—that is, as *professors of orthodoxy*—provided much of the ecclesiastical status and institutional-religious self-conceptions of late medieval and early Reformation universities.

Much research remains to be done on individual controversies, and many valid distinctions must elsewhere be drawn between the activities of different universities, in different countries or different centuries. Here we must limit our consideration to some general perspectives on how universities as institutions (and how certain faculties of theology in particular) came, both by conscious assertion and by gradual practice, to be a major link in the chain of authority; how, in a time of confusion and widespread debate about the nature and locus of such authority, the universities and faculties proliferated in number and laid claim to even wider authority and respect; how they exercised such authority and power; and finally, on what grounds their authority was challenged, undermined, and fragmented in the early days of the Reformation. The story of how the whole process reemerged, in some ways even stronger, after the establishment of book censorship, the decisions of the Council of Trent, and the development of Protestant "scholasticism" in its own universities, must await another occasion.

Until recently, far more historians of this period have concentrated on the problem of the *reform of authority* than on the attitudes and means of the *authority to reform* (i.e., to restore something which had become deformed). But in a still strongly hierarchical society, one which in addition generally accepted the notion of the existence of one objective truth, those in authority (civil, ecclesiastical, and intellectual) had obligations to establish orthodoxy and to defend proper beliefs against any threat whether from the mis- or badly-informed or the nefarious deviationist.

Theologians had a role in society. It was not that of the priest (although most were so ordained) who must relate the powers of salvation and reassurance inherent in the sacraments to those who could receive them. It was not that of the village cunning man who tapped the potency of the supernatural world for the purposes of the here and now. Rather the university theologian had the task of explaining to mankind, in as coherent a fashion as possible, the nature of the deity and the verities of revelation. It was a role fraught with danger and, quite possibly, with arrogance. A lifetime in conversation with ultimate questions was likely to render many theologians incapable of casual discourse and, perhaps at times, of many manifestations of tolerance and kindness. They were not pastors. Theologians were there to make sure that, when laymen or priests or their colleagues thought and spoke about God and Christian belief, they got it right. It was the theologians' Christian duty to educate where possible; but, in any case, to use the oft quoted words of Luke 14:23, they were to "compel them to come in." The penalties imposed on those who continued in the ways of unacceptable error or inexcusable disobedience were meant to serve two purposes: in the first place, *educational,* to the culprit himself and to those who observed his correction; and in the second place, *motivational,* to give a person who was insensitive to other considerations, a compelling reason for compliance.

As we have said, all of this implies an attitude toward the existence of *truth* and the positive value of *orthodoxy*. The intense concern about these things among late medieval and Reformation theologians was compounded of two things: care for souls and respect for the *magisterium* and spiritual tradition. Doctrines could change in light of new knowledge or careful reinterpretation, but it was hard to set aside old ways without some compelling authority to do so. Holy ideas, like sacred places, were to be protected from defilement. Tradition was one means to affect this protection. Rigidity, repression, and censorship were others. Sometimes a threatening situation could lead to hostility and obstructionism toward any new methods, new questions, and new languages which others sought to apply to old truths. The humanist critics, however much they have been misunderstood by modern minds, did have some valid objections to late medieval university scholasticism. But the proliferation of concerns about orthodoxy and heresy, about purity and contagion of mind and belief, does not necessarily denote the existence of a rigid mental outlook or a stable social context.

The contrary may very well be true, since orthodoxy relates to a psychology of truth, power, and commitment which historians of the late medieval and early modern periods have not yet fully worked out. But it is clear that new paradigms of orthodoxy, unlike traditions, can come into articulated being virtually overnight, and that rival orthodoxies can be the most virulent of antagonists. This was the world the theologians had, in part, created: one which they both lived in and policed.[2]

Universities as institutions and theology as a science and an academic discipline developed simultaneously and with considerable interacton in the twelfth and thirteenth centuries.[3] The position of theologians and theological faculties as experts and authorities in the later Middle Ages would be inconceivable without this foundation.

---

[2] I am obviously somewhat indebted both to the writings of T.S. Kuhn, esp. *The Structure of Scientific Revolutions* (Chicago, 2nd ed. 1970) (as well as to the considerable debate this book has provoked) and to those of Mary Douglas, esp. *Purity and Danger* (New York, 1966). On *heresy*, see both the texts and the bibliographies of G. Leff, *Heresy in the Later Middle Ages* (Manchester, 1967); M.D. Lambert, *Medieval Heresy* (London, 1977); and J. Le Goff (eg.), *Héresies et sociétés dans l'Europe pre-industrielle, 11ᵉ-18ᵉ siecles* (Paris, 1968). On *orthodoxy* in its late medieval context, see, e.g., R. Kieckhefer, *Repression of Heresy in Medieval Germany* (Philadelphia, 1979) and L.G. Duggan, "The Unresponsiveness of the Late Medieval Church: a reconsideration," *Sixteenth Cent. J.*, 9 (1978), 3-26. (Although they may perhaps be somewhat related, my conception of "orthodoxy" and its psychological, as well as intellectual, influence is distinct from the new sense of *accuracy* (in textual transmission and thought) which developed with the invention of the new medium of print: see E.L. Eisenstein, *The Printing Press as an Agent of Change* (Cambridge, 1979), 2 vols. Despite the importance of these volumes, much still remains to be done on the relationships between universities and print.) On the closely related concept of *tradition*, see Y.M.-J. Congar, O.P., *Tradition and Traditions* (London, 1966); J.L. Murphy, *The Notion of Tradition in John Driedo* (Milwaukee, 1959) (and the review in *Theologische Zeitschrift*, 17 (1969), 231-234); and G.Tavard, *Holy Writ and Holy Church* (New York, 1959) (and the rev. art. by R. McA. Brown, " 'Tradition' as a Problem for Protestants," *Union Sem. Q. R.* (Jan., 1961), 197-211). See also, R.E. Davies, *The problem of Authority in the Continental Reformation* (London, 1946); J. Lecler, *Toleration and the Reformation* (London, 1960), 2 vols.; and C. Russell, "Arguments for Religious Unity in England, 1530-1650," *J. Eccl. H.*, 18 (1967), 201-226. Finally, for a compelling statement of the mental world I am trying to suggest, see Sir Isaiah Berlin, *Against the Current* (ed. H. Hardy; London, 1979), 333f.

[3] For the development of universities as institutions, see refs. in notes 1 and 4. For theology as a science and an academic discipline in the twelfth century, see the recent volume by G.R. Evans, *Old Arts and New Theology* (Oxford, 1980), as well as, e.g., M.-D. Chenu, *Nature, Man, and Society in the Twelfth Century* (Chicago, 1968), esp. chapter 8. For the thirteenth century, see the book-length article by P. Glorieux, "Techniques et Méthodes en usage à la Faculte de Théologie de Paris, au XIIIᵉ siecle," *Archives d'Hist. doctrinale et Litt. du M.A.*, 32 (1968), 3-186; and Chenu, *La théologie comme science au XIIIᵉ siecle* (Paris, 1957). (See also note 26 below.) For a perspective very similar to mine on the relationships between the institutional and intellectual spheres, see the paper by Prof. Peter Classen (Heidelberg), "*Libertas scolastica:* scholarly privilege and academic freedom in the Middle Ages" (presented at the U. of London, March, 1980) which I hope he will publish soon in some form.

Their emergence as formal, legal corporations in the early thirteenth century gave universities official identities, continuity, the ability to make rules to govern their own affairs and members, and the power to certify intellectual competence by granting degrees. They were able to assert their freedom from control of local bishops and their officials, a necessary step toward recognition as independent authorities. By exercising their right, as a corporation, to impose *oaths* of loyalty and obedience on members, an obligaton which did not end when the student or master left the university geographically, they gained a substantial measure of control over the beliefs, or at least the public teaching or publishing, of intellectuals throughout their lives.[4] Universities, notably Paris, provided permanent gatherings of experts, whom popes and kings could consult and who could receive and authenticate opinions reached and decisions rendered elswhere.[5] In part the growth of the role of universities in the thirteenth century (again especially Paris) was due to an efflorescence of genuine intellectual brilliance, but historians have long stressed the importance of their institutional development which guaranteed the permanence of the high medieval renaissance.[6] The professionalization of the roles and status of the theologians and the definition of the nature of theology as a science, a curriculum of fairly set textbooks, and a methodology acted in a smiliar way to build the cohesion of theological faculties and to define their purposes.[7] Conflicts occured, as they always

---

[4] G. Post, "Parisian Masters as a Corporation, 1200-1246," *Speculum,* 9 (1934), 421-445; and, "Alexander III, the *licentia docendi* and the Rise of the Univerities," in *Anniversary Essays in Mediaeval History by Students of Charles Homer Haskins* (ed. C.H. Taylor and J.L. LaMonte; Boston, 1929), 255-277; A.B. Cobban, "Episcopal Control in the Mediaeval Universities of Northern Europe," *Studies in Church History,* 5(1969), 1-22 and refs. there; P. Kibre, "Academic Oaths at the University of Paris in the Middle Ages," in *Essays in Medieval Life and Thought Presented in Honor of Austin Patterson Evans* (eds. J.H. Mundy, *et al.;* New York, 1955) 123-137; A.E. Bernstein, "Magisterium and License: corporate autonomy against papal authority in the medieval University of Paris," *Viator,* 9 (1978), 291-307.

[5] See, e.g., P.R. McKeon, "The Status of the University of Paris as *Parens scientiarum:* an episode in the development of its autonomy," *Speculum,* 39 (1964), 651-675; and "Consilium Generale and Studium Generale: the transformation of doctrinal regulation in the Middle Ages," *Church History,* 35 (1966), 24-34; and examples below.

[6] See, e.g., G. Leff, *Paris and Oxford Universities in the Thirteenth and Fourteenth Centuries* (New York, 1968); M.-M. Dufeil, *Guillaume de Saint-Amour et la polémique universitaire parisienne, 1250-1259* (Paris, 1972); and the articles ed. by A. Zimmermann, *Die Auseinandersetzungen an der Pariser Universität im XIII Jahrhundert,* in *Miscellanen Mediaevalia,* 10 (1976).

[7] J. Leclercq, "L'idéal du théologian au moyen âge," *Revue des Sciences Religieuses,* 21 (1947), 121-148; R. Guelluy, "La place des théologiens dans l'Église et la société médiévals," in *Miscellanea historica in honorem Alberti De Meyer* (Louvain/Bruxelles, 1946), 571-589; G. LeBras, *"Velut Splendor Firmamenti*: le docteur dans le droit de l'Englise médiévale," in *Mélanges offerts à Etienne Gilson* (Toronto/Paris, 1959), 373-388. (Also see note 3 above.)

would, as rival faculties, masters or orders struggled for positions. The excitement inherent in new ideas and intellectual debate could produce divergent, even heretical, views which had to be corrected.[8] But even in the midst of these problems, especially in the late thirteenth century, the role of the universities as religious authorities was increasingly acknowledged. In his treatise against the mendicants in the 1280s, the imperial publicist Alexander of Roes wrote:

> Antichrist will never come as long as the Church has the (Holy) Roman Empire as a defender in things temporal and the University of the Gauls (Paris) as an adjunct in things spiritual. But when these are destroyed, when the Church, after the destruction of the Empire and the secular militia in Germany shall wish to defend herself against tyrants (or) after the University has been wrecked . . . she shall prove incapable of defending herself against heretics, then . . . that son of Perdition will come and with impunity wreak havoc on Christendom . . . . (Now) the science of the University is being converted into heresy, and these developments are the forerunners of Antichrist.[9]

Eternal vigilance, within the faculty or university itself as well as in the world outside the cloister and lecture hall, was essential if the theologians were to fulfill their religius duties adequately.

The rapid rise of universities to positions of intellectual and spiritual preeminence naturally provoked some resentment from those with commitments to other authorities. In 1290, for example, Cardinal Gaëtani (the future Boniface VIII) denounced the Parisian masters:

> You sit here in your (academic) chairs and think that Christ is ruled by your reasonings . . . . They have filled the whole world with their pestiferous teaching.[10]

But paeans of tribute, some genuine and some intended merely to flatter, were far more common. At about the same time, Ramon Lull addressed the University of Paris as the

---

[8]For the most famous case, see refs. in note 6 above, plus — most recently — J.F.Wippel, "The Condemnations of 1270 and 1277 at Paris," *J. Med. and Ren. Studies,* 7 (1977), 169-201 and E. Grant, "The Condemnation of 1277, God's Absolute Power, and Physical Thought in the Middle Ages," *Viator,* 10 (1979), 211-244 and the refs. contained in each. For a comparison, see D.A. Callus, *The Condemnation of St. Thomas at Oxford* (London, Aquinas Papers #5, 1955).

[9]H. Grundmann and H. Heimpel (eds.), *Die Schriften des Alexander von Roes* (Weimar, 1949), 98 (*Noticia seculi,* cap. 20).

[10]See J.N. Hillgarth, *Ramon Lull* and *Lullism in Fouteenth-Century France* (Oxford, 1971), 152 and n. 12.

fountain of supernatural wisdom, which has with marvellous doctrine intoxicated so many teachers at Paris (who are endowed) with such great authority . . . . Happy is the university which has brought forth so many defenders of the faith.[11]

Many similar tributes would be heard throughout the later Middle Ages.

This institutional and intellectual evolution, along with the general acceptance by contemporary men of learning of the hegemony of the universities over the trade in ideas, was certainly very important. But some quite practical considerations also enhanced the role of the *studia general* as religious authorities. If no one had needed their services, if no one had sent questions to be resolved or writings to be judged, the ambitions of the universities for such power would simply have withered. Theologians were willing to pronounce opinions on virtually anything, including tyrannicide, usury, the occult, diplomacy, ecclesiastical politics, and much else.[12] Some of the topics of their concern appear to us to be more naturally in the provenance of the legal or medical faculties. But to minds embued with religion, everything has a theological dimension. And despite the stereotype of the scholastic, hardly any late medieval intellectuals sought the luxury of pure, isolated speculation.

Of course involvement in public issues meant controversy and almost guaranteed direct intervention, or at least pressure, by kings, popes, bishops, and other interested parties. Since the privileges and immunities enjoyed by the universities relied to a large extent on continued royal and papal favor, the masters were vulnerable.[13] Still they seldom rendered totally craven decisions. In 1308, Philip IV of France arrested the Templars and sought support for his illegal action from the Paris Theology Faculty. The latter body commended him for asking their opinion

following the praiseworthy customs of your holy predecessors, inflamed with zeal for the faith, yet wishing to defend even the faith with the proper rule of reason and without usurping the right of another power, although you might command us as your clients, yet of your great condescension have preferred to ask our opinion in friendly fashion by your letters . . . .

[11]*ibid.*, 151, cf. p. 152, nn. 13-14.
[12]The chief printed source is C. duPlessis d'Argentré (ed.), *Collectio judiciorum de Novis Erroribus* . . . (Paris, 1728), 3 vols. Detailed analyses of these and other case studies, with full primary and secondary documentation, will appear in my forthcoming book, *Professors of Orthodoxy.*
[13]See P. Kibre, *Scholarly Privileges in the Middle Ages* (Cambridge, Mass.; 1962) (and note 4 above).

After a lengthy delay (due to "the importance of the affair and the absence of some of our chief members"), the faculty ("having held careful and mature and frequent deliberation over the said articles") replied. While their conclusions gave little substantive support or justification to the king's infringement of clerical immunity from secualar arrest, they applauded his attacks on heresy and scandal and couched it all in words that sound very cautious and subservient.[14]

Open disagreements with the papacy were more frequent. In 1331, the Faculty of Theology at Paris, "the permanent council of the Gauls," refused to accede to the opinion of John XXII concerning the beatific vision of the saints. In this decision, they had the support of the King, who wrote to the Pope:

> Our doctors know what ought to be believed in matters of faith better than the jurists and other clerks who inhabit your court and who know little or nothing of theology.[15]

Universities clearly lacked both ultimate spiritual authority and sufficient earthly power to enforce their own judgments without help, but they were important *practical* authorities. Like the early parliaments, they could be consulted for advice when necessary, they could articulate rhetorical and intellectual justifications for royal (or ecclesiastical) policies, and they provided a forum to try and condemn those who troubled the spiritual (and sometimes the temporal) realm. But the universities, and especially the doctors of theology, certainly considered themselves to be more than mere handmaidens; and, on more than a few occasions, their sense of their wide-ranging spiritual responsibilities combined with their limited powers to compel acceptance of their views (sometimes even on all of their own members) resulted in frustration, vindictiveness, arrogance, and impotence. But the universities had unquestionably become integral parts of the authority structure of the later Middle Ages.

During this period, universities were influential through their own actions and through the careers of their graduates who reached prominent offices. By the later fourteenth century, the higher clergy were almost all university men. Then, as now, relatively few students either wanted to stay on at the universities or were forced to choose academic careers: more money, more power, more comfort, and even perhaps less work attracted them elsewhere. Even those who did remain professors usually had at least one foot out-

---

[14]H. Denifle and A. Chatelain (eds.), *Chartularium Universitatis Parisiensis* (Paris, 1889 ff.) (=*C.U.P.*), ii. 125 ff.; M. Barber, *The Trial of the Templars* (Cambridge, 1978), esp. 81-85.

[15]d'Argentré, i. (pt. i) 316-320.

side academia, advising all and sundry or guiding a religious order. Doctors of theology influenced a variety of policy decisions, based on theories they had learned or conceived at the univrsities, from power bases as royal chaplains, diplomatic representatives to Councils, masters of the Sacred Palace, inquisitors, or just generally recognized experts on religion, politics, or the causes of floods or plagues.[16]

To analyze such activities fully would require a comprehensive social and intellectual history of the whole late medieval educated elite, but one type of theological business is worth noting in passing. From the frescoes in the cloister chapel of Sta. Maria Novella in Florence in the 1360s to a guild altarpiece in St. Peters, Louvain, a century later, theologians were quite often employed to prescribe the iconographical content and to authenticate the orthodoxy of the finished *oeuvre*.[17] Theologians and theological faculties were generally considered to be the guardians against the introduction of unwarranted novelties into Christian dogma and the confuters of heretical depravity. According to Heinrich von Oyta, the church had established universities in order to

---

[16]For a new perspective on the careers of university men, see my "The Later Careers of Oxford Students," in J. Kittelson (ed.), *Universities in Transition, 1300-1700* (Columbus, 1981) and my book *University Scholars and English Society*. Much indirect, but relevant, material is contained in A. Murray, *Reason and Society in the Middle Ages* (Oxford, 1978). For the place of university men in the church, see my "Patronage Patterns and Oxford Colleges, c. 1300-c. 1530," in *The University in Society* (ed. L. Stone; Princeton, 1974), 111-149 and the debate provoked by this article: esp. T.H. Aston, "Oxford's Medieval Alumni," *Past and Present*, 74 (1977), 3-40; Aston, G.D. Duncan and T.A.R. Evans, "The Medieval Alumni of the University of Cambridge," *ibid.*, 86 (1980), 9-86; W.J. Courtenay, "The Effect of the Black Death on English Higher Education," *Speculum*, 55(1980), 696-714; B. Dobson, "Oxford Graduates and the so-called Patronage Crisis of the later Middle Ages," in *The Church in a Changing Society* (Proceedings of the C.I.H.E.C. Conference, Uppsala, 1977) (Uppsala, 1978), 211-216. This Uppsala volume and the Louvain proceedings (see note 1 above) also contain other relevant articles about Continental universities.

[17]I am now embarking on a fairly large-scale iconographical project dealing with the relationships between theologians and patrons and artists during the later Middle Ages, Renaissance, and Reformation. For the specific examples here, see E. Bonechi, *Florence* (Florence, 1970 ed.), 150 (for directions by Fr. Zenobi da Guasconi, O.P., for Andrea di Bonaiuto); W. Stechow (ed.), *Northern Renaissance Art, 1400-1600: sources and documents* (Englewood Cliffs, N.J., 1966), 10-11 (for prescriptions by Masters Jan Vaernacker and Gillis Bailluwel, professors of theology at Louvain, to Dirk Bouts, as specified in the latter's contract with his guild patrons.) See also, S.N. Blum, *Early Netherlandish Triptychs* (Berkeley/Los Angeles, 1969), chpt. 6 and *passim*; R. Hatfield, *Botticelli's Uffizi "Adoration"* (Princeton, 1976); F. Hartt, *A History of Italian Renaissance Art* (New York/London, rev. ed. 1980), esp. 9-10 and refs. there. For another aspect, see my "Religion and the Lay Patron in Reformation England," in Guy Fitch Lytle and Stephen Orgel (eds.), *Patronage in the Age of the Renaissance* (Princeton, 1981).

nourish, increase and make acceptable true and catholic doctors who have sufficient knowledge and are able to extirpate heresy and to sow sound doctrine.[18]

One can find considerable contemporary evidence of theologians and theological faculties taking their roles very seriously and of society generally encouraging their function.

For the most part, the edicts of the universities fell into two main categories (both of which included proscriptions and prescriptions): keeping their own theological houses in order and responding to overt or perceived threats (whether intellectual or political) from outside. Success at the first of these tasks was essential for the latter. As Oxford found out, to its lasting humiliation, the taint of heresy largely silenced a university's religious influence.[19]

Purity could be preserved and encouraged in a number of ways: control over textbooks; the assignment of specific questions to be covered in lectures; close supervision, and if necessary correction, of the teaching of young bachelors.[20] Masters could gather together to hear a public reading of a new work by one of their colleagues and, if all was well, "authenticate" its publication either by crowning the author with laurel or in some other symbolic way.[21] Theologians on several occasions found it necessary to forbid members of the Arts Faculties to discuss matters pertaining to faith and, at Paris, even went so far as to impose an oath to this effect. And, of course, the universities could specifically ban unacceptable theories and propositions and force those masters who held them to recant, resign, or face excommunication.[22] At Paris, in 1525, the Theology Faculty, having received complaints "that said that many of the masters were Lutherans or favored this pernicious sect and revealed the Faculty's secrets to it," had to demand a formal oath denying the rumor from each master.[23]

---

[18]G. Sommerfeldt, "Zwei politische Sermone des Heinrich von Oyta und des Nikolaus von Dinkelsbühl (1388 und 1417)," *Historisches Jahrbuch*, 26 (1905), 321.
[19]I examined this problem in my paper "Heresy and Humanism in Early Tudor Oxford" (see note * above), which I hope to publish shortly.
[20]For the best general discussion of these matters, see M.M. McLaughlin, *Intellectual Freedom and Its Limitations in the University of Paris in the Thirteenth and Fourteenth Centuries* (New York, 1977), esp. 192ff and 208ff.
[21]L. Thorndike, "Public Readings of New Works in Mediaeval Universities," *Speculum*, 1 (1926), 101-103.
[22]See, e.g., *C.U.P.*, i. 499-500. Among many examples generally discussed in McLaughlin and elsewhere, see now esp. W.J. Courtenay, "John of Mirecourt and Gregory of Rimini on Whether God Can Undo the Past," *Recherches de Théol. anc. et. med.*, 39 (1972) and 40 (1973); and R.J. Van Neste, "A Reappraisal of the Supposed Skepticism of John of Mirecourt," *ibid.*, 44 (1977), 101-126.
[23]L. Delisle, "Notice sur un registre des procès-verbaux de la Faculté de théologie de Paris pendant les années 1503-33," *Notices et extraits des manuscrits de la Bibliohèque nationale*, 36 (1899), 375-376.

But the universities were not intellectual islands. Substantive theological issues (the nature of the Eucharist; the Immaculate Conception; Apostolic poverty) required frequent discussions and determinations in the universities. Theological faculties received (from bishops, princes, former masters, and other concerned people) lists of suspect teachings and copies of doubtful books (in Latin and the vernaculars), and verdicts were duly issued. In the fourteenth century, we know of more than two dozen such rulings issued by Paris alone.[24] The most common concern was the threat posed to the Catholic faith by magic, sortilege, prophecies, and the occult in general. The condemnation of the magical arts at Paris in 1398 gives us some insights into the minds and self-conception of the theologians: Addressing "all the devotees of the orthodox faith, the Chancellor of Paris and the Faculty of Theology" urged their hearers to "have hope in the Lord and not look upon vanities and false insanities":

From olden darkness a foul flood of errors newly emerging has warned us to recall, that often catholic truth which escapes others is quite clear to those studious in sacred writ, since certainly every art has this property of being clear to those trained in it . . . . Hence that line of Horace, which Jerome quotes writing to Paulinus, "Physicians utter what is medical, smiths handle tools." To this in the case of sacred writ is added something special which neither experience nor sense can give as in the other arts, nor can readily be apprehended by eyes wrapped in the mist of sin . . . . Others have been turned astray by proud curiosity and the dire desire to investigate the occult. Others . . . hanging breathless on the morrow, are driven into most superstitious and impious observances . . . Perceiving, therefore, that the nefarious, pestiferous, and monstrous abomination of false insanities with its heresies had developed more than usual in our times, lest perchance the monster of such horrid impiety and pernicious contagion avail to inflect our most Christian realm, which once was free and by God's protection shall be free from monsters, desirous of checking every attmept, *mindfull besides of our profession* and burning with zeal for the faith, we have decreed to brand with the cautery of damnation a few articles bearing on this matter, lest henceforth they deceive unawares, recalling among innumerable others that saying of the most sapient doctor Augustine concerning superstitious observances, that those who believe in these . . . should know that they have belied their Christian faith and baptism and become pagans and apostates . . . and enemies of God, and have incurred the wrath

---

[24]d'Argentré, i. (pt, i.) 267-400; i. (pt. ii.) 1-158.

of God gravely for eternity, unless, corrected by ecclesiastical penance, they are reconciled to God . . . Not that it is our intention in any way to derogate from lawful and true traditions, sciences and arts, for it will keep us busy to extirpate and uproot, in so far as we may, the insane and sacrilegious errors of the foolish and fatal rites that harm, contaminate, infect the orthodox faith and Christian religion, and to restore its due honor to sincere truth.[25]

And through all of these discussions and actions, theology as a science was becoming ever more sophisticated intellectually (too much so for some contemporaries), as well as more subtle in its understanding of the different types and degrees of heresy and more confident in dealing with their challenge.[26]

During the later fourteenth and early fifteenth centuries, when schism and conciliarism, learned and popular heresies, political and religious nationalism, lay piety and anti-clericalsim, and other forces were combining to challenge the structure and authority of the medieval church, universities came to play even more important and more self-confident roles within the Christian community. It is hardly surprising that at a time when the very nature and locus of religious authority were topics of fervent debate, those theological experts, who had for so long acted as advisers and judges in the employ of others, should make greater claims for themselves.[27] New universities and new theology faculties proliferated as rival popes during the Schism sought general support and intellectual adherents to shore up their causes. Within universities, new colleges

---

[25]*C.U.P.*, iv. 32-35; L. Thorndike (ed.), *University Records and Life in the Middle Ages* (New York, 1944), 261ff.; see also R. Kieckhefer, *European Witch Trials: their foundations in popular and learned culture, 1300-1500* (Berkeley/Los Angeles, 1976), 22.

[26]See, e.g., J.F. Kelly, "The Place of Pierre d'Ailly in the Development of Medieval Theological Sources and Censures," *Studies in Medieval Culture*, VI-VII (Kalamazoo, 1974), 141-150; and S.F. Brown, "Peter of Candia's Sermons in Praise of Peter Lombard," in *Studies Honoring I.C. Brady, Friar Minor* (ed. R.S. Almagno and C.L. Harkins; St. Bonaventure, N.Y., 1976), 141-176. I plan to deal with the question of the "science of theology" during the Renaissance in a forthcoming paper, "The Mind of Man and the Science of God." Also important are R. Guelluy, *Philosophie et théologie chez Guillaume d'Ockham* (Louvain/Paris, 1947); G. Leff, *William of Ockham* (Manchester, 1975), chpt. 5; and P. De Vooght, *Les sources de la doctrine chrétienne d'après les théologiens du XIVe siècle et du début du XVe* (Bruges, 1954).

[27]On these developments, see esp. R.N. Swanson, *Universities, Academics and the Great Schism* (Cambridge, 1979); S. Ozment, *the Age of Reform 1250-1550* (New Haven, 1980), esp. chpts. 2-4; F. Oakley, *The Western Church in the Later Middle Ages* (Ithaca, 1979); A.E. Bernstein, *Pierre d'Ailly and the Blanchard Affair* (Leiden, 1978); the forthcoming book by Margaret Harvey; and my article (which is, in part, a review of the above and other books) "Universities and the Church in the Later Middle Ages," *History of Universities, 2 (1982).* (See also the essays by Morrissey and Schuessler in the present volume.)

were endowed and new religious houses of study were established. Many of the colleges were founded explicitly to train men in theology to counteract the forces of heresy and error; or, in the words of Bishop Fleming's early fifteenth century preface to the statutes of Lincoln College, Oxford,

to overcome those who with their swinish snouts imperil the pearls of true theology.[28]

Theology masters like Raoul Glachard, d'Ailly, Gerson, and others all exalted the place of universities, sometimes even above popes and councils, as the chief seat of Christian truth and the principal bulwark against heresy.[29] Universities had matured in important, if not always attractive ways. In his brief, interesting remarks on the self-conceptions of the medieval university from Abelard to Gerson, Jacques leGoff saw that by the latter era the

université n'etait plus qu'une caste. Sans doute était elle ouverte encore . . . a toutes les classes, representait bien l'ensemble de la société. Mais elle était une caste par sa mentalité et sa fonction. La corporation des manieurs des livre se changeait enun groupe de théologiens rabacheurs s'erigeant en policiers de l'esprit et des moeurs, des brûleurs de livres.[30]

But whatever our modern judgment may be, the prestige of academics was high. In 1414, King Charles VI formally declared that

the members of the Paris Faculty of Theology hold the first rank in the science of sacred letters . . . . The people recognize this fact, and the court of Rome has itself admitted this when, on several occasions, both in the past and more recently, when some ambiguity or doubt had arisen concerning the doctrines of the Christian religion, it has not disdained to address itself to this council of the faith residing in Paris, in order to obtain a clear decision on these points.[31]

---

[28]*Statutes of the Colleges of Oxford* . . . (Oxford/London, 1853), i. (Lincoln College) ∴ See also refs. in note 32 below, plus A.L. Gabriel, *Garlandia: studies in the history of the mediaveal university* (Notre Dame/Frankfurt am Main, 1969), esp. chpt. X; and E.F. Jacob, *Essays in Later Medieval History* (Manchester, 1968), chpt. VIII.

[29]*C.U.P.*, iii. 487, 595-6; McLaughlin, esp. 302-303, but chpt. 5 passim; Swanson, chpt. 1 and *passim;* S.E. Ozment, "The University and the Church: patterns of reform in Jean Gerson," *Medievalia et Humanistica*, n.s. 1 (1970), 111-126; Bernstein, 157-158, n. 41; and the current Stanford University dissertation of Douglass Taber, to whom I am very grateful for sharing his as yet unpublished work.

[30]J. Le Goff, "Quelle conscience l'Université médiévale a-t-elle eue d'elle même?" in his *Pour un autre Moyen Age* (Paris, 1977), 197.

[31]Crevier, *Histoire de l'Universite de Paris* (Paris, 1761), iii. 379.

82 REFORM AND AUTHORITY

How well did this prestige translate into power? The activities of fifteenth century universities were similar to those of the previous century, but more extensive. In Germany, for example, five new universities were created during the Schism (Cologne, Heidelberg, Wurzburg, Erfurt, and Leipzig).[32] Modeled in large part on the University of Paris, it is not surprising that they all assumed anti-heretical functions in their society. Cologne, which along with Paris had been referred to by the Roman cardinals in 1406 as one of the "shining stars of infinite learning,"[33] reacted to a variety of perceived threats. In 1445, it raised the spectre of heresy against those of its own members who still believed in the superiority of councils over popes.[34] A year later it condemned Ferdinand of Cordova for denying free will.[35] Toward the end of the century, the theological faculty proceeded against several astrologers and their writings.[36] Again following Paris, it exercised its *pre*scriptive role by decreeing that all those who graduated in theology must uphold the doctrine of the Immaculate Conception in lectures, disputations, and sermons.[37] And in a case which became infamous in its own time, Cologne led the fierce campaign against the books of the humanist Hebrew scholar Johann Reuchlin.[38] The advent of Luther could thus easily be viewed by these scholars on the lower Rhine as just another problem of a type they had encountered and dealt with frequently in the century before.

At Paris, the Theology Faculty was even busier than in the previous century.[39] The plague of nominalism and the ever-popular occult tracts called for numerous denunciations. The theologians

---

[32]On the spread of universities, see Rashdall, vol. ii., *passim;* Swanson, esp. chpt. 1 and appendix 2; and P.W. Knoll, "The Papacy at Avignon and University Foundations," in *The Church in a Changing Society* (C.I.H.E.C. Conference, 1977), (Uppsala, 1978), 191-196. For the German context, see Kieckhefer, *Repression of Heresy in Medieval Germany* (note 2 above) and the more detailed Ph.D. thesis on which it is based, "Repression of Heresy in Germany, 1348-1520" (U. of Texas, 1972).

[33]E. Martène and U. Durand (eds.), *Thesaurus novus anecdotorum* (Paris, 1717), ii. 1286 ff.

[34]H. Keussen, *Die alte Universität Köln. Grundzuge ihre Verfassung und Geschichte* (Cologne, 134), 74 ff.; see also, J.W. Stieber, *Pope Eugenius IV, the Council of Basel and the Secular and Ecclesiastical Authorities in the Empire* (Leiden, 1978), 85 ff.

[35]Keussen, 79; R.W. Scribner, "Why was there no Reformation in Cologne?", *B.I.H.R.*, 49 (1976), 229. Two of its theologians were also involved in the 1479 condemnation of Johann Rucherat von Wesel, who had claimed that Holy Scripture was the only authority in theology: *ibid.*, 229 and E. Kleineidam, *Universitas Studii Erfordiensis* (Leipzig, 1964-9), ii. 114.

[36]H. Keussen, *Regesten und Auszuge zur Geschichte der Universität Köln 1388-1559* (Cologne, 1918), ## 1901, 1987.

[37]*ibid.*, # 2016a; Scribner art., 229 and n. 5.

[38]The best discussion of Reuchlin is J.H. Overfield, "A New Look at the Reuchlin Affair," *Studies in Medieval and Renaissance History*, 8 (1971), 167-207.

[39]d'Argentré, i. (pt. ii.), *passim.*

even asserted their authority (and perhaps their offended dignity) against the annual celebration of the "feast of fools" and refused to accept "the law of custom" as a valid defense against their ruling which was based "on the testimony of Holy Writ."[40] Throughout Europe, all universities were issuing similar decrees on major theological problems and minor local disputes.[41]

Procedures for reaching these collective decisions varied enormously. Sometimes one master or a few prominent individuals would be asked to respond on behalf of the university.[42] Sometimes faculties (and especially whole universities) were unable to reach a viable consensus, and no formal judgment could emerge. Sometimes universities split into rival factions. In the late fifteenth century, a defender of the ostensibly banned nominalism, explained the reasons for its "persecution" by the other theologians at Paris. They were envious of the nominalists' fame and were frustrated at their inability to defeat them in disputations, so they

---

[40]*ibid.*, i (pt. ii.) 286 ff.; *C.U.P.*, iv. 652 ff.

[41] I am at present compiling a comprehensive list of these university edicts and actions which I will analyze in my forthcoming book. In addition to the bibliographies of medieval universities above, several recent detailed studies of particular theology faculties, editions of registers, etc., have significantly advaned our knowledge: see, e.g., C. Piana, O.F.M., *La Facoltà Teologica dell'Università di Firenze nel Quattro e Cinquecento* (Grottaferrata, 1977); H.A. Oberman, *Werden und Wertung der Reformation* (Tubingen, 1977); R.L. Harison, "The Reformation of the Theological Faculty of the University of Tubingen, 1534-1555" (Vanderbilt Ph.D. diss., 1975); J.K. Farge, "The Faculty of Theology of Paris, 1500-1536: institution, personnel and activity in early sixteenth-century France" (Toronto Ph.D. diss., 1976); E.J.M. Van Eijl (ed.), *Facultas S. Theologiae Lovaniensis 1432-1797* (Louvain, 1977), with refs. therein to the numerous older studies of late medieval and early Reformation Louvain; and the Ph.D. dissertations of two of my former students at Catholic University: Sr. Justina M. Grothe, S.M.I.C., "Cistercians and Higher Education in the Late Middle Ages with a special reference to Heidelberg" (1976) and Franz-Bernard Lickteig, "The German Carmelites at the Medieval Universities" (1977). I am particularly appreciative of Dr. Lickteig's continued active collaboration in my research. In addition to the actual proceedings by universities, their role is often discussed in theoretical and literary sources: see, e.g., *Four English Political Tracts of the Later Middle Ages* (ed. J.-P. Genet; Camden Soc., London, 1977), 52, 156; and *Mum and the Sothsegger* (eds. M. Day and R. Steele; London, E.E.T.S., 1936), 36-38; P. Chaplais, "Some documents. . . of the Treaty of Bretigny (1360-1369)," in *Camden Miscellany* (Camden Soc., London, 1952), 53. Also, J.W. Baldwin and R.A. Goldthwaite (eds.), *Universities in Politics: case studies from the late Middle Ages and early modern period* (Baltimore, 1972); and Swanson, chpt. *l*.

[42] Again the specific case studies in d'Argentré and elsewhere will be analyzed in my book for the procedures as well as for the content of the university responses. For an example of an individual being asked to respond on behalf of a university, see the case of Edward Powell's refutation of Luther's *Babylonian Captivity* in his *Propugnaculum summi sacerdotij euangelici, . . . aduersus M. Lutherum* (London, 1523). I have given the full context of this controversy in my "Heresy and Humanism in Early Tudor Oxford" (see note * above).

try to get rid of them entirely. The third cause comes from a heresy concocted at the University of Louvain. For a certain teacher at Louvain composed a treatise in which he denied certitude and divine prescience concerning contingents, asserting that propositions concerning the contingent future, even though contained in the Bible and set forth by Christ, were not true. This treatise, full of these heresies, the University of Louvain approved and sent its promoter to Paris to solicit the Faculty of Theology to approve the said treatise. When many doctors of the said faculty were favorable to him, and those especially who are intent on the extermination of the doctrine of nominalists, those who are called nominalists objected and opposed this strongly, fearing no peril in their defense of the faith, and the prevented the Faculty of Theology from approving the said treatise. Those who are called realists took this very hard and to the number of twenty-four subscribed to the said treatise and approved it. The author of this treatise was cited before the apostolic see . . . and produced in his justification the signatures of the twenty-four doctors of Paris . . . . Their support notwithstanding, the said Louvain professor . . . was condemned and his treatise decleared heretical. Because of which condemnation the said approvers of these heresies were moved with anger and hatred to disturb, molest, and harass the defenders of the faith . . . . A regent in Arts at Paris from somewhere in Germany publicly sustained these Louvain heresies . . . and when he was accused before the Faculty of Theology of having called Christ a liar, he was defended by the doctors who had approved the said heresies from Louvain . . . . Nevertheless we do not wish to say that the nominalists are wholly immune from errors. "For if we say that we have no sin, there is no truth in us." For neither can the Thomists assert this concerning St. Thomas, against whom while still living many articles were drawn up at Paris, against whose errors in the name of the Faculty of Theology a treatise was composed and sent to Rome. Nor can the followers of the *Sentences* assert this of master Peter Lombard, since there are commonly listed against him twenty-six articles in which he is not to be followed. But we will say that, among all doctors, they erred least and followed the truth of the faith more integrally than others.[43]

Late medieval theology, even university scholasticism, was far from being a monolithic ideology. Many of the personal and institutional

---

[43]d'Argentré, i. (pt, ii.) 286-288; Thorndike, 358-360.

tensions, as well as the nuances of the rival doctrinal positions themselves, will be much more clearly delineated by detailed case-histories of particular condemnations.

The early sixteenth century was a curious time for universities as religious authorities. Their jurisdiction was still widely acknowledged and their activities largely the same as before. In 1518, in the Augsburg encounter with Cajetan, Luther himself had praised the University of Paris (for its revived conciliarism) and had said that

> since I am a man who can err, I have submitted and now again submit to the judgment and the lawful conclusions of the holy church and of all who are better informed than I .... I am even prepared ... to hear the judgment and opinion ... of the doctors of the famed imperial universities of Basel, Freiburg, and Louvain, or, if this is not satisfactory, also of Paris, the parent of learning and from the beginning the university which was most Christian and most renowned in theology.[44]

Recent work has shown that, up to this time, the young Luther was indeed quite conventional in his views about heresy and the need for unity of faith.[45] But a year later, immediately after the debate at Leipzig, Eck wrote to Jakob von Hochstraten that

> at first Luther did not want to have any university in the world as a judge. But the most Christian prince, Duke George of Saxony, would not permit any disputation concerning matters of faith unless competent teachers would judge. Thus Luther was forced into it, urged by supporters. If he had not debated and agreed to have judges, all would have left him. When I left the selection of universities up to him, he chose Paris and Erfurt. I do not know the University of Paris ... but I would cordially ask you ... for the sake of the Christian faith to write to your friends or, if you please, to the entire university so that, upon receiving the disputation from the beloved ruler, George, with a request for a decision, they do not refuse it, but courageously attack the opponents. We both recognize them as judges. I hope the matter is clear enough that it does not need a long examination. May they at once give their judgment according to the ruler's request and affirm what is in accord with our faith ....[46]

---

[44]*Acta Augustana* (1518), in *D. Martin Luthers Werke, Kritische Gesamtausgabe* (Weimar, 1883-　　) (=*WA.*), 2:7-9.

[45]U. Mauser, *Der junge Luther und die Häresie* (Gütersloh, 1968).

[46]N. Weiss, "Martin Luther, Jean Eck et l'Université de Paris d'après une lettre inedite, 11 Septembre 1519," *Bull. Soc. de l'hist. du protestantisme français*, 66 (1917), 35-48.

The continued acceptance of the authoritative role of universities was reflected in Duke George's approach to the universities for a ruling on the debate "for the sake of public peace and pure doctrine."[47]

Erfurt declined the request on the grounds that they did not believe that both disputants really wanted their opinion or would abide by it and, in a show of faculty cohesion, because two orders (the Dominicans and Augustinians) had been explicitly excluded from voting in the conditions set by the Duke's letter.[48] However, Paris and other universities, notably Louvain, did later condemn some different writings by Luther, despite the fact that, as Froben had told Luther in early 1519, many of his books

> are sold at Paris, and are even read and approved by the doctors of the Sorbonne, as certain of our friends have assured us; for some of the most learned say that they have hitherto missed among those who treat Scripture the same freedom that you show.[49]

We need not examine here the details of the Sorbonne or Louvain proceedings against Luther (or, in something of the same mood but in a rather different context, against Erasmus), since those events have been exhaustively studied by others.[50] Rather we would like to conclude with some further considerations of the reactions of those who faced university censure.

The opinions of the universities did not always meet with immediate or docile acceptance. Legal ploys, difficulties of communication, the intervening hand of a powerful patron, or countless other practical considerations often frustrated all attempts to en-

---

[47]*Akten und Briefe zur Kirchenpolitik Herzog Georgs von Sachsen* (ed. F. Gess; Leipzig, 1905-17), i. 92-94, 100.

[48]*ibid.*, i. 113.

[49]*D. Martin Luthers Werke: . . . Briefwochsel* (ed. K. Burdach, *et al.;* Weimar, 1930), i. 332. (=*WA.*, Br.)

[50]For recent studies, which also contain references to older, but still important, works, see esp. D. Hempsall, "Martin Luther and the Sorbonne, 1519-21," *B.I.H.R.*, 46 (1973), 28-40; F.T. Bos, *Luther in het oordeel van de Sorbonne* (Amsterdam, 1974); and F.M. Higman, *Censorship and the Sorbonne* (Geneva, 1979). An interesting and often overlooked work is C.Garside, Jr., " 'La Farce des Theologastres': humanism, heresy, and the Sorbonne, 1523-1525," *Rice University Studies* (1974) 45-82. For Erasmus, see esp. J. Etienne, *Spiritualisme érasmien et théologiens louvanistes* (Louvain/Gembloux, 1956); F. Bierlaire, *Les Colloques d'Érasme: réform des études, réforme des moeurs et réforme do l'Église au XVIe siecle* (Paris, 1978); M. Gielis, *Kritiek van Leuvense theologen op Erasmus' Kerkopvatting: de conflicten tussen Erasmus en theologen van de leuvense faculteit aangaande de strucuur van de kerk (1521-1524)* (Louvain, 1976), 2 vols. Also see the exhaustive bibliography covering all of these issues in J.-P. Massant, *Josse Clichtore, l'humanisme et la réforme du clergé* (Paris, 1968), i. 29-96. For an interesting Catholic attitude, see J. Wicks, S.J., *Cajetan Responds* (Washington, 1978), 9 ff. (esp. p. 10, n. 29 and 30, n. 63).

force university decrees. Sometimes the very things that fostered the growth of universities and their power, later caused ambiguities which undermined their role as religious authorities. The charters of priveleges granted to the universities by popes and princes made them largely autonomous institutions, except with regard to their exalted protectors. The multiplication of universities had produced more theologians and more activity, but it also resulted in a Babel of voices: no unified university perspective would be heard on any issue. The conciliar movement had provided a stage on which the universities had acted quite successfully; yet their achievement in ending the Schism brought the virtual demise of the movement and the ending of an international forum for university actions and theories. The invention of printing inaugurated a new era for universities and faculties as censors and bookburners, while at the same time it meant that it would now be impossible to contain heterodox ideas.

But whatever force these external conditions might exert on specific cases, virtually all the "victims" of university condemnations felt compelled to respond with some sort of defense. Humanist lampoons of blithering scholastics have tended to make late medieval and early Reformation professors seem bigoted and ridiculous. To contemporaries, they were much more substantial opponents, who had to be answered. We should not, however, look for many lengthy, point-by-point responses to the specific criticisms or even for extended rational debate. Rather, on the one hand, the late medieval sermon and the humanist satire mingled forces to cultivate the genre of *character assassination;* and, on the other hand, late medieval piety, with its strong anti-intellectual elements, combined with Christian humanist emphasis on the primacy of Holy Scripture to produce the defense *appeal to a higher authority.*

A real master of ridicule in the middle of the fourteenth century, Peter Ceffons of Clairvaux, blasted those Paris theologians who had censured John of Mirecourt and Nicholas of Autrecourt as envious, pompous, egocentric, and sanctimonious persecutors of serious, hard-working thinkers. In elegant Latin, Peter called these Parisians boors, dullards, and brutal authoritarians, who were hostile to all good letters and a menace to the traditions of the Church Fathers.[51]

If Peter represents the sophisticated reaction of a learned wit, others raised the standard of simplicity and conformity to the Gospels. For Thomas à Kempis

---

[51]D. Trapp, "Peter Ceffons of Clairvaux," *Rech. Théol. anc. et med.,* 24 (1957), 147 ff.

What will it profit thee to dispute profoundly of the Trinity, if thou be void of humility and are thereby displeasing to the Trinity? . . . I would rather feel compunction than to understand the definition thereof . . . . Truly, at the day of Judgment, we shall not be examined on what we have read, but on what we have done, not how well we have spoken, but how religiously we have lived . . . . There is a great difference between the knowledge of an illuminated and devout man and the knowledge of a learned and studious clerk.[52]

John Wyclif was quite ambiguous about the worth and even the authority, of universities;[53] but most later medieval heretical movements were generally hostile to the traditional erudition of the schoolmen and believed that, instead of being proclaimed by some theological faculty, "every doctrine needs to be tested by Christ's words and life, to see if it accords with His example and teachings."[54] Still, the Bohemian Petr Chelicky could admit:

I acknowledge all the holy doctors, those of today too, so far as they can point out to me through their learning the path of true understanding . . . and I follow them thankfully and regard them as right when they provide real understanding and enlightenment or explain faithfully some hidden truth.[55]

Both of these defensive strategies were prominent in the writings of the reformers and humanists of the early sixteenth century. The *Letters of Obscure Men* or almost any of Erasmus' treatises could provide many useful examples whose implications have scarcely been fully understood by modern commentators.[56] But to conclude this short consideration of universities as religious authorities, it might be worthwhile to glance at two less well-known pieces:

---

[52]Thomas à Kempis, *De Imitatione Christi* (Oxford, 1874 ed.), esp. pp. 5 ff. See also R.R. Post, *The Modern Devotion: confrontation with Reformation and Humanism* (Leiden, 19678), 80-83, 143-145, and *passim*.

[53]I have examined in some detail Wyclif's attitude toward universities (and viceversa) in "Heresy and Humanism in early Tudor Oxford" (see note * above), but for now see his *Tractatus de Ecclesia* (ed. J. Loserth; London, 1886), 370-376; *Select English Works of John Wyclif* (ed. T. Arnold; Oxford, 1869) i. 13; *Opera minora* (ed. J. Loserth; London, 1913), 303-304.

[54]Cited in P. Brock, *The Political and Social Doctrines of the Unity of Czech Brethren in the Fifteenth and early Sixteenth Centuries* ('s-Gravenhage, 1957), 67.

[55]*ibid.*, 67.

[56]Ulrich von Hutten, *et al.*, *Letters of Obscure Men* (Eng., ed., London, 1909; Philadelphia, 1972). Among literally hundreds of possible Erasmus citations, see esp. the *Praise of Folly* (many eds.) and the *Paraclesis*, which is most readily available in D. Erasmus, *Christian Humanism and the Reformation: selected writings* (ed. John C. Olin; New York, 1965), 92-106. (For secondary studies, see refs. in note 50 above.)

Melanchthon's *Against the Furious Decree of the Parisian Theologasters* and Luther's *Against Latomus.*[57]

Luther, for all his extravagant rhetoric, was not unconcerned about the opinions of his peers at other universities. He was relieved when Erfurt did not rule against him; and he felt the need to make various attempts to refute the verdicts of "the asses of Paris and Louvain" right up to the end of his life.[58] But he was also glad when Melanchthon entered the lists against their common opponents.[59]

Melanchthon's purpose for writing was clearly stated:

Christian reader, I have wanted to warn you of these things lest you be frightened away from the Lutheran doctrine by the authority of the Sorbonne.[60]

He did not seek the abolition of the universities or even deny them their place as religious experts. He was rather profoundly sorry that they were doing their noble task so poorly, that their methods of theological reasoning and argument were so faulty, that they lacked charity, and that they had wrongly asserted their own authority above the ultimate authority of the Bible. The Sorbonne had accused

Luther of heresy, not because he disagrees with Scripture, but with the universities, the holy fathers, and the councils. And then they call the opinions of the universities, . . . holy fathers, and . . . councils the primary principles of faith.[61]

But all of these authorities can err, and

since there are no articles of faith except those which have been prescribed by sacred Scripture, why is it wicked for us to differ either with the councils or the universities, provided we do not differ with Scripture.[62]

---

[57]Melanchthon, *Selected Writings* (transl. C.L. Hill; eds. E.E. Flack and L.J. Satre; Minneapolis, 1962) (=*S.W.*), 69-87; *Luther's Works, American Ed.* (eds. J.J. Pelikan and H.T. Lehmann; St. Louis/Philadelphia, 1955 ff.) (=*LW.*) vol. 32: *Career of the Reformer II* (ed. G.W. Forell; Philadelphia, 1958), 177 ff. (and see note 74 below).

[58]See *LW.* 48: 136-137; on Luther's concern with this problem right up to his deathbed, see *WA.*, 54: 417 ff.; *LW.*, 34: 346 ff.; *LW.*, 50: 316-318; A useful introduction to Luther's attitudes toward universities is in J. Headley, *Luther's View of Church History* (New Haven, 1963), 207 ff. A convenient collection of sources on the subject is J. Dillenberger (ed.), *Martin Luther: selections from his writings* (Garden City, N.Y., 1961), 178, 186, 253-254, 279, 296, 364, 472-476. On the development of Luther's conceptions of his task as a theologian, see L. Grane, *Modus Loquendi Theologius: Luthers Kampf um die Erneuerung des Theologie (1515-1518)* (Leiden, 1975) and H. Steinlein, *Luthers Doktorat* (Leipzig, 1912).

[59]*LW.*, 48: 270.

[60]Melanchthon, *S.W.*, 87.

[61]*ibid.*, 72.

[62]*ibid.*, 72-73.

Not only were the theologians mistaken to claim that Scripture could only be interpreted through their scholastic traditions, in fact their whole approach was wrong. When the scholastic method

> began to consider the divine Law according to the philosophy of Aristotle, it abrogated for the sake of lust whatever laws of God it wanted to annul.[63]

Interestingly, despite this continuous attack on scholasticism throughout the treatise and his emphasis on Scripture as the sole authority, Melanchthon does not quote the Bible very often or very effectively and, indeed, allowed the Sorbonne decree to set the structure and the issues for his *Defense*. Still his theme is repeatedly reitereated:

> It is not about universities that we labor, for scholastic theology . . . has proved that all the schools are heretical. At this point, cry out, my masters: "He has blasphemed. He accuses the schools of heresy." Rightly so, if they teach things that differ from the Gospel. And the scholasticism of the Parisians does differ . . . . Moreover, I ask you, masters, what do you call the Church? Is it (the same as) the French Sorbonne? But how can that be the Church which is foreign to the Word of Christ . . . ?[64]

If "the Sorbonne alone is not the Church," how is it that they claim to

> exclude Luther from the communion of the devout? You should have accused him, not condemned him. You should have written down the testimonies of Scripture, not set forth naked articles.[65]

They had proved to be a "false faculty" by their failure to rely on Scripture and for saying that "Luther must be destroyed by fire rather than conquered by reason."[66] In addition, Melanchthon believed that the condemnation had been issued by only a small minority of the whole faculty.[67] He concluded

---

[63]*ibid.*, 75.
[64]*ibid;* 79, 81.
[65]*ibid.*, 81-82.
[66]*ibid.*, 72.
[67]*ibid.*, 71.

O wretched France to have been polluted by such censors and judges of sacred matters, who are really more worthy to deal with sewers than to treat sacred letters. . . . You may find Christ among the carpenters far more quickly than in that class of men.[68]

The Parisians reacted slowly (1523) and to some extent in kind, but in terms that we would expect from doctors of theology with by now several centuries of tradition behind their words. It was preposterous and presumptuous for a mere "boy" of twenty-four, a "married man," a "layman," and only "a Greek teacher" to claim to "know so much" and to challenge the entire Sorbonne. The professors of orthodoxy reasserted their attitude on the question of the Bible: "Because Scriptures are obscure, they must be interpreted by Masters, especially the Masters of Paris."[69] The universities had not yet been forced onto the defensive.

On July 13, 1521, Luther wrote to Melanchthon that "I have decided to translate your *Defense* against the Parisian asses, together with their nonsense, and all notes to it."[70] Two days later, he told George Spalatin that he had

seen the decree of the Parisian sophists, together with Philip's *Defense*, and I wholeheartedly rejoice. Christ would not have made them so blind had he not decided to use these affairs to bring about the end of their tyranny. I have already sent the book against Latomus to the press.[71]

James Masson, better known by his humanist name Latomus, was a Louvain Doctor of Theology and a bitter opponent of both Luther and Erasmus.[72] He wrote a sharp defense of Louvain's condemnation of Luther's teaching, to which the latter felt obligated to reply, unwillingly, because, "I have already set my soul on quiet study . . . (and) there is the disgust of having to read his verbose and badly written stuff."[73] The resulting work appeared in late September, 1521; but the problem was still in Luther's mind a month later when he mentioned his own and Melanchthon's

---

[68]*ibid.*, 86-87.
[69]*WA.*, Br. 2: 357 ff, 365.
[70]*LW.*, 48: 257-258.
[71]*ibid.*, 270.
[72]On Latomus, see Étienne, *Spiritualisme erasmien*, 163 ff. His most relevant works for us are *Articulorum doctrinae fratris M. Lutheri per theologos Lovaniensis damnatorum ratio ex sacris literis et veteribus tractoribus* (Louvain, 1521) and *De trium linguarum et studii theologici ratione dialogus* (Louvain, 1519).
[73]*LW.*, 48: 229.

writings in a letter to Nicholas Gerbel and added: "I am eager to launch a public attack against the universities, but I have not yet made definite plans."[74]

Although he apparently never completed the latter project, Luther made his attitude toward universities who opposed him quite clear in a number of writings, especially in his reply to Latomus. The Louvain theologian had accused Luther of renegging on his original promise to submit to the findings of the academic authorities when their judgment went against him. Luther answered that

> to be sure, I regret that I did quite seriously submit (my writings) to them, for my sincere opinion of the pope, councils, and universities was no different from the common one. Although much of what they had said seemed absurd to me and completely alien to Christ . . . . I always believed that there were theologians hidden in the schools who would not have been silent if these teachings were impious. I then still believed that scarcely anywhere were there fewer stupid blockheads and asses . . . (and) scoundrels than at Louvain. However, in view of what has happened, knowledge of the true situaiton—as well as courage—has grown . . . . I give thanks to my Lord Jesus Christ who, on account of this assault, has repaid me . . . with the knowledge—of which I am now convinced—that the pope is the Antichrist . . . and that the universities are indeed the ultimate in the synagogues of Satan, in which the rule belongs to those Epicurean swine, the sophistic theologians.[75]

Latomus had claimed that Luther, by relying on his own opinions against the corrections offered by Louvain and by his intemperate reply to their condemnations, lacked "evangelical modesty." But Luther held that

> the sophists have no right to judge me, for they themselves see that my work does not disagree with the apostles, Christ, and the prophets . . . . (Yet) if you tell them (the theologians) what they are—ignorant, stupid, godless blasphemers against God's Word, doing incalculable damage to the service of God and souls—then you are called one who offends against the whole gospel. . . . Evidently evangelical moderation or excess depends exclusively on whether one venerates papal idols and sophistic idiots![76]

Luther granted "that one ought to respect superiors, but not the extent of offending against the Word of God."[77] He would even

approve and agree that erroneous books must be burnt, but not—as is foolishly maintained by these arrogant new prophets—those which have not yet been proved to be in error.[78]

Luther was furious that Latomus and the Louvainians refused to debate him on the substance of his beliefs, but rather simply condemned him outright: "in the beginning I disputed with complete sincerity, until I realized that our (i.e., the scholastic) professors are idiots and swine."[79] According to Luther

the main point. . . described by Latomus. . . was this: "We are the teachers, the judges; we cannot erri, the world obeys us, and whatever we say is an article of faith, evangelical and prophetic.". . . Were the prophets and evangelists from Louvain? Truly, (I) did not know this. . . This infallible judge and evangelist (i.e., Latomus) means by "truth" the opinions of the Louvanians.[80]

Luther charged them with a "pride, conceit, rashness, ignorance, dullness, . . . malice, . . . haughtiness, arrogance, . . . villainy, . . . superciliousness,. . . . and stupidity that there is nothing to surpass. . . ."[81] He concluded by alleging that the Louvain Faculty must believe that the

human word must rule, all must approve it . . . . But the divine thunders must be silenced and cast down, and one must accept just any arbitrary interpretation of any rascal whatsoever. The word of man is sacred and is to be venerated, but God's Word is handed over to whores . . . . The sophists have imposed their tyranny and bondage upon our freedom to such a point that we must not resist that twice accursed Aristotle, but are compelled to submit. Shall we therefore be perpetually enslaved and never breathe in Christian liberty, nor sigh out from this Babylon for our Scriptures and our home? . . . I am commanded to believe the Word of God, not their fancies. There is one teacher, even Christ . . . . But doesn't obscure Scripture require explanation? Set aside the obscure and cling to the clear.[82]

---

[77]*ibid.,* 146.
[78]*ibid.,* 150.
[79]*ibid.,* 148.
[80]*ibid.,* 149-150.
[81]*ibid.,* 150, 160.
[82]*ibid.,* 215-217.

Luther's advice was to

> avoid scholastic philosophy and theology like the very death of
> the soul. The Gospels are not so difficult that children are not
> ready to hear them. How was Christianity taught in the times
> of the martyrs when this . . . theology did not exist? . . . In all
> these hundreds of years up to the present . . . . the universities
> have not produced, out of so many students, a single martyr or
> saint to prove that their instruction is right and pleasing to
> God . . . .[83]

What about St. Thomas? Luther was not at all sure whether

> Aquinas is among the damned or the blessed . . . . (He) wrote a
> great deal of heresy, and is responsible for the reign of
> Aristotle, the destroyer of souls.[84]

The same themes, with Luther's usual exuberant rhetorical
flourishes, occur throughout his writings and were echoed in
numerous early Reformation debates.

The terms of debate were similar in Switzerland. During the first
Zurich disputation, the Catholic advocate Johannes Faber initially
balked at a public airing of theological matters: in "my opinion
whatever such things as one would discuss should be brought before
the universities, as at Paris, Cologne, or Louvain."[85] Here everyone
laughed when his opponent, Zwingli, interrupted to propose: "How
about Erfut? Would not Wittenberg do?"[86] According to Faber,
only in the universities "can one find many taught in the Scriptures,
who have the ability to handle such great subjects."[87] Zwingli made a
counter-proposal:

> since reference is made to the judges which my Lord Vicar
> thinks cannot be found outside the universities, I say that we
> have here infallible and unprejudiced judges, that is the Holy
> Writ, which can neither lie nor deceive. These we have present
> in the Hebrew, Greek, and Latin tongues; let us take these on
> both sides as fair and just judges.[88]

---

[83]*ibid.*, 258.
[84]*ibid.*, 258.
[85]Ulrich Zwingli, *Selected Works* (ed S.M. Jackson; Philadelphia, 1901; new ed.,
1972), 51-52.
[86]*ibid.*, 52-53.
[87]*ibid.*, 52.
[88]*ibid.*, 56-57.

But Faber responded with the traditional argument that it is

not . . . sufficient that one . . . bring forward Scripture, but . . .
that one understand Scripture correctly. With that in view
perhaps one should attend to such matters at the universities
. . . .[89]

To Zwingli's repeated charge that "you present nothing from the
Scriptures," Faber answered

I will do that and prove it before the universities, where learned judges sit. And choose a place, be it Paris, Cologne, or
Freiburg, whichever you please; then I shall overthrow the
articles presented by you and prove them to be wrong.[90]

Zwingli would not be enticed:

No judge do I want except the Scriptures, as they have been
. . . spoken by the Spirit of God; no human being, whosoever it
may be . . . . That at various times such matters . . . have been
brought before human judges and universities is the reason
priests no longer desired to study, and paid greater attention
to wantonness . . . than to reading the Bible . . . . One considered as scholars and chose as judges those who had attached to themselves only the appearance or diploma of wisdom,
and who knew nothing concerning the right spirit of God or the
Scriptures. But now through the grace of God, the divine . . .
Scriptures have been born and brought to light by means of
print . . . , so that . . . every pious Christian who can read . . . can
easily inform himself and learn the will of God.[91]

Higher education was still respected, but the role of the universities
was severely undermined. As we have shown elsewhere, some conservative opponents of Luther and the other Protestant apologists
understood that they could only convince them of their errors by
fighting on Biblical grounds.[92] Faber, too, was forced to give in. But
here and on other occasions the result was seldom a rout for either
side. Catholic theologians were learned men and astute debaters,
with a long tradition and a strong sense of purpose. But never had
the theologians, collectively in the universities or as individuals,
faced a more serious threat to their own status and function or their
paradigm of faith.

---

[89]*ibid.*, 67.
[90]*ibid.*, 102.
[91]*ibid.*, 102-106.
92One of the best examples of this is Edward Powell's refutation of Luther (see
note 42 above).

Just as there were many problems for universities on the way to reaching their decisions and many strategies and tactics of defense for those attacked by them, so there were many reasons for the rejection of universities as final authorities. They lacked power, especially the power to enforce their decrees. When the matters involved were of great significance, as many both political and ecclesiastical aspects of the Reformation were, the consequences were too important to be left in the hands of intellectuals. The universities could be consulted, for genuine expressions of their opinions or simply to bolster rhetorically an already determined cause; they could be used as part of the censorship process; and they would always be valuable as training grounds for necessary experts and administrators. But in the final analysis, there was always some more weighty authority, even on strictly religious grounds. Popes, Councils, the Church Fathers, and—increasingly—Holy Scriptures were more universal in their claims to possess truth than were the universities. The universities continued to issue condemnations, lists of prohibited books, and opinions on law, public policy, and even economic affairs.[93] The theology faculties remained vigilant over the orthodoxy of their own members and any others they could control; and their intellectual impact in this way was far from negligible.[94] But the old orthodoxy was fatally fragmented; and, despite the force of the rival paradigms of religious truth competing in the sixteenth and seventeenth centuries, the very concept of "orthodoxy" (with its moral requirements on those who believed to enforce it on those who did not) was gradually coming under attack. The self-conceptions held by late medieval and early Reformation university theologians and theological faculties of their role as religious authorities could not survive the demise of that ideal.

---

[93]For a few of the wide range of university edicts and judgments, see, e.g., Higman, *Censorship and the Sorbonne, passim;* L. Hanke, *The Spanish Struggle for Justice in the Conquest of America* (Boston, 1965 ed.); A. Hyma, "Calvinism and Capitalism in the Netherlands, 1555-1700," *J. Mod. Hist.*, 10 (1938), 325 ff.; H.E.C. Midelfort, *Witch Hunting in Southwestern Germany, 1562-1684* (Stanford, 1972), esp. 49 ff.; the enormous literature on Henry VIII's consultation of the English and Continental universities about his divorce plans (see G. deC. Parmiter, *The King's Great Matter* (London, 1967), chpt. 7; J.J. Scarisbrick, *Henry VIII* (London, 1968), 163 ff.; E. Surtz, S.J., *Henry VIII's Great Matter in Italy* (Ann Arbor: Univ. Microfilms Monograph Ser. # LD 00025; 1975); and H.A. Kelly, *The Matrimonial Trials of Henry VIII,* (Stanford, 1976) chpt. 10); and N.Z. Davis, *Society and Culture in Early Modern France* (Stanford, 1975), 17 ff.

[94]For Paris, e.g., in addition to Pascal's *Provincial Letters* and Descartes' "Preface" to the *Meditations of First Philosophy*, see L. Thorndike, "Censorship by the Sorbonne of Science and Superstition in the first half of the Seventeenth Century," *J. Hist. Ideas*, 16 (1955), 119-125; T. McClaughlin, "Censorship and Defenders of the Cartesian Faith in Mid-Seventeenth Century France," *ibid.*, 40 (1979), 563-581; Y. Poutet, "Les Docteurs de Sorbonne et leurs opinions théologiques au XVIIe siècle," *Divus Thomas*, 81 (1978), 213-348; H. Gouhier, *Cartésianisme et Augustinisme au XVIIe siecle* (Paris, 1979). For England, see J.L. Axtell, "The Mechanics of Opposition: Restoration Cambridge v. Daniel Scargill," *B.I.H.R.*, 38 (1965), 102-111.

⁹⁵Since completing this study, I have seen James K. Farge's very interesting article, "Self-Image and Authority of Paris Theologians in Early Reformation France," in Miriam U. Chrisman and O. Gründler (eds.), *Social Groups and Religious Ideas in the Sixteenth Century* (Kalamazoo, 1978), 68-75, which generally supports the position I have suggested. I have benefitted from several discussions with Professor Farge and eagerly look forward to his future publications.

NOTES

*Slightly different versions of this paper were given as lectures at the Catholic University of America (1976) and at Oxford (1980). It is one of a series of studies in which I have attempted to change our understanding of the learned culture of the later Middle Ages, Renaissance, and Reformation: "Fools and Knaves in Solomon's Houses: a humanist theme from Petrarch to Swift" (Washington, Folger Shakespeare Library, World Petrarch Congress, 1974); "A University Mentality in the later Middle Ages: the pragmatism, humanism, and orthodoxy of New College, Oxford" (Oxford, 1975, and Avignon, 1978; now published in *Genèse et Débuts du Grand Schisme d'Occident* (Paris, Éditions du Centre National de la Recherche Scientifique, 1980), 201-230; "Scholastic Latin, Humanistic Latin, and the Vernacular in the Age of the Reformation" (Tours, IIIᵉ Congrè International des Études Néo-Latin, 1976); "The Concept of '*vera theologia*' in Erasmus and Luther" (Folger Shakespeare Library, Renaissance Institute, 1975; and Oxford, 1976); "Church Fathers and Oxford Professors: a new interpretation of Christian Humanism" (Dallas, A.H.A. Convention, 1977; Bologna, IV International Congress of Neo-Latin Studies, 1979 — scheduled to appear in the proceedings of that gathering); and "Heresy and Humanism in early Tudor Oxford" (St. Louis, Sixteenth Century Studies Conference, 1980). This work will culminate in a book, tentatively entitled *Professors of Orthodoxy: universities, theologians and heresy during the late Middle Ages, Renaissance and Reformation*, which will contain the case-studies, full documentation, and further analysis necessary to support many of the points made here. I would like to thank the American Council of Learned Societies, the American Philosophical Society, the Centre National de la Recherche Scientifique, the Folger Shakespeare Library, the Catholic University of America, and the University of Texas at Austin for grants in support of this research.

I am, of course, not alone in attempting to reformulate the relationship between humanism and scholasticism and other related questions: see, most recently, C.G. Nauert, Jr., "The Clash of Humanists and Scholastics: an approach to pre-Reformation controversies," *Sixteenth Cent. J.*, 4 (1973), 1-18; J.H. Overfield, "Scholastic Opposition to Humanism in pre-Reformation Germany," *Viator*, 7 (1976), 391-420; S. Ozment, "Humanism, Scholasticism, and the Intellectual Origins of the Reformation," in *Continuity and Discontinuity in Church History: essays presented to G.H. Williams* . . . (eds. F.F. Church and T. George; Leiden, 1979), 133-149; J.W. O'Malley, *Praise and Blame in Renaissance Rome* (Durham, 1979); W. Kölmel, "*Scholasticus Literator:* die Humanisten und ihr Verhältnis zur Scholastik," *Historisches Jahrbuch*, 93 (1973), 301-335; and, of course, P.O. Kristeller, *Renaissance Thought* (New York, 1961), especially chapter 5. (See also notes 27, 29, and 41 below.) While my emphases on the social, ecclesiastical, and institutional roles of late medieval, Renaissance, and early Reformation theologians and theology faculties, as well as on their *mentalites*, may differ somewhat from the concerns of these scholars, I am very grateful to each of them, as well as to my colleagues in the History of the University of Oxford project (especially Sir Richard Southern, Jeremy Catto, and James McConica), to John Wipple, William Wallace, Alaistair Crombie, R.N. Swanson, M.M. Harvey, Douglass Taber, and to the other contributors to the present volume, for numerous conversations, countless references, sharp (and generally accurate) criticisms, and continuous encouragement during my research.

 **The Fifth Lateran Council:**

its partial successes and its larger failures

by Richard J. Schoeck
University of Colorado

The Fifth Lateran Council (1512-1517) was the last council before the Reformation, and thus from one point of view it can well be called, as it has been by Jedin, "the last attempt at a papal reform of the Church before the break-up of Christian unity." But this is by no means the whole story, though in this respect as in certain others the Fifth Lateran was the last medieval council. Whatever else it was, this remains the most neglected of councils. Even the source materials and modern scholarship are deficient. The generally useful though at best introductory manual by H. J. Schroeder, *Disciplinary Decrees of the General Councils* (1937) of course omits many of the important decrees and bulls, yet even the more scholarly and more recent *Conciliorum Oecumenicorum Decreta* (edited in 1962 by Alberigo and others under the guiding consultantship of Jedin) is far from complete, though the *COD* does go behind Mansi to the 1521 edition of the conciliar degrees. However, in collating 1521 texts with those of 1515, I have observed marked differences in punctuation, spelling, and even paragraphing: it must be declared *ab initio* that we have nothing like a definitive text for the decrees and bulls of this council. The archival material is scant: there is much less than what survives from the Fourth Lateran, and it is of a totally different order of magnitude from what we have for the Council of Trent, where the materials are so voluminous and the problems in ordering and interpreting them so complex that we have reached the stage of essays on Tridentine historiography.[1] To my knowledge the chief document is not fully available, for the diary of

---

[1] Jedin remains the incomparable account of the history of reform up to Trent, but he does not treat all aspects of the Councils immediately preceding Trent. It is to be observed that there is no record available of the actual debates at Lateran V; we have only summaries completed after the event. See Jedin, I, 128. Cf. Nelson H. Minnich, "Concepts of Reform Proposed at the Fifth Lateran Council," *Archivum historiae pontificae*, 7 (1969), 253-286.

the papal court for this period by Paride de' Grassi is still incompletely edited.[2] But the relative paucity of modern scholarship is astounding: there is nothing extensive on it in English, and not a book devoted to it in any language; even a listing of articles and monographs would be relatively small, expecially if we look beyond discussions of Luther and the controversy over the definition of the immortality of the soul in the Eighth Session.[3] One cannot assume therefore that degree of familiarity with the Fifth Lateran that everyone has of Trent or even of the Fourth Lateran, and so I propose first to locate the council in its historical context.

A vital dimension of the context is of course the century of intensive conciliar activity and thought which preceded the convocation of the Fifth Lateran.[4] For now, let us simply rehearse the immediate background chronology. All of the bishops of France had been summoned to meet in Orleans in September, 1510, to consult on their liberties and privileges of the Gallican Church.[5] While this

---

[2]Paride de'Grassi, or Paris De Grassis (1470-1528), brother of Achilles (cardinal of S. Sisto, chaplain to Julius II, canonist), was master of ceremonies for both Julius II and Leo X. Also a canonist, he was made bishop of Pesaro in 1515, it is said, "for the admirable way in which he had organized and conducted the function (the solemn opening of the Council) in St. John Lateran" (R. L. Foley, in *NCE*, VI, 705). His *Diarium* is a major source for the Fifth Lateran, especially for the day-to-day narrative history of the two popes he served; edited in part in the nineteenth century (by Döllinger, *Beiträge zur politischen, kirchlichen und Kulturgeschichte der sechs letzten Jahrhunderte*, 3 vols., Munich, 1862-82) and used by Pastor, it is now being fully edited by Msgr. José Ruysschaert of the Vatican Library.

[3]For introduction to the events, see 'Le Drama de Martin Luther' in Daniel-Rops; Jedin, I, *passim*. For the immediate context of the 'posting' of the theses, see K. Honselmann, *Urfassung und Drucke der Ablassthesen Martin Luthers und ihre Veröffentlichung* (Paderborn, 1966). Cf. C. Stange, *Luther und das 5. Laterankonzil*(Gütersloh, 1928), for a general discussion.

[4]The bibliography on the conciliar period is very large (see C.M.D. Crowder, *Unity, Heresy, and Reform, 1378-1460* (London, 1977), 190-205), but the following are still central studies: Brian Tierney, *Foundations of the Conciliar Theory* (Cambridge, 1955); W. Ullmann, *The Origins of the Great Schism* (London, 1948; rptd. 1967); E. F. Jacob, *Essays in the Conciliar Epoch*, 2d. ed. (Manchester, 1963); and Martin. One may echo the conclusion of Knowles: "above all the schism, by loosening the bonds of spiritual discipline while retaining, and even increasing, the burden of papal taxation, brought a new urgency into the demand for reform in head and members. This demand grew as the years passed and reached its height in the early period of the Council of Basle. If any lesson was learnt by Europe at large from the 'conciliar epoch' it was that councils could not, and that popes as yet would not, satisfy that demand." David Knowles in *The Middle Ages* by David Knowles with Dimitri Obolensky (vol. II in *The Christian Centuries*) (London, 1968), 425. M. Seidlmayer, *Die Anfänge des grossen abendländischen Schismas* (Münster, 1940) views the work of Heinrich von Langenstein as traditional rather revolutionary: see Jedin, I, ch.i, "The Victory of the Papacy over the Reform Councils;" and on Heinrich, see n. 52 below. Now cf. R. N. Swanson, *Universities, Academics and the Great Schism* (Cambridge, 1979).

[5]For the French background to Pisa, see Pierre Imbart de la Tour, *Les origines de la réforme*, 4 vols. (Melun, 1905-46), esp. II, 1 ff.; Renaudet; and Martin. In 1509

assembly, which actually met at Tours, not Orleans, marked one threat to the Court of Rome, there was still another. In May, 1511, the delegates both of the Roman Emperor Maximilian I and of the King of France, Louis XII, were notified that a council was to open in Pisa on September 1, 1511, an action which was said to be in compliance with the decree *Frequens* of the Council of Constance,[6] which called for a council to meet at least every ten years. But no council had been called, owing (as the French King and the Emperor thought) to the negligence of the pope, who upon election in 1503 had sworn to summon a general council within two years, at a place to be determined by the Pope and two-thirds of the College of Cardinals.

The Council of Pisa was to be convoked in the name of nine cardinals: Carvajal, Briçonnet, Francesco Borgia, Adriano de Castello, de Prie, Carlo del Caretto, Sanseverino, Ippolito d'Este, and Philip of Luxembourg.[7] King Louis XII and Maximilian I supported these dissident cardinals in their open defiance of the authority of the pope. That there was an active rebellion being plotted is indicated by the protest of three cardinals that their names had been affixed by the others to the citation, without consultation or permission — Philip of Luxembourg, Adriano de Castello, and Carlo del Caretto — and another backed away from the plot, eventually to be reconciled.

The document announcing a *soi-disant* universal council at Pisa

---

Julius had issued the Bull *Suscepti Regiminis* which forbade appeals from the pope to a future council. At that time Venice was under attack by Louis XII, among others. Another turning point was the death on May 25, 1510, of Georges d'Amboise, Cardinal de Rohan, who had been granted legatine power for life over the French Church (not unlike the administrative powers which Wolsey was shortly to enjoy in England). Without the leadership of Amboise, Louis summoned a meeting to study reform of the Church and the liberties of the realm, with Louis himself coming to the convening of this session at Tours in September, 1510. All of these events prepared for the calling of the council by the French bishops, which was done in April 1511 at Lyons; and on May 19 from Milan the two French Cardinals, De Prie and Briçonnet, with one Italian, Sanseverino, and two Spaniards, Borgia and Carvajal, convoked the Council of Pisa, claiming the added support of four more members of the Sacred College (who later were to withhold their approval), to meet at Pisa on September 1, 1511. See also A. Deneffe, "Die Absicht des V. Laterankonzils," *Scholastik*, 8 (1933), 359—79; and E. Guglia, "Zur Geschichte des zweiten Conciliums von Pisa, 1511-1512," in *Mitteilungen d. Instituts f. österr. Geschichtsforschung*, 31 (1910), 593-610.

[6]The number of cardinals is not beyond question, but nine is the consensus, counting the four who later withdrew or renounced support. On *Frequens*, see n. 76 below.

[7]The Pisan documents are conveniently collected by A. Renaudet, *Le Concile Gallican de Pise-Milan* (Paris, 1922); on the announcement of this council see p. 29. Jedin notes that Cardinals Carvajal, Sanseverino, Borgia, De Prie and Briçonnet were "apparently acting in collusion with four other members of the Sacred College" (I, 107).

was issued on May 16, 1511.[8] On the 25th of July (although dated
the 18th), Julius II published a bill summoning a true universal
council to Rome on April 19, 1512 — thereby smothering the abortive revolt, or potential schism, of the cardinals named.[9] The preamble to this 1511 bull contains much of interest, for Julius sets forth
the supreme dignity of the Roman Catholic Church and its primacy,
which entailed (so it declared) the duty of withstanding all
schismatic attempts to destroy her unity. Julius then asserted that
he had done his best to convoke a council and that the long delay
was not his fault. A council, the bull maintained, could lawfully be
summoned only by a pope, and so, "with the approval of the loyal
cardinals and by the plenitude of his apostolic power, [he] pronounced the edict of a convocation of a synod by the cardinals in
revolt to be, in both its contents and effects, illegal, null and void;
that its authors and their aides are deprived of all dignities, and that
all cities and districts which harbor and support them are laid under
interdict."

I. The context of criticism and opposition

In attempting to understand the setting of the Fifth Lateran
Council, we want to gauge the dynamics of thoughts, feelings and
actions, and for this effort three contemporary documents will serve
to suggest the violence and depths of those dynamics, indeed the
contradictory or counter-balancing currents of the moment.

First, we have a document completed on October 12, 1511, by the
influential Dominican theologican, Cajetan: his *De Comparatione*

---

[8]To my knowledge there is no bibliographical study of the promulgation of bulls,
but Dr. R. Hirsch of the University of Pennsylvania Library is engaged upon such a
study. These bulls apparently circulated in two ways: one, copies sent to all dioceses,
and two, copies nailed to churches in Rome.

[9]The Bull *Sacrosanctae Romanae Ecclesiae* of July 18, 1511 convoked a General
Council for 19 April 1512 at the Lateran. Beginning with a display of traditional
titles bestowed on the Pontiff, the Bull inveighed against the 'headless lobsters
(*locustae acephali*) who had dared to launch the spurious enterprise of a factitious
council (*conventiculum* and *conciliabulum* are the scornful terms employed) without
papal authority. Reproaching the fractious cardinals and ridiculing the haste of the
proposed council in Pisa (a place unfit, it was declared, to accomodate the leaders of
the world), Julius announced that the Fifth Lateran Council would extinguish
smouldering heresies, extirpate new schisms, and fight the infidels who now
possessed Jerusalem and were attacking the kingdom of Sicily--all conventional
intentions--and that all of this would be discussed 'in alma Urbe nostra, communi
omnium patria, loco optissimo et tutissimo' (§18). On the convocation of a Council
there was not complete agreement as to procedures or tests for authenticity.
Domenico Jacobazzi in *De concili* (written during the period of the Fifth Lateran
Council) declared that a Council could in a state of emergency be convoked without
the authorization of the Pope. See the discussion by Jedin, I, 97-9.

Acutoritatis Papae et Concilii,[10] which refutes the theories of the conciliarists, putting aside the arguments of the canonists and placing the question of papal power and authority within dogmatic theology, to which Almain, a young theologian of Paris, made his reply in 1512.[11] Among those also supporting Julius II must be mentioned the name of Gianfrancesco Poggio, also a Dominican. This traditional line of argument for papal power underscores the argument and rhetoric of the preamble to the 1511 bull of Julius.

Second, a satirical document appeared soon after the death of Julius in February 1513 and described the dead pope as praying for admission through the gate of heaven, while he boasted of his papal supremacy, of being above a council, and related quite cynically how he had managed to derail the *conciliabulum,* the Pisan assembly. This lampoon, *Iulius Exclusus e Coelis,* is now generally (though not universally) accepted as the work of Erasmus: however, he steadfastly denied authorship.[12] It and like literary texts give wider testimony to the force of anti-curial feelings and anti-papal thought, much of it produced during the century-long background of conciliar-papal struggles, as well as by public scandal of the private lives of the latest of the popes themselves. By 1512 the papacy had suffered an immense, perhaps an irrecoverable, loss of moral prestige at the hands of men who were more busy being Italian princes than they were vicars of Christ.

The third document is essential to indicate how much of a desire there was for the reform of the church from within. The document, *Libellus ad Leonem X,* prepared by two Venetians who had just entered the Order of Camaldoli (itself a reform order), and who in 1513 presented a massive plan for the *aggiornamento* of the Church, a plan characterized by Jedin as "both the widest and the boldest of all the many reform programmes drawn up since the conciliar era."[13]

---

[10]For a convenient summary of the career of Cajetan, see *NCE*, and notes 24 and 30 below. It must be remarked that some neglected writings of Cajetan are most relevant to debates in the Fifth Lateran, especially those concerning the *Monte Pietatis.* Cajetan's *De Eleemosynae Praecepto* (1496, reprinted in 1511, and again in 1541 and 1588), together with his treatise on *De Monte Pietatis* (1498, reprinted 1511), are central documents in the study of the full canonical as well as theological context of these debates. See also *De Cambiis* (1499; 1506 and 1511), *Responsio ad Tria Dubia* (1514), *De Societate Negotiatoria* (1515), *De Emptione Rerum Raptarum in Bello Iniusto* (1529): these all manifest his concern with ethical aspects of commerce, exchange, and the booty of war, and they have all been edited by P. P. Zammit, *Scripta Philosophica-Opuscula Oeconomico-Socialia* (Rome, 1934).
[11]Jacques Almain (c. 1480-1515) wrote *De Auctoritate Ecclesiae et Conciliorum Generalium adversus Thom. de Vio* (1512), which is a refutation of Cajetan concerning the temporal power. See O. de la Brosse, *Le Pape et le Concile* (1965), pp. 185-315.
[12]So distinguished an Erasmian historian as James K. McConica is dubious of Erasmus' authorship, but the work will be included in the Toronto Edition of the *Complete Works of Erasmus.* See Jedin, I, 115.
[13]Jedin, I. 128.

In their brief to the pope, these two, Giustiniani and Quirini, stressed the challenge of the American missions and of union with Eastern Christians; they exposed the ignorance both of the regular clergy and the religious (estimating that only two percent understood liturgical Latin), and of the laity (who needed instruction in the fundamentals); they struck at superstition, which touched every public and private activity; and they charged the popes with responsibility for neglect of their duties by the clergy. They were looking to the council to renew the whole life of the Church.[14]

It cannot be too strongly emphasized that there was across Europe a strong movement for renewal, of genuine attempts to purify the liturgical and institutional life of the Church, and that there were in fact real fruits of renewal before 1515. There were several popular or new religious groups and movements: to single out one, the *Oratorio del Divine Amore*.[15] There were also many individuals who cried out for reform before 1512 — individuals as diverse as John Colet in England, Giles of Viterbo in Italy, Ximenez of Spain — and it is to be remarked that many of these in the generation born before 1470 would become backward-looking by the 1540s: that some of the reformers of the Fifth Lateran became the older men charged with responsibilities of authority, which so many of them saw as requiring a defence of the integrity of the Church against heretics and schismatics, against all criticism and all critics (witness Thomas More, even, after 1529). Indeed, as Evennett has provocatively remarked, "it is interesting that so many of the first Protestant leaders should — like Luther himself — have come from the ranks of reformed and observant friars."[16]

I offer, then, these three kinds or groups of documents to suggest the dynamics of the situation. But it must be made clear that all such documents need to be read with care and with a sense of the contexts — as the modern theologian Chenu has suggested in addressing the need to apply to documents like ours the same spirit with which scriptural scholars have been reading biblical texts — for all of the documents in Denzinger and the *COD* (bulls, encyclicals, briefs, etc.) are not univocal; they must be read as unique documents, each with its own special context.[17]

---

[14]Giustiniani, it may be remarked, was a friend of humanists. See Jedin, I, 128 ff., and Evennett, *NCMH*, II, 277.

[15]Cf. D. Cantimori in *NCMH*, II, ch. viii, "Italy and the Papacy," 251-74.

[16]Evennett, *ibid.*, ch. ix, 'The New Orders,' 275-300.

[17]There are of course other documents of great significance in a fuller study; cf. Cantimori's suggestive, and quite lovely, discussion in ch. 2 of his *Eretici Italiani*; and, further *L'attesa dell' età nuova nella spiritualità della fine del Medioevo* (in *Attide III covegno . . . dell'Accademia Tudertina*, Todi, 1962).

II. The Opening of the Council

Against so complex and dark a background, delayed by the French victory at Ravenna on April 11, 1512, the Fifth Lateran Council was formally opened on May 3, 1512. Present were sixteen cardinals, one hundred other prelates (mostly Italians, of whom about seventy were bishops, twelve patriarchs, and three generals of religious orders); in addition, there were envoys of Spain, Venice, and Florence, as well as a certain number of the Roman nobility. The Mass in honor of the Holy Ghost[18] was sung by Cardinal Riario,[19] after which the Master-General of the Augustinians, Giles (Aegedio) of Viterbo,[20] delivered an address in classical Latin on the theme of reform. This oration was universally applauded by members of the Council and others, and it was published in at least two separate editions. Then the Pope bestowed the customary solemn benediction and announced the standard plenary indulgences. After prayers, Cardinal Farnese[21] read the Pope's address, in which the reasons inspiring Julius to summon the Council were set forth, these being the same as declared in the Bull of 1511, convoking the Council. These introductory ceremonies having been concluded, the Pope fixed the 10th of May as the day of the first session.

We know little about the discussion which preceded the drafting of the conciliar documents, but it is known that the Curia decided what was to be dealt with in the individual sessions. Although the bishops were allowed to elect a committee of twenty-four to discuss these drafts, the group was dominated by curial officials.

To follow the convenient summary of procedure by Hughes, "The twenty four were formed into three groups of eight, according to the matter to be studied: the question of the schism and of international peace; the reform of the Church; the faith, and the problem of the French law, called the Pragmatic Sanction....To each of these commissions of eight the pope added eight cardinals and two Generals

---

[18]On the significance of the Mass of the Holy Ghost see my studies: for the historical account, "Medieval Lawyers and the History of the Red Mass," *St. Louis University Law Journal*, (1959), and for a devotional commentary, "The Mass of the Holy Ghost," *American Ecclesiastical Review*, 142 (1960), 387-9. Trent too was begun with a Mass of the Holy Ghost: see note 50 below.

[19]Raffaele Riario (1461-1521) was created cardinal in 1477. Julius II was his uncle, and he became, ironically, a notorious pluralist (see *NCE*). On Ficino's letters to Riario, urging that reform be initiated, see E. Garin, *G. P. della Mirandola* (Florence, 1937); cf. Jedin, I, 155,54.

[20]On Giles of Viterbo--Aegidius, sometimes called Canidio--see further F. Secret, *Scechina e Libellus de Litteris Hebraicis*, (Rome, 1959). The work of John W. O'Malley, *Giles of Viterbo on Church Reform* (Leiden, 1968) is now standard.

[21]Alessandro Farnese (1468-1549) was made cardinal in 1493 and ordained in 1519; as Paul III (1534-49) he convened Trent in 1545. For a number of years he was dean of the Sacred College (officially styled Cardinal Nipote). See *NCE*, and Jedin, I, 288 ff.

of religious orders — a means of securing that the bishops should not overdo the business of radical reform in, say, the practice of the Curia or the life of the mendicant orders. Finally, the whole body of the bishops debated the draft at a 'general congregation'...[22]

III. The Work of the Twelve Sessions

(1) The First Session opened on May 10, 1512, presided over by the Pope. The sermon by Bernardino Zane dealt with the Turkish question,[23] and with the problem of the unity of the Church, which was defined as consisting in first the union of the members with each other, and second in their subordination to the Head, the Vicar of Christ; and that therefore all who did not obey the Head were schismatics. (The language of this council, one might remark, has many echoes of Constance, with its great concern with the heresies of Wyclif and Hus, and it no doubt cast its long shadow on the polemical writings of Luther, Eck, Erasmus, Dolet, Thomas More and the hosts of others who produced the groaning bookshelves crammed with the heavy folios and quartos of sixteenth-century controversies.) In a short address the Pope stated the object of the Council to be, first, the rooting out of schism; second, the reform of the Church; and third, the Crusade against the Turks.

(2) In the Second Session (May 17, 1512) the Hungarian Cardinal Backocs celebrated the High Mass, and the Sermon was preached by Cajetan.[24] His was a powerful sermon, for it remains a remarkable analysis of the Church as the Holy City of Jerusalem seen by John in *Apocalypse* xxi, with her healing powers (the sacraments), her apostles, pastors, teachers, and gifts. The sermon expounded the closeness of mutual union among the inhabitants of that city as like the union which must exist between all members of the same body[25] — again, the familiar medieval analogy of the human body. Cajetan went on to say that the Church is governed by the Vicar of Christ to whom all owed allegiance; by contrast, the Pisan Synod did not possess (it was asserted) any of the notes of the true Church, being neither holy nor lawfully convoked and, in fact, being stained with error in subordinating the head to the members, the pope to the rest of the Church. Both in the First and Second Ses-

---

[22]Philip Hughes, *The Church in Crisis: A History of the General Councils, 325-1870* (New York, 1961), 291. On the composition of the sub-committees, see Hefele, VIII, 810 ff.

[23]I have provided a convenient summary of some humanistic attitudes towards the Turks in "Thomas More's 'Dialogue of Comfort' and the Problem of the Real Grand Turk," *English Miscellany*, 20 (1969), 23-36. See further, E. Guglia, "Die Türkenfrage auf dem laterankonzil," in *Mitteilungen d. Instituts f. österr. Geschichtsforschung*, 21 (1900), 679-91.

[24]For Cajetan's career and importance, see refs. in notes 10 and 47.

[25]Medieval political thought is of course, dominated by the organic metaphor: see note 51 below.

sions we have seen the stress on the authenticity of this Council, developing points made either briefly or only implicitly in the papal bull of 1512 which summoned the Council.

After Cajetan's address, a letter from Henry VIII of England was read which professed his alliance with the Pope;[26] then this was followed by a similar epistle from the King of Spain. The papal bull which confirmed the censures the pope had proclaimed against the pseudo-Council of Pisa (*Cum inchoatum*[27]) was also read.

(3) At the Third Session (December 3, 1512), the sermon was once again on the unity of the Church; and a letter from Maximilian was read which repudiated the pseudo-council set up at Pisa and declared the Emperor's adherence to this council. At the conclusion of the session a papal bull was read by the Bishop of Forli which declared once again that all acts of the Pisan Synod were null and void and pronounced the interdict upon France.[28]

(4) At the Fourth Session (December 10, 1512), there was a larger number present than at the First Session. At the pope's order, the secretary of the Council read letters abrogating the Pragmatic Sanction of Bourges and summoning all protagonists of the Pragmatic Sanction to appear before the Council within sixty days.

(5) At the Fifth Session (February 16, 1513), a bull was read which confirmed prior papal decrees concerning the Pragmatic Sanction. This was the last session presided over by Julius, and it is somewhat ironic that in this session an address had been delivered by the Apostolic Notary, Marcellus of Venice, which was a panegyric on the Pope. The adulatory tone is suggested by these phrases: *Tu enim Pastor. Tu medicus. Tu gubernator. Tu cultor. Tu denique Deus in terris.* While there is little new in the individual figures of praise, the cumulative effect of the rhetoric is something of a landmark in the history of the papal style. The Fifth Session also produced a bull which condemned simony in papal elections and declared (in an inserted constitution, *Cum tam divino*) papal elections null and void if tainted with simony: *Si summus rerum opifex.*

On the 21st of February Julius died, and it was said that "Rome felt that the soul which had passed from her had been of royal cast." The Council was of course suspended, awaiting the election of a new pope and the necessary act of summoning the Council anew. On the 11th of March 1513, the Cardinal Deacon John de'Medici was

---

[26]Christopher Bainbridge, Archbishop of York, who was made Cardinal by Julius II in 1511, was the orator of Henry VIII in Rome. He was anti-French, whereas Silvestre Gigli, absentee bishop of Worcester and resident English ambassador at Rome, was pro-French. See D. S. Chambers, *Cardinal Bainbridge in the Court of Rome, 1509-1514* (London, 1965).

[27]*Cum inchoatum, COD,* 571.

[28]*Ad Illius, COD,* 573.

elected pope and assumed the name of Leo X.[29] He announced that the Council would continue with a minimum of delay.

(6) The Sixth Session (April 27, 1513), over which Leo presided, heard his address which communicated to the Council members his resolve to continue working until complete peace for Christendom was secured.[30]

(7) The Seventh Session (June 17, 1513) heard and approved the constitution *Meditatio Cordis Nostri*, which set the date for the next session.[31]

Cardinals Carvajal and Sanseverino repudiated the Synod of Pisa and recognized the legitimacy of the Fifth Lateran Council.[32] After long discussion, absolution from the censure previously incurred was granted to them. The form of their abjuration and the fact of their reception back into the College of Cardinals is perhaps more interesting to historians of the cardinalate than to us today, but set against his later tactics in dealing with Luther, Leo's actions here are worthy of further study.

(8) The Eighth Session (December 19, 1513) continued to focus on French matters. The ambassadors of Louis XII presented the king's renunciation of Pisa, then in session at Lyons, and his recognition of Lateran. Further, it was resolved to send legates to all Christian sovereigns to seek arms against the Turks, and there was an effort to achieve peace among Christians (in *De pace inter christianos principes componenda*[33]). This was the session which dealt with the pressing question of the immortality of the soul and condemned (in the bull *Apostolici regiminis sollicitudo*[34]) the doctrine that the soul of man is mortal, as well as the teaching that there is one and the same soul in all men. There was also some discussion of reform (although largely restricted to the Curia's taxation system), producing the bull on reform, *In apostolici culminis*.[35] A prominent layman, Giangrancesco Pico della Mirandola was present during these debates. Afterwords he wrote his *De Reformandis*, a copy of which was sent to the Pope, in which he urged that a combination of Scripture and the tradition of early Christianity was sufficient and that later accretions to Christianity were superfluous.[36]

---

[28]A*Si summus rerum opifex*, COD, 576.

[29]Leo X was born Giovanni de' Medici in 1475, and was taught by Ficino, Poliziano, and Pico; in 1492 he was made Cardinal and in 1513 received Holy Orders, after his election to the Papacy.

[30] See *COD*, 579, *Supernae illius ordinatione*. It might be observed that the absence of Cajetan during this period raises questions concerning his contribution to and his influence upon the work of the Council in its final phases. On Cajetan see notes 10 and 47.

[31]*Meditatio Cordis Nostri*, COD, 581; cf. Mansi XXXII, 815.

[32]*Ibid.*

[33]*De pace inter christianos principles*, COD, 582.

[34]*Apostolici regiminis sollicitudo*, COD, 581.

[35]*In apostolici culminis*, COD, 584.

[36]NCE, XI, 345; E. Garin, *La Filosofia* (1947), II, 72-7.

(9) At the Ninth Session (May 5, 1514) the French bishops were still absent, and they were thus charged with contumacy. But after it was shown that these bishops had in fact started their journey to the Council, but had been detained by the Duke of Milan,[37] the Pope extended the time allowed for them to appear at the Council. The Ninth Session witnessed another exhortation of the Pope for peace, *Postquam ad universalis ecclesiae,*[38] which repeated the platitudinous expressions of the Eighth Session. It also produced the important *bulla reformationis curiae, Supernae dispositionis arbitrio,*[39] which is discussed further below.

At this point one may note that two years have now gone by, and the delays and confusion caused by the Pisan Council are still coloring the deliberations and weakening the work of Lateran. It is not generally realized how seriously this pseudo-council (which had concluded in early 1512, after holding several sessions, and which had decreed among other things the suspension of Julius II) impaired the viability of the Fifth Lateran. This impairment must be put alongside the tactics of the fragmentation of all discussion of reform; both are vital dynamics of this Council.

(10) The Tenth Session (May 4, 1515) came a full year later, and it is difficult to understand why there should have been such an interval. During this session three important questions were discussed, and on two of them decrees of the greatest importance were passed. Before this, on March 31, 1515, Leo X had issued the bull authorizing the indulgence to support the building of St. Peter's to be preached in the Archdioceses of Mainz and Madgeburg; and Tetzel began preaching in January 1517. This action is obviously of paramount importance in Lutheran studies, but it is important here both as an indication of the failure of Leo to comprehend the urgent need for reform and also of his preoccupations with other matters.

Of the Council's activities, first, sanction was given to the 'Monti de Pieta.'[40] In the latter half of the fifteenth century, Franciscans had taken the lead in a crucial area of social reform. In order to prevent the exploitation by money-lenders who demanded exorbitantly

---

[37] Milan, of course, rivalled Rome as one of the most ancient sees in Italy. It should be noted that a daughter of Galeazzo, duke of Milan until his death by assassination in 1476, was Bianca Maria, married to Maximilian I in 1493. The Duke of Milan in 1514 was Massimiliano, a son of Ludovico II Moro (son of Francesco, d. 1466, and uncle of the young Gian Galeazzo who succeeded Galeazzo Maria, who had usurped the rule of Milan in 1478). Such rivalries, accompanied by the fierce loyalties of the powerful families which produced so many cardinals (and popes) almost in defense against their rivals, provide the 'figure in the carpet' for the politics of the times.

[38] *Postquam ad universalis ecclesiae, COD,* 585.

[39] *Supernae dispositionis arbitrio, COD,* 590.

[40] 'Monte' was commonly used in the sense of a 'community chest' or 'bank' long before the first monte di pietà was founded (cf. Rizasco, *Dizionario . . . storico e administrativo*). Cf. note 10 on Cajetan above, and Jedin I, 132.

high interest on loans, yet to provide loans where they were desperately needed by destitute townsfolk, and the poor everywhere, the Franciscans founded institutions which were really benevolent banks (rather than pawn shops, as some have called them), whose capital came from voluntary contributions, gifts and legacies; and these would supply money in exchange for a pledge, without interest, but with a small charge imposed. First opened in the Papal States in the 1460s, these institutions spread rapidly through Italy and to other countries (Bavaria, France, England). But their very success was a problem: to meet the increasing administrative expenses, the Monti had had to make a small charge on each loan, and to this the Dominicans objected violently, calling the imposition of anything more than the amount of the loan usury. Although the foundation of the Monti had been approved by popes from Pius II to Julius II, the charging of expenses was under criticism. In this decree of 1515, *De reformatione Montium pietatis: Inter multiplices nostrae solicitudinis curas,*[41] the Franciscans finally won a complete victory: a small percentage of interest on loans, sufficient to defray expenses, was permitted, but there was to be no profit in the transaction. Those who asserted this to be unlawful thereby incurred excommunication.

Another weighty matter at this session was that of the printing of books, this being the first General Council to consider printing.[42] It was forbidden by *Super impressione librorum* to print books without the approbation of the ordinary and the inquisitor, and in Rome of the Cardinal Vicar and the Master of the Palace, under pain of excommunication and the imposition of heavy fines. Every book printed contrary to this decree was to be burned.

Another item with a different kind of importance was the reform of the calendar, but opinions were so divergent that Leo X withdrew the question as not yet rip for action. Still another problem was the further regulation of friars, but this was carried over into the Twelfth Session.[43]

(11) The Eleventh Session (December 19, 1516) was one of immense consequence for the relations between the Eastern and Western Churches, although this issue of greater importance is usually overlooked because the Pragmatic Sanction of Bourges once again surfaced.

At this session, envoys of the Patriarch of the Maronites of the Lebanon, Simon Peter, were admitted to tender their obedience to the Pope, and the Patriarch's letter was delivered. This epistle contained a profession of faith in which the Maronites stated their belief in the procession of the Holy Ghost from the Father *and* the

---

[41]*Inter multiplices nostrae . . . curas, COD,* 601-2.
[42]On printing: cf. *Super impressione librorum: Inter sollicitudines, COD,* 608.
[43]On reform of the calendar, see *NCE.* On regulating the friars, see *COD,* 621.

Son, in the doctrine of Purgatory, and in Easter Communion. The Patriarch thanked the Pope for having sent the Guardian of the Franciscan Monastery at Beirut to instruct the Maronites. There are no references to this important profession either in Denzinger or in the *COD*.[44]

Also at this session, a concordat made between the Pope and the King of France was read to the Council, along with bull *Pastor Aeternus* (which formally abrogated the Pragmatic Sanction, with the approval of the Council.)[45] And, this was the session that legislated, with far-reaching effects, on preaching, in *Circa modum praedicandi*.[46]

(12) At the Twelfth and concluding session (March 16, 1517), a bull was read that, in effect, closed the Council on the grounds that since peace had now been established among Christian princes there was no need to prolong this Council. The reform of morals, the bull declared, had been attended to by salutary canons; and, finally, the schism of Pisa had been repaired.

In further studies, it would be well to inquire further into the mind of the Council—insofar as that is possible, given the archival and documentary limitations that obtain—to establish whether this decision to close the Council was made by the Pope alone, or by the Pope in consultation either with his cardinals or with the Council. Certainly it can now be seen to have been premature to suppose that reform had been accomplished, not only in the light of the thunder-and-lightning which issued from Wittenberg on the following October 31st, but also in the light of the general failure to enforce the reform of the Roman curia or diocesan organizations (for the success of some cardinals like Ximenez in pre-Tridentine reform was not general).

It remains to be indicated that the Twelfth Session imposed a three-year tax on all benefices, to be used for a war against the Turks. Thus, it would seem, the external threat to Christendom, that of the Turks, was never entirely lost from sight between the First Session and the Twelfth; but the threat from within was rarely faced again after the moving oration of Giles of Viterbo. Twenty

---

[44]Professor Peter Bilaniuk (University of Toronto) is developing a study of this profession and its history.

[45]*Pastor aeternus, COD*, 616. Cf. *NCE*, VI, 266 d.

[46]There is, disappointingly, no discussion of Lateran V or of *Circa modum praedicandi, COD*,610, in J. W. Blench's recent *Preaching in England in the late 15th and 16th Centuries* (Oxford, 1964). There is nothing published on Lateran V as a whole to compare with P. Arendt, *Die Predigten des Konstanzer Konzils* (Freiburg, 1933), though a certain amount has been written on Giles of Viterbo. For the post-Lateran V period, see J. Rainer, "Entstehungsgeschichte des Trienter Predigtreformdekretes," *Z. Kath. Theol.*, 39 (1915), 256-317, 465-523; and cf. Jedin, I, *passim*. See n. 69 below.

years later, in his *Dialogue of Comfort* Thomas Moore would structure his consolation around this bitter irony and would contrast the
inner and the external threats.

It is obvious that much work needs to be done on this council and
its problems. One kind of research must deal with the individuals involved: Cajetan, Bembo, Sadoleto, and others who were in positions
of ecclesiastical power or influence, or who might be regarded as
career diplomats; there has been some notable study of this kind.[47]
An even more fundamental need is a full catalogue of the documentation, published and unpublished. Yet another kind of study should
focus on the reaction of some key minds to the Council. Stange's
work on Luther, for example, now needs reevaluation[48].

We can summarize by saying that the Fifth Lateran Council gave
that ultimate stamp to the inflation of papal claims against which
Luther was to react so violently. By encouraging the curialists to
overplay their hand, the Council in its most general influence intensified and accelerated Luther's alienation from the medieval Church
of Rome. More specifically, two decrees of the Council were of
notable influence upon the German reformer's development: the
one, the product of a serious political threat to the papacy, the other
the product of an equally threatening philosophical issue. In its condemnation of the Council of Basel, the Lateran achieved the effect of
encouraging and justifying Luther in his right to ignore councils except insofar as they agreed with his understanding of scripture. In
its decree on immortality,the Lateran helped to convince Luther
both that the Papacy was the Antichrist and that his own age was
that of the last times.

IV. A Council of Reform?

Jedin has written, "the notion that before the Schism the Church
was sunk in worldliness, superstition and abuses, which used to
prevail in Protestant circles, has long been known to be untenable.
On the other hand [he goes on], we should refrain from viewing
Catholic attempts at reform in the period of the Middle Ages as a
mighty stream which, by its own momentum, would have led to a
general reform even if there had been no schism. The latter event did
more than merely tamper with its course or divert it. The Protestant

---

[47]See, for example, R. M. Douglas, *Jacopo Sadoleto, 1477-1547, Humanist and
Reformer* (Cambridge, Mass., 1959); Cecil H. Clough's various published and
continuing work on Bembo; and now a new book by Jared Wicks, *Cajetan Responds*
(Washington, 1978).

[48]In an aborted volume on the Fifth Lateran Council which was being planned at
Toronto, there were essays contributed by J. K. McConica on Erasmus, John
Headley on Luther, and Fr. von Gunten on Cajetan. I should like to express publicly
to these and other active contributors to that proposed volume my regrets that,
owing to problems in finding support for publication, the volume never saw print.

Reformation owed its success to the fact that the attempts at reform which sprouted from the soil of the Church did not come to maturity. They nevertheless constituted the preliminaries and even the beginning of that regeneration of the Church in the last years of the sixteenth century which is usually referred to as the Catholic Reformation. The reform decrees of the Council of Trent are the most notable fruits of this transformation. The Schism did much more than provide the occasion for the Council of Trent. Not only were its dogmatic definitions called for by the errors of the Reformers, but even its reform decrees might not have been promulgated but for the Schism. This is the lesson of the story of the conciliar idea and reform from the days of Basle which we have followed up thus far...."[49]

But Jedin does not go far enough, even from a Roman Catholic point of view, and he does not put enough questions to the body of data subsumed in his splendid narrative. The Fifth Lateran Council was opened with a Mass in honor of the Holy Ghost—as was the Reformation Parliament in England in 1529, and the Council of Trent[50] — and some theologians might now want to ask (in the ecumenical spirit possible four centuries after these shattering events) whether the pattern of meaning into which those event of the Reformation and its sequellae have developed, cannot best be understood in the light of an operation of the Holy Ghost?

Above all else, and it is a vital matter both to historians of political thought and those of the papacy and conciliar relations, there is the immensely troubling question of responsibility for reform. To the extent that men really thought of the total structure of *ecclesia* in the metaphor of John of Salisbury—the familiar medieval metaphor of the head and its members—that metaphor has its limiting force: one tends to reduce or limit the role and responsiblity of the members according to the analogy.[51] In point of fact, Durandus had written in the earlier *De Modo Concilii Generalis Celebrandi* that "the reform of the Church must proceed from the head, that is, from the Roman Church"; the pope, he said further, must be a pattern for all. To be sure, conciliarists would have put the responsibility upon a council; as early as 1381 Heinrich von Langenstein in his *Epistola Concilii Pacis* "had already asserted that the reform of the Church would be one of the tasks of

---

[49]Jedin, I, 165.

[50]On the Mass of the Holy Ghost, see n. 18 above. Trent was of course begun with a Mass of the Holy Ghost, as was the so-called Reformation Parliament of 1529 in England.

[51]John of Salisbury has generally been credited with the metaphor of the human body for political concepts, but as with all such metaphors the problem of attribution is vexed. See H. Liebeschütz, "John of Salisbury and Pseudo-Plutarch," *J. Warburg & Court. Inst.*, 6 (1943), 33-9; and , further, A. Momigliano, *ibid.*, 12 (1949), 189 ff. Cf. E. H. Kantorowicz, *The King's Two Bodies* (Princeton, 1957), p. 199 & *n.* See n. 25 above.

the Council of reunion."[52] But by 1517 there had been a triumph of the papacy in the struggles for power between pope and councils, and councils were reduced to instruments of the pope. The Italian popes had then concentrated a great deal of their energies upon Italian politics. The price was double: the unification of the Italian state was set back centuries behind that of the rest of Europe, and the Western Church was still dependent upon an Italian papal court for the intitiative to reform. The focus of responsibility was the same as the focus of power: the Roman pontiff. Jedin has sketched this portrait of Leo X and his court at the time of the Lateran Council, and it carries the color-tones I would also want to give:
"Surrounded as he was by the most brilliant court in Europe...exalted to the sky by the humanists who enjoyed his favour, Leo X might well have persuaded himself that schism and Council were but a bad dream, the anti-Roman opposition of those beyond the Alps and the cry for a reform of the Curia no more than a protest of late-comers, malcontents and everlasting fault-finders. His was a dreadful mistake. The fire of a religious revolution broke out in the house before its inmates were aware of it.... For more than a century and a half men had devised plans for a reform of the Curia and the Church. It had been discussed and written about, but never had a liberating step been taken by which the Papacy would have placed itself at the head of a movement for the Church's renewal. A grand opportunity had been missed.[53]

Perhaps the greatest opportunity manqué was that of the reform of the canon law, which was so vital to the life of the Church and whose reform proceeded less than almost any other area. For the canon law came to be the very image of all that the Reformers hated about the Church of Rome—other than the sometimes exaggerated charges of corruption and ignorance and simony—and had canon

---

[52]Heinrich von Langenstein, *Epistola concilii pacis* (1381) in Gerson, *Opera omnia*, ed. L. Dupin (Antwerp, 1706), II, 239 ff.; cf. Jedin, I, 11 & n. Also, G. Durandus, *De modo concilii generalis celebrandi*, in *Tractatus illustrium iurisconsultorum*, xiii (Venice, 1584), fols. 173-5v. For discussion of this significant treatise, see A. Posch, "Der Reformvorschlag des Wilhelm Durandus jun. auf. dem Konzil von Vienne," in *Mitteilungen des Instituts für österreichesche Geschichtsforschung, Ergänzungsband,* 11 (1929), 288-303; cf. Jedin, I, 8 *n.* For other tracts to be considered: Marsiglio of Padua, *Defensor pacis*, ed. R. Scholz (Hanover, 1932), and Alan Gewirth, *Marsiglio of Padua and Medieval Political Philosophy*, vol. I. (New York, 1951): cf. Jacob, *Essays in the Conciliar Epoch*, pp. 85-105. Marsiglio's work was condemned by John XXII in 1327, in the Bull *Licet iuxta doctrinam.* The printing of Marsiglio in 1522 was an event that threw a long shadow on sixteenth century political thought, especially in England. Finally, Ockham's *Dialogue* (1343): cf. R. Scholz, *W. von Ockham als politischer Denker und sein Breviloquium de principatu tyrannico* (Leipzig, 1944). The circulation of the ideas of Heinrich von Langenstein, Durandus, Marsiglio and Ockham among the participants in the Fifth Lateran Council is a matter that needs further study.
[53]Jedin, I, 137-8.

law, theology, and the devotional life of the Church been brought into more meaningful relationship, much that did happen in the sixteenth century, and subsequent centuries, would not have happened: much pain and expenditure of energy would have been obviated. A vital link with the long medieval centuries of Christian traditions would not have been lost, or blurred, by the Protestant Reformation, and so oppressive a weight of orthodoxy, with its concomitant fierce searching out of heresy, would not have been assumed as a Catholic character: the gap between Protestantism and Roman Catholicism would likely not have become so great. But I am building speculation upon a structure that has little solid research to support it, for in the history of canon law in the West, no period has been so neglected as that after 1500.[54] There is as yet little evidence to testify to attempts towards reform legislation which the Council did enact. There are many areas where further research is necessary.[55]

The massive programming of the *Libellus ad Leonem X* was of course not remotely put into actuality, nor was very much of the conciliar work a translation of the high moral exhortation put forward in the opening oration of Giles of Viterbo. In part, the inherited form of a Lateran synod dominated by an Italian pope and his court was not adequate to the monumental pressures of new demands and responsiblities: the times had changed (if ever that form had been appropriate to the needs of the Church), and the pressure of social, intellectual and ecclesiastical problems were now too great. Julius and Leo had won the century-long war with councils and conciliarists, but the Church, the whole Church, paid the price. But, more concerned as they were with recovering fiscal and administrative powers, jurisdictions, than with restoring spiritual integrity and authority, the pre-Reformation popes (and these two especially) did not understand what reform meant and could not,

[54]S. Kuttner is continuing his work on the reform of the canon law. For the period immediately preceding the Lateran Council, see R. J. Schoeck, "Canon Law in England on the Eve of the Reformation," *Mediaeval Studies*, 25 (1963), 125-47.

[55]One might comment on the following as further areas where research is needed: enforcement of the Lateran councils, the continuity between Lateran and Trent, and later citations of Lateran. One wishes for study of the influence of certain quattrocento figures, most notably Savonarola. He is reported to have urged Charles VIII in 1494 to go on to Rome, to convene the Council, and to "dispose the usurper who bought the tiara but was never a true pope . . . ." On the relation between Savonarola and Pico, with respect to reform, see Jedin, I, 155 *n*. As against Savonarola's urging to call a Council there was Torquemada, who held the idea that a Council was a danger to the Church: see Jedin, I, 28 (and for a suggestive statement of the influence of Torquemada's *Summa de ecclesia*, Jedin, I, 27 ff.). Much more needs to be done with the role of individual orders and their representatives: the Dominicans were conspicuous, with Prierias, Cajetan, among others (Jedin, I, 28). There is evidence that Nicholas of Cusa was a strong influence upon many council participants: see A. Posch, *Die Concordantie catholica des Nicolaus von Cues* (Paderborn, 1930). See general studies cited in note 4 above.

even had they so intended, quicken into life what little reform they permitted to be legislated in Lateran V; that the decrees of the Council were published as papal bulls, with the papal coat of arms in large on the title-page, did not help the cause of reform across the Alps. Too much the Italian princes, Julius and Leo were too little the vicars of Christ. Little wonder that for all of his being a man of good will, Adrian VI would fail in his reform efforts: so much integrity had been lost, few could believe in the sincerity of a pope.

The last of the medieval councils came to an end with its twelfth session on the 16th of March 1517. Seven months later, on October 31st of the same year, Martin Luther promulgated his ninety-five theses in Wittenberg, and the initiative for reform had passed from Rome to Germany.

V. A Retrospective View

The Council failed. Even if Martin Luther had not so dramatically published his theses seven months after the closing of the final session,[56] it would be obvious that the Council had not achieved its purpose of reforming the Church. With our historical hindsight of that event in Wittenberg at the end of October 1517, and against the unfolding drama of the Reformation that moved with increasing swiftness, one must view the Council as a masterstroke of Sophoclean irony: it was not enough to have failed, but the Council must think that it had done its work and congratulate itself.

But the nature of the failure, and the reasons for it, are vital problems for study. As historians we must ask, *why?* in order to understand that age more fully. And in our own times it will become heuristic—as we move in time away from the immediacy of Vatican II—to compare two such different reform-councils. With Lateran V in mind, we may well ask how much of the gay optimism that attended the closing of Vatican II was well-founded? Then can Christians in the summer of 1517 all be thought foolishly optimistic?

For matters of Church reform the key manifesto of European humanists of the early sixteenth century may well have been the *Libellus Ad Leonem X* presented to the Fifth Lateran Council by Tommaso Giustiniani and Vincenzo Quirini.[57] But optimism and

---

[56]The 95 Theses were nailed up on 31 October, 1517, and printed, so that they were easily distributed. The sources were gathered by W. Köhler, *Dokumente zum Ablasstreit* (Tübingen, 1902) The argument over whether the theses were tacked to the church door still goes on: see E. Iserloh, *The Theses Were Not Posted* (London, 1968), and R. L. McNally, "The Ninety-five Theses of Martin Luther," *Theological Studies*, 28 (1967) 439-80. What is clear and important is that they were written, printed and circulated; what is to the point here is that the Fifth Lateran Council had ended on the 16th of March 1517, eight months earlier.

[57]See Jedin, 128 ff. On the *Libellus* as a humanist document see James K. McConica, *English Humanists and Reformation Politics* (Osford, 1965), 2; and H. O. Evennett in *NCMH*, II, 275 ff.

hope were not universal. Erasmus' *Iulius Exclusus* expresses much of the cynicism one finds increasingly in such works as the *Letters of Obscure Men*, a cynicism that is both general and at the same time specific, often finding its target in the bitter anti-papal feelings and attitudes. The way from 1512 to 1517 seems to have been a painful road for many humanists: More's *Utopia* (as I have elsewhere urged[58]) was in 1516 a last-ditch appeal for the use of reason towards the solution of urgent problems in Christendom, and such diverse writers as Skelton in England and Machiavelli in Italy testify to the sharpness of criticism, or indeed cynicism, concerning professed public values. Yet at the same time there were strong currents of piety, and both spiritual and institutional reform, as Hughes and Evennett have stressed.[59]

Perhaps the final paradox of the Fifth Lateran Council is that its major achievement was theological: the definition of the immortality and essential individuality of the soul. And this was a definition clearly and vigorously asserted against strong neo-Aristotelian (and like contemporary) views, and in the heat of a still-continuing flood of philosophical and theological treaties on the burning issue of immortality.[60] As a result of this definition, the soul can be declared (as by modern Catholic theologians) to be "immortal, though this immortality is not to be considered mere continuance as before but a supratemporal fulfillment of the spiritual person who has finished the period when he was free to act in time, and though revelation testifies that ultimately this fulfillment will be manifest as the completion of the whole man."[61]

a. Mendicants and Bishops

The story of this conflict is of great importance in its own right, but it can also be said to have permanently obstructed the central problem of Church reform for many generations, "the reconstruc-

---

[58] In *NCE* (s.v., More, 'Utopia') and in "'A Nursery of Correct and Useful Institutions': Reading More's *Utopia* as Dialogue," *Moreana*, 22 (1969)--(rptd. in *Essential Articles for the Study of Thomas More*, ed. R. S. Sylvester and G. Marc'hadour (Hamden, Conn., 1977), 281 ff. and 627-30). See now the chapter on *Utopia* in my *Achievement of Thomas More* (University of Victoria, 1976).

[59] Philip Hughes, cited above, and H. Evennett, *NCHM*, also as cited above.

[60] On the Bull of Leo X, *Apostolici Regiminis* (Session VIII), see above. On the question of the immortality of souls, see E. Gilson, "Autour de Pomponazzi: Problématique de l'immortalité de l'âme en italie au début du XVIe siècle," *Archives d'Histoire Doctrinale et Littéraire du Moyen Age*, 36 (1961) 163-79; see also Cajetan "On the Immortality of Minds", in Leonard A. Kennedy (ed.) *Renaissance Philosophy* (The Hague, 1973), 41-54.

[61] Thus Karl Rahner and Herbert Vorgimler, *Theological Dictionary*, trans. R. Strachan (New York:, 1965), 433.

tion of the Church's apostolic efficiency."[62] The Council addressed itself to this long-standing problem of the friars and their exemptions, but it could not solve it. Behind the Bull of 1516 lay nearly three centuries of bitter quarrels over jurisdiction and theology,[63] since the granting to the mendicant Orders of the right to preach anywhere without prior permissions from bishops—granted by Clement IV and Martin IV in the thirteenth century.

Frequent conflicts arose, and to the scandal of the Church Benedict VIII was obliged for the sake of peace to restrict the prerogatives of the mendicant Orders. Henceforth, without the permission of the Ordinary the mendicants could not hear confessions, nor preach in parish churches and administer the last sacraments without the permission of the pastors. In the ensuing decades, the fortunes now of the seculars, now of the mendicants, rose and fell: the regulations of Boniface VIII were suppressed by Benedict XI, then reinstituted by Clement V at the Council of Vienne (1311-1312).[64]

The case for the seculars was pushed to its extremes by Jean De Pouilly, master of the University of Paris during the pontificate of John XXII; he taught that because the jurisdiction of bishops and pastors derived immediately from God, no one (not even the pope) could deprive them of it. Hence, it was argued, absolution conferred by the regulars—even when they possessed proper Apostolic indults—were invalid. Summoned by John XXII to Avignon, Jean was defeated in a theological debate and compelled to recant. His errors were formally condemned in the Bull *Vas electionis* of July 21, 1321.[65]

But the mendicant case was argued equally extremely; some mendicants asserted that their powers in matters of confession had no limitations. Sixtus IV (a former Superior General of the Franciscans and a member of the powerful della Rovere family) dispensed the mendicants from the payment of the *quarta funeralium*, that quarter of the funeral stipend required by Boniface VIII to be paid to the parish, when conducting funeral services in their own churches. In other ways Sixtus favored the mendicants, and in 1474 and 1479 he granted them power to absolve from cases reserved to bishops.[66] His is a notable instance of the paradox of personal piety

---

[62]See H. Evennett, "The New Orders," in *NCMH.*, II, 276.

[63]For a convenient summary of the rivalry of friars and seculars, see Arnold Williams, 'Chaucer and the Friars,' *Speculum,* xxviii (1953), 499-513, and D.W. Robertson, Jr. *A Preface to Chaucer* (Princeton, 1962). See also P. Hughes, *Reformation in England* (1963), I, 69; and *DTC,* 'Freres mineurs'.

For the early development of the controversy, see D. L. Douie, *The Conflict Between the Seculars and the Mendicants of the University of Paris in the Thirteeth Century* (London, 1954).

[64]See Denzinger No. 458, 'Errores Guilelmi de Sancto Amore.' There are echoes, of course, in the writings of Erasmus, More, and Rabelais.

[65]Denzinger No. 491.

and public corruption in one person.

The problems were manifestly complex, and the causes fervently and at times violently argued. The matter of the mendicants and the bishops was introduced, as we have seen, into the Tenth Session of Lateran V, and in 1515 Leo X issued the Bull *contra exemptos* (later, in 1516, *Super religiosos*), with a number of stringent regulations, which mollified the seculars only minimally, although it did regularize certain practices; yet the mendicants, while not dissolved (as some extremists among the seculars had hoped) were not altogether placed under the jurisdiction of the ordinaries; the identity and essential functions of the mendicants were preserved. Now the mendicants could neither bless a marriage nor administer the Last Sacraments without the pastor's permission; further, they were accountable to their own Ordinary in the matter of ordinations and the consecration of their own churches; and, finally, they were subject to episcopal visitation of all parish churches served by them. The problems were not all solved, but the moderating compromise of these Leonine regulations must be measured against not only the violence and antiquity of the quarrel but also the phenomenon of the establishment of many new orders and communities, both of men and women, and of diverse structures and devotional ends. Again, many in the period found it easier to move outside the existing orders to found new ones than to reform the old or to modify their structures.[67]

b. Other Matters

There were other aspects or activities which must be recognized. The Council did deal with printing, albeit three-quarters of a century after its beginnings. It was the first General Council of the Church to receive a representative from the New World, the bishop of Santo Domingo; not until Vatican II would there be a like expansion of the fixed horizons of the Church. And it would prove to be the one council in four centuries to have lay representatives, for not until Vatican II would laymen again be present at the proceedings of a Council of the Roman Catholic Church. These are not triumphs, even of a minor order; yet they are a part of the total history of the Council, as are the approval of the *Monti pietati* (the work of Ses-

---

[66]It must be remarked that Sixtus IV, who died in 1484, was Francesco della Rovere, and Cardinal Riario (who is cited in an earlier section) was his nephew; and it was Sixtus who canonized Bonaventura. A century later, another Franciscan pope, Sixtus V ranked Bonaventure among the 'primary doctors': *NCE*.

[67]See H. O. Evennett, *The Spirit of the Counter-Reformation* (London, 1968) for a general survey.

sion X[68]), and the reform of preaching (in Session XI[69]). Both were vital to the role of the Church in the changing world.

We may pause here to glance at the New World insofar as the Church and its reform are being considered. The conquest of New Spain was, as J.H. Parry has put it, "a spiritual as well as a military campaign,"[70] and the early Franciscans were like the first Dominicans who were sent out from Spain in 1524 and 1525: "They were picked products of Church reform in Spain, representing both the radical churchmanship of Cisneros and the humanism and learning of Erasmus." While some of the problems of the pre-Reformation Church in the Old World were not carried over—national churches and the struggle between papalists and conciliarists, for example—others were, and a fight between the friars and the seculars would inevitably arise to parallel that of the Old World. But these matters, like larger relationships between Lateran V and the missionary activities throughout the world, must remain for future studies in the working and influence of Lateran V.[71].

It would be a mistake, surely, to consider that there were no results or lasting effects of the Fifth Lateran Council. One measure of the effect of this Council is the fact that soon after 1517 there was a widespread and continuing call for another general council: if there had been total cynicism, there would have been little hope in still another council. It must be remembered that except for the abortive and invalid Council of Pisa there had been no council for sixty-seven years (from 1445, the end of the Council of Florence, to 1512, the beginning of Lateran V). In his *Appellatio ad Concilium a Leone X, denuo repetitia et innovata* (1520), Luther appealed for a council, and his appeal was largely to a general council committed to the primacy of scripture in matters of faith and unrestricted by pope or curia.[72] Others, too, called for a council after 1520.

Into this context must be placed the extraordinary document drawn up by Pope Adrian, the *Instructio* read to the Diet of Nürn-

---

[68]On *De reformatione Montium pietatis*, see note 40 above.

[69]On *Circa modum praedicanci*, see note 46 above, and the forthcoming works of John W. O'Malley on preaching at the papal court; J. W. Blench, *Preaching in England in the late 15th and 16th centuries* (Oxford, 1964) is useful as a study of English sermon style and content, but it does not address the question of the reform of preaching (as noted by L. Boyle in *RES,* n.s. XVII [1966], 308-9).

[70]*NCHM,* II, 565.

[71]I have spoken earlier of the collection of studies made at Toronto in the late 1960s, which, unfortunately, did not see print; I am now preparing a bibliography of studies on Lateran V and would welcome hearing from others at work in this field.

[72]*WA,* 7: 75-82. But Luther finally considered--at least by 1539--that ecumenical councils were less effective for reformation than the work of individual schools and parishes; he continued to claim that a general council was superior to a pope: see John M. Headley, Introduction to the *Responsio Ad Lutherum,* (Yale Edition of the Complete Works of St. Thomas More, vol. 5) (New Haven, 1969), II, 969. For a full discussion, see C. Stange, *Luther und das 5. Laterankonzil* (Gütersloh, 1928); however, there is much that needs to be updated and revised.

berg on the 3d of January 1523, for not only did the Pope himself set forth his plans for a complete reform of the Church but he candidly confessed that the present lamentable state of the Church stemmed from the sins of both clergy and Curia.[73] Few questioned Adrian's sincerity or doubted that he wished for an honest and thorough-going reform of Curia and Church, but many questioned whether Adrian had the strength to reform his own Curia; Luther, it is clear, reviled Adrian as the Anti-Christ, and other reformers saw the document only as the last of a series promised but never achieved reforms. And, in any case, Adrian died soon afterwards (September 14, 1423), and for any carrying-out of his dreams for reform one must look past his immediate successor to the architects of the Council of Trent.

c. Reform of the Canon Law

Perhaps only such an honesty and humility as Adrian's could have successfully engaged the reform of the canon law, for so much of the late fifteenth-century presentation and functioning of canon law was addressed to the papacy and curia, and anything like complete revision, much less reorganization, of canon law and its systems could have involved much examination of papal and curial authority. Yet surely among the more profound consequences of Lateran V, perhaps in its long-run effects upon not only the discipline but also the very life of the Church, was the failure of the Council to address itself to reform on the canon law. But this is a most complex problem, which must be left entirely for future investigation.[74]

---

[73]The *Instructio* was read by the papal legate, the astute Francesco Chieragati; he had been sent to Nürnberg specifically to implement provisions of *Exsurge Domine* and the Diet of Worms--see Pastor, IX, 132. As Jedin declares, "the action [of admitting publicly sins of clergy and Curia] was without precedent and was never repeated": op. cit., I, 210. For the text of the *Instructio*, see Carl Mirbt und Kurt Aland, *Quellen zur Geschichte des Papsttums und des Römischen Katholizismus* (Tübingen, 1967), I, 504 ff.

[74]Recent studies of canon law and reform in the Council of Trent have been to some extent retrospective: see, e.g., S. Kuttner, "The reform of the Church and the Council of Trent," The *Jurist*, 22 (1962), 123-42. But there has been little close reading of the question of canon law in the Fifth Lateran Council, and close study is called for the memorandum on abuses and for reform of canon law in the sixth session of Lateran V. Historians must now examine a number of specific issues, such as the first printing of the *Corpus Juris Canonici* by Jean Chappuis (whose *oeuvre* I am now examining), as well as questions with wider implications. See my "Canon Law in England on the Eve of the Reformation," *Mediaeval Studies*, 25 (1963), 125-47 for an introductory survey; and my discussion of the interlocking roles of canon and common law in the case of Richard Hunne in *St. Thomas More: Action and Contemplation*, ed. R. S. Sylvester (New Haven, 1972), 15-55. Further study is also

d. Conciliarism

Finally, it must be accepted that Lateran V was a triumph of papacy over council, but a costly triumph of a very personal concept of papalism for which, unwittingly, Pisa had set the stage, and this triumph is imaged by the coat-of-arms of Leo that graced and nearly filled the title-pages of the bulls which issued forth from Rome during the Council.

At Constance—a valid general council of the Church, whose decrees, there can be little question, received papal confirmation—two major principles had been enunciated, but never observed or absorbed into the life-stream of the Church. The first was a decree establishing the supremacy of general councils,[75] and the second a decree establishing both the principle of and the machinery for the summoning of councils every ten years.[76] Perhaps because he had experienced the Council of Basle, Pope Eugenius IV fought against the doctrine of conciliar supremacy, and he staunchly refused, as did his successors, to summon another council. Only the Gallican sponsoring of a pseudo-council (a *conciliabulum*) at Pisa in 1511, as we have seen, forced the hand of Julius and compelled him to summon the Fifth Lateran Council in 1512 as a counter-measure. Historians will largely agree with Denys Hay that the refusal to hold a general council against the will of a majority in the Church and at a time when everywhere men cried out for reform, "resulted in the further development of heresy, near-heresy, and indifference"[77] —although we must also observe, with Evennett, that at the same time a record

needed not only of the leaders in Lateran V, but of such lesser known cardinals as Jacobazzi (on whom, see Jedin, I, 97); and I echo Jedin's observation that "in view of the proofs adduced in Book I, chapters II and V, of the conciliarist opinions of some Italian canonists, it would be expedient to examine, on the basis of the registers of Padua, Pavia, Bologna, etc., which bishops and jurists of the Reformation period had studied law in Italy and under which professors." For an introduction to these complex questions of law and religion, see ch. ix, 'Les Aspects Juridiques la Controverse', in Olivier de la Brosse, *Le Pape et Le Concile* (Paris, 1965); and on the congruence of canon law with natural law, see A. - M. Stickler in Hölbock and Sartory, eds., *El Misterio de la Eglesia* (Barcelona, 1966), II, 127-224. For the relationship of universities and reform, see the forthcoming work of Guy Lytle. See also n. 54 above.

[75]*COD*, 384 (*Haec sancta*); Session XXXIX, October 1417. See Jedin's convenient summary of the "Survival of Conciliar Theory," *op. cit.*, ch. ii.

[76]*COD*. 414 (*Frequens*): Sessions XLIII, March 1418. It is true, to be sure, that *Execrabilis* (1460) declared null and void both *Sacrosancta* and *Frequens*, but conciliarism continued; and not only the conciliarism of the conciliabulum of Pisa but also the writings of Almain and Major (among others) are significant in calling attention to the fact that conciliarism continued to draw theological as well as canonist supporters; see H. O. Oberman, *Forerunners of The Reformation* (N.Y., 1977). 214

[77]Denys Hay, in *NCMH*, I, 11.

number of new orders and communities came into being for achieving local reform or for providing institutional structures for greater
spirituality among individuals.[78]

It may well be argued that the failure to call a general council for
so many years contributed to the emergence of national churches;
for many of the bishops turned to the kings and princes for that support which Rome would not give, and the rulers found it timely to
adopt and foster ecclesiastical policies which gave them a greater
measure of control over their clergy.

Nowhere were these developments more congenial than
in Germany. There a prolonged hatred of popes was a sentiment that occasionally could even bind the emperors
and the princes together. The Germans, both lay and ecclesiastical rulers, were naturally amongst the warmest
supporters of the conciliar reform programme, which promised them the greatest possible independence in ecclesiastical matters. Here (as in the case of the reception
of Roman law) the conciliarism of the Germans redound-
ed to the advantage of the prince, not the emperor. As
many of the German prelates were also temporal rulers,
their attitude is hardly to be distinguished from that of
the secular princes, to whom they were frequently
related; indeed, the bishops had even more to gain than
the lay lords from a reduction in papal power.[79]

But what has been said, so rightly, of Germany was in lesser
degrees also true throughout Europe. In all countries, no insignifi-
cant factor was the discontent of great numbers of the diocesan
clergy, the lowest part and under-privileged members of the hierarchical structure of the sacerdotal and administrative Church; and
reform denied by reference to a general council, it is no wonder that
when the call to reform Rome came from Wittenberg, thousands
were ready to follow a new leader. (Concomitantly, many of the
younger and more reform-minded of the orders were frustrated by
the failure to achieve reform within their orders as within the
Church as a whole: small wonder that they too flocked to join the
Reformation.)

It is important to inquire why conciliarism died so quickly,
although we must recognize that even in the 1520s, after Luther's
attacks upon the papacy had already begun, so loyal a Roman
Catholic as Thomas More felt that Henry VIII had overstated papal
claims to power; he did not surrender his conciliarist ideas easily.
Clearly, however, once the institution of the papacy was under
massive direct attack, conciliarist positions were increasingly difficult to maintain, and the long quarrel between conciliarists and

---

[78]Thus H. Evennett, in NCMH.
[79]Denys Hay in the Introduction to Vol. I of the *New Cambridge Modern History,
The Renaissance* ed. by G. R. Potter (Cambridge: Cambridge University Press,
1957), pp. 12-13.

papalists was progressively pushed to the sidelines as the battle between the Lutheran North and Rome intensified. In each nation a different picture developed, each separate development a function of differences of traditions, milieux, problems and personalities.

By the time of Trent, conciliarism was already, very largely, past history, and there was little place for it in the Counter-Reformation Church. Not until Vatican II and its documents on collegiality would anything like a full and serious re-examination of balancing structures within the Church (or, indeed, of the very structure of the Church itself) be taken up again. A number of theologians have quickly recognized that the roots of Vatican II collegiality go very deep, well beyond Vatican I—and, I would urge, back to Lateran V, and earlier.[80]

VI. Conclusion

We end by returning to the inaugural oration of Giles of Viterbo and to his famous norm for reform: *homines per sacra immutari fas est, non sacra per homines.*[81] Perhaps the oration was reprinted and widely read because it said the things men wanted, or expected, to have said: wanted to have said only, for they were not ready for the call both to reform the individual and to launch an *aggiornamento* of the institution. The rhetorical features of Giles' oration indicate that the speaker assumed a conventional response from his sympathetic audience; and for all its reception and popularity, it is conventionally exhortatory, and its thinking about Church and reform are essentially conservative.[82]

We must reflect on the extent to which a cast, a particular style of historical thinking, conditioned—or even so limited as virtually to preclude—serious and structural reform thought.[83] Perhaps we need

---

[80]Hans Küng, in *Structures of the Church* (N.Y., 1964), is one of the few contemporary theologians who writes with a sufficiently viable sense of the history of the Church. In the nineteenth century one can identify Cardinal Newman, or Lord Acton, as two of a small number of Roman Catholics who either were historians or who developed a deeply historical sense of tradition.

[81]"Men must be changed by religion, not religion by men" (Mansi, xxxii, 669); cf. John W. O'Malley, S.J., "Historical Thought and the Reform Crisis of the Early Sixteenth Century," *Theological Studies*, 28 (1967), 531-548, esp. 533.

[82]Cf. John W. O'Malley, S. J., *Giles of Viterbo* (Leiden, 1968), 142, with its stress on Gile's conservatism and his clear statement of reform policy; "We are not innovators" (Non enim nova facimus). Cf. also G. Signorelli, *Il Cardinale Egidio da Viterbo* (Firenze, 1929), 52.

[83]Cf. O'Malley, "Historical Thought and the Reform Crisis," 537: "It is hard to imagine an intellectual atmosphere in which reform through a program of bringing things up to date would have received a more startled and uncompromising hearing."

to be reminded that to a critical degree the society of western Christendom was in 1517 a closed society, and that the mind of western man was very much a closed mind. I have suggested elsewhere that part of the achievement of More's *Utopia* was to create a model that would compel men to use reason in thinking about and moving to achieve reform;[84] and the comment of More's contemporary Budé—that the *Utopia* offered a 'seminarium' of good and useful institutions which men could now adapt and impart into their own commonwealths—would confirm this approach. By such a boot-strap effort of imaginative writing, More made it possible for European Christians to view their society from outside, to criticize their own institutions and indeed Christian society as a whole. But it was too much of a last-minute appeal, a last-ditch call to the use of reason, and there is no evidence that a reading of More's *Utopia* influenced any of the Council fathers (even though More knew a certain number of clerics and ecclesiastics who were in attendance at different times).

Yet by understanding Giles and his role in the Council, and such contemporaries as More (especially when we bear in mind that his *Utopia* is a work written during the sessions of the Council), we are enabled to understand the failure of the curial and hierarchical mind to see its own limitations and shortcomings, and the more general failure of minds in the crucial years from 1512 to 1517 to comprehend the condition of the Church, to criticize its abuses and corruptions, and to begin to answer even the muted clarion call by Giles to reform. Opportunities there were, but all the major gambits were declined.

It must, then, be finally concluded in the terms and light here considered, that the Fifth Lateran Council was a failure. Yet historically it can be said that it laid the groundwork (albeit in curiously complex and frequently counter-poising or opposing ways) both for the protestant Reformation and for Trent. For in a real sense it cleared the air for reformers: after 1517, what answer could be given to the charge, and a just charge, that a council of the Church has so recently failed? Providentially, then—and this is written after Vatican II, at a time when ecumenicism has become viable, and it was begun in a university (Toronto) where ecumenicism has for half a century been a part of the structure of the humanities—one can only meditate upon the fact that Lateran V began, as did the Reform Paliament of 1529 in England, with a validly celebrated Mass of the Holy Ghost. *Ecclesia semper reformanda.*

---

[84]See note 58 above.

[85]The book *Latran V et Trente* by O. Brosse, J. Lecler, H. Hostein, and Ch. Lefebvre (Tome 10 of *l'Histoire des Conciles Oecumeniques*, sous la direction de G. Dumeige (Paris, 1975) was not available to me at the time this essay was completed in 1975.

The following general sources carry the abbreviations indicated:

COD = *Conciliorum Oecumenicorum Decreta,* ed. J. Alberigo *et al.,* H. Jedin consultante (Freiburg-Rome, 1962)

Daniel-Rops = Daniel Rops, *L'Eglise de la Renaissance et de la Reforme* (Paris, 1955)

DDC = *Dictionnaire de droit canonique* (1935 to Reg), VI (1957), 353-6

DTC = *Dictionnaire de théologie catholique* (1907-50), VIII (1925), 2667-86

Fliche & Martin - *Histoire de l'Eglise,* by A. Fliche and V. Martin, cont. by J. B. Duroselle and E. Jarry

Hefele = K. J. Hefele and H. Leclercq, *Histoire des Conciles,* 8 vols. (1907-21), esp. VIII

Jedin = H. Jedin, *A History of the Council of Trent,* trans. Ernst Graf, 2 vols. (New York and London, 1957-61)

LexThK = *Lexikon für Theologie und Kirche,* 2d ed. (Freiburg-i-Br., 1930-8), VI (1961), 817-8

Martin = Victor Martin, *Les origines du Gallicanisme* (2 vols., Paris, 1939)

Martimort = Aime-Georges Martimort, *Le Gallicanisme de Bossuet* (Paris, 1953), ch. i.

Mansi = J. Mansi, *Sacrorum conciliorum nova et amplissima collectio ,* 31 vols. (1759 ff.), esp. vol. XXXII

NCE = *New Catholic Encyclopedia,* 15 vols. (Washington, 1967)

NCMH = *The New Cambridge Modern History,* vol. II, *The Reformation, 1520-1559;* ed. G. R. Elton (Cambridge, 1958)

Pastor = L. Pastor, *Geschichte de Päpste,* 16 vols. (Freiburg-i. Br., 1885-1933)

Renaudet = Augustin Renaudet, *Préréforme et Humanisme à paris pendant les premières guerres d'Italie*: 1496-1517 (2nd ed., Paris, 1953)

Incipiat Iudicium a Domo Domini:

The Fifth Lateran Council and the Reform of Rome*

by Nelson H. Minnich
The Catholic University of America

For five years from 1512 to 1517, under two popes Julius II (1503-13) and Leo X (1513-21), and with the official participation of over four-hundred leading ecclesiastics and laymen representing the nations of Latin Christendom, the Fifth Lateran Council was celebrated amid the splendors of Renaissance Rome.[1] Its agenda included the healing of schism, eradication of heresy, pacification of Christian princes, preparation of a crusade, and reformation of Christendom.[2] Although this council tended to shy away from the traditional formula used by the rival council at Pisa of "a reformation in head and members," the mentality encapsulated in that phrase was prevalent among the conciliar fathers meeting at the Lateran. The tears many shed when the inaugural homelist, Egidio Antonini, predicted the success of their reforming efforts were not unrelated to an awareness that earlier councils had labored mostly in vain and popes had drawn up but never promulgated various bulls to bring about this renewal of the Church's head, that is, of the papal court, the Curia, and in an extended sense, the city of Rome.[3] The importance of initiating such a reform was also recognized by the two popes associated with the council.

The official documents, by which Julius II convoked the Lateran Council and Leo X continued it, spoke only in general terms about

*An earlier version of this paper was delivered at a joint session of the American Catholic Historical Association and American Historical Association conventions meeting in San Francisco on 28 December 1978.

[1]The official acts of the council edited by Antonio del Monte are reprinted in *Sacrorum conciliorum nova et amplissima collectio*, ed. Giovanni Domenico Mansi *et alii*, vol 32 (Paris, 1902 reprint), cols. 665A-999C, hereafter cited as Mansi. The most recent general study of this council is that by Olivier de La Brosse in *Latran V et Trente*, vol. 10 of *Histoire des conciles oecuméniques*, ed. Gervais Dumeige (Paris, 1975), 12-114, an up-to-date bibliography is provided on 471-73.

[2]Mansi, 667D, 687BC, 688D, 692B, 695B.

[3]*Acta primi concilii Pisani celebrati ad tollendum schisma anno Domini M.CCCC.IX et concilii Senensis M.CCCC.XXIII. ex codice MS. Item constitutiones sanctae factae in diversis sessionibus sacri generalis concilii Pisani ex bibliotheca*

the need for universal Church renewal. In his allocution to the sixth session, however, Leo X singled out Rome as an appropriate object of the council's reforming efforts. In a bull read at the eighth session, Leo claimed that his predecessor Julius had convoked the council "both for many reasons and because of the frequent complaints about the Roman Curia."[4] In practice both pontiffs used the council as an occasion for curial reform. Before the council opened Julius charged the preparatory commission of cardinals to cleanse the city of Rome--its people, Curia, and papal court--lest the prelates coming to the council be easily scandalized. Based on the cardinals' recommendations the pope issued at the end of March 1512 a decree reforming the curial officials and reducing their fees. At the fourth session Julius had the council give its formal approval to this decree.[5] Leo followed a similar procedure at the eighth session. He had earlier urged the conciliar reform deputation to address itself to a reform of his own office, of his household, and of the lives of members of the Curia.[6]

A dominant theme in many of the reform proposals from the time of the council was the necessity of initiating church renewal at Rome. In their *Libellus* (1513) addressed to Leo X, the two Venetian patricians, Camaldolese hermits, and papal confidants, Paolo Giustiniani and Pietro Quirini, enunciated a principle implicit in the writings of many others: reform should begin at the top. According to their metaphysical model, what happens at the apex of the ecclesiastical hierarchy will necessarily influence the lower orders. The Hungarian bishop and preacher at the council, Šimum Bejna-Kožičić, insisted that the church of Rome be first restored, because from that head as from a fount flows health or illness into

regia (Paris, 1612), 25, 36, 101, etc.; the phrase rarely if ever appears in the documents of the Lateran Council; Odocio Rainaldi, *Annales Ecclesiastici post Baronium ab anno 1198 ad annum 1565*, rev. and ed. G.D. Mansi and A. Theiner (Paris, 1877) ad annum 1512, nr. 35, 40, hereafter cited as Rainaldi; Léonce Celier, "L'idée de Réforme à la cour pontificale: du concile de Bâle au concile de Lateran," *Revue des questions historiques* 86 (1909), 418-435 and his "Alexandre VI e la Réforme de l'Eglise," *Mélanges d'archéologie et histoire de l'Ecole Française de Rome* 27 (1907), 65-124. For the centrality of Rome in the thinking of this prominent reformer at the council, see John W. O'Malley, "Giles of Viterbo: A Reformer's Thought on Renaissance Rome," *Renaissance Quarterly* 20 (1976), 1-11.

[4]Mansi, 667D, 687BC, 688D, 692B, 695B, 783AB, 845E; Rainaldi, 1513, nr. 24; Paride de Grassi, *Diarium Leonis*, Bibliotheca Apostolica Vaticana (hereafter cited as B A V) Vat. Lat. 12275, fol. 38r.

[5]Mansi, 753AB, 772E; Rainaldi, 1512, nr. 29-31; Paride de Grassi, *Diarium Julii*, BAV, Vat. Lat. 12412, fol 151v, 206v.

[6]Mansi, 845D-47A; Rainaldi, 1513, nr. 27, 97; Nelson H. Minnich, "Concepts of Reform Proposed at the Fifth Lateran Council," *Archivum Historiae Pontificiae* 7 (1969), 245; Raffaele Lippo Brandolini, *Dialogus Leo Nuncupatus . . .*, ed. Francesco Fogliazzi (Venezia, 1753), 121.

the other members. Antonio Pucci, the cleric of the Camera and servant of Medicean interests from Florence alluded to the statement of this theme found in 1 Peter 4:17 when he observed in his sermon at the ninth session that judgment most fittingly proceeds from the House of the Lord and spreads to the world: "Urbem primum, ut judicium incipiat a domo Domini, inde orbem . . . restitue.[7]

Appeals were made that the pope begin the reform with himself. The two Camaldolese and the court humanist, Gianfrancesco Poggio Bracciolini, urged the pope to be a model of virtues and sound teachings since others will follow his example. While Poggio stressed his role as inspirer, another court humanist, Raffaele Lippo Brandolini, portrayed Alessandro Farnese (the future Paul III) as hoping that Leo will not neglect severity and justice, should his kindness and clemency fail to inspire a reform. The same message was found in the oration sent to Leo by Gianfrancesco Pico della Mirandola. This humanist prince claimed that only the pope can reform the Church and to be successful Leo should add rigor to his accustomed mildness.[8]

The papal household was singled out to be among the first to experience the pontiff's zeal for reform. Leo's personal friend, Quirini, gave specific recommendations. Let the pope's relatives who are not engaged in necessary tasks be sent back to Florence. His personal staff should be reduced by a third and the attire of its members be simple and befitting clerics. Precious metals and fabrics ought not adorn his retainers, horses, mules, or halls, but be dedicated to liturgical purposes. The papal table should serve a simple fare and the meals be accompanied by spiritual reading or edifying conversation.[9]

Together with Giustiniani, his fellow Camaldolese, Quirini also urged the pope to investigate and correct the conduct of the cardinals and to assign them salaries rather than benefices. The royal instructions for the Spanish ambassadors to the council were also concerned about the cardinals, insisting that financial offerings

---

[7]Paolo Giustiniani and Pietro Quirini, *Libellus ad Leonem X. Pontificem Maximum* in *Annales Camaldulenses Ordinis Sancti Benedicti*, ed. G. -B. Mittarelli and A. Costadoni, IX (Venezia, 1773), col. 698, hereafter this work is cited as *Libellus;* Mansi, 803B, 897D.

[8]*Libellus*, 691-92; Gianfrancesco Poggio Bracciolini, *De veri pastoris munere liber,* B A V, Vat. Lat. 3732, fol. 6ʳ, 10ʳ; Brandolini, *Dialogus Leo, 124;* Gianfrancesco Pico della Mirandola, *Ad Leonem Decimum Pontificem Maximum et Concilium Lateranense . . . de reformandis moribus oratio*, App. 146 in William Roscoe, *The Life and Pontificate of Leo the Tenth*, 2nd ed. rev. (London, 1806), VI, 69.

[9]Pietro Quirini, "Fragment eines Reformgutachtens für Leo X (1513)," in Hubert Jedin, "Vincenzo Quirini und Pietro Bembo (1946)," reprinted in *Kirche des Glaubens, Kirche der Geschichte: Ausgewählte Aufsätze und Vorträge*, (Freiburg, 1966), I, 165-66.

have no influence in their appointment or in their election of the pope.[10]

A reform of the Curia was urgently demanded by writers from many countries. The Venetian Camaldolese hermits warned Leo soon after his election that if he failed to correct the Curia, nothing great could be expected from his reign. The Florentine humanist, Brandolini, educated at Naples and Rome, denounced the widespread immorality, greed, and ambition of the Curia.[11] Both Diego de Deza, the Dominican archbishop of Seville, and Jakob Wimpfeling, the Alsatian humanist and ardent defender of the council, lamented that those who were rejected by their local ordinaries as unfit either for ordination or for holding a benefice easily obtained from the Roman Curia authorization to be ordained and appointment to church office. Among the abuses to be remedied by the council, according to Deza, was the appointment by Rome as cathedral canons of those who were uneducated and ignorant of church doctrine, not even tonsured and mere children. The Curia did not honor its agreement with the Spanish Church to reserve at least two canonries in each cathedral for university graduates. The royal instructions for the Spanish ambassadors to the council repeated this accusation. The archbishop also complained of the Curia's appointment of absentee, unsuited, and negligent clerics to benefices in Spain.[12] The French ambassador at the Lateran Council, Claude de Seyssel, observed that curial connections and favoritism advanced the careers of ambitious and unqualified men. The correction of these abuses will come, according to the Venetian hermits, when Leo insists on a strict observance of curial regulations.[13]

Spanish prelates advocated an end of various curial practices. Pascual Rebenga, the ascetical bishop of Burgos appointed as delegate of Castile to the council, denounced Rome's granting for a fee all kinds of dispensations from church law. Deza attacked in particular those dispensation's allowing *conversos* to have their own confessors and the Mass celebrated in their homes. He also wanted exemptions from local jurisdiction to be effective only in Rome or within the confines of a monastery's walls. Religious should not be permitted to transfer to laxer orders nor should Rome grant to prelates the administration of religious houses and their revenues.

---

[10]*Libellus*, 694-96; José M. Doussinague, *Fernando el católico y el cisma de Pisa* (Madrid, 1946), 539-40, hereafter this work is cited as Doussinague.

[11]*Libellus*, 711; Brandolini, *Oratio ad Lateranense Concilium excogitata*, BAV, Ottob. Lat. 813, fol. 24r-v, 25v, 51r.

[12]L. Dacheux, *Un réformateur à la fin du XVe siècle. Jean Geiler de Kaysersberg, prédicateur à la Cathédrale de Strasbourg 1478-1510. Etude sur sa vie et son temps* (Paris, 1876), 153, n.1; Doussinague, 533, 536-38, 541.

[13]Claude de Seyssel, *La grand monarchie de France* (Paris, 1541), 21r; *Libellus*, 712-13.

The archbishop also enumerated a host of curial practices which must be terminated: appointment to almost all the major and minor benefices of Spain in disregard of local rights, reservations, untimely expectatives, coadjutorships, commendations, fraudulent provisions without open hearings, lengthy litigations, dispensations from residency and ordination, pluralism, and confiscation of the spoils and legacies of deceased prelates. Many of Deza's complaints were incorporated into the instructions for the Spanish ambassadors.[14] With the exception of the *conversos* question, complaints similar to these of the Spanish would probably have been registered across Europe had other Christian princes also solicited the opinion of their subjects in preparation for the council.

The curial abuse most harshly criticized was simony. Rebenga wanted its practitioners declared heretics and punished accordingly. The Spanish ambassadors were instructed to denounce its pernicious presence in the election of popes, bishops, canons, and other church officials. The eminent curial canonist and bishop, Domenico Giacobazzi, noted that due to the simoniacal purchase of church office, Rome had become the prize of prostitutes--an elusive but suggestive statement.[15]

The city of Rome both papal bureaucracy and local residents was also the subject of a few reform proposals. The bishop of Burgos who had visited this capital of Christendom on a number of occasions and died there during the council denounced the terrible turpitude and outrageous public sins of both the clergy and laity of Rome. Such conduct, he claimed, blasphemed God and confirmed infidels in their opposition to the Faith. Of particular concern to Rebenga were the tolerance shown toward the idolatrous practices of pagans and the religious rites of Jews, the protection given to apostate *conversos*, and the conferral on them of Roman citizenship with the right to hold public office and rule over the lands of the Church. The Camaldolese hermits made much of the numerous prostitutes, claiming that they swarmed the City's streets in broad daylight, even around the papal palace, that priests and prelates had not one but many concubines on whom they lavished church revenues, and that so prevalent was the problem that the City had become a stinking and sordid brothel. The solutions recommended were the expulsion of these ladies from Rome or at least their restriction to a remote corner of the City. These measures were, however, felt by these hermits to be inadequate, and new, more serious and efficacious remedies needed to be devised.[16]

---

[14]Doussinague, 531, 533-41.

[15]Doussinague, 530, 539-40; Domenico Giacobazzi, *De Concilio tractatus* (Roma, 1538), 228B: "Hodie, autem, propter hoc, perdita est omnis devotio: quia Roma facta est frons meretricis."

[16]Doussinague, 530-31; Joaquín Luis Ortega, "Un reformador pretridentino: don Pascual de Ampudia, obispo de Burgos (1496-1512)," *Anthologica Annua* 19 (1972), 413-35; *Libellus,* 706-07.

Some of the writers were insistent that the pope embrace their reforms. Giustiniani and Quirini were remarkably blunt. If Leo did not see these widespread abuses under his very nose, it was questionable that he would ever fulfil his function as overseer of the Church. If he saw, but ignored them, he shared in the guilt of the sinners he tolerated and should beware lest he also incur the dreadful punishment God inflicted on Eli, the priest of Siloh, for a similar negligence.[17] Bracciolini warned Leo that men in high office are prone to forget their virtuous past and claim a license for sin. Alert to his own frailty, let Leo surround himself with wise councillors. A doctor once grown ill is not likely to cure others.[18] The current civil and ecclesiastical powers of the pope in Rome are such, according to Rebenga, that Julius II has no excuse for failing to correct the evils there.[19] These admonitions were not lost on the popes.

Both Julius II and Leo X used the Lateran Council to issue decrees reforming various aspects of Rome. The papal office was, however, virtually untouched by the council. As he lay on his deathbed, Julius had the conciliar fathers reaffirm his bull of 1505 which prescribed detailed measures for preventing simony in the election of a successor as bishop of Rome. In spite of his instructions to the Lateran's reform deputation that it reform his own office, Leo X failed to promulgate a single conciliar decree affecting specifically his own personal life or performance of duty. That Leo gave some thought, however fleeting and fuzzy, to self reform is suggested by a statement he made soon after his election. On refusing to wear certain vestments of his predecessors, Leo affirmed that he wished to reform himself first both internally and externally in order the better to reform others. There is no evidence, though, that he undertook any significant personal reform.[20] His commissioning of the conciliar deputation to reform his own household resulted in an important sentence inserted into the bull *Supernae dispositionis arbitrio* of the ninth session. It stated that all the provisions of this decree also applied to the members of the papal household, with the exception that they could continue to wear traditionally red garments.[21]

The cardinals were the subject of some of the prescriptions of this same bull. These papal advisors were forbidden to act as special advocates of political interests or to divulge anything said or done

[17]*Libellus*, 707; 1 Samuel 3:13-14, 4:11-18.
[18]Bracciolini, *De Munere*, 10r - 11v.
[19]Doussinague, 530.
[20]Mansi, 768A - 72D; de Grassi, *Diarium Leonis*, Vat. Lat. 12275, fol. 36r.
[21]Minnich, "Concepts of Reform," 245; Mansi, 880A.

in secret consistory. In processing consistorial provision to major benefices, they were to follow set procedures. While obliged to maintain their residence in Rome, they were also to become knowledgeable about conditions throughout Christendom and keep the pontiff properly informed. After appointment as legate, they were bound to betake themselves within five months to the region assigned. Fixed portions of the revenues from their consistorial benefices were designated for specific purposes. Qualified clerical and religious staffing, plus funds for its support and the maintenance of church property, were to be provided in the cardinals' major commendatory benefices. Their titular churches in Rome required an annual visitation either in person or through a vicar, and careful provision for the pastoral needs of the people and for the material maintenance of the buildings. Distinguished persons seeking the cardinals' assistance at the Curia were to be dealt with in a kindly and courteous manner. Special concern was to be shown to the cases brought by the poor, by religious, and by those oppressed and unjustly burdened.[22]

The cardinals were to give attention to the personnel of their households. If they employed a bishop, they were to treat him as a brother and not assign him menial tasks. Clerical members of their staffs were to wear the attire proper to their status, keep their hair trimmed and scalps tonsured, and avoid costly coverings and ornaments on their beasts of burden. When absent from Rome and not engaged in official business or recreation, these staff members lost their exemptions from the jurisdiction of their ordinaries. Cardinals were to concern themselves with the moral integrity of their servants lest the faithful be scandalized by them. Their households were to be havens of hospitality for the learned and upright, especially for impoverished nobility and men of high repute. But care was also to be taken lest the number of their retainers be beyond their means or judged excessive. Moderation and frugality were to be exercised, too, regarding the material aspects of their households: its building, furnishings, table, and stable.[23]

The personal lives of cardinals were the subject of a series of exhortations. These prelates were to conduct themselves with moderation, sobriety, chastity, and piety, abstaining not only from evil but even from its slightest appearance. They were to have their own chapels and be devoted to the recitation of the divine office and celebration of the Eucharist. Their revenues were to be spent on good and pious purposes and not consumed in extravagant, wasteful, and thoughtless expenditures. When providing for their

[22]Mansi, 875C - 77A, 877E - 79A, 880B - 81C.
[23]Mansi, 877E-78A, 879A-80A, 909BC.

relatives, especially those who were worthy and in need, cardinals should not so enrich them with church revenues that others sustain losses. And finally, the total expenses for a cardinal's funeral were not to exceed one and a half thousand florins.[24]

A reform of the Roman Curia, first of the functions and then of the lives of its officials, was promulgated in the council. At the fourth session, Julius had the conciliar fathers reaffirm his bull of March 1512 which reduced fees and eliminated some of the more scandalous practices of the Curia.[25] Leo followed the same procedure. The findings of his reform deputation became the basis for various changes in the number and functions of curial officials and in the fees they could charge for their services.[26] A lengthy bull covering a wide range of curial officials was issued by Leo six days before the eighth session. This document known as *Pastoralis officii* mandated a return of curial practices to the time of Paul II, reduced taxes, fixed service fees, listed prices for various absolutions, and prohibited such abuses as writing with white ink and keeping transactions secret. It also required a careful examination of all candidates for holy orders who requested of the Curia letters authorizing their ordination. When Leo sought conciliarly mandated sanctions to secure its enforcement, the council fathers gave a reluctant approval complaining that the bull failed to reform the reformers, that is, the curial officials who had helped in the composition of the bull. Leo promised to tackle that problem in the following session.[27] The other reforms of curial practice which Leo legislated through the council were prohibitions on special reservations and on the division and union of benefices, limitations on pluralism, reaffirmations of the canonical requirements for promotions, transfer, or deprivation of bishops and abbots, and restrictions on exemptions and appeals to Roman tribunals.[28]

The personal lives of curialists were treated both explicitly and implicitly in the bull *Supernae dispositionis arbitrio.* The third and

---

[24]Mansi, 877DE, 878DE, 881A.

[25]Julius II, *Bulla reformationis officialium Romanae Curiae:* "Et si Romanus Pontifex," B A V, Raccolta I. IV. 961, int. 11 and in the Bibliotheca Angelica, Y.10.39/1; Mansi, 753 AB, 772E, 846A.

[26]Mansi, 816E, 846B; Walther von Hofmann, *Forschungen zur Geschichte der kurialen Behörden vom Schisma bis zur Reformation,* vols. 12 and 13 of *Bibliothek des kgl. preuss. historischen Instituts in Rom* (Roma, 1914), II, 54-64, 240-48, e.g., nr. 239, 248-50, 260; Guilelmus van Gulik and Conradus Eubel, *Hierarchia catholica medii et recentioris aevi sive summorum pontificum S.R.E. Cardinalium ecclesiarum antistitum series,* Vol. 3: *Saeculum XVI ab anno 1503 complectens,* rev. Ludovicus Schmitz-Kallenberg (Münster, 1923), 81-84; *Bullarum diplomatum et privilegiorum sanctorum Romanorum pontificum Taurinensis editio,* ed. Francisco Gaude *et alii* (Torino, 1860), V (1431-1521), 566-67, Leo X, nr. IV.

[27]*Bullarum Taurinensis editio,* V, 571-601, Leo X, nr. V.

[28]Mansi, 875A-76A, 877A-C, 907E-10B.

final section of this conciliar decree specifically prohibited the practice of simony in the Roman Curia and ordered a careful investigation of the Curia for the presence of any persons ill-disposed toward the Faith or feigning to be Christian, especially heretics, those tainted with heresy, and those practicing the Jewish religion. If found and convicted, they were to be duly punished. The bull concluded with a statement affirming that even those of its prescriptions regarding life, customs, and ecclesiastical discipline which did not explicitly mention curialists were also binding on them whether dwelling then in the Roman Curia or elsewhere. The measures which most likely affected these officials were those which made mention of clerics. Those failing to recite their breviary or engaging in blasphemy were liable to deprivation of benefices. Those found guilty of fornication, sodomy, or concubinage were to be punished according to canon law. Deposition, imprisonment, and removal from church office awaited any cleric who once reprimanded continued to invoke demons or practice incantations, divinations, or other superstitions.[29]

Attempts to enforce the Lateran's decrees reforming the procedures and fees of the Curia were not successful. In his desire to please all, to keep papal finances solvent, to protect the investment curialists made in their offices, to reward their labors, and to remove reasons for illicit exactions, Leo allowed questionable practices to continue, granted many exemptions from the conciliar decrees, and raised the fees curialists could legally charge for their services.[30] Given the sporadic nature of his threats and imposition of penalties, unqualified candidates continued to be approved for ordination by the Curia.[31] The piecemeal efforts of his successor Hadrian VI to reform curial practices were opposed by the bureaucrats and undone when his brief pontificate was followed by that of Clement VII. The one area in which reform did make some headway and triumphed for a while under Clement was the careful examination and certification in the Curia of candidates for holy orders. This is attributable to the zeal of Giampietro Carafa whom both pontiffs entrusted with this responsibility.[32] Clement, unfortunately, lacked the determination

[29]Mansi, 881D-82A, D-E, 883A-C, 884D-85A.
[30]Leo X, *Bulla super societatibus officiorum Romanae curiae:* "Romanum Pontificem" (12 January 1514), aiiʳ, in B A V, Raccolta I.IV.961, int. 15; Hofmann, *Forschungen,* I, 275,314; Ludwig von Pastor, *Storia dei papi dalla fine del medio evo,* Italian version by Angelo Mercati, IV-I (Roma, 1960), 545-47—hereafter cited as Pastor-Mercati.
[31]G. Pelliccia, *La preparazione ed ammissione dei chierici ai santi ordini nella Roma del secolo XVI* (Roma, 1946), 53-76, 82-84.
[32]Robert E. McNally, "Pope Adrian VI (1522-23) and Church Reform," *Archivum Historiae Pontificiae* 7 (1969), 283-84; Antonio Caracciolo, *Vite e gesti di Giovanni Pietro Carafa, cioè di Paolo IIII. Pont. Mas.,* B A V, Barb. Lat. 4953, fol. 53ᵛ-54ʳ. Pastor-Mercati, IV-II, (Roma, 1956) 29, 77-78; Mandell Creighton, *A History of the Papacy from the Great Schism to the Sack of Rome,* new ed. (New York, 1897), VI, 242; Pelliccia, *Preparazione ed ammissione,* 90-92.

of Carafa. In spite of the complaints of the German diets, the exhortations of the Emperor, and the advice of such loyal Catholics as Eck, Clement like his cousin Leo did not enforce with vigor the Lateran decrees reforming curial taxes and practices. In its response of autumn 1530 to the twenty-nine complaints of the German diet, a commission of eight cardinals, half of whom had attended the Lateran Council, made thirteen explicit references to the Lateran's decrees which if enforced would remedy abuses often current in the Curia.[33] Serious reform had to wait until Paul III. Soon after his election, he ordered the observance of the conciliarly mandated bull *Pastoralis officii* and subsequently issued other measures which echoed at times the decrees of the Lateran Council.[34] The prudence and resolve of this pontiff accomplished much for the reform of the Curia.

By following the attempts at enforcing the conciliar bull *Supernae dispositionis arbitrio*, some indications can be gathered as to the seriousness of papal efforts at reforming the lives of curialists and other residents of Rome. The same month that the bull was issued (May of 1514), Leo entrusted to cardinals Lorenzo Pucci and Bernardo Dovizi da Bibbiena responsibility for enforcing its provisions against Marranos and Jews respectively.[35] In spite of the bull's stern language about imposing rigorously the penalties prescribed by canon law for fornication, sodomy, and concubinage, Leo seems to have tolerated lax sexual mores in Rome. The census taken three years after the decree's promulgation reveals large numbers of courtesans, mostly female but some male, spread throughout the City and no longer confined to their former district along the Tiber between the Aventine and Capitoline hills. Instead of relegating prostitutes to a corner of the City and imposing stiff penalties, Leo made provision for prevention and repentance. On the feast of the Annunciation he distributed alms to poor girls so that they would have the dowry needed for a respectable marriage. The convent of Santa Maria Maddalena for penitent prostitutes was founded with the financial support of the Compagnia della Carità under the direction of the pope's cousin, cardinal Giulio dei Medici. On the advice of the imperial ambassador, Alberto Pio, who had

---

[33]Gerhard Müller, *Die römische Kurie und die Reformation 1523-34: Kirche und Politik während des Pontifikates Clemens' VII.*, Vol. 38 of *Quellen und Forschungen zur Reformationsgeschichte* (Gütersloher, 1969), 53-54, 172; *Concilium Tridentinum diariorum actorum epistularum tractatuum nova collectio*, ed. Societate Goerresiana, Vol. 12: *Tractatuum pars prior (1513-1548)*, ed. Vincent Schweitzer (Freiburg im Breisgau, 1930), 59:18, 52; 60:7, 33; 61:1, 15 bis, 31, 57; 65:12, 41-66:2—hereafter this collection is cited as *C.T.*

[34]Stephan Ehses "Kirchliche Reformarbeiten unter Papst Paul III. vor dem Trienter Konzil," *Römische Quartalschrift* 15 (1901), 153-74, 395-409, esp. 154 and 168; *C.T.*, IV, 451-57, esp. 451 n.3.

[35]Marino Sanuto, *I Diarii*, ed. Federico Stefani, Guglielmo Berchet, and Nicolò Barozzi (Venezia, 1879ff), XVIII, 210.

seen similar institutions in France, Leo gave it an Augustinian rule modeled on the French and imposed a strict, perpetual cloister, closed even to cardinals. The money left by curial prostitutes who died without wills was assigned to this convent; and when making their wills, prostitutes were required, under threat of having their legacies confiscated, to bequeathe at least a fifth of their wealth to this house of refuge.[36]

When the conciliar bull, *Supernae dispositionis arbitrio*, was initially ignored at Rome, Leo X ordered his official, Amadeo Berruti, to secure observance. Berruti was given exceptional powers as governor in the City and vice-camerlengo in the Curia with jurisdiction over both civil and ecclesiastical cases. Lest anyone claim ignorance of Latin as an excuse for non-compliance, Berruti issued in Italian an edict summarizing the measures contained in the bull. He warned that the penalties therein mandated would be imposed according to the degree of disobedience.[37] Another edict was promulgated on 1 October 1516 by Girolamo de Ghinucci, who in virtue of his office as general auditor of cases in the apostolic camera was the ordinary executor in the Roman Curia of apostolic decrees. He demanded observance of the council's bulls and noted that they were available for consultation in the office of the notary Guglielmo de Vergio and included specific reforms of the practices and officials of the Curia. Leo, he claimed, was resolved on getting compliance everywhere, but especially at Rome which must be freed of its unsavory reputation as teacher of sin to the rest of Christendom.[38] Twelve days later the vicar general for spiritual affairs in the diocese of Rome, Domenico Giacobazzi, issued his edict requiring those in his jurisdiction, whether lay, clerical, exempt, or Jews, to comply with the decrees of the council. He affirmed that it was fitting that the renowned city of Rome which divine mercy established as the head of the world, should put these decrees into immediate execution.[39]

---

[36]Mariano Armellini, "Un censimento della città di Roma sotto il pontificato di Leone X tratto da un codice inedito dell'Archivio Vaticano," *Gli Studi in Italia: Periodico didattico scientifico e letterario*, Anno IV, Vol. II (1881), 890-909, esp. 897 and Anno V (1882), Vol. I., 69-84, 161-92, 321-55, 481-518, but esp. 162-84 and 328-29; Emmanuel Rodocanachi, *Courtisanes et bouffons: Etude de moeurs romaines au XVIe siècle* (Paris, 1894), 21-22, 59-64, 69-71; *Histoire de Rome: Le Pontificat de Léon X 1513-1521* (Paris, 1931), 195, n. 3; Leo X, *Bulla Monasterii Sanctae Mariae Magdalenae Ordinis Sancti Augustini Convertitarum de Urbe:* "Salvator Noster" (19.V.1520), in Archivio di Stato di Roma, Bandi e buste, nr. 293, int. 34, fol. Aii^{r-v}; Peter Partner, *Renaissance Rome, 1500-1559: A Portrait of a Society* (Berkeley, 1976), 97-111.

[37]Amadeo Berruti, "Monitorio per la observatione de la reformatione del sacro concilio Laterano," in Mansi, *Sacrorum conciliorum collectio*, vol. 35: *In quo continentur reliqui textus ab anno MCDXIV ad annum MDCCXXIV pertinentes* (reprint Paris, 1902), 1586A-88B.

[38]Mansi, XXXV, 1584A-85D.

[39]Mansi, XXXV, 1582B-83D.

These edicts of the papal vicars were not without effect. In mid-January of 1517 Alessandro Gabbioneta wrote from Rome to the Marquis of Mantova that a reform of the clergy was evidenced by their wearing of priestly attire. Clerics who came to the City on business bringing with them expensive and colorful wardrobes were surprised to discover that they were required to wear ankle-length robes closed at the collars with large hoods in the style of a canon. Girolamo Aleandro, former rector of the University of Paris and now agent of the prince-bishop of Liège, Evrard de La Marck, conformed externally to these reforms lest he hinder his negotiations; but beneath the approved robes, he wore more stylish ones even in the summer heat of the City. Much to his relief, the rigors of this reform which lasted several months finally abated.[40] That reports from Rome singled out for comment the phenomenon of ecclesiastics wearing the attire prescribed by the council, as if this dress code constituted a central element in church reform, suggests that the principal papal concern was for a visual symbol of the restored clerical order: withdrawn from secular affairs, dedicated to its spiritual mission, and obedient to the mandates of the hierarchy. Had not Leo soon after his election described reform in terms of wearing a set of priestly robes not associated with the attire of his delinquent predecessors and thereby signaling an interior renewal? His efforts to enforce effectively, even if only temporarily, the other provisions of this bull are not easily documented.

That the reforms of the Lateran Council did not become a permanent feature of Leonine Rome is suggested by their absence from a collection of statutes compiled for the governance of the City. The first three books are basically Paul II's 1471 codification of civil, criminal, and administrative legislation. While the preface claims that these laws were revised,[41] there is no evidence that they were brought into line with the council's decrees. The stiffest penalties for blasphemy in the Roman code were a ten pound fine and eight days of detention. The council allowed judges to condemn repeated offenders to life imprisonment or the galleys.[42] Although detailed civil legislation prohibited concubinage, fornication between single consenting adults was not made illegal; indeed, the code provided protection for prostitutes: from rape and kidnapping, and from having their doors set aflame or manure deposited at their windows and doors. Imprisonment, torture, and exile awaited

---

[40]Pastor-Mercati, IV-I, 546, n.7; IV-II, 650; Léon Dorez, "Une lettre de Gilles de Gourmont à Girolamo Aleandro (1531) suivie de documents nouveaux sur Aleandro," *Revue des Bibliothèques* 8 (1898), 214.

[41]*Statuta et novae reformationes urbis Romae eiusdemque varia privilegia a diversis romanis pontificibus emanata in sex libros divisa novissime compilata* (Romae: per Stephanum Guilereti de Lunarivilla Tullensis diocesis, 1523), A_{ij}r, A_{jjj}r; Creighton, *History of the Papacy*, VI, 31.

[42]*Statuta*, Book II, chp. 102; Mansi, XXXII, 882B.

the perpetrators of such crimes. The conciliar fathers directed their legislation not to the protection of these ladies, but to the severe punishment of their clerical clients.[43] The Lateran's decree against false Christians of Jewish descent did not apparently affect provisions in the code condemning heretics or regulating Jewish life in the City.[44] A partial explanation for these discrepancies may be found in the composition of the commission entrusted with revising the code.[45] Of its six members, only one (provided Bishop Farnese is cardinal Alessandro) ever attended the council and by the time the revised code was promulgated Hadrian VI was pontiff.

Reform-minded prelates urged Leo's successor, Hadrian Florenszoon Dedel who had never attended the council, to bring about church renewal. The Swiss cardinal and former member of the conciliar reform deputation, Matthias Schiner, wrote the new pope advising him to begin his reforms with Roman officials, their households, and their venal performance of curial functions. A knowledgeable curialist, cardinal Lorenzo Campeggio, lamented the fact that the Lateran Council's decrees regulating clerical life were approved by all, but thus far observed by few. He exhorted the Dutch pope to obtain enforcement not only of these conciliar measures but also of those prohibiting a plurality of benefices.[46] A former member of both the Pisan and Lateran Councils and now bishop of Guardialfiera, Zaccaria Ferreri, directed the pope's attention to the city of Rome, especially the Curia. Like Christ with whip in hand, His vicar was to drive from the Temple those who bought and sold spiritual favors and also those who scandalized the faithful by their lewdness. If Rome, the head, mother and teacher of the other churches were reformed, the other churches would follow: "Purge Rome, and the world is cleansed; restore and reform Rome and the whole world is restored and reformed."[47]

The new pontiff accepted this criticism of Rome. In his allocution to the cardinals following his coronation, Hadrian solicited their help in correcting the vices, injustices, and immoral conduct of the Curia so that once again it would become a model of righteousness and norm of proper conduct. His instructions to the bishop of Feramo, Francesco Chieregati, sent as papal nuncio to the imperial diet at Nürnberg in September of 1522, promised to begin church reform with the Curia "from which has come perhaps all this evil." Illness has spread from the head to the members and must be cured

---

[43]*Statuta*, II, 60, IV, 22-23; Mansi, 882DE.
[44]*Statuta*, I, 2, III, 159-61; Mansi, 884E-85A.
[45]*Statuta*, A$_{iii}$$^{r-v}$
[46]*C.T.*, XII, 8-9; Pastor-Mercati, IV-II, 693-94.
[47]*C.T.*, XII, 23,27.

at its source. Christ also began his work of reform by purging the Temple.[48]

Hadrian began his reform with the Curia. Instead of issuing a sweeping set of regulations, he took up each question as it came to his attention and after mature reflection issued the appropriate corrective measure. The curial cardinals resented his curtailment of their privileges. He brought to Rome, housed in the Vatican palace, and appointed as his agents for the reform of Rome two men he had met in Spain: Giampietro Carafa, bishop of Chieti, and Tommaso Gazzella, a jurist from Gaeta. It seems they were charged to move especially against blasphemers, usurers, simoniacs, fictive *conversos*, despisers of the Faith, corrupters of youth, and ordainers of unworthy candidates.[49] They, thus, became in effect the enforcers at Rome of a number of the Lateran's decrees.

Soon after his election as pope Clement VII, Giulio dei Medici, who had figured prominently at the Lateran Council and had applied its decrees to his archdiocese of Florence, took measures to reform the city and Curia of Rome in accordance with these same decrees. On 24 February 1524 he urged the cardinals gathered in consistory to see that members of their households wore clerical tonsure and garb, that prelates were attired with rochet (*rochetto*) and felt cap (*pileo*), and that the cardinals, especially Lorenzo Pucci (the grand penitentiary) and Pompejo Colonna (the vice-chancellor) warned the curial officials subject to them to observe the Lateran decrees.[50] Clement appointed men like Giampietro Carafa, Jacopo Sadoleto, and Matteo Ghiberti to a commission charged with bringing the City into compliance with the council. On learning from their report about the abuses and corruptions practiced by curial officials, the pope registered his official displeasure. In hopes of eliminating continued disregard of the conciliar decree governing promotion to sacred orders, Clement put the officials in charge of examining and certifying candidates under the sole authority of Carafa whom he appointed as his special vicar.[51] At the consistory of September ninth, the cardinals agreed with the pope's proposal to

---

[48]*C.T.*, XII, 31; Creighton, *History of the Papacy*, VI, 254-60; John C. Olin, *The Catholic Reformation: Savonarola to Ignatius Loyola. Reform in the Church 1495-1540* (New York, 1969), 125.

[49]See above note 32 and Rainaldi, 1523, nr. 117.

[50]Fondo Consistorialia, Acta Miscellanea, Vol. 20, fol. 13v in Archivio Segreto Vaticano; Müller, *Römische Kurie*, 17-19, 26; Richard C. Trexler, *Synodal Law in Florence and Fiesole 1306-1518*, vol. 268 of *Studi e Testi* (Città del Vaticano, 1971), 10-11; Mansi, XXXV, 215-318, esp. 232D-34B, 270E-72B, 274D-75D, 283B-D, 290B-D, 304B.

[51]A. Caracciolo, *Vite e gesti*, fol. 54v-55v, 57r-v; Pelliccia, *Preparazione ed ammissione*, 90-91, 462; Richard M. Douglas, *Jacopo Sadoleto 1477-1547, Humanist and Reformer* (Cambridge, Mass., 1959), 36-37. Douglas's assertion that Carafa was vicar-general is not, however, supported by the partial list found in Konrad Eubel, "Series vicariorum Urbis a. 1200-1558," *Römische Quartalschrift für christliche Alterthumskunde und für Kirchengeschichte*, 8 (1894), 499.

prepare Rome for the Holy Year. All churches were to be visited and corrected, parish clergy to be examined and those found unworthy prohibited from celebrating the Mass at least during the Jubilee, and regular clergy to be prepared as confessors. By the end of October the zealous Carafa had produced notable results: candidates for the priesthood were strictly examined free of charge, ordained priests were carefully checked before being allowed to celebrate the liturgy, religious services were put on a regular basis and churches filled. Carafa was soon hailed as the reformer of the papal court.[52]

In November Clement renewed his efforts at a reform of the City. At a consistory on the seventh he ordered the cardinals to correct their households, especially the attire and morals of their retainers. The decrees of the Lateran Council were to be applied and the Curia reformed. Lorenzo Pucci was charged with preparing the minutes of a bull on this subject. After mature deliberation and with the advice and consent of the college of cardinals, Clement published on the twenty-first of that month, almost a year to the day of his election as pope, the bull *Meditatio cordis nostri.*[53]

In this document, Clement recalled the efforts of his cousin Leo X to reform morals and secure observance of canon law by his bull *Supernae dispositionis arbitrio* of the ninth session of the Lateran Council. Clement affirmed his own chief desire to see that decree observed. He recounted its contents generally by repeating verbatim its provisions with minor stylistic changes in the text and a rearrangement of some of its sections. The only exception from its provisions he explicitly mentioned was an exemption for non-resident curialists from the obligation of wearing the capuche.[54] A comparison of Clement's account with the original Lateran decree, however, reveals a number of more important alterations. Over one-half of the conciliar bull has been dropped. Deleted were those sections dealing with curial procedures in the provision of benefices and any measures directly affecting the cardinals' personal life style, consistorial or curial duties, legations, limitations on benefices, and responsibilities for informing the pope about conditions throughout Christendom. Also dropped were: prohibitions against lay interference in clerical affairs; condemnations of sodomy, sorcery, superstition, and feigned belief, especially in the

---

[52]Letters of Valerio Lugio to Francesco de Zuane de la Seda, 21·X·1524 and of Di Marin da Pozo to Francesco Spinelli, 21·XII·1524 in Sanuto, *I Diarii,* XXXVII, 88-89, 357; Müller, *Römische Kurie,* 37; Hubert Jedin, *A History of the Council of Trent,* trans. Ernest Graf (New York, 1957) I, 422.

[53]Fondo Consistorialia, Acta Miscellanea, vol. 20, fol. 15ᵛ; Clement VII, *Meditatio cordis nostri assidue,* (Romae, XI Kal. Dec. 1524), Bᵢʳ in BAV, Raccolta I.IV, 1680, int. 14, fol. 58ʳ-63ʳ.

[54]Clement VII, *Meditatio cordia,* Bᵢʳ.

Roman Curia; and requirements that youths be given religious instructions and clerics recite the divine office.[55] The only thing Clement added to the Lateran decree was a prohibition against beneficed and ordained clerics wearing linen shirts with effeminate ruffles and pleats, insisting instead that clerical garb be simple and decent in style and somber in color, and thus witness to a priestly dignity, purity of mind, and fitting service in the heavenly militia of Christ. This bull *Meditatio cordis* was to be published as soon as possible in Rome and elsewhere and observance in the City was to be secured by the vice-camerlengo, the governor, the auditor, and other competent judges.[56]

These actions of Clement in the first year of his pontificate would seem to indicate that the Lateran decrees were considered central to his plan for a reform of Rome. The alterations he made in the bull of the ninth session suggest a desire to deal with higher prelates in private, to reissue only those portions of the Lateran decree which he could realistically hope to enforce, and to eliminate the more obvious sources of scandal by insisting on externals.[57] Observance of this decree seems to have lasted at least until the Sack of 1527 temporarily removed Carafa, its zealous enforcer, from the Roman scene.[58]

This brief survey of the first decade at Rome following the council has shown that the Lateran decrees were not forgotten in the wake of the Wittenberg theses. The papacy in the person of Hadrian and Clement saw them as tools for correcting some of the abuses in the head, in the church at Rome, which had given added force to the Protestant critique. In some sense a culmination of the pre-Lutheran Catholic Reform, the Lateran decrees went on to become an element in the Counter-Reformation program for Rome. In the edict on the reform of the clergy of Rome issued after the Council of Trent, echoes of the Lateran legislation can be detected, there is even a specific reference to the Lateran Council in this edict.[59] The Lateran's reforms, especially those touching clerical garb, tonsure, and livery had become part of the Roman patrimony. They had helped in a limited way to bring about a reform in the head, in the House of the Lord, which would eventually affect the members, and spread to the world, *ab urbe ad orbem*.

---

[55]Sections dropped by Clement include the following: Mansi, 874D-79D, 881CD, 882E-85B.

[56]Clement VII, *Meditatio cordis*, B$_i$v - B$_{ii}$r

[57]In his undated memorial, Tommaso Campeggio acknowledged the possible need to revise this Lateran decree: "In primis videtur innovanda Bulla reformationis edita per felicis recordationis Leonem X in nona sessione novissimi Lateranensis concilii sed prius in consultatione posita an aliqua sint moderanda addenda vel minuenda propter quae forte non fuit usu recepta." - see his *Consilium quoddam de reformanda ecclesia*, BAV, Cod. Reg. Lat., 451, fol. 225r.

[58]Pelliccia, *Preparazione ed ammissione*, 92.

[59]Jacobus Sabellus, *Edictum super reformatione cleri Urbis* (Romae, 30.X.1566), fol. 1r-2r in BAV, Stamp. Chig. II. 1073, int. 15.

8 Reforming the Roman Curia:

Emperor Ferdinand I and the Council of Trent

by Robert Trisco
Catholic University of America

From the time of the Great Western Schism the cry for a
reformatio in capite was raised ever more insistently in the Church.
When the councils of Constance and Basel tried to satisfy this demand, the popes resisted attempts at reform which were grounded
on the conciliar theory. Around the middle of the fifteenth century,
however, some attention was given to the problem in Rome. At the
request of Nicholas V in 1449 Cardinal Domenico Capranica drafted
a project, *Advisamenta super reformatione Papae et Romanae
Curiae*, in which he depicted the illness of the head as the cause of
the illness of the rest of the body; and at the behest of Pius II in
1458 Domenico de' Domenichi, referendary of the Signatura, papal
theologian, and member of the commission appointed to study ways
of reforming the Roman Curia, submitted a memorial, *Tractatus de
reformationibus Romanae Curiae*, in which he censured the behavior
of the cardinals and other high prelates and recommended the institution of a board that would inspect the operations of the curial
officials, especially in financial matters. If the popes of the
Renaissance had adopted proposals such as these, they could have
removed many of the *gravamina* that the clergy and laity of Europe
eventually came to think could be eliminated only by a general
council. Actually, no reform of the Curia was effected before the
turn of the century.

Between 1500 and the opening of the Council of Trent several pontiffs acknowledged the need for reform. In 1512, shortly before the
Fifth Lateran Council, Julius II published a bull directed against
the most glaring abuses in the Curia, and in the following year his
successor, Leo X, received the extensive memorial, the *Libellus ad
Leonem X*, in which two prominent Venetian Camaldolese monks,
Tommaso Giustiniani and Vincenzo Quirini, proposed positive
measures for the renewal of the whole Church. Although Leo X promulgated a bull (which was accepted by the council in 1514) imposing a partial reform on the Curia, he manifested little earnestness in
enforcing it. Even after Martin Luther and his followers made
"reform" their shibboleth, the successive popes were content with

143

promises and gestures for many years. It was only after Paul III elevated several advocates of Catholic reform to the cardinalate that the movement gained strength. In 1536 he appointed a commission to draw up a reform program for the council that he had just summoned to Mantua and for the pope to pursue in the meantime; in the following year this body produced the famous *Consilium delectorum cardinalium et aliorum praelatorum de emendanda Ecclesia*, in which the evils afflicting the Church were unsparingly denounced and the necessary remedies were boldly prescribed. Conservative reformers criticized this plan, partly because a radical reform of the Curia might appear to confirm the Protestants' accusations against the papacy, partly because it would be easy to abolish the existing system but difficult to substitute a better one that would still yield adequate revenue, and partly because they thought it would be sufficient to enforce the old laws. In view of the determined opposition of many curialists, Paul III proceeded to consider the reform of the Datary, the Penitentiary, and the Chancery on a conservative basis; although he did improve the administration of some departments of the Curia and did choose some upright officials, he was not single-minded enough in such efforts to bring about a thorough or substantial reform. Because of his failure to correct abuses at Rome to a noticeable degree, he was less able to convince observers north of the Alps of his seriousness in convoking a council which, once assembled, might independently take up the question of *reformatio in capite* in a hostile mood, and he was in a weaker position to prevent the Council of Trent, when it finally convened at the end of 1545, from embarking on that dangerous course which could lead it into a devastating struggle for supremacy over the pope.[1]

For this reason the second of the three papal legates at Trent during the first period of the council, Cardinal Marcello Cervini, repeatedly urged the pope to take the initiative promptly in the reform of the Curia and thus to cut the ground from under the feet of those bishops or ambassadors who otherwise would eventually insist on taking the matter into their own hands. As the council became more conscious of its own responsibility, Paul III understood that he had to allow it to co-operate with him in the general work of reform. Accordingly, on March 23, 1546, he informed the legates that the council was not to be forbidden in principle to deal with the reform of the Curia, but he added several restrictions. This policy remained substantially in effect until the

---

[1] For a convenient summary of the background to the Council of Trent see Hubert Jedin, *A History of the Council of Trent*, trans. Ernest Graf, Vol. I (London, 1957), pp. 12-19, 117-135, 349-351, and 410-445. For the "Progetto di riforma ecclesiastica disciplinare" dealing with the reform of the Curia and probably dating from the beginning of the pontificate of Paul III see Döllinger, *Beiträge*, III, xx-xxi and 208-236. A list of abbreviations and short references used in the footnotes may be found at the end of this article (pp. 334-337).

end of the council. By this prudent concession Paul III did not imply, however, that he would be subject to reform measures passed by the council, nor did he intend to leave further efforts entirely to that body. In fact, heeding Cervini's advice, he promised to promote the reform at Rome *via facti*, without decrees, and he began with the Datary, the office most resistant to change. When the council came to consider the pivotal problem of church reform, that is, the duty of bishops and pastors to reside in their dioceses and parishes respectively, it could not avoid adverting to the curial practices which hindered the fulfillment of this obligation, such as the granting of dispensations for the union in one hand of several benefices with the care of souls, the bestowal of bishoprics on men holding high curial offices which were sold, and the employment of bishops of residential sees as nuncios at the courts of princes, as well as limitations on the authority of ordinaries which discouraged those who would wish to remain at their posts if they could be more than helpless spectators, such as the exempting of cathedral chapters, religious orders, and even individual clerics from episcopal jurisdiction, the giving of licenses to unfit men to have themselves ordained for a diocese *a quocumque*, the dispensing of the holders of pastoral benefices from residence, the accepting of all appeals from the local tribunals, and the exclusion of the bishop from legal cases pertaining to his diocese tried by the Curia (often through judges delegate). When it was proposed in the council to include cardinals in a decree enjoining residence on bishops, the commission of cardinals for the affairs of the council, which advised the pope in Rome, expressed its firm opposition. The debates which ensued at Trent, especially those concerning the retroactive effect of reforms, pointed up the fundamental problem regarding the extent to which the council was competent to curtail the papal prerogatives or to modify the curial practices. Paul III met some of the demands of the bishops with a great reform bull dated December 31, 1546, in which he restricted certain exemptions and prohibited certain dispensations previously granted by the Curia, and on February 18, 1547, he decided in consistory to forbid the cardinals to hold more than one bishopric, although they would still not be able to reside in the one diocese that they would retain because they were obliged to remain at the papal court. With the pope's permission, moreover, the council included various provisions affecting the Curia in its reform decrees approved in the seventh session (March 3, 1547), such as the ban on the accumulation of bishoprics. Even these modest achievements produced no practical results, however, because the conciliar decrees were never confirmed before the death of Paul III.[2]

---

[2]For details regarding the attempts to reform curial practices during the first period of the council see Jedin, *A History of the Council of Trent*, trans. Ernest Graf, Vol. II: *The First Sessions at Trent, 1545-47* (London, 1961), pp. 33-36, 126-131, 317-367.

During the council's first period at Trent and its continuation at Bologna it became clear to Cardinal Cervini and like-minded participants that the heart of the general reform of the Church had to be the self-renewal of the papacy and the Curia and that this could not be separated from the reform work of the council, for most of the abuses hindering the care of souls could not be eradicated without altering many curial usages. The first president, on the other hand, Cardinal Gianbattista Del Monte, was determined to reserve any structural reforms to the pope. When Del Monte succeeded Paul III on the papal throne, he initiated some projects for reform, especially of the Datary and the *Signatura gratiae*. He appointed in succession two cardinalitial commissions to propose reforms; the second, larger one, which he named on February 18, 1551, included several earnest reformers such as Cardinals Cervini, Gian Pietro Carafa, Reginald Pole, and Giovanni Morone, but it made little progress before the council was reopened at Trent on May 1. Then Julius instructed his legate, Cardinal Marcello Crescenzio, to follow the same policy as he himself had maintained during the first period. By his method of governing the council Crescenzio aroused the dissatisfaction of the Spaniards and Germans, who concluded that he desired only to safeguard the rights and claims of the Curia. In fact, he succeeded in keeping the reform decrees free of any grave infringement on curial prerogatives. Then when Julius III issued the bull permitting the council to pass a decree of suspension, he attempted to revive his predecessor's plan of holding a convention of bishops in Rome to advise him in regard to the needed reform of the pope and the Curia, but so strong was the aversion of the imperialist party to collaborating in such a mummery that the plan materialized no more after the second period of the council than it had after the first.

Thereupon Julius renewed the deliberations of the reform commission of cardinals but, probably because of political events which demanded his attention, as well as the opposition of the curial bureaucracy, he did not pursue the work assiduously. Finally, in the winter of 1553-1554 a bull entitled *Varietas temporum*, containing a comprehensive program for the reform of the whole Church, was drafted. The first two of the 150 chapters, dictated by Julius himself, dealt with the pope and the cardinals but were limited to general principles; other chapters would have modified the curial practice regarding absolutions and the bestowing of favors reserved personally to the pope, and still others laid down guidelines for the Grand Penitentiary and other officials of the Curia. The bull was conceived of as a substitute for and extension of the reform work of the council; it was to be only a beginning and to be completed when the council would reconvene. In the following spring the draft was revised; some parts were made sharper, and a consistorial decree of 1547 forbidding the accumulation of bishoprics by cardinals was renewed. The bull was still being discussed by the cardinals, however, when Julius died, and it was never promulgated.[3] The two immediate successors of Julius III were better known as champions of ecclesiastical reform before than they were to be after they donned the tiara. As soon as Cardinal Cervini was elected pope (Marcellus II), he began to prepare the reform bull for publication, and he ordered the *Signatura* and the Penitentiary not to grant any more favors or dispensations until the new regulations would be put into effect. But he accomplished nothing permanent because he died of a stroke of apoplexy only three weeks after his election.[4] Then Paul IV, formerly Cardinal Gian Pietro Carafa, with his impetuous Neapolitan temperament, started his four-year reign with a rigorous enforcement of existing decrees, but he had no intention of continuing the Council of Trent, nor did he resume consideration of Julius III's reform bull. Instead, in January, 1556, he unveiled in a consistory his plan for a thorough reform of the Roman Curia and for this purpose promptly appointed a large, special commission as a tractable substitute for an unpredictable council. Regardless of the losses that he would suffer in consequence, he was resolved to eradicate simony, which he judged to lie at the root of all the abuses. He actually carried out a radical reform of the Datary, which cost him two-thirds of his personal income, and he forbade by decree some of the worst abuses related to ecclesiastical benefices, especially the regress (the reservation whereby a resigned benefice should revert to the original holder under certain conditions). It was mainly with a view to reform, moreover, that Paul IV chose new cardinals. Soon, however, he became engrossed in the war with Spain, and later he devoted his attention to the Inquisition. Apparently he was also planning to broaden the reform commission into a general council at Rome similar to the Fifth Lateran, but he could never have persuaded the non-Italians that such an assembly would effectively reform the Church; in fact, he did not seriously attempt to hold a council. The declining strength of this austere octogenarian sufficed for little more than the moral improvement of Rome and the expulsion of the bishops who did not hold offices in the Curia. Thus Paul IV with his lack of a systematic approach, his negative measures,

---

[3]For the most recent general treatment of the continuation of the council at Bologna and the second period at Trent see Jedin, *Geschichte des Konzils von Trient*, Band III: *Bologneser Tagung (1547/48), Zweite Trienter Tagungsperiode (1551/52)* (Freiburg, 1970), esp. pp. 139-140, 213-214, 285-287, 292, 330-336, 369-370, and 388-394; and *Geschichte*, IV/1, 2-6. For a favorable judgment of the pope's reforming intentions and activities see Pastor, Vol. XIII: *Julius III (1550-1555)*, ed. Ralph Francis Kerr (St. Louis, 1951), pp. 158-170.

[4]On Marcellus II's reforming efforts see Pastor, Vol. XIV: *Marcellus II (1555), Paul IV (1555-1559)*, ed. Ralph Francis Kerr (reprinted Nendeln, Liechtenstein, 1969), pp. 33-48; and Jedin, *Geschichte*, IV/1, 10. On the reform memorial of Girolamo Seripando, Archbishop of Salerno and quondam general of the Hermits of St. Augustine see Jedin, *Seripando*, pp. 497-498.

and his draconian harshness failed to realize the expectations that his earlier career had raised, but he left a lasting mark on the face of Roman Curia.[5]

It was during Paul IV's pontificate, moreover, that decisive changes occurred in the Empire. By the Religious Peace of Augsburg permanent rights were accorded to the Lutheran princes and states and any further Catholic claims in those territories were excluded. This settlement had been accepted by the King of the Romans, Ferdinand I, who was acting with the full authority of his brother, Charles V, and who was so hard pressed between the Protestants and the Turks that he had no alternative. Paul IV, nevertheless, not only protested solemnly against the agreement of 1555 but also thought of deposing both the Hapsburg brothers for having made such concessions to heretics. In the following year Charles V abdicated the imperial throne in favor of his brother, but not until February, 1558, did the electors consent to this act and go on to elect Ferdinand as Roman Emperor. Having been ignored in all these proceedings and shocked by Ferdinand's oath to uphold the Religious Peace of Augsburg, Paul IV refused, with the support of many curialists, to recognize the validity of Ferdinand's title to the imperial dignity until certain conditions would be met. Although the tension between the two heads of Catholic Christendom—the ecclesiastical and the secular— was somewhat eased later in the year by Charles V's death, which eliminated the question of the legality of his resignation without papal approval, relations between them were never normalized before the death of Paul IV.

Ferdinand was suspected in Rome not only because of the participation of Lutheran electors in his elevation to the imperial throne but also because of his concessions to the Lutheran nobles of his hereditary lands and his toleration of the heterodoxy of his eldest son and heir, Maximilian.[6] Actually, Ferdinand was pained by his helplessness in both respects, for he was deeply pious and genuinely loyal to the Holy See. All contemporary witnesses agreed that he was a fervent Catholic. For example, Giacomo Soranzo, who was Venetian ambassador at the imperial court from 1559 to 1561, described Ferdinand in these words:

... He is most religious, and it can truthfully be said that he has not separated himself an inch from the Catholic religion; he hears two Masses every day. . . .
On all vigils and feast days he hears vespers, and on the morning of the feast day he hears high Mass and the ser-

[5]On Paul IV's attitude toward reform of the Curia see Pastor, XIV, 90-91, 175-209, 215-216, and 233-235: and Jedin, *Geschichte*, IV/1, 10-16.
[6]On Maximilian's attitude toward the Catholic Church at this time and Ferdinand's efforts to reconvert him see Robert Holtzmann, *Kaiser Maximilian II. bis zu seiner Thronbesteigung (1527-1564). Ein Beitrag zur Geschichte des Ubergangs von der Reformation zur Gegenreformation* (Berlin, 1903), pp. 316-331.

mon in the company of his ambassadors; every Friday he takes part in a procession and hears a high Mass, and he goes to confession and communion ten times a year.

The ambassador also asserted that Ferdinand had always shown himself to be most devoted to the Apostolic See but that he did not maintain close friendship with any cardinal at the Court of Rome nor had he ever wished to interfere in papal elctions or in the creation of cardinals.[7] Similarly, the papal nuncio at the imperial court in 1560, Stanislaus Hosius, wrote to the Archbishop of Salzburg: "I have no doubt that he is a truly Christian and sincerely Catholic prince, greatly imbued with the fear of God."[8] Peter Canisius, too, one of the Jesuits whose work Ferdinand had fostered in his lands throughout the 1550's, expressed to the general of his society his regret that the emperor was spoken of badly in Rome and was counted among the heretics while actually he had never before been "more concerned about making his conscience agreeable to God and having it acknowledged by good men than at this time." Canisius believed that Ferdinand would soon give brilliant proofs of his upright intentions and that the chief obstacle to harmony between the emperor and the pope was that neither one trusted the other.[9]

Ferdinand's reverence for the Holy See, however, did not blind him to the abuses rampant in the Roman Curia or deter him from advocating a serious reform. As early as 1541 at the Diet and Colloquy of Regensburg he had insisted during a visit to Cardinal Gasparo Contarini that a reform should be carried out before a council be opened, and he complained that although Paul III had often promised a reform, nothing had been done. In reply Contarini explained the need for time and enumerated the reforms already made, adding that experience would show him how different the morals of the papal court were then from what they had been in times past under other popes. Ferdinand, nevertheless, went on to deplore the papal dispensations which had caused enormous scandal in Germany, and in particular the dispensing of men appointed bishops from the obligation of receiving sacred orders.[10] Later King Ferdinand told the nuncio, Giovanni Morone, that he had little hope for

---

[7]"Relazione di Giacomo Soranzo, tornato ambasciatore da Ferdinando I. nel 1562," Albèri, Series I, Vol. VI (Florence, 1862), pp. 148-149, 155-156; also in *Relationen venetianischen Botschafter über Deutschland und Österreich im sechzehnten Jahrhundert*, ed. Joseph Fiedler ("Fontes Rerum Austriacarum. Österreichische Geschichts-Quellen, Zweite Abtheilung: Diplomataria et Acta, Vol. XXX [Vienna, 1870]), pp. 215, 221.
[8]September 12, 1560, Steinherz, I, 112.
[9]Canisius to Laìnez, Augsburg, May 27, 1559, Braunsberger, II, 425 (No. 354).
[10]Contarini to Cardinal Alessandro Farnese, Regensburg, June 27, 1541, in "Die Correspondenz des Cardinals Contarini während seiner deutschen Legation (1541)," ed. Ludwig von Pastor, *Historisches Jahrbuch*, I (1880), 487 (No. 104).

the projected council in view of the few preparations made till then in regard to reform which it was necessary to accomplish before going to a council lest anyone have reason to say, "Physician, heal thyself."[11] Since neither Paul III and his three successors nor the first two periods of the Council of Trent had brought about the thorough reform at Rome that Ferdinand desired, he was especially eager to know who the next pope would be after the death of Paul IV.

II. Preparing for the Council, 1560-1561

When the emperor learned in July, 1559, that the pope was succumbing to dropsy, he wrote to his ambassador at Rome, Franz von Thurm, that he knew that there were not lacking good cardinals, one of whom could take the dying pontiff's place and then, as soon as possible, convoke "the longed-for free and ecumenical council" as well as institute and carry into effect the supremely necessary reform of the whole Church, since this was the shortest way to bring divided Christendom back to the one and true understanding of religion.[12] Thus he already insinuated that the Council of Trent was not the kind of council that could achieve that result. After the conclave opened, von Thurm sent Ferdinand a copy of the election capitulations that all the cardinals had signed. Each one promised that if he should be elected pope, he would with all zeal and diligence, both by a general council and by all other lawful means, see to it that heresies and other abuses in the Church and in Christian society should be wiped out and, furthermore, that the universal Church and the Roman Curia should be reformed, beginning with the tribunals of the city because of the widespread outcry against them; the one elected, moreover, was to elevate to the cardinalate only men who were properly qualified by age, probity of life, reputation, and learning.[13] After Cardinal Gian Angelo de' Medici was elected, he confirmed these promises almost verbatim in a bull.[14]

Ferdinand was pleased by the election of the man whom he had known in 1542 as apostolic commissary with the papal troops

---

[11]Morone to Farnese, Regensburg, June 27, 1541, in "Die Nuntiaturberichte Giovanni Morone's vom Reichstage zu Regensburg 1541," ed. Franz Dittrich, *Historisches Jahrbuch*, IV (1883), 625-626 (No. 36).

[12]Ferdinand to Franz von Thurm, Augsburg, July 15, 1559, Sickel, *Concil*, p. 6 (No. III).

[13]Sickel, *Concil*, pp. 12-13 (No. VII), where mention of the tribunals is omitted; *CT*, VIII, 1-2 (No. 1); cf. Raynaldus, 1559, No. 37, p. 41, and Le Plat, IV, 612. The date of September 8, 1559, was established by Stephan Ehses, "Die letzte Berufung des Trienter Konzils durch Pius IV., 29. November 1560," *Festschrift Georg von Hertling* (Kempten, 1913), p. 139, n. 1.

[14]*Decet Romanum Pontificem*, January 12, 1560, *CT*, VIII, 3 (No. 2); Raynaldus, 1559, No. 38, p. 42; Le Plat, IV, 613-614.

fighting in Hungary against the Turks,[15] and even more so by Pius IV's recognition of his imperial title and the pope's restoration of the nunciature at the imperial court. The emperor was also reassured by the reports that his ambassador sent him from Rome. Pius told von Thurm that he intended to summon and complete a council as soon as possible and to prepare expeditions against the Turks; these statements led the ambassador to hope that the emperor "would gain everything from this holy pontiff."[16] Twelve days later von Thurm wrote that Pius had discussed in a meeting with the cardinals, among other topics, the reform of clerics throughout Christendom and had told them that he would begin that reform with himself.[17] In another congregation of cardinals held three days afterwards, according to von Thurm, this reform of the pope's person and household was treated again, and it was stated that gradually all the cardinals would have to suffer a similar reform. A cardinalitial commission consisting of three Italians, one German, and one Frenchman was appointed; it was to report to the pope the things needing correction; he would then present the proposals to all the cardinals and with their consent would institute the reform.[18] Finally, Pius appointed a permanent reform commission consisting of fourteen cardinals with Angelo Massarelli, Bishop of

---

[15]Soranzo to the Doge, Vienna, January 10, 1560, Turba, III, 131 (No 57). Cf. Soranzo's "Relazione," Albèri, VI, 155.

[16]Thurm to Ferdinand, Rome, January 1, 1560, Sickel, *Concil,* p. 23 (No. XVII).

[17]Thurm to Ferdinand, Rome, January 13, 1560, Sickel, *Concil,* pp. 25-26 (No. XIX).

[18]Thurm to Ferdinand, Rome, January 16, 1560, Sickel, *Concil,* p. 26 (No. XXI). Cf. *CT*, VIII, 34, n. 1. On February 25, 1560, the Spanish envoy in Rome, Francisco de Vargas, wrote to Philip II that Pius IV had proposed a reform and had held some meetings but that there would not be lacking people who would set up impediments in regard to the council; Vargas advised the king to urge the convocation and not to let the matter drop out of respect for the pope. Quoted by Wilhelm Voss, *Die Verhandlungen Pius IV. mit den katholischen Mächten über die Neuberufung des Tridentiner Concils im Jahre 1560 bis zum Erlass der Indiktionsbulle vom 29. November desselben Jahres* (Inaugural-Dissertation der Hohen Philosophischen Fakultät der Universität Leipzig zur Erlangung der Doktorwürde [Leipzig, 1887]), p. 29, n. 56. In the consistory of February 14, 1560, to which all the bishops living in Rome were summoned and at which about seventy were present, Pius IV told them to go after Ash Wednesday to their dioceses as by divine and human law they were obliged to do and to remain there and arrange matters until they would be called to the council which the pope intended to celebrate. "Excerpta ex Actis consistorialibus anni 1560," *CT,* VIII, 6-7. When some of them asked him to remove the hindrances to residence, he issued a decree *De residentia episcoporum* (April 25, 1560, *ibid.,* pp. 15-16), which not only reaffirmed his earlier order but also made its execution more attractive by granting certain privileges to those residing in their dioceses. Massarelli, as secretary of the reform congregation of cardinals, recorded on June 20, 1560, however, that the pope had deferred for a little while sending them to their dioceses because it would be dangerous to their health to leave the city in the heat of the summer, especially since many of them were from the Kingdom of Naples (*ibid.,* p. 35).

Telese, as secretary.[19] Thus the pope manifested his intention to fulfill one of the important obligations that he had assumed in his election capitulations and had ratified in a solemn document,[20] but he did not indicate much awareness of the obstacles that he would have to surmount in this undertaking.

Pius IV had also promised to convoke a council as soon as possible. Accordingly, he directed his nuncio, Bishop Hosius,[21] to tell the emperor that he was resolved to hold the council and was merely awaiting news from France and Spain. Ferdinand replied that there was no better way to relieve the distress of the Church than a general council, but that the place and time of the council had to be considered at greater length.[22] Thereupon the emperor referred the matter to his privy council.[23] In the *consultatio* held on June 5 the

---

[19]Massarelli's Diary, VII, March 6-15, 1560,*CT*, II, 343. Massarelli had been secretary of the Council of Trent during its first two periods.

[20]Guido Gianetti, however, an informer in the service of the English government who had settled at Venice in the assumed character of a merchant, reported to William Cecil on January 20, 1560, that Pius IV had conceded "the conditional resignation [*i Regressi*] to churches and benefices" which his predecessor had refused to allow. *CSP, 1559-1560*, p. 292 (No. 598).

[21]Hosius has been characterized as a conscientious, conservative ecclesiastic who feared that a change would all too easily be interpreted as a justification in principle of the theoretical and practical criticizing and that all too easily people would become accustomed to throwing out the fire with the ashes, authority with abuses. He always distinguished between the office and the incumbent. See Joseph Lortz, *Kardinal Stanislaus Hosius. Beiträge zur Erkenntniss der Persönlichkeit und des Werkes* (Braunsberg i.O., 1931), pp. 76-85.

[22]Hosius to Pius IV, Vienna, May 13, 1560, Steinherz, I, 23-24. Marcantonio da Mula, the Venetian ambassador in Rome, in his dispatch of May 27, 1560, quoted Pius IV as saying: "Volemo che riformino quello che accade, che si riordino le cose etiam nella persona nostra et cose nostre; ben volemo mantener le cose della fede et questa santa sede." On May 31 he reported that the pope had said that he wanted all freedom and reform to be used in the council, even in his own affairs, and that it must be free. Quoted by Eduard Reimann, "Unterhandlungen Ferdinands I. mit Pius IV. über das Konzil im Jahre 1560 und 1561," *Forschungen zur deutschen Geschichte*, VI (1866), 595, n. 1.

[23]Constant called the imperial councilors "all good Catholics," although he admitted that like all statesmen and the majority of the bishops in Germany and France they adhered to the principles of the Council of Basel on the authority of the pope and that of the bishops. He asserted that their contemporaries certainly did not regard them as narrow adversaries of the Curia, and he gave evidence of their orthodoxy. These convinced and avowed Catholics formed part of a movement for reunion which tried to restore religious peace in Germany by non-violent means. See *Concession*, I, 117-127. It is necessary to distinguish among them, however, because conciliarism was more dominant in the minds of some than of others. Richard, on the other hand, betrayed a special animus against Ferdinand and his councilors, asserting that the latter knew and cared only about their own country and had a narrow, exclusive, and purely legal manner of governing, while the former, who depended on them in all matters, subordinated everything to the needs of Germany-- the council, the reform, the pope, and the Church of Rome. See P. Richard, *Concile de Trente* (Vol. IX, Pt. 2, of Hefele-Leclercq, *Histoire des Conciles* [Paris, 1931]), pp. 816-817.

pope was blamed for not satisfying his obligation in religious matters, being interested only in the advancement of his relatives; his proposal regarding the council was called very jejune because he would not subject himself to the council as he was bound to do according to the decrees of the Councils of Constance and Basel and as the adherents of the Confession of Augsburg would demand.[24] Although Ferdinand had originally recommended the speedy convocation of a general council, he now feared that a council such as the pope had in mind—a continuation of the Council of Trent—not only would fail to attract the Protestants but also would provoke them to armed opposition and even to invasion of his dominions if they thought that it threatened to alter the Religious Peace of Augsburg; if the emperor could not obtain the kind of council that the Protestants would attend and accept, he would prefer none at all for the time being.[25] Hence, he had one of his councilors, Georg Gienger,[26] compose a long memorandum which in its original version was handed to the nuncio on June 20. In this document the emperor set forth six objections to the immediate convocation of a council and then added a jeremiad about the corruption of the clergy which was the principal cause of the present schism: "For if the priest, who is anointed, should sin, he will make the people fall away too." Hence, he implored the pope to proceed to a reform of the clergy without waiting for the gathering of the council.[27] Here the reform *in capite* was not mentioned explicitly, but it was implied in the urgent demand for a reform of the clergy in general.

Taking up the topic of the pope's activity in Rome, Hosius asked the emperor whether anyone could say that a reform was not happening there when not even the cardinals were spared, thus alluding to the recent arrest and imprisonment of Cardinal Innocenzo Del Monte, the dissolute favorite of Julius III, and Cardinals Carlo and Alfonso Carafa, the nephews of Paul IV. If no account was taken of cardinals in Rome when it was a question of reform, argued Hosius, much less would be taken of bishops who, he recalled, had sometimes been cast into the Castel Sant'Angelo for their discipline

---

[24]Sickel, *Concil*, pp. 49-50 (No. XXXIV).

[25]See Henry Outram Evennett, *The Cardinal of Lorraine and the Council of Trent* (Cambridge, 1930), pp. 152-153, 173.

[26]Gienger, Burgvogt von Enns, formerly vice-chancellor, a very cultured man and a fine Latin stylist, enjoyed Ferdinand's confidence and respect and possessed great influence over him. Although in some ways he was a conciliarist, he was never a crypto-Lutheran, as some Catholics, then and subsequently, suspected him of being. See Eder, p. 36. Loewe was the first to show that Gienger was the author of this anonymous memorial, pp. 72-78; cf. pp. 15-19.

[27]"Primum Ferdinandi Imperatoris circa concilium indicendum responsum," Vienna, June [20 and] 26, 1560, *CT*, VIII, 45-46; a less accurate version in Le Plat, IV, 632. The memorandum was revised at Hosius' request and handed to him in its final form on June 26. Cf. Wolfgang P. Fischer, *Frankreich und die Wiedereröffnung des Konzils von Trient 1559-1562* (Münster Westfalen, 1973), pp. 110-117 and 154-162.

because of sins of the flesh, and much less still of other priests of lower rank.[28] Apparently Ferdinand was not entirely convinced by this argument, for he wrote to his nephew, Philip II, that he had urged the pope to carry out a reform before convoking a council because, besides being so necessary in all Christendom, it could serve as an example to the heretics who kept the sights of their firearms on the bad example of ecclesiastics, and it could move them to desire the council; or, failing that, it could avail at least to set the council right and bring it to its proper effect and execution.[29]

When Cardinal Carlo Borromeo, who directed the papal secretariat, replied in the name of his uncle, the pope, to the emperor's objections to the projected council, he wrote that as far as reform was concerned, Pius had already partially attended to it by taking various measures for what was needed in Rome, but that in regard to northern lands Ferdinand would have to consent to a council in which his demands for the chalice for the laity and marriage for the clergy could be discussed.[30] This response was brought to Vienna by a second nuncio whom the pope sent to Ferdinand, Zaccaria Delfino, Bishop of Lesina (in Dalmatia), a more skilful diplomat than Hosius and an old friend of the emperor and his family. In the instructions that he gave to Delfino on the advice of Cardinal Morone, Borromeo elaborated on the pope's answer to the emperor's memorandum. In regard to the question of reform, the new nuncio was to tell Ferdinand that Pius was not failing to do something every day as the occasion arose and was causing the bishops to reside in their dioceses; for this purpose he was conferring many favors on them and increasing their authority; little by little he would continue to do what he could; he would still be pleased, nevertheless, that this reform should be treated in the council; and, it was added, "if in the very person of His Holiness there will be anything deserving of being reformed, he will be the first to allow himself to be reformed and will give an example to the others." In the event that the emperor should reject Trent or any

---

[28]Hosius to Borromeo, Vienna, June 27, 1560, Steinherz, I, 64. Later Hosius reported to Borromeo in cipher without further elaboration that the French ambassador (Bernardin Bochetel, Bishop of Rennes) had spoken to him about reforming the pope (Vienna, July 31, 1560, Steinherz, I, 84).

[29]Ferdinand to Philip II, Vienna, June 27, 1560, *CDI*, II (1843), 561, and XCVIII (1891), 154.

[30]"Carolus Borromaeus Pontificis nomine respondet de difficultatibus . . . ," Rome, August 30, 1560, *CT*, VIII, 62 (No. 33); also Le Plat, IV, 636, and Raynaldus, 1560, No. 56, p. 80. Borromeo, an inexperienced youth in his early twenties, was the faithful and tireless executor of his uncle's wishes but had little direct influence on papal policy and made no important decisions on his own authority. See Pio Paschini, "Il primo soggiorno di S. Carlo Borromeo a Roma, 1560-1565," in *Cinquecento Romano e Riforma Cattolica* ("Lateranum," N.S., Vol. XXIV [Rome, 1958]), pp. 107-109. Cf. Hubert Jedin, *Carlo Borromeo* ("Bibliotheca Biographica," 2 [Rome, 1971]), pp. 8-10.

place in Italy as the site of the council and should reiterate his demand for reforms and concessions, Delfino was to propose that bishops and theologians should be assembled in Rome to seek solutions to these problems.[31] Delfino observed these instructions and presented the pope's written reply when, along with Hosius, he was received in audience by the emperor on September 29, 1560. Ferdinand declined to give the nuncios immediately a definite answer regarding the proposed resumption of the council at Trent. Instead he entrusted the Bishop of Vienna, Anton Brus von Müglitz,[32] with the task of composing a reply to the pope's letter. The draft was approved by Ferdinand on October 8, when the news arrived from Rome that Pius had decided to lift the suspension of the Council of Trent in order to preclude a national council in France which might lead to the separation of that whole country from the Holy See or to the concession to the Huguenots of rights similar to those accorded to the Lutherans by the Religious Peace of Augsburg. On the next day Ferdinand granted the nuncios an audience during which he handed them his official reply. He declared that he was opposed to continuing the Council of Trent because of the expected reactions of the Protestants, but would be content with a convocation to some other place such as Innsbruck. He also stated in the written reply that he was pleased to hear that the pope had to some extent already come to commence the reform by making various provisions for the needs at Rome, and he asked the pope to apply himself with the greatest earnestness to the prosecution and completion of that salutary and necessary undertaking and especially to see to it that that kind of reform be begun not only at Rome but also in those places in which

---

[31]Borromeo to Delfino, Rome, August 15-30, 1560, Steinherz, I, 104-109. Delfino (1527-1583), a Venetian, had been nuncio to Ferdinand from 1553 to 1555 and again in 1556 and had been present at the Diet of Augsburg during his first nunciature. After returning to Rome in the autumn of 1556 he had maintained close relations with Ferdinand until Paul IV forbade him to correspond with the Hapsburgs. This time he remained at the imperial court, wielding great influence, until 1565, when he was elevated to the cardinalate at the request of the emperor and of Duke Cosimo I of Florence. For a sketch of his career and an appraisal of his character see Helmut Goetz (ed.), *Nuntiaturberichte aus Deutschland*, Erste Abteilung: *1533-1559*, 17. Band: *Nuntiatur Delfinos, Legation Morones, Sendung Lippomanos (1554-1556)* (Tübingen, 1970), pp. vii-xv and xli-liv. Goetz defends Delfino against the traditional accusations of excessive ambition and avarice but notes that he had placed himself at the service of two masters and thus came into conflict with almost all the later popes.

[32]Brus, a native of Mohelnice (Müglitz) in Moravia, had been named Bishop of Vienna by Ferdinand in 1558, but Paul IV refused to confirm his appointment, and even Pius IV waited until December, 1560, to do so. In 1561 he was promoted to the metropolitan see of Prague, which had been vacant since 1431. For a biographical sketch see S. Steinherz (ed.), *Briefe des Prager Erzbischofs Anton Brus von Müglitz, 1562-1563* (Prague, 1907), pp. 5-16.

religious discord prevailed.[33] Besides this written reply, Ferdinand
discoursed at length about reform. When Hosius said that a beginning had already been made, the emperor rejoined, "Such a reform
is not sufficient; there is need of another both in Rome and in these
lands." He also affirmed that it would be most advantageous if the
pope, who had himself made the suggestion, would summon learned,
pious, and practical men from the whole Christian world to Rome
and with them determine what kind of reform would be best suited
to the customs of each country.[34] Ferdinand also ordered the nuncios to make known to the pope alone that it would be advisable to
correct the abuses pertaining to the creation of cardinals, taking
into account their number and age and the status of the persons
chosen, as well as having regard for the nations which he wished to
honor, and, said the emperor, honor would be shown by placing men
in that dignity not for worldly interests but according to their
merits.[35] In this oral statement to the nuncios he expressed the contents of a confidential letter to the pope that had been planned but
was never completed. It seems that Ferdinand chose the form of an
address instead for the communication of these thoughts in order to
soften their harshness.[36]

Lest his exhortations be weakened through transmission by the
nuncios, however, the emperor included them in their full strength
in the instructions that he sent his new ambassador at Rome, Prospero d'Arco.[37] In regard to reform he wrote that he had told the
nuncios:

> ... with our zeal and burning desire to aid religion and
> the commonwealth we could not help but be astonished at
> the delay and hesitation that is caused to so necessary a
> task which is handled so coldly and at the way in which
> the reform is commenced on the surface only, when we
> saw with the greatest sadness of our spirit that while on
> the one hand it is said that a reform is being undertaken
> in the Church, on the other a great deformation is

---

[33]"Ferdinandi I Imperatoris responsum secundum traditum RmisDnis episcopis
Warmiensi et Delphino," Vienna, October 9, 1560, CT, VIII, 84; also Le Plat, IV,
643. On the reactions of the Protestant princes to rumors of a reopening of the
council see Voss, op. cit., pp. 84-86; cf. pp. 118-119.

[34]Hosius and Delfino to Borromeo, Vienna, October 14, 1560, Steinherz, I, 137.

[35]Delfino to Pius IV, Vienna, October 18, 1560, Steinherz, I, 148. On January 31,
1560, Pius had elevated to the cardinalate his nephew Carlo Borromeo (who was
twenty-one years of age), his cousin Gian Antonio Serbelloni, and Giovanni
de'Medici, the seventeen-year-old son of Cosimo I, Duke of Florence, who had helped
to procure his election to the papacy.

[36]This is the conclusion of Eder, pp. 60-61.

[37]Count Prospero d'Arco had replaced Franz von Thurm toward the end of June,
1560. See Gerhard Rill, "Prosper Graf von Arco, kaiserlicher Orator beim Hl. Stuhl
1560-1572," Mitteilungen des österreichischen Staatsarchivs, XIII (1960), 1-106,
esp. 11-33.

actually happening, leading to the worst contempt of His
Holiness and the Apostolic See and to the harm of
religion itself and of the Christian commonwealth—
especially in the creation of cardinals. For according to
the sacred constitutions their number should not exceed
twenty-four, and those cardinals should be beyond compare in terms of piety, integrity, learning, and prudence
and should be of legitimate age, so that they may be able,
as is their duty, to assist and advise the supreme pontiff
in matters concerning the welfare of the whole Christian
flock and to elect a fit pope.[38] Yet by bad example and
wicked abuse it has been brought to pass that there are
more than sixty cardinals and that in the choice of many
of them no account is taken either of the age or of the
other qualities which are required in a cardinal. For mere
boys are created cardinals, and when they grow up they
cast themselves into every kind of disgraceful and
shameful conduct, and finally they have to be punished
and basely put to death to the great dishonor both of the
popes by whom thery were admitted to so lofty a rank
and of their family. Although no law or decree prohibits
it, still with little advantage for the Church there are
likewise appointed the sons of princes, who, supported by
their clients, relatives, power, and money, and corrupting
the minds of others by their bribes, aspire to the papacy
and afterwards stir up wars and throw the whole world
into disorder. . . . It is also a cause for astonishment that
this abuse is excused on the pretext of dispensation, and
so the popes take to themselves the authority and power
of dispensing without a council in those matters in which
private advantage is attended to, the good-will of princes
is won, wihtout any public advantage entering in, while in
other matters in which many thousands of souls could be
gained by this sort of dispensation, it is so inflexibly
denied without a council. And because the present pope
too has a bad reputation in that respect, although otherwise we do not miss in him any honesty or sagacity or any
of those qualities that belong to a good and capable pontiff, it is our wish that His Holiness would show himself
to be irreproachable in this respect too. What is said in

---

[38]The Council of Basel limited the number of cardinals to twenty-four, set a
minimum of thirty years for their age, prescribed other qualities, restricted the appointment of the sons, brothers, or nephews of kings or great princes, and forbade
the choice of nephews of the pope, in its Twenty-Third Session (March 26, 1436). See
COD, p. 501. At the time of the conclave in which Pius IV was elected there were
fifty-two cardinals.

defense of this deed of the pope—that he could not do otherwise than gratify his relatives—does not stand up, for Christ was not willing in this way to gratify the sons of Zebedee. . . . And so it grieves us very much that in this way an occasion of scandal is given to those who are of the other religion, as well as material and cause for ridiculing both his Holiness and us together with all Catholics. And this evil cannot help but affect other Catholics also with extraordinary sadness.[39]

This sharp admonition, marked by references to the reform councils of the fifteenth century, seems to have been composed by Francisco de Córdoba, a Spanish Minorite of the Strict Observance, the confessor of Philip II's sister and Maximilian's wife Mary; he was a convinced conciliarist, a relentless critic of the Roman Curia, a persistent advocate of the intervention of the secular powers in the cause of ecclesiastical reform, and a champion of episcopal authority as opposed to the centralized absolutism of the pope.[40] Whether or not he was the author, the emperor himself took responsibility for this protest against abuses in the College of Cardinals and against papal nepotism, since he felt obliged in conscience to press for reform in this area also. Later he was to return to these points in earnest. For almost a year, however, he was content to observe the

---

[39]Ferdinand to Arco, Vienna, October 18, 1560, Sickel, *Concil*, pp. 113-114 (No. LX). The imperial ambassador was to see to it that Pius IV should not misinterpret Ferdinand's intention or take offense (*ibid.*, p. 115). For a graphic description of the Court of Rome, especially of the cardinals, and of the conclave see the lengthy report of Luigi Mocenigo composed upon the termination of his ambassadorship in the summer of 1560, in Albèri, Vol. X (Series II, Tome IV [Florence, 1857]), pp. 31-32, 42-44.

[40]Loewe excluded the authorship of others at the imperial court and proposed that of Francisco de Córdoba in the light of similarities in the instruction to his written opinion of October, 1561, addressed to the emperor, and his share in the emperor's letter to the pope of March 3, 1563 (pp. 63-71). Eder supported this opinion as far as the section quoted and translated here is concerned; he supposed that the Franciscan's draft was combined with drafts of other parts of the instruction and edited by the emperor's secretary, Marcus Singkhmoser, in keeping with the previous direction of the privy council and the vice-chancellor, Sigismund Seld (pp. 65-66). After living an exemplary life as a friar for thirty-three years in Spain, Francisco was chosen by Philip II in 1559 to be the confessor of the Queen of the Romans and future empress. At the imperial court he soon gained considerable influence over Ferdinand as an adviser on religious affairs. It is not certain whether he acquired his conciliarist opinions in his native country or in Central Europe. See Bohdan Chudoba, "Las relaciones de las cortes habsburgesas en la tercera asamblea del Concilio Tridentino," *Boletin de la Academia de Historia*, CIII (1933), 297-368; (I have used an offprint with separate pagination), pp. 30-31. Hosius, who employed Córdoba as an intermediary with the Spanish ambassador, Don Claudio Fernández de Quiñones, Count de Luna, called him a "pious and learned man." Hosius to Borromeo, Vienna, February 6, 1561, Steinherz, I, 209.

extent of the reform being carried out by Pius IV.[41] During this period the relations between the imperial and papal courts hinged mainly on the bull of convocation for the council with its designed ambiguity regarding the question of a *nova indictio* or a *continuatio*.[42] Ferdinand was preoccupied more with the reactions of the Protestants to the convocation than with the preparation for the council through reform in Rome.

Once it was decided to proceed at once to the opening of a council, the proposal of a reform convention at Rome was abandoned.[43] When Giovanni Francesco Commendone, Bishop of Zante, delivered the bull of convocation to the emperor, he explained to him why the pope had not acted on the suggestion of assembling prelates from several countries in Rome to discuss reform; the pope, Commendone said, was afraid that by doing so he would appear to impede the council, the speedy progress of which he earnestly desired; but if the emperor and the other princes should judge such an assembly to be expedient anyway, the pope was ready in this way too not to be wanting to his office. The emperor replied that since the pope had made provision by means of the council, he deemed it good to promote it, but if by chance obstacles should ensue, then they could

---

[41]On September 3, 1560, Otto von Truchsess, Bishop of Augsburg, wrote from Rome to Duke Albrecht V of Bavaria that the pope would not be idle with the reform there ("Ir Hayl. werden och hie entlich mitt der Reformation nitt feyren"), and three days later he wrote that in the consistory on September 4 the pope had ordered all bishops who did not have offices in the Curia to reside in their sees "onnachlässig mitt ernst." Edited by Joseph Baader in *Archiv für die Geschichte des Bistums Augsburg*, II (1859), 206-207, 210. I have been unable to find Ferdinand Siebert, *Zwischen Kaiser und Papst. Kardinal Truchsess von Waldburg* (Berlin, 1943). Peter Canisius reported the encouraging news from Augsburg to his confrère, Leonard Kessel, rector of the Jesuit college in Cologne, on September 17, and a week later he wrote to another member of the Society of Jesus at Cologne, Nicolaus Goudanus, that the pope was diligently at work on the reform of the Roman Curia and the convocation of a council (Braunsberger, II, 726, 735). For the bull *De salutis gregis dominici*, on the residence of bishops, the privileges of those who resided, and the penalties for those who did not, September 4, 1560, see *Bullarum*, VII, 55-58 (No. XII).

[42]For the bull *Ad Ecclesiae regimen*, November 29, 1560, see *Bullarum*, VII, 90-92 (No. XXVII).

[43]Although Philip II at first had endorsed his uncle's recommendation of a reform convention of ecclesiastics of various nationalities in Rome, upon further deliberation he took a contrary position for several reasons, the first of which was that "although the reform might be as complete as could be desired, it could not satisfy either the strayed (*desviados*) or even many other persons who desire it, because it would appear that the reform was being made in that place from which in their opinion the disorder and bad example arise and by the very ones who have need of being reformed." The king had so informed the nuncios at his court and his ambassador at Rome. He was opposed only to any attempt to prescribe reforms for the universal Church in this way before the council; he did not mean that the pope should have his hands tied if he should deem it proper to remedy one thing or another. See Philip II to Vargas, Toledo, November 22, 1560, Döllinger, *Beiträge*, I, 344-346 (No. 92).

have recourse to the other remedy.⁴⁴ Nothing further was heard of this proposal.

While the emperor procrastinated the sending of his representatives to Trent throughout 1561, his theological advisers were not idle. In the early autumn of that year Francisco de Córdoba submitted to him a memorial consisting of sixty-two articles on the subject of ecclesiastical reform.⁴⁵ Proceeding in the same direction as he had pointed out a year before, the Spanish friar defended the divinely constituted position of the bishops in the Church against the encroachments of the pope, the cardinals, and the Curia. Thus he called it tyrannical and contrary to the order established by God for a cardinal priest to take precedence over a bishop. According to the same order, he asserted, bishops are the primary counselors of the pope and of the Church in all matters pertaining to faith and morals; cardinals, on the other hand, who are not officials *(praelati)* or shepherds of the Church, are, as advisers of the pope, substitutes for and vicars of the bishops. When a general council, moreover, has been canonically convoked, the College of Cardinals has no function, because at that time the bishops represent the universal Church. He reminded the emperor that the pope and officials of the Church are not its lords and masters, nor is the Church the pope's handmaid; the pope, therefore, should not bear rule over the Church but should render it service for the glory of God and the advantage of the Church. The Franciscan confessor also stated boldly that the Church was not edified by the pomp of the cardinals, in which they surpassed many secular princes, and he recommended that they be brought back into order lest they be a scandal to the people of God, and that many privileges which had been granted to them should be annulled by the general council so that they might understand that they were on a lower level than the bishops. He said the same about the ostentation of the pope and other prelates, and he thought that the honor and reverence paid to the pope, for example, the kissing of his feet by the faithful and even by priests and the wearing of the cross of Christ on his shoes, were excessive and improper. He even recommended that the universal Church, gathered in council, with the aid of the princes should set up a different manner of electing a pope and should take this power away from the cardinals if it wished to remove scandals from the Church and change its ways for the better. He went so far as to say that it should take away the pope's power of creating cardinals, because in doing so he did not seek the good of the Church; the pope chose many unworthy men whose promotion was scandalous to the Church and through whom the Church of Rome was brought into ill repute. Instead Córdoba

---

⁴⁴Commendone to Borromeo, Vienna, January 13, 1561, *CT*, VIII, 132.

⁴⁵Loewe was the first to determine the date of composition--between the end of September and October 10, 1561--and the author (pp. 43 ff.). Eder confirmed his arguments (pp. 103 ff.).

proposed that the princes and prelates in the several nations should choose upright men, skilled in God's law, who would be counselors of the pope and would also elect the pope according to a procedure that the council would establish. If the pope with the college of cardinals should resist this decree of the council, the Franciscan did not shrink from asserting that the pope ought to be regarded as a schismatic and a tyrant, because, in administering the Church, he would not be following the advice of the universal Church (represented by the council) but would be acting on his own opinion and thus would separate himself from the unity of the Church. Fearing, moreover, that if the pope, possessing supreme power and authority, could not be judged by anyone, he could become a tyrant, Córdoba wanted the council to declare how the Church could resist without schism a pope destroying the Church and to declare also when his sentence of excommunication was not to be feared and in which abuses, tyrannies, and superstitions he was not to be obeyed. The writer also commented on the fact that because the pope distributed benefices, many unworthy men obtained them, since the pope, being busy with many affairs, could not find out who were fit, and since he conferred several benefices on the same person with a dispensation, which the Spaniard called a dissipation; furthermore, since the benefices were conferred at Rome, they pretended that they were resigning or exchanging benefices when actually they were selling them. If the council should wish to abolish such simony, it should first, he thought, remove from the Church the "tyranny of benefices," so that the pope would confer only those of the Church of Rome and not those of other dioceses and the College of Cardinals would not confer any at all. Finally, the queen's confessor wished to have the council define that the administration of ecclesiastical affairs whould be performed without charge, for at that time, he said, without money nothing, and with it everything, was done at Rome.[46] In these and many other articles Padre Francisco vigorously set forth the ideal of the early Christian Church as he conceived it and gave further evidence of his own rigid conciliarism. Powerful as his presentation was in its simple, direct, unpolished Latin style, it was not apt to induce Ferdinand to adopt such extreme theories and proposals, nor does the friar's attitude toward the papacy seem to have been characteristic of all the emperor's councilors.

It is clear that at least the imperial vice-chancellor, Georg Sigmund Seld,[47] did not share the Franciscan's opinion regarding

---

[46]*CT*, XIII, 489-500 (No. 79), esp. articles 18, 20, 23, 27, 32, 40, 43, 45, 54, and 56.

[47]Seld wielded great influence over Ferdinand, especially in matters pertaining to the council. He was a very good Catholic and was considered by papal diplomats to be loyal to the Holy See. See the article on him by A. von Druffel in *Allgemeine Deutsche Biographie*, XXXIII (Leipzig, 1891), 673-679, and Helmut Goetz, "Die geheimen Ratgeber Ferdinands I. (1503-1564). Ihre Persönlichkeit im Urteil der Nuntien und Gesandten," *Quellen und Forschungen aus italienischen Archiven und Bibliotheken*, XLII/XLIII (1963), 483-487.

reform *in capite* as the most pressing need of the time and the indispensable prerequisite for all other reform when he drafted instructions for the emperor's envoys to the council. Here it was said that the reform of both estates—the secular and especially the spiritual—was to be fostered with all earnestness, but since it was not to be attained so soon at the Court of Rome or in Italy beyond all human diligence, it should not be flouted for another day or hour in Germany, where it was so urgently required.[48] Although the privy council approved these instructions on October 20, 1561, no envoys were appointed yet. The instructions were again discussed in the privy council at Prague on December 6 in the presence of the emperor, who showed intense interest in the question of reform. He wished the fathers of the council to take up this matter without delay, and he intended to bring all his influence to bear on it. Hence, he asked his councilors when and how his desires should be presented to the council. He thought of arranging an agreement with the kings of Spain, France, Portugal, and Poland for the purpose of countering any attempts by the Curia to frustrate the demands for reform by breaking the council off or suspending it or by using the preponderance of Italian votes to overwhelm the pious desires of the other nations. The councilors at this meeting, however, argued against any plan of trying to unite the secular powers because it would arouse the suspicions of both the pope and the Protestants and would encounter other obstacles; they recommended instead that the question of reform be left to the council. A definite decision was deferred, nevertheless, until the emperor's trusted adviser Gienger, who was absent from Prague, could be heard.

Accordingly, Ferdinand had a letter sent to Gienger, informing him of the deliberations and requesting his opinion. The emperor's mind is clearly revealed in the first sentence:

> First, since it is idle to hope for any fruit from this imminent council unless the causes of God's wrath and of the evils by which the whole Christian commonwealth is now being brought to ruin, namely, our sins, are removed by a strict and canonical reform of all the estates and ranks in the Christian people, and therefore since it seems that every effort should be made with the fathers in the council to have the reform undertaken and brought into effect without any hesitation or tergiversation, we earnestly desire to learn your judgment about pressing and enforcing the reform, lest so pious a work be longer delayed to the detriment of Christendom and lest, on the other hand, if it be urged too importunately or overhastily, by so odious a matter which the pope with the

---

48Sickel, "Libell," pp. 35-36 (par. 14).

whole Roman Curia and clergy, no less than the secular order, so greatly dread and reject, an occasion and grounds be furnished to the pope or others to interrupt or abandon the council completely, so that all [our] toil would be rendered utterly ineffectual.[49]

Five days later Gienger replied to the emperor. He considered the instructions for the envoys to the council to have been so wisely and carefully thought out and weighed that no addition or modification was necessary. If the matter was to be seriously carried on, he commented, there was no need for lengthy instructions; if not, not even a directive of a thousand pages would help. Then he continued:

But who can believe that the Roman Curia, on which all the other churches of the western world depend, is seriously and sincerely seeking or pressing for a council when all its actions are diametrically opposed to the most salutary decrees of the sacred councils? Who can hope that the Roman Curia can bear a reform when it steadily affirms that the Church is without wrinkle or stain and when it doggedly *(mordicus)* denies that errors or abuses or corruption or superstitions exist anywhere?

The writers recalled that the "most Christian Gerson" had complained that the whole Church had become brutish and carnal in his age and had urged that it be brought back to the times at least of Sylvester and Gregory, if not to those of the Apostles. In response to the emperor's question about the policy to be adopted, Gienger wrote that since the reform of the Church *in capite et in membris* was one of the purposes for which general councils were regularly held and was also a principal part of this council (as the bull of convocation expressly stated), it should frequently and seriously be urged by the imperial envoys, and neither the pope nor anyone else concerned about the good of the Church could or should be offended thereby. Although he recommended that Ferdinand's ambassadors should communicate and collaborate with those of other kings in promoting the reform as the need or occasion might arise at the council, he thought that it would be safer to eschew any agreement with the kings themselves for the time being and better to await patiently the progress of the council. Realistically he observed that it would be very difficult amid the current conditions of mutual mistrust to obtain the co-operation of the emperor as the supreme advocate of the Church and of the other kings and princes that would be necessary to force the pontiffs and the prelates both north

---

[49]Ferdinand to Gienger, Prague, December 10, 1561, Sickel, *Concil*, pp. 243-244 (No. CXLII).

and south of the Alps to accept reform. Concluding his reply, Gienger suggested that if the council should fail, Ferdinand might go to Rome to restore order immediately as Emperor Henry III had done in 1046.[50] Although this last reference to precedents for direct intervention illustrated his conviction of the need for a thorough *reformatio in capite*, no concrete ways of achieving this goal were proposed.

In his letter Gienger also suggested that one or more theologians who were not too obstinate or haughty, as for the most part theologians were wont to be, should be attached to the ambassadors. The emperor replied that he and his councilors had discussed this suggestion and deemed it expedient but could not carry it into effect because of the grave lack of suitable theologians. Excluding several men by name, he first mentioned the Jesuits Peter Canisius and Nicholas Delanoy but added that both seemed to be excessively rigid in making certain concessions and perhaps would be more remiss than necessary in urging the reform of the Roman Curia. In the end he chose a Hungarian bishop, Andrew Dudić Sbardelato de Horehonica (Horehowitz), who had already set out for Trent; this man could assist the ambassadors until a more learned theologian could be appointed.[51] Later, nevertheless, the emperor was to employ Canisius as a theologian at his own court.

After being discussed for several months by the emperor and his privy council, the instructions for the ambassadors to the council were completed on January 1, 1562. Keeping in contact with the envoys of the other kings and governments, particularly of Philip II, they were to admonish the fathers of the council, whenever it would be opportune or necessary, to effect "a rigorous and canonical reform of morals," especially in the clerical state. Then it was stated explicitly: "Since Italy and also the Roman Curia itself, as well as Germany and the other nations of Christendom, have extreme need

---

[50]Gienger to Ferdinand, Vienna, December 15, 1561, Sickel, *Concil*, pp. 244-249 (No. CXLIII). On Gienger see the comments of Alois Kröss, S.J., "Kaiser Ferdinand und seine Reformationsvorschläge auf dem Konzil von Trient," *Zeitschrift für katholische Theologie*, XXVII (1903), 460.

[51]Ferdinand to Gienger, Prague, December 28, 1561, Sickel, *Concil*, p. 249. Peter Canisius was engaged mainly in preaching and writing at Augsburg; Delanoy was rector of the Jesuit college at Ingolstadt. On Canisius' interest in the council see Brodrick, pp. 476-482. Ferdinand was aware of their attitude toward communion *sub utraque* and marriage for priests. At this time Dudić (also spelled Dudith, Dudics, and Dudich) was Bishop of Knin (in Dalmatia); he and the bishop-elect of Csanád were designated by the bishops and clergy of the ecclesiastical province of Gran on January 14, 1562, as their procurators at the council. After the death of the bishop of Csanád on November 24, 1562, Dudić succeeded him in that see. He was named bishop of Pécs in 1565 and was sent by the emperor as ambassador in Poland. There he married and consequently was deposed and excommunicated in 1568. It is not certain that he formally became a Protestant. See the biographical article by Hubert Jedin in *Dictionnaire d'Histoire et de Géographie Ecclésiastiques*, XIV (1960), 988-990.

of this reform, an effort must be made among the fathers in the council that without any further delay or hesitation it be undertaken in all places and lands and especially in Germany."[52] But in spite of Ferdinand's determination to promote reform from top to bottom, a definite program was still lacking as the council opened, partly because detailed demands had not been decided upon and partly because the initiative was being left to the fathers at Trent.

These protracted deliberations at the imperial court might seem to imply that reform was meanwhile being entirely neglected at the papal court. As the time for the reopening of the council drew near, however, reform activity was intensified there. On the very day on which the bull of convocation was issued, the imperial ambassador at Rome reported that a congregation of cardinals had been appointed for matters pertaining to the council and to reform; it was expected that the first thing that would be reformed was the procedure for papal elections.[53] A fortnight later he wrote that all the cardinals, theologians, and doctors were meeting twice a week to reform the Penitentiary, the Chancery, the Datary,[54] and the

---

[52]"Instruction für die kaiserlichen Oratoren auf dem Concil," Prague, January 1, 1562, Sickel, *Concil*, pp. 258-259 (No. CXLVI).

[53]Arco to Ferdinand, Rome, November 29, 1561, Sickel, *Concil*, p. 242. On the same day Cardinal Francesco Gonzaga wrote from Rome to his uncle, the Cardinal of Mantua (Ercole Gonzaga), who had been sent to Trent as the first legate, that the pope had declared that to reform the Court of Rome he wished to take the reforms already made by Leo X, Clement VII, Paul III, and Julius III and from all these to extract one that would meet the need; as far as he was concerned, the pope said that he was already resolved to restrict and reduce in another form the principal offices of the court such as those of the Penitentiary, the Vice-Chancellor, and the Camerlengo; he would make this intention public little by little and not wait to do everything at once; he added that it was his wish that the same cardinals who felt some inconvenience because of the restrictions on those offices should be the ones to reform him in regard to the Datary; later he also spoke about his intention to reform the conclave. Giovanni Drei (ed.), "Carteggio del cardinal Ercole Gonzaga sul Concilio di Trento (1561),"*Archivio della R. Società Romana di Storia Patria*, XLI (1918), 216-217. On the scandalous abuses of the last conclave, which lasted from September 5 to December 25, 1559, see Pastor, Vol. XV: *Pius IV (1559-1565)*, ed. Ralph Francis Kerr (London, 1928; repr. 1951), pp. 6-65. Pius suggested that in papal elections the form of voting used in electing the doge of Venice be introduced, but the cardinals did not agree with him; hence, the idea was abandoned. Jedin, *Geschichte*, IV/l, 77-78.

[54]According to Mocenigo, the pope's entire income, aside from what he received from the spoils of benefices, came through the Datary either by the composition of benefices (by which those wishing to resign in favor of others had to bargain with the head of this office over the regress or reservation of profits) or by the sale of offices which were vacated. In these ways the popes had formerly received from 10,000 to 14,000 scudi a month, but Paul IV had stopped the composition of benefices and the sale of offices which carried judicial authority and thus had reduced the revenues from the Datary to 3,000 or 4,000 scudi a month. The ambassador added, "while now that the present pontiff has reopened the road to the regresses and reservations of profits, and is also willing that all the offices be sold, one may believe that the Datary will return to its former amounts; then it will be able to supply for all the extraordinary expenses with the money derived from it, as all the other popes have done . . . ." Mocenigo estimated that the capital value of the

Apostolic Camera.[55] The Spanish ambassador revealed Pius IV's strategy when he informed Philip II that with respect to reform the pope had said "that the legates would concur in everything that would be just but that the reform of the Curia and that which touched his person he wished to carry out himself and that the council would not have reason to treat of it."[56] In the end it was the Roman Rota for which a reform bull was published first,[57] and this was the only one to appear before the council was reopened at Trent on January 18, 1562.

---

salable offices was approximately 3,000,000 in gold and that they all became vacant every fifteen years on the average. See Mocenigo's report (cited *supra,* n. 39), pp. 28-29. See also Felice Litva, S.I., "L'attività finanziaria della Dataria durante il periodo tridentino," *Archivum Historiae Pontificiae,* V (1967), 79-174. See further Nicola Storti, *La storia e il diritto della Dataria Apostolica dalle origini ai nostri giorni* (Naples, 1969), pp. 252-261; this author explains that by the sixteenth century the term "composition" meant simply a financial contribution which was required for the granting of a favor or benefice by the pope and which was intended to satisfy the general economic needs of the Holy See; the principal source of revenue which came under the heading of "compositions" consisted of the reserved benefices, that is, benefices scattered throughout the Church which were conferred directly by the pope (instead of the diocesan bishop) according to clearly defined legislative norms.

[55]Arco to Ferdinand, Rome, December 14, 1561, Sickel, *Concil,* p. 242. In the following month the ambassador frankly stated his opinion of the need for reform in the Curia when he reported that Cardinal Morone had spoken to the pope about the awaited confirmation of the bishops of Csanád (in Hungary) and Knin (in Dalmatia) and the dispatching of the bulls for them gratis, as the emperor had requested; Pius obligingly ordered Morone to propose their names in the next consistory for preconization, but the dispatching of the apostolic letters free of charge would displease the cardinals. Arco added: "They beg and make themselves very surly and peevish (*admodum difficiles et morosos*), and it takes much effort for anyone to wrest anything away from them without paying." Arco to Ferdinand, Rome, January 10, 1562, Kassowitz, p. 49. The English government was informed that the cardinals had objected to being shut up in the Castel Sant'Angelo and to being given only bread and water if they failed to agree in the conclave by a certain time, as Pius had proposed. Rome, December 13, 1561, *CSP, 1561-1562,* p. 453 (No. 738); cf. December 19, 1561, *ibid.,* p. 466 (No. 758).

Pius appointed two cardinals and two prelates for the reform of the Camera and of the Penitentiary with the charge to reduce their competencies; he entrusted the reform of the Datary to two other cardinals, the Grand Penitentiary and the Camerlengo. In this way, he asserted, he himself (that is, the Datary) would be reformed by the heads of those offices whose reform he was carrying on through the deputies he had named. His remark about the reciprocity of the reforms in the Datary on the one side and in the Penitentiary and the Camera on the other indicates that he was not contemplating radical changes and was merely trying to forestall action by the council. Jedin, *Geschichte,* IV/l, 78, and 311, n. 7. News of these reform efforts, nevertheless, was received with satisfaction at Trent; Cardinal Seripando was quoted as saying that the council could be concluded a month after its opening if it did not have to occupy itself with matters of reform. Calini to Cornaro, Trent, November 6, 1561, Marani, p. 56.

[56]Vargas to Philip II, Rome, December 25, 1561, Manuel Ferrandis Torres (ed.), *El Concilio de Trento. Documentos procedentes del Archivo General de Simancas* ("Archivo Histórico Español. Colección de Documentos inéditos para la Historia de España y sus Indias," publicados por la Academia de Estudios Histórico-Sociales de Valladolid, Vol. VI [Valladolid, 1934]), Vol. II: *1560 y 1561,* p. 341 (No. CII).

[57]*In throno iustitiae,* December 27, 1561, *Bullarum,* VII, 155-158 (No. LIV).

III. Reforms Demanded and Decreed, January-June, 1562

Neither Ferdinand's ambassadors nor those of any other king were present at that solemn ceremony in the Cathedral of St. Vigilius, although the date had been continually moved back to ensure their participation. On the same day, however, there arrived in Trent George Drasković, Bishop of Pécs (Fünfkirchen), who was to represent Ferdinand as King of Hungary.[58] As emperor, Ferdinand was to be represented by two ambassadors, an ecclesiastic and a layman. The former, Archbishop Brus von Müglitz, arrived on January 31, and the latter, Count Sigmund von Thun,[59] on February 10. Three days later the three ambassadors presented to the legates a note in which they requested, among other things, that the council take up questions of reform. The legates forwarded the note to Rome, where the pope discussed it with the commission of cardinals for the affairs of the council.[60] Then Borromeo informed Cardinal Lodovico Simonetta, the legate who most enjoyed the pope's confidence,[61] that it would be "apropos to mix with the safeconduct [which the imperial ambassadors had requested for the Protestants] some articles on the reform of the universal Church (not, however, of

---

[58]Drasković was Hungarian but his family had originally come from Dalmatia, and he had studied at the University of Padua. He had been named bishop in 1557 and was later transferred to other sees. He became a cardinal in 1585 and two years later died at Vienna at the age of sixty-two. See Eder, pp. 114-115.

[59]For remarks on the piety and wisdom of the elderly von Thun see the letter that Muzio Calini, Archbishop of Zara (Zadar), wrote from Trent on February 12, 1562, to his protector in Rome, Cardinal Luigi Cornaro, in Marani, pp. 114-115.

[60]Petition of the imperial ambassadors to the legates, February 13, 1562, and the reply of the legates, February 17, 1562, CT, VIII, 325-328 (No. 228).

[61]Like Pius IV, Simonetta came from a prominent Milanese family and was a canonist rather than a theologian. As datary, he had increased the revenues of this office to the pope's satisfaction. He was determined to guard the rights of the papacy and the Curia against any infringement by the council. He had attended the first period of the council as Bishop of Pesaro and had been transferred to the see of Lodi in 1560. The author of a biographical sketch of Simonetta has stated: "He seemed to the foreign prelates to be *too Roman*. In fact, his principle was to have the council take up immediately the examination of only minor reforms and of questions of a quite particular character. It was necessary, he said, that the Supreme Pontiff should give his opinion on the reforms of a general nature before the fathers could discuss them." Thus he came into conflict with his colleagues Gonzaga and Seripando. This writer maintained that Simonetta assumed that attitude only out of caution (*prudenza*); since the pope had supreme authority in the Church, Simonetta deemed it risky to let the council consider a general reform (including also the Court of Rome) without having received from the Roman Pontiff an express commission, which, in the most important affairs, would be sufficient only if it were special. Eugenio Sol, "Il Cardinale Ludovico Simonetta, Datario di Pio IV e Legato al Concilio di Trento," *Archivio della R. Società Romana di Storia Patria*, XXVI (1903), 213-214. Although he often revealed a lack of critical judgment, Sol criticized Simonentta for having, in his secret reports to Rome, attributed to the foreign prelates the most subversive sentiments in regard to religion for the sole reason that in a disputed question (on the origin of the obligation of episcopal residence) they held an opinion different from his (p. 227).

the affairs of Rome, because Our Lord [Pius IV] is doing that here)
and His Holiness is pleased that they should do so." Borromeo also
sent Simonetta a copy of the bull that Paul III had wished to issue
for the safeguarding of the bishops' authority, as well as a list of
subjects that had not yet been treated by the council. If the need
should arise, it would be left to the wisdom of the legates to select
from the bull and the list the most suitable proposals—those that
would be least vexatious to the Curia.[62] In the event Simonetta
made no use of his special authorization.

As time went on without any attention being given to questions
of reform in the council, the imperial ambassadors sought a way to
implement their instructions in this regard. On March 5 they submitted a note in which they proposed "a rigorous and canonical
reform"; although they were willing to pass over in silence the
ecclesiastical conditions in Italy, they insisted that in Germany the
danger of a radical destruction could be averted only by a thorough
reform of the clergy.[63] The legates politely rejected this request

---

[62]Borromeo to Simonetta, Rome, February 20, 1562, Susta, II, 33 (No. 12a); cf.
Borromeo to the legates, same date, *ibid.*, p. 31 (No. 12), and Borromeo to the
legates, Rome, March 8, 1562, *ibid.*, p. 49 (No. 18), where Simonetta was expressly
instructed to determine which reform articles in the bulls of Paul III and Julius III
not yet treated could be handled without much prejudice to the Court of Rome.
Meanwhile Seripando had asked some reform-minded bishops for suggestions and
probably collaborated personally in drafting a memorial consisting of ninety-three
articles. The ninety-second, cautiously couched in the form of a wish, touched on the
reform of the Roman Curia: "Would that what the cardinals chosen by Paul III of
happy memory [that is, the authors of the *Consilium de emendanda Ecclesia*]
recommended (*excogitarunt*) might be put into execution." *CT*, XIII, 612 (No. 95);
cf. Jedin, *Geschichte*, IV/l, 110, 112. This so-called Italian reform memorial carefully
avoided any attempt to interfere in the exclusive competence that the pope claimed
to reform the curial offices by himself. It may be regarded as a product of the
humanistic reform group from northern Italy. Although it was not presented to the
council or made known publicly, some of its articles (though not the ninety-second)
were laid before the fathers by the legates.
    Prospero d'Arco reported that on February 16 Pius IV had published a *motu
proprio* for the reform of the attire of priests in Rome; this raised an uproar, and
some cardinals protested that many priests were involved in lawsuits over their
benefices and many others were poor--some were prevented from complying in one
way and others in another--so that the limit of nine days which was set in the papal
document for dressing in priestly fashion was extended to the next consistory in
which the pope promised to declare his will more clearly. Kassowitz, Anhang No. 17,
p. xvii.
    [63]Musotti Scripturae conciliares (A). *CT*, III, 101, and legates' reply of March 10,
p. 102. Although the ambassadors recognized that both the clerical and the lay
orders had to be called back to true discipline, they recommended that the council
take up the reform of the clergy first. The legates promised that when the bishops of
Germany and the other countries with whom it would be necessary to deal in regard
to reform would arrive, the council would satisfy this and any other just desires of
the emperor. Loewe maintained that the ambassadors submitted two memorials to
the legates, one between February 26 and March 3, and the other on March 9, that
Pallavicini erred in speaking of only one, and that the legates' reply should be dated
after March 10 (pp. 79-85). Eder denied the existence of the earlier note and showed
that the only one is that given by Le Plat, V, 102, where it is dated March 6, but that
it should be dated the 5th (pp. 147-150).

because it concerned a particular country and could not easily be fulfilled by the council in the complete absence of bishops from Germany. The ambassadors had not acted entirely in vain, nevertheless, for on March 11 the legates submitted to the fathers of the council a dozen reform propositions, some of which not only corresponded to the emperor's desires but even anticipated his future demands for remedies to the Church's troubles in Germany. The first of the twelve dealt with the bishops' duty of residence.[64] The ensuing debate illustrated how closely the interests of the Curia were interwoven in all questions of reform, for it was argued that if the council should define such an obligation to be of divine right, it would implicitly condemn the dispensations from residence previously given by the pope and would furnish the Protestants an opportunity to attack the Curia for this violation of divine law. The curialists were greatly disturbed by the reports sent by bishops at Trent about the conciliar discussion of this question. Cardinal Francesco Gonzaga informed his uncle, the president of the council, that the cardinals at Rome who held dioceses and the courtiers who held parishes were holding their breath and that if the council could get by that rock, it would be the best news for the whole court. To this end Francesco had been asked by many friends of the Gonzaga family to use his good offices with his uncle.[65] The pope, in fact, was thinking of replacing the two legates who tolerated critical speeches, Cardinals Ercole Gonzaga and Girolamo Seripando, with canonists like Simonetta who would defend the prerogatives of the Curia and stifle free discussion of reform.

Before the emperor and his councilors learned of the reform articles proposed by the legates on March 11, they were becoming disillusioned with their policy of leaving the initiative to the council in this regard. Some time after March 4 the tenacious Franciscan, Francisco de Córdoba, composed his *Considerationes de ecclesia reformanda et de concilio*, in which he manifested more mildness toward the papacy and the cardinals than he had shown in the previous autumn, but still boldly denounced abuses at Rome in the following paragraphs:

II. 7. "Freely give what you have freely received." It is amazing that the Church complains that the bishops and their officials and notaries accept something for ordination, while the Church does not complain that the pope accepts money for ordination, confirmation [of elec-

---

[64]Acta, March 11, 1562, *CT*, VIII, 378-379 (No. 244). See Hubert Jedin, "Der Kampf um die bischöfliche Residenzpflicht 1562/63," in *Il Concilio di Trento e la Riforma Tridentina* (2 vols.; Rome, 1965), I, 1-25; also in Jedin, *Kirche des Glaubens, Kirche der Geschichte* (2 vols.; Freiburg, Basel, and Vienna, 1966), II, 398-413.

[65]Francesco Gonzaga to Ercole Gonzaga, Rome, April 11, 1562, Drei, XVII, 227 (No. XXI).

tions or appointments], dispensations—in short, not one thing can be found for which the pope and his officials do not accept money—and that when the pope sells offices he accepts money. It is necessary, therefore, that the pope freely give what he has freely received; it is also necessary that he not sell offices or accept money for the confirmation or consecration or dispensation of bishops or for any ecclesiastical business . . . . For if the pope did not call so many affairs to himself, he would not need so many ministers, and if he did not sell offices, the notaries would not charge such a high price for papers and similar things. It is expedient, therefore, that the bishops, especially the pope, be content with their stipends.

III. The supreme council demands supreme freedom.

Fourthly, the freedom which is wanted in the council in these calamitous times is that the council have free and full power to reform the Church both in head and in members. I do not, however, attribute this power of correcting the pope to a general council, because it has not yet been defined that it belongs to the Church. But it is to be desired by the Church, the spouse of Christ, that the pope, who is the vicar of Christ and the minister and servant of the Church, should subject himself to the judgment of an ecumenical council for love of him whose vicar he is . . . . For what a great thing the supreme pontiff would do if he would subject himself to the judgment of a general council, as he has deigned to subject the schismatics and heretics, in order to gather together the children of God. For this would be the surer way of bringing all back to one faith and it would be most pleasing to God.[66]

Whether or not this paper was written before March 17, it certainly belonged to the preparation of the petitions for reform which it was decided in the privy council at Prague on that day should be drawn up for presentation in the Council of Trent.[67] This decision marks a step in the imperial policy from indirect action through vaguely instructed ambassadors to direct proposal of specific measures. It was due to the impetus of Ferdinand himself, who felt obliged in conscience to promote reform for the good of religion and

---

[66]*CT*, XIII, 618, 622. Jedin give arguments for the authorship of Francisco de Córdoba, p. 613, n. 1.

[67]The genesis of the imperial reform *libellus* has been studied by Sickel, "Libell," pp. 37 ff.; by Loewe, pp. 33 ff.; and most thoroughly by Eder, pp. 172 ff. Sickel and Loewe supposed a causal connection between the twelve reform articles proposed by the legates and the *libellus*, but Eder demonstrated that since the articles were not sent from Trent until March 17, they had no bearing on the discussion which took place in Prague on the same day.

the salvation of his subjects' souls. Thus three experts at Maximilian's court—Urban Pfaffstetter, Bishop of Gurk,[68] Francisco de Córdoba, and Georg Gienger—were to be commissioned to submit their opinion as to whether and how the fathers at Trent should be induced to treat questions of reform and certain other matters. Urban and Gienger were chosen, no doubt, because they were respected exponents of the conciliatory tendency at the court; Francisco, although more extreme in his views, was known for his interest in problems of reform, and the fact that he was included may suggest Ferdinand's seriousness about striving ˙for a reform *in capite*. None of the memorials submitted by these consultants has been preserved.

Francisco de Córdoba was not content to answer the privy council's request but spontaneously offered his advice during this spring of 1562 also to two prominent personages outside the imperial court. To the president of the council, the Cardinal of Mantua (Ercole Gonzaga), he proposed three ways of reuniting those separated from the Church: reform *in capite et in membris*, reform of ecclesiastical administration, and reform of the monks; he wrote that the reform of the clergy was a sure means of bringing heretics back to the faith and schismatics back to the Church, and that Mantua, like a second Paul, should withstand the pope, the successor of the Apostle Peter, to his face if the latter should act against the truth of the gospel in the administration of the Church; he said that people had a low opinion of the reform as it had been decreed in Rome and Trent thus far; it should begin not with the dress and tonsure of clerics but with that of the cardinals since the latter served as a model for the clergy; he also thought that the conciliar reform article by which the bishops and their ministers were not to be allowed to take anything for conferring holy orders should be recommended to the pope and the Curia, for the bishops in their dioceses imitated what they saw the pope doing in the universal Church.[69] Later Córdoba sent certain reform articles to Philip II and implored him to have them proposed at Trent.[70] In the absence of his memorial for

---

[68]Pfaffstetter was the name of the village in which Urban as a child was found among the dead after the retreat of the Turks; he was also called Sagstetter after his foster-father. He had been bishop of Gurk in Carinthia since 1556, and when Brus was promoted to the metropolitan see of Prague in the autumn of 1561, Urban was appointed administrator of the Diocese of Vienna in addition to his own see. Ferdinand had appointed him his court preacher in 1556, and Maximilian did the same at the beginning of 1562. The favor that Urban enjoyed with the emperor and especially with his son shows that the bishop was broad-minded and disposed toward concessions such as communion *sub utraque*.

[69]Córdoba to Ercole Gonzaga, Linz, April 14, 1562, Steinherz, III, 38-39 (No. 18).

[70]Córdoba to Philip II, Linz, May 22, 1562, Döllinger, *Beiträge*, I, 426 (No. 125). The articles to which he referred are not printed here. The Spanish bishops who accepted the leadership of Pedro Guerrero, Archbishop of Granada, had already formulated their own reform articles, sixty-seven in number, and had presented them to the legates at some time prior to April 6, when Simonetta forwarded them to Rome. They demanded a change in the whole practice of the curial offices, not only

the privy council, it may be assumed that his favorite themes—the need of reforming the pope and the Curia, of restricting papal dispensations, reservations, and taxes, and of changing the manner of electing the pope (even to the extent of taking the right away from the cardinals)—were included therein. Few of them, however, were to be incorporated in the emperor's reform *libellus*.

Francisco de Córdoba's practical recommendations could not easily be reconciled with those of Gienger, with whom Bishop Urban collaborated in a subordinate capacity. Although the layman also emphasized in principle the necessity of a reform *in capite*, he expressed it with caution in documents intended for publication. He too regarded the Roman Curia as the enemy of thorough reform, but he also recognized the realities of the situation and did not wish to jeopardize concrete plans for reform by making exorbitant demands.[71]

Gienger's position was closer to that of the vice-chancellor, who was not only a moderate conciliarist but also a skilled statesman. For him a reform of the papacy was less urgent than that of the Church in Germany. As a *Realpolitiker,* Seld appreciated the value of friendly relations with the Curia, which he foresaw would be disturbed by any determined demand for reform in Rome; yet his respectful attitude was not motivated merely by diplomatic considerations but also by a desire to obtain what he deemed most important for the care of souls. He expressed these ideas in the memorial that he composed at the emperor's behest after he had read those by Gienger and Córdoba. Ferdinand had asked Seld to consult his confessor and court preacher, Matthias Cithardus, a Dominican from Aachen. Apparently this friar could not agree with Seld on a common position, probably because he went farther in demanding the reforms which he judged necessary for the restoration of unity, though he did not go so far as his Franciscan colleague. In any case, he produced his own memorial in which he declared that just as the emperor would gladly and promptly undergo a severe reform of himself first and then of his court (*suos*)

---

of the Datary but also of the entire procedure of bestowing benefices, without which no effective reform was conceivable. They also demanded that cardinals should be incapable of holding dioceses, ecclesiastical benefices, and pensions and should receive equal salaries from the Patrimony of St. Peter so that they would not be beholden to any king or country and would more freely advise the pope; their number should be reduced, and they should always reside in Rome. "Reformatio ab Hispanis concepta Tridenti sub Pio IV," *CT*, XIII, 624-628 (No. 97).

[71] For example, when the emperor heard of Pius IV's illness, he asked Gienger on March 21 whether in case of the pope's death the election of his successor belonged to the council or to the College of Cardinals. Gienger replied that in the light of the councils of Constance and Basel the council had the right to elect the new pope, but since there were only five cardinals in Trent against fifty in Rome, the latter would not surrender their right; hence, to prevent a schism, it would be good if the council handed its right over to the College of Cardinals. Gienger to Ferdinand, Linz, April 2, 1562, Sickel, *Concil*, pp. 288-289 (No. CLXIII).

if anything in him or them should need to be corrected, so also the pope with his cardinals ought not to flee from it, for in them "the privilege of honors should be the teachings of uprightness, lest their official dignity be exalted and their private life be base, their function honorable and their conduct disgraceful."[72] In spite of his high moral tone, the Dominican dealt only in generalities which were of little use in the development of the emperor's reform *libellus*.

On May 2, 1562, the four memorials of Córdoba, Gienger and Urban, Seld, and Cithardus were laid before the privy council which then decided that they should be combined in a unified text by the emperor's secretary, Marcus Singkhmoser. Since his was to be the task of editing, not of revising, the various proposals of the several writers were left intact and to some extent can be identified in his draft. The first part of this document concerns the urgency of reform in general, and the second part contains fifteen articles proposing specific reforms. The first three articles read as follows:

1. Our most holy Lord Pope Pius is to be exhorted and entreated through the sacred council that wherever around His Holiness's person, condition, or curia he may perhaps perceive some things that seem to need correction, he benignly suffer them to be reformed for the better. For only then will His Holiness judge rightly about the errors of others when he does not have anything to be condemned in himself. For His Holiness knows that neither Blessed Peter nor his successors received with the privilege of the see a license to sin and that it is not easy to stand in the place of Peter and Paul, that is, to hold the chair of those reigning in Christ, since it is not the sons of the saints who hold the places of the saints but those who perform their deeds. Our most holy Lord will also remember that the Roman Church is indeed the mother of the churches but not the mistress, just as His Holiness is not the master of the bishops but one of them and, moreover, the brother of those who love God and a sharer with those who fear him, so that under the happy government of His Holiness we may see the Church of God purified, beautiful as a dove, of the same mind, and agreeing as one body with the eternal glory and memory of His Holiness.

2. It was once and still is for many a grave complaint that the frequent multiplication of lord cardinals is in many ways hurtful and burdensome to the Church of God, and therefore our most holy Lord is to be begged to deign to restrict and reduce this rank, if not to the

---

[72]The name "Cithardus" came from the town of Sittard in the Duchy of Jülich, in which he was born; his family name was Esche. His memorial is given in part by Sickel, "Libell," pp. 47 ff.

number of the twelve Apostles, at least to double that number, namely, twenty-four and two supernumerary cardinals—a number sufficient for governing the universal Church—as it is said was solemnly decreed in the Council of Basel.

3. Although the supreme pontiffs, by the plenitude of their power, above the law, indeed even against the Old Testament and the four councils and the Apostle himself, usurp the authority to dispense, since such dispensations seem to be very scandalous and connected with the staining of the condition of the Church and therefore should be considered dissipations rather than dispensations, [it may be good] if our most holy Lord together with the sacred council should see to it that this scandal be removed from the Church and that such moderation be used that what is permitted by dispensation be done by law and what cannot be done by law not be permitted by dispensation.[73]

It seems likely that the first part of Article 1 and all of Article 2, which are gentler in tone, were taken from the draft of Gienger and Urban, and the rest of Article 1 and all of Article 3, which are marked by a sharper anticurial tendency, were taken from that of Córdoba.[74] In any case, at Seld's suggestion Friedrich Staphylus, a lay theologian and councilor of the emperor, was summoned to court and directed to revise Singkhmoser's draft.[75] He proceeded to make more or less extensive changes in all but two of the articles. In the first he retained only the first sentence and substituted the following wording for the rest;

. . . For then will His Holiness be able to judge about the errors of others with greater authority when he will have shown himself to all to be a blameless judge. There is no doubt that His Holiness frequently meditates on this alone that neither St. Peter nor any successors of this Apostle, when they reached the highest dignity in the Church of God, should have thought that at the same time they acquired all license to sin together with so great

---

[73]Eder, pp. 239-240.

[74]This was Eder's opinion, although he expressed reservations about the attribution of Article 3 to Córdoba because of stylistic reasons (pp. 187-193). Loewe had asserted that all three articles were copied from Gienger and Urban's work (p. 36), and Eder tended toward the same conclusion in his final summary (p. 210).

[75]Staphylus had once been a professor of Protestant theology and a friend of Luther and Melanchthon but had been reconverted to the Cathoic faith in 1552; Ferdinand had appointed him a participant in the Colloquy of Worms in 1557, and in the following year he became a professor at Ingolstadt and a ducal councilor of Bavaria at the recommendation of Peter Canisius. See Johannes Soffner, *Friedrich Staphylus, ein katholischer Kontroversist und Apologet aus der Mitte des 16. Jahrhunderts, gest. 1564* (Breslau, 1904), pp. 57-73.

a privilege, or should have supposed that it was enough to sit in the chair of Peter and Paul, since those who occupy the places of the saints are not immediately the children of the saints but those who imitate the deeds of the saints by their conduct. His Holiness will also remember that just as the Roman Church is the mother, not the mistress, of the other churches, so also the Roman pontiff is not the master of the other bishops but both their brother and their father, who considers that his sons should not only be corrected by the stern discipline of the laws but much rather lovingly instructed and healed by the example of his own praiseworthy life. For in this way he will cleanse of wrinkles and make beautiful the Church which can rightly be called the sole most dear spouse of Christ.

In the second article Staphylus rewrote the first part as it was to appear in the final version, and deleted the mention of the two supernumerary cardinals in what remained. The third article too he completely recast in a form which, with some modification at the end, was to be definitive.[76] It is clear, therefore, that Staphylus kept the main contents of Singkhmoser's draft but dressed them in new and more comely and copious language. The general effect of his labors was to mellow the bitter passages of the earlier draft and to increase its length.

Staphylus' draft was in turn reviewed by the vice-chancellor, who wrote a number of brief amendments. Regarding the first article he objected to the very hard words"which would be twisted by the unlearned and the malicious as if the emperor were charging the pope with claiming for himself every license to sin," with neglecting the works and morals of Peter and Paul, and with not being the son of the saints or imitating their deeds, while, in Seld's opinion, Pius IV was not noted for any important vice except the one that was common to almost all popes, that is, he was a little too eager to advance his own relatives. Seld added: "For many reasons I would not wish the emperor to set himself up as the accuser of the pope; others do this—and let them do it whose character it better suits." The vice-chancellor admitted little liking for the second article because he thought that it was not pertinent to the reform of the German Church, which till then had shown slight concern over the number or the authority of the cardinals. he feared that the third article would remove all power of dispensing, and he doubted that such a thing was advisable, for the Apostles themselves had dispensed in many matters; besides, contemporary conditions did not allow the severi-

---

[76]Sickel, "Libell," pp. 62-67. Loewe (p. 37) thought that Staphylus played a more important role in the development of the *libellus* than Sickel (p.96) gave him credit for; Eder too maintained that Staphylus imparted to the work a coloring, a character, of his own (pp. 215-220).

ty of the ancient canons, and the greatest monarchs could not permit the pope to be shorn òf his dispensing power, especially when it
came to contracting marriages in a forbidden degree. It seemed better to him to remove the misuse of dispensation than the use.[77]
Staphylus agreed with most of Seld's comments and found new
ways of phrasing the objectionable articles.

The final draft of the reform *libellus* was then discussed by the
emperor and the privy council on May 17. Almost all of Seld's
amendments were accepted, and after some minor additions were
made on the following day, the whole memorial was approved. Instructions for the ambassadors at Trent were also composed; here
reference was made more vaguely to the reform *in capitibus et membris* which could very conveniently be carried out in the council,
since it had been reported that the pope had left to the conciliar
fathers the business of reform, like everything else that pertained to
faith and morals, and had granted them the most ample power of
deciding and decreeing. Hence, the ambassadors were ordered to
present the petition to the legates and fathers of the council with
due courtesy and to press it on them with the greatest zeal.[78] The instructions and the memorial were finally dispatched to the ambassadors on May 22.

In the definitive form of the *libellus* the first two sentences of the
first article read as they had read in Staphylus' draft, but the rest
was now reworded thus:

> . . . For we see that these times are such as require
> uprightness of life and behavior, especially in ec-
> clesiastical leaders, so that it hardly seems to be enough
> to keep oneself clear of all guilt of any infamous crime but
> it is also necessary to avoid, if possible, the suspicion of
> any transgression. . . . Therefore there is no doubt that
> our most holy Lord Pope Pius, in view of his fatherly af-
> fection and the weakness in the misled people, will take
> every measure to correct and remove, as soon as possible,
> whatever he may notice in his Curia that could turn aside
> the people and the other nations and render them more
> averse to love for and obedience to the Apostolic See, for
> this especially behooves a loving father who believes that
> his children should be instructed and corrected not so
> much by the stern discipline of laws as by the example of
> fatherly virtue.

The next three articles also concerned the papacy and its practices.

> II. It was once and still is a grave complaint of many
> pious people that the too frequent multiplication of car-

---

[77]Sickel, "Libell," pp. 88-89.
[78]Sickel, "Libell," pp. 39-40.

dinals is burdensome and hardly becoming to the Church. For the wealth of the Church is exhausted by so many cardinals, and not rarely men who are hardly suitable are appointed to that rank with the consequence that they are more a stumbling-block than fit for the necessary functions of the Church. And so our most holy Lord is to be begged to deign to restrict and reduce this class, if not to the number of the twelve Apostles, then at least to double that number, of the twelve Apostles, then at least to double that number, that is, twenty-four, with two supernumerary--a number of cardinals sufficient for the government of the universal Church. . . .

III. Although the Roman pontiff has the greatest power of dispensing, especially in matters of positive law, nevertheless, it has been remarked that sometimes there are issued from the city [of Rome] to foreign nations dispensations which are full of public scandal and which not only diminish the authority of the Apostolic See but also disgrace it and bring it about that all other dispensations, even those legitimately granted, are cheapened and despised. And so let our most holy Lord Pope Pius and the rest of the most reverend fathers gathered in this council dutifully and diligently see to it that this scandal be removed from the Church and that in the future nothing be dispensed from, which would seem to deprive the sacred canons completely of their authority or imply any offensive misuse unworthy of that dispensing power.

IV. The same is true of exemptions granted indiscriminately against the common laws, that by the authority of the council they may be revoked, and all basilicas and monasteries of both sexes may stand under the power of that bishop in whose territory or diocese they are located, according to the dispositions of the sacred canons.[79]

While this list of respectful but forceful petitions for reforms and concessions was being composed at the imperial court, Cardinals Gonzaga and Seripando had become so concerned about the attitudes of the conciliar fathers and the biased and alarming secret reports being sent to Rome by Simonetta that they sent the former's servant, Federigo Pendaso, to Rome on April 11 with in-

---

[79]"Petitiones a S. Caes. Mtis consiliariis et aliis a S. Mte deputatis exhibitae, ut earum a S. Synodo Tridentina aliqua habeatur ratio et consideratio," *CT*, XIII, 666-667; also in Le Plat, V, 238-239; Le Plat also prints the "Syllabus praecipuorum postulatorum quae Imperatori Ferdinando, si fieri posset, in concilio Tridentino urgenda videbantur," V, 260-261. Pallavicini commented that the *libellus* was composed of sentiments that those who made every effort against the honor of the council and of its presidents and against the splendor of the papacy had instilled into the misinformed zeal of some good men (XVII, i, 6).

structions composed principally by the latter. In this document
they stated that in the year elapsed since they had arrived at Trent
they had learned, both from their own conversations with a good
number of the prelates and from information about the bishops' conversations among themselves, that it was their intention and desire
that the council should attend "to a true, sincere, and substantial
reform." On this alone, the bishops thought, could be based some
hope of remedy for the controversies of belief, which were ir-
remediable by means of conciliar decrees. The bishops confirmed
this opinion with the experience of the first two periods of the Council of Trent, in which many good decrees regarding faith were passed
but in regard to reform only a few, feeble, weak ones, measured in
terms of the prevailing evils and the good remedies that the world
expected. To this experience they attributed the increase of heresy
and the ineffectiveness of those few reform measures. The prelates,
furthermore, made it understood that no true reform could be
brought about unless the affairs of Rome were taken in hand
without any exception whatever. They were willing, to be sure, to
leave untouched the immediate decisions of the pope, but for the
rest they wanted to lay their hands on the College of Cardinals and
all the offices of the Curia, by which they complained of having been
badly treated with unjust provisions obtained solely for money. It
was the legates' understanding that the points which the prelates
wished to reform were the collations of benefices and especially of
preferments *(dignità)* and other cures, appeals which let crimes go
unpunished, and the nuncios and other commissions which tied an
ordinary's hands and caused great and sometimes righteous
grumbling against the Holy See; above all, the bishops disliked the
numerous exemptions which meant that a good number of exempt
men had neither superior nor anyone to correct their failings. According to the legates, the conciliar fathers were further upset because
the report of a reform being carried out in Rome, which was spread
also by the legates, was something that suddenly disappeared
without either good or apparent effect. They manifested an "un-
bridled desire" for the reform measures which were recommended to
Paul III in the *Consilium de emendanda Ecclesia*. In view of this
widespread discontent Gonzaga and Seripando suggested that the
pope should decide which of those reforms could be treated in the
council and send them all together to the legates, who could have
them distributed opportunely and decreed in the sessions; in this
way too they could silence the murmurings against their having to
wait for orders from Rome. To urge the pope to act without delay,
the two legates added that the fathers were awaiting the French
bishops, who would be in agreement with the considerable number
of Spaniards already present in regard to reform and complaints
against the Court of Rome; the Portuguese and the imperial ambassadors, moreover, would concur with them, as well perhaps as
not a few Italians; all these could still be overwhelmed by the votes
of the Italians subservient to the pope, but it would not be without

scandal, the cardinals observed, that the decrees would be passed by
one nation alone in opposition to all the others.[80]

Pius IV thanked the legates for having sent Pendaso to Rome. He
alleged his recent illness as an excuse for the delay in the reform, for
since important and interested persons of the court were involved,
he had to listen to them and then impose a decision with his own
authority. This he had done first for the Penitentiary, which, he
said, "we have destroyed and reduced almost *ad forum conscientiae
tantum* amid loud cries and complaints of all the officials." Now he
was at work on the Apostolic Camera, and he promised to attend to
all the abuses in due time. He added:

> If the world is not reformed now, it will never be, and we
> will do something real and not mere talk, as may be said
> has been done by others. It is quite true that we would
> like the reform and not the destruction of this see, as
> some would wish. So it seems to us that we should go lit-
> tle by little and not do everything all at once, and we
> should bear in mind (as we know you do) that there are
> some persons who, when one offers them his hand, want
> to take the whole arm and after the arm the whole body.

Pius promised to send Pendaso back to Trent with the bull for the
reform of the Penitentiary and other things pertaining to the reform
as well as with oral instructions.[81] When, a few days later, he gave
Pendaso his credentials, he repeated his promise to do what could be
expected of a good pope, a good gentleman, and a good Christian.
The proceeds from the compositions of the Datary, which, he affirmed, would be made according to justice and honesty and not
otherwise, would be devoted to pious purposes. "Every day you will
hear something new from us," he concluded, "and perhaps it will appear to you too strict a reform."[82]

On his way back to Trent Pendaso was so seriously injured in falling from his horse that he could not complete the journey. Hence, he
dictated the oral instructions for the legates that he had received
from the pope. Here Pius reaffirmed his determination to carry out
the reform both of the universal Church and of Rome, even though
in reforming the offices of the Curia he would lose 50,000 scudi a

---

[80]"Instruttioni date al Pandasio che fu mandato a Roma alli ll. d'Aprile 1562," in
"Hieronymi Seripandi de Tridentino concilio Commentarii, C. Fragmenta ad
historiam annorum 1561 et 1562 pertinentia," *CT*, II, 483-484. Another version with
numerous variations and the date of April 9, Susta, II, 79-81 (No. 27). See Giuseppe
Alberigo's remarks on "the myth of the solidarity (*compattezza*) of the Italian
prelates" at the council; according to this author, "The dominant motives that
determined their different positions in the council were essentially on the religious
level." *I vescovi italiani al Concilio di Trento (1545-1547)* (Florence, 1959), pp. 458,
460.
[81]Pius IV to the legates, Rome, April 28, 1562, Susta, II, 99-100 (No. 34).
[82]Pius IV to the legates, Rome, May 3, 1562, Susta, II, 107-108 (No. 37).

year. He also promised from then on to send some significant reform
measure to Trent before each session. Although Pius again professed his desire to have the reform of the universal Church done in
the council, he expressed some reservations; the legates should not
try to satisfy every request made by the Spanish, French, German,
and other prelates, "especially when their requests tend to end in
the destruction of the Court of Rome, as one may suspect that some
of them are thinking"; secondly, when it would be necessary to
make decrees touching on his own person, the pope wished the
legates to send them to Rome so that he might issue them with the
words *"Nos Pius, sacro approbante concilio."* In regard to the proposals of the *Consilium delectorum cardinalium,* the pope disapproved of the one that would deprive cardinals of the right to hold
bishoprics and curacies. He would not allow bishops free collation of
benefices with the care of souls but would permit them to examine
and nominate candidates. He had already abolished the collection
for the building of St. Peter's Basilica, and he stated his will regarding many other points. Finally, he exhorted the legates to be
stouthearted and united among themselves.[83] Obviously, the area in
which Pius left the legates free to act was narrowly circumscribed.
From this time on, moreover, he lost confidence in Gonzaga and
Seripando and relied on Simonetta's advice to an ever greater
degree than before.[84]

The pope's claims about reforms in Rome were corroborated by
other witnesses. In a letter to his uncle Ercole, the Cardinal of Mantua, Cardinal Francesco Gonzaga repudiated the suspicion that
might have occurred to any of the other legates, namely, that the
pope did not wish to reform the court, for, said the writer, Pius had
not been thinking of anything else or attending to other business
than meetings about the curial offices. The reform of the Penitentiary was already dispatched and that of several other departments
was to follow shortly. Francesco added: "Let your most illustrious
Lordship not believe that [the reforms] do not touch the principal
things, because I promise you that they shave down to the skin, as
you will be able to see from the bull for the Penitentiary."[85] The
Mantuan agent Bernardino Pia wrote three days later that the bull
which was being prepared would take away more than two-thirds of
the revenues of the cardinal penitentiary; the latter did what he

---

[83]"Riporto dell'Arrivabene dal Pendasio," Susta, II, 109-113 (No. 37a). Gonzaga
and Seripando must have been disturbed to learn that some of the cardinals whom
the pope had consulted were even less disposed to make concessions than he was.
The strongest opposition to a determined program of reform came from cardinals
who would be directly hit by an alteration of the existing curial system.

[84]See Jedin, *Seripando,* p. 609. Simonetta thought that the existence of the papacy
would be jeopardized if the existing curial system were to be touched in the council.
Hence, he raised the specter of the "ruin of the Roman Curia." It was only to be
expected that the pope would favor his side against Gonzaga and Seripando.

[85]Francesco Gonzaga to Ercole Gonzaga, Rome, April 22, 1562, Drei. XVII, 232
(No. XXIV).

could by his own means and through others to have the severity of the reform mitigated, but accomplished nothing because the pope was too firmly resolved. According to Pia, the camerlengo would also get a queer blow since the dispatching of many things would be taken away from him and the payments would be greatly reduced, but the heaviest loss would be suffered by the *Audientia Litterarum Contradictarum.*[86]

The bull for the reform of the Apostolic Penitentiary was actually published on May 4, 1562.[87] On the same day the Spanish ambassador at Rome reported to his king that eighty per cent of the income had been taken away from the Penitentiary and if that amount would not be increased for the Datary, as many thought it would, it would be very good, for it would support the officials of that tribunal who were reputed to be ruined, since Pius and his predecessors had sold those offices as long as those uses or abuses lasted; thus those officials were whining and saying almost whatever came to their mouths about the Datary and other offices of which a reform could be foreseen, although the pope's intention in this respect was to be regarded as very good. The ambassador, Francisco de Vargas, had heard that Pius wished to send this reform bull to the council, not to be enacted or accepted but to be read there; in the ambassador's opinion, it would be another injury if the council were not to do more than canonize the pretensions of Rome.[88] Later in the month Vargas conveyed directly to the pope a caution from Philip II against the great harm that would result from limiting the council in matters of reform and from ordering what was to be done at Trent, for this would directly take away its freedom and give scandal; he also took up the question of the briefs and all the rest as a very substantial matter in which the council had

---

[86]Pia to Ercole Gonzaga, Rome, April 23, 1562, Drei, XVII, 232, n. 2

[87]*In sublimi beati Petro solio, Bullarum,* VII, 193-197 (No. LXV). Emil Göller stated that this reform bull produced a sudden change in the development of the institution of the Penitentiary but did not yet lay the axe to the root. The Penitentiary still retained a certain amount of authority in the area of the external forum. It underwent a more thorough reform during the pontificate of Pius V. *Die päpstliche Pönitentiarie von ihrem Ursprung bis zu ihrer Umgestaltung unter Pius V.,* Band 2: *Die Päpstliche Pönitentiarie von Eugen IV. bis Pius V.,* I. Teil: *Darstellung* ("Bibliothek des Kgl. Preuss. Historischen Instituts in Rom," Band VII [Rome, 1911]), p. 128.

[88]Vargas to Philip II, Rome, May 4, 1562, Döllinger, *Beiträge,* I, 425 (No. 124). On the same day Pius IV's nephew informed the papal nuncio to Philip II about the bull which he hoped would give such proof of the pope's "good and holy intention that the world will remain fully satisfied with it." For the king's enlightenment Borromeo stated that the pope was "attending to a rigorous reform of all the tribunals and offices of this court"; that morning in the consistory he had abolished the regress, access, the restricted distribution of benefices, and all other procedures of similar nature which needed reform; he had also abolished the faculties of the *fabrica di S. Pietro et di S. Spirito.* Borromeo to Crivello, Rome, May 4, 1562, Susta, II, 441 (Beilage XVIII).

received considerable injury; he feared that if, for lack of anything else, only the reform of the Court of Rome would be read in the next session, which had been prorogued from May 14 to June 4, the council would be further embarrassed; and he warned the pope that the fact that he had excepted the reform of the Curia and the rest which tended to the same end and which weakened the authority of the council would never be forgotten and would be written and published in large letters. Hence, Vargas strove to prevent the reading in a session of the council of any bull for the reform of the Curia, for this, he said, would certainly be an "intolerable grievance in that they would not wish the council to speak or make use of any authority but rather keep silent and put up with it, and in that all would understand that by that act the council would disqualify itself in this regard."[89] Few observers penetrated the designs of the Curia better than the Spanish ambassador.

Pius IV hastened to revise the impression that he knew Vargas had left on Philip's mind. He wrote to the king that he had made and was making a very harsh reform which would be the salvation of the world. He had already carried out, he averred, a most rigorous reform of the court at a cost of more than 200,000 scudi to himself in capital for the (salable) offices, besides what was lost every day in the revenues of the Datary and other offices—a considerable sum.[90] A week later, in an autograph letter, he assured Philip that the council was free; in fact, some fathers had become insolent and seemed to be aiming at the destruction of the Roman see. Pius promised, nevertheless, to proceed calmly and to bring about every appropriate reform, even with great severity, so that the whole court would cry out.[91] Pius was well aware of the importance of retaining the confidence of the mighty monarch, who otherwise might insist that the council undertake the reform of the Curia.

Unlike his colleague from Spain, the imperial ambassador at Rome did not attempt to influence papal policy. He merely reported the reforms that the pope was making as well as his promises to restore order and to correct whatever needed correction. Arco also related the rumors that if these reforms were actually followed up, they would cost 150,000 scudi between what the heads of the main departments—the grand penitentiary and the camerlengo—and what the other officials would lose.[92] Besides these reports, the

---

[89]Vargas to Philip II, Rome, Döllinger, *Beiträge*, I, 434-435 (No. 127), where the date is given as May 23, 1562, and *CDI*, IX (1846), 203-204, where the date is given as May 25. There is also a variation in one passage: "ni infamase mas el Sínodo" in Döllinger's edition, and "ni infirmase mas el Sínodo" in the other.

[90]Pius IV to Philip II, Rome, May 23, 1562, *CDI*, IX (1846), 198. Eder remarks of Pius IV: "What could be expected of him was sympathetic appreciation of desires, correction of individual abuses, and concessions under the viewpoint of opportuneness--in short, reforms but not reform" (p. 33).

[91]Pius IV to Philip II, Rome, June 1, 1562, *CDI*, IX (1846), 243-244.

[92]Arco to Ferdinand, Rome, May 9, 1562, Sickel, *Concil*, pp. 298-299 (No. CLXVIII). On the same day the French envoy in Rome, Gilles de Noailles, Abbé de l'Isle, informed the French ambassador to the council, Louis de St. Gelais, Sieur de

emperor also received copies of the bulls, including the one for the reform of the offices of the corrector of the Apostolic Chancery and of the *Audientia Litterarum Contradictarum* and another for the reform of the tribunal of the Apostolic Camera, after both of these were published on May 27, 1562.[93] At the same time the pope saw to it that Ferdinand was apprised of the "rigorous reform of all the tribunals and offices of this court" through the nuncio, Bishop Delfino. Borromeo expressed the hope that the bull for the Penitentiary would give "such a sample of the good and holy intention" of his uncle that the world would be fully satisfied with it. He also informed Delfino for the emperor's benefit that recently in consistory the pope had prohibited for the future the various lucrative practices connected with benefices and, said Borromeo, "he has also taken away and abolished the faculties of the fabric of St. Peter's and of the Holy Spirit, and in short he will act so that it may be better known every day that he desires more than anything else that the reform should go ahead indeed, as he has always desired and procured the good progress of the council."[94]

In the spring of 1562, however, the council was entering upon a crisis. The discussion of the source of the obligation of episcopal residence—whether it was divine law or not—got down to the basic question of the papal primacy and resulted in a sharp division of the fathers. Hence, on May 8 Pius decided to forbid the council to continue the debate on the obligation of episcopal residence for the present; he apparently feared that the old controversy over the relationship between the pope and the council would flare up again. The pope, moreover, was indignant at some remarks that Drasković was reported to have made during this debate. According to Borromeo,

---

Lansac, that the pope was carrying out new reforms day by day and that the Penitentiary, which had received the first attack, now lacked power to issue a single dispensation outside the common law. De l'Isle also wrote that Pius had apprised him of the revocation of all quaestors and collectors bearing indulgences throughout Christendom for the fabric of St. Peter's, for St. Anthony, St. Sebastian, and other communities. The pope had said that he did not wish to entrust the dispensation and distribution of such graces to anyone any more and wished to confer them gratis in order to abolish the abuses which were committed in that regard. Dupuy, p. 184.

[93] *Universi gregis dominici, Bullarum*, VII, 200-203 (No. LXVII), and *Romanus Pontifex, Christi vicarius, ibid.*, pp. 203-207 (No. LXVIII). A bull for the reform of the tribunal of the judge of the causes of the curia of the Apostolic Camera, *Inter multiplices*, followed on June 2, 1562, *ibid.*, pp. 207-210 (No. LXIX).

[94] ". . . levò de futuro i regressi, gli accessi, le confidentie, et tutte le altre espeditioni di simil natura." Borromeo to Delfino, Rome, May 16, 1562, Steinherz, III, 51 (No. 23). Likewise the nuncio in Paris, Prospero Santacroce, assured the Constable of France, Anne de Montmorency, that the pope was disregarding his own interests in making so rigorous a reform that it was prejudicial not only to his court and to many of his subjects but also to his finances by diminishing the revenues of the papacy at a time when it was necessary to increase them because he was obliged to make expenditures which exceeded his means. Santacroce to Borromeo, Paris, June 1, 1562, "Lettres de Prosper de Sainte-Croix au Cardinal Borromée," in L. Cimber and F. Danjou (eds.), *Archives curieuses de l'histoire de France*, 1st series, VI (1835), 102.

he had said "many things unworthy of an ambassador and also of a bishop, among others that in Rome bishoprics are given to cooks who make good soups and to persons who work in the stable." The cardinal nephew assured Delfino that the greatest possible care was exercised in the conferring not only of bishoprics but also of inferior benefices.[95] The pope was also applying pressure on Ferdinand to hasten the termination of the council. The Cardinal of Mantua described to his nephew Francesco the master stroke that the pope had performed in letting the emperor know that he could not help him with the military operations against the Turks in Hungary as long as the council lasted because of the heavy expenses it entailed. Ercole Gonzaga was convinced that in order to obtain promptly the money that the pope was spending on the council, the emperor would propose no more delays and that the council would be finished in less than a year, provided that the pope would wish it to undertake the reform of the universal Church and would himself carry out that of his court and of Rome; otherwise, the president feared, nothing good or speedy could be done.[96]

After nothing more than a decree of prorogation was passed in the session on May 14, four persons who were considered most trustworthy were chosen by the legates—"all creatures of that court [of Rome] and vassals of the Church," as Seripando called them—and were charged with collecting matters for reform, provided that they would not impinge upon that part of the reform that the pope had reserved to himself. After a few days, however, all four told the legates that they had not found anything that seemed appropriate or that had not been decreed in the first two periods of the council.[97] By June 10 three Spanish prelates at Trent complained to their king that there was little or no hope of bringing about a reform of the Church, which was so necessary, and that this situation was unworthy of a council. As for the reform that the pope was undertaking, beginning with the Penitentiary, the writers had no illu-

---

[95] Borromeo to Delfino, Rome, April 28, 1562, Steinherz, III, 43 (No. 20). Cardinal Truchsess later assured the pope that Drasković had been falsely accused of insulting the Holy See and Pius himself by malevolent men and slanderers who had fabricated those remarks. Truchsess adduced in support of this denial not only the previous life of Drasković, who was always most respectful of the Holy See and the pope, but also the opinion of all who knew him; Truchsess asserted, moreover, that the legates were witnesses to Drasković's innocence. Pius replied that he believed those witnesses and had more trust in Drasković than in those who reported the story. Truchsess also commended the ambassador for promising not to be silent when the correction of morals would be discussed, and informed him that the reform was being carried out seriously in Rome and that Pius was very ardent about it so that no occasion was left, even to the most wicked critics, to accuse him in this matter. Truchsess to Drasković, Rome, June 10, 1562, Poggiani, III, 83-85 (No. XXXIX of 1562). Giulio Poggiani was Truchsess' Latin secretary at this time.

[96] Ercole Gonzaga to Francesco Gonzaga, Trent, April 20, 1562, Drei, XVII, 230-231 (No. XXIII).

[97] Seripando to Borromeo, Trent, May 17, 1562, Sickel, *Röm. Ber.*, II, 109; *CT*, III, 183.

sions: "it is transparent that it is no more than [a way] to stop the outcry and clamor that are and will be [raised] here for bringing about a reform, and it is clear that what is done in that way will not be in matters of much substance or last long."[98] These incidents and comments illustrate the sense of frustration that many sincere promoters of reform felt around the time when the emperor's petitions were delivered to his ambassadors at Trent.[99]

IV. The Fate of Ferdinand's Reform *Libellus,* June—November, 1562

Ferdinand had previously ordered his ambassadors to preclude any mention of the continuation of the council at the forthcoming session, which was set for June 4.[100] When they presented this demand, the legates requested direction from the pope. No answer had been received from Rome by the time that the emperor's *libellus* was brought to his ambassadors in Trent. Hence, they decided to postpone submitting this document to the legates and bishops lest it interfere with their other request and perhaps disturb the progress of the council. If the pope had ordered an explicit mention of continuation, however, they would have been unable to present the emperor's petitions, because they had been further instructed in that case to absent themselves from all subsequent meetings or acts of the council.[101] Ferdinand approved of his ambassadors' decision to defer presentation of his reform memorial, but he repeated his prohibition to attend any further public act of the council in the

---

[98]Pedro Guerrero, Archbishop of Granada, Gaspar Cervantes de Gaeta, Archbishop of Messina, and Martin Pérez de Ayala, Bishop of Segovia, to Philip II, Trent, June 10, 1562, *CDI,* IX (1846), 265-266. On the first of the three see Antonio Marin Ocete, *El Arzobispo Don Pedro Guerrero y la política conciliar española en el siglo XVI,* Vol. II ("Monografías de Historia Eclesiástica," Vol. IV [Madrid, 1970]), Chap. XIX: "La Reforma en el Concilio," pp. 569-675. Jedin pronounces this judgment on Pius IV: "His great error--at least at this point--was that he still believed that the reform of the Church could be neatly separated from the reform of the Curia; having grown up in the workings of the curial bureaucracy, he lacked the deeper insight into the connection between the abuses outside and the practice of the Roman authorities" (*Geschichte,* IV/1, 129).

[99]Augustin Paumgartner (or Baumgartner), the ambassador of the Duke of Bavaria (who was Ferdinand's son-in-law), also increased the prevalent uneasiness when he was presented in a general congregation of the council; he demanded communion *sub utraque,* the marriage of priests, and the reform both of the head and of the members of the Church. Calini to Cornaro, Trent, May 11, 1562, Marani, pp. 172-173.

[100]The imperial ambassadors to Ferdinand, Trent, May 12 and 13, 1562, Sickel, *Concil,* pp. 302-305 (No. CLXX), and Ferdinand to the imperial ambassadors, Prague, May 22, 1562, *ibid.,* pp. 314-318 (No. CLXXIV). The Spanish ambassadors and bishops at Trent were insisting on an explicit statement of continuation because their king had so commanded them and the bishops did not wish to reopen certain questions settled in their favor (especially regarding their relations with their cathedral chapters) in the earlier periods of the council.

[101]The imperial ambassadors to Ferdinand, Trent, May 29, 1562, Sickel, *Concil,* pp. 320-323 (No. CLXXVI).

event that continuation was to be expressly declared in the next session.[102] At the last moment Pius directed the legates to put the declaration off as long as possible. Then they succeeded in arranging a compromise by which no mention of continuation was included in the decree of prorogation adopted by the council in its fourth session under Pius IV.

Two days after this crisis was overcome, Ferdinand's envoys handed the legates his *libellus*[103] and requested permission to present the petitions in a public congregation of the council. The legates were amazed because they had not previously been informed about the emperor's scheme either by the nuncio at his court or by anyone else. The normal procedure for the emperor to submit his requests to the council would have been to communicate them to the nuncio and then with the mutual agreement of the pope and the emperor they would have been transmitted to the legates. Under the actual circumstances, however, the legates foresaw that two kinds of disorder would result from submitting the emperor's petitions to the council. One would be a "great and dangerous disagreement among the fathers, a good part of whom undoubtedly would not accept the things proposed to them and would not wish to have the regard for them that reasonably ought to be had for everything that comes from His Majesty's own mind and hand." The legates also feared that these petitions would encourage the French and others to propose similar and even worse ones. The minority which would accept the emperor's proposals, in the opinion of the legates, was weaker and less esteemed and would be motivated by a longing for novelty and a desire to disturb the order and progress of the council and to put some shadow or even open disagreement between the pope and the emperor that would give rise to a great disturbance in the Catholic Church. (It is not clear whom the legates were judging so harshly.) The second danger, connected with the first, was that the council might break up, to the infinite joy not only of the heretics but also of the other worldly and turbulent people who wished to see every hope of remedying the present evils dashed. Adverting to the fact that the petitions had ostensibly been submitted to the emperor by his advisers, the legates hoped that Delfino could turn Ferdinand's mind away from such proposals, which, they said, "in appearance seem to be good and praiseworthy but secretly contain some kind of pernicious poison contrary to the good designs and holy plans of His Majesty." In the first pages of the *libellus* the legates found some seeds of discord, some things contrary to the proper procedures of legitimate councils, and some things which ought not be proposed to the council because it lacked the power to

---

[102]Ferdinand to the imperial ambassadors, Prague, June 4, 1562, Sickel, *Concil*, p. 326 (No. CLXXVII).
[103]Two summaries of the articles are given in Le Plat, V, 264 and 266.

investigate and judge them. The legates detected in this memorial a "longing for a renewal of the pestiferous Council of Basel, condemned by the common agreement of the whole Catholic Church." They also directed the nuncio to explain to the emperor why they had not permitted the presentation of his petitions to the council; they needed more time to study the memorial and to submit their opinion to the pope. They promised, nevertheless, that whatever they might find in it that was appropriate and good they would willingly accept and submit to the fathers according to the regulation laid down for the council, and that such things would receive their remedies either in Trent or in Rome from the pope, who had already begun to set the affairs of his own house in order, sparing neither himself nor others.[104] The legates, of course, did not understand the emperor's conscientious determination if they really thought they could deflect him from his carefully plotted course by such arguments and assurances, but perhaps they were merely playing for time.

While awaiting replies from the imperial and papal courts, the legates used every means to dissuade the ambassadors from presenting the *libellus* to the council. Hosius impressed on Brus that they would be extremely displeased if something so unworthy of the good and right-minded emperor and so contrary to their expectations were presented in his name. The Polish cardinal succeeded to such an extent that Brus not only agreed not to communciate the *libellus* to the council but also promised to make every effort to convince the emperor (when he would go to Prague for the coronation of Maximilian as king of Bohemia) that the *libellus* should not be presented or even mentioned any more. The legates were understandably proud of their apparent success in winning this am-

---

[104]The legates to Delfino, Trent, June 8, 1562, Steinherz, III, 61-64 (No. 28). The legates sent a copy of this letter to Borromeo and requested the pope's judgment; same date, Susta, II, 184 (No. 52). Cardinal Seripando's secretary, Filippo Musotti, recorded in his diary for June 7, 1562, that the legates thought that Ferdinand wished to interfere in the council and "had at hand good reason to be able to do it without being able to be blamed for it." Döllinger, *Ungedruckte*, II, 18.

On June 7 the three French ambassadors to the council reported to their king that the imperial ambassadors had that day communicated to them Ferdinand's memorial requesting that the council begin with a reform of morals and, in the first place, of the abuses of the Court of Rome which it did not identify. In the reply sent to the French ambassadors reference was made to the legates' statement that the estate of princes would have to be reformed even in regard to the disposition of benefices; the ambassadors were instructed that once the abuses of the Court of Rome would have been reformed, the king would willingly submit himself to every holy reform for the provision of the benefices of his kingdom but only on condition that the privileges, franchises, and liberties of the Gallican Church would be respected as far as reason demanded. Dupuy, pp. 225, 229. Obviously the French crown had no intention of loosening its grasp on benefices in the name of reform.

bassador over to their side.[105] After Brus's departure from Trent the other two ambassadors reported to the emperor that while awaiting his final decision, they had yielded to the legates' objections, partly because they did not wish to be responsible for disturbing the tranquility of the council and partly because the legates had consented to propose for discussion in the council one of the emperor's principal requests, namely, communion under both kinds.[106] By this time the ordinary members of the council had learned of the existence of the emperor's memorial though not of its exact contents, and rumors were circulating that Ferdinand was scheming to break up the council in order to keep his oath to the Protestant princes to uphold the Religious Peace of Augsburg and thus to win the support of the Protestant electors for the candidacy of his son Maximilian as King of the Romans, while the blame for disrupting the council would fall on others.[107] Such suspicions hardly presaged a favorable reception of his *libellus* in the event of its eventual presentation to the council.

Ferdinand defended himself against the imputation of any wrong motive or improper conduct when he discussed the matter with the nuncio in Prague. To the reproach that he had contravened the established order of the council which required that he should have first communicated such thoughts to the pope, he replied that he had not thought of that nor had he acted from malice and he had supposed that the legates would make it known to the pope. Answering the charge that he had gone beyond the custom of the Catholic emperors who had no other part in councils than to aid and defend the assemblies, he said that when Delfino would read his

---

[105]The legates to Borromeo, Trent, June 11, 1562, Susta, II, 190-191 (No. 53). Hosius had written directly to the emperor on June 8, begging him to withdraw the libellus; this letter is no longer extant. See Henry Damien Wojtyska, C.P., *Cardinal Hosius, Legate to the Council of Trent* ("Studia Ecclesiastica," 3, Historica, 4, Dissertationes, 5 [Rome, 1967]), pp. 122-123. The ease with which Hosius persuaded Brus to intercede personally with the emperor made this author suspect that in return Hosius had promised to strive for the granting of the chalice to the laity, for from that time on he was favorable to this concession. In Wojtyska's opinion, Hosius deserves more recognition for his contribution in the field of doctrine than in that of reform; although he was a reformer in his own diocese, at Trent he considered even the slightest disagreement with the papacy in matters of discipline to be a case of conscience (pp. 266-267).

[106]Thun and Drasković to Ferdinand, Trent, June 16, 1562, Sickel, *Concil*, p. 331 (No. CLXXIX). On the same day the French ambassador to the council, Lansac, wrote to the French ambassador at the imperial court, Bernardin Bochetel, Bishop of Rennes, asking him to hasten Brus's return to Trent, "because [of] the other two ambassadors who are here, one [Sigismund von Thun] is a good old man *de robbe courte*, who, in my judgment, serves no purpose in this position but for show, [and] the other, who is the Bishop of the Five Churches [Pécs], although he is a noble and virtuous person and a good man in my opinion, does not intervene so much or with such authority in the affairs of His Imperial Majesty as does the Archbishop of Prague. . . ." Meyenhofer, p. 315 (No. 5).

[107]Calini to Cornaro, Trent, June 18, 1562, Marini, pp. 202-203.

libellus he would find that its tone was modest and its contents were only opinions given by various persons; the whole affair had been referred to the council, and he continued: "I am so far from pretending to lay down law for the council that I do not even wish this paper to be called advice or proposal but merely a reverent communication to the sacred council of what has been represented to me by pious and practical men desirous of seeing the Church reunited, pacified, and reformed, and with the condition that I shall approve only the things that are approved by the council." Ferdinand was sorry that if his *libellus* were read in a public congregation it might cause restless men to plot novelties, for he had always striven to repress turbulence, and he desired the fruitful progress of the council; he denied that he would bring about the disruption of the council, though if others were seeking an occasion for this purpose they would not lack one. Delfino not only continued to voice the legates' objections but even exceeded their harshness, ending by threatening the emperor with eternal infamy and the perpetual damnation of his soul. Provoked to equal candor, Ferdinand replied:

> I am grieved by such severe remarks. . . . You and the Most Reverend [Bishop] of Ermland [Cardinal Hosius] know how it weighs upon me to see His Holiness promote the scandal that the world receives when it sees young men without virtue made cardinals because of relationship and other reasons, not because of their merits, and in such great number that it is a disgrace *(un'infamia)*.

The emperor dilated on this subject, maintaining that from the neglect of his articles there resulted enormous harm to the Church. The nuncio rejoined that granted the justice of his complaint, he should have spoken about it with the pope himself, and that whoever advised him otherwise showed that he did not know that

---

[108]Delfino to the legates, Prague, June 22, 1562, Steinherz, III, 69-73 (No. 30). In his comment on the scandal of the cardinals, Ferdinand was probably referring to the creation of eighteen at one time on February 26, 1561; some of these, such as Girolamo Seripando and Stanislaus Hosius, were excellent men; others were elevated to please Philip II, Cosimo I, and the French government; several were chosen because of their allegiance to the Gonzaga family in opposition to the Carafas; and Mark Sittich von Hohenems, a young, worldly, ignorant man, was singled out not because he was a German but because he was the pope's nephew--the third relative of his to receive the red hat. Four of the new cardinals--Seripando, Hosius, Sittich, and Simonetta--were destined to be legates when the Council of Trent reopened.

According to the Venetian ambassador to the emperor, when Delfino threatened that the council would be broken up if Ferdinand insisted on the presentation of his *libellus*, the latter replied that if the council were broken up for that reason, he would protest. Giovanni Micheli to the Doge, Prague, June 29, 1562, Turba, III, 210-211 (No. 105).

the first see could not be judged by anyone and did not admit that its privileges could be increased or decreased only by God.

Delfino returned to the theme of the inviolability of the Holy See when he resumed his discussion with the emperor on the following day. Ferdinand expressed his agreement and declared that he would never tire of serving the pope and would show himself obedient to him with all gratitude. Embarrassed before the legates and the Curia for not having learned of the existence of the *libellus* before its transmission to Trent, the nuncio begged the emperor not to issue anything else pertaining to the council without first communicating it to him, and Ferdinand consented to do so. Hence, Delfino tried to set the legates' minds at ease and predicted that good would result from this evil; unreservedly he vouched for the emperor's obedience to the pope. Finally, he asserted that Seld shared his views.[108] With all these reassurances the nuncio had good reason to expect that he would ultimately persuade Ferdinand to withdraw the *libellus*.

In a later audience, in fact, Delfino saw success within his grasp. Again Ferdinand deplored the extremely harsh interpretation that the legates and the nuncio had placed on his memorial, and he insisted that neither its authors nor he himself nor anyone in his privy council had ever dreamed of the things to which exception had been taken, especially in regard to the person of the pope. He called God to witness that he regarded the pope as his father and lord and that he always wished to be obligated to him and would never be separated from him. He promised that Delfino would be pleased with his written reply to the legates.[109] Thus the nuncio had won this battle by taking an aggressive stance from the beginning and putting the emperor on the defensive.

At his second audience Delfino presented to the emperor a *libellus supplex* in which the reasons for not having read his memorial publicly in the council and for referring the matter to the judgment of the chair of Peter were set forth. He wanted Ferdinand to know that the pope was so intent on the reform of the Roman Curia and was devoting all his interest and activity to that end so diligently and seriously that the emperor and all men would judge that the pope would spare no one, not even himself, in fully ordering and

---

[109]Delfino to the legates, Prague, June 29, 1562, Steinherz, III, 77-78 (No. 32). The nuncio also related a conversation he had had with Seld, who offered a similar defense of the *libellus;* when its authors asked that the council reform the Court of Rome, they did not think they were saying anything wrong, because Eugene IV, after being recognized as the rightful pope, had convoked a council for the reform of the Church in head and members; when reform was first being treated in this council, moreover, Pius IV declared a laissez-faire policy. The vice-chancellor also told Delfino that in the end the *libellus* would be left to the legates so that they might at the proper time lay before the council whatever articles in it they considered worthy of being proposed.

steadily retaining that reform.[110] When Ferdinand wrote to his ambassador at Rome on the next day, he commended the remarkable efforts that the pope was making in the matter of reform about which the nuncio had informed him, for he deemed the reform so necessary that without it the unity and peace of the Church could hardly be recovered. But while he praised the reform of several offices in the Roman Curia, especially the Datary, the Penitentiary, and the Chancery, he pointed out the extraordinary difficulty of limiting the faculties of the nuncios, as the pope had also decreed; he feared, for one thing, that many Catholics living among Protestants who could previously obtain apostolic favors and dispensations from the nuncio at the imperial court at modest and bearable expense and labor would not bother themselves to apply to Rome for them; the result would be a heavier loss to the Catholic religion and a slighting of the authority of the Holy See. Almost apologizing for having his ambassador inform the pope about this matter, he denied any intention of watching all the pope's actions so that if he might dislike one he would have something to note or even to prescribe a measure or law for the pope and thus to put his sickle in another man's harvest; he wished only to aid the pope in advancing and completing the reform just as in other matters where it would be necessary, nor did he ever wish to appear to be lacking in filial reverence toward him. Acceding to this request, Pius IV restored the nuncio's faculties which he had restricted at the petition of the conciliar legates.[111]

Such amicable relations between the imperial and papal courts did not mean, however, that Ferdinand's advisers would let him abandon his reform *libellus* entirely. In fact, he exercised his usual caution and thoroughness in preparing replies to his ambassadors and to the legates at Trent. After Archbishop Brus arrived in Prague, he was asked to submit a report in writing. Contrary to the expectations of the legates, this ambassador recommended that the emperor should ask that the cardinals themselves lay the reform articles in order before the fathers or permit the imperial ambassadors to do so. He maintained that it was proper for the emperor to take such action when he was moved by dangers to his subjects' souls, and he observed that the emperor had in writing and in print examples of the abuses of the Roman Curia, as could be seen in the *Consilium de emendanda Ecclesia*, which was submitted to Paul III and at his behest by certain cardinals, one of whom (Gianpietro Carafa) later became pope.[112] Apparently the complaisance

[110]Delfino to Ferdinand, Prague, June 19, 1562, Le Plat, V, 328-329.
[111]Ferdinand to Arco, Prague, June 20, 1562, Sickel, *Concil*, pp. 335-336 (No. CLXXXI). Arco to Ferdinand, Rome, July 8, 1562, *ibid.*, pp. 336-337.
[112]"Summa relationis de moderno statu S. generalis Tridentinae synodi," June, 1562, Sickel, *Concil*, pp. 333-334 (No. CLXXX). Although this document is unsigned and incomplete, Sickel attributes it to Brus.

that Brus had shown to Hosius at Trent was merely a diplomatic gesture.

Brus's report was then subjected to extensive comment by the vice-chancellor. Seld agreed that the emperor should reply to the legates, but at greater length, and should accept their benevolent interpretation of his initiative, since indeed he was not moved by any private advantage or sentiment but was seeking only the glory of God and the welfare of the afflicted Church. Justifying the *libellus,* Seld reminded Ferdinand that as Roman emperor he was the supreme advocate and defender of the Church, and therefore it could not be considered improper for him to promote by virtue of his office whatever pertained to the honor of the universal Church. In the vice-chancellor's opinion, among the articles that belong to the business of a council not the last is that which regards the reform of the Church both in head and in members, and sometimes councils were convoked by popes of the preceding century (when things were less confused) for this very purpose. In case one or another article of the *libellus* should be handled outside the council, the legates would see that the emperor was not so stiff-necked as to insist that his opinions be preferred to others or that he alone be obeyed; it would be enough for him to do what he considered to be his duty, that is, to admonish diligently and frankly on each point. Seld suggested that the emperor should express his regret that the legates had not declared in greater detail which articles they had found offensive. If they were alluding to those touching on the pope, the emperor should assert that it was never his intention to accuse the pope; on the contrary, it was his opinion, as he often and clearly stated, that in many years there had not been a better pope or one more attached to public tranquility and peace, not to mention the extraordinary and paternal benevolence with which Pius IV had always embraced Ferdinand, so that the latter would have to be considered the most ungrateful of all mortals if he should try, beyond all reason, to denigrate the pope. In his reply the emperor should admit, Seld advised, that some reference was made in the *libellus* to the reform of the Roman Curia, but this subject was broached only conditionally and so briefly and moderately that the emperor would have supposed that the heavens would fall before anyone would be offended by it. Ferdinand could say that he understood that paragraph in the same way as the legates interpreted it, that is, that the pope himself should take the obligation of that reform upon himself if and insofar as there was need for it. If the legates should judge, nevertheless, that the presentation of the *libellus* would provide grounds for disrupting the council, the emperor would not wish to be responsible for such an evil; in that case, although the reform of the Roman Curia would undoubtedly contribute very much to the splendor of the universal Church, the emperor did not care about it to that extent; on the contrary, since he had recently learned that the pope himself was devoting his full attention to it, the emperor would trust that Pius would perform the function of a conscientious shepherd in this regard. Thus Seld would have had the emperor merely pray that God would further the pope's pious efforts and that Pius would win such praise from this work as none of his predecessors had been able to attain.[113] These observations reveal once again the statesmanlike attitude of the vice-chancellor, who was prompt to defend the emperor's right to intervene but reluctant to press it beyond the limits of expediency and who always considered the reform of the Church in Germany more important to the emperor than the reform of the Roman Curia.

Friedrich Staphylus, to whom both Brus's report and Seld's advice were then submitted for further reflection, was more inclined to take a stand on what he considered to be right. He expressed his general agreement with the vice-chancellor's recommendations but added some comments of his own. Taking up the legates' objection that just as the emperor would hardly permit his subjects to reform him, so also the Roman pontiff, being the head of the whole Church, could not be reformed by his bishops, Staphylus admitted no doubt that if the emperor had committed to certain princes a general reform of the Roman Empire, he would not take it amiss but would willingly permit it if some reform of his imperial court seemed to be necessary. Why, he asked, should the supreme pontiff of Rome not be able to bear this zeal for reform when he wrote to the fathers that he did not want the council to be dependent on him and when he entrusted to the council the power of reforming the universal Church, from which the head could not be separated? The counselor went on to cite the historical example of a pope (Sixtus III) who asked an emperor (Valentinian) to assemble a council to judge him, and he wondered why Pius IV should refuse to do the same in order that his innocence might become publicly known. According to Staphylus, hardly any other cause could move the Protestants more effectively to send representatives to the council than their hearing that the pope did not wish the council to be dependent on his own direction; on the other hand, he did not have to state their reaction if they were to learn that the legates wanted the council to be so dependent. Resolutely the converted theologian upheld his position, quoting from the Bible and giving examples from history such as the actions of Constantine, Theodosius, and Charlemagne. Staphylus resented the threat of a disruption of the council for which the presentation of the emperor's *libellus* would be alleged to be the cause, since it was meant to be a means of restoring harmony. "What is there," he asked, "in that whole paper that has the note not of sedition but of some bitterness? Why, therefore, is it forbidden to be presented in a public session?" He wanted to know who the seditious men were to

---

[113]"Sententia Seldii de propositione archiepiscopi Pragensis," between June 14 and 24, 1562, *CT,* XIII, 688-691 (No. 105).

whom the legates referred; they were not Protestants or Calvinists, who were not in the council; all who were there were Catholics. He pointed out the opinion of many serious and pious men that the very word "reform" seemed to many to be seditious; he thought that the name of the supreme pontiff would be used as a pretext, as if not only did he not wish to pass a severe judgment of reform on his Curia, but if anyone made mention of it he was to be regarded as guilty of sedition and responsible for the dissolution of the council. "For those good men believe," he remarked with sarcasm, "that the papal dignity is being oppressed if Pope Pius lowers himself to the point of submitting the correction of his Curia to the severe judgment of an ecumenical council." Staphylus recalled that St. Peter did not lose the honor of the apostolic primacy just because an inferior, his colleague Paul, withstood him to his face;

> . . . the inferior corrected the greater; the head allowed himself to be called to task by a limb. Was Paul, therefore, seditious? Did Peter, therefore, cease to be pontiff? Did the dignity of the Apostolic See thereby become worthless? . . . But it is a seditious question for the fathers in full council to alert our most holy Lord that he paternally order the correction of anything that he might notice in need of it in his Curia, as if, if this is done, one must immediately conclude that the ecumenical council as the body is over the pope himself as over the head of all.

Staphylus was not in favor of resolving the question of the relative superiority of the pope and the council "in those narrow passes of the Tridentine Alps," but he admitted no connection between that question and the emperor's *libellus*.[114] The more intransigent attitude of Staphylus would have to yield to the more realistic advice of the vice-chancellor.[115]

It was, in fact, in accordance with Seld's observations and with the approval of the privy council that the emperor's reply to the legates was composed. Obviously Ferdinand dreaded the danger of a dissolution of the council so much that he decided to take a different tack from the collision course recommended by Staphylus. As he had done in conversation with the nuncio, so also in his letter to the conciliar legates Ferdinand defended his right to propose reform articles to the council. It had always been his understanding, he

---

[114] "Sententia de propositionibus archiepiscopi Pragensis," *ante* June 27, 1562, *CT,* XIII, 696-699 (No. 106).
[115] On these proceedings see Steinherz, III, 84-87. Kassowitz remarked: "The good sense of the statesmen of the privy council could not overtake the undeniable jump of the curial policy that Delfino had gotten on the emperor in personal discussions through the formal withdrawal of the reform *libellus*" (p. 89).

declared, that among the articles that belonged to the agenda of a council, not the last was that which concerned the reform of the Church both in head and in members, and he recalled that in the past, popes convoked councils expressly for the sake of reform. He also expressed his disappointment that the legates had not stated specifically which articles in the *libellus* were so offensive that they might cause a disruption of the council. For as far as the pope was concerned, he said,

> it has never been our intention to accuse or censure him; indeed, we have such feeling for His Holiness' very great conscientiousness (*pietate*), uprightness, and spotless-ness of life and morals as well as his devotedness to Christendom that we have been wont to bear witness to it often and openly in the presence of many. . . . In a long series of years we have not had a better pope or one more zealous for public peace and tranquility . . . so that we would deservedly be considered the most ungrateful of all mortals if, beyond all reason, we would try to denigrate His Holiness.[116]

Ferdinand, no doubt, did not think it prudent to commit to writing what he had said to Delfino about Pius IV's appointment of cardinals.

The reply to the legates was entrusted to the imperial ambassadors at Trent for delivery. They were also ordered to try to obtain a reply as soon as possible. Since the emperor had exhorted the legates to let the *libellus* be proposed to the fathers of the council with equanimity, he directed the ambassadors to encourage the legates to comply with his desire. If the legates should find any "pious and salutary" points in his memorial and should let the fathers discuss them, the ambassadors were to demand that this discussion not be postponed but that the articles which were not disapproved or rejected be laid before the fathers to be examined at least one by one. Most of all, the ambassadors were to make every effort that the legates should protect the freedom of the council against any infringement. In performing these tasks, the ambassadors were to seek the support of the ambassadors of the kings of Spain and France and of the other princes who shared the emperor's view.[117] This last directive meant an important change in the imperial policy. The two ecclesiastical ambassadors, Brus and Drasković, did not need more than these instructions to justify their

[116]Ferdinand to the legates, Prague, June 30, 1562, Le Plat, V, 351-360, esp. 355-356; Baluze, IV, 446-451, esp. 448-449.
[117]Ferdinand to the imperial ambassadors, Prague, June 29, 1562, Sickel, *Concil,* pp. 343-344 (No. CLXXXIV). The Spanish ambassador at the imperial court also ad-

own personal desires for the council's action on the emperor's reform petitions.

To the nuncio, however, Ferdinand could hardly have been more obliging. In another audience he declared: "I believe that you are satisfied with my reply to the most reverend legates, but I tell you moreover that I leave everything to them, and I am content that they should let all or part [of the *libellus*] be proposed at whatever time they choose, because I do not wish to be the cause of anything but good." Delfino commented to the legates that great princes were not wont to retract so easily or to condemn themselves, especially when the negotiations were conducted with permanent records and such great and important interests were involved as in the present affair. For even if the emperor did not write the memorial himself, he sent it and deemed it worthy of being proposed to the fathers, and he did all this with the customary advice of his councilors. To Delfino it was no surprise that they now defended their action, retracted only little by little, and did not wish to scatter all of a sudden and appear inconsistent. In the nuncio's opinion, not only was the emperor convinced that it behooved him to promote what was necessary for the council, but perhaps he had also been advised that it would be advantageous for him to follow this route, because the French, who informed the Protestants of all that happened, could always say that the heat which came from the emperor's court to the council was not going against the Protestants but was directed only at that kind of reform which could not harm them. Hence, the nuncio was certain that Ferdinand would

---

vised his sovereign to insist on reform and to persuade the pope to let the council proceed freely and treat the things necessary for the good of Christendom, without giving an account to anyone. Luna to Philip II, Prague, June 25, 1562, *CDI*, XCVIII (1891), 342.

The French ambassador in Trent expressed the hope that God would maintain the emperor's will and give him the means to attend the council in person, for otherwise he did not expect the good which was necessary, "not that I do not have a very high opinion of the Pope's good intention, but I know well that it is turned aside by certain evil persons aroused for their own interest, . . . by his relatives who are tired of the expense of this council and would only like to be relieved of it in order to save the profit that they can from the pontificate, not troubling themselves about the ruin that can later happen to it." Lansac to Bochetel, Trent, June 23, 1562, Meyenhofer, p. 317 (No. 6).

After Lansac had made remonstrances to the legates and the latter had reported them to Rome, the pope complained to De l'Isle, reminding him of the reforms that Pius had already carried out in his court and of others that he was pursuing day by day. The pope asserted that the estate and living conditions could not be more regulated than they were, not only in the person of the cardinals but also in his own, to such an extent that everywhere their life had become an example, considering the time when the cardinals went about the city in lay attire and the halls and antechambers of the popes, his predecessors, were filled with bishops making up the court; abhorring the offensive life style and former luxury of the court, the pope, according to his own claim, had provided as far as possible for the correction of morals and had issued a decree to subject all bishops to residence in their dioceses, anticipating and satisfying the intention of the council and terminating the long disputes begun in it. By these means, De l'Isle wrote, the pope implied that the

regard it as sufficient to have made this sham and from then on would be quiet in similar cases, for his heart *(l'intrinseco suo)* was

world should be content with his efforts in regard to the desired reform of the head of the Church and that not only should the prelates assembled in the council show him this respect but also the ambassadors of all princes should withdraw their demands for anything to the contrary. In particular Pius directed De l'Isle to write to his king that if anything which depended on the pope's authority should be demanded and pursued at the council in the king's name, the pope would revoke all aid that he had promised for the king's affairs but he would willingly treat with the king and handle separately both the annates and all the other rights that were being contested. De l'Isle to Charles IX, June 15, 1562, Dupuy, pp. 238-239. In order to ward off any challenge to his authority from the French ambassadors in Trent, Pius did not hestitate to threaten the French government which needed his financial assistance in the war against the Huguenots. For details on the papal gift and loan see Pastor, XVI, 183-184.

De l'Isle had also written to Lansac that the pope wanted the council to leave to him alone the reform of his estate and of the Court of Rome, suggesting thereby that the ambassadors should refrain from proposing anything concerning the reform *in capite.* Lansac replied that the ambassadors would be careful not to say anything or to pursue such matters for which they had no express commission or charge, and when they would receive it they would not fail to do the duty of gentlemen and faithful ministers, since they did not have to render an account of their actions to anyone except the king alone, who would punish them if they exceeded his order. Lansac also assured his colleague in Rome that until then they had in no way entered into those proposals or into anything approximating them; if they had spoken of reform, according to their charge, they merely meant the entire reform of the Church, without specifying or particularizing any part of it. Lansac added his own opinion that provided the reform be done well and thoroughly and be lasting, it was all the same to him whether it be done by the pope or by the council. But he avowed that he found it extremely strange that when he had recently been in Rome the pope had assured him of his good-will toward the council to which he wished entirely to leave the settlement of everything, whether of doctrine or of the reform of morals without any particular concern. Now Lansac thought that the pope was in fear and doubt regarding the council as if it would treat or put into practice something to his prejudice--which Lansac professed not to see or know anything about, and if he would notice it he would not permit it insofar as he could prevent it. As he was to write to Bochetel a week later, Lansac declared that he did not believe that such doubts arose in the pope's own mind but rather he was persuaded by some malicious persons who wished to arouse this fear in him for some evil purposes of their own. Lansac to De l'Isle, Trent, June 16, 1562, Dupuy, pp. 244-246.

In the following month Catherine de Médicis wrote to Lansac that she was not surprised by the pope's displeasure at his conduct, because one who is to be reformed ordinarily complains; she reminded the ambassador that he was not at Trent to favor the pope's cause but to promote the honor of God and the reform of the abuses in the Church, "of which the Court of Rome causes a large part"; if the pope had reason to complain, she added, it would be rather of the emperor and his bishops and ministers, who, until then, had urged the reform more severely and rigorously than the French had, and yet in a Catholic and religious manner. Catherine to Lansac, n.p., July 11, 1562, *Lettres de Catherine de Médicis,* ed. Hector de la Ferrière, Vol. I: *1553-1563* (Paris, 1880), p. 355. In this regard the queen mother also wrote to her ambassador to the emperor that the pope had no reason to complain about Lansac, because although he repeatedly affirmed that he desired nothing so much as a rigid reform, "he intended it for others and not for himself"; she feared that unless he was adroitly handled, he would not readily let himself get involved in the reform. She was glad that the emperor knew him and was resolved to stand fast. Catherine to Bochetel, Vincennes, July 22, 1562, *ibid.,* p. 363. The papal legate in France, Cardinal Ippolito d'Este, warned Borromeo that the French at the council would always support the emperor's demands; hence, he thought that it

really good, and if he saw hope of being able to do some good, he would make any sacrifice for the Church *(per noi)* and against the heretics.[118]

Confident though the nuncio was of the emperor's attachment to the pope, he thought it advisable to obtain some sign of reciprocity. Hence, he informed Borromeo that Ferdinand had been hurt by the rumors and suspicions spread about him, and Delfino suggested that the pope assure the imperial ambassador in Rome that he was satisfied with the emperor's letter and was aware of his good-will toward him; above all, the pope should demonstrate that he interpreted well everything that came from the emperor. Otherwise, every particle of doubt that would appear to have entered the pope's mind because of this affair would cause the emperor to doubt about his intention, and thus one grudge would beget another, and a mutual lack of trust would be created.[119] The nuncio apparently believed that victors can afford to be magnanimous.

Pius IV, however, had already determined to squelch the rumors about his intention of dissolving the council rather than letting it reform the Curia. He ordered the legates to reply that such reports were groundless and that he could not hold the tongues of others although he could show that they were telling a lie, as he believed

---

would be more effective for the pope to induce the emperor to moderate his requests than for the legate to ask the queen to restrain her envoys, because it would be easier to influence a prince possessing authority and a good disposition than the Kingdom of France, "which at present does not have a strong head." Este to Borromeo, Bois de Vincennes, June 18, 1562, Baluze, IV, 421. Later he informed the papal nephew that the only instructions given to the French envoys were to carry out the wishes of the imperial ambassadors at Trent, for they though that they could not be blamed or err if they followed that prince who was held to be so good and Catholic. Same to same, Bois de Vincennes, July 8, 1562, *ibid.,* p. 432.

[118]Delfino to the legates, Prague, July 2, 1562, Steinherz, III, 81-83 (No. 33). The nuncio was aware that not all the emperor's councilors were so well disposed, for one of them had asked him: "If he [Ferdinand] sees that he cannot now restore the Catholic faith, why should he, by attempting it in vain, at the wrong time, and without compromise, put himself in the risk of losing his states?"

[119]Delfino to Borromeo, Prague, July 2, 1562, Steinherz, III, 83 (No. 33). On the same day the French ambassador at the imperial court reported to Catherine de Médicis Ferdinand's reply to the legates and added that the emperor had ordered his ambassadors to communicate all the reform articles to the French and Spanish ambassadors so that if the latter were of the same opinion, they could insist together that the legates propose the articles to the council as they had promised. Bochetel told Ferdinand that many prelates who were good men and important persons would speak their mind more frankly on matters of reform if they saw the articles proposed by the emperor and thus knew that they themselves were supported by him than if the same proposals were made in other ways. Ferdinand replied that it would be sufficient if it were understood that the articles came from him and the other princes to whom his ambassadors would communicate them. The emperor also said that the words in those articles which angered *(fasché z)* the legates were that reform *in capite et in membris* was necessary, being terms used by the councils of Constance and Basel which were not pleasing to Rome. Bochetel to Catherine, Prague, July 2, 1562, Meyenhofer, pp. 321-322 (No. 8).

that he had done and was still doing by his actions, which were indicative of his mind and intention. He boasted to the legates that since his elevation to the papacy, in the important matters and especially in those that concerned the service of God and the public welfare, he never counted the cost. He added:

> In regard to the loss to the court on account of the reform, it is well known that this could never happen to make us dissolve the council, because we have already made and executed a rigorous reform of the affairs of the court with loss to ourselves of more than 200,000 scudi of capital in the [salable] offices besides what is lost every day of the emoluments of the Datary and other offices, which is a sizable sum. This loss, however, we count a very great gain, seeing that it tends to the public benefit and the edification of God's Church.[120]

It was understandably difficult for the pope to establish his credibility along the broad front of reform, where failure to advance at some points brought the whole campaign under suspicion.

When the legates received the emperor's letter regarding his reform memorial, they postponed a reply until they could learn the pope's will.[121] Meanwhile Ferdinand complained to his ambassadors that treatment of reform was being deferred in the council, and he ordered them to busy themselves with the legates in order that the articles of his *libellus* be laid before the fathers for discussion at least one by one and at an appropriate time.[122] Fearing, however, that they might hinder the granting of the chalice to the laity if they made too many requests at one time, Drasković and Thun thought

---

[120]Pius IV to the legates, Rome, June 29, 1562, Sickel, *Röm. Ber.*, II, 118-119. The Mantuan agent Bernardino Pia reported on July 8, 1562, that the pope had said that he wished to make such a reform that there would be nothing more to say either inside or outside; the Datary would be reformed so that the pope would no longer have any emolument in the world; if it would go on thus, it would exceed the ideas of those who had requested it. Jedin, *Geschichte*, IV/2, 306, n. 6.

[121]The legates to Borromeo, Trent, July 13, 1562, Susta, II, 243 (No. 67).

[122]Ferdinand to the imperial ambassadors, Prague, July 16, 1562, Sickel, *Concil*, p. 358 (No. CXCI). On the same day the emperor directed his ambassador in Rome reverently to express his concern to the pope about the lack of freedom in the council; one instance that he cited was that the fathers who, at the dictation of their conscience, spoke more freely about reform and other matters of that kind were delated to the pope and incurred his hatred and indignation. Ferdinand to Arco, Prague, July 16, 1562, *ibid.*, p. 356 (No. CXC). In response the pope contended that the council was too free and its freedom was verging on license, for many men in it dared to speak ill of his person, while he remained silent. Arco to Ferdinand, Rome, August 5, 1562, *ibid.*, p. 367 (No. CXCVII). Ferdinand also directed the Spanish ambassador at his court to ask his king to support the liberty of the council in order that it might proceed more boldly to remedy the ills of the Church. Luna to Philip II, Prague, August 29, 1562, *CDI*, XCVIII (1891), 362-363.

that it was not opportune to urge the presentation of the *libellus* just then.[123] They did, nevertheless, press the legates to answer their master's letter without further delay. The legates offered excuses for their slowness without admitting that they were awaiting word from Rome, but the ambassadors recognized the true reason.[124] Before the legates sent their second request for directions to Rome, Borromeo had already dispatched the pope's answer. It was Pius IV's wish that the legates not speak about the *libellus* any more because in effect the emperor had left it in their hands; indeed, they should cause it to be forgotten entirely and should try to soothe the emperor and show that they remained satisfied with his good intention, making use of Delfino and speaking with the imperial ambassadors at Trent just as the pope had done with the ambassador at Rome.[125] According to his nephew, Pius had spoken with Prospero d'Arco with appropriate "sweetness and assuagement," and he now hoped that this affair would not make any more stir and everything would go ahead quietly without any alteration.[126]

After receiving the legates' second and more urgent appeal, however, Pius decided to follow their advice. Hence, Borromeo directed them to extract from the *libellus* all the reform articles that could be treated honorably and without prejudice to the Holy See and let them be discussed along with the other reform proposals on a given day—to be disposed of in whatever way the Holy Spirit

---

[123]Thun and Drasković to Ferdinand, Trent, July 17, 1562, Sickel, *Concil*, p. 360 (No. CXCII). Meanwhile the French ambassador to the council was growing impatient at the failure to make progress on the way of the reform and to relax some positive laws in order to pacify the troubles in his country. Hence, he suggested to the French ambassador at the imperial court that the imperial ambassadors at Trent should invite the French, Spanish, and other ambassadors to a meeting in order that together they might deliberate on joint action to press the legates to proceed, before all else, to make "a good and thorough reform"; as a means to this end he recommended that the reform articles drawn up by the emperor and others be urged on the legates, and he was confident that the imperial ambassadors would find the others ready and willing to co-operate with them in every respect. Lansac to Bochetel, Trent, July 14, 1562, Meyenhofer, pp. 326-327 (No. 10). In expecting the imperial ambassadors to take the initiative in uniting the other ambassadors for "such a holy and just pursuit," Lansac apparently was not aware of the reasons for not insisting at that time on the reform measures that he deemed necessary.
[124]The legates to Borromeo, Trent, July 20, 1562, Susta, II, 261-262 (No. 70). Thun and Drasković to Ferdinand, Trent, July 27, 1562, Sickel, *Concil*, p. 363 (No. CXCIV).
[125]Borromeo to the legates, Rome, July 18, 1562, Susta, II, 270 (No. 73). Arco had reported to the emperor from Rome on July 8 that the pope had complained to him a little about the reform *libellus* but then calmed down when he saw that it was not so bad as it had been depicted; he asked, however, that whenever anything relating to his person might be necessary, the emperor confer with him first, for the pope would always try to satisfy him. Meanwhile meetings on reform were being held every day. Sickel, *Concil*, p. 350 (No. CLXXXVII).
[126]Borromeo to Delfino, Rome, July 18, 1562, Steinherz, III, 94 (No. 36).

might inspire. As for the articles of the *libellus* that would remain undiscussed, the legates were not to make any issue or long-worded excuse to the emperor, since he had left the matter to their discretion; it would be enough to write him "four sweet words in excuse" and then to rely on Delfino's dexterity to pacify him. Borromeo still hoped, nevertheless, that the legates would find it possible to fulfill the pope's earlier wish, not mentioning the *libellus* nor taking the trouble to write about it, but simply extracting the articles that could be treated in the council.[127] The papal nephew also ordered Delfino to make some appropriate, modest excuse to the emperor with respect to the neglected articles of his memorial and to make him feel satisfied and even edified by the desire of the pope and of all his ministers to please and serve him in every possible way.[128] To strengthen at the imperial court the impression of continuing reform activity at Rome, Borromeo sent the nuncio ten days later printed copies of the bull for the reform of the judges of the Apostolic Camera.[129]

Once they were apprised of the pope's will, the legates composed their long-delayed reply to the emperor's letter of June 30. They had no choice but politely to reject the articles on the reform of the Church *in capite*. Although they admitted that there was no more salutary medicine for the present ills than that all the parts of the Church should be called back to a better mode of life by the authority of the council, they warned that by insisting too much on this matter they might go too far and cross the boundaries set by their forebears. They asserted that a council had no right over a pope, and whenever his conduct seemed to be in need of correction in some respect, a council could never legitimately take cognizance of the case, which had to be reserved intact to the judgment of God. After citing the ancient Fathers and ecclesiastical history in support of their position, they asked: "But if now in matters pertaining to reform the order of affairs should be so inverted and exchanged that all [the sheep] dare to go ahead of the shepherd, and all the limbs dare to command the head, what other outcome of this sacred assembly could we hope for than that at the earliest possible time it be dissolved without having finished the business?" Then the legates complimented Ferdinand for having up till then shown that his will was inclined to defend and enhance the dignity and authority of the pope.[130] It is clear from this letter that what the legates

---

[127]Borromeo to the legates, Rome, July 22-23, 1562, Susta, II, 273-274 (No. 74). Borromeo repeated his instructions to the legates on July 29, 1562 (*ibid.*, p. 289), trusting that the emperor would acquiesce in this line of action.

[128]Borromeo to Delfino, Rome, July 22, 1562, Steinherz, III, 99-100 (No. 38).

[129]Borromeo to Delfino, Rome, August 1, 1562, Steinherz, III, 103 (No. 40). Cf. n. 93 *supra*.

[130]The legates to Ferdinand, Trent, July 28, 1562, Le Plat, V, 427; Baluze, IV, 452 (with date of July 22, 1562). At the same time the French ambassador was still chafing at his inability to steer the council toward reform. He wrote in cipher: "I

feared most was a renewal of the discussions of the Councils of Constance and Basel regarding the question of the superiority of a council over a pope and the attempt of the secular power to execute the claims of the council in a sense hostile to the papacy. Even though they probably recognized that Ferdinand had no such objects in mind, they did not wish to jeopardize the progress of the council in this way.[131]

In their report to Rome the legates stated that they had decided to select some articles from the emperor's *libellus* from time to time and to have them treated in the council with other reform matters, as the pope had permitted them to do; they would also deal with the emperor in the manner prescribed by Borromeo.[132] This compliance of the legates naturally pleased the pope, who had nothing to reply except to command that whenever they had to account to the emperor for their handling of these or other matters, they should write him very briefly and send the letter in care of Delfino, and also explain to the nuncio what he would have to say to the emperor in their name, because a live presentation would make a greater impression than a letter and a letter might not be understood or interpreted in the way in which it was written. In this way they would also get around the ambition of some of the emperor's councilors, who, according to Borromeo, liked "to reply and attack, perhaps to flaunt their wisdom."[133] Whatever justification Borromeo may have

---

know well that the Pope seeks nothing else than to end this council as soon as possible, having it decide the matters that had been treated and proposed previously and having it disperse *de facto* without touching, any more than it can help, the reform of morals and the abuses of his court, and he would like the council to leave to him the decision of matters that are in some difficulty here." Lansac repeated his suggestion that Bochetel should dispose the emperor to order his ambassadors at Trent to make a remonstrance to the legates along with the French ambassador, demanding that the council defer the treatment of doctrine until the arrival of the French bishops and in the meantime deal with reform according to the memorials which the emperor had sent and others which might be proposed by the Christian princes. He thought that if the various ambassadors acted jointly and earnestly, it could turn out to their advantage. Lansac to Bochetel, Trent, July 28, 1562, Meyenhofer, p. 336 (No. 13). A week later Lansac wrote that Drašković had told him that he had received letters from the emperor ordering him to pursue actively with the other ambassadors the reform of morals. They replied to him that they were all ready to assist him "en toutes ses actions et poursuittes" and that they had waited till then to do it only in order to do it jointly and had discussed meeting together to decide what ought to be done. Same to same, Trent, August 4, 1562, Meyenhofer, p. 339 (No. 14).

[131]This judgment is in agreement with Bucholtz, VIII, 457. Kassowitz, on the other hand, expressed a very negative opinion of the legates' reply: "Essentially the imperial *libellus* was a brilliant refutation of those quibbles with which the legates, in their zeal worthy of a better cause, sought to cover up the inability to reform of the Tridentine council directed from Rome" (p. 89).

[132]The legates to Borromeo, Trent, July 30, 1562, Susta, II, 278 (No. 75).

[133]Borromeo to the legates, Rome, August 6, 1562, Susta, II, 303-304 (No. 81); cf. p. 306.

had for this unfavorable opinion of the councilors, he was not averse to courting their good-will. In fact, nearly a month earlier he had told Delfino that the pope understood how important it was for the council to have the councilors fond of the Holy See. Hence, the pope wished Delfino to make every effort to win them over, and if for this purpose the nuncio would think it opportune to give them, or some of them, some presents, the pope would send him the means, and he could assure them that what they desired was already on the way.[134] Following this advice, Delfino proceeded to become intimate with the councilors, but the only gifts they would accept were certain Italian delicacies—pistachio nuts, salamis, botargos, Malmseys, and similar things of small value.[135] Apparently the councilors did not feel that they would be suborned by such trifling bribes.

Whatever little presents may have delighted the councilors' palates did not change their minds regarding the need of reform decrees. They advised the emperor, therefore, to hold his ground in replying to the legates' letter. He stated in it, accordingly, that he did not take it amiss that they had not presented his *libellus* to the council, and he repeated that he did not advocate reform to upset the proper order of things or to put on trial the life, conduct, or deeds of the pope. But in that affair he was looking especially to the peace and quiet of the Church, the public well-being of the Christian world, and the extreme necessity, recognized by all good men, of improving morals and removing abuses. Consequently, he again besought the legates to be intent on reform legislation.[136] He did not know that about the same time the pope was admonishing the legates to defer no longer extracting some suitable articles from the emperor's reform *libellus* and proposing them in the council among other reform matters.[137] To bring more pressure to bear on the

---

[134]Borromeo to Delfino, Rome, July 11, 1562, Steinherz, III, 92 (No. 35).

[135]Borromeo to Delfino, Rome, August 22, 1562, Steinherz, III, 110 (No. 42). Borromeo promised to order some of these things from Naples, but since they were not always available, nor were the orders ever filled promptly, and the distance was great, he doubted that they would be delivered to Delfino on time.

[136]Ferdinand to the legates, [Prague,] August 12 and 22, 1562, Le Plat, V, 450-451. The ambassadors held this letter back, however, until September 11. When Catherine de Médicis directed the French envoy in Rome, Gilles de Noailles, Abbé de l'Isle, to urge the pope to have reform put ahead of doctrine at the council, she used language so similar to Ferdinand's that a concerted effort of the two rulers must be suspected; she wrote that the purpose was "not to upset and change the order of things, nor any desire to call into question and judgment the life, customs, and actions of His Holiness, by which we are so edified that we have great reason to praise God for having given us so good a common father, but it is in order to reach more easily the point that he himself desires, which is to see union in the Church in the preservation and strengthening of his authority and that of the Holy See . . . which it is impossible to bring about without without coming to an improvement of morals and to the correction and reform of the abuses. . . . " Catherine to De l'Isle, Bourges, September 6, 1562, La Ferrière, *op. cit.*, I, 396-397.

[137]Borromeo to Ercole Gonzaga, Rome, August 15, 1562, Sickel, *Röm. Ber.*, II, 124.

legates, however, Ferdinand sent Arco a copy of his letter to them
and directed him to give it to the pope. Pius replied to the ambassador that he had handled and was handling the reform of his
own person and of his court with some cardinals at Rome, but he
would write to the legates to have the reform in general handled by
the council.[138] True to his word, the pope again told the legates that
just as he was not failing to carry out a strict reform in Rome, so
they should accompany the discussion of dogma with that of
reform, choosing some articles from the *libellus* of the emperor,
whom the pope wished to satisfy in whatever way he honorably
could. He assured them that not only did he not shrink from such a
reform but even liked it, provided it would not be destructive of the
Holy See.[139]

Pius had promised to write to the legates at greater length about
the reform work of the council, but after having considered all the
articles proposed by the emperor, he did not think it necessary to
send the legates comments on any of them for presentation to the
council, because outside of those that he deemed exorbitant and unworthy of being presented, he found that all the rest were in one way
or another contained in the other reform articles that he had already
sent to the legates several times.[140] Meanwhile the legates
themselves had selected certain articles and had submitted them to
the pope for his approval before proposing them to the council.
Since none of them touched the pope's person or Curia, his nephew
praised the legates' good judgment.[141] Thus the way was cleared for
the enactment of several reform decrees in the twenty-second session (the sixth under Pius IV), which was held on September 17.
Among those strengthening the authority of the bishops within
their dioceses, for example, one provided that dispensations, by
whatever authority they might be granted, if they were to be sent

[138]Arco to Ferdinand, Rome, August 26, 1562, Steinherz, III, 116.

[139]Pius IV to the legates, Rome, August 26, 1562, Susta, II, 328 (No. 89).

[140]Borromeo to the legates, Rome, September 2, 1562, Susta, II, 350 (No. 94).

[141]Borromeo to the legates, Rome, September 5, 1562, Susta, II, 355 (No. 96). Two
of the articles, nevertheless, did directly affect the Curia's interests; chapters 3 and
4 would have set limits to the extent to which bishoprics and parishes could be
burdened with the obligation to pay pensions to third parties (including those who
resigned such benefices) when they were conferred on new holders; since these
pensions often swallowed up a large part of the income, it was proposed to protect
the holders of such benefices by decreeing that pensions could not take away more
than half of the revenues; 500 gold ducats would have to be left free in the case of
bishoprics and fifty in the case of parishes; if the income was less, no pension at all
could be imposed. *CT*, VIII, 924 (No. 422). Since cardinals, relatives of the pope, and
even laymen for whom financial provision was to be made were frequently the
beneficiaries of such pensions, the curialists at Trent naturally objected to these
chapters. On the other hand, the Spanish bishops wished to abolish such pensions
altogether or at least to guarantee to the holder of the benefice a larger portion of
the income. In the end the curialists prevailed. In the revised draft, which was
brought in on September 15, these two chapters were omitted. For a summary of
this episode see Jedin, *Geschichte*, IV/1, 201-203.

outside the Roman Curia, were to be entrusted to the ordinaries of those who obtained them; then those which were granted as a favor would not take effect until the ordinaries, as delegates of the Apostolic See, should have ascertained that the terms of the original petition for each dispensation were free from fraud and deception.[142] To that moderate extent the abuses connected with the papal dispensing system were corrected. That the bishops were also given certain other powers as delegates of the Apostolic See meant that while the papal rights in such matters were acknowledged in theory, they were to be exercised by the local bishops rather than by the Roman Curia. By the juridical device of delegation, therefore, some slight limits were set in practice on Rome's interference in the administration of dioceses.[143]

This reform decree marked a defeat for the French ambassadors at the council, who had been instructed to procure the complete cessation of papal dispensations in their kingdom. They had requested the support of the three imperial ambassadors for their reform demands in return for the help that the French had given them in their petition for communion *sub utraque*.[144] Ferdinand ordered his ambassadors to aid the French in urging that reform be placed before dogma on the conciliar agenda. Lest excessive in-

---

[142]Sessio XXII, *de ref.*, cap. V, Schroder, p. 428; English translation, pp. 155-156. The imperial ambassadors were not the only ones in the council disappointed by the meagerness of the reform decrees. In the congregation of September 13, 1562, the Bishop of Coimbra, João Soarez, stated that to treat reform according to the needs of the Church it was necessary to enact more serious provisions, as had been done in the Council of Basel, especially in regard to papal elections, the number and quality of cardinals, and other things; he thought that the proposed canons did not correspond to the dignity and the expectation of so great a council. Calini to Cornaro, Trent, September 14, 1562, Marani, p. 270.

The Bishop of Orense, Francisco Blanco, also argued that the pope was obliged by the laws of the council, not indeed by their constraining force but by their directive force, for the council did not have power over its head but the head was bound by the natural law to conform to the other members in whatever was not improper for him because of his special condition of being head. Pallavicini, XVIII, vii. 1.

[143]See Hubert Jedin, "Delegatus Sedis Apostolicae und bischöfliche Gewalt auf dem Konzil von Trient," in *Die Kirche und ihre Ämter und Stande. Festgabe Joseph Kardinal Frings* (Cologne, 1960), pp. 462-475; also in Jedin, *Kirche des Glaubens*, II, 414-428.

[144]The imperial ambassadors to Ferdinand, Trent, August 18, 1562, Sickel, *Concil*, pp. 369-370 (No. CIC). On the relations between the French envoys and the imperial ambassadors at this juncture see Meyenhofer, pp. 186-189. He concludes that in this coalition France was not powerful enough to influence the emperor's policy and could only support him in his controversies with the Curia.

Giovanni Strozzi, the Florentine ambassador to the council, expressed to his master his own opinion, which he said was confirmed by persons of importance, namely, "that these ultramontane prelates always have an eye on the greatness of the Pope, of the Court of Rome, and of the Italian prelates, and under this pretext of reform which at first sight appears to be a good and holy thing, their intention is to reduce that greatness and that authority and to diminish the splendor of that college." Strozzi did not deny that the reforms were necessary, but he doubted that

sistence on this point provoke a suspension of the council, however, the imperial ambassadors decided to proceed cautiously, at least until the outcome of the deliberation on the lay chalice would be known. They were resolved, nevertheless, to press for consideration of reform alone, in conjunction with the French ambassadors, after the session of September 17.[145] When the emperor learned that his ambassadors had not even deliverd his letter of August 12 to the legates, he reprimanded them, for he saw nothing in it by which the legates could be reasonably offended, just as not even the pope was offended but rather had commended his eagerness to promote reform. He also ordered them to acquaint the legates with the pope's approval and promise of assistance.[146] In their defense Draskovic and Thun explained their fear that the delivery of the letter before the session of September 17 would have prevented favorable action by the council on their petition for the lay chalice; as it was, they managed only to have a majority of the fathers agree to refer the matter to the pope for a decision rather than reject it outright. As the ambassadors viewed the situation, the majority of the bishops at the council consisted of Italians and those for the most part educated at Rome who aspired to the cardinalate; nothing more odious to them could be devised than the word "reform," not even the thing itself; for they had heard from the cardinals that among the other reform articles in the emperor's *libellus* was one about limiting the number of cardinals; and the ambassadors asked, "Could anything more bitter than that have befallen them?"[147] After receiving the emperor's reprimand, however, Draskovic and Thun delivered his letter to the legates with a convenient excuse on September 11; of course, they did not doubt that the legates had already seen copies of it sent from Rome or by Delfino, but for the furthering of their immediate cause they judged it very important that the legates had not received the letter from them any earlier.[148]

A few days after the session, on September 21, the imperial and French ambassadors visited the legates; the French demanded that dogmatic discussion of the sacraments of Holy Orders and Matri-

---

"the enfeebling and, so to speak, degrading (*l'avilire*) of that Holy See" was useful to Italy, "which, perhaps, is what the ultramontanes envy." He averred that he was very much attached to Italian things and to the majesty of the Holy See and in particular was most devoted to the pope. Strozzi to Cosimo I, Trent, September 3, 1562, D'Addario, pp. 182-183 (No. XCI). Apparently the ambassador was so afflicted with xenophobia that he had no contact with any non-Italians in Trent.

[145]Draskovic to Ferdinand, Trent, September 8, 1562, Sickel, *Concil*, pp. 373-374 (No. CCII).

[146]Ferdinand to the imperial ambassadors, Prague, September 14, 1562, Sickel, *Concil*, pp. 381-382 (No. CCIV).

[147]On the attitude of the Italian ecclesiastics toward a reform *in capite et in membris* see Alberigo, *op. cit.*, p. 29.

[148]Thun and Draskovic to Ferdinand, Trent, September 18, 1562, partly in Sickel, *Concil*, pp. 382-383 (No. CCV), and partly in Bucholtz, IX, 698.

mony, on which decrees had to be ready by the next session (November 12) according to the determination of the last session, be postponed until the French bishops would arrive in Trent and that in the meantime reform be discussed. In spite of this impressive delegation, the legates refused to alter the established order of business in the council.[149] Afterwards the imperial ambassadors lamented this intransigence in a conversation with the legates' secretary, Filippo Musotti; they also reminded him that for the coming session the emperor desired that if not all, then a half or a third of his reform *libellus,* according to the judgment of the legates, be submitted to the conciliar fathers. If some of the articles would be rejected, they told Musotti, they would not care much, because they had already thought that there could be in the council many fathers who perhaps desired to be cardinals and who, upon hearing the proposal that there should not be more than twenty-six in the Sacred College, would all vote *non placet.* Offering another motive for acting on Ferdinand's memorial, the ambassadors said that they understood that it was already in the hands of many in Rome, in Germany, in the council, and in other places and from one minute to the next they expected to hear that it was printed; hence, if it were not proposed in the council, the world would assume the reason to be that since the emperor's petitions were honorable it was feared that the fathers would accept them; but if it were proposed, the world would calm down, saying that the fathers did not like the part that they were not pleased to grant, and thus a great harm that the *libellus* could cause would be remedied. Finally, they said that the emperor and the whole world wondered why there was so much delay in beginning to treat of reform.[150]

When the legates reported to Borromeo this *démarche* of the imperial and French ambassadors acting in concert, they said they were sure that it was not desire for reform or zeal for religion that moved the ambassadors but only a plan to prolong the council, with what intention and to what purpose only God knew. They alleged proof of this conclusion from the fact that when they had said to Drasković that they would never propose or allow to be proposed some articles of the emperor's *libellus,* such as the marriage of priests, which not even the Lutherans themselves would dare to ask and which would besmirch the august name of His Majesty and make it odious to the council and the whole world, Drasković replied that this did not matter but that they should propose the articles also to show that they had regard for the emperor's requests, but if they were not granted he did not care; he said the same thing about

[149]Thun and Drasković to Ferdinand, Trent, September 22, 1562, Sickel, *Concil,* pp. 385-386 (No. CCVI).
[150]"Philippi Musotti Scripturae conciliares (C)," Trent, September 22, 1562, *CT,* III, 162-163; also Susta, III, 355-356 (Beilage IV).

reducing the number of cardinals to twenty-six. The ambassadors would achieve the end that the legates imputed to them—prolonging the council—for it would take no less than two or three years to treat the things contained in the *libellus*. However, since the ambassadors would never be quiet unless some part of it were treated in the council (and likewise the French unless something were taken from their Assembly of Poissy)—and something of importance, because till then they had laughed at the articles that the legates proposed under the name of reform and regarded them as worthless and unworthy of the council—the legates thought it necessary that the pope consider the *libellus* (and the French articles), see what could be granted without prejudice to religion and the dignity of the Holy See, and send it to them; then they could close the mouths of those who were saying that the legates only wanted a reform of trifles. It was the legates' suggestion, therefore, that leaving aside the articles of the *libellus* (and of the Assembly of Poissy) that touched on the authority of the pope and of the Apostolic See, and those so exorbitant that the Lutherans themselves would be ashamed to ask for them, they could grant for the rest what the ambassadors were requesting. To the legates this seemed to be the way to confound and make liars out of those who had the impudence to say that the pope did not want a reform sincerely. Even if the pope would thus not have granted all the petitions of the emperor or of the king of France, he would have granted so many that the world would know that the others were not worthy of being granted. The legates urged that if the pope should consent to this plan, he act without delay, so that the reform articles could be given to the ambassadors while the fathers were still discussing the dogmatic decrees, because the ambassadors had complained till then that they received the drafts so late and had asked to be given them a few days before the fathers, in order to be able to give their opinions of them according to the instructions that they had from their princes. The legates begged Borromeo, therefore, to take this matter to heart, for they were waiting "with infinite desire," wishing to remove the cause of the ambassadors' indignation.[151] This dispatch reveals that the ambassadors had made a greater impression on the legates than they realized.

---

[151]The legates to Borromeo, Trent, September 24, 1562, Grisar, I, 394-399 (Appendix, No. 1). On the same day the Cardinal of Mantua wrote from Trent to his nephew in Rome, Francesco Gonzaga: "Let our Lord [Pius IV] carry out the reform of himself as head of the Church and order that that of the members be carried out here, and the Council will be ended qickly and with much praise for His Holiness and with infinite advantages for the Church of God, which in truth has much need of it." Drei, XVIII, 108 (No. LXXI). On September 28 he wrote again that he had heard that the pope which to take in hand again the bull for the conclave and improve it in order to be able to publish it. He was pleased by this news because (after his personal experience of three years previously) he thought it most necessary to make some dispositions "about the abuses of the conclave, which are infinite." *Ibid.*, pp. 108-109 (No. LXXII).

Before Borromeo received the legates' urgent request, he related to them his uncle's opinion of the reform proposals made by them. The pope thought that the prelates and envoys who criticized the proposals were imagining such a strict reform that they themselves did not know how to express it in words; he pointed out that all the reforms which they called frivolous were advocated by themselves and were not in fact of so little substance as they seemed to the critics. As for papal elections, about which the ultramontane prelates grumbled, Borromeo announced that the pope had completed a bull which would leave nothing to be desired and which would be published in a week or so. The cardinal secretary also promised that the pope would make opportune provisions for the creation of cardinals.[152] A few days later, when Borromeo replied to the legates' report of their meeting with the ambassadors, he conveyed the pope's praise for their having rebuffed the ambassadors, especially Drasković, who had requested that the emperor's *libellus* be read in the council. He reminded the legates that the pope had always said to the imperial and French ambassadors that he was more willing to attend to reform than any of his predecessors in the Holy See but that he intended that the things that touched on himself and his court should be left to him, as he had already done in large measure and was continuing to do. If they should desire anything more, either in the reform of Rome or in that of the universal Church, they ought, wrote Borromeo, to ask it of His Holiness as a pure favor and not presume to force it, as those ambassadors and some of the fathers wished to do. He suggested that if they had approached the pope in the right way, they would have found him more ready to satisfy and oblige them in all reasonable things than they thought. After asserting that the pope was more amenable to humble petitions than to insistent demands, he proceeded to show that the opposite was true, for he said that the pope had approved most of the reform articles desired and sent by a majority of the fathers, and Borromeo promised to send the list to the legates promptly.[153]

---

[152]Borromeo to the legates, Rome, September 26, 1562, Grisar, I, 399-400 (Appendix, No. 2).

[153]Borromeo to the legates, Rome, September 30, 1562, Grisar, I, 404-405 (Appendix, No. 5). In an audience the French ambassador said to the pope that if the council could find a way of putting the reform decrees into such firm and stable execution that they could not be altered, it would confer a great benefit on the world. Pius replied that for his part he would provide for the observance of the decrees and was reducing as much as he could all the parts of his court with great harm and loss to many of its officials; the pope said that he would proceed farther if he were not aware that by diminishing his estate more severely he would give his adversaries a great advantage and would be more exposed to their injury and thus would endanger his position and that of all Catholics under his protection. As for controlling the countries outside his temporal jurisdiction, he said that the kings and princes perverted the discipline of the Church by seeking extraordinary dispensations and provisions so insistently that the pope could not refuse them. De l'Isle to Charles IX, [Rome,] September 28, 1562, Dupuy, p. 300.

Although the ambassadors blamed the legates for failing to promote serious reform measures in the council, the latter had not been negligent or idle. After they received the pope's admonition of August 15, they directed Gabriele Paleotti, an auditor of the Rota who had been sent to Trent as adviser or counselor to the college of legates, to examine the emperor's *libellus* carefully. Paleotti proceeded to classify the individual requests of the emperor in two distinct categories—those that were acceptable, albeit conditionally and with restrictions, and those that were not acceptable either because they were contrary to the rights of the council or of the pope or because they were already discussed or superfluous.[154] In the first category he included the limitation on dispensations to hold several benefices, especially those with the care of souls. He rejected, on the other hand, the proposed reform of the pope and of the Curia by the council, because this reform was already being set in motion in Rome; the pope had already published many reform bulls, and he was known to be applying himself to this matter zealously. Paleotti also rejected the proposed reduction of the number of cardinals, because the number could not be rigidly fixed since it had to vary according to the needs of the Church, and of this the pope was the judge; indeed, said Paleotti, even if the pope should bind himself by an oath not to exceed a certain number, he would not be held by the bond of his oath if the benefit of the Church should afterwards require otherwise. Likewise the Rotal judge was opposed to the petition regarding dispensations sent outside the Curia; he observed that dispensations were necessary even for civil governments, as all admitted; if it was desirable to be more sparing in granting them, although no law could be laid down for the pope, he pointed out that the whole office of the Penitentiary, which issued very many dispensations, and some other offices of this kind also had been adjusted by the pope of his own accord; a decree to be enacted in the forthcoming session of the council would deal with many other dispensations. Finally, he called it unfair to demand that exemptions contrary to the common law be abolished, because they were granted for very just reasons and inserted into the *corpus juris*. According to a recent biographer of Paleotti, this memorial shows his eagerness to promote serious reform without abandoning the ecclesiastical tradition of Rome, and this was the course that the council was to follow in its final phase.[155]

---

[154]Steinherz, III, 132-133, n., gives the first part of Paleotti's comments and completes the second part, which was previously edited by Le Plat, V, 385-388, who spoke of it as a memorial sent to Rome by the legates; it was indeed sent to Rome by the legates but was not composed by them.

[155]Paolo Prodi, *Il cardinale Gabriele Paleotti (1522-1597)* (2 vols.; Rome, 1959, 1967), I, 144-145. The Bishop of Salamanca, Pedro Gonzales de Mendoza, had

The legates sent Paleotti's memorial to Rome on August 27, but they received no reply about it for five weeks. On September 24, as seen above, they pleaded for permission to present some of Ferdinand's reform proposals to the council, and only then did the pope re-examine the proposals individually. Finally, on October 3, Borromeo sent Paleotti's analysis back to them with the pope's animadversions on a separate sheet. Pius IV's views coincided almost completely with Paleotti's; for example, in regard to the requested reform of the pope and the Curia, the pontiff remarked that the legates in their letter of July 28 to the emperor had sufficiently demonstrated the reasons for not taking it up in the council; since the pope's zeal in this matter was also evident, this article should be put aside.[156]

At the same time the pope left it to the discretion of the legates to submit to the council the proposals of which he approved. Still, if Draskovič should insist that the emperor's whole *libellus* be read to the council, Pius permitted the legates to do so, provided that it be simply read and that all understand that it was not being proposed to the fathers to be voted on; in this case the pope suggested that when it would be read, a proposal should be made to appoint a committee of several prelates—canonists rather than theologians—who, together with one of the legates, should select from the *libellus* the articles worthy of being proposed in the council. It was Borromeo's hope that with this response from Rome the legates would be completely freed from the trouble and travail that the ambassadors had caused them on the score of reform, and that these ambassadors would learn from the results that however much the pope had promised in this regard, he had promised much less than he intended to do in order to restore the Catholic Church to its pristine splendor.[157] The cardinal secretary, however, also wrote separately to the pope's confidant among the legates, Cardinal Simonetta, asking him to pay close attention lest anything contrary to the pope's

---

received from one of the legates and was sending to his king a copy of the summary of the articles in the imperial *libellus* with the response to each one; he thought that among the things that were asked four were very scandalous and would cause the emperor much grief (*sentimiento*), but he was probably referring to such things as the marriage of priests rather than the reform of the pope. See his letter to Philip II, Trent, September 28, 1562, *CDI*, IX (1846), 289.

[156]"Summarium Responsi jussu Pii IV per Cardinalem Borromaeum ad legatos concilii missi, quo probatur responsum per eos datum ad petitiones Imperatoris Ferdinandi," Le Plat, V, 388. Paleotti noted that his replies to the emperor's *libellus* were all approved by the pope, who wrote back to the legates that one could not give a better answer and that he found it satisfactory. "Paleotti Acta concilii Tridentini,"October 3, 1562, *CT*, III, 440.

[157]Borromeo to the legates, Rome, October 3, 1562, Sickel, *Röm. Ber.*, II, 126-127, and Grisar, I, 407 (Appendix, No. 6); see also Pius IV's letter to the legates, attached to the preceding, in which he said that if the *libellus* had to be read in the council, the

dignity be decreed and that the reforms be made at the least possible expense to the Roman Curia.[158] It could be concluded that the pope would allow no more reform of Roman affairs in the council than he absolutely had to.

Spurred by demands from Trent, Pius continued his own reform work, especially related to the conclave and the cardinals.[159] To prevent a recurrence of the abuses that marred the conclave of 1559 and to forestall any claim of the council to elect his successor if he should die while the council was still in session, the pope issued the bull *In eligendis* on October 9, 1562.[160] This has been called "a statesman's masterpiece," not only because the papacy out of its own resources announced a reform of papal elections, anticipating the suggestions of the council and thus retaining its own determination of the nature and extent of the reforms, but also because it thereby proved that it took reality into greater account than the powers consulting together in Trent did when they devised projects that could never be put into execution.[161] This bull alone, however, did not promote any improvement of the quality of the papal electors, from whose number the man elected also normally came. Pius IV, therefore, entrusted new reform projects to a commission of cardinals, but what he had foreseen happened; the cardinals hesitated to approve more thorough reform measures and declared it impossible to satisfy the demands of the secular powers. In fact, the bull for the reform of papal elections was the last important decree of this kind issued by the papacy during the Council of Trent.

Pius IV did not conceal his own growing impatience with the importunate demands for the reform of the Curia. While he was discussing with Cardinals Morone and San Clemente (Gianbattista

---

emperor's letters, especially the latest ones, which made his petitions somewhat more moderate, should also be read. Grisar, I, 407 (Appendix, No. 7). On the same day Borromeo also wrote a separate letter to the Cardinal of Mantua, in which, after recalling the pope's approval of the president's recommendation of reading the *libellus* to the fathers, directed him to manage the affair with his own good judgment and that of the other legates, since the pope left it in their hands. Sickel, *Röm. Ber.*, II, 130.

[158]Borromeo and Pius IV to Simonetta, Rome, October 3, 1562, Sickel, *Röm. Ber.*, II, 131-133. Cf. "Paleotti Acta concilii Tridentini," October 3, 1562, *CT*, III, 440. In spite of this advice to Simonetta, Paleotti thought that the letters from Rome were written with such moderation and good judgment that nothing in them would offend the reader, and the pope's whole mind seemed to be turned toward the public welfare.

[159]Prospero d'Arco reported to the emperor from Rome on October 3, 1562, that the pope was holding daily meetings on reform; in regard to the creation of cardinals he wished to require the age proper to each rank. Kassowitz, Anhang, No. 38, p. xxviii.

[160]*Bullarum*, VII, 230-236 (No. LXXV).

[161]Paul Herre, *Papsttum und Papstwahl im Zeitalter Philipps II.* (Leipzig, 1907), p. 71. Cf. Pallavicini, XVIII, xvii, 1.

Cicada) the last of the reform proposals sent from Trent, he said that with these the whole reform should finally be finished and he should at last escape from that annoyance. He indicated that he did not wish to hear it mentioned any more, for he thought that he had reached the last step that he could take without ruining the Court of Rome. Turning to Cardinal Francesco Gonzaga, he hinted that Cardinal Ercole Gonzaga with his adroitness and prudence could refute those who wished to ask more and thus could relieve the pope of this trouble which displeased him so much.[162] Such an attitude boded ill for any further efforts at Trent to obtain a reform *in capite*. In addition, the pope was vexed by a report that the imperial ambassadors had attempted to conspire with those of France, Portugal, and the Catholic cantons of Switzerland and the Spanish bishops (having invited in vain the Venetian and Florentine ambassadors); they had appointed three of their number to go around secretly intriguing for the purpose of bringing reform before the council. Through the ambassador at Rome Pius admonished the emperor not to continue such practices which might easily cause a schism but to deal openly with the legates; he also warned him against letting his ambassadors enter into any intrigues with the French who were soon to arrive in Trent. Otherwise the pope could retaliate by withholding his confirmation of the expected election of Ferdinand's son as King of the Romans or by refusing to grant the lay chalice.[163] With his back to the wall, Pius was now letting his political instincts prevail over his religious sense of duty.

When the legates received Borromeo's letters of October 3 and the pope's own animadversions on the reform proposals of the emperor and of the Assembly of Poissy, they agreed that Pius had thereby demonstrated his benignity, "conceding perhaps more than many would have imagined he should have conceded." Thereupon Simonetta with four reliable assistants (including Paleotti) was to draft reform decrees on the points approved by the pope.[164] This group of curialists, of course, from which "any foreigner" was excluded as untrustworthy, could not fail to protect the interests of their friends in Rome. The pope advised them, nevertheless, not to

---

[162]Francesco Gonzaga to Ercole Gonzaga, Rome, October 12, 1562, Drei, XVIII, 113 (No. LXXVI).

[163] Arco to Ferdinand, Rome, October 14, 1562, Sickel, *Concil*, p. 391 (No. CCXI).

[164]The legates to Borromeo, Trent, October 12, 1562, Susta, III, 19-20 (No. 6). In spite of their praise of Pius IV's generosity, the legates must have been deeply disappointed by his decision, for twenty of the thirty-three articles had been stricken; among them were the reforms designed to strengthen the episcopal power in the conferring of benefices, against the accumulation of benefices, and against the imposition of pensions. Jedin comments that it was not understood in Rome that this old tactic of trying to have the Curia reformed by the pope and not by the council was no longer practicable and "that at least a part of the national reform demands had to be satisfied by the council, as then happened a year later in the great reform proposal of Cardinal Morone" (*Geschichte*, IV/1, 220).

present all the canons at the same time but to divide them according to their good judgment.[165]

Knowing nothing about this correspondence between Trent and Rome, the imperial ambassadors to the council and their master in Prague grew more and more impatient. On September 30 and October 4 Ferdinand again directed his envoys to have the council discuss reform in preference to doctrine, at least reform related to his own domains and the Empire,[166] but Drasković and Thun could not persuade the legates to alter the established order of the council.[167] Although they maintained their diligence, the Bishop of Pécs had to admit toward the end of October that he had not heard a word about the reform proposals, and early in November he expressed his disappointment at the legates' failure to submit even the first article to the council. He observed, however, that more Italian bishops were arriving in Trent every day, and he, along with many others, suspected that the purpose was that the efforts of the imperial ambassadors and the Spanish bishops, together with the French who were expected, on behalf of reform might be resisted and obstructed.[168] Brus and Drasković recognized, however, that it was not entirely the legates' fault that reform was being neglected by the council, since the legates could not exceed the limits of their orders. The imperial envoys advised Ferdinand, therefore, to make his efforts in Rome, for that was where those who held the rudder of the council were, and as long as they were unwilling, the ambassadors at Trent would labor in vain, there being so few bishops who sincerely desired reform.[169] In the autumn of 1562, however, while the council was agitated by vehement debates on the divine institution of the episcopal office and later on the episcopal obligation of residence, the emperor ceased to press for the submission of his proposals, because he had to devote his attention to other matters.

---

[165]Borromeo to the legates, Rome, October 21, 1562, Susta, III, 37 (No. 11).

[166]Ferdinand to the imperial ambassadors, Prague, September 30, October 4, 1562, Sickel, Concil, pp. 387-388 (Nos. CCVII, CCVIII).

[167]Thun and Drasković to Ferdinand, Trent, October 19, 1562, Sickel, Concil, p. 392 (No. CCXII).

[168]Drasković to Ferdinand, Trent, October 27, November 3, 1562, Sickel, Concil, pp. 395-397 (No. CCXV, CCXVI). After the Archbishop of Prague returned to Trent, he insistently demanded, in the name of all the other oratores, that reform be discussed. Carlo Visconti (Bishop of Ventimiglia) to Borromeo, Trent, December 14, 1562, Baluze, III, 434-435.

[169]Brus and Drasković to Ferdinand, Trent, November 24, 1562, Sickel, Concil, p. 404 (No. CCXX). The emperor was displeased by this advice, because he wished the council to proceed in proper order, but he was resolved to continue to do what would appear to be his duty. Ferdinand to the imperial ambassadors, Freiburg im Breisgau, December 31, 1562, ibid., p. 416 (No. CCXXVII).

He was especially preoccupied with procuring the election of his son Maximilian as King of the Romans at the Diet of Frankfurt. Only with the coming of 1563 did his relations with the council enter upon a new phase.

V. The Critical Period, November, 1562—March, 1563

On November 13, 1562, the long-awaited French bishops, abbots, and theologians, led by Charles de Guise, the Cardinal of Lorraine, arrived in Trent. As the foremost exponents of conciliarism in the Church, the French alarmed the papalists with a possible demand for a radical reform of the Roman Curia, whose financial and administrative practices they detested, as well as of the manner of electing the pope. The ultramontane bishops and envoys, on the other hand, had looked forward to the coming of the French with impatience, and within a few weeks they coalesced around the Cardinal of Lorraine as the center of the opposition.[170] Seeking a weapon for a counter-attack, the curialists decided to promote the idea of reforming the princes through the council. The pope gave the legates free rein to accede to all the just desires of the conciliar fathers in this regard, remarking that the princes could not reasonably complain about the correction of some of their disorders since the pope was not looking to his own interests in many reforms that were being carried out in Rome and at the council, although, as Borromeo reminded the legates, he preferred that the council not treat his own affairs without his participation, in keeping with the great reverence owed by all to the Holy See.[171] In reply the legates expressed their surprise that the pope heard that every day things prejudicial to him and his court were being said and proposed in the council, because they remembered that the only time they had ever interrupted anyone was when the speaker touched on the pope or the Holy See. Hence the legates concluded that "great lies" were being written from Trent to Rome and were being believed, with no less annoyance to them than displeasure to the pope.[172] This ex-

---

[170]On the early reform activities of the French at Trent see Jedin, *Krisis*, pp. 48-55, 61-69. The Cardinal of Lorraine and the bishops accompanying him had been advised by an assembly of notables convoked by the regent after their departure not to insist too stubbornly on the reform of the abuses of the Court of Rome at the beginning and until after reaching agreement on other points; it was feared that otherwise they might give the pope an occasion to try to dissolve the council before they had reaped from it the fruit necessary for the good of Christendom. "Mémoire baillé à M. le Cardinal de Lorraine," Le Plat, V, 561.

[171]Borromeo to the legates, Rome, December 5, 1562, Grisar, I, 453-454 (Appendix, No. 37). Cf. same to same, Rome, December 12, 1562, *ibid.*, p. 457 (No. 39).

[172]The legates to Borromeo, Trent, December 17, 1562, Grisar, I, 459 (Appendix, No. 41).

change of letters further illustrates the pope's lack of confidence in the two senior legates, Gonzaga and Seripando, who had been accused to him of allowing the bishops in the council too much freedom of speech.

Apprised of the disgust with the Roman Curia that the Cardinal of Lorraine had expressed to Seripando, Pius wrote to him after his secretary, Gurone Bertano, had arrived in Rome. He reminded the French cardinal how licentious the Court of Rome had always been and how he could not do enough to reform it unless he tore it away from his own person; the real remedy, he thought, was for him to do better as others spoke worse about it. Pius pleaded with Guise to have confidence in his good intentions and *malignum spernere vulgus*, for one who listened to those deceitful and wicked tongues would never have anything else to do.[173] Such attempts to win Lorraine over to the papal side, however, could not be successful when the pope's fair assurances were belied by the actions of his legates in the council.

The Cardinal of Lorraine had alarmed the papalists the previous spring by telling the nuncio in France, Prospero Santa Croce, Bishop of Cisamus, that he believed that the German Protestants in a projected conference would return to the Catholic Church provided that one point on which they were insistent be conceded, namely, a change in the manner of electing the pope. Guise had assured the nuncio that this demand would not affect the past election, of which all Christendom approved, but he said that for the future a different procedure should be found, because the existing one, by which the cardinals elected the pope, was not good, as past conclaves showed; he added that it was not fitting that this dignity should always be in the hands of Italians.[174] This dispatch deeply disturbed Pius IV. In a general congregation of cardinals he declared cryptically that they should be alert to a terrible and momentous thing that had happened and should realize that some of those who most proclaimed themselves devoted sons of the Apostolic See were moving to take the papal election away from the College of Cardinals. Pius added that he was not personally concerned, but that the cardinals were threatened with this great injury to their rights. They were greatly surprised, and since the pope offered no further explanation they began to speculate who these

---

[173]Pius IV to Lorraine, Rome, December 30, 1562, Grisar, I, 463-464 (Appendix, No. 44). Sebastiano Gualterio, Bishop of Viterbo, had reported to Borromeo on December 10 that the Cardinal of Lorraine had intended to condemn the reservation of the papal months, but Gualterio after a conversation of two hours had dissuaded him. Jedin, *Krisis*, pp. 134-135 (No. 18).

[174]Santa Croce to Borromeo, Paris, April 27-28, 1562, Susta, II, 438 (Beilage XVII).

false friends might be.[175] This episode makes it easier to understand why Pius adamantly refused to let the council have any part in the reform of the conclave. Half a year later, after arriving in Trent, the Cardinal of Lorraine was informed by friends in Rome that Pius was so ill that he could not live beyond the following March. In the opinion of the Cardinal of Mantua, the French prelates' expectation of a proximate vacancy in the Holy See was very harmful to the affairs of the council for two reasons. One was that since the council would still be in session, the papal election could be drawn out by various means, for example, by having the College of Cardinals and the council together elect a pope, or by having each elect a different pope. But what in his judgment was most important was that not only the French but also the Spaniards and the imperialists would hope during the interregnum to be able to reform the whole Church in their own way, believing that a genuine reform could not be carried out while the pope was alive because of his own interests and those of the Court of Rome. The second reason was that as long as the Cardinal of Lorraine supposed that within two or three months he would have to leave Trent to take part in the conclave at Rome, he was not interested in working more than with his fellow Frenchmen, the Spaniards, and the imperialists to resolve the differences among the fathers of the council; being new and opposed to the authority of the Apostolic See and of the pope, most of these questions, in Mantua's opinion, would not deserve to be treated if it were not for a desire to bring about peace and a good and speedy end of the council.[176]

While some bishops at Trent expected the pope's imminent demise to alter the course of the council, others heard the false rumor that the emperor was procuring its suspension at Rome.[177] Meanwhile the council itself was making no progress. By the beginning of January, 1563, Brus and Drasković were convinced by their long experience that they would accomplish nothing by dealing gently with the legates. They reported to the emperor that the French ambassadors and many of the fathers openly blamed them for dealing too slowly and mildly with the legates. Since all who desired reform looked to them for leadership, the two prelates asked the emperor whether they should continue to remain within the

---

[175]Vargas to Philip II, Rome, May 23, 1562, Döllinger, *Beiträge*, I, 427 (No. 126). Before long Vargas learned from conversations with cardinals and others that it was the "French and the Cardinal of Lorraine" who, it was feared, would attempt to change the form of election so that it would not belong to the cardinals. Same to same, Rome, July 1, 1562, *ibid.*, pp. 443-444 (No. 131).

[176]"Istruzione di Mantova per mons. Carlo Visconti inviato a Roma il 27 Dicembre 1562," Drei, XVIII, 122-123 (No. LXXXIII). The legates sent Visconti, in whom the pope had great confidence, to enlighten him about the situation in Trent.

[177]Brus and Drasković to Ferdinand, Trent, November 24, 1562, Sickel, *Concil*, p. 410 (No. CCXXIV).

bounds of meekness or should become somewhat more vehement (*acriores*).[178] In his reply Ferdinand attributed his lack of success in urging reform to the failure of other kings and princes, as well as of prelates, to come to his aid, for at the beginning the French and the Spaniards were not present and other nationalities—by which he obviously meant the Italians—were not sufficiently disposed and inclined to promote reform at the risk of offending anyone. Now he ordered his ambassadors to renew and continue their activity, informing the legates of their support of the French reform petitions which were similar to his own. He declared that as emperor and a Catholic prince he could not and should not neglect his duty of admonishing the legates to propose for discussion first his proposals and then those of the French. Though he did not exclude the Roman Curia, he emphasized the need for reform of the Church in his own domains and in other countries.[179] Applying pressure at Rome as well as at Trent, Ferdinand informed the nuncio at his court that he liked the French reform proposals and that he had directed his ambassadors to the council to urge the discussion of his own articles and to support also those of the French.[180]

As far as the French proposals were concerned,[181] Pius IV had already communicated them to the curial cardinals and requested

---

[178]Brus and Drasković to Ferdinand, Trent, January 5, 1563, Sickel, *Concil*, p. 418 (No. CCXXVIII). A fortnight later the three ambassadors were to acknowledge that most of the credit for whatever good would be accomplished in the council would be owed to the Cardinal of Lorraine. The imperial ambassadors to Ferdinand, Trent, January 19, 1563, *ibid.*, p. 422 (No. CCXXX).
[179]Ferdinand to the imperial ambassadors, Constance, January 17, 1563, Sickel, *Concil*, pp. 419-421 (No. CCXXIX).
[180]Delfino to Borromeo, January 21, 1563, Steinherz, III, 171-172 (No. 63).
[181]For the thirty-four reform articles of the French see Raynaldus, 1562, Nos. 86-88, pp. 244-247, and Le Plat, V, 631-643. Although the French did not mention the reform of the Curia explicitly, they requested many changes in its practice, for example, that benefices could not be conferred any more on foreigners or by vicars but only by ordinaries (art. 20); that orders for provisions, expectancies, regress, resignations in trust, and commendams be revoked and kept away from the Church (art. 21); that resignations in favor of a particular person be entirely eliminated from the Roman Curia (art. 22); that pensions not be placed on benefices and that those that have been imposed be removed (art. 25); that ecclesiastical jurisdictions be restored to bishops within each diocese and that all exemptions, except the chapters of orders and those that are subject to monasteries, be abolished (art. 26); that legal controversies over benefices be not only made shorter but even ended by ordering the bishops to confer benefices not on those who seek them but on those who flee from them and are well deserving of the Church (art. 32); and that in suits over the power of conferring a benefice or presenting to it, the rights of the bishop be respected and appeals be limited (art. 33). The legates replied without mentioning the articles that affected curial practice; they merely cautioned against those that could of necessity lead to a discussion of the power and authority of the pope, which they thought it imperative to avoid like a reef, lest there arise a dispute over the superiority of the pope over the council or of the council over the pope. The legates to Borromeo, Trent, January 9, 1563, Grisar, I, 464 (Appendix, No. 45).

their advice in writing. Some recommended that the pope have the
council ask the princes to yield their right of presentation to
benefices and of placing pensions on benefices; they thought that in
this way the princes would be induced not to demand reform any
more. Others advised the pope to ask that the princes put all their
requests regarding reform in writing; these cardinals assumed that
the princes would never agree among themselves and thus would
furnish the pope with a good excuse for not executing these
reforms.[182] It is ironic to recall that Pius had complained about the
alleged intrigues of the ambassadors at Trent, when his own cardinals would resort to such wiles.

Even before the emperor's reply to his ambassadors was written,
they had begun to act in its spirit. Having obtained an audience
with the legates on January 12, they presented several requests,
and on the following day the legates replied through Seripando; on
the 14th the ambassadors in turn handed their written answer to
the legates. They had asked first that the reform articles presented
by the *oratores* of the Most Christian King, which for the most part
were in harmony with the emperor's, be proposed to the council. The
legates replied that they had not yet had time to compare the two
papers but would respond as soon as they would have done so. The
ambassadors' rejoinder was that the legates should do so as soon as
possible. Secondly, the envoys reminded the legates that nearly
seven months previously they had asked that the emperor's *libellus*
be taken into consideration and that both the emperor and his ambassadors had been promised that some of the main articles would
be set before the fathers. In this regard the legates repeated the
distinction that they had made before, namely, that some points
were unworthy of the emperor while some were above the council,
touching on the supreme power in the Church, so that it was not fitting to propose them, and others were such as could be safely
handed to the fathers for discussion; these last the legates promised
to present. Answering these assertions, the ambassadors denied
that anything in the *libellus* detracted from the emperor's piety,
good judgment, or authority; secondly, they wished to be told which
articles neither could nor should be treated or defined in the
council.[183] These negotiations were not kept entirely secret, but
became known to at least some of the bishops at Trent.[184] The
legates' formal reply, which was delivered to Archbishop Brus by

---

[182] Arco to Ferdinand, Rome, January 20, 1563, Sickel, *Concil*, p. 425 (No. CCXXI).
The Cardinal of Augsburg confirmed the impression given by the imperial
ambassador, writing, "The reform goes on more in words than in deeds." Truchsess
to Canisius, Rome, January 23, 1563, Braunsberger, IV, 33 (No. 768).

[183] Seripando's remarks, January 13, 1563, Susta, III, 167. "Scriptum oratorum S.
Caes. Mtis Rev. DD. legatis exhibitum," January 14, 1563, *ibid.*, pp. 169-170.

[184] Calini to Cornaro, Trent, January 14, 1563, Marani, pp. 374-375.

the secretary of the council, Bishop Massarelli, ten days later, reiterated their position. They insisted that the emperor's reform proposals regarding the pope could not be handled by the council without providing an occasion for a debate about the relative power of the pope and the council—something against which the imperial counselors themselves in the *libellus* had "piously and prudently" warned the legates; hence, the latter were merely following this advice in deciding to abstain from any discussion of this sort.[185] After receiving this reply, Drasković left Trent and set out for the imperial court, which Ferdinand, after returning from the Diet of Frankfurt, established in Innsbruck in order to be nearer to Trent. Some of the conciliar fathers supposed that the Bishop of Pécs was going to the emperor not merely to convey the mind of the legates on the question of reform, as he could have done easily enough by letter, but especially to report in general on the affairs of the council so that the emperor might be better prepared to reply to the legates. Such fathers feared that Drasković with his great influence would persuade the emperor to interfere in the council's proceedings in some way.[186]

In spite of their firm rejection of all proposals to reform the pope's personal affairs or his court, the legates were aware of the importance of treating reform in the council. The president expressed his thoughts and fears to Sebastiano Gualterio, Bishop of Viterbo, whom Pius IV had sent to Trent in November, 1562, because of his knowledge of French affairs and his intimacy with the Cardinal of Lorraine, and whom the latter had sent back to Rome on January 6 to explain his position to the pope. If Pius IV would allow the council to treat that part of the French petitions which touched on his power and authority with the restraints that Lorraine had proposed to him, the Cardinal of Mantua said that he would have no reason to comment; but if Pius refused to let such things be discussed in the council lest he lead the world to believe that the council was superior to the pope, Mantua thought that one of two possible results would necessarily follow: either the French with the imperial ambassadors would leave that part of their petitions aside and would urge the rest pertaining to the Church in general, co-operating with the pope for the universal reform, or, if they insisted on the part that was unacceptable to the pope, the council would be disrupted, for it would not be proper for the legates to preside in a place where the pope's power was being discussed against his will; in case of a disruption, furthermore, the cardinal predicted that either the

---

[185]"Responsum Rev. DD. legatorum ad scriptum DD. oratorum Caes. Mtis nuper oblatum Rev. D. Pragensi die 24 Januarii . . . per Rev. D. episcopum Tylesinum sacri concilii secretarium redditum," Susta, III, 182. See Seripando's similar comments, *ibid.*
[186]Calini to Cornaro, Trent, January 28, 1563, Marani, pp. 389-390. Cf. "Advices from different places," Trent, February 1, 1563, *CSP, 1563,* p. 132 (No. 311).

Spaniards and the French would remain in Trent to continue the reform *in capite et in membris* in their own way, or in many countries national councils would be held. Confronted with this crisis, the legates decided to recommend to the pope that the experienced diplomat, Bishop Commendone, be sent to the emperor in their name to beg him to direct his ambassadors at the council not to propose anything from his *libellus* related to the pope's power and authority; instead he should deal directly with the pope in regard to such matters. The legates thought that Ferdinand would acquiesce in their suggestion because he had written them several months before that he left to them the choice of both the time and the articles of his *libellus* for submission to the council. If they would succeed in persuading the emperor, the legates were almost certain that the French ambassadors would be willing to remove from their petitions everything touching on the pope's power, because of the understanding between them and the imperialists. Then there would remain the question of church reform in general which the pope could settle in whatever way he might judge proper for his office and the discharge of his conscience. The legates' immediate concern was that the council should not be disrupted by the desire of the emperor and the French to meddle in the reform of the pope. But if their efforts would not suffice to bring about the emperor's withdrawal, they believed that the pope would be justified in ordering the legates to depart from Trent with the majority of the prelates, regardless of the consequences, because then the disruption would not be caused by the pope but by the princes who wished to usurp more authority than belonged to them, in spite of the warnings and entreaties of the legates.[187] This grim analysis indicates the turbulence of the waters into which the fragile bark of the council had drifted.

With Pius IV's consent the legates sent Commendone to the emperor immediately after Drasković had set out for Innsbruck. In their instructions they directed the nuncio to give Ferdinand their excuses for not having presented his *libellus* to the council. Commendone was to convince him that in order that the council might achieve the progress and conclusion which every good Christian and especially a prince such as the emperor, "first-born and advocate of the Church," should desire, it was necessary to leave aside the points pertaining to the authority of the pope and the convenience of his court, because the pope knew what it behooved him to do and he had not only done much already but every day was thinking of doing more; however, not everything could be done at once when the disorders were so extreme. The nuncio was to induce the emperor to

---

[187]Ercole Gonzaga to Gualterio, Trent, January 9, 1563, Grisar, I, 465-467 (Appendix, No. 46).

deal directly with the pope regarding anything touching on the pope's authority that he deemed to be in need of reform rather than with the council, because in this way he could be certain that the pope would do everything that he ought, "being very well disposed and by nature most inclined to the good and to satisfy his duty entirely," provided that one had recourse to him and asked him as head of the Church, and with the proper means. But if one intended to act otherwise and to wish in any way to diminish the reputation and the authority given him by God and to make superior to him those who were and had to be subject to him, the pope would not tolerate it, nor would the legates consent to it. From this there would arise the danger of a great disorder that might easily in a short time cause the ruin of God's Church and of the world along with it. Hence, the legates implored the emperor to deign, by his natural goodness and what he owed to the rank and title he held, to consider this danger carefully and to take care that such evils might not follow in the Christendom of which he was emperor and defender. If the emperor would wish to deal with the pope through them rather than through his ambassadors, the legates offered to exert themselves willingly to obtain from the pope whatever he would honorably desire and request. As far as the rest of the *libellus* was concerned, the nuncio was to promise that the legates would do what they could but to explain that they could not do everything at once because of the many different and important obstacles in the way, especially those raised by the French in the recent debates on the sacrament of Orders. Appealing again to Ferdinand's sense of duty, they begged him to help them to overcome the existing obstacles rather than to increase them, for otherwise the council would never end, the scandal in the world would grow worse, and the dioceses without their bishops would incur greater danger of ruin. Although the legates suggested to Commendone all the arguments that they could conceive, they left it to his discretion to use whichever ones he would think most effective.[188] The range of their tactics, however, extending from lofty motives to flattery, cajolery, and threats, shows how critical they perceived their situation to be.

The assurances of Pius IV's good intentions with which the legates wished to impress the emperor appeared less credible when there reached Trent and Innsbruck the news of two new episcopal promotions completely contrary to the decree of the previous session and of the creation of two cardinals who lacked even the qualification of age. Paleotti recorded in his *acta* that these actions of the pope disturbed everyone, "for during a council in which reform is being seriously treated, when no need was pressing,

---

[188]The legates to Commendone, Trent, January 28, 1563, Döllinger, *Beiträge*, III, 317-320.

it did not seem right to create these cardinals, one of whom [Federico Gonzaga] is eighteen years of age, and the other [Ferdinando de' Medici], of Florence, eleven." Some excused the pope, asserting that he not only wished to create cardinals during the council (following the example of Paul III and Julius III) lest the papal power seem to be subordinate to the council, but also wished to console the duke of Florence, two of whose sons (one of them a cardinal) and whose wife had recently died; they also alleged that he wished to show his gratitude to Ercole Gonzaga by making his nephew a cardinal, for Ercole had requested permission to leave Trent if the slanders against him were continued or renewed. Insufficient as all these alleged motives were, the promotion would not have caused such dismay if the new cardinals had been older. Paleotti, however, was mistaken about their ages by a few years.[189] The episcopal appointments seemed scandalous to the Rotal judge because the see of Torcello was conferred on a man who had neither a doctorate nor sacred orders, and the see could not bear such a large pension, while the see of Turin was given to a cardinal who would, perhaps, never see it, at a time when the council was so concerned about residence.[190] The Cardinal of Lorraine spoke candidly to Cardinals Hosius and Simonetta about the loud complaints that the ambassadors and prelates at Trent were making "against the abuses of the Court of Rome" and in particular against its daily contravention of the conciliar decrees; hence, they were saying that it was futile to hold a council and that some prelates, moreover, were compiling a list of many things that had been done and were still being done against the council.[191] Their resentment in turn alarmed the pope. Borromeo, to whom the legates had reported the sentiment growing in Trent, pretended that there was no need to justify what had been done because the reform which was being carried out

---

[189] Federico Gonzaga was actually twenty-three years old at this time. See Gaetano Moroni, *Dizionario di Erudizione Storico-Ecclesiastica,* XXXI (Venice, 1845), 285 (s.v.). (The red hat which Francesco Gonzaga had received from Pius IV less than two years previously had been a reward to the Mantuan family for the marriage of the pope's niece, Camilla Borromeo, to Cesare Gonzaga, Duke of Molfetta and Guastalla.) Ferdinando Medici was actually fourteen. See *ibid.,* XLIV (1847), 92 (s.v.). These higher ages are in keeping with Borromeo's explanation sent to Delfino on February 6, 1563 (see n. 193, *infra*). Jedin, however, maintains that Gonzaga was only eighteen (*Geschichte,* IV/1, 248).

[190] "Paleotti Acta concilii Tridentini," January 10,1563, *CT,* III, 537-538. The new bishop of Torcello was Giovanni Delfino; the pope reserved a pension of 1,300 ducats for persons whom he would name. See Guilelmus Van Gulik and Conradus Eubel, *Hierarchia Catholica Medii Aevi,* Vol. III: *Saeculum XVI ab anno 1503 complectens* (Münster, 1910), p. 335. The new archbishop of Turin was the Cardinal of Aragon, Inigo Avalos, whom Pius had raised to the cardinalate on February 26, 1561; two years later he resigned the see in favor of Girolamo della Rovere. See *ibid.,* p. 329.

[191] The legates to Borromeo, Trent, January 18, 1563, Grisar, I 485 (Appendix, No. 51).

day by day in Rome adequately demonstrated the pope's sincerity.[192]

The cardinal nephew also rationalized the creation of the two young cardinals for Ferdinand's benefit. Writing to the nuncio at the imperial court, he maintained that Federico Gonzaga was of the legitimate age, being already an ordained priest besides being of good morals and learning. Borromeo stated further, with exceptional naïveté if he was sincere, that although he had not been asked by the emperor, the pope elevated Federico to the cardinalate all the more willingly because he thought that he was doing something pleasing to Ferdinand because of the relationship between the houses of Hapsburg and Mantua (Federico's brother, Duke Guglielmo, having married the emperor's daughter, Eleonora of Austria). An additional excuse offered by Borromeo was that the House of Mantua would have been completely upset if Federico had not been made a cardinal (even though two Gonzagas—Ercole and Francesco—were already in the Sacred College). As far as the other new cardinal was concerned, the cardinal secretary asserted that he was sixteen years old—an age close to that required for the diaconate—and he added that if it seemed that the cardinalitial dignity should not be bestowed on anyone below that age, still the person of his father, Duke Cosimo I, warranted some difference and respect as well as some assuagement of his grief (Ferdinando's brother Giovanni, whom Pius IV had made a cardinal at the age of seventeen in 1560, having died on November 22, 1562).[193] The actual reason for these appointments seems to have been Pius IV's policy of drawing the Italian princely houses closer to himself because he felt insecure as long as the council was in session.

The emperor was indeed disturbed by the creation of the two cardinals, one a boy and the other a youth, as he called them. "And by this," he wrote to Philip II, "one sees whether [the pope] has the intention of making such a great and good reform as would be necessary. . . ." He also drew his royal nephew's attention to the disorder in the council and its lack of freedom and authority, as well as to the pope's great desire that the council vanish without positive results. For this reason Ferdinand asked the king to order his ambassador, the Count de Luna, or his bishops at Trent to put themselves in agreement with the Cardinal of Lorraine and the other bishops and the ambassadors of France, as well as with the imperial ambassadors, to prevent the destruction of the council and

---

[192]Borromeo to the legates, Rome, January 27, 1563, Grisar, I, 499-500 (Appendix, No. 57).

[193]Borromeo to Delfino, Rome, February 6, 1563, Steinherz, III, 175-176 (No. 66). Pius IV had insisted, in spite of Prospero d'Arco's contradiction, that he had been asked by Ferdinand, Maximilian, and Albrecht of Bavaria to promote Federico Gonzaga to the cardinalate. See Sickel, *Concil*, p. 426.

to promote its progress in freedom according to custom and reason; they should also strive to have the council proceed with the reform sincerely, treating the main points (which he did not specify) and not beating about the bush (*no anden por las ramas*). In this way Philip would perform a deed worthy of his person and title of "Catholic King" and would give Ferdinand the greatest pleasure and happiness that could be given him in this world.[194]

In his letter of February 6 Borromeo authorized the nuncio to say to the emperor that the pope was not displeased to have reform matters proposed, for no one excelled him in desiring that "a genuine and holy discipline be restored in the Catholic religion," as he had demonstrated by the many reforms that he had made and was still making every day in Rome. But he could not approve the emperor's having praised the French petitions so unreservedly and having ordered his ambassadors to support them, since there were many things in them that were neither honorable nor reasonable.[195] It was mainly his own reform proposals, however, that Ferdinand discussed with Delfino and Commendone after the latter arrived in Innsbruck. The two nuncios interpreted the emperor's intention differently. Delfino thought that Ferdinand had acquiesced in letting the legates lay before the council only that part of his *libellus* that they judged proper and that the legates' order would have to be carried out by the execution of the reforms previously accepted and desired by the emperor. Commendone, on the other hand, concluded that in his letters Ferdinand had never agreed that only the part of the *libellus* that pleased the legates should be proposed to the council, or that all that they thought touched the pope should be left aside; although the emperor had disavowed any intention of impugning the pope's morals, he had expressed, nevertheless, an intense desire for reform; as for the presentation of his *libellus* to the council, he had merely consented that the legates could begin with any chapter and proceed step by step rather than present all at once, and this had always been the demand of his ambassadors at Trent. Summing up his analysis, Commendone ventured the opinion that

[194]Ferdinand to Philip II, Innsbruck, February 11, 1563, *CDI*, XCVIII (1891), 398. A week earlier the general of the Society of Jesus, Jaime Laínez, had expressed to Francisco Borja, the Jesuit commissary for Italy and Sicily, his joy that their king, uniting himself with the pope, had declared that he did not wish anything to be treated which would prejudice the pope's authority, although it was to be desired that the council not fail for this reason to treat matters of reform; Borja had written about the pope's reforming activity, and Laínez replied skeptically that they would see whether the results would be in keeping with the words. Trent, February 4, 1563, *Lainii Monumenta*, VI, 675 (No. 1775).

[195]See n. 192 *supra*. On January 30, 1563, Arco had reported to Ferdinand the reform measures that Pius IV had proposed in a consistory that day and had said that he intended to promulgate. Kassowitz, Anhang, No. 50, p. xxxi; this author remarks that exclusively harmless articles or those conducive to the interference of the Curia were discussed. (p. 156.).

the affair could not be brought to an end there but that every time the emperor would ask which chapters had to be left aside as pertaining to the pope, it would be necessary to do one of two things: either to declare that the greater part of the *libellus* was to be omitted or to allow many chapters to be laid before the council, thus falling back into the same difficulties in which they then found themselves. When Commendone during his audience discoursed on the disorder and extreme danger that would follow from any discussion of reforms touching the pope's authority, the emperor replied that he wished to have in writing what the nuncio had said in order that he might ponder and answer it better, adding that it was very necessary to remove abuses.[196]

Ferdinand did not intend to ponder the nuncios' arguments alone, for he had summoned three theologians--Peter Canisius, Francisco de Córdoba, and Friedrich Staphylus--to Innsbruck in addition to his counselors. Delfino felt little confidence in any of them. He thought that although Canisius was in every respect truly Catholic and pious, he was not very well versed in those doctrines in which one who wished to defend the power of the pope had to be particularly expert. He said that Córdoba had "many fantastic opinions" and a "too free tongue." Staphylus, in the nuncio's estimation, when treating the power of the pope, always spoke in such a way as to reveal himself as a student of Jean Gerson, and in such matters he was "certainly dangerous," so much the more that he differed much from Drasković, who in this area had "terrible ideas." Since Delfino recognized that his and Commendone's advice would be suspect to the emperor, he decided to do two things. One was to induce Ferdinand to add to his body of theologians Delfino's own theologian, Daniele Barboli, O.P., whom the emperor had recently presented to the episcopal see of Pedena (a town of Istria) and whom he had praised after hearing him preach. The other was to beg the legates to send to Innsbruck Jerónimo Nadal, who had recently been a visitator of the Jesuits' houses in France and could pretend to have come to recommend the Jesuits' other colleges to the emperor. Delfino believed that if these two theologians were appointed to the emperor's board, they would docilely follow the nuncio's directions; he also supposed that Ferdinand, being favorably impressed with Nadal, would appoint him, but if not, the Spanish Jesuit could still render many useful services at the nuncio's direction not only with the emperor but also with his fellow Spaniard, Francisco de Córdoba, and perhaps even with Staphylus. Delfino was to be disappointed in his hope of persuading Ferdinand to make Nadal one of his theological advisers and of thereby "pack-

[196]Delfino and Commendone to the legates, Innsbruck, February 8, 1563, Steinherz, III, 180-185 (No. 67). Cf. Giovanni Micheli to the Doge, Innsbruck, February 10, 1563, Turba, III, 218-219 (No. 110).

ing the court." The nuncio soon became less sanguine; he alerted the legates to the fact that some of those at the court were striving to keep Ferdinand convinced that whatever the pope did in regard to reform was of little or no importance for that true reform which the present state of affairs required, because they said, and even presumed to demonstrate, that the only way was for the council to decree the reform, and that meant that the emperor would insist on a reform by the council.[197]

Delfino not only wrote about Canisius but also spoke with him. Although the Jesuit was eager to return to Augsburg as early in Lent as possible, the nuncio dissuaded him from insisting that he be permitted to depart. Delfino also convinced him of the desirability of having Nadal sent to Innsbruck. Hence, Canisius presented this request to the father general, supporting it with only one argument, namely, that with Nadal's aid he could offer more effective opposition to the other two theologians, who would easily agree between themselves, as he feared, and he could defend the rights of the Church more appropriately. He thought that Córdoba and Staphylus followed their own opinions too freely and like hypercritical judges (Aristarchi) made imprudent pronouncements on things concerning the common good of the Church in the spirit of those who were silently contemplating a separation (discessionem). At this time the emperor was planning to have the theologians consider three points: (1) whether the articles of his libellus which the legates maintained should be suppressed ought to be proposed to the council; (2) whether the freedom of the council should be asserted, as if it were wrong that everything should be referred to the pope and approved by him before being published; and (3) reform, of which the patrons and defenders of the Roman Curia were thought to be entirely intolerant. Dreading the possibility of schism, Canisius understood how pessimistic the emperor and the other princes were about the council, and he feared that the Cardinal of Lorraine, who was to arrive at Innsbruck in a short time, would add fuel to the fire so that the flames would blaze up out of

[197]Delfino to the legates, Innsbruck, February 11, 1563, Steinherz, II. 188-190 (No. 69); also Braunsberger, IV, 952—953 (Monumenta tridentina, No. 542). Same to same, Innsbruck, February 12 and 14, 1563, Jedin, Geschichte, IV/1, 356, n. 12. On Nadal see Miguel Nicolau, S.I., Jerónimo Nadal, S.I. (1507-1580). Sus obras y doctrinas espirituales (Madrid, 1949), pp. 47-48. Miquel Batllori, S.I., Catalunya a l'època moderna. Recerques d'història cultural i religiosa, ed. Josep M. Benítez i Riera ("Col·lecció estudis i documents," 17 [Barcelona, 1971]), pp. 250-252; this chapter (IX) was originally published as "Jerónimo Nadal y el concilio de Trento" in the Bolleti de la Societat Arqueològica Lul·liana, 29 (1944-1947), 377-424; the Tridentine studies of this volume were published separately under the title Mallorca en Trento: Miscelánea conmemorative del IV centenario tridentino (Palma de Mallorca, 1946), pp. 11-58. Manuel Ruiz Jurado, S.I., "Cronología de la vida del P. Jerónimo Nadal S.I. (1507-1580)," Archivum Historicum Societatis Iesu, XLVIII (July-December, 1979), 248-276 at 267-268.

control.[198] From Canisius' observations too, one can judge how grave the situation had become by the middle of the winter.

When the rumors had first reached Rome that the Cardinal of Lorraine would go to Innsbruck for conferences with the emperor and that Ferdinand was planning some strange move regarding the council, the fearful curialists aroused great suspicions in the pope's mind. To remedy "such great jealousy," Cardinal Cicada and Bishop Gualterio recommended that Pius IV ask the Cardinal of Mantua to go to Innsbruck under the pretense of visiting the emperor as a relative (the cardinal's nephew, Duke Guglielmo, being the emperor's son-in-law); then he could use this opportunity to explore Ferdinand's attitude and to dispose him to consent to the closing of the council and to content himself with the rigorous reforms that the pope was making.[199] Although Cardinal Francesco Gonzaga argued against this proposal, the pope ordered him to ask his uncle to make the journey. Borromeo also composed a letter to the same effect to which both Pius and he added autograph postscripts stressing the importance of the mission and the seriousness of the pope's desire for a rigorous reform.[200] It was later decided, however, to let Cardinal Ercole Gonzaga himself choose the appropriate time, since Commendone had already gone to the imperial court.[201] The cardinal, however, declined the undertaking, probably because he considered himself ill-suited for such negotiations and possibly because he recognized that his health was failing and he did not feel well enough to travel, especially through the mountains in the winter.[202] As it turned out, he was dead within a fortnight.

The Cardinal of Lorraine's visit to the emperor at Innsbruck, where Maximilian, King now not only of Bohemia but of the Romans as well, Duke Albrecht of Bavaria, and the Archbishop of Salzburg were sojourning, was also the object of Visconti's speculation. He was sure that it would bring some new move in view of the emperor's dissatisfaction with the council and his collaboration

---

[198]Canisius to Laínez, Innsbruck, February 11, 1563, Braunsberger, IV, 49-51 (No. 778). Nadal arrived in Innsbruck within a week. For a justification of Canisius' practice of revealing the emperor's confidential negotiations to Laínez and Nadal see *ibid.*, pp. 40-42, and Brodrick, p. 528.

[199]Francesco Gonzaga to Ercole Gonzaga, Rome, February 10, 1563, Drei, XVIII, 142 (No. XCIII). The possibility of sending Hosius, the former nuncio at the imperial court, to Innsbruck was also discussed. On the same day the Mantuan agent Pia reported that the pope intended to annul the previously conceded regresses and to make the planned decree retroactive; consequently, many were frightened. Jedin, *Geschichte*, IV/2, 306, n. 6.

[200]Pius IV and Borromeo to Ercole Gonzaga, Rome, February 10, 1563, Susta, III, 224-225 (No. 62a).

[201]Vargas to Philip II, Rome, February 14, 1563, Döllinger, *Beiträge*, I, 486 (No. 144).

[202]Gonzaga's reply of February 19, 1563, has not been preserved, Susta, III, 229.

with the French. Visconti reported that some thought the purpose of Guise's visit was to consult Ferdinand so that, if they did not obtain what they desired from the council--the chalice for the laity, reform *in capite et in membris*, and a guarantee of the observance of the conciliar decrees--they might seek a pretext for departing and providing by themselves for the needs of their countries.[203] The seriousness of the situation also appears in other diplomatic dispatches. The Venetian ambassador reported that Maximilian had shown him letters from Rome and Trent intimating that one of the legates was to be sent to the emperor to discuss a suspension of the council; then, speaking of the council, the king said that since neither the pope nor the others on his side wished to be reformed, the emperor would "not fail to proceed to something which would be to the pope's dissatisfaction," and if the pope would not let himself be persuaded to take measures for the common good, some great disorder could result.[204] Simultaneously in France a messenger of the emperor told two English envoys, Sir Thomas Smith and Somers, "that the Emperor intended shortly to make a general meeting or Council, whereto all Princes might freely come. And that the Pope should not be master there, nor have other voice than any other Prelate had." In reply Smith warned him against the pope's subtlety and unwillingness to "abide any reformation"; he pointed to the last period at Trent as an example of what a council could do where the pope was a part of it. The messenger admitted that "those of the Council amused themselves about trifles," but he contended that "even there the Cardinal of Lorraine, and divers Bishops of Spain, France, and Germany, began to talk openly for the reformation of the Pope; and that the Italian prelates made pasquils of it." With bigoted incredulity Somers replied "that small credit was to be given to the Cardinal of Lorraine or to any Papist Prelate."[205] It is hard to conceive, nevertheless, of any messenger being authorized by Ferdinand to make such radical suggestions unless he was merely trying to draw the English out.

Without awaiting the arrival of the Cardinal of Lorraine, whom he met on his way back, the special nuncio, Commendone, left Inns-

---

[203]Visconti to Borromeo (memoire to Letter III), Trent, February 11, 1563, Aymon, I, 24, and Baluze, III, 440.

[204]Micheli to the Doge, Innsbruck, February 15, 1563, Turba, III, 219-220 (No. 111). Maximilian may have been referring to Prospero d'Arco's letter of February 3, in which suspension was said to be regarded as the only escape because to conclude the council without carrying out the reform would be to condemn the Protestants without aiding religion, while, on the other hand, to carry out a reform such as the princes demanded appeared to the curialists to be impossible; a suspension was not expected to offend either side. Sickel, *Concil,* p. 433.

[205]Smith to the Privy Council, Blois, February 17, 1563, *CSP, 1563,* p. 139 (No.323).

bruck and returned to Trent. He then submitted to the legates a long report in which he stated:

> I hold it as certain that His Majesty is so well disposed that if his goodness could be divided among the ecclesiastical and secular princes of Germany, it would be sufficient for the restoration of the Catholic religion in that land. Everyone sees how exemplary and holy the life and habits of His Majesty are. His zeal has always been great, but now, on the occasion of the council, it seems to me that it is becoming greater every day, both because His Majesty devotes much thought and effort to this and because he has and will have many who exhort him to it. On this goodness of his and on his many pious and holy words many ground a very sure hope that the emperor will never wish or hold *mordicus*, as they say, anything that may not be to our lord's [the pope's] satisfaction. In particular they add three reasons: one is that His Majesty is very firm in believing that the pope is superior to the council and that Seld, His Majesty's chief minister, holds the same; the second [reason] is that His Majesty not only is, but confesses to be, much obligated to His Holiness; the third reason is the close union of the Catholic King [Philip II] and of other princes with His Beatitude.
>
> As for his goodness, I for my part believe that the emperor, by that same goodness, is rather partly persuaded already by himself and partly can be more easily persuaded by others that in Christendom's extreme need it behooves him to take care of this common demand for reform in an ecumenical council, especially since the situation in Germany is peaceful enough and after such a long truce with the Turks and the election of the most serene king, his son. And the words that he is wont to use in his letters have given an indication of his intention--"Pro officio nostro caesareo" and "agnoscimus nos imperatorem" and "supremum ecclesiae advocatum" and other similar words worthy, in my opinion, of consideration.
>
> As for the second basis of His Majesty's many pious and holy words, I certainly deem it of great importance, since His Majesty is a man of much faith and truth. But precisely for this reason I think it is sometimes more dangerous to interpret his words more broadly than what His Majesty is accustomed to say sincerely and very modestly. As far as the discussions that I have had with him are concerned, I have been considering that some of his words are general, and these, in my judgment, can with difficulty be alleged in proof against what His Ma-

jesty says particularly and expressly he is obliged by his conscience to do and in fact orders his ambassadors to do . . . .

Of His Majesty's love and reverence for our lord [Pius IV] I have no doubt. Nevertheless, I have read in His Majesty's latest letters to his ambassadors: "For the sake of reform we have supposed that we should not have regard for any man but [only] for our imperial office, that we might urge the matter as forcefully as possible," and a little farther on: "And so we wish and strictly enjoin you to renew this activity."[206]

Commendone did not take up the third reason for the complacency of many curialists, namely, the pope's good relations with Philip II and other princes. He continued:

I have not heard His Majesty or Seld or any other counselor speak about the opinion of His Majesty and Seld that the pope is superior to the council. I have heard that the most serious and principal complaint that they are making in that court is [based] on the persuasion that they have that here [at Trent] nothing can be done without express and explicit orders from Rome; and moreover, I have heard that in these days His Majesty has complained about some decrees recently made in Rome prejudicial to the council, as if one were declaring through them that the pope is superior to the council . . . .

Commendone concluded that he had seen not only in the emperor but also in his principal ministers, such as Seld, a most ardent desire for reform and for the progress of the council, as well as a firm impression that many at Trent did not wish any reform. Consequently, he suspected that the confidence that had been placed in the emperor's good-will up till then by those who delayed the opportune remedies had done more harm than good and had only confirmed Ferdinand's opinion that on the papal side there was no desire to act sincerely. From this opinion, the nuncio feared, the emperor could be led to go beyond what he would have done in the beginning. In view of the rumors about a suspension or dissolution of the council, Commendone quoted those who were trying to persuade the emperor that in such a case it was incumbent on him "to take up the

---

[206]These quotations are taken with some variations from Ferdinand's letter of January 17, 1563, to his ambassadors at Trent, Sickel, *Concil,* pp. 419-420 (No. CCXXIX). Cf. n. 179 *supra.* Cf. his reply to the pope's remonstrances against his support of the French petitions: Ferdinand to Arco, February 22, 1563, *ibid.,* pp. 426-427.

cause of the Church of which he is the advocate and protector," and the nuncio cautioned that it might be difficult to remove this notion from his mind, although Ferdinand professed not to lay down laws for the council but to accept them from it. To Commendone the assembly of theologians at Innsbruck was also a source of disquietude, for perhaps it would only serve to reassure the emperor in his own inclinations. One of the principal points proposed to the theologians, furthermore, was to what extent and in what way the council should handle the problem of reform, and at that juncture the Sorbonists, as he called the Cardinal of Lorraine and the nine French bishops and other theologians in his suite, arrived at the imperial court. Commendone feared that the imperialists and the French would expand the petitions of the *libellus* to fashion in their own way a greater and more complete reform. In the nuncio's opinion, it was fortunate that Canisius, "a man of very great goodness and learning and a great defender of the papal power," was among the theologians at Innsbruck, but Commendone feared that in this respect the Jesuit was alone or almost alone.[207] This realistic analysis of the mentality prevailing at Innsbruck, along with the nuncio's unstated but evident failure to obtain any definite answer from the emperor, must have increased the legates' apprehensions.

While Commendone was composing his report, the permanent nuncio at the imperial court was endeavoring to prevent the Cardinal of Lorraine from concluding with the emperor any agreement prejudicial to the Holy See. In a conversation with Delfino held before the cardinal began his discussion with Ferdinand he stated frankly that a few cardinals who wished to be pope and a few bishops who wished to be cardinals were ruining the world, and he added that if the reform were not undertaken by the council it would not be accepted by France. Delfino tried to show him that it should not seem strange that the pope wished to preserve the privileges of the Holy See and neither should nor could yield those he held by the grace of God and his predecessors had possessed for so many centuries. Since Lorraine insisted that whatever was not decreed by the council could be altered at any moment, Delfino endeavored to dispel that fear, arguing that the present state of affairs had made Pius IV and every pope very firm, and that without very great and more than sufficient grounds Pius would not disregard any part of the reform he had issued.[208] These unsupported assertions must have made little impression on the French cardinal. Delfino was soon to learn how closely the emperor's views on these matters coincided with Guise's.

---

[207]Commendone to the legates, Trent, February 19, 1563, Poggiani, III, 243-245; also Steinherz, III, 198-204 (No. 73).

[208]Delfino to the legates, Innsbruck, February 18, 1563, Steinherz, III, 196-197 (No. 72).

While awaiting the outcome of Commendone's discussions with the emperor, however, the legates had not forgotten the urgency of proposing reform measures to the council. On February 15 they implored the pope to send them as soon as possible his decision regarding both the French petitions and those of the emperor. To explain their importunity they said that since nothing had been done yet, the ambassadors were extremely discontented and were murmuring that the legates took no heed of the emperor and the princes and that the rulers would have to look after these matters themselves. Such talk greatly annoyed the legates, who told Borromeo that if he knew the ways and maneuvers to which they had resorted to arrive at that point without presenting or allowing to be presented any of those petitions, he would say that it was impossible to withhold them any longer. They feared that otherwise some disorder would occur to their prejudice and dishonor.[209] On that same day, however, they recieved the oral communication that the Bishop of Nola, Antonio Scarampi, brought from Pius IV and Borromeo. In response they declared themselves pleased with the pope's favorable disposition toward the council and his readiness for reform, and they prayed that it could be carried out promptly to the full satisfaction of all parties so that Christendom might be set in order and the pope relieved of vexation and expense with lasting glory.[210] When Borromeo received the legates' first letter of February 15 repeating their request for advice, he threw the blame back on them and rebuked them sharply, saying that the pope had sent the French petitions back to them and had not expected any more trouble about the emperor's *libellus* because four and a half months previously he had sent them his annotations attached to a summary of the *libellus* and had then left everything to their judgment. The cardinal nephew suggested that if the legates would reread his letter of October 3, 1562, they would understand that they had nothing more to expect from the pope and that rather the pope and Borromeo were the ones to expect that the legates would have done something about the presentation of the *libellus*, since the pope had agreed that they might present even the whole document as it stood if they considered it advisable. Now, however, that Delfino had reported that the emperor would be content if the legates extracted certain articles and proposed them to the council without the others, Borromeo advised them not to present the whole *libellus*.[211] At this time, of course, Borromeo had not seen Commen-

---

[209]The legates to Borromeo, Trent, February 15, 1563, Susta, III, 219 (No. 61).

[210]The legates to Borromeo, Trent, February 15, 1563, Grisar, I, 508 (Appendix, No. 62).

[211]Borromeo to the legates, Rome, February 21, 1563, Susta, III, 239-241 (No. 66). Cf. Borromeo to the legates, Rome, February 25, 1563, *ibid.*, p. 245 (No. 67), where the legates were instructed not to propose the chapters from the French petitions and the emperor's *libellus* that they had selected as good and reasonable.

done's interpretation of the emperor's attitude, which differed so essentially from Delfino's on this point. The cardinal secretary was also unfair in reproving the legates for neglecting their duty when he knew that they were paralyzed by the division fomented within the legatine college by the pope's own lack of confidence in Gonzaga and Seripando and his secret correspondence with the reactionary curialist, Simonetta. In these matters Hosius sided with Simonetta not out of self-interest but out of religious conviction.

When Commendone returned to Trent he brought along a letter from Canisius to Hosius. The cardinal legate's dejected spirit is evident in his reply. He deplored the danger that under the specious name of reform a deformation would be effected, for there were some even of the household of faith who longed to call back to order the one through whom, till then, order and unity, as well as the majesty of princes, had been preserved in a large part of the world. He lamented, "What we expected from the Protestants we now see being done by those who profess themselves to be sons of the mother Church."[212] Hosius was undoubtedly alluding to those, among others, with whom Canisius was discussing matters pertaining to the council at Innsbruck.

On the following day Hosius unfolded his thoughts on the same subject at greater length to Canisius. (There was no one, he said, to whom he wrote more confidently than to this correspondent.) The fire has indeed been kindled, he exclaimed, and would that the flames not be increased by those by whom they ought to be extinguished! Even those adorned with the sacred infulae and those who seemed to surpass others in religion drove this matter on with uncontrolled force. He cited the example of Constantine, who burned the booklets in which the crimes of bishops and priests were contained, saying that he should be judged by them, not they by him. He added:

> Now certain persons are suggesting to pious, orthodox, and Catholic princes, not that they themselves judge, but that they let be judged not just any bishop or priest, but him who is the prince of bishops, by those who come to be judged by him; that members judge the head, sheep the shepherd, and subjects him to whom by divine law they are subject. What is this but to overthrow all order and to wish him to be forced into order, when if his dignity is preserved all order in the Church is preserved.

Then Hosius offered another example illustrating the principle that the first see is not judged by anyone. He denied that he was one who

---

[212]Hosius to Canisius, Trent, February 18 or 19, 1563, Braunsberger, IV, 63 (No. 785).

would present a defense for the sins of the Roman Curia, to which he professed himself to be as opposed as was St. Bernard, who detested them but still wished the authority and dignity of the first see to be preserved. He admitted that the wrongdoings of the Curia should be corrected, but he asked by whom they should be corrected. He would say to the pope, "Judge your own case and that of your Curia yourself," and would beg him to root out all the vices, for to invert the proper order seemed to him to be no less a sin than those sins because of which that would be done. It would mean the establishment of anarchy and not so much the reform which was being demanded with loud cries as a deformation. He thought that he would not be rash in affirming that there was more danger in this mode of reforming than in dissimulating the evils that the Church had tolerated till then. Asserting that anyone who refused reform was worthy of reproach, still he could not see how a new way of reform could be sought with a great confusion of everything and an upheaval of the whole world. In his opinion it was a question of the dignity and authority not only of the pope but of all those in a position of power, for some day the subjects of the latter might wish to be permitted to do the same to them as they wished to be permitted to those who were subject to his power.[213] Although Hosius' ecclesiology may have been vitiated by his monarchical theory, his integrity shone forth. His position proves that not all those who were opposed to any attempt to reform on the pope were motivated by selfish considerations.

The recipient of these letters, Peter Canisius, was meanwhile involved in the deliberations of the emperor's theological commission. The foundation for their work was laid by Drasković, who, after his arrival at Innsbruck, first reported to Ferdinand orally in an audience on January 31 and then at his behest set forth in a paper the principal requirements for a fruitful celebration of the council. Weighing the relative advantages of a continuation and a suspension of the council, he said that he would recommend the latter if he knew that the pope, the emperor, and the other princes did not wish to undertake a serious reform, for it would be better for the council to be suspended with some hope of future reconciliation and reform than to be concluded without fruit and with the loss of hope. If the council, on the other hand, was to be continued, it had to have due freedom from Roman dictation, and the exclusive right of the legates to propose matters for deliberation had to be abrogated. In Drasković's opinion, the more necessary articles of the *libellus* and of the French list should, at the emperor's choice, be laid before the fathers, so that not one or another of the legates would judge them but rather the whole council would give its verdict and would pro-

---

[213]Hosius to Canisius, Trent, February 19 or 20, 1563, Braunsberger, IV, 68-73 (No. 786).

nounce what it judged to be expedient for the *respublica christiana*. If there were some petitions that deserved to be rejected, then everyone would understand that that was done not by the connivance of the pope and the emperor, as the heretics claimed, but by the authority of the whole ecumenical council. This could be done all the more easily since the *libellus* was already in everybody's hands. Among his other recommendations the Bishop of Pécs also exhorted the emperor to go to Trent as his pious predecessors had gone to ecumenical councils.[214] Obviously the episcopal ambassador regarded the emperor's intervention as the only means of rescuing the council.

With Draskovič's help the imperial vice-chancellor then compiled seventeen articles on the affairs of the council for study. Some of them dealt with the questions of adjourning, suspending, or continuing the council and of winning its due freedom. Article VI asked whether the business of reform should still be urged vehemently, and which points in particular. Article VII read:

> Whether those articles [of the *libellus*] which regard the person of the Supreme Pontiff and the Roman Curia are to be omitted? And in case it should seem good that they be pressed, whether and how precaution should be taken that the minds of His Holiness and the Roman Curia may not be offended thereby so that they seize the occasion to break off the council. In this place let the reform articles proposed by His Majesty be carefully examined, together with the notes composed on them, especially as regards restricting the number of cardinals and limiting the license of dispensations.[215]

Each member of the commission was to reply in writing.

The chairman of the commission, Bishop Draskovič, reiterated the views that he had expressed in his earlier report. To the sixth question he replied that the matter of reform should be urged most earnestly (*vehementissime*) lest the majority of the fathers in the council and the Christian world itself be scandalized; this should be done by urging the presentation and examination of the emperor's *libellus* and the French petitions, which together contained the whole of a universal reform; but he recommended moderation. In response to Article VII the Bishop of Pécs thought that what pertained properly to the reform of the pope's person should not at all be urged in the emperor's name, since even with his silence it could not be omitted. Regarding the reform of the conclave and of the

---

[214]Draskovič to Ferdinand, Innsbruck, February 2, 1563, Sickel, *Concil*, pp. 427-430 (No. CCXXXII).
[215]Seld to Canisius, Innsbruck, February 15, 1563, Braunsberger, IV, 58-59 (No. 783).

Roman Curia, the Hungarian ambassador believed that the emperor could deal with the pope much more successfully in private than in public in order that in this way "that odious and pernicious discussion of the superiority of the pope and the council," which seemed to be imminent, could be avoided. He also stated his desire that the number of cardinals be limited, but if this could not be done, he saw no reason for failing to take up the age and ability of those to be elevated to that dignity; specifically he wanted the requirements for them to be the same as those decreed by other councils and by the present one for candidates for the episcopate, and he did not think that by determining this the council would prejudice the pope's authority since it did not do so by prescribing qualifications for episcopal candidates.[216] In general it seems that Drasković's former ardor had been tempered with a good measure of prudence; in some respects his vision of reform was to be realized by the end of the year.

Two other members of the commission submitted contradictory opinions. Francisco de Córdoba recommended that the emperor's reform articles be treated by the council altogether and in order. Barboli, on the other hand, insisted that the pope remain outside the council's reforming activity "as an absolute lord not recognizing any superior on earth." To determine the number of the cardinals or to limit dispensations would tie his hands. Since the demands of the French and the Spaniards aimed at a restriction of the papal power, they were inadmissible.[217] Delfino had been wise to strengthen his side by having this Dominican bishop-elect added to the commission in order to counterbalance the weight of the Spanish Franciscan.

The fourth member of the commission, Peter Canisius, reduced all the questions to two categories--those dealing with the preservation and advancement of the council and those dealing with the reform of ecclesiastics. In the former category he recommended that the emperor strive to fix a place--either Bologna or Mantua or some other neighboring town--where at the earliest possible time he could meet the pope, for there much more agreeably than in Trent matters pertaining to the council and reform could be negotiated; this would be the occasion to propose and urge whatever was desired for the reform of the pope and his Curia. Canisius could think of no more convenient and efficacious way by which the wounds that were then felt could be healed and the even greater dangers which were feared could be dispelled both from the council and from all of Christendom. Answering the question about the omission of the reform

---

[216]"Gutachten des Bischofs von Fünfkirchen," Innsbruck, February 22, 1563, Sickel, *Concil,* pp. 442-444 (No. CCXXXV).

[217]Sickel, *Concil,* p. 445. Singkhmoser put the same date, February 22, 1563, on all four responses.

articles regarding the pope's person and Curia, Canisius replied that
these articles should not be omitted but still should not be pressed
before the fathers of the council. For this advice he gave several
reasons: first, lest the emperor who by divine right was subject like
a sheep to the supreme shepherd and pontiff might seem to wish to
prescribe laws for him through the council; secondly, lest, if that
were done, the opinion would be confirmed that the council's
authority was greater than the pope's, and the holders of that
opinion would then obey the pope less and would more and more
withdraw themselves from his authority; thirdly, lest some might
appeal from the government of the pope to the decision of the council and might more easily make a legal exception against the Roman
Church; fourthly, because that procedure, which was in many ways
dangerous in that time of turbulence and sedition, would make the
pope's authority, which was otherwise attacked and widely despised, even more unpopular; finally, because there were many ancient and approved canons and many councils held under popes
from which a similar or still greater reform could have been demanded, but nothing of the sort was proposed or done in them; on
the contrary, both the canons and historical facts showed that the
pope could not be judged by anyone. Canisius recognized, nevertheless, that the reform, if there was to be any, should begin with
the head and the primary see, and that therefore it would be worth
the trouble to bring it about that the shepherd of shepherds apply
his mind to the necessary reform. Hence, the emperor would merit
well of the Church if he were to take it up in person with the pope
who was most friendly to him; but if the emperor were prevented by
other affairs from meeting the pope in the near future, he should
send to him some wise and God-fearing men who would undertake
this project for the common advantage and need of the Church.
Among the things that should be proposed to the pope Canisius
wished to have explicit mention made of the removal of the abuses
which were customary at Rome during the conclave; he recommended that a very severe bull prohibit the crimes of those who engaged
in dishonorable practices at the time of a papal election and often
gave scandal to others. As far as the number of the cardinals was
concerned, the Jesuit believed that the responsibility for reducing it
belonged not to the council but to the Apostolic See and the Roman
Church. It was his advice, therefore, that this matter be taken up
with the pope, whose authority it was neither right nor proper to
limit so that he could not choose more or fewer cardinals according
to the needs of the Church and the merits of the candidates. He
observed that if the pope were to enact any regulation in this regard,
it would be a matter of human, not divine, law and consequently
liable to dispensation. Passing on to the question of dispensation,
Canisius admitted the great corruption that had become prevalent.
The emperor would act wisely and piously, he stated, if he used his
influence so that dispensations might not be granted at Rome so frequently and easily, without restraint or legitimate grounds, and for

the sake of profit, for thus it happened that ecclesiastical laws were violated and generally relaxed and as a result came not only to be neglected but even brought into open contempt, while the lawlessness of the common people raged. He uttered the caution, however, that the pope's dispensing power could not be taken away because of such abuse, for it was not only useful but even necessary in the Church as in any human polity. On the other hand, Canisius endorsed the articles of the *libellus* requesting moderation in the granting of exemptions and the inflicting of excommunications.[218] The whole paper bespoke the anxiety of a conscientious churchman to solve the religious problems of the age, but it also betrayed his lack of personal familiarity with the Roman Curia.

In composing his memorial, Canisius was assisted both by Nadal, whom Ferdinand had consulted but had not appointed to the commission, and by Antonio Maria Graziani, Commendone's secretary, who had remained behind in Innsbruck after the special nuncio's return to Trent. Canisius at first intended to let the wording of the *libellus* stand to the effect that the pope should be asked "*ut patiatur reformari,*" but when Graziani objected that that phrase was offensive and unjust, Canisius changed it to read that the pope should be asked to reform himself and the Roman Curia. Graziani reported that at his request the Jesuit also revised many other passages, but he remarked that Commendone could imagine the animadversions of the other theologians when Canisius, who could be called a saint, was willing to have things that would offend Rome. In Graziani's judgment, however, the Jesuit's final paper was "very pious and full of learning" and could not help but please the emperor. Canisius also told Graziani that the Cardinal of Lorraine had communicated to him that Delfino had complained to him that the cardinal and the other Frenchmen wanted to be the "cause of the ruin of the Church" with their demands that aimed at nothing but attacking the authority of the Apostolic See; the nuncio also said that such things should be treated directly with the pope. Canisius feared that this disagreement would injure the nuncio's cause, for the cardinal would unite with the emperor in a common move.[219] The nuncio was also hard pressed to rationalize Pius IV's recent creation of two unqualified cardinals. From Canisius and Barboli he

[218]Canisius to Seld, Innsbruck, February 22, 1563, Braunsberger, IV, 75, 83, 85-91 (No. 788). For an English translation of large portions of Canisius' memorial see Brodrick, pp. 531-540.

[219]Graziani to Commendone, Innsbruck, February 19 and 21, 1563, Döllinger, *Beiträge,* III, 324-329, and Braunsberger, IV, 98-99. While praising Canisus' "great piety and prudence," Graziani commented that the Jesuit had treated all the articles "with many words, according to the custom of German writings." After learning of Seld's seventeen articles from Canisius, Graziani reported them to Commendone as well as he could remember them.

heard that the emperor had said many things about the case and could not forget what had been done against his liking; moreover, he had called so many dispensations "dissipations," and almost with tears had said that if reform were not carried out in a lasting manner and if it could be altered every day, Christendom would remain without a remedy. Ferdinand had reminded them that Paul IV too had made a great reform in the affairs of the Court of Rome but that everything went up in smoke. Having been previously instructed by the nuncio, Canisius and Barboli replied to the emperor that the pope had remedied these ills by himself and was still at work; as for finding a way to make the reforms permanent, they said that such a thing could be done only by the pope and that one should not think of involving the authority of the council but rather could beg the pope to take all the measures; they assured the emperor that then the pope, without prejudice to the privileges of the Holy See, would not fail to do what he could.[220] Such assurances must have had a hollow ring after the promotion of the young cadets of the ducal families of Florence and Mantua.

The pope was annoyed by the significance that the emperor attached to this deed, not admitting that his credibility should be affected by his conduct. Borromeo repeated the arguments and came closer to the real motive when he mentioned the importance of the dukes of Florence and Mantua in Italy. Since it was also rumored that Pius intended to create several more cardinals, his nephew authorized the nuncio to assure those at the imperial court that "for now" the pope did not have any such thought but preferred to see a good end to the council and to attend to such a reform that all good men would have to be satisfied with it "forever." In earnest of this pledge Borromeo sent the nuncio a list of the restrictions imposed on the Datary in the last consistory.[221] The outcome of what has been called the emperor's bye-council at Innsbruck, however, was not affected by such promises.

The nuncio meanwhile was striving to convince Ferdinand that no discussion *de reformando capite* should ever be held in the council and that whatever would be related to this subject, such as the reform of the Court of Rome, should be left to the pope. Delfino

---

[220]Delfino to the legates, Innsbruck, February 20, 1563, Steinherz, III, 210 (No. 74). A week earlier the cardinal nephew had ordered the nuncio to repeat to Ferdinand that the pope would execute the reform much more strictly than others would expect or perhaps desire, for he did not wish to fail to do all the right things requested by the emperor and the French and many others besides; but he could not tolerate any attempt, under the guise of words, to prejudice the authority that God alone had given to that see. Ominously the cardinal added: "We shall always do what will be possible so that progress may be made with peace, harmony, and charity, but if we will be paid with such bad coin, no one will be able to accuse us if we try to protect and defend our duty." Borromeo to Delfino, February 13, 1563, *ibid.*, p. 194 (No. 71).
[221]Borromeo to Delfino, Rome, February 21, 1563, Steinherz, III, 214-215 (No. 75).

warned him against "restricting or diminishing the absolute and free privileges of the Apostolic See" by having things done in the council or hastening the firmness of the reform. The nuncio predicted to the legates that the emperor's conclusion would be far from prejudicing the pope's authority; although he would continue to demand a severe reform, he would acquiesce little by little and in the end would be content with what he could get.[222] This forecast was not to be verified so easily as Delfino expected.

Being less well informed, the bishops at Trent entertained grave misgivings about the resolutions of the theologians assembled at Inns-bruck. Some feared that the fundamental question being discussed there concerned the proper role of an emperor in a general council and that this would cause trouble because Ferdinand had "some bad counselors" who made the imperial authority much greater than it really was in matters pertaining to the care of the Church.[223] Others supposed that since the imperialists and the French were thinking about nothing but reform, which was also desired by the princes and the whole world, it would be necessary to enact it and to make it strong and general so that even the princes would have reason to fear it; they believed that this would be the real way to make them keep silent and to remove the malicious opinions spread about.[224] This may have been the brave talk of those who concluded that they could ward off reform no longer. When the Cardinal of Lorraine returned to Trent, however, he let it be known that as long as the pope would carry out a good and vigorous reform, the emperor and the French would not ask anything touching on his authority. Guise asserted, furthermore, that Philip II would also concur in this decision.[225]

This answer to one of the most vital questions studied at Inns-bruck was the first result not only of Lorraine's conference with Ferdinand and Maximilian but also of the consultation of the

---

[222]Delfino to the legates, Innsbruck, February 24, 1563, Steinherz, III, 217-218 (No. 76). Delfino also told the Venetian ambassador that the emperor would limit himself to four or five points and would not ask that anything be treated which would diminish the pope's authority. Micheli to the Doge, Innsbruck, March 1, 1563, Turba, III, 223 (No. 113).

[223]Calini to Cornaro, Trent, February 25, 1563, Marani, p. 411.

[224]Visconti to Borromeo (memoire to Letter VII), Trent, February 24, 1563, Aymon, I, 62-72, and Baluze, III, 444.

[225]Visconti to Borromeo (memoire to Letter VIII), Trent, March, 1, 1563, Aymon, I, 84, and Baluze, III, 445-446. Meyenhofer (*op. cit.*, p. 196) remarks that Lorraine's success found its literary expression in Ferdinand's letters of March 3 to the pope and the legates (see notes 228 and 229 *infra*). The cardinal succeeded in bringing it about that France and the emperor were at last pursuing a common conciliar policy and were even supported by the King of Spain in it. But the Curia quickly found the weak spot in the alliance, namely, that the two partners held different opinions on the primacy of jurisdiction and the person of the pope, and thus Cardinal Morone could restore Ferdinand's trust in the management of the council in the spring of the same year.

theologians. Their four memorials could be spread out in this order from left to right: Córdoba's, Drašković's, Canisius', and Barboli's. Between the radical reformism of the Spanish Franciscan and the extreme curialism of the Italian Dominican stood the Hungarian bishop and the Dutch Jesuit. The two in the middle, however, had assumed independent standpoints; Drašković represented a moderate form of Ferdinand's reform Catholicism, and Canisius an enlightened conservatism, though the views of both corresponded in principle to a strongly ecclesiastical position.[226] Writing to Hosius after he had returned to Augsburg, Canisius lamented that some of the reformers wished to be deformers and to increase the diseases rather than heal them. He attributed to a temptation of Satan the fact that some tried to attack and weaken the authority of him who alone had always been and had to be the foremost judge of the Church, established by Christ himself. Next to this effort he set the plans of the princes, who did not care to be sheep of the shepherd but had to set themselves up as judges and reformers of pontiffs, fathers, and the whole clerical order. Hence, he sympathized with the legates because the imperialists were such captious (*morosi*) and unfair appraisers of things.[227] These harsh comments suggest the intensity of the struggle waged at Innsbruck.

The final decisions issuing from all these deliberations were embodied in three letters dated March 3, 1563. Two were addressed to the pope--one open and the other confidential--and the third to Drašković and the other imperial ambassadors to the council. In the open letter the emperor described the alarming plight of the council and enumerated the evil consequences that would result from its dissolution or suspension. He urged that the freedom traditional in ecumenical councils--whether of the fathers and ambassadors to make proposals or of the participants to speak and vote as they wished--be respected and safeguarded. Attempting to disarm the pope in advance, he stated that he was not making these requests in order to lay down a law for the pope or to instruct him how to discharge his pastoral duty or to weaken or question the dignity and authority that rightly belonged to him. But since he had been apprised of various facts by which people were being alienated from the pope and the Apostolic See, Ferdinand considered it his function, ''as the first-born and most obedient son of the Church and its advocate,'' to inform the pope about these evils and to beg him to

---

[226]Cf. Kassowitz, p. 166.
[227]Canisius to Hosius, Augsburg, March 11, 1563, Braunsberger, IV, 113-114 (No. 797). This was a reply to Hosius' letter of February 19 or 20 (see n. 213 *supra*). Canisius was soon informed that he and Nadal were held in high repute at the Court of Rome for their good offices in aid of religion and of the authority of the Apostolic See. Polanco to Canisius, Trent, March 14, 1563, *ibid.*, p. 118 (No. 799).

apply an apt remedy to them with his good judgment. For this purpose the emperor promised to stand by him with his filial assistance
and to render every service proper to his office.[228]

In the secret letter, on the other hand, the emperor spoke in more
pointed language about the matters that his counselors had advised
him to treat directly with the pope and that he had mentioned only
lightly or had passed over in silence in the open letter out of respect
for the pope. He stressed the need of beginning the reform at the
head and source, but while he complained about the delay of reform
work, he excluded from this censure the person of the pope, in
whom, he said, he did not find missing either dutifulness (*pietatem*),
conscientiousness (*religionem*), virtuousness (*sanctimoniam vitae*),
or any of the things that could be sought in a holy and uncorrupted
shepherd. The first requirement for reform, in his opinion, was to
establish a mode of electing the pope by which every way of aspiring
to that dignity be closed in the future to those who were not fit for
it. Going on to a delicate subject, Ferdinand pleaded that simony
and all illegal intrigues which had occurred in past conclaves in
spite of the cardinals' oath be completely eliminated in the future.
He expatiated on the need that the electors be such as would be willing and able to choose a pope to whom Christ's Church could be
safely entrusted; he reminded Pius of the very serious complaints
heard at that time, namely, that sometimes cardinals were created
who partly were still lacking sound judgment because of their youth
and partly were unlearned, so that they could not advise the pope in
regard to the government of the Church and would follow their
"private passions" in a papal election and obstruct the votes of
good and learned men. Since the unsuited cardinals aspired to the
papacy just as the most learned and experienced one did, they had
recourse to improper and unlawful means to achieve their goal. To
Ferdinand it was obvious what was to be expected of a pope elected
by such cardinals through simony or other illicit machinations.
Hence, he drew the lesson of the importance of appointing to the
cardinalate men outstanding for their learning, piety, wisdom, and
experience. The emperor did not reprove the pope for sustaining,
guarding, and preserving his authority and dignity, which belonged
to him and his successors according to God's commandment and
Sacred Scripture as well as the sacred canons and many approved
councils, because he could not do otherwise in keeping with his
pastoral duty. With a candor that would sound condescending in
Rome, nevertheless, Ferdinand counseled Pius to adopt that
method of preserving his apostolic authority which would evidence
that the pope was seeking "nothing but the honor of the divine majesty and the increase of the faith and the Church, as well as the

---

[228]Ferdinand to Pius IV, Innsbruck, March 3, 1563, Raynaldus, 1563, No. 34,
p.331-334, and Le Plat, V, 690-694, with corrections in Sickel, *Concil,* pp. 449-450.

edification of Christ's people," lest someone be able rightly to object that the pope was striving not for Christ's glory but for his own, regardless of the needs of the Church. Ferdinand trusted that in the exercise of his pastoral office the pope would always keep in mind that "by his vigilance, care, and effort" many thousands of souls should be gained for Christ, and he promised that in this way the pope would have in him a most ardent (*acerrimus*) defender of his apostolic authority and power.[229] The fact that the emperor conveyed these exhortations in a secret letter rather than in public would seem to confirm his claim to be acting out of conscientious motives.

On the same day the emperor issued fresh instructions to Drasković and his other two ambassadors at Trent. They were to communicate to the legates a copy of his open letter to the pope and to ask them not only to press upon the pope that he give the emperor's admonition his benign consideration but also to accede to his advice and conform their conduct to it. The ambassadors, moreover, were to take the greatest care that "that very odious question about the superiority of the council over the pope or of the pope over the council be avoided." Drasković was also to relate to the Cardinal of Lorraine what had happened at Innsbruck after the cardinal's departure, give him a copy of the open letter and intimate the contents of the secret one, and promise to communicate to him any further instructions that the emperor might send his ambassadors after receiving the pope's reply. He recognized that he might seem to be harsher in some points than the pope had expected.[230] On the day before all these letters were dispatched, an event occurred at Trent, unknown, of course, to the court at Inns-

---

[229]Ferdinand to Pius IV *(arcanae litterae),*Innsbruck, March 3, 1563, Raynaldus, 1563, No. 37, pp. 336-338, and Le Plat, V, 697, 701, with corrections in Sickel, *Concil,* p. 450; also Steinherz, III, 223-234 (No. 79). Loewe has tried to trace the influence of Francisco de Córdoba on this letter and has pointed out some striking similarities to the thoughts and views expressed in the friar's writings (pp. 61-63). Jedin comments that both letters, especially the second, bespoke the deeply Catholic ruler's burning concern about the fate of the Church which he believed was seriously endangered by the Curia's conciliar policy. The sending of these letters was an act of high politics. The emperor did not interfere directly in the conduct of the council; he respected the pope's supreme power of direction and did not wish to touch his authority. But he knew—or at least thought that he knew—that the cause of the crisis of the council in the final analysis did not lie in the ecclesiological differences which had emerged in the debate over the decree on Orders but rather in the pope's fear of a conciliar reform of the entire curial system. The emperor desired that this reform should be accomplished by the council, because otherwise it would remain superficial like all previous starts at reform. To the pope such an invasion by the council of his personal sphere appeared to be an attempt to carry out the conciliarist doctrine of the superiority of the council over the pope. *Geschichte,* IV/1, 263.

[230]Ferdinand to Drasković and his colleagues, Innsbruck, March 3, 1563, Sickel, *Concil,* pp. 446-449 (No. CCXXXVI). Ferdinand also wrote a brief letter directly to the Cardinal of Lorraine, Innsbruck, March 3, 1563, Le Plat, V, 690.

bruck, which was to entail profound consequences; this was the death of the Cardinal of Mantua, which opened the way for the appointment of a new president of the council, Cardinal Morone.

Before leaving Innsbruck, Drasković assured the nuncio of his desire for the calm and fruitful progress of the council, and he swore that he would prove himself to be most obedient to the pope and most respectful to the legates. Staphylus also affirmed that the resolutions could not offend the papal side in any way, stating, "You have emerged the victor in the more important articles." Delfino believed that if Staphylus had not given faithful counsel, the advice of the Franciscan, a "dangerous Gersonist," would have caused much trouble.[231] Two days after he sent this consoling news to the legates, the complacent nuncio wrote them that Drasković had been ordered not to demand for the emperor things that would offend them and that the Hungarian bishop would never again utter another word either about having the council reform the Church *in capite* or about limiting the number of the cardinals or about similar matters which Delfino considered injurious to the pope's authority. During the consultation, the nuncio reported, the emperor had told each one clearly to live unswervingly under the obedience of the pope.[232] Delfino might have had misgivings, however, if he had been aware of Ferdinand's secret letter to Pius IV.

---

[231]Delfino to the legates, Innsbruck, March 4, 1563, Steinherz, III, 235-236 (No. 80).

[232]Delfino to the legates, Innsbruck, March 6, 1563, Steinherz, III, 242-243 (No. 83). Three days later Ferdinand gave the nuncio his reply to the pope's request for protection against the Spanish and French bishops in the council who were calling into question the pope's due power and authority to rule and shepherd the universal Church. The emperor declared that he had no doubt about this matter; in his letters he had always addressed the pope with that title and had never hesitated to call him the supreme pontiff of the holy Roman and universal Church. He also assured Pius that as far as he could, mindful of his imperial duty, he would alawys protect, defend, and maintain the due and competent authority and power of the pope as behooved him. He had already ordered his ambassadors at the council to discuss this matter with the Spanish and French bishops and to dissuade them from all unnecessary disputations. Nevertheless, the emperor "reverently and courteously" warned Pius that if he would attempt to extend his authority and power and thereby to weaken and diminish the authority of the council or would wish all to admit tacitly what many denied openly (that is, the pope's superiority over the council), he would arouse a very difficult and serious controversy which it would be advantageous at that turbulent time to avoid. Hence, the emperor in turn asked the pope to respect the due and competent authority of the ecumenical council. "Responsum ab Imperatore Ferdinando datum nuntio pontificis," March 9, 1563, Le Plat, V, 716-717.

According to the Florentine ambassador to the council, after Drasković returned to Trent he presented the emperor's letters to the legates, but finding Seripando ill, he told some confidant that he did not wish to deal with the other two legates (Hosius and Simonetta) and preferred to wait to see what decision the pope would make. The imperial ambassador was observed to be in close contact with the French ambassadors but it was not known what intrigues they were planning. Strozzi to Cosimo I, Trent, March 11, 1563, D'Addario, pp. 280-281 (No. CLX).

Equally unsuspecting that a courier was on his way from Innsbruck, the pope sent a brief to the emperor on March 6. He maintained that he had done everything that could have been expected of him to facilitate the progress of the council, but he grieved that some were so hostile to the Holy See. Hence, he exhorted Ferdinand to take up the cause and defense of that see in keeping with the duty of his imperial office. Pius gave full assurance that not only those who were fair but also the biased would readily understand that "with a straightforward, upright, and sincere will and with an ardent eagerness of mind" he desired the abrogation of evil customs, the improvement of habits, and the very strict reform of everything that needed correction; he also promised to satisfy fully the laudable desire of the emperor and of all good men in this regard as well as his own duty.[233] Pius IV's profession of reforming zeal would not have convinced the Spanish ambassador in Rome, who wrote to his king the next day: "The reform that His Holiness is making of this Curia and most recently of the Datary, besides being prejudicial to the authority of the council, is something fruitless and which will last only as long as the council [since the pope has introduced it] because of pressing and difficult situations and in order to appear to be doing something; [but] it will all pass in twenty-four hours like something ephemeral, and there is no one here and in Trent and elsewhere who is not disillusioned with it."[234] The Spanish ambassador was more censorious than the imperial ambassador in Rome was.

---

[233]Pius IV to Ferdinand, Rome, March 6, 1563, Raynaldus, 1563, No. 67, pp. 362-363, and Le Plat, V, 709-710; also Steinherz, III, 237-238 (No. 81); CT, IX, 1137-1138. In his reply to this brief the emperor professed his surprise at the report that some conciliar fathers had called into question the power which God had granted to the Holy See to rule and shepherd the universal Church, for he himself had never doubted it; hence, he had ordered his ambassadors in Trent to dissuade the Spanish and French prelates from all unnecessary disputations. He acknowledged not only his duty to defend the dignity and authority of the Holy See but also his obligation of gratitude to Pius IV. He warned the pope, nevertheless, against trying to expand his authority by weakening that of the council or to have all admit what many openly denied (that is, the pope's superiority over the council). In conclusion the emperor thanked Pius for the assurance of his desire for reform and called God to witness the purity of his intentions in urging the reform. Ferdinand to Pius IV, Innsbruck, March 23, 1563, Sickel, Concil, pp. 468-470 (No. CCXLI); cf. n. 232 supra.

[234]Vargas to Philip II, Rome, March 7, 1563, Döllinger, Beiträge, I, 488 (No. 146): "por emplastar y verse apretado Su Santidad y parecer que hace alguna cosa. . . ." Later that spring the departing Venetian ambassador, Girolamo Soranzo, who had spent nearly three years in Rome, reported to the Senate that the pope's income from the Datary, which had previously amounted to 25,000 or 30,000 scudi a month, and in some months 40,000, had been reduced by the abolition of regress and by other reforms to 8,000 at most; this was the privy purse which the pope used to make up ordinary expenses, to build, and to give his relatives and retainers. "Relazione di Roma . . . letta in Senato il 14 Giugno 1563," Albèri, Vol. X (Series II, Tome IV), p. 87.

It was to the latter, Prospero d'Arco, that Pius IV revealed his initial reaction to Ferdinand's admonitions. After reading the open letter, he remarked that he recognized in it many things characteristic of the Cardinal of Lorraine, and he added that he took everything in a good spirit. As far as the reform of the conclave was concerned, he had already prepared a bull, which he would willingly have sent to the council so that it could be seen by it and the words *"sacro approbante concilio"* could be inserted; but he had not done so because the conciliar fathers would have raised difficulties over the provision allowing only ten days after the death of the pope for the cardinals to assemble in Rome, as if this showed little respect for the cardinals outside Italy. He had not yet sent the bull, he said, lest the election of a new pope be placed in doubt as to whether it pertained to the cardinals or to the council, and he believed that little agreement could be expected from the council. Pius also promised to supply a copy for Ferdinand so that the latter could see that provision was made in it for all the disorders; the pope was dubious only about the execution of the bull, for even though many canons and severe laws had been laid down regarding simony, nevertheless, some of his predecessors had arrived at the papacy by means of simony. As for the cardinals, Pius IV averred that he had done nothing to regret if one would consider those whom his predecessors had made; some of those whom he had appointed he had appointed because he knew that they would be servants of the emperor, who ought not take it amiss to have someone attached to himself in the Sacred College. The pope insisted that necessity had forced him to choose the last two, explaining how otherwise there would have been dissension in the House of Gonzaga and how necessary it was to show regard for the duke of Florence, whose state was so near to Rome; he alleged, furthermore, the custom of the popes to give their own red hats to whomever they wished as often as the places in the College of Cardinals became free; finally, although he admitted that Ferdinando de' Medici was not old enough to advise him, Pius denied that the young cardinal could do any harm in a papal election since he would not have a vote until he would reach the diaconal age. Going on to the topic of reform, Pius affirmed that he had reformed what pertained to his own person and even in part what pertained to the universal Church. He claimed to be greatly displeased that the legates had not laid Ferdinand's petitions before the council. At the end of his dispatch the imperial ambassador wrote that the pope had given this extemporaneous reply but was holding the courier so that he might reply in writing after more deliberation.[235] As it turned out, this dispatch acquired special value from the fact that in spite of repeated promises the pope never replied to the emperor's

---

[235] Arco to Ferdinand, Rome, March 10, 1563, Sickel, *Concil,* pp. 452-454 (No. CCXXXVIII). Pius also said that he had chosen Morone as president, knowing that he was a confidant of the emperor. Later in the month Pius again told the am-

two letters in writing and in the end conveyed his further response through Cardinal Morone. That Pius IV sincerely intended at first to write back to Ferdinand, nevertheless, is evident from the drafts that he had his chancery prepare.[236] First, the emperor's open letter was summarized, and after each proposition a rejoinder was set down. Where the emperor had said that a suspension would be interpreted as indicating a desire to impede the reform, the pope was to deny that he had ever thought of suspending the council, because he had always had and still had the intention of reforming what ought to be reformed. Where the emperor had reminded the pope to carry out the reform, the pope was to assert his desire for reform and to prove it by giving an account of the bulls already printed; he was also to take this occasion to mention the reform of the secular princes. These ideas were even incorporated in a letter addressed to Ferdinand and dated March 18 but never sent. Here the pope expressed his pleasure at the emperor's exhortation but also brought to his attention the care and diligence with which he had already corrected whatever seemed to need correction in the Roman Curia, disregarding any interests of his own or of his subjects. Pius argued that since he had begun the reform with himself and his Curia (as his bulls proved), everyone could understand how sincerely he wished the rest of the abuses in the Church to be eliminated.[237]

Ferdinand's secret letter of March 3 was likewise summarized and answered by the papal chancery. Where the emperor had stated that the council was convoked because of heresies and the abuses of the clergy and people, the pope was not only to express his agreement but to go a step further, saying that not only the clergy and people should be reformed but also the princes as leaders (*capi*) of the people, as Ferdinand himself had said that the reform should begin "*a capitibus et fontibus.*" The slowness of the reform about which the emperor complained was to be excused by blaming the representatives of the princes for requesting delays. In response to Ferdinand's recommendations for the reform of the conclave, the pope was to mention his new bull and to express his willingness to have it approved by the council; he was also to emphasize as a "great remedy" that the princes should not meddle in the conclave with intrigues and might even be made liable to excommunication. To all the emperor's remonstrances regarding cardinals the pope was merely to reply that he would choose properly qualified men but was not thinking of appointing any more; he was also to add the irrele-

---

bassador that he had composed the bull on the reform of the conclave in Rome, because if he had left it to the council, nothing would have been done, but if Ferdinand wished, it could be sent to the council and approved by it. Same to same, Rome, March 23, 1563, *ibid.*, p. 471 (No. CCXLII).

[236]"Projets de réponse du Pape aux lettres impériales du 3 mars," Rome, March, 1563, Constant, *Légation*, pp. 16-29 (No. 5).

[237]Raynaldus, 1563, Nos. 35-36, pp. 334-336, and Le Plat, V, 761-765, esp. 763.

vant comment that even in the college of the Apostles there was *aliquis reprobus*. Ferdinand had also adverted to the impropriety of referring conciliar matters to a few cardinals at Rome who were reasonably suspect in the reform of the conclave and the freedom of the council. In the envisioned reply the pope was to say that even if he consulted some cardinals, he did not thereby deprive the council of the freedom to treat and determine what it deemed expedient; furthermore, even if the pope listened to the opinions of certain cardinals, he did not leave the decisions to them. The emperor had also exhorted the pope to put more credence in the council than in the cardinals in regard to the conclave, the choice of cardinals, and other matters, because the Holy Spirit assisted the council but was not always conspicuous in the Sacred College. The rebuttal to this was to deny that it was good advice to refer to the council reform matters that needed prompt solutions, as was clear from the prolonged controversy over the episcopal duty of residence. The pope would let the council approve the bull for the reform of the conclave, however, to please the emperor; this bull, it was asserted, was drawn up in conformity with older bulls, some of which were passed by councils in which the Holy Spirit had been no less present than he was at Trent; whoever would propose an entirely new form of papal election, therefore, would contravene the orders of the councils. Finally, although the emperor had recognized the pope's right to preserve for himself and his successors all the authority granted him by God's precept or by Sacred Scripture or by the sacred canons or by the approved ancient councils, he admonished the pope not to arrogate to himself authority not granted to him in those ways nor to let the world believe that he was seeking his own, instead of Christ's, interests. With these ideals, of course, the pope was to state his agreement and, furthermore, to accept all the assistance that the emperor offered him. In this sense a formal reply to Ferdinand's confidential letter was drafted. At the end the pope said that lest he make his letter too long, Cardinal Morone, his legate, would enlighten the emperor on these matters at greater leisure.[238] In fact, although the two replies were never sent to Ferdinand, they and the notes of the chancery on which they were based served as instructions to the new president of the council who was soon to visit the emperor at Innsbruck. The fact that the replies were not sent indicates the embarrassment of the pope and his fear that the answers to the individual points might appear less convincing in the humanist script of a curial amanuensis than they would sound on the lips of the new president.

While the pope and his intimate advisers were planning their strategy, the other members of the Roman Curia, having heard inac-

---

[238]Pius IV to Ferdinand (*litterae arcanae*), Rome, March 18, 1563, Raynaldus, 1563, No. 38, pp. 341-342, and Le Plat, V, 765-768, esp. 766.

curate rumors about the emperor's demands, were terrified. It was being said that King Maximilian, as his agent in Rome reported to him, had gone to Bohemia and Hungary to get the bishops to attend the council "in order to be able to outweigh the pope's votes and to reform him in such a way that the popes and cardinals would have to return to the manner of the primitive Church." According to another dispatch of the same agent, the pope was improving the defenses of Rome because he feared that the council might investigate the validity of his election; many cardinals were supposed to wish to see the emperor go to the council and to induce the pope to go so that they would have a legitimate cause to prove his election simoniacal, as it was known to be "not only to cardinals but to many others"; the Cardinal of Augsburg, Otto von Truchsess, was quoted as asserting that it would be proved and the pope would certainly be deposed if he went to the council.[239] Such wild rumors inevitably heightened the tension between the papal and the imperial courts.

Meanwhile Cardinal Borromeo was receiving intelligence and advice from his special agents at Trent. Visconti suggested that since the emperor by his reform articles and his letter to the pope had not only shown his intention of infringing on the pope's authority but had also given the impression of wishing to go beyond what his predecessors, who were more powerful than he, had done, and since he had sent copies of his letter to the princes in order to justify his action, the pope should issue a brief in which he would show some resentment against the emperor and against those who had persuaded him to meddle in the pope's affairs; this brief would serve as a justification of the pope before the world, because copies of it could be sent to the nuncios at the princes' courts. Whether Visconti was really disingenuous or was merely resorting to flattery, he said that he could not understand why Pius IV's "good and holy intention in all matters of the service of God and particularly in what pertained to reform" was not recognized; in any case, he saw the need for removing the bad opinions that were held at Trent and elsewhere and thought it a pity that no way was found to undeceive the princes and their ministers, for if they were well informed, they would be satisfied with the pope's "holy attitude (mente)."[240] The advice of such a narrow-minded curialist could hardly have benefited the pope.

Gualterio, on the other hand, kept Borromeo informed about the Cardinal of Lorraine, who complained that the pope did not trust him and was convinced that Guise was aiming at reducing the

[239]Galeazzo Cusano to Maximilian, Rome, May 10 and 13, 1563, Sickel, *Concil*, p. 455.
[240]Visconti to Borromeo (memoire to Letter XIV), Trent, March 13, 1563, "Scrittura indrizzata al Bendone," Aymon, I, 134-136, and Baluze, III, 450-451.

pope's authority or ruining his court, toward which Guise showed himself to be very well affected. The French cardinal even criticized some of the pope's reforms as too rigorous; he feared that if they were pursued by the council, the pope would soon be aware of his error, because in every kingdom they would be modified by pragmatic sanctions, so that he would not succeed in the design, attributed to him by many, of returning the things in his vicinity to their previous laxness.[241] Visconti, however, was less sanguine about Lorraine's favorable disposition toward the Curia; he reported to Borromeo that he had heard from the Bishop of Vercelli (Guido Ferreri) that Guise desired that everyone should speak freely of the pope's person and so on, beginning with the cardinals.[242] Later Visconti himself had an interview with Guise, who said that he had been informed that Luis d'Avila, an envoy extraordinary of Philip II, had asked the pope in the name of his king for a reform "from head to foot" and for the freedom of the council; pleased with the position assumed by the Spanish monarch, the cardinal dilated on the question of reform, remarking that it was necessary to make it from alpha to omega and that it would be good if as many as fifty bishops who were always opposed to all the good resolutions were removed from the council. Lorraine also told Visconti that the emperor had informed him about the pope's reply concerning the reform of the cardinals as regarded age and number; Lorraine thought it necessary to attend to this matter also. In general he believed that in all the time that had passed since the beginning of the council the pope had made enough promises of reform, even more than were asked of him, but had accomplished nothing. Hence, he explained, the emperor and the other princes concluded that if the pope were really reform-minded, the legates would not have failed to carry out his will. In rejoinder Visconti tried to defend the pope's sincerity and reminded the cardinal that in the Council of Basel Juan de Torquemada had said that the abuses should be removed but not the use; the Bishop of Ventimiglia also tried to excuse the failure to execute the pope's good intentions by alleging the sole reason of not interruping the established order of treating reform in connection with dogma; he added, finally, that the legates already had in hand many reform articles which, if they were published, would make clear "how good and holy" the pope's intention was.[243] The bishop,

---

[241]Gualterio to Borromeo, Trent, March 13, 1563, Jedin, *Krisis*, p. 191 (No. 51).
[242]Visconti to Borromeo (memoire to Letter XVIII), Trent, March 22, 1563, Aymon, I, 160, and Baluze, III, 453-454.
[243]Visconti to Borromeo (Letter XIX and "Scrittura mandata al Bendone"), Padua, April 2, 1563, Aymon, I, 178, 180, and Baluze, III, 454-456. When Luis de Avila arrived in Rome on March 14, he presented almost the same complaints and admonitions as the pope had just heard from the emperor and the Cardinal of Lorraine; Pius IV, who, relying on the optimistic reports of his nuncios in Spain, had expected reassurances of Philip's support, was extremely disappointed.

of course, could not claim that he had convinced his interlocutor. To obtain more accurate information about the pope's attitude toward reform, the Cardinal of Lorraine sent to Rome Filippo Musotti, whom he had engaged as his own secretary after the death of Seripando. In the report that he composed afterwards, Musotti quoted Pius IV as saying that he desired reform more than anyone else did and would enjoin it on himself, his court, and all who needed it. According to the pope, the French ambassador who had just departed had sometimes talked about reform as necessary and desirable, but only in general terms without specifying anything. Pius boasted:

> We have reformed our Datary, which has meant for us a loss of 100,000 or 150,000 scudi of income per year, which, however, we could have taken without doing any evil, as did our predecessors, whom we do not intend to blame. . . . We have reformed the Camera, the Rota, the Penitentiary, the office of the *Contradictae*, the clergy of Rome, and our own officials, so that in the end all are crying out and already many have asked permission to go off in search of another way of life, and we are assured that an immense number of those in our court and of the lord cardinals bear us a grudge. And it is necessary that we should have done it. *Patientia!* Let them show us a single reform that they have made!

Obviously savoring the irony of the situation, Pius stated that the French ambassadors asked that he no longer give benefices *in commendam* and then they requested the opposite on behalf of their king who every day nominated incompetent men who lacked the qualifications required for the provision of bishoprics, abbacies, and other similar benefices. The pope declared that he was pleased not to confer benefices in this way any more and had recently refused one to the bastard of King Henry II, but then the French were extremely dissatisfied. Pius continued:

> It is the same ones who have 150,000 scudi worth of benefices and whose brothers have as much, who desire reform in the plurality of benefices, and then say: *retrotrahatur. Fiat, fiat!* We wish it and we are content with it. They shall see how they stand. As for ourselves, we intend to safeguard the archbishopric of Rome; then we shall begin with our nephew Borromeo and all the others without allowing a single exception, requiring that each one who has a diocese go to reside in it, even the cardinals, and we would already have sent those who have dioceses if it were not that we are not yet resolved whether we should first send them to the council. . . .

Musotti concluded:

To sum up, this word "reform" was so displeasing to His Holiness that he dwelt on it for nearly three quarters of an hour, repeating the same thing again and again, without getting excited or angry, saying that His Holiness felt it an incredible pleasure to have this honor of having the reform done in his time, that he will approve everything that will be said at the council, and that he has not found wrong any article proposed by the ambassadors of France on the subject of reform.[244]

If the inconsistencies of the French irked the pope, they must also have nourished his sense of moral superiority. He did not succeed, nevertheless, in convincing Musotti of his complete sincerity.

Even observers at Trent whose loyalty to the Holy See could not be questioned did not conceal in confidential letters their discontent with the pope's handling of the reform issue. Juan de Polanco, secretary of the Society of Jesus, who had accompanied the general, first praised "the good emperor" for having done what he could, by his letters to the pope (copies of which he had sent to Trent), to help the council to go forward and attend to the reform which the pope also *said* he wished to promote without prejudice to the authority of the Apostolic See.[245] With more explicit skepticism he related to the Jesuit commissary in Spain that they had understood that the pope desired reform and considered it already done and more severe than many had wished; Polanco added: "May God Our Lord let us see it in deeds and in truth, as until now we have heard it many times in words."[246] One day earlier Paleotti wrote to his brother that some printed provisions for reform from the pope had been circulating at Trent; he thought that if they had been made many months before, they would have been much more helpful but now that the emperor

---

[244]"Musotti de rebus 22. Aprilis 1563 cum Pio IV gestis relatio," in "Musotti scripturae conciliares (C)," No. VII, *CT*, III, 164-165.
[245]Polanco to Canisius, Trent, March 24, 1563, Braunsberger, IV, 124 (No. 806). On Polanco see Constancio Gutiérrez, S.J., *Españoles en Trento* (Valladolid, 1951), pp. 670-687.
[246]Polanco to Antonio Araoz, Trent, April 6, 1563, *Polanci Complementa. Epistolae et Commentaria P. Joannis Alphonsi de Polanco e Societate Jesu* ("Monumenta Historica Societatis Jesu" [2 vols.; Madrid, 1916-1917]), I, 361 (Ep. 77). When Polanco had been at Saint-Germain in January, 1562, with the legate, Cardinal Ippolito d'Este, he had been confident that the pope would allow the council to discuss reform *in capite* and would submit to its decrees, prescinding from the question of his superiority over the council or the council's over him: "Remedia instantium Ecclesiae malorum a Lainio proposita," *Lainii Monumenta*, VIII, 787. On Polanco's authorship see Mario Scaduto, S.I., *L'Epoca di Giacomo Lainez, 1556-1565. L'Azione* ("Storia della Compagnia di Gesù in Italia," Vol. IV [Rome, 1974]), pp. 131-132.

254   REFORM AND AUTHORITY

and the French were insistently asking that their petitions, in which there were some similar proposals, be presented to the council, it was doubtful that the pope's reforms would produce the intended effect; moreover, there was a danger that since the council was to treat the same subjects, it might decide something different from what the pope had laid down. Hence, in Paleotti's opinion, for the future it would be better that the pope have whatever he deemed deserving of reform carried out in practice and leave to the council the task of putting it in writing. The Rotal judge also quoted several prelates (with whom he obviously agreed, since he called them prudent and right-minded) as saying that since the council had gone on so long fruitlessly and with increasing scandal, it was too late for an ordinary remedy and it was necessary to take an extraordinary resolution, namely, a meeting between the pope and the emperor which could bring a genuine settlement to Catholics and terror to their enemies as well as infinite esteem to all Christendom.[247] Paleotti and like-minded prelates at Trent rightly discerned the need for some new *démarche* to overcome the crisis, but it was to be the new first legate, not the pope himself, who would meet the emperor.

Between the sending of the emperor's letters of March 3 and the arrival of Cardinal Morone seven weeks later, those at Innsbruck continued to watch carefully the developments at Trent. When the French and Spanish bishops, in the course of the discussion of the sacrament of Orders, appeared to be reopening the controversy over the pope's authority and over his relationship to the council, the nuncio tried to win Ferdinand over to the Curia's point of view. Since Canisius had by then returned to Augsburg, Delfino asked Nadal to collect "some authorities" demonstrating that the pope was the shepherd of the universal Church, and these helped to convince Staphylus and other counselors of the emperor. At the nuncio's request Nadal also prepared some arguments to dissuade the emperor from asking of the council the reform of the Church *in capite*. From what Draskovic and others had said, Polanco gathered that Ferdinand would maintain a proper respect for the pope's authority and that his requests in the council would be as moderate as Nadal expected.[248]

After receiving from the emperor's ambassadors the copy of his open letter to the pope, the two remaining legates, Hosius and Simonetta (Seripando having died on March 17), praised Ferdinand, in an obvious *captatio benevolentiae*, for having done something becoming "a Christian, Catholic, and orthodox emperor and the

---

[247] Gabriele Paleotti to Camillo Paleotti, Trent, April 5, 1563, in Prodi, *op. cit.*, I, 168 and 171, n. 6.

[248] Polanco to Christopher Madrid (superintendent of the Jesuit college in Rome), Trent, March 11, 1563, *Lainii Monumenta*, VI, 716-717 (Ep. 1791).

first-born son of the Church," and they acknowledged his "most righteous grounds for complaining that the affairs of the council had come to such a pass that great scandal and offense had been given to the whole Christian world." They attributed the current situation, however, to the fact that those to whom it did not belong had arrogated to themselves the power of proposing matters to the council. They stated that if their authority had been respected, the council would have been finished by then or nearly so, and almost all the reform proposals of the emperor and the other princes would have been handled.[249] While they offered explanations for the past, they gave no assurances for the future.

Disturbed by the proceedings of the council, Ferdinand sent further instructions to his ambassadors at Trent on March 21. In case the pope would allow the envoys of the princes the power of making proposals to the council, the emperor wished his ambassadors to give priority to the reform petitions that concerned his own lands and those of the Empire. Among these he included restricting the granting of dispensations, taking into account the age and abilities of candidates for the cardinalate, the episcopate, and other prominent ecclesiastical dignities, reform of the conclave and papal election, moderation of the practice of reservations, and abolition of commendam, regress, and coadjutorship with the right of succession. Considering these proposals in part useful and necessary for the state of affairs in Germany and in part just and holy in themselves, the emperor directed his ambassadors to ponder ways of bringing them before the council with the aid of the envoys of other kings and princes. These articles he distinguished from others which in the recent consultation had been judged to be in part dangerous and in part not necessary or at least not pertinent. In his view it was indeed to be desired that the articles touching on the person of the pope and on the Roman Curia and requiring a limit on the number of cardinals should not be overlooked or neglected; indeed, they could be fruitfully urged, especially so that from then on, the popes might be hindered from enriching and promoting their nephews. But after the emperor had ascertained that such proposals would be so disagreeable (*gravia*) and intolerable to the pope that, if anyone would make such admonitions publicly, he might prematurely break off or dissolve the council, Ferdinand decided to refrain from pressing such demands until he could learn what the envoys of other kings and princes thought about the matter. The emperor would also have liked, by means of a collection in every country, to compensate the pope and the officials of the Curia for the loss of the fees charged for dispatching documents; he feared, however, that this idea would be so far-reaching and complicated

---

[249]The legates to Ferdinand, [Trent, March, 1563,] Raynaldus, 1563, No. 32, pp. 328, 331, and le Plat, V, 755-756.

that it should not be brought before the council. Among his many other injunctions he cautioned his ambassadors against providing any occasion for a discussion of "that odious and most difficult question" of the relative superiority of the pope and the council; but if it could not be avoided, he did not see how the German nation could allow itself to be moved away from the decrees of the Councils of Constance and Basel; therefore, if the ambassadors should notice that an effort was being made to have the pope do all the council's work and to leave the whole business of reform to his judgment so that nothing could be done in the council except what he might think appropriate for it, then the ambassadors were to seek further instructions from the emperor.[250] By not insisting on the presentation of all his reform proposals to the council, in particular of those concerning the pope and the Curia, the emperor demonstrated his desire to avoid an acute conflict with the pope and to enable the council to resume its work.

Commenting on Hosius and Simonetta's implied promise to lay the emperor's *libellus* before the council as soon as possible, Drasković and Thun expressed their incredulity, because the legates, they said, had always kept them in suspense with such fine-sounding promises but also maintained that some proposals could not be presented to the fathers without infringing on the pope's dignity or encroaching on his authority. The ambassadors assured the emperor, nevertheless, that if the legates should keep their word, the ambassadors would not let any part of the *libellus* be proposed to the council without Ferdinand's explicit consent. But they were sure that nothing would be done before the arrival of Cardinal Morone, who, according to a rumor originating in Rome, would go immediately to confer with the emperor before assuming the actual direction of the council.[251]

---

[250]Ferdinand to the imperial ambassadors, Innsbruck, March 21, 1563, Sickel, *Concil*, pp. 456-463 (No. CCXXXIX). In another instruction, dated March 23, the emperor again ordered them to try to persuade the Spanish and French prelates to avoid a discussion of the pope's superiority over the council. *Ibid.*, pp. 463-465 (No. CCXL). Considering the sum of the emperor's proposals in his letters of this month to the pope and to his ambassadors at Trent, Helle observes that it forms a transition from the first imperial *libellus* (of June 7, 1562) to the second (of June 5, 1563) (p. 47).

[251]Thun and Drasković to Ferdinand, Trent, March 28, 1563, Sickel, *Concil*, p. 474 (No. CCXLIII). Brus had gone to Innsbruck just as the Cardinal of Lorraine and many other bishops had temporarily left Trent because they knew that nothing important would be done at the council until the new legate would take over the reins. Meanwhile the Curia was considering ways of winning Drasković, the most feared of the imperial ambassadors. Borromeo wrote to Simonetta that if he could not be brought over in any other way, he could be promised the cardinalate, and the pope would not fail to fulfill his promise. April 13, 1563, Susta, III, 306 (No. 83).

VI. Cardinal Morone and the Emperor, April--June, 1563

The rumor about Morone's plans were correct. Having reached Trent on April 10, he set out six days later for Innsbruck, where he arrived on the 21st and began his negotiations on the following day. Morone had enjoyed Ferdinand's esteem for his seriousness, wisdom, and moderation ever since he had been sent as nuncio to the court of the King of the Romans in 1536, when he was only twenty-seven years old; consequently, he did not now have to spend time in winning the emperor's confidence. During his four-hour private audience he answered all the points contained in the emperor's ostensible and confidential letters of March 3 to the pope, adhering to the position stated in the unsent briefs of March 18. In regard to the reform *in capite*, the legate asserted that it could not be treated in the council unless one also wished to treat the authority of the pope, and this was contrary to the emperor's intention. As far as the pope was concerned, said Morone, he had no need of such means because he was resolved to pursue the reform already partially achieved. It had never been the custom, moreover, for a council to wish to lay down laws for the pope--all the more so now, when Pius IV was ready to do it by himself. It was not possible for a council to prescribe a law for the pope, because only what the pope confirmed, and when and insofar as he confirmed it, was valid. To wish to prescribe laws for the pope, argued Morone further, would be much worse than for the subjects of the Empire to wish to prescribe laws for the emperor. The princes had even less right than the council to involve themselves in legislating for the pope, nor should they under the pretext of reform and religion engage in bargaining and trading over the council. Finally, the president of the council admonished the emperor that as advocate and defender of the Church he ought to protect his head and not go along in any way with anyone who was opposed to him directly or indirectly.

In regard to the conclave and papal election Morone did not deny that some cardinals sometimes gave scandal, but he affirmed that for the most part the scandals of the conclave resulted from the interests and intrigues of the princes who introduced divisions. Likewise he did not deny that among the cardinals were still some who were not good, but he thought it no cause for wonder, for the same thing had happened among the Apostles and in every collegiate body. To remedy the abuses at papal elections as far as possible, the pope had issued a new bull restricting and reforming the conclave and would have consented to have it read and accepted in the council if he had not feared more prolonged debates than other matters had caused, because of the designs of some and the curiosity of many. Morone observed, finally, that the true remedy for the conclave would be that the princes not interfere by means of letters or embassies and that even penalties and excommunications be inflicted on them.

In regard to the promotion of cardinals Morone first explained why Pius IV had created the last two, and then added that the pope did not have any new promotion in mind but if he were to think of one he would choose fit persons. The legate argued that it was not possible to reduce the cardinals to a certain number, for it was not reasonable that a pope should be constrained to make use of his predecessor's counselors (nor were secular princes obliged to do so); moreover, since the cardinalitial dignity had also been for life, it was not reasonable that a pope who would dismiss his predecessor's cardinals as counselors should also deprive them of the cardinalate. The legate asserted that it was necessary sometimes to gratify with such dignities persons who were well deserving of the Holy See and to satisfy the requests of princes, even though the Sacred College might be full. Often, he said, the Apostolic See had need of a greater number and different abilities of ministers. He promised, finally, that Pius IV would always be careful to make worthy and good appointments and in order to provide for the future as much as possible would issue a bull on this subject.[252] Although individual arguments offered by Morone might have seemed questionable, the accumulation of them must have made a deep impression on the emperor.

Reporting to the pope on this initial conversation, Morone described some of Ferdinand's reactions. In regard to the reform *in capite* the emperor declared that to preserve the pope's authority he was ready to give his blood and his life; he added, nevertheless, that one should not wish to defend this authority, instituted by God for the salvation of the world, in such a way that scandal and ruin would follow. He also admitted that the pope's dispensing power was necessary but he insisted that it should be used with moderation and only for serious reasons. Morone replied that the pope was neither able nor willing to tolerate any limitation on the papal power, for since he had not acquired it for the Church, he did not wish to lose it for the Church, and since it was given by God, it could not be restricted by men even though all should conspire together. As for the use of the power and the granting of dispensations, the legate assured Ferdinand that the pope wanted the reform to be effective and to restrict himself to such an extent that he would perhaps displease the princes themselves, who were wont to extort from Rome the first transgressions of good and holy laws. The emperor listened attentively and affably and impressed the legate as continuing in his customary goodness and piety. He replied, however, that there were many in Rome and in Trent who watched everything that the pope did contrary to the decrees of the council

---

[252]"Sommaire de la réponse de Morone à l'empereur," Innsbruck, April 23, 1563, Constant, *Légation,* pp. 39-44 (No. 9), and Steinherz, III, 274-275. Although written on April 23, it summarizes the arguments presented orally on the previous day.

and reported it to the princes and that from this failure to observe the decrees some disorder could occur.[253] Ferdinand did not make any definite commitments to Morone at that first interview. Afterwards the emperor enumerated, as well as he could remember them, the several points discussed with Morone. Then Seld compiled fourteen articles of which only the third pertained to reform *in capite*; it read: "That the reform both of the pontiff's person and of the Roman Curia, especially insofar as it regards the papal conclave and the creation of cardinals, should be permitted to His Holiness alone, and the council should not get entangled in it."[254] This formulation indicated Seld's inclination to the papal side. The next step was to solicit the advice of the emperor's theologians on each of these articles.

In preparation for the negotiations with Morone, Ferdinand had again assembled a number of theologians at his court. This commission was composed of Canisius, Staphylus, Francisco de Córdoba, Conrad Braun (a jurist and canon of Augsburg), and Francis Forgách, Bishop of Nagy-Warad (Grosswardein), and possibly also Cithard, the emperor's confessor, and Brus, who had come from Trent.[255] Forgách was the chairman of the commission, and Braun the secretary. Staphylus, the most forceful member, had a definite and negative opinion of the papal attitude toward reform. In reply to a number of questions on which he had been consulted at the beginning of April, he had expressed doubt that the pope and the Curia were really willing to reform themselves; often enough had such reforms been begun, he observed, but they were never completed; sometimes one got the impression that the Romans would rather see no council take place forever than to hear a reform of the head through the council even only spoken of. Can one expect, he asked, the nations that have turned away from the pope to return to obedience when he, to be sure, takes action against others but does not wish to reform himself and his Curia? In regard to the relationship of the pope to the council Staphylus developed a theory of his own: the Apostolic See, which possesses the privileges of Peter, is to be distinguished from its temporary occupant; this incumbent may not evade reform through the council that represents the universal Church. Nevertheless, one might first wait to see whether the self-reform announced by the pope would be sufficient. "Hence, I believe that no mention of the *reformatio capitis* should be made by the imperial ambassadors in the public assembly of the fathers before it has become clearly known what both the pope and the cardinals and

---

[253]Morone to Borromeo, Innsbruck, April 23, 1563, Steinherz, III, 267-268 (No. 93).

[254]"Articuli quos C. Mtas theologis suis proposuit deliberandos," [Innsbruck,] April 24, 1563, Sickel, *Concil,* p. 491 (No. CCXLVIII).

[255]Pastor considered it "very important that Gienger was not at Innsbruck." XV, 319, n. 3.

other prelates are willing to conclude and do in a serious way." This opinion resembles the later answer of the emperor.

Similarly the imperial vice-chancellor had presented several questions to Braun, who enjoyed the emperor's esteem; the last one was what position should be adopted if the disagreeable dispute regarding the pope's superiority over the council could not be avoided. Braun replied that the council should settle the old controversy by declaring that the pope possesses greater and higher authority than the general council. Obviously Braun was not a conciliarist, but he was also not far-sighted if he did not foresee the consequences of such a conciliar decision. When Morone commented on Braun's answer under the guise of "a theologian," he advised against wishing to let the question of relative power be decided by the council, for then an endless controversy would arise. It could have been predicted that this heterogeneous group of theologians would not easily come to agreement.[256]

On April 24 the imperial vice-chancellor handed them the list of fourteen points, and for the next fortnight they deliberated on them. One of the theologians passed a copy to Morone, who then composed *avertimenti* and gave them secretly to certain trusted members of the commission--probably to Canisius, Staphylus, and Braun. Regarding reform *in capite*, he wrote: "Because the first see is judged by no one, and sheep do not accuse the shepherd, it seems that the reform of the pontiff's person and of the Roman Curia pertain to the pontiff himself if he is prepared to execute the reform of which there is need." Morone recommended likewise that the emperor deal with the pope in regard to the creation of cardinals so that provision might be made for the appointment of suitable men in the future.[257] Although Morone did not know what answer he would receive in the end and foresaw difficulties in some respects, he assured the other legates that he had found in Ferdinand "extreme good-will and very great devotion to the Apostolic See and in particular to the person of His Beatitude."[258] A few days later the president of the council drew up more *avertimenti*, this time on four questions submitted to the theologians. They had been asked for their

---

[256]Jedin, *Geschichte*, IV/2, 15-18 and 263, nn. 9 and 10.

[257]Constant, *Légation*, p. 70. On March 20, 1563, Pius IV had informed Canisius that Morone was about to visit Ferdinand and would explain certain things to him in the pope's name; he also directed the Jesuit to trust the cardinal's words. Braunsberger, IV, 121 (No. 803). A brief in the same words was also sent to Staphylus. *Ibid.*, p. 122.

[258]Morone to the legates, Innsbruck, April 24, 1563, Constant, *Légation*, p. 47 (No. 11). Pallavicini stated that Morone always disliked the procedure of these discussions "not only as prolix but as dangerous," and besides the difficulty of restricting the conclusions to the subject proposed, he always feared "that stormy and seditious questions might be raised, as about the pope's authority." Pallavicini attributed the outcome in large measure to Ferdinand's old and now renewed confidence in the legate. XX, xv, 2.

opinion of the bull issued by the pope forbidding the council to involve itself in the papal election. Morone deprecated any discussion of this subject, saying that in a papal election the papal decrees and ancient customs of the Church simply had to be obeyed; no council had ever interfered in this matter except during a schism and with the consent of the cardinals, as in the Council of Constance. Otherwise, if the council wished to have a role in the election of a pope, the result would be schism and the overthrow of the whole Church. Secondly, the theologians were to suggest ways by which the votes in the conclave should not be announced and the princes should not corrupt the voters with their intrigues. In Morone's opinion sufficient provision was already made for these abuses in the bull, but if a more effective remedy seemed to be needed, the pope could be so advised; as far as restraining the princes was concerned, Morone conceded that the pope could threaten them with excommunication unless he was afraid of offending them.[259] Thus the resourceful legate tried to influence the deliberations at the imperial court.

As time went on, Morone was confirmed in his high regard for Ferdinand, who, he wrote, was as pious and Catholic as one could desire. But he observed that the agreements made with other princes were making a satisfactory solution more difficult to achieve, especially since he could not alter the conviction prevailing in Innsbruck that the Romans did not want reform; it was this conviction that had given rise to agreements with other princes and helped to maintain them. The legate strove to convince the emperor and his ministers that the pope really wished reform not only in the form of decrees and conciliar canons but in their execution and observance, but he had to confess frankly to Borromeo that not only the ministers but even the emperor himself had told him that they had taken note of the pope's dispensations and transgressions against the decrees of the council. Morone defended Pius by asserting that one would never find in the pope's documents any clause annulling even in part the Tridentine decrees, notwithstanding the fact that the council was not yet concluded or approved by the Holy See.[260] Ferdinand always listened to the legate with courtesy, if not with credulity. When Morone was confined to bed with gout for eight days, the emperor even paid him the honor of a visit. When the theologians also called on him, he continued his efforts to convince them of the pope's determination regarding the reform of himself and his court and to show them the impropriety of wishing the council to reform the head of the Church. He contended that whoever would not be content with letting the pope proceed in canonical and

---

[259]This set of *avertimenti* is dated by Braunsberger (IV, 154-155) April 22-24 and by Constant (*Légation*, p. 73) after April 26.

[260]Morone to Borromeo, Innsbruck, May 2, 1563, Steinherz, III, 282-284 (No. 95).

correct ways and would try to find another route, would show that
he desired confusion and not reform.[261] In keeping with contemporary diplomatic usage, Morone employed every means, including
gifts of money, to obtain or confirm the support of the theologians
and lay advisers of the emperor.

Meanwhile the theological commission produced the first draft of
a reply to the legate. Here it was not denied that the fullness of ecclesiastical power resided in the successor of St. Peter alone, but it
was affirmed that this power should be confined within definite
boundaries of divine and natural law. Hence, the pope should
observe moderation in dispensing and should not remit anything in
matters of natural and divine law. In the theologians' opinion the
greatest abuse of all was that the Curia and other major and minor
prelates accepted or demanded something for the exercise of ecclesiastical and spiritual power, either from voluntary donors or
from the unwilling. According to the commission, moreover, it was
obvious to all that discipline had long been neglected in the Roman
Curia. The commission also enumerated the abuses that occurred in
papal elections. First, since boys and profane men, such as soldiers
and fools (moriones), were appointed cardinals to advance certain
families to great honor, power, and wealth, and since these persons
had an active and passive vote, it often happened that through
unlawful canvassing (ambitum), simony, and other intrigues either
they themselves or other unworthy men were elected to the papacy.
The second abuse was the large number of cardinals electing. The
third was that kings and other secular princes interfered in the
papal elections and corrupted the cardinals by various practices.
The fourth was that cardinals striving for the papacy by various
pretexts and clever tricks drew votes away from worthy candidates
and often transferred them obliquely to themselves. To correct
these abuses the theologians recommended that the legal prescriptions be observed, that cardinals not be younger than twenty-five
years of age from then on, that the number of cardinals be definite,
that the ambassadors of kings and princes be bound by oath not to
intrigue with any cardinal or his servants, and lastly that if any cardinal should be elected for whom kings or others interceded or who
traded votes or had them cast for himself, the election should be ipso jure null and void, and the elect should not be put in possession of
the papacy.[262] This draft was then revised by Seld, who deleted
many passages, recast others, and added an introduction. The

[261]Morone to Borromeo, Innsbruck, May 6, 1563, Steinherz, III, 286-287 (No. 96).
[262]Kassowitz, pp. xl-xlii (Nos. 71, 72, 79, 80, 85-93). The Venetian ambassador who
concluded his term at Rome about this time commented in his final report to the
Senate that the number of cardinals was larger than what had been customary, that
as a result their dignity was diminished since some were very poor and many were of

revised text was then submitted to the commission of theologians for their final approval.

Canisius was dissatisfied with the proposed reply but understood that he could not obtain what he considered to be right from the other theologians. Hence, he went to the emperor to present his views on two matters. First, he set forth the difficulties that he found in the document composed by his colleagues. He thought that it was not necessary or solid, extemporaneously written by a few persons not entirely fit for such a task, persons who were hampered in judging by their sentiments and their lack of experience. (Here he must have meant Córdoba and Staphylus). It was not fitting, he believed, for the emperor to deal harshly with a pope devoted to him; the pope might be offended and his eagerness for reform slowed down; his promises should not be distrusted, but rather his efforts should be fostered. Canisius feared that when the commission's paper would come into the hands of the doctors, it would stir up new disputes and would hinder rather than advance the cause of the council. Many would equate the emperor's assiduity with the constant outcries of the Church's adversaries against abuses and with the attitudes of those who wished to lay down laws rather than accept them and who were unwilling to look at their own misdeeds while they disparaged only the ecclesiastical superiors. The Jesuit also detected the danger that this exertion, resulting from excessive zeal, would not only be useless but would even irritate the spirits of the sick in the Roman Curia who were to be cured, for they would notice that they and the abuses of their Curia were being censured in so hateful and false a manner, laws were being laid down for the cardinals, the pope was being made subject to the council for reform, and so on. Consequently, he feared that while they wished to cure the diseases at Rome and Trent they might aggravate them, especially when spirits were so inclined everywhere to withdraw from the obedience due to the supreme shepherd and vicar of Christ. Considering the circumstances, Canisius did not expect the council to last much longer and therefore recommended that not so much at-

---

little value and of no nobility. These all followed the pope's wishes and no one dared to oppose his will; hence, in the consistories and congregations of cardinals independent opinions were not heard but only simple consent to, and approval of, whatever the pope proposed or whatever they knew would be useful to the princes to whom they were obligated. The ambassador added that the idea of Pope Marcellus II to have a fixed number of cardinals and to give each a decent income without letting them have bishoprics or other benefices was regarded by the most intelligent as very good and helpful to the Holy See in all respects and particularly in papal elections, when the effects of the cardinals' dependence on the princes became evident. "Relazione di Roma di Girolamo Soranzo, letta in Senato il 14 Giugno 1563," Albèri, Vol. X (Series II, Tome IV), pp. 96-97. It is clear that some of the reform ideas being discussed at Innsbruck were also current in Rome.

tention be paid to what was being done at Rome as to what was being done in Germany. Then he proceeded to expound the ways in which the emperor could use this occasion to promote the council and reform. He exhorted Ferdinand not to lose the opportunity that the visit of the great Cardinal Morone furnished him for dealing with a friendly person not in writing but in conversation and for hearing his opinions about the obstacles to the progress of the Church and the council. It would be safer, he suggested, to begin with lesser matters; they could appropriately consider ways of strengthening and executing the reform decrees passed by the council. The pope should be encouraged to continue in the reform activity that he had undertaken and be asked for certain things for the restoration of Germany. When Canisius finished his presentation, Ferdinand did not say much in reply but indicated that he would think about the whole question, and he would labor to have some things stated more gently and less offensively in that paper. Canisius, however, was not satisfied with this answer.[263]

True to his word, Ferdinand noted with his own hand what he wished to be changed, and he had Seld submit fifty-eight amendments to the theologians. Certain words, which especially referred to the pope, were to be used for the sake of courtesty, and the same

---

[263]Canisius to Laínez (epistula prior), Innsbruck, May 8, 1563, Braunsberger, IV, 174-176 (No. 846); partially translated in Brodrick, pp. 552-555. Rupert asserts that Canisius did and said, in the meetings of the commission and in conversations with the emperor, almost nothing that Laínez had not suggested to him from Trent. Hence, Rupert credits the general with most of Canisius' influence (p. 32).

When Laínez received from Canisius at the end of April a copy of Seld's fourteen articles which had been submitted to the imperial theologians, he composed a brief commentary for Canisius' use. Regarding the third article he stated many reasons proving that it belonged to the pope to reform his own person and Curia. If the pope wished to find out what needed to be reformed in the Curia he could do so, with the advice of the cardinals and other experts of that body, more easily than the council could. Being comparatively few in number, moreover, the curialists could deliberate more quickly, and they would not lack the assistance of the Holy Spirit, while in the council there were many bishops and among them many were not very learned or familiar with the affairs of the Curia, for they hardly knew what pertained to their own dioceses. The pope, furthermore, had already begun and in large part accomplished the reform; hence, there was no reason for the council to snatch this business out of his hands. Finally, these things would have to be changed, in keeping with the requirements of the common good of the Church, as times and circumstances would change; the pope could do this if he determined the reforms, but if the council decreed them, those who held that the council was above the pope would deny that he could change them. Laínez admitted, nevertheless, that princes and others could suggest to the pope out of charity and without acrimoniousness or impudence whatever might occur to them, and the pope ought to listen to whatever proper suggestions they might make. They should be content, once they would have unburdened their consciences, and should be more alert to see their own faults than those of others, especially of superiors. Miguel Roca Cabanellas, "Diego Laynez en la última etapa del Concilio," in Il Concilio di Trento e la Riforma Tridentina, I, 107.

was to be done with respect to the appointment of cardinals. The reform of the conclave was to be omitted because of the bull, which was quite acceptable to the emperor, provided that it be faithfully carried into execution thereafter.[264] When the theologians resumed their consultations, however, Canisius was still dissatisfied. He asked Morone not to blame him or the Society of Jesus for whatever he would find displeasing in the emperor's reply. The emperor, on the other hand, promised to listen gladly to the opinion of Morone and Delfino.[265] The final task of revision was then entrusted to Singkhmoser, who condensed and shortened the text so that the original form of the theologians' draft disappeared almost completely. Ferdinand then made some further corrections and additions, and Seld added the finishing touches. Finally, Ferdinand himself handed the formal reply to the ailing legate while visiting him on May 7.[266]

In this lengthy document the emperor stated that the article regarding "the universal reform of the whole Church" was not only difficult in itself but also the most important among all the other articles. This reform,[267] he asseverated, was extremely necessary because of those manifest abuses which long before had crept into the Church and had produced all the evils then prevailing. Among the abuses of ecclesiastical jurisdiction and power he enumerated "indiscriminate dispensations, unjust decisions (constitutionibus),

---

[264]Kassowitz, p. xlii (Nos. 94-96).

[265]Canisius to Laínez (as in n. 263 supra), pp. 176-179. Canisius prayed and asked others to pray that Christ might either put a stop to the emperor's plans in this reply or turn them to the advantage of the Church. He declined to name the person who was said to be daily suggesting this stern advice to the emperor about the reform of the Church in capite et membris, the abuses of the Roman Curia, etc., but the Spanish Franciscan would fit the description. Canisius also remarked that those at the court twisted the fact that the pope was issuing reform bulls as if his effort were a subterfuge to avoid the judgment of the council, and he was shocked that evil men would calumniate what good men were doing.

[266]Canisius to Laínez (epistula secunda), Innsbruck, May 8, 1563, Braunsberger, IV, 182 (No. 847). Canisius was happy because he had obtained most of what he had requested of the emperor, namely, that the long and contentious paper conceived by his colleagues and approved by the emperor had been cut down and reduced to a sort of compendium. Hence, he raised his hope that Ferdinand would incur less unpopularity and hatred by his reply and would better safeguard the authority of the pope and the council. Both of Canisius' letters of May 8 to Laínez were sent to Rome to be shown to Pius IV. On the same day he confided to Hosius his hope that Morone would not depart from Innsbruck before the obstacles that some persons had caused or increased were removed. He also complained about unnamed "false brethren, more culpable (nocentiores) than external enemies," whom Satan suborned to throw domestic affairs into confusion, perplex men's minds, and foment new disturbances. Braunsberger, IV, 185-186 (No. 849). Braunsberger points out how little concrete information Canisius gave Hosius about the theologians' consultations and how carefully he kept the emperor's confidence.

illegitimate summonses, unreasonable exemptions, frivolous excommunications, unworthy collations, provisions, and confirmations of
benefices, excessive pluralities of benefices, and a thousand others
of that kind" which were practiced in the Roman Curia, mostly out
of cupidity for profit and money. In consequence the heretics not
only despised and ridiculed all ecclesiastical jurisdiction and power
but also established their own regulations and courts. The emperor
lamented that negligence and even sluggishness (*torpor*) and, as it
were, lethargy (*veternus*) had so overcome those who were charged
with building up the Church that "while Peter sleeps, Judas
wakes," and the foundations of the Church were being undermined.
After listing the vices of the clergy, Ferdinand asked where or
through whom the reform could and should most conveniently be
undertaken. As far as the person of the pope was concerned, he
perceived no difficulty and thought that the whole world would
agree with him. Nor did he regard the city of Rome and the temporal
state to be objects of much concern, for he supposed that the pope
either by himself or with the advice of the College of Cardinals had
already set everything in order or would do so in the future insofar
as might be needed. But the reform of matters that affected both
the Church and the Curia, he affirmed, pertained by ordinary law to
the pope as head and to the council as body (insofar as it was connected with the head). From the acts of the ancient councils and
from the books and unanimous opinion of experts he asserted that
universal reform was not the least of the reasons for which councils
were convoked, but he did not wish to enter into an elaborate discussion of these matters with the pope. Although he conceded that the
pope was not bound by strict law to share the labor of reform with
the council, the emperor thought that considering the needs of that
most perilous age, the pope ought to show some condescension. Ferdinand then proceeded to set forth arguments for his position. First,
in this way, he said, the pope would free himself of this occupation
in the place where, because of the large number of holy and learned
fathers, there would be little suspicion of treating the matter
carelessly or faithlessly, while if it were done in Rome, such suspicion could hardly be avoided, because of the human weakness of
those who would have to assist the pope and perhaps also because of
the self-interests of some, that something which ought to be done
would be passed over, or vice versa. Secondly, if the pope lowered
himself in this way, imitating the example of him whom he

---

[267] Here in the original draft, reform not only in the members, of which the council
had already begun to treat, "but also *in capite ejus*, which is the Roman Church and
its prelate, the Roman pontiff," was explicitly stated, but in the final version the
wording was changed to "this universal reform of the Church about which frequent
mention is made in the ancient councils." Constant, *Légation*, p. 91, n. 9. This
emendation had been requested by Morone with particular insistence. The same
change was also made a little farther on.

represented, he would acquire immense glory not only throughout the present world but also among all posterity. Furthermore, many persons handle the case of another better than one or a few handle their own (as Ferdinand proved by citing various maxims). Finally, by this means the pope would greatly enhance the council's authority which was to be considered the strongest bulwark against the heretics of the age. One part of this whole affair, namely, the reform of the conclave, Ferdinand granted had been prudently determined by Pius IV, but still he believed that if it would be referred to the council, the machinations that usually threw conclaves into disorder could more effectively be prevented, because they were caused by the kings and princes (and their ambassadors or agents) who would in the future have more respect for the decisions of the council in this regard. Summing up, the emperor wrote that many upright and loyal Catholics judged that the pope should be begged to take into account not so much his own authority as the condition of the afflicted Church; hence, Ferdinand would not like to see imputed to the pope by anyone excessive negligence or severity, either of which could appear to have inflicted ultimate destruction on the Church.[268] Although somewhat softened in language, the emperor's message even in this final form remained hard in substance.

On the very next day Morone went to Ferdinand to reply particularly to three points on which he was not satisfied. One of these was the reform *in capite* which the emperor wished to have the council decree. The legate was of the opinion that this disagreement consisted more in words than in substance, for all the abuses that Ferdinand had enumerated (such as dispensations) and many others which touched the pope's person more closely (such as the appointment of bishops) had already been proposed and settled in the council or had at least been drawn up in canons and would be laid before the fathers and decided at the first opportunity. From this fact Morone concluded that the pope did not really refuse to have this kind of reform carried out in the council; indeed, with a very few exceptions regarding the persons and choice of cardinals and of the pope, Pius had submitted and would submit almost all the rest to the examination and decision of the council. But the legate asked that the expression "reform *in capite*" be removed from the emperor's reply, not because he did not approve of Ferdinand's intention (which, he said, appeared very pious and Catholic in that document), nor because the pope did not approve of that reform being carried out in the council, but because the reply could easily fall into the hands of others who would understand the expression in a different sense and would think that the emperor wished not only to suggest the things contained in his reply but especially to cen-

---

[268]"Responsum Sacrae Caesareae Majestatis ad propositionem Rmi Cardinalis Moroni," Innsbruck, May 7, 1563, Constant, *Légation*. pp. 90-94.

sure the person and conduct of the pope. The main reason alleged by Morone for deleting the expression was that it could easily give rise to the treatment of the question of the relative superiority of the pope and the council, which the emperor had always wisely advised should be avoided. Morone, nevertheless, invited Ferdinand to suggest to the pope any details that he wished to see included in the bull for the reform of the conclave, and he promised that the pope would accept them all in a calm and fatherly spirit. Pius would not even take it amiss that the bull be presented to the council if he did not fear the diverse exertions of the fathers and their ignorance of the subject as well as the great loss of time and the cases that could arise meanwhile outside the council with the great danger of schism. (Here he was apparently alluding to France.) Since these misfortunes should be forestalled, Morone was opposed to presenting the bull to the council, reminding Ferdinand that, as acknowledged in his reply, the settlement of matters proposed to the council pertaining to religion and the reform of morals resided principally in the supreme pontiff as the head and from him was channeled to the conciliar fathers as the members; hence, it did not seem right that what the pope as head had already decided, the fathers, who were members, should judge and dispute.[269] At the end of the audience, which lasted about three hours, the emperor said that he wished to consult his theologians again before replying. Through all the mists of words there shone clearly two different ecclesiological assumptions which lay at the base of the differences about modes of reform--one in which the pope alone was head of the Church and the other in which the pope along with the body of bishops in council was the head. It was not necessary, however, that this basic divergence be resolved in order to bring about the desired reform.

Among the theologians whom Ferdinand consulted Francisco de Córdoba was the most intransigent on the question of reform *in capite*. From the legate's reply he gathered that the pope did not wish to do what was right and consonant with his duty, because he was unwilling to grant anything that the emperor had requested. The Franciscan took it as a bad sign that the pope wished to drag out the business of the reform *in capite*, which was the main issue. Instead of the full authority that Morone was supposed to have, Francisco doubted that he had any. Concluding that those of Rome

---

[269]"Moroni replica ad Sacrae Majestatis Responsum in materia concilii," Innsbruck, May 8, 1563, Constant, *Légation*, pp. 101-111. This was a series of notes that Morone used to aid his memory during his long conversation and then at the emperor's request handed over. The request for a "reform *in capite*" to which Morone objected is not to be found explicitly in the emperor's *Responsum* of May 7, but it must have been in an earlier text, as the emperor's *Responsum* of May 12 indicates (see n. 271 *infra*); cf. Jedin, *Geschichte*, IV/2, 264, n. 13.

abhorred reform, the Spanish confessor urged the necessity of placing more insistence on the reform of the Church.[270]

After the theologians deliberated on Morone's reply, the emperor's secretary, Singkhmoser, used their conclusions in drafting a response. In this document the style was gentler and the thought more veiled than in the minutes of the theologians' discussions, as might have been expected of a diplomat. Substantially, nevertheless, the ideas remained unchanged, especially in the article dealing with reform. Here the emperor confirmed the legates' assumption that in recounting the abuses of the Roman Curia, he did not mean to limit himself to those mentioned but set them down as examples; hence, if there were other things likewise in need of reform, he expressed his confidence that Morone, together with his colleagues at Trent, would see to it that nothing was overlooked. As for the reform of the conclave, Ferdinand declared that the longer he thought about that article, the more he believed that norms for the appointment of cardinals should be taken up, because this would not prejudice Pius IV's rights but would only curb his successors lest they give scandal as the popes of the preceding century had done. Ferdinand did not consider his proposal a novelty, for popes in the past, he said, had often reformed in councils not only matters pertaining to the Roman Curia but also the conclave itself. He even cited the ancient practice of the Roman Church of referring to ecumenical councils matters pertaining to faith and other political issues which had been settled in Roman synods, and he said that nevertheless the authority of the Roman pontiff remained safe and unimpaired. Supposing that some discussion of this question should arise among the fathers because of their different inclinations, Ferdinand countered Morone's argument by insisting that a discussion undertaken not out of eagerness for display or contradiction but for the sake of disengaging the truth should not be considered superfluous but rather extremely appropriate and salutary, so that even if some time might be lost it should not be a source of concern in such serious and necessary matters. Finally, Ferdinand stated frankly that he did not see the urgent reason for expunging the words "reform in capite" as Morone had requested, especially since it was clear enough from his whole reply what kind of opinion he had of the pope's person as regarded his integrity and holiness. Anyone would have to be extraordinarily impudent to try to twist his mean-

[270]Córdoba to Ferdinand, [Innsbruck, between May 8 and 12, 1563,] Constant, Légation, p. 114, n. 2. Morone later called Córdoba "the most severe (acerbo) and pertinacious in his opinions" of all the imperial theologians. Steinherz, III, 296 (No. 98; see n. 274 infra). Brodrick passionately attacked him for lack of vision and inability to take into consideration any views other than narrow national ones, but thereby the English Jesuit betrayed his own myopia and partiality (pp. 555-556). In any case, it was too late for Córdoba to change the direction of the emperor's policy.

ing. Moreover, Ferdinand had been informed that this expression was very common in the sacred canons and their interpreters, and he would not wish to reject either expressly or tacitly what had been sanctioned so often by venerable antiquity, especially since he did not see how this would lead to the difficult dispute about the pope's superiority over the council. Nor would it follow that the council was superior to the pope from the fact that the Roman Curia, insofar as it was joined to the head, that is, the Roman pontiff, had to be reformed by the council, because the pope was included in the council, and it would be understood in that case that the reform was not done by the council distinct from the pope but by the pope on the advice of the conciliar fathers. The greater part of the emperor's arguments was meant to show, furthermore, that even if the pope was superior to the council, still he could permit this reform to the council out of courtesy (ex urbanitate). All these considerations notwithstanding, the emperor said that he willingly complied with Morone's advice and had ordered that those words be expunged and others be substituted. He assumed, however, that in any case there was no difference of opinion and intention between himself and the legate.[271] Whether his yielding to Morone's firmness on this point really amounted only to a verbal concession or also to a surrender of his position would soon be seen.

This second reply of the emperor (called the *duplica*) was handed to Morone as the latter was getting ready to leave Innsbruck. Interrupting his preparations, he immediately conferred with Ferdinand again for two hours, and he also spoke with Seld and Singkhmoser. Finally, he composed a rather long paper and left it with the nuncio, whom he directed to deliver it to the emperor. In this reply the departing legate first alleged his esteem for, and attachment to, the emperor as reasons for his having spoken so freely with him about the three chapters which he was striving to have him suppress. But while he acknowledged and praised Ferdinand's truly Christian intention, he feared that the emperor was not sufficiently informed about the affairs of the council and did not judge them rightly. Hence, besides arguing against the proposals of forming deputations by nations and of modifying the exclusive right of the legates to determine the agenda of the council, Morone tried to dissuade Ferdinand from insisting that the bull for the reform of the conclave be laid before the fathers at Trent. Attempting to refute Ferdinand's arguments, the legate asserted that the bull had been drawn up by the pope with the assistance of experts while none or very few of the fathers in the council were familiar with these mat-

---

[271]"Duplica Sacrae Caesareae Majestatis ad replicam Cardinalis Moroni," Innsbruck, May 12, 1563, Constant, *Légation*, pp. 114-116 (No. 23), and Sickel, *Concil*, pp. 499-500 (No. CCL).

ters; moreover, the subject of papal elections was never treated in a council unless the pope was present, and Pius IV had merely renewed what such popes had decreed; this practice, which was not then in use, could not be introduced without prejudice to the Holy See, which could not give to anyone else the authority granted to it by God. Morone conceded, however, that if the emperor thought the bull was not sufficient to remove the obstacles created by kings and princes, he could recommend that the council treat these questions pertaining to the secular rulers. Perhaps insinuating the need for compromise, Morone expressed his regret that his visit to Innsbruck would not entirely satisfy the emperor or the pope, and he urged Ferdinand in regard to the disputed questions to show the same affection for the pope as he did in other regards so that no disagreement would remain between them.[272] The legate must indeed have been a formidable, though urbane, adversary.

After Morone's departure from Innsbruck Delfino delivered his reply to the emperor's *duplica* and added other remarks orally. On the next day Ferdinand replied again. Before taking up the three contested points in order, he assured Morone that he had not taken any of his statements amiss and that there was no one with whom he would more willingly confer about matters of such great importance in view of his long-standing good-will toward him. In regard to the reform of the conclave the emperor repeated that he was wonderfully pleased with the bull. Hence, for the present he asked only that the pope exert himself zealously, partly that the bull be surely executed and partly that not only the cardinals together with the conclavists (for whom he thought that sufficient dispositions had been made in the bull) but also the ambassadors in Rome and the custodians of the conclave, along with all the people of the city, be deterred and restrained by the most drastic penalties from the machinations customary in papal elections. Thus he took up the legates' offer to let the council, with the deliberation and advice of the ambassadors of the kings and princes present in it, issue a decree on this topic. Finally, Ferdinand declared his hope that in promoting and handling matters pertaining to the public welfare of all Christendom, he and the pope might always have "one and the same permanent and constant will."[273]

---

[272]"Scriptum Cardinalis Moroni super duplica Caesareae Majestatis praesentatum per nuncium apostolicum, post discessum Cardinalis Moroni," Innsbruck, May 12, 1563, Constant, *Légation*, pp. 116-119 (No. 24). Cf. Raynaldus, 1563, No. 91, p. 375. Morone probably assumed that Ferdinand would not wish to grasp the thorny issue of the hindrances to the freedom of papal elections arising from the secular powers and therefore would not insist that the bull for the reform of the conclave be submitted to the council.

[273]"Responsum S. C. Majestatis super scripto Cardinalis Moroni per nuncium apostolicum Majestati S. C. exhibito," Innsbruck, May 13, 1563, Constant, *Légation*, pp. 123-124 (No. 27), and Sickel, *Concil*, pp. 500-502 (No. CCL). Cf. "Punctation über die persönliche Verhandlung des Kaisers Ferdinand und des

Quoting loosely this last wish and professing his joy at Ferdinand's attitude, Morone acknowledged receipt of the emperor's letter which the nuncio had forwarded to him. Since he was sure of the pope's good intentions and was now apprised of the emperor's adherence, he trusted that as a consequence of this union of minds great things could be done in the council.[274] Morone also asked the nuncio to present to Ferdinand a note requesting that he direct his ambassadors at Trent to support the legates and to favor their worthy decisions, desires, and efforts.[275] Acceding to this request, Ferdinand wrote immediately to his ambassadors, apprising them of the conclusions reached with Morone and ordering them to help the legates to make the freedom of the council observed and to ward off idle and temerarious questions. If anyone refused to abide by the regulations governing councils in general and this one in particular, he was to be checked by the legates; to ensure the observance of good order, the ambassadors were to lend the legates all timely aid and were to agree with them in all matters related to the advancement of God's glory and the Church's unity and peace and to make themselves available to the legates at all times and places.[276] Thus the emperor appeared to have succumbed to Morone's diplomatic charms.[277]

To what extent, then, it may be asked, did Morone achieve the objectives of his visit to Innsbruck? Canisius thought that the legate had accomplished some remarkable things that hardly anyone else could have accomplished, because he was so dear to, and familiar with, the emperor. Among these feats Canisius mentioned in particular the expunction of the frequently repeated phrase, "reform *in*

Legaten Moronus," Innsbruck, April [wrong month; it should be May] 13, 1563, Bucholtz, IX, 688. Here Ferdinand recorded that he had expressed to Morone his pleasure at the many decrees enacted at Trent under Paul III and Julius III as well as Pius IV, especially in matters concerning the abuses of the Roman Curia, but he also asked that if there were other things that similarly needed reform, the legates see to it that nothing be neglected. Morone not only promised this but also showed the emperor many canons which in this business of reform were to be proposed in the council at an early date. When Morone also showed him a copy of the bull for the reform of the conclave, the emperor admired its wise and holy provisions and continued to speak as in the *Responsum* just cited.
[274]Morone to Ferdinand, Matrei, May 13, 1563, Constant, *Légation*, pp. 125-126 (No. 28). Matrei was about ten miles from Innsbruck.
[275]Delfino to Ferdinand, Innsbruck, May 15, 1563, Constant, *Légation*, p. 126 (No. 29), and Sickel, *Concil*, p. 505.
[276]Ferdinand to the imperial ambassadors, Innsbruck, May 15, 1563, Sickel, *Concil*, p. 504 (No. CCLI).
[277]At this point in his narrative Sarpi inserted a rumor that was spread in Trent at that time and was regarded as certain by the most sensible people. It was said that Morone had treated more secret matters with the emperor and his son Maximilian and shown them that because of the divergent purposes and contrary interests of the princes and prelates it would be impossible to obtain from the council what any of them desired. In regard to reform he was supposed to have said that every class

capite et membris." The emperor, moreover, had approved what the
pope had begun to do in the area of reform.[278] Morone himself, in
reporting his conversations with Ferdinand to Borromeo, wrote
that the emperor's statement was considerably modified in the
three points to which he had objected; mention was no longer made
of the reform *in capite*, and the pope was spoken of with due
reverence; even where the question of carrying out the "universal
reform" in the council was taken up, the word "universal" was
restricted to the practice of the ancient councils in order to exclude
the Councils of Constance and Basel. Although Morone was inward-
ly pleased with his success, he showed little satisfaction to the
emperor.[279] Upon reading this dispatch, Pius IV shared his legate's
contentment. "In truth I can assure you," replied Borromeo, "that
in his whole pontificate he has never received greater satisfaction
from any minister; hence, the more arduous and difficult the
negotiations have been and the more important and primary for
public peace and for the preservation of the Apostolic See, the
greater praise and merit is due to Your Illustrious Lordship." Acting on Morone's suggestion, the pope had also expressed to the imperial ambassador at Rome his pleasure at Ferdinand's goodness
and piety and at his resolutions given to Morone, especially his
desire to be united with the pope in all public affairs and in looking
forward to the execution of the reform.[280]

---

wished to preserve itself in its present state and to reform the others; hence, a
greater number was opposed to each reform article proposed than was in favor of it,
and everybody wished to make the pope the minister of their own intentions without
thinking that others might thereby be offended. Where it was a question of
reforming the pope, the cardinal did not pretend to declare Pius IV's mind, but he
asked with what reason anyone could convince himself that in what did not and
could not touch the pope, Pius did not comply, because such a person did not know
what was not known to all, since to the pope alone were the desires of all referred.
Hence, Morone was said to have argued that since the council could not be fruitful it
should be concluded in the best way possible. According to the story, Ferdinand and
his son understood that it would be better to bury the council with honor, and they
promised to connive with him for its early termination. Sarpi did not advert to the
fact that Maximilian was not present for the discussions at Innsbruck, but he mentioned reasons for believing and disbelieving the rumor; trying to find a middle way,
he himself presented the thesis that those princes abandoned the hope of securing
any good result from the council and agreed not to obstruct its conclusion, but
thinking it not honorable to make a sudden retreat, they decided instead gradually
to abate their demands lest they advertise their lack of judgment in having ever conceived any hope of good from the council. Sarpi, ed. Gambarin, II, 895-896; ed.
Vivanti, II, 1091-1093. Such an interpretation, of course, was colored by the Venetian Servite's bias against the Romans.
[278]Canisius to Laínez, Innsbruck, May 12, 1563, Braunsberger, IV, 193-194 (No.
854), partially translated in Brodrick, pp. 557-558. The writer complained again
about his colleagues on the theological commission who did not accommodate their
rigid resolutions to the times or listen gladly to his admonitions.
[279]Morone to Borromeo, Matrei, May 13, 1563, Steinherz, III, 296-298 (No. 98).
[280]Borromeo to Morone, Rome, May 18, 1563, Constant, *Légation*, pp. 137-138
(No. 33). Cf. Borromeo to Alessandro Crivelli (nuncio in Spain), Rome, May 19, 1563,

In a later report, however, Morone made clearer to the pope exact-
ly what the emperor still desired in spite of his deletion of the phrase
"reform *in capite.*" The most troublesome point that they had
discussed was precisely this reform, which came down to papal elections and the appointment of cardinals, since the pope had already
left almost all the other matters to the council. First, for all his per-
suasiveness the legate had not induced the emperor to withdraw his
request that the bull for the reform of the conclave be proposed in
the council and that the council be permitted to make some addition
to it insofar as the princes were concerned. Morone shrewdly observed that if Ferdinand should persist in this request, it would be
something for the ambassadors of the secular princes to contradict,
not for the ministers of the pope; in fact, the more effective a remedy
the emperor would find to obstruct the intrigues of the princes, the
more reason the Romans would have to be obligated to him. Secondly, in regard to the reform of the cardinals, although the emperor
finally had dropped his request for a limit on their number, he had
continued to demand that some requirements be set down for their
qualifications and that this matter should be treated in the council.
In the end, nevertheless, Ferdinand was reduced to declaring that
he would be satisfied if the pope made provisions separately for the
creation of cardinals with his own bulls and if some mention of them
be made in the council, not in order that the council might pass
judgment on the bulls but that the measures might be more public
to the world and that Pius IV's successors might show more respect
for them and not contravene them.[281] It seems that Morone did not
consider the emperor's remaining requests unreasonable and was
implicitly seeking the pope's consent.

Susta, IV, 470, where the cardinal praised the emperor for having shown in his
negotiations with Morone "an infinite reverence" for the Holy See and for the
person of the pope.

[281] Morone to Borromeo, Trent, May 17, 1563, Steinherz, III, 309-310 (No. 99). In a
summary report on his mission to Innsbruck which was probably composed in
January, 1564, and possibly not by Morone himself but by someone else such as his
friend and confidant Filippo Gherio (it is narrated in the third person), it was said
that after the early discussions the emperor yielded on all but three points, viz., the
legates' exclusive right of proposing matter for conciliar action, voting by nations,
and the reform *in capite.* "Each of these subjects had many consequences and
opened the door to everyone to be able to propose whatever he wanted in the council
in regard to reform and dogmas, and to grant one of them would mean to grant them
all." Since the emperor could not be diverted from them, it was necessary to find a
compromise (*temperamento*) which would satisfy him in some way and at the same
time not prejudice the authority of the pope or of the legates. On the third subject it
was agreed that in drafting the decrees all the essential points set down by the
emperor would be treated, but the expression "reform *in capite*" would not be used,
in order to avoid the troubles that could follow, "especially the dispute of the
Sorbonne over the authority of the pope and the council." Constant, *Légation*, pp.
134-135 (No. 32). Ranke greatly exaggerated the importance of this document (of
later date and dubious authorship), calling it the most important he knew of
regarding the negotiations at Innsbruck.

Pius and his nephew were quick to observe that this final report on Morone's negotiations with the emperor cast a somewhat different light on the situation. The pope was still most satisfied with the conclusions that Morone had reached with Ferdinand and still expected from him all the good that could come from this affair. Pius had expressed his contentment to all the ambassadors at Rome and in particular to the imperial ambassador, to whom he had praised the emperor's piety and zeal. He also ordered Arco to assure Ferdinand that he should not remain deceived by his opinion of the pope, who wished to be sincerely united with him in everything concerning the service of God and public peace. Then the pope took up each of the three points on which a difference of views perdured. In regard to the reform *in capite* and the promotion of cardinals, the pope still refused to send the bulls for the reform of the conclave and other matters to the council so that they could then be published with the clause "*sacro approbante concilio.*" He asserted that he would be willing to do so if he were sure that the conciliar fathers would not make this reform a subject of dispute, as he thought would easily happen because of the difference of tendencies and interests reigning among them; then too, they would drag the council out indefinitely. To explain his failure to forbid expressly, in the bull for the reform of the conclave, the maneuvers and intrigues of the ministers of the princes, Pius said that he had wished thereby to show his respect for those princes, especially since he deemed it sufficient to prohibit all dealing to the cardinals, for if they obeyed, the ministers would not have anyone to deal with. If the emperor were to insist, however, that this matter be treated by the council, the pope would not be opposed to such an addition to the bull. As far as the appointment of cardinals was concerned, the pope merely promised to make provision for the qualifications required in each grade. He also promised to prepare a bull on this subject immediately and to send it to both the legates and the emperor within a few days.[282] A few days later, however, Borromeo confided to Morone that the pope was doubtful about the proposal in the draft of the

[282]Borromeo to Morone, Rome, May 27, 1563, Susta, IV, 33 (No. 6a), and Constant, *Légation*, pp. 152-155. Borromeo also related the strange divergence between what the imperial ambassador and what Morone had stated regarding the emperor's position on the appointment of a new archbishop of Mantua. Arco had requested the see in the emperor's name for. Cardinal Federico Gonzaga, brother of Duke Guglielmo and nephew of the late Cardinal Ercole, whose promotion to the Sacred College had caused so much turmoil in January; Arco had even shown letters to this effect from Ferdinand. Morone, on the other hand, had written to Borromeo (May 17, 1563, Steinherz, III, 305 [No. 99]) that Ferdinand did not wish to make an absolute request, doubting that he could obtain it from the pope because it was contrary to the decrees of the council. Morone believed that Ferdinand would be more satisfied with a refusal than with a granting of the favor. Pius, however, was not unwilling, said Borromeo, to give a bishopric to a cardinal of twenty-four years who was already a priest and had said many Masses and was not only of good life and habits but also brother of the duke, for he thought that such factors largely

bull to prohibit the elevation to the cardinalate of the brother of any cardinal; although this was also forbidden by the capitulations of the conclave, Pius was afraid of offending two brothers who were already cardinals. Hence, he did not know whether to make the reform in Rome or in the council, but he promised not to let this difficulty retard such a good work and rather to leave it to the legates and the council to do what might seem best to them.[283] Thus Pius would have been willing to let others assist him with problems that he could not solve by himself.

In assessing the significance of Morone's visit to Innsbruck, historians have agreed that the event was a turning point but have disagreed over the direction in which the turn was made. Ferdinand's admiring biographer believed that the negotiations strengthened in the pope the feeling of trust that mightily contributed to accelerate the progress of useful reforms of the ecclesiastical order, as, on the other side, the emperor's zeal contributed essentially to promote the same goal. Hence, for this author the visit produced positive results: the pope thereafter entrusted more of the reform to the council and consented to the inclusion of the cardinals in the conciliar decrees.[284] For a more recent writer, on the other hand, Morone's negotiations in Innsbruck meant the turning point at which the failure of the greatest part of the emperor's reform proposals was sealed. Before Morone's arrival Ferdinand with French and Spanish collaboration could have carried the reform of the Church through the council in his own way because of the fear of national councils. But the clever diplomat

counterbalanced what Federico was lacking in age. (Constant, Légation, pp. 155-156.) Accordingly, the pope promoted the cardinal to the see of Mantua in the consistory of June 6, although, being only twenty-three, he had not yet reached the age required by the conciliar decrees. (In its Seventh Session [de ref., cap. 1, Schroeder, p. 333; English translation, p. 55] on March 3, 1547, and again in its Twenty-second Session [de ref., cap. 2, ibid., pp. 425, 153] on September 17, 1562, the council had renewed the decree of the Third Lateran Council which prohibited the choice of anyone as bishop who had not completed his thirtieth year [COD, p. 212]. The Fifth Lateran Council had prohibited dispensations for age to anyone below his twenty-seventh year [COD, p. 615].) Afterwards Pius protested that he had only yielded to the emperor's demands. But though he thus tried to excuse his own deed by blaming the emperor and at the same time perhaps tried to discredit the emperor's demand for reform, Pius's real motives were the same as those he had had for creating Federico a cardinal at the beginning of the year, this is, to bind the House of Gonzaga more closely to himself.

[283]Borromeo to Morone, Rome, May 30, 1563, Constant, Légation, pp. 156-157. The two brothers were Alessandro Sforza di Santa Fiore, Bishop of Parma, and Guido Ascanio Sforza di Santa Fiore, the camerlengo. Borromeo also authorized Morone to win over Drašković, Brus, and the Bishop of Calahora, Juan de Quiñones, by promising them whatever might be necessary, even a cardinal's hat. The cardinal nephew also assured the legate that the pope gladly approved of all that he would do or would have Delfino and others do in the way of "presents," for, he added, "His Holiness knows well that no money is better spent than that."

[284]Bucholtz, VIII, 558.

from the Curia achieved his essential aim of averting a coalition of the emperor with Spain and France in the council which could have forced a reform.[285] The editor of the nuncios' reports accepted the belief of Morone's contemporaries in his triumph at Innsbruck, whether they were pleased by it (as Pius, Borromeo, and Canisius) or displeased (as Maximilian and, to some extent, Lorraine), and the latest historian of the council called the legate's journey to Innsbruck a complete success, for Morone not only convinced Ferdinand of the pope's good intentions, for which he vouched, but he also detached the emperor from France and Spain, thus obviating the danger to the papacy that had arisen from the common dissatisfaction of the three main Catholic powers and from their consequent cooperation at the council.[286] Yet it has appeared to other historians that Morone and Ferdinand reached genuine agreement only in regard to the dogmatic difficulties raised by the French and Spaniards but in other respects the legate's mission was unsuccessful; the emperor's partial complaisance was but a momentary obligingness.[287] Certainly, those who credit Morone with a resounding victory in this encounter cannot explain why Ferdinand did not desist from demanding a reform *in capite* (without using those words any longer) after the president of the council returned to Trent.

After Morone's departure from Innsbruck Ferdinand ordered that a summary be made of the conclusions on which he and the legate had agreed. While the other records of the conference were to be kept secret, copies of this summary were sent to the Cardinal of Lorraine and the Count de Luna for their information.[288] Ferdinand also communicated the various papers connected with Morone's visit to his sons Maximilian and Ferdinand; he asked Maximilian, who was in Vienna, to discuss this matter with four privy councilors and to send back his opinion. He probably did not expect so forthright a reply as he was to receive. After noting his father's extraordinary meekness and humility toward the pope, the King of the Romans said he did not doubt that the emperor, by abjectly soothing the pope, intended to induce him and the cardinals to scrutinize the forsaken and torn face of the Church, recognize themselves from their innermost depths, take the pious advice to heart, and pursue their occupation more sincerely than before. From his father's transactions with Morone, nevertheless, Maximilian concluded that very

---

[285]Kassowitz, pp. 186-187, 189. Kassowitz also remarks that at least in his old age Ferdinand was not a far-sighted statesman, for his zeal relied on the general promises of a reform that Morone gave him orally and that he, out of modesty, did not demand in writing (p. 216).

[286]Steinherz, III, 313. Jedin, *Geschichte,* IV/2, 25.

[287]Helle, pp. 61-62, following his master, Moritz Ritter.

[288]"Summarium eorum quae acta sunt inter Caesaream Majestatem et Cardinalem Moronum," Innsbruck, n.d. [May 14, 1563], Constant, *Légation,* pp. 128-133 (No. 31); also Le Plat, VI, 15-18.

little or almost no hope of obtaining any result or benefit from the Council of Trent was left. He thought that the negotiations had revealed the purpose of the papalists, for Morone, having removed his mask sufficiently, allowed himself and his followers to be clearly examined. The very fact that he worked so hard to have the word "head" expunged from the article on reform was enough; it was a most evident token of what the Roman Curia was hoping for, for that expression was not only frequently used by the holy Fathers of the Church but also by the councils themselves, which earnestly pressed it although it was not so urgently demanded in those times as it was in the present corrupt state of the Church. However, since the deed was done and the emperor had yielded to Morone in those and many other matters, they could not be sought again or called back into question. But since, in Maximilian's opinion, the other side hardly took into account the emperor's paternal and extreme good-will, and thus less advantage could be expected from the council from then on, his son advised him not to let himself be detained in Innsbruck any longer but rather to betake himself to Vienna, where he had other difficult and important affairs of no less concern to Christendom. For if the council should turn out to be fruitless, it would be more advisable for the emperor to be far away from it, especially, as Maximilian feared, if it should be dissolved without completing its business. In a postscript the king approved of the list of abuses of the German bishops, canons, and clergy which his father had sent him, especially those from which the opportunity was closed to Roman bird-catching. He thought it would be highly advantageous if, with due heed to equality, the head and its members were censured with the same severity as the prelates of the Empire, and if the members separated from the head were subjected to reform. Otherwise Maximilian feared that the emperor would be blamed for not having prevented this injustice and that the German prelates would not only disregard the council's judgment but would also despise the authority of the Holy See. For how would the German archbishops, especially the electors, who were equal to the cardinals in ambition, feel, he asked, if they saw themselves subjected to a rigorous, thorough reform while the cardinals continued with impunity in their licentious freedom? They could not easily be induced to bear it, and if no universal reform were undertaken, they would be given an occasion to protest against the council as partial, just like the Lutherans. Hence, he concluded again that the council would produce nothing of value unless an equal and universal reform were instituted from the top of the head to the soles of the feet.[289] It is obvious that the King of the Romans had not experienced Morone's sweet reasonableness which the emperor had not been able to resist.

---

[289]Maximilian to Ferdinand ,Vienna, May 24, 1563, Bucholtz, IX, 689-693. The Venetian ambassador who had been recalled from Rome about this time shared Maximilian's pessimism. In his final report to the Senate Girolamo Soranzo said

Replying to his son, the emperor tried to justify his concessions to the president of the council. He wrote that in their conversations he had kept back none of the things that needed correction in the clergy and especially in the Roman Curia. He also denied that he had easily yielded to all of Morone's requests without frankly contradicting him; hence, the legate seemed to be not entirely content and satisfied when he departed, as his final statement revealed. Ferdinand, however, did not want all the matters that were orally and secretly discussed between the two of them to be set down in writing, nor did he think it fitting, when the pope had sent him such a distinguished and well-affected man, to dismiss him with a reply in which nothing would be granted him at least for the sake of goodwill but all his requests would be denied. In Ferdinand's opinion, however, his benevolence had not extended to the point of conceding anything by which prejudice was done to the Church or the fathers of the council or other Christian kings and princes. For even though he had removed from his first statement the express mention of instituting a reform not only in the members but also *in capite*, nevertheless, such words were substituted as meant the same thing substantially, namely, that there was necessary a universal reform of which there was express mention in the ancient councils, since the ancient councils mentioned reform *in capite et membris*. (Apparently the emperor interpreted this reference differently from Morone.) Ferdinand admitted no reason for being able or obliged to oppose so obstinately the pope whom he had to acknowledge as his superior *in spiritualibus* and who had clearly shown his paternal affection for him. Adding a personal motive for complaisance, the emperor reminded his son that if the pope were exasperated, he could easily raise very numerous and serious difficulties in the matter of confirming and approving the election of Maximilian as King of the Romans and next emperor. In the troubled state of their affairs Fer-

---

that Pius IV was now trying to end the council by prolonging the deliberations so that the emperor would leave Innsbruck and the French, "by nature impatient and very little disposed to endure any inconvenience," would decide to return to their dioceses, and in this way the council would be dissolved but it would appear that the dissolution was not caused by Rome but rather by the disagreements of the fathers. He observed that many in Rome were displeased by the intention of many persons at the council to establish the reform in such a way and form that it would no longer be in the pope's power to alter it; Pius IV especially resented this attempt to make him the simple executor of the decisions of the council instead of universal head of the Church. The ambassador accepted the opinion of the best-informed men of Rome that in those circumstances the council could have no other effect than that produced by a strong medicine in a weak body--instead of curing, it kills--"and that thus when the world is in such disorder and turmoil, by wishing to apply such a powerful remedy, one runs the risk not of putting the Apostolic See in order but of bringing it to ruin." "Relazione . . . letta in Senato il 14 Giugno 1563, Albèri, Vol. X (Series II, Tome IV), pp. 118-119.

dinand naturally preferred to obviate such an eventuality.[290] It
seems that Ferdinand attached more importance to the pope's confirmation of Maximilian's election than Maximilian himself did.

Ferdinand also rejected his son's advice to leave the neighborhood
of the council at the first opportunity and thus abandon all hope for
its success. Instead he assigned to the theological commission the
task of reviewing the reform *libellus* of the previous year. The nuncio reported to the legates that it would be modified to the extent
that the mention of reform *in capite*, of limiting the number of the
cardinals, and of some other similar things, as well as of those
already treated by the council, would be removed; what would be
left would be sent to the imperial ambassadors at Trent for proposal
to the council.[291] The nuncio was more sanguine about the expected
outcome of these deliberations than Canisius, who was a member of
the commission. The Jesuit narrated to his general an audience in
which the emperor condemned the stubborn endeavor to refuse the
judgment of council in matters pertaining to the reform of the
Roman Curia. Canisius called this attitude "the old and com-
monplace song of many" which his colleagues on the commission
seemed to have increased. He feared that when they would come to
the chapter on reform, his colleagues would defeat him, offering in-
flexible counsel to the emperor and advising him to make demands
which it was not expedient to grant.[292] Canisius had previously informed the general of the grievances that the imperialists felt
against Rome. For example, the contrary of what was decided in the
council was declared in deeds at Rome, as had happened when
questors of alms were sent to the Kingdom of Naples after the council had forbidden this practice. Moreover, although bulls had recently been issued at Rome, the imperialists thought that due concern
was not shown for their execution, as if the reform of the Roman
Curia were not being seriously considered. Canisius was reporting
these complaints to the general, he said, partly that he might know
how to reply to such objections and partly that the scandals which
could result and the troubles for those who could help the Church at

[290]Ferdinand to Maximilian, Innsbruck, June 2, 1563, Sickel, *Concil,* pp. 517-518
(No. CCLVII). Kassowitz remarked that it was not a question of empty words, "and
if Ferdinand meant that the expression substituted at the legate's request did not
mean less than the one previously used and [if he] did not correctly notice that the
softening of individual words in this case meant the abandonment of the position
hitherto held by the emperor in his reform policy and the renunciation of the
traditions of Constance and Basel, then this self-deception of the emperor is a
striking proof of the diplomatic skill with which Morone understood how to get the
better of his political opponent in this difficult question" (p. 209).
[291]Delfino to the legates, Innsbruck, May 17, 1563, Steinherz, III, 315 (No. 100).
[292]Canisius to Laínez, Innsbruck, May 23, 1563, Braunsberger, IV, 213 (No. 866);
also given with some variations in a more impersonal form as "Bericht eines
Ungenannten" in Steinherz, III, 320-321 (No. 102).

the imperial court might be averted.[293] In other words, Canisius did not wish to be held responsible at Rome for any of the emperor's eventual decisions that the Curia might resent. At the same time he probably foresaw that copies of his letters with their gentle criticisms of certain curial attitudes and practices would be sent to Rome. In fact, the pertinent parts of his letters were communicated to Morone and to Rome although his authorship of the suggestions for more fruitful negotiations with the emperor was concealed.

The same complaints as Canisius had reported to Laínez as being raised at the imperial court were made known to Borromeo directly by the legates at Trent. In the council rumors and whispers were heard that at Rome the decrees of that very council were being violated every day. The legates said that such things caused them very great distress and compelled them to beg the pope again to have due regard given to the decrees in order to avoid any trouble. They warned him also that some would seize on this occasion to bind his hands by asserting divine right in every matter, by seeking the reform *in capite*, and by trying to maintain that the council was superior to the pope. In the legates' opinion, this was what primarily scandalized the conciliar fathers and the princes. Like Canisius, the cardinals added that a particular cause of complaint was that in spite of the council's decree abolishing all questors of alms, those of St. Anthony and perhaps also those of the fabric of St. Peter's were going through the Kingdom of Naples. The legates suggested that if this was true, Borromeo should take some appropriate action.[294] It was clear that the council's patience with the Roman Curia was wearing thin.

Meanwhile the general and secretary of the Society of Jesus at Trent were awaiting some action of the council on reform. Morone had indicated that something worthwhile would be done. Once again Polanco concluded, "May God Our Lord let us see it not only in writing but also in effect."[295] The emperor too was waiting for the pope to complete the reform which remained to be done; he told the nuncio that he would not seek anything from the council beyond what the pope would have done. He also said that his theologians and counselors often asked him whether the pope had yet issued a bull on the required qualifications for the cardinalate, and he made it clear that he himself desired to see strict measures laid down in

[293]Canisius to Laínez, Innsbruck, May 17, 1563, Braunsberger, IV, 203 (No. 859), partially translated in Brodrick, pp. 559-560. The name and services of questors of alms had been abolished on July 16, 1562, in the Twenty-first Session, *de ref.*, cap. 9, Schroeder, p. 415; English translation, p. 142.
[294]The legates to Borromeo, Trent, May 28, 1563, Susta, IV, 24 (No. 4).
[295]Polanco to Canisius, Trent, May 25, 1563 (a reply to his letters of May 17 and 23), Braunsberger, IV, 220-221 (No. 869).

this regard.[296] Thus Ferdinand maintained pressure on the Holy See. At the same time the emperor was also waiting for his theological commission to complete the task that he had assigned to it, namely, to review all his previous instructions, his *libelli*, and his agreements with Morone, to compare them with the demands presented in the council by the French and the Spaniards and with the conciliar decrees, and to recommend what should be done and proposed in the council in the emperor's name. Because of the diversity of views of its members, the commission's progress was slow,[297] and its report, compiled by its secretary, Conrad Braun, was not completed until June 5. Here were set down several articles to be proposed in the council anew in the emperor's name. Among those on the advancement of the council the tenth (and last) read as follows: "that the universal reform of the Church be done in the council before its dissolution, not only in the particular inferior churches but also in the first patriarchal church of Rome and its Curia." After enumerating other reforms in various areas, the commission returned to the universal reform of the Church, "which they call the reform *in capite et in membris*"; this, they affirmed, was the most necessary of all, for unless it would precede, no reform of the members could conveniently be accomplished or be useful. The commission acknowledged that in the judgment of many persons "the universal reform of the Church *in capite et membris*" ought to be done by the authority not only of the Roman pontiff but also of the ecumenical council, for this was said to be one of the reasons for which a council had of necessity to be convoked. Although, according to the commission, the emperor would leave that dispute to more sagacious men (*prudentioribus*), nevertheless, he believed that the reform *in capite*, even if it ought to belong to the pope alone, would be much more beneficial and easy if it were done together with the council, for several reasons: (1) in this way the matter of reform would be brought to a conclusion more promptly; (2) because of the large number of holy and learned fathers all

<hr/>

[296]Delfino to Borromeo, [Innsbruck,] May 26, 1563, Steinherz, III, 318. Five days later the nuncio reported to the president of the council that he was not failing to "exorcise the Franciscan every day" and had made him so gentle (*addolcito*) that Canisius was amazed. Delfino to Morone, Innsbruck, May 31, 1563, Steinherz, III, 323 (No. 103). The nuncio's efforts to win Córdoba over to the Curia's side by means of little presents, however, were unsuccessful.

[297]Under the heading "Syllabus praecipuorum postulatorum, quae imperatori Ferdinando, si fieri posset, in concilio Tridentino urgenda videbantur," and under the year 1562, Le Plat (V, 260-264), borrowing from Schelhorn (*Amoenitates*, I, 587 ff.), printed the articles that Córdoba handed to the commission before June 1, 1563, according to Sickel, *Concil*, p. 528. Here are included various demands, e.g., that the reform of the Church be done in a general council (VI), that the pope humble himself after the example of Christ and endure a reform of his person, state, and Curia (VII), and that the reform of the conclave and of the election of cardinals be done in the council (VIII). Here too are many other points that were adopted in the commission's final report.

suspicion would cease, while it could not be avoided if the reform were done in Rome, because of the various and perverse interests of those who would have to assist the pope; (3) this humbling of himself, in keeping with the example of many of his predecessors, would win great glory for the pope throughout the world and in the eyes of posterity; (4) many handle the case of another person better than one or a few handle their own, for where there is much advice, there is safety; (5) a reform decreed by the whole council would have more weight among kings and princes and would be executed more easily than one done by the pope alone in Rome; and (6) in consequence, the authority of the council, which ought to be regarded as the strongest bulwark against the heretics, would be immensely enhanced. Referring to the reform of the conclave, the commission observed that although some things contained in the papal bull were said to have been already reformed, certain other things in the Curia itself, aside from the matters of the conclave, were supposed to need reform, and it quoted the following list drawn from the Council of Constance: the number, qualifications, and nationality of the cardinals, reservations to the Holy See, annates, *servitia communia et minuta*, collations of benefices and expectative favors, confirmations of elections, cases to be treated in the Curia or not, appeals to the Curia, the duties of the Chancery and Penitentiary, commendams and fruits of the *medium tempus*, the alienation of the property of the Roman church, the extirpation of simony, dispensations, the support of the pope and the cardinals, the sale of offices, the huge sums paid for the pallium and for confirmations of elections, resignations and exchanges of benefices, and the arranging of peace between princes. Although Ferdinand, in discussing the reform of the conclave with Morone, had said that it seemed advisable to refer some of these matters to the council too, the commission refrained from prescribing any "law" for the emperor in this regard and did not consider itself competent to reconsider what he had already done.

This response of the theological commission, although it was approved by the chairman and the other members, did not fully satisfy all of them. The secretary appended a note in which he submitted its contents "to the judgment of the Holy, Catholic, Roman, and Apostolic Church."[298] Córdoba, on the other hand, addressed two letters to the emperor on the following day, asking him to press for

---

[298]"Liber in materia reformationis C. Mti a theologis deputatis oblatus," June 5, 1563, Sickel, *Concil*, pp. 522, 525-527 (No. CCLVIII). On the reforms demanded by the Council of Constance, Fortieth Session (October 30, 1417), see *COD*, p. 444. Comparing the sum of the anticurial proposals of this second *libellus* with those of the first (of June 7, 1562), Helle points out the greater number and sharpness of those in the second. Instead of asking the pope to reform his person and his Curia, it was now demanded without much ado that the council undertake the reform of the universal Church, and the positive proposals were increased by the list taken from the Council of Constance. The same tendency appeared in the demand for the right of proposition and in others (pp. 21, 27-29).

the reform of the Church with determination and to permit the individual members of the commission to submit separate memorials. On June 7 Ferdinand transmitted the commission's report, along with Córdoba's comments, to his envoys at Trent and requested their opinion.[299] In their response the Archbishop of Prague and the Bishop of Pécs stated that although they had always striven to carry out the emperor's commands, still they praised the work of the theological commission for putting all these matters in proper order. They agreed with the imperial theologians that the universal reform of the Church and especially of the Roman Curia was necessary and desirable, but they feared that although this had been promised to them in a public congregation, only words had been given them. They entertained this suspicion especially because it was often said both privately and publicly that articles for this kind of reform had been sent from Rome to Trent and yet none of the persons with whom they had spoken could mention even one of the reform articles to them. The legates had promised to communicate any such matters to them, however, before proposing them to the council, as their predecessors, Cardinals Gonzaga and Seripando, had been accustomed to do. The two episcopal ambassadors likewise expressed their ardent desire that the reform *in capite et membris* be done in the council rather than in Rome, and they said that they had sought after that one object in particular from the beginning with great earnestness and diligence, especially since they understood that the reforms done by the popes at Rome were wont to perish with the popes themselves. Hence, they exhorted the emperor to write about this matter both to the pope and to the legates and to bring it about that all these reforms be enacted in the council for their more constant and lasting observance. Finally, they asked Ferdinand whether they should continue to urge these matters according to the commission's report and their own animadversions on it.[300]

Ferdinand must have received this reply shortly before he departed from Innsbruck on June 25, having learned from experience, Sarpi says, "either at this time or two months before when Morone was with him, that his nearness to the council not only failedto produce the good results that he had expected but even brought about contrary effects, in as much as the prelates of the papal party, suspecting that His Majesty had designs against the authority of the Roman Court, took umbrage at everything; hence, the difficulties and suspicions were increasing in bitterness and

[299]Sickel, *Concil*, p. 528. Cf. Steinherz, III, 326, on Córdoba's insistence that the emperor not drop the reform of the papacy and the College of Cardinals but rather commission his envoys to propose to the council a motion that "the council not be dissolved or concluded until the reform be accomplished in the *patriarchal* church of Rome."

[300]Brus and Drasković to Ferdinand, Trent, June 18, 1563, Sickel, *Concil*, pp. 528-530, 532-533.

growing also in number.''[301] Although such an attitude might have
been justified to some extent, the Servite historian of the council did
not substantiate his interpretation with any documentary evidence,
while other grounds for the emperor's departure from the vicinity of
the council are well known.

VII.   The Council's Reform Work, June--December, 1563

The explanation of the emperor's partial loss of interest may be
sought in the developments that occurred at Trent after Morone
returned from Innsbruck and took in hand the reins of the council.
He did not attempt to prevent the fathers from bringing up certain
aspects of the desired reform of the cardinals during the discussion
of the abuses of the sacrament of Orders. The Cardinal of Lorraine
recommended that the council go back to the discipline of the first
500 years of the Church, when dispensations were unknown, and he
said that if the popes had abstained from granting them fifty years
before or would abstain for a few years even then, there would be no
need for so many new laws. To support his position he quoted part
of the *Cosilium delectorum cardinalium* presented to Paul III, and
he urged that dispensations not be granted without extreme
necessity. Lorraine was also in favor of compelling bishops to go to
live in their dioceses within six months as an antidote to commendams. He considered this to be the worst abuse, especially in cardinal deacons, who were sometimes created at the age of twelve and
were given sees which should have been given only to men of mature
age (at least thirty); he even thought it was shameful (*indignum*) to
give sees in commendam to cardinal priests, but he deemed this
practice more tolerable, although they too should reside in their
dioceses unless they would be called away by the pope; nevertheless,
he believed it better that priests be priests and not bishops.[302] The
pope's own nephew was one of the cardinal deacons whom Lorraine
criticized (without naming him), for he was perpetual administrator
of the Archdiocese of Milan although he had not received any sacred
order higher than that of deacon.
    Substantially agreeing with these opinions, another speaker,
Pedro Guerrero, Archbishop of Granada, declared that it was
reasonable to deliberate in the council on the manner of choosing

---

[301]Sarpi, ed. Gambarin, II, 923; ed. Vivanti, 1125-1126. Perhaps the Servite had
seen the diary of the secretary to the Venetian ambassadors to the council, who
believed that since Cardinal Morone had negotiated in person with the emperor,
"His Majesty seemed no longer to be so ardent about the affairs of the council; also
his ambassadors withdrew their demands for the reform of the pope and of the
cardinals." [Antonio Milledonne,] *Journal du Concile de Trente rédigé par un
secrétaire vénitien présent aux sessions de 1562 à 1563*, ed. Armand Baschet (Paris,
1870), p. 134.
[302]General Congregation, May 14, 1563, Acta, *CT*, IX, 492 (No. 169), and "Paleotti
Acta," *CT*, III, 615-616. Borromeo was ordained a priest two months later, on July
17, 1563.

cardinals and on the qualities to be sought in them, because the
council had power over every potentate except the pope and because
all the decrees of the council could be regarded as having been made
by the pope, who would have to approve them. This Spaniard also
censured the cardinals, who were obliged to remain close to the
pope, for having the care of dioceses with such danger to their souls.
Guerrero spoke at length against the exemptions and reservations
granted by the Holy See, which were unknown to the ancient
Church; he pointed out the absurdity of the situation of a priest or
canon in Spain or India who could not be judged by anyone except
in Rome, and he urged that the bishops be given back their proper
authority.[303] Another Spaniard, Diego Enrico de Almanca, Bishop
of Coria, insisted that since the council was trying in its decrees to
give good form to all the other orders and ecclesiastical dignities, it
should do the same for the cardinals.[304] Calini commented that such
a reform seemed to be expressly desired by all the ultramontanes
who regarded it as the main foundation of the reform of the Church;
he added that it was also tacitly requested by many Italians who
left it without any exception to the requests of the ultramontanes.[305]
A few days later another Spaniard, Antonio Corrionero, Bishop of
Almería, explicitly declared the reform of the cardinals to be the
main foundation of the universal reform, because they elected the
pope and were accustomed to choose one from their own college.
Then, to propose a model that could be used in creating cardinals for
the benefit of the whole Church, he recommended that the council
give the pope the advice that Jethro gave Moses when the latter was
to choose assistants in governing the people of Israel. Thus, cardinals should be chosen from every country, should be learned, wise,
and at least forty years old, not adulators who would agree with the

---

[303]Gualterio to Borromeo, Trent, May 16, 1563, Jedin, *Krisis*, pp. 239-240 (No. 78);
cf. Acta, *CT*, IX, 494 (No. 170), where Guerrero answers the objection that since the
pope creates cardinals, the council must not say anything about them, remarking:
"the Pope also creates bishops, and if the cardinals wish to have churches [dioceses],
let them have them, but not in commendam, but let them be true bishops," and
reside in their dioceses.

[304]General Congregation, May 24, 1563, Acta, *CT*, IX, 526 (No. 183). Domenico
Mellini, the secretary who reported to Cosimo I after the departure of the Florentine
ambassador (Giovanni Strozzi) from Trent, wrote that he had heard that in the
general congregations awful things (*cose grandissime*) were being said, especially
about reforming the pope and the cardinals. He had been told that it had been said
by someone besides the bishop of Paris that there were those--and they were
numerous enough--who wished to maintain the abuses of the Roman Curia and
Court and who reported to Rome especially the speeches that they did not like and
slandered those who spoke the truth and desired what was good; they would not fail
because of that, however, to demand justice, to defend the truth, and to bear witness
to their conscience; it was said that these threats of informing Rome were improper
means and that soon they would ruin those who used them rather than others. In
conclusion the secretary lamented that the council was "in a state where it seems
that nothing can be seen but the darkness of discord, if darkness can be seen."
Mellini to Cosimo I, Trent, May 21, 1563, D'Addario, p. 311 (No. CLXXXVI).

[305]Calini to Cornaro, Trent, May 27, 1563, Marani, p. 457.

pope in every case, nor men who would fear kings or seek pensions from them.[306]

The deputation which the legates appointed to draft the reform decree for the next session made good use of the petitions of the emperor and of the Spanish, French, and other nations. Since it dealt with important matters, especially the cardinals, the legates sent the earliest version available to the pope, imperfect though it was. At the same time they reminded him that since there were few fathers who did not mention the age and qualifications that should be required of cardinals and who did not request their reform earnestly, it would not be a bad idea to issue as soon as possible the bull that he was preparing. Even at that, they added, it would still be difficult to close the mouths of the fathers and to stop them from crying out for the reform of the cardinals.[307]

Responding to this pressure, Pius IV in the consistory of June 9 appointed a commission and ordered it to prepare a bull for reform of the Sacred College with respect not so much to the number and other conditions of the cardinals as to their morals. His nephew explained to the nuncio in Spain that if the pope had thought that the reforms undertaken at Rome would be properly understood in the council, he would not have put his hand to it, but knowing that

---

[306]Calini to Cornaro, Trent, May 31, 1563, Marani, p. 461. General Congregation, May 29, 1563, Acta, *CT*, IX, 546 (No. 195). About the same time Drasković, speaking on the proposed reform chapters, enumerated various kinds of abuses, one of which was the confirmation in the Roman Curia of the elections and nominations of bishops on the basis of the bare decisions of the chapters and recommendations of the princes without any previous inquiry into the truth or falsity of the decisions or recommendations or into the ability of the persons elected or nominated but solely on payment of the fee. The Bishop of Pécs stated that the council could remedy this evil if it would declare that before any action would be taken in Rome, the pope should depute trustworthy commissioners who would inquire into all circumstances of the election or nomination and faithfully report to the pope on them all. In this recommendation Drasković certainly showed no hostility to the Holy See; on the contrary, he would have effectively increased its power. "Votum episcopi Quinqueecclesiensis de 16 capitibus reformationis," May 28, 1563, *CT*, IX, 543. On this subject see Robert Trisco, "The Debate on the Election of Bishops in the Council of Trent," *The Jurist*, XXXIV (1974), 257-291.

On May 31, 1563, the Venetian ambassadors to the council reported that Morone had said that the pope wished a reform without mention of the Apostolic See in order to preserve all its authority, and Lorraine replied that one should not cover the abuses with the mantle of the Apostolic See. Milledonne-Baschet, *op. cit.*, pp. 233-234.

[307]The legates to Borromeo, Trent, June 4, 1563, Susta, IV, 42 (No. 8). Several days later the legates warned Borromeo that the affairs of the council were taking a turn toward demanding a reform of the Court of Rome and an increase of the faculties of bishops; there were few congregations, they wrote, "in which there is not talk about reforming the cardinals whom they would wish not to have bishoprics but to stay in Rome and serve their titular churches, so to speak, like parishes, and on the other hand they aim only at raising the dignity of the bishops whom they would not wish to have to go to Rome either for dispensations or for collation of benefices; they would wish them to have so much authority that their rank would be greater than that of the cardinals." Same to same, Trent, June 10, 1563, *ibid.*, p. 54 (No. 11).

because of the variety of whims and opinions at Trent, especially of those who were not familiar with the affairs of Rome, and, not having diagnosed the malady, did not know what medicine to apply and who perhaps would conduct themselves with passion and maliciousness according to their own interests, the pope had decided to do by himself what pertained to him; thus he had always believed that by his good example he would give cause for edification rather than for scandal to the whole world, and this he would do in the other reforms that remained to be carried out and especially in that of the cardinals, which was then under study. Borromeo promised that soon a bull would be issued which would prescribe the qualities required in candidates for that dignity. Although Pius was decreeing these reforms by himself, fearing that the council would never agree on making them, nevertheless, he would always send them to the council for approval. "So great," he concluded, "is the desire of His Holiness to see a genuine and very rigorous and strict reform."[308]

If by this message Pius intended to anticipate Philip II's collaboration with the imperialists and the French for the reform of the Sacred College, he was too late, for a few days earlier the king had informed his uncle that he had strongly urged the pope to leave the reform to the council, arguing that the pope could do so without prejudice to his authority and without any danger or inconvenience whatsoever, and that while in those times a reform that he would make at Rome would be of little effect, no matter how great and good it might be, a reform made in the council would have much more authority and give much more satisfaction. Notwithstanding all the arguments with which Philip had tried to persuade and mollify him, Pius did not reply to him in such a way as to give hope that he would do as Philip had requested; he had extolled the reform and the amount that he was losing in revenue as a result of it, and he had said that when it would be finished it could be confirmed by the council. The King of Spain recognized that this reply was an expedient and an attempt of the pope "to excuse himself with general and ambiguous words" rather than comply with what was so rightly asked of him; he saw little reason to doubt that the council would do what was desired. After receiving this reply, the king decided to ask Ferdinand what course they could take, besides once again urging the pope, as they were both doing; he suggested that if the pope should still refuse to acquiesce, the ambassadors of the princes, each for his own country, should present in the council very long and complete memorials about everything that needed to be remedied;

---

[308]Borromeo to Crivello, Rome, June 15, 1563, Susta, IV, 499-500 (Beilage X), and Constant, *Légation*, pp. 469-470 (Appendix, No. XIV), and n. 3. The pope asked the legates also to express their opinions regarding bulls for the reform of the cardinals and of the conclave (as far as the sovereigns and their envoys were concerned). Borromeo to the legates, Rome, June 12 and 16, 1563, Susta, IV, 83-84, 89 (Nos. 16 and 18).

in them were to be set forth the injuries and disorders that originated in the Roman curia, and it was to be asked insistently that the council treat all of this without delay.[309] No doubt, when Pius came to realize that he could not count on the support of the Catholic King, he recognized the inevitability of allowing the council some share in the reform of the cardinals.

The first indication of this change of attitude was intimated by the legate appointed at the same time as Morone, Cardinal Bernardo Navagero, to the Cardinal of Lorraine, who communicated it to Brus and Drasković. The new legate expressed high hope for the reform since he had heard that the pope was willing to let the age, qualifications, and choice of cardinals be discussed in the council; the reason for referring this matter to the council was that the pope was gravely offended by the disagreement of the cardinals at Rome over this

---

[309]Philip II to Ferdinand, Aranjuez, June 9, 1563, *CDI*, IX (1846), 334-335. Ferdinand replied to this letter more than two months later. He assured his royal nephew that both on his part and on that of his ambassadors at Trent he had always taken care to preserve and defend the dignity and authority of the pope and to hold it in due esteem, especially in those times when the pope was so defamed and debased by his enemies. Hence, he did not believe that the pope had any legitimate cause to complain about him, all the more so because for that same respect he had labored to have the old controversy over the superiority of the pope and the council stayed, in consideration of the scandal that could result to the detriment of the dignity and authority of the Holy See. In case, nevertheless, the pope should wish to use his power for the destruction rather than for the edification of the Church, and in disregard of the sacred canons and councils observed up till then in all times and places, Ferdinand affirmed his obligation, "as supreme protector and defender of the Church," to oppose the pope, and he promised to exercise that office as often as he would deem it proper and necessary; he would also see to it that by some "new example of pretension" the pope would not seek to apply or attribute to himself what did not belong to him and could not be proved from the usual sources. In regard to reform, the emperor complimented Philip on his efforts to move the pope. He said that in his negotiations with Cardinal Morone he had concealed nothing pertaining to the manifest abuses of ecclesiastics, especially "the various abuses of ecclesiastical jurisdiction and power in the Court of Rome, and all to extract money legally and illegally," which caused heretics to hold all such jurisdiction and power in contempt and up to mockery. Ferdinand had also told Morone that although he had always had a good opinion of the person of the pope and had no doubt about the temporal government of the Papal States, he considered that matters related to the Court of Rome which were common to all of Christendom had to be treated in the council, because their reform according to ordinary law pertained to the pope as head and to the council as body joined to it, and this was not one of the least causes for which councils were wont to be convoked. Ferdinand said that he had given Morone a statement of the abuses that should be corrected in the council and not by the authority of the pope alone or of the cardinals (for he did not know what could be expected if the reform depended on them alone); but Morone had shown him many decrees touching on the abuses of the Roman court, made in the two previous periods of the council at Trent, and some made in the current one, as well as drafts of bulls and canons to be proposed; hence, Ferdinand had decided to wait to see what the cardinal would do--he had promised to do it earnestly (*encarecidamente*). Ferdinand to Philip II, Vienna, August 12, 1563, *CDI*, IX, 359-362.

reform.[310] The good news, which the envoys at Guise's request forwarded to the emperor, brought him extraordinary pleasure. He replied that this was one of the topics that he had discussed with Morone with the greatest contention, but he had not been able to obtain any promise or hope from him even though he kept up his insistence to the end. Since this occasion was now presented, Ferdinand directed his ambassadors to press the matter unremittingly.[311]

The reason alleged for the pope's change of plan was corroborated by the dispatches of the imperial ambassador at Rome. According to Arco, when Pius announced in the consistory on June 9 that the bull for the reform of the conclave was to be revised at the emperor's request so as to prohibit the secular princes from interfering in the election and to specify the qualifications of candidates for the cardinalate, the cardinals were not pleased because they saw that if the secular princes would no longer meddle in the conclave, neither would they give the cardinals pensions, abbacies, and other dignities as the kings of Spain and France had previously done; indeed, they would even be forced to give up such emoluments. Hence, it was thought to be difficult or even impossible that the cardinals should bring themselves to this point by themselves, and even if they did so, it was feared that the French would not be satisfied, because they wanted everything pertaining to reform to be concluded by the council and not by those in Rome, in order to give it more firmness.[312] A few days later the ambassador reported that some cardinals wished to leave the bull as it was without adding anything to it; others argued against reducing the cardinals to a definite number; according to one of these arguments, if this were done, many bishops at the council would be deprived of the hope of becoming cardinals, and this could harm the pope by removing the possibility of rewarding many who were defending his side. As for their sources of income, some thought that the princes could be deterred from interfering in the conclave by a threat of excommunication. Still others advised the pope to do whatever the emperor asked, because later he could abrogate whatever was decreed.[313] At the end of the month Arco wrote that the cardinals even refused to come to the consistory if the emperor's proposals were to be discussed; hence, the pope threatened to refer the reform of the Sacred College to the council.[314] Obviously, no results could be expected from the Roman cardinals.

Meanwhile the long discussion of the abuses of the sacrament of orders was drawing to a close at Trent. The legates had appointed a

---

[310]Brus and Drasković to Ferdinand, Trent, June 9, 1563, Sickel, *Concil*, pp. 538-539 (No. CCLX).

[311]Ferdinand to the imperial ambassadors, Innsbruck, June 14, 1563, Sickel, *Concil*, p. 544 (No. CCLXIII).

[312]Arco to Ferdinand, Rome, June 12, 1563, Sickel, *Concil*, p. 542 (No. CCLXII).

[313]Arco to Ferdinand, Rome, June 16, 1563, Sickel, *Concil*, p. 542-543.

[314]Arco to Ferdinand, Rome, June 30, 1563, Sickel, *Concil*, p. 543.

deputation to collect the opinions of the fathers who had spoken on this subject and to draw up appropriate canons. The deputies, however, reflected the division in the whole assembly; some wished to include the reform of the cardinals in the forthcoming session because a large number of the speakers had requested it, while others wished to omit it because it had not been requested by a majority of the speakers and because that did not seem to be the proper place to treat it. Hence, the two French members of the deputation asked the legates to appoint three additional fathers who they thought would agree with them in this regard. The legates used this disagreement to remind Borromeo that every reform which the pope would make could only be good, and the sooner he would make it, the better it would be, especially if it would be substantial. They frankly commented that they had found little of substance in the proposals that Borromeo had sent them. Even if the pope enacted a substantial reform, it would be difficult, they foresaw, to keep quiet those who wished to decree the reform in Trent and who could not be induced to believe that the pope sincerely desired it. "They are even saying openly that we are deferring and putting off the business of reform with the intention of settling the other matters and going off with God, leaving the reform to whoever wants it."[315] Pius must have understood that it would be foolhardy to ignore the legates' warnings much longer.

The last speaker in the debate on the abuses of the sacrament of Orders was the general of the Society of Jesus, Diego Laínez.[316] A few days previously he had written to Francisco Borja in Rome that the reform which was hoped for from Rome, instead of being kept under wraps, ought to be published and put into effect by order of the pope, because the affairs at Trent necessarily went more slowly and much time was required to treat them. Although they could be concluded shortly, he thought it more becoming that the pope than the council should handle the matters which touched the papal court more closely.[317] When he prepared his speech he believed that the pope had already sent a rather severe reform decree to Trent many

---

[315]The legates to Borromeo, Trent, June 14, 1563, Susta, IV, 66 (No. 13).

[316]On Laínez's participation in the third period of the Council of Trent see Scaduto, *op. cit.*, pp. 137-267. Scaduto states that the fear of a schism dominated Laínez's thoughts to such an extent as "to make him sacrifice his theoretical positions and to make him pursue, in the concrete field of reform, as much as could be realized without danger to the unity of the Church and prejudice to the authority of the Apostolic See." He concludes: "The conduct of Laínez and his men, therefore, was inspired not by opportunistic calculation but by a realistic evaluation of the development of events" (p. 153). See also Feliciano Cereceda, S. J., *Diego Laínez en la Europa religiosa de su tiempo, 1512-1565* (2 vols.; Madrid, 1946), II, 93-282. This author remarks that Laínez's support of the papal side was not due to toadyism (*lacayismo*) but to a deeper feeling for the life of the Church which a good number of his compatriots at the council lacked (II, 157).

[317]Laínez to Borja, Trent, June 10, 1563, *Lainii Monumenta*, VII, 136-137 (No. 1850).

days before and that the current discussion was being hastened to a close in order to make room for the papal project.[318] Perhaps he intended in his remarks on reform to set the stage for the debate that he thought was soon to follow. Calini commented that Laínez "said in truth many good things but also several that he could have kept quiet," since they were offensive to others. He boldly expressed his opinion that it was in no way fitting that the reform of the Court of Rome should be undertaken by the council in view of the pope's desire to do it, because inferiors could not lay down laws for the superior, nor would the pope be bound by any decrees of the council since they would be of merely positive law; he added that if the pope did not want the council to take up this question he could all of a sudden suspend and dissolve it so that all its acts would be null and void, or else not confirm it, or at his pleasure dispense from its decrees as he had done in regard to the Council of Basel. The general warned the French in particular not to seek an occasion to break the unity of the Church and separate themselves from obedience to its head, because that would entail their complete ruin.[319] It is hardly surprising that the French were extremely indignant at his impolitic remarks and that some took notes with the intention of adverting to

---

[318]Polanco to Canisius, Trent, June 15, 1563, Braunsberger, IV, 258 (No. 895).

[319]Calini to Cornaro, Trent, June 17, 1563, Marani, p. 474; also *Lainii Monumenta*, VIII, 821-822 (Appendix, No. 70). For the text, "Primum votum de reformatione," see Grisar, II, 214-220. Cf. Acta, *CT*, IX, 589-590, and "Paleotti Acta," *CT*, III, 665-666. See also the brief treatise, "An pontifex reformandus sit per concilium" (Grisar, II, 74-88, with comments in the "Prolegomena," pp. 42*-44*), which Grisar assumed that Laínez composed at Trent early in 1563; Cabanellas contends that the author was really Nadal (*op. cit.*, pp. 104-105). Scaduto agrees that the treatise was written by Nadal at Innsbruck at Delfino's request (*op. cit.*, p. 204). The purpose of the treatise was to prove that the council should not seek to reform the Church *in capite* because (1) it could not be done *de jure*, (2) *de facto* it would never and could not be done, (3) there was no need for it to be done, (4) nor was there any advantage, and (5) many troubles would follow if it were done. Rupert, regarding Laínez as the author, contrasts this position with the one that he maintains the general held when he was in France (at the Colloquy of Poissy and afterwards) before coming to Trent; at that time, according to Rupert (pp. 6-23), he wished to commit the reform of the whole Church--also and even primarily of the head--to the council, and he proposed two ways in which that could be done, as well as ways to which the pope could be induced to accept a reform imposed by the council. Rupert (pp. 27, 40) believes that the main reason for Laínez's change of mind was the danger of schism because of the conciliaristic consequences that he came to perceive, probably during the last months of his sojourn in France; previously he had mistakenly thought that the pope would allow the council freedom to correct abuses in the Curia and that this could be done without raising the question of the relative superiority of the pope and the council and without settling it in favor of the latter. He always urged, nevertheless, that the pope reform the Curia.

This interpretation has been disputed by Cabanellas (*op. cit.*, p. 95), who asserts: "The thesis of a radical, or almost radical, revolution of Laínez's thought in regard to the reform of the pope by the council lacks a positive foundation because the documents on which it could be supported cannot be attributed with certainty to the general of the Jesuits. Furthermore, there exist serious reasons for thinking that these documents are the work of Polanco and reflect only his mentality, which could

them when their turn to speak would come. According to Visconti, the French and Spanish prelates thought that Laínez had not expressed those opinions without the command or the consent of the legates, who had done many favors for him.[320] According to Paleotti, the legates were embarrassed by the general's remarks about reform, because they feared that others would suppose that he had spoken thus at their behest or even at that of the pope, as if these were averse to letting the council do anything about reform and were shrinking back from the whole matter for which all men ardently longed. At that time, moreover, when the legates were seeking a basis of understanding with the French and the Spaniards, they would not have wished Laínez to speak in such a way as to insult them lest the legates' efforts appear to be a scheme for doing nothing at all.[321]

When the legates themselves reported to Borromeo on the contents and effects of the general's discourse, they expressed regret at what he had said, because the council believed that it was at their

---

well be different from that of Laínez." On the contrary, Cabanellas believes that Laínez's position on this question was constant: "Laínez desired the reform of the Roman Curia, but he always judged that this reform should be realized by the pope." In effect this author agrees with Rupert, nevertheless, in recognizing Laínez's fear of conciliarism as the motive for his stand in the council: "The tense situation created at Trent by the disputes over the origin of episcopal jurisdiction (in which the problem of the relations between the primacy and episcopacy was becoming involved), and especially the presence in the council of a theological current anchored to the positions of the Council of Basel, reinforced and hardened this posture of the general of the Jesuits" (ibid., p. 114).

Scaduto also believes that Polanco composed the main document in question, "De universa Ecclesiae Reformatione" (Lainii Monumenta, VIII, 800- 805), at Trent late in 1562. Although Scaduto distinguishes the proposals of this program for general reform from the doctrinal position of conciliarism, he seems to concede that the document reflected the opinion that Laínez held on the subject before the Spanish party at Trent unleashed the raucous dispute over the divine right of bishops, for he says that "it was precisely this reality which subsequently opened Laínez's eyes on the spot and induced him to change his course energetically, abandoning, as if it were an erratic boulder, what on French soil he had fondly looked upon as a realizable and decisive program" (p. 143). Indeed, Scaduto considers it very probable that Laínez had asked his secretary to draft a position paper, and Polanco's memorial has the characteristics of a draft; but after mature reflection the general did not accept his secretary's suggestions (p. 197).

[320]Visconti to Borromeo, Trent, June 17, 1563, Aymon, II, 68, 70 & 72 (Letter XLIII and Poliza), and Baluze, III, 471-472; the letter (without the poliza) also in Lainii Monumenta, VIII, 819-820 (Appendix, No. 68), with the date of June 16. Three weeks previously the secretary of the Society had recognized that its service to the Holy See, especially at the council, had rendered it odious to various nations as being "too papist." Polanco to Christopher Madrid, Trent, May 27, 1563, Lainii Monumenta, VII, 109 (No. 1840).

[321]"Paleotti Acta concilii Tridentini," June 16, 1563, CT, III, 666. Paleotti added that Laínez said some things that perhaps could have been left unsaid but had affirmed that he feared nothing more than God and said those things as his conscience dictated. Paleotti concluded that this should be believed because of the long-evident holiness of his life, his example, and his other virtues.

persuasion; they denied that this was so and affirmed that it was all done without their knowledge.[322] Thereafter Morone became more and more estranged from the Jesuits in Trent and hardly ever consulted them.[323] Not foreseeing this reaction, the secretary of the Society, while admitting that Laínez had touched many men of every nation on the sore spot, claimed that the majority felt very great satisfaction, and he hoped that the benefit would also be great.[324] In a letter to Vargas the general defended himself against the complaints and wrong information that he knew had been given to Luna and to the Spanish ambassadors at various courts. He questioned the good faith of those who asserted that the Jesuits were obstructing the reform in order that they might reign. Until then, he remarked, the weight of the reform had hung over the pope and the poor clergy (*sobre el que no tiene capa*), for the princes had their ambassadors who said *Noli me tangere*, and the bishops regarded reform as cutting from the lapfuls of others and putting it in their own sleeves.[325] This was hardly the climate in which a dispassionate discussion could take place.

Several fathers had submitted suggestions for the reform of cardinals which they wished to discuss in the council. From this

---

[322]The legates to Borromeo, Trent, June 17, 1563, Susta, IV, 69 (No. 14), and *Lainii Monumenta*, VIII, 820 (Appendix, No. 69).

[323]Rupert, pp. 35-36. This author admits that "perhaps" Laínez expressed his opinion too freely and inveighed against others too harshly.

[324]Polanco to Nadal, Trent, June 22, 1563, *Epistolae P. Hieronymi Nadal, Societatis Jesu*, Vol. II: *1562-1565* (Madrid, 1899), p. 312 (No. 286). On June 17 Polanco wrote to his confrère Madrid that the Cardinal of Lorraine, with whom he had spoken on the preceding day, showed that he resented the general's remarks, and on the 17th Laínez went to give him an explanation. The cardinal complained about his statement that if the fathers should insist on reforming the Curia and matters that touched the pope, the latter could dissolve the council or its decrees would not be valid. Laínez replied that he had spoken conditionally, that is, if the fathers would attempt to treat these matters against the pope's will, as some had let it be known that they intended; but he did not say that the pope did not wish these things to be treated in the council, as some French bishops had understood him; he assumed that it was understood at Trent that the pope wished the reform, and if he did it as the Cardinal of Lorraine had indicated the day before, he would relieve the council of much labor. *Ibid.*, n. 3 After the council Polanco found it necessary to explain the actions of the Jesuits at Trent to the members of the Society in Spain, because some of the bishops returning to that country had made known their displeasure especially at Laínez's opposition to the proposed reform of the Curia and many other matters which seemed to the bishops to be advantageous to the Church but which were not decided because of the resistance of the Jesuits. Polanco affirmed that those who made such complaints had been striving, on the pretext of reforming the Curia (something that the general fully supported, speaking severely about reforming it), to deprive the pope of the authority which God had given him and to assume it for themselves, claiming that that was the only means they held to be good for the reform. The secretary acknowledged that in this respect the bishops were contradicted by the Jesuits, as was right. But he refuted the charge or suspicion that the Jesuits at Trent were hired, asserting that they did not even receive enough to live on from the pope. Rome, July 6, 1564, *Polanci Complementa*, I, 462, 464.

[325]Laínez to Vargas, Trent, July 19, 1563, *Lainii Monumenta*, VII, 215 (No. 1874).

material the legates selected certain points and composed the draft of a decree which they sent to the pope for his approval. At the same time they informed Pius that however much he might do in Rome, many of the bishops in Trent would not wish to stop doing their own part in the reform of the cardinals. Some of the bishops, such as Andrew Dudić Sbardelato, had made demands especially regarding the income, number, and nationality of the cardinals that alarmed the legates. They feared that the fathers intended to go farther than was proper and in time "to take this supreme dignity away from Italy" by requiring that all nations be equally represented in the Sacred College. The legates suggested, therefore, that instead of instituting a special reform for the cardinals, which they thought would be more disrespectful and troublesome, they extend to the cardinals, especially cardinal priests, the conditions to be required of candidates for the episcopate, and to the cardinal deacons, those to be required for ordination to the diaconate, and so on.[326] In spite of the many advantages that this ingenious solution to the problem offered, the pope was not yet quite ready to accept it.

In spite of the rumors about the pope's having sent to the legates reform articles for discussion in the council, there was no evidence of such an intention on their part. On June 19, therefore, the Cardinal of Lorraine informed the legates that the emperor and the kings of France, Spain, and Portugal had resolved to ask jointly that the reform of the cardinals be undertaken by the council by all means. Thereupon the legates considered that it would be better *(manco male)* to do it voluntarily than to wait to be obliged to do it at the insistence of others. They reminded Borromeo that if the pope should decide to do it himself at Rome, he would have to make it such as would satisfy those at Trent so that they would not consider putting their hand in it and by that act not only do little honor to the pope but also indicate that the council was superior to him.[327] Thus the legates under Morone's guidance put their own pressure on Pius.

Along with their dispatch the legates sent to Rome fourteen reform articles which were desired by almost the whole Spanish nation at the council. These concerned various practices of the Curia, especially of the Chancery and the Datary, regarding benefices, as well as exemptions and the qualities of episcopal candidates. It was also proposed that cardinals be made incapable of holding any diocese or benefice besides their own titles and be given a definite and equal income from the Patrimony of St. Peter so that they would not be subservient to any king or nation or republic but would be free to advise the pope; they should always reside in Rome

---

[326]The legates Borromeo, Trent, June 17, 1563, Susta, IV, 73-74. On Dudić's *votum* see Acta, *CT*, IX, 577-578 (No. 210), and "Paleotti Acta," *CT*, III, 658-659.
[327]The legates to Borromeo, Trent, June 19, 1563, Susta, IV, 75-76 (No. 15). Cf. Visconti to Borromeo, Trent, June 19, 1563, Aymon, II, 74 & 76 (Letter XLIV), and Baluze, III, 472.

or in the legations entrusted to them, and their number should be reduced.[328] It was becoming a question of how long the pope and the cardinals in Rome could withstand the flood of demands for reform rushing down upon them from Trent.

Morone and his colleagues were shrewdly advocating the strategy of including the cardinals in the other reform decrees to be enacted by the council instead of drafting a separate decree for them alone. They thought that the reform bull which the pope intended to issue would not simply be received by the council without any modification, because "almost all the Spaniards and French, the ambassadors, and some Italians" wanted to decree the reform at Trent and insisted that such was the mind of the princes. Besides, if the council were to treat, for example, the plurality of benefices or regress or to determine the age and other qualifications of candidates for the episcopate, it would be necessry to include the cardinals. The legates assured the papal nephew that they would have preferred to have the reform done by the pope, but they understood how difficult it would be to prevent the council from taking part in it. They added in their letter:

> And they are saying already that as long as the side of
> the cardinals is not reformed, they do not believe that
> there would ever be anything else to do, for that is the
> main side after that of our Lord [the pope], but the
> princes are content that there sould be no discussion of
> the latter.

The legates concluded with an indirect but none the less daring criticism: "And since the news of those twenty-four cardinals deputed for this purpose has come from Rome to various persons here, they have begun to say that from that number and from the profession of many of them it can be regarded as certain that nothing will be done."[329] Pius could hardly have been pleased to be informed so bluntly of the commonly felt lack of confidence in those whom he had chosen for this task.

While waiting for some word from Pius IV, the legates privately showed Cardinals Guise and Ludovico Madruzzo some articles for the reform of the cardinals drawn from previous councils.[330] Guise, however, replied that he would have no part in this affair and would

---

[328]"Capita aliquot reformationum missa ab Illmis legatis die 19 Junii 1563," Jedin, *Krisis*, pp. 293-294 (Abhang VI).

[329]The legates to Borromeo, Trent, June 22, 1563, Susta, IV, 91-92 (No. 19).

[330]All the reform measures which had been decreed since the time of Martin V or had at least been proposed but not yet carried into execution had been sent from Rome. "Paleotti Acta," June 24, 1563, *CT*, III, 673-674. By his way of recording these events Paleotti suggested his belief that it would be advisable to abandon the project in the Curia and to leave it to the judgment of the fathers at Trent, because, he pointed out, otherwise the fathers might not be satisfied with the measures decreed in Rome and might demand still more as if to revise them--which would be unbecoming (*indignum*).

not give his opinion before learning whether the pope had decided that it could be treated in the council.[331] The unusual movement of the ambassadors also made the papal observer Gualterio suspicious, though he doubted what his friend Lorraine had hinted, namely, that the emperor, who was about to leave Innsbruck, would soon return from his journey and come to Trent with a band of Protestants or at least apply great pressure on the council.[332] A few days later the French cardinal told Gualterio that the emperor had left to him the charge of having the reform decreed because he wished that it be done *"in totum et per totum"*; then, to be sure that he was correctly understood, Ferdinand added that by those words he meant *"in capite et in membris."*[333] Meanwhile Calini had heard that the emperor had again strongly insisted that his reforms be proposed to the council, and since they dealt especially with the cardinals, Calini thought that this subject would have to be examined by the council. The fact that those in Rome had begun to treat this matter would bring little advantage, in his opinion, unless they hurried so that this reform would be issued and published there before it would be proposed in the council.[334] Thus it seemed to many at Trent to be inevitable that this topic would eventually be aired.

Yielding to the demands from the council, Pius IV on June 24 sent the legates several proposed canons on the reform of the cardinals. In the second it was stated that only mature, learned, virtuous men who were well versed in ecclesiastical discipline should be appointed

---

[331]Visconti to Borromeo, Trent, June 24, 1563, Aymon, II, 94 (Letter XLVI), and Baluze, III, 474, with the date of June 27. Visconti had heard that while speaking later with some other prelates, the Cardinal of Lorraine let it be understood that he did not desire too strict a reform, and he said in particular that he did not deem it improper for a cardinal, provided he was *in sacris*, to hold a bishopric, but he did not think a cardinal deacon should be a bishop. On June 24, however, Guise wrote to his agent in Rome, Nicole Breton, to whom Cardinal Alessandro Farnese had expressed his displeasure at Guise's position on reform questions. He commissioned the agent to deny that he wished to increase the power of the bishops at the expense of the papal authority in an unbecoming way or to lessen the dignity of the College of Cardinals; nor was there any such intention in the ranks of his adherents. He did, however, consider thorough-going reforms to be necessary. He admitted that he had declared that a cardinal deacon should not hold a bishopric, for it was shocking to see a bishop who not even a priest. He had never consented that his brother, Cardinal Louis de Guise, should hold a bishopric while he was only a deacon. Lorraine asked Farnese to indicate more precise details in his speech that appeared offensive; he declined Farnese's invitation to settle down in Rome, for he was thinking about returning to his diocese in France. It is significant that Farnese wished to allure the Cardinal of Lorraine to Rome, where his reforming ardor would soon be dampened. Birkner, pp. 350-351.
[332]Gualterio to Borromeo, Trent, June 24, 1563, Jedin, *Krisis*, pp. 258-259 (No. 88).
[333]Gualterio to Borromeo, Trent, June 28, 1563, Jedin, *Krisis*, p. 261 (No. 89).
[334]Calini to Cornaro, Trent, June 28, 1563, Marani, p. 483. Calini seems to have been misinformed about the purpose of the imperial ambassadors' visit to the legates. Besides the silence in Ferdinand's instructions and their dispatches see Morone to Borromeo, Trent, June 28, 1563, Constant, *Légation*, pp. 186-187 (No. 50).

cardinals, and their number should not be increased without a reasonable cause; in their appointment the canons regarding the age required for each order should be observed. Next it was laid down, for the good government of the Church and the successful straightening out of the Sacred College, that no one should be appointed a cardinal who was a brother of a living cardinal, and brothers of living cardinals were to be completely ineligible; not even for the most urgent reason was any dispensation from this canon to be permitted. Then it was prescribed that cardinals should strive to illuminate the Church like burning lamps, give a good example to all men, govern their household, prudently and lovingly aid and advise the pope, shun the courts of secular princes unless some pious and honorable cause would require their presence, see to it that other dioceses entrusted to their administration be governed by suitable vicars and suffragans, and not abuse the privileges granted them. Lastly, it was proposed that cardinals should not have several dioceses, should not enjoy the privileges when absent from them, and should visit them at some time during the year; if a cardinal should obtain more than one by title or commendam or administration or any other means, he should retain only one and give up the rest and not have more than one in the future, exception being made for the six cardinal bishops.[335] Apparently the pope thought that these measures should satisfy the reform-minded prelates and princes.

Probably Pius also believed that the cardinals would not tolerate more stringent reforms. At the end of June Arco informed the emperor that the pope had told the cardinals that he wished to hold a meeting on the subject of reform, but they could not be induced to give up the bishoprics, benefices, curacies, and abbacies that they had in commendam, and the pensions that they drew from the secular princes. Hence, to bring them to accept reform, the pope stated that if he could do nothing else, he would leave the matter to the council. A few days later the same ambassador reported that in Rome there was much talk of the reform of the cardinals but no action had yet been seen.[336]

Meanwhile the legates seem to have been trusting that eventually the pope would recognize the wisdom of their strategy.[337] On July 5 they wrote to Borromeo that they were thinking of giving out the reform articles that they had previously sent him; their purpose

[335]Le Plat, VI, 113-115.
[336]Arco to Ferdinand, Rome, June 30, July 3, 1563, Kassowitz, p. xliv (Anhang, No. 100). On July 21 the ambassador wrote that the reform of the cardinals was not mentioned any more at Rome and the pope said that he had referred it to the council (ibid.).
[337]The legates to Borromeo, Trent, June 30, 1563, Constant, Légation, p. liii, n. 1. They said they were becoming more certain day by day that the princes wanted the reform of the cardinals from the council and not from the pope. Cf. same to same, Trent, June 21, 1563, Susta, IV, 86 (No. 17).

would be to dispel the suspicion of many a father that they wished to concentrate on the dogmatic decrees in order to exclude reform. At the same time they repeated that although they were, of course, pleased that the pope was making the reform of the cardinals in Rome, nevertheless, at least in regard to their age and qualifications it would give great satisfaction to the emperor and the fathers to leave the reform to the council, in the sense that whatever would be decreed about the age and qualifications of bishops would be extended to the cardinals, and the latter would be included also in the chapter on the plurality of benefices.[338] On the same day Pius at last began to approve the legates' plan. Borromeo wrote them that although the reform of the cardinals was still awaited in Rome, when reform articles for deacons, priests, and bishops which could appropriately be applied to cardinals were treated in the council, the legates could mention them expressly, since it was the pope's mind that cardinals be reformed as well as others. According to his nephew, the pope was thinking of more severe reforms at Rome than would be made at Trent, for example, that no bishopric would be given to a cardinal who was less than thirty years of age, that such a cardinal would be obliged to reside in his see like any other bishop, and that the ages for cardinal priests and deacons would be twenty-five and twenty years respectively. Pius also left the decree on residence to the discretion of the legates, because, said the cardinal nephew, since he wanted even a cardinal who had a see to reside in it, he did not care whether the decree was drawn up in one way or another.[339]

Finally, recognizing the futility of his own plan, Pius yielded completely to the petitions of the legates. He had Borromeo inform them that since those chosen to discuss the reform of the cardinals had not yet been able to agree on anything that the pope thought would satisfy the fathers of the council and the others who so vehemently demanded this reform, and since he thought that the matter could be deferred no longer, the legates should not await anything further from Rome but should proceed with the council to whatever might seem best to them; they could either mention the cardinals expressly in all the reform chapters already composed or to be composed or draw up a separate decree for them. The legates were instructed not to be sparing, for whatever reform might be devised, it could never seem to the pope to be too severe, for he wished to satisfy the council and the princes in this as well as in all other becoming matters. Borromeo admitted that this order would

---

[338]The legates to Borromeo, Trent, July 5, 1563, Susta, IV, 109 (No. 23). Laínez was still hoping for a bull for the reform of the cardinals and even more for the effect intended by it, and he supposed that the legates had not published the reform articles which the pope had sent them because they understood that many prelates would not agree. Laínez to Borja, Trent, June 28, 1563, *Lainii Monumenta*, VII, 167-168 (No. 1863).

[339]Borromeo to the legates, Rome, July 5, 1563, Susta, IV, 116-117 (No. 25).

not have been delayed till that day if there had not been a hope of ac-
complishing anything satisfactory in Rome.[340] A more candid confession of the Sacred College's inability and unwillingnes to reform
itself could hardly be imagined.

In the consistory at the end of the month Pius IV gave a
somewhat different explanation of his decision. According to Cardinal Francesco Gambara's notes, he spoke of the necessity of
reform and of his will to reform himself first, then the Sacred College, the rest of the Church, and the secular princes. In this matter
he left free rein to the legates and the council, he said; anyone who
might be caused any inconvenience as a result should console
himself with the thought of the need for, and public benefit of, the
reform. The pope declared that he had originally intended to have
the reform of the cardinals carried out at Rome, but then when he
observed that several princes desired to have it done in the council,
which had begun to discuss it from the outset, he decided to refer it
to the council lest some divergence arise if it were treated at the
same time in Rome and in the council. He urged the cardinals to accept it willingly, for the reform which would be decreed by the council would be more in keeping with their views than one done in
Rome, especially since the legates would be careful to safeguard the
dignity and interests of the Sacred College. Pius dissented from the
opinion that the decree on residence would be an injury to the cardinals, because previously a legal doubt had existed as to whether
they could be made bishops of dioceses, but a decision in their favor
seemed to be implied in the council, and this was a greater gain than
the trouble of residence, which in any case should not seem burdensome to the cardinals, for it was a highly honorable thing, as was
also the obligation for those who were bishops to receive episcopal
consecration.[341] The sequel was to show that the pope failed to convince many of the cardinals with these arguments.

In fact, the reasons of expediency that he alleged in the consistory, even when added to his disappointment at the cardinals'
failure to take advantage of the opportunity that he had given them
to reform themselves, would not by themselves alone seem enough
to outweigh his earlier reasons for forbidding the council to reform
the Curia. Previously he had feared the ever threatening discussion
of the question of the relative superiority of the pope and the council; this danger was always latent in the debates over the divine

---

[340]Borromeo to the legates, Rome, July 10, 1563, Le Plat, VI, 139; Pallavicini,
XXI, vi, 7. The letter was so composed that the legates could exhibit it as authorization for their future policy.

[341]Cardinal Gambara's Consistorial Diary, July 30, 1563, Susta, IV, 127-128. The
legates had pointed out to Borromeo immediately after the session that the
cardinals were included in the chapter on episcopal residence because previously it
had appeared to be incompatible, but now the thesis that cardinals could have
bishoprics and observe residence was in legal possession. Trent, July 15, 1563,
Susta, IV, 124.

obligation of residence. At the beginning, moreover, the reform of the College of Cardinals was connected with the reform of the conclave; hence, consideration of the former could have led the council to attempt a revision of the whole procedure of papal elections and even, pehaps, to claim the right of choosing Pius IV's successor if he should die while it was in session. But now the debate on residence was concluded, and the reform of the conclave had been decreed by the pope alone. The emperor, furthermore, had assured Morone that he did not desire a discussion of the superiority question and had instructed his ambassadors accordingly. Philip II had nothing to gain from weakening the pope's authority since the king's power over the Church in the Spanish Empire stemmed from papal concessions. Under these circumstances, therefore, it must have seemed to Pius much less dangerous than before to refer the reform of the cardinals to the council.[342]

The pope's authorization arrived in Trent in time to permit a modification of the reform decree which was to be enacted in the Twenty-Third Session (July 15). In the last general congregation preceding the session the legates themselves proposed that the cardinals who held bishoprics be expressly mentioned in the decree. Accordingly, in the first chapter such cardinals were bound to personal residence in their dioceses and could lawfully absent themselves only for reasons approved by the pope. Since the obligation of residence was thus not declared to be of divine law, the pope could dispense from it whenever he judged that Christian charity, urgent necessity, or manifest advantage to the Church or the commonwealth required a cardinal's absence from his see. According to the second chapter, cardinals as well as others who were named bishops of dioceses were to be consecrated within three months under penalty of restoring the income received, and if they neglected this duty for more than three months, they were to be *ipso jure* deprived of their dioceses.[343] In Chapter XII, however, which prescribed the ages of candidates for the three major orders, cardinals were not mentioned lest it appear that the age of twenty-two years required for ordination to the diaconate would be considered sufficient also for cardinal deacons. In a modest way these provisions exemplified the wisdom of Morone's policy for handling the reform of the cardinals.

Only a part of the reform in which the cardinals were to be included was enacted in that session.[334] While the council then pro-

---

[342]Cf. Birkner, pp. 349-350.

[343]Schroeder, pp. 436-437, 439; English translation, pp. 164-165, 167.

[344]At Borromeo's behest, for example, Visconti discussed with Morone the abolition of reservations of dioceses. Morone thought this desirable as far as the cardinals were concerned, since they had paid nothing for the dispatch of the bulls, but he wished the pope to do it in Rome because if the council were to take up the question, it would extend the abolition to other churches as well, and then many would complain that they were deprived of the favors conferred on them by the pope

ceeded with the drafting of further decrees, Morone looked ahead to the closing of the whole assembly after the general reform (pertaining to all countries) and the dogmatic decree on matrimony, the last of the sacraments to be treated, would be completed. He was being pressed by Pius IV, who was impatient to be relieved of both the anxiety and the expense that the council caused him. To effect a prompt conclusion, the president needed the consent of the various nations represented at Trent. Having won the Cardinal of Lorraine to the idea, he turned next to the emperor and asked the pope to persuade Philip II. In approaching the emperor, he used the good offices of Dudić Sbardelato, now Bishop of Csanád, who had been summoned to the coronation of Maximilian as king of Hungary. Morone explained to him that Spain wished to draw the council out but that an early closing would be advantageous for Germany. The legate's strategy was to combine the emperor, the French, the Portuguese, and the Italians in order to overcome the weight of the Spaniards. To convince the emperor, Morone argued that the concessions which he wanted most, namely, communion under both kinds and the marriage of priests, would never be granted by the council nor could they be granted by the pope as long as the council remained open, but that once it would be closed, the pope would be free to make such concessions. Hence, the president of the council asked the emperor to direct his ambassadors at Trent to urge that once the so-called general reform would be completed, the matters pertaining to the welfare of individual countries be referred to the pope.[345] Morone also wrote directly to Ferdinand, pointing out that in the last session mention was made of the cardinals in the reform article pertaining to residence because it was especially desired by the emperor. He promised to continue to fulfil his duty and averred that he would seek the common good and the unity of the Church not only by his own desire but also at the pope's command. In conclusion he urged Ferdinand to support the plan for an early closing of the council.[346] At the same time the president endeavored to win the good-will of Ferdinand's ambassadors at Trent.[347]

---

without being refunded the money they had paid for the dispatch of the bulls. Visconti to Borromeo, Trent, July 19, 1563, Aymon, II, 182 & 184 (Letter LVI), and Baluze, III, 482-483.

[345]Morone to Borromeo, Trent, July 19, 1563, Susta, IV, 132-133 (No. 28a), and Constant, *Légation*, pp. 195-197 (No. 56). "Summarium eorum quae episcopus Chanadiensis proposuit S. C. Mti et Sermo regi Romanorum nomine Rmi D. Moroni," July 26, 1563, Sickel, *Concil*, p. 564.

[346]Morone to Ferdinand, Trent, July 20, 1563, Sickel, *Concil*, p. 563 (No. CCLXIX) (first part), and Le Plat, VI, 161, and Raynaldus, 1563, No. 170, p. 414 (second part).

[347]In the oral instructions that Morone gave Gualterio before the latter departed for Rome, July 23, 1563, he told him to report to the pope that he had won over Drasković and Brus, "although the former more than the latter." Jedin, *Krisis*, p. 277 (No. 98). A few days later Borromeo urged Morone to win friends for the Curia with money, "especially pursuing the web (*tela*) begun with the [Bishop of] Pécs." Rome, July 28, 1563, Constant, *Légation*, p. 207 (No. 61).

Morone's request arrived in Vienna during a religious conference summoned by the emperor and attended by his delegates and those of the electors of Cologne, Mainz, and Trier, of the Archbishop of Salzburg, and of the Duke of Bavaria. The imperial representative stated that in Ferdinand's opinion the reform must be universal—*in capite et in membris*. But the conference recognized the manifold difficulty of reforming the head, by which were understood "the pope, cardinals, his clergy, and, *in summa*, the whole Roman court." The delegates merely recalled that the pope had offered a reform of the Roman Curia, while the emperor would have preferred to see him leave this to the council.[348] Apparently there was no expectation at the imperial court that the council could accomplish much in this respect and therefore there was one less reason for prolonging it. Hence, in his reply to Morone, Ferdinand said that he was not displeased by the desire of the pope, along with the Italian and French bishops, to close the council as soon as possible, as long as it not be brought to an end precipitately. He wanted to see accomplished first all the things for which the council had been convoked, for otherwise great scandal would be given to the whole Christian world and an occasion for still more widespread defection would be provided, "especially," he added, "since there does not appear to be any need for headlong haste."[349] Undoubtedly the emperor perceived that if the council were closed without completing its reform work, he would have no leverage to constrain the pope to complete it afterwards.

Pius IV, however, knew that both sides could play the game of using the council to apply pressure.[350] Hence, he declared that not only

---

[348]"Protocollum colloquii ecclesiastici Viennae habiti mense Augusti [1563]," Constant, *Concession*, I, 445, n. 5. No resolution concerning reform *in capite* was adopted by this meeting.

[349]Ferdinand to Morone, Vienna, July 31, 1563, Raynaldus, 1563, No. 139, p. 405, and Constant, *Légation*, pp. 211-212 (No. 63). Morone forwarded this letter to Borromeo, Trent, August 9, 1563, *ibid.*, p. 224 (No. 69). The emperor was still eager to obtain the pope's confirmation of his son's election. See Ferdinand to Morone, Vienna, August 18, 1563, *ibid.*, pp. 226-228 (No. 71). See also Ferdinand's letter to Luna, Vienna, July 30, 1563, Sickel, *Concil*, p. 569 (No. CCLXXI), where he refers to his past efforts to have a "universal reform" instituted at the earliest possible time.

[350]Previously the Curia and the legates had held themselves officially aloof from any scheme to reform the princes, considering it too risky and dangerous, but they had let those bishops who so wished agitate the question and even encouraed them more or less indirectly, especially through Visconti, to prepare memorials on the subject. See Visconti to Borromeo, [Trent,] April [not "October"] 22, 1563, Baluze, III, 459 (Letter XXV). Thus during March and April at least three Italian bishops wrote down their observations on the abuses of the secular princes and on the need to abolish their pragmatic sanctions in regard to ecclesiastical affairs and either sent them to Rome or presented them to the legates. Only toward the end of June, however, when the secular powers urged more strenuously that the council reform the Curia, did the pope put forward the reform of the princes in order to curb their excessive zeal for correcting ecclesiastical abuses. See Luigi Prosdocimi, "Il progetto di 'Riforma dei Principi' al Concilio di Trento (1563)," *Aevum*, XIII (1939), 7-9.

the cardinals but also the lay princes should be reformed by the council in the sense that the encroachment of the latter on the rights and goods of the Church should be prohibited.[351] Toward the end of June the pope had ordered the legates to allow or induce some of the fathers to complain *(cantare)* about the reform demands *(il libro)* of the secular princes; the legates, however, were to see to it that this plan did not appear to originate with them.[352] Toward the end of July forty-two articles on universal reform were drafted and communicated to the ambassadors, who were invited to submit their comments. Brus and Drašković were the first to respond; they thought that some of these provisions were not suitable and would cause disturbances so that they should be partly corrected and partly rejected entirely.[353] In particular they made such suggestions as the following: that the legates should see to it that a serious and durable reform of the conclave be made at Trent; that the alienation of ecclesiastical property should be regulated, especially in the Church of Rome; and that laymen should not be cited to Rome in the

---

[351]After Commendone had returned from Germany in 1562, he submitted to Pius IV a report in which he recommended the fourth of four possible ways of remedying the ecclesiastical situation in that country without violence, that is, to correct the abuses and usurpations of the lay princes. He assumed that this reform should follow that of the Curia, so that after the pope would bring about a "true, general, and lasting reform" or at least would make it clear to the world that he would not fail to remove all the abuses from his court in order to restore health to the Church, it would be evident that that health could not be recovered or preserved unless the lay princes would give up what they had no right to. Döllinger, *Beiträge*, III, 313; also *Nuntiaturberichte aus Deutschland, 1560-1572*, Vol. II: *Nuntius Commendone 1560 (Dezember)-1562 (März)*, ed. Adam Wandruszka (Graz, Cologne, 1953), pp. 53-54. Morone had told Visconti before going to Innsbruck that it was necessary to reform the princes too, for too much regard was had for them. Visconti to Borromeo, Trent, April 15, 1563, Aymon, I, 210.
[352]Borromeo to the legates, Rome, June 26, 1563, Susta, IV, 100-101 (No. 21).
[353]Brus and Drašković to Ferdinand, Trent, July 27 and August 3, 1563, Sickel, *Concil*, pp. 573-574, 572 (No. CCLXXII). According to a letter lacking indication of the sender and the addressee but received at Florence, some prelates who had visited the writer at Trent feared that the proposed reform of the princes would stir up a hornets' nest and would incite the princes to demand a very strict reform of the pope and of the Court of Rome, which they would do all the more readily as many of them were believed to be looking for such an occasion. He continued: "And among the others who are supposed to desire it, the emperor is thought to desire it very much and the king of the Romans much more; the latter, I have understood from a very good party, is not very well disposed toward the Court of Rome and has sometimes spoken some words full of scorn *(sdegno)*, such as that it cannot be tolerated that for the abuses of that [court] the states should be divided upside down in so many sects and the world should go to perdition, and that it will be necessary to attend to it with more than words. It is also the opinion of intelligent persons that if the reverence of the emperor, his father, did not restrain that prince, one would have already seen some big decisions *(grandi risolutioni)*. But the emperor, as far as is known, does not wish that any way other than that of the council be tried until it becomes clear that by this route no good can be done. All this I have learned from persons worthy of faith, but I have not been able to verify it." Trent, July 26, 1563, D'Addario, pp. 359-360 (No. CCXVIII).

first instance of a case at law.[354] The other ambassadors at the council also protested against the proposed reform of the secular princes. The Bishop of Salamanca remarked that as they asked that the pope reform himself, so he asked that the kings and princes who kept the state and freedom of the Church oppressed reform themselves. The Spanish prelate noted that the legates were very resolute in proposing these things to the council and in insisting that those who so desired and demanded reform should be the first to be reformed.[355]

The imperial ambassadors also sent a copy of the proposed reform articles to Vienna with a request for further instructions. Before the emperor received their dispatch, however, he had ordered them to urge the reform, especially of the cardinals and the conclave. To that they replied that the cardinals would be included in the canon that would require for bishops certain qualifications and the age of thirty years. They could not bring about a reduction of the number of cardinals, however, because all the fathers and ambassadors, even Luna, agreed that it would not be to the Church's advantage if no pious and learned man of any country could be appointed until the nearly sixty living cardinals would be reduced to twenty-four or twenty-six—which could hardly happen in the space of several pontificates. With respect to the cardinals as well as to the conclave Morone maintained that he had already reached an agreement with the emperor at Innsbruck, and he promised only out of special regard for him that at the next session the pope's bull for the reform of the conclave would be published, so that it could be given the consent of the council and entered among its acts. Later the ambassadors reported that twenty-one articles for the universal reform had been proposed by the legates and were being discussed in several *classes* into which the fathers had been divided; the articles were substantially the same as those that had previously been sent to the emperor but had in the meantime been revised in form—some for the better and others for the worse, in the ambassadors' opinion.[356] By that time, however, all the parties involved were most concerned about the proposed reform of the princes.

---

[354]July 31, 1563, Sickel, *Concil*, p. 575.

[355]Pedro Gonçalez de Mendoça, "Lo sucedido en el concilio de Trento," July 28, 1563, *CT*, II, 691.

[356]Ferdinand to the ambassadors, Vienna, August 8, 1563, and the ambassadors to Ferdinand, Trent, August 24 and September 6, 1563, Sickel, *Concil*, p. 584 (excerpts and summaries). Before making this draft the basis of the formal discussion in the general congregations, the legates wanted to consult the prelates, besides the ambassadors, in this informal manner and to receive their suggestions of changes in advance in order to prepare a final draft that might be voted on without a long debate.

An anonymous correspondent reported to Florence that the imperial and French ambassadors had given some notes about the reform, more or less the same in

Ferdinand had instructed his ambassadors in Trent about this proposal on August 23. He both suspected its motivation and rejected its provisions. On the former he wrote:

> It certainly seems to us that the intention of those at Rome who devoted their attention to composing and collecting those articles was that, being sick of our very frequent appeals in the matter of universal reform *in capite et membris*—which the clergy of our times and especially the Roman Curia so much refuse—they would propose to us such a scheme of reform as they knew could by no means be allowed or executed by us, and thus frustrate all the labors and efforts that we have until now undertaken in this affair, and afterwards they would transfer to us all the blame for not having made a reform . . . .
>
> Surely it was proper that the reform should begin with the head, that is, the Roman pontiff and his cardinals and the Roman Curia, who ought to furnish an example of reformed life both to the lower ecclesiastical ranks and especially to the secular states. But they have thought it best to launch this kind of attack, and we have decided not to remain silent about it in order that we may exonerate our conscience and defend our honor and dignity.

As far as the substance of the proposal was concerned, Ferdinand maintained that he had never attacked or oppressed, but had rather defended, the jurisdiction and freedom belonging to ecclesiastics; still he could not permit their immunity and exemption from all contributions, impositions, and other financial burdens. Hence, he ordered the ambassadors to dissuade the legates from proceeding with those articles which were so prejudicial to him, to the Holy Roman Empire, to his kingdoms and dominions, and to other kings and princes. If in spite of all such arguments the council should pass and publish those articles, the ambassadors, after communicating with the Spanish and French ambassadors, were to enter a solemn protest.[357] Ferdinand apparently did not understand that even

---

substance though very different in words and order, all admissible except two or three; among the latter were the proposals regarding the reduction of the number of cardinals, the exclusion of nephews of the pope and of relatives of living cardinals as well as of two from the same region or diocese, their age, experience, and attendance on the pope, their incapacity to hold dioceses or benefices, the equality of their income, and the representation of all countries among them. The writer declared such demands to be honorable (*honeste*) in appearance but asked who disclosed the most unjust consequence. Trent, August 10, 1563, D'Addario, p. 377 (No. CCXXX).

[357]Ferdinand to the imperial ambassadors, Vienna, August 23, 1563, Sickel, *Concil,* pp. 585-586 (No. CCLXVII).

honorable bishops wished to be freed from the oppressive control of the secular princes in order to be able to govern their dioceses for the good of souls. He was certainly mistaken in regarding the demand for a measure of ecclesiastical independence as nothing more than a device invented by incorrigible clergymen.

The curialists who designed this reform project may indeed have foreseen just such a vehement reaction on the emperor's part, but Morone seems to have been sincerely indignant when Brus apprised him of it. He expressed amazement that the emperor would wish to impede the council's liberty and hinder the universal reform—both of them the very things he had demanded from Rome. The president upheld the need for the proposed reform in places such as the Kingdom of Sicily and Naples and asserted that the fathers of the council insisted on it. At first the legates refused not only to acquiesce in Ferdinand's request but even to postpone the discussion in the council. But after Brus returned to explain the situation in Germany in greater detail, Morone, having consulted his fellow legates, agreed to send a revised version of the articles to the emperor and then to wait no longer than eight days for a response before presenting them to the council.[358] At the same time Morone in a letter to Ferdinand complained about the request conveyed by Brus and asserted that the legates could not omit or postpone treatment of the whole draft without very great scandal and disturbance. "For it is fair and demanded by almost all the bishops who have assembled here that if they remove those obstacles which are supposed to spring from the Supreme Pontiff, and if a true reform is being made of the whole ecclesiastical order, likewise the obstacles which spring from secular [rulers] and directly hinder the government of the churches committed to the bishops should also be removed." Morone denied that the proposed reform would affect the persons or courts of the princes themselves. Having added many

---

[358]The legates to Borromeo, Trent, August 28, 1563 (two letters), Susta, IV, 201-205 (No. 46), and Constant, *Légation*, pp. 237-239; the excerpts from the ambassadors' letters to Ferdinand, Sickel, *Concil*, pp. 586-588. According to Paleotti, after the legates, yielding to Ferdinand's vehement and pressing demands, promised to defer consideration of the chapter on the reform of the princes for ten or twelve days until they would receive an answer from the emperor, many prelates openly stated to the legates that they would not discuss the other chapters in the congregations unless the last one (on the princes) was joined to the rest. Some were even so inclined to interpret everything wrongly against the pope and the Roman Curia, asserted Paleotti, as to say that this was done by the legates on purpose so that when they added the chapter on the princes to the other reform articles, they calculated that it would easily happen that the princes would cry out against it and thus the whole reform would be thrown into confusion and nothing would be proposed any more. Paleotti, however, defended the legates' decision to allow ten days lest disturbances occur in Germany. "Paleotti Acta," August 28, 1563, *CT*, III, 707.

other reasons, he begged the emperor to consider in how many ways the Roman Curia or rather the pope himself had been reformed even though the latter could not be made subject to the laws of the council. In conclusion he tried to placate the emperor by saying that he had written to the pope in support of Ferdinand's proposal regarding the desired confirmation of Maximilian's election.[359]

Pius IV was less eager than his legate to have the council enact the so-called reform of the princes. He had Borromeo inform Morone that this would be a "good thing" if it could be obtained, but if this issue would delay the closing of the council, perhaps it would be better to disregard it for the present, because these things were all contained in the ancient councils and in the canons; if the princes were unwilling to observe these, neither would they observe the decrees of this council. If the council were to pass over this question, after its conclusion the pope would carry out the same reform and do it more boldly than at that moment. (It is remarkable that the pope thought that he would be just as effective without a conciliar decree in slapping the profane hands that the domineering and grasping princes would lay on the Church's rights and goods.) Pius left the matter, nevertheless, to the legates' discretion.[360]

Meanwhile Ferdinand had gone on to Bratislava (Pressburg), where his son was to be crowned king of Hungary. From there he first directed his ambassadors to insist that more time be allowed to himself and the other princes to consider the proposed reform and to reply. If the legates would refuse to postpone the council's deliberation of this matter, the ambassadors were to enter his reservations (instead of his express protest).[361] In the same vein he replied to Morone, repudiating the false motives alleged for his opposition to the draft decree and presenting specific objections related to the prelates of the Empire.[362] After receiving this unyielding reply,

---

[359]Morone to Ferdinand, Trent, August 28, 1563, Sickel, *Concil*, pp. 588-590 (No. CCLXXVIII), and Constant, *Légation*, pp. 243-244 (No. 77). Borromeo wrote Morone (Rome, September 4, 1563) that the pope was pleased with the decision to wait eight days for the emperor's opinion and especially with the legates' letter to Ferdinand. Constant, *Légation*, pp. 248-250 (No. 80).

[360]Borromeo to Morone, Rome, September 8, 1563, Constant, *Légation*, pp. 250-251 (No. 81).

[361]Ferdinand to the imperial ambassadors, Bratislava, September 4 and 5, 1563, Sickel, *Concil*, pp. 595-597 (No. CCLXXX).

[362]Ferdinand to Morone, Bratislava, September 12, 1563, Constant, *Légation*, pp. 253-256 (No. 83). After the French ambassador at Trent, Arnaud du Ferrier, had delivered in the council on September 22 an insolent diatribe against the proposed reform of the princes, Ferdinand wrote to Morone again, insisting that his opinions should be heard before anything would be decided in the council on this question. Bratislava, October 2, 1563, *ibid.*, p. 285 (No. 94).

Morone could have had no doubt about the emperor's determination to forestall any action that he considered prejudicial to himself or other secular princes. In his best diplomatic style Morone replied that neither the pope nor the legates nor the council fathers had ever thought of prejudicing his rights and that if any decree on the reform of the secular rulers would be enacted, it would merely revive some of the ancient canons, especially those the neglect of which caused bishops either not to reside in their dioceses or to reside there in a useless way. He added: "We are already pressing the business of reform; we are not at all sparing the Roman Curia; many things are being granted to the prelates; they themselves are being quite strictly reformed; the secular [princes] are being barely touched unless they are an obstacle to us." Finally, Morone begged the emperor to support the great reform work and to promote the closing of the council.[363]

Before Ferdinand's stern letter of September 12 was delivered in Trent, the reform proposal to which he objected so firmly had been modified insofar as several offensive clauses were deleted, the tone was softened, and the nature of the chapter was described as an admonition. In this milder form it had been made public on September 14 at the insistence of a large group of council fathers, though it was still not formally presented as the basis of discussion.[364] Since the emperor and the French ambassador persisted in their opposition, however, Morone, to avoid an impasse, persuaded the fathers to postpone treatment of this chapter. He argued that in this way everyone would see that they were really eager for ecclesiastical reform. If any thought otherwise, believing that this chapter had been devised in order to force the princes (who wished to have it omitted) to spare the ecclesiastics, such persons would now have to lay aside their false suspicion and judge the fathers' piety correctly.[365] Meanwhile, at the pope's bidding, Delfino was arranging an agreement whereby Ferdinand would consent to the closure of the council in exchange for papal confirmation of Maximilian's election.[366] In a session of the Privy Council on September 28 the emperor decided to acquiesce in Morone's requests. To solve the problem of the reform of the princes he suggested secretly to Morone that certain ancient canons and decrees regarding ecclesiastical immunity should be renewed.[367] With the pope's consent

---

[363] Morone to Ferdinand, Trent, September 23, 1563, Sickel, *Concil*, pp. 604-605 (No. CCLXXXIV).

[364] The series of fourteen reform articles made public on September 14, 1563, *CT*, IX, 766-774 (No. 270).

[365] Massarelli's Diary, October 8, 1563, *CT*, IX, 880-881.

[366] On these negotiations see Steinherz, III, xlii-lviii, and Holzmann, *op. cit.*, pp. 451-502.

[367] Ferdinand to the imperial ambassadors, Bratislava, October 3 and 4, 1563, Sickel, *Concil*, pp. 619-625 (No. CCLXXXIX).

the president of the council adopted this suggestion,[368] and in the end the secular rulers were merely admonished, without threat of censure or penalty, to respect and defend the rights of the Church.[369] Once he had forged an agreement on this delicate matter, Morone was mainly concerned with bringing the council to a speedy close. In this endeavor he was to encounter the opposition not of the emperor but rather of the Spaniards at Trent.

Philip II's ambassador, Count de Luna, was to be the unflagging leader of those who wished to continue the council until it would have decreed a thorough reform of the Church. When he had received from the legates the proposed reform articles in the summer, he made various observations in his reply but the only request he made was that the council also treat of the conclave; he indicated, moreover, that he was awaiting an answer from Rome on this subject.[370] Actually, he informed the pope by letter a few days later that some of the ambassadors at the council were demanding that the question of reforming the College of Cardinals and the papal election be considered, because it was commonly suspected that there were some faults to be corrected. Luna declared that he did not wish to express his opinion on these matters until he would be apprised of the pope's mind and will; this he would then promote. He was confident, he added, that what the pope would decide would be apt both to maintain God's religion and piety and to preserve and increase the dignity of the College of Cardinals.[371] This letter greatly puzzled Pius IV, who noted two things in particular, namely, (1) the count's professed desire to do nothing that might displease the pope without mentioning his stubborn demand for changes in the procedure of the council, and (2) either his unawareness of the consequences of letting the mode of papal elections be treated in the council or his intention to render a most remarkable disservice to his master, since the King of Spain always interfered in papal elections more than any other prince. The Pope had Borromeo send a copy of this strange letter to the legates and ask their opinion; if the ambassador should raise any question about these two points, the

---

[368]See Morone's letters to Borromeo, Trent, October 10 and 18, 1563, Susta, IV, 307-309 (No. 69a), and 326-327 (No. 73a); also Constant, *Légation*, pp. 305-306 (No. 101), and p. 335 (No. 108); and Borromeo's replies to Morone, Rome, October 15 and 27, 1563, Susta, IV, 330 (No. 74a), and 359-360 (No. 82); also Constant, *Légation*, p. 326 (No. 105), and p. 335, n. 3; Borromeo to Delfino, Trent, November 2, 1563, Constant, *Légation*, pp. 356-357 (No. 117).

[369]Twenty-fifth Session, December 3, 1563, *de ref.*, cap. 20, Schroeder, pp. 517-518; English translation, pp. 251-252.

[370]Visconti to Borromeo, Trent, August 8, 1573 (*Poliza*), Aymon, II, 248 (Billet to Letter LXII), and Baluze, III, 488.

[371]Luna to Pius IV, Trent, August 12, 1563, Constant, *Légation*, pp. 530-531 (Appendix, No. XLI).

legates were to reply that the pope had already permitted them to handle the reform of the cardinals as they saw fit and that if the pope's bull for the reform of the conclave had any defect it was the respect that it showed for the kings who meddled in the elections; however, the council was free to remedy this abuse as it wished. Borromeo assured the legates, furthermore, that the odd behavior *(le stranezze)* of the Spanish ambassador was not according to the mind or command of his king, who had told the nuncio that he desired the earliest possible closing of the council; Philip had also expressed his friendship for the pope.[372] The papal party's tactic was to isolate Luna as much as possible.

Knowing that he had been criticized in Rome for wishing to prolong the council, Luna attempted to justify himself to the Spanish ambassador in that city, Luis de Avila. He said that the emperor knew that he desired and requested the reform of the cardinals and of the conclave, but he did not wish to speak until he might learn the pope's will. It was being said at Trent that the pope had left the matter to the council, and Luna believed that this course would serve to free him from importunity.[373] When Pius IV finally replied to Luna, he tersely advised him to inquire of the legates, who were fully aware of all the pope's plans regarding the reform of the College of Cardinals and of the conclave.[374] Borromeo commented on this brief in a letter to the legates of the same date, saying that the latest maneuvers of the count to insist that the Church be reformed *in capite* and that the council discuss by what right the pope conferred benefices as well as to hold private gatherings in his house and to forbid the subjects of the Catholic King to attend those of the legates, were so contrary to his duty that they caused little annoyance to the pope, for he supposed that one of two explanations was true: either that the count was not so imprudent as to intend really to enter upon this course, although out of anger or for his own plans he might say so a thousand times, or that the legates would not find it difficult to discover a remedy, since they certainly did not have to tolerate his starting this fire in the council. Borromeo then directed the legates to tell Luna that the pope had entrusted the reform of the cardinals to the council and would let it be done there; the reform of the conclave was sufficiently done in the pope's bull besides the decrees of so many previous councils that nothing needed to be added unless the council would wish to attach a chapter against the secular princes and their ambassadors who wished to in-

---

[372]Borromeo to the legates, Rome, August 21, 1563, Susta, IV, 205-207 (No. 47), and Constant, *Légation*, p. 530, n.

[373]Luna to Avila, Trent, August 19, 1563, Constant, *Légation*, p. 537 (Appendix, No. XLV).

[374]Pius IV to Luna, Rome, August 28, 1563, Constant, *Légation*, p. 540 (Appendix, No. XLVII).

terfere in papal elections. If Luna were to insist that such a chapter be added, he was to be advised not to offend his master, who meddled in papal elections more than anyone else.[375]

Pius was not so naïve as to suppose that the legates' admonition would restrain the obstinate Count de Luna. Hence, he also had his nephew direct the nuncio in Spain to complain to King Philip about his ambassador, who was making impossible demands at Trent and was fiercely opposing the reform of the princes. Luna, wrote Borromeo, was proposing "things more filled with rage and poison than with good sense and judgment"; besides scandalizing all good men, they made the ambassador odious to the whole council and were diametrically opposed to the interests of his king. As far as the pope's right to bestow benefices was concerned, Borromeo argued that if it did not exist, the right to name bishops and abbots that the Apostolic See had given to the King of Spain and to other Christian princes would also not exist. "But the poor count," he added, "does not know the import of these things and lets himself be advised and governed by three or four prelates who, for their own passion and interest, would like to see evil come to us and worse to His Majesty, provided the result be each one's own greatness of being pope in his own diocese." The king, therefore, should order his ambassador and bishops to promote the closing of the council.[376]

Although Philip II was generally well disposed toward Pius IV, he was not at all displeased with Luna's conduct at the council. He deemed it proper that if matters concerning himself and other secular princes were proposed, matters related to the pope and to his authority and power should also be treated. Hence, he commended Luna for having opposed this move, just as he had commanded Luna to do from the beginning. Philip expressed surprise that in spite of his earlier representations the pope had authorized the council to treat this matter, especially with the intention of inducing the king to agree with what they wanted.[377] Obviously, for

[375]Borromeo to the legates, Rome, August 28, 1563, Susta, IV, 220-221 (No. 50), and Constant, *Légation*, p. 539, n.

[376]Pius IV and Borromeo to Crivello, Rome, August 30, 1563, Susta, IV, 559 (Beilage XXVII), and Constant, *Légation*, pp. 542-543 (Appendix, No. XLIX). In the consistory of August 18, 1563, Pius IV observed that he had already issued many reform bulls, but it did little good to know the law if there was no one to enforce it. He named four cardinals (Borromeo included), therefore, to see to it that the bulls would be enforced and to punish those who did not obey them. Cardinal Gambara's Consistorial Diary quoted by Paschini, *op. cit.*, p. 157.

[377]Philip II to Luna, Monzón, October 10, 1563, *CDI*, XCVIII (1891), 511-512. The king had already informed his uncle that he had instructed his ambassadors at Rome and Trent to make earnest representations against a premature termination of the council. Philip II to Ferdinand, Monzón, September 21, 1563, Sickel, *Concil*, p. 603 (No. CCLXXXIII).

Philip the demand for a reform of the pope was merely a foil with which his ambassador could parry the thrust for a reform of the princes.

Count de Luna had not succeeded, however, in persuading the emperor to support his demand for a reform of the papacy through the council and for a slower pace. In regard to the latter Ferdinand merely replied that the affairs of the council should not be handled with precipitate haste but should be finished with good order so that nothing which ought to be determined there would be omitted. The emperor also expressed a caution against useless delays which disgusted the people who longed for a happy outcome of the council and which kept the fathers away from their dioceses in those disturbed times. If Ferdinand perceived no reasons for unduly prolonging the council, neither did he see how he could or should urge the reform of the Roman Curia more strongly, because the pope himself had promulgated many constitutions for this purpose. He admitted that since he did not have exact information about all the offices and the condition of the Curia, he could not easily point out what was still missing in those constitutions. As for the reform of the conclave, he was quite satisfied with the pope's bull, provided it be carefully observed; if anything were to be added, he continued with irony, it would be that the kings and princes of Christendom, especially the kings of Spain and France, should not disturb the order of the conclave or hinder or corrupt the votes of the cardinals by entreaties, payments, or other wiles. In regard to the reform of the cardinals, he approved of some provisions in the articles recently proposed, but he liked much more what the French ambassadors had added about the number, nationality, age, way of life, conduct, and other qualifications of candidates for the cardinalate. He had ordered his own ambassadors to assist the French in promoting those additions, and he trusted that Luna would do the same. The emperor concluded that since the reform business was at that stage, nothing else remained to be done except to await its settlement; he believed that since a question of such magnitude could not be easily and quickly discussed and since until it would be finished the council could not be concluded, there was no reason to fear for its untimely dissolution.[378] No words could have indicated more clearly Ferdinand's resolution not to press for the reform *in capite*. Even the idea of having the bull *In eligendis* read in the council was quietly abandoned.

In spite of the lack of encouragement from Vienna, Count de Luna continued to pursue his own objectives. More disruptive of the legates' plans for the reform of the cardinals, however, were the

---

[378]Ferdinand to Luna, Vienna, August 31, 1563, Sickel, *Concil,* pp. 591-592 (No. CCLXXIX). Cf. Chudoba, *op, cit.,* pp. 54-56; this author continually refers to Ferdinand as unstable, vacillating, and never definitive, and he accuses the emperor's counselors of being inclined to heterodox opinions.

machinations of their colleagues in Rome. Late in August the Cardinal of San Clemente, Gianbattista Cicada, told Borromeo that Morone had asked him to send the chapters for the reform of the cardinals which had been discussed in Rome. When Borromeo reported this to his uncle, the latter asked him to inform Morone that those reform chapters had been drafted by cardinals who were more interested in increasing their revenues and privileges than in reforming themselves in any way. According to the cardinal nephew, this was the reason why the pope, after seeing those chapters, immediately resolved to refer this reform together with the others to the council. Hence, Morone was directed to disregard their contents and to do what would seem to him and the other legates to be proper and fitting and what would be satisfactory to the council and beneficial to all Christendom, without any worldly regard. In this way, the president was assured, he would be pleasing the pope, who would always be ready to favor and honor the cardinals without their trying to get it by force.[379] Morone was amazed by this communication, because neither he nor any of the other legates to his knowledge had asked San Clemente for those reform chapters. He supposed, therefore, that those cardinals at Rome had taken this tack in order to make the legates less ardent, but he promised that this would not deter them from doing their duty.[380]

Meanwhile another powerful Roman cardinal resisting reform, Alessandro Farnese, whose grandfather, Paul III, had elevated Morone to the sacred purple, tried to sway him directly. He alerted the president to the intense dissatisfaction felt within the Sacred College because Morone was not defending its dignity. Morone, he wrote, could not excuse himself by alleging the will of the pope, because the pope desired only the prompt conclusion of the council, not the ruin of the College. Farnese professed to sympathize with him because of the great difficulties that confronted him in the council; he could see how Morone was mastering them. But, he concluded mockingly, to say that Morone could not achieve more vis-à-vis the council was useless, because no one would believe it; he had already won such an ascendancy over the council that what he did not achieve was to be ascribed not to inability but to lack of goodwill.

Morone replied with a letter the dignified calm of which contrasted with the aggressive sarcasm of Cardinal Farnese. It would never have come to this, he wrote, if a reform of the Curia and of the cardinals had been provided in time, but now it was impossible to withstand the pressure of the princes. When he had accepted the legation he had foreseen that he would be slandered from all sides;

---

[379]Borromeo to Morone, Rome, August 25, 1563, Susta, IV, 219 (No. 49a), and Constant, *Légation*, p. 236 (No. 75).

[380]Morone to Borromeo, Trent, September 2, 1563, Susta, IV, 219, and Constant, *Légation*, p. 236, n. 8.

he wished to use his authority to fulfill the will of the pope and not to serve his own private interests. The dignity of the College of Cardinals meant nothing, he said, when the authority of the Holy See was tottering; but not even for the latter did he succeed in inserting two words in one of the decrees passed earlier. It was not what the fathers wanted that counted, but only what the courts dictated. Hence, Farnese could see that Morone's influence was not omnipotent. With irony Morone added that it would have been better if someone such as Farnese who had excellent relations with all the courts were at the head of the council. He also assured Farnese that the legates were keeping the interests of the Sacred College in mind. In fact, in Trent he was even reproached for having forestalled further decisions of the council on the conferral of bishoprics on cardinals by having them mentioned in the decree on residence, and thus of having represented the cardinals' interests unduly. In the reform plan drafted at Rome it was set down that no cardinal should have an income of less than ;&&& scudi and fewer than forty servants; in Trent, wrote Morone, there were prelates—and not the most radical—who proposed that a cardinal could have no more than a determined income and a determined number of servants. Thus caution was recommended. It would be better in any case to throw a part of the ballast overboard than to wait until the whole ship sank. It was not feasible to leave the whole reform of the cardinals to the pope again, as Farnese had written to one of the bishops. In the long-disputed question of clandestine marriages, which touched the bishops personally much less, that suggestion was vehemently rejected, and Laínez, who expressed the same opinion on this matter in a general congregation, was shouted down by all the fathers. The best thing to do then, concluded Morone, was to discuss the reform of the cardinals in connection with that of the bishops; the result would not be too bad.[381] Morone would have been wasting his paper and ink if he had laid spiritual motives before Farnese, but even his practical appeal to common sense was unavailing.

Farnese and other Roman cardinals averse to reform also tried other means to avert the impending change in their way of life. They wrote to various bishops at Trent that the pope and Borromeo did not approve of the reform under consideration and asked those bishops not to consent to it. Morone and the other legates were much annoyed by this scheme, for they were not trying to make the reform any more rigorous than was necessary to satisfy the princes and their ministers and were striving to reach the most honorable

---

[381]Farnese to Morone, Rome, September 1, 1563, and Morone to Farnese, Trent, September 9, 1563, paraphrased in Birkner, pp. 351-352. These two letters were shown by Morone's agent in Rome, Pierluigi Fedele, to Borromeo, who expressed his indignation at Farnese's words and praised Morone's candid reply.

mean possible *(la più honesta mediocrità che si possa)*. Now they foresaw that if the reform articles that they had proposed would be disputed, not only would the council be prolonged but harder things would be asked by the secular princes, because, Morone said, "experience has shown that the more one temporizes in the council, the more this blessed reform stirs men to action." Hence, the president lamented that from Rome, whence one ought to expect help, there came this obstacle, but he promised to go ahead, trusting more in Borromeo's instructions than in the warnings sent deviously by those cardinals.[382] In reply Borromeo conveyed the pope's order to pay no attention to whatever might be written by any of those cardinals and not to trust them in anything that was not in keeping with what Morone knew to be the mind of the pope and his instructions, for he could always excuse himself by pleading the obedience that he owed to the pope. Referring to the Roman cardinals Borromeo wrote: "This reform vexes *(cuoce)* them a great deal, and not only if one looked to them would it never be made but they will try to obstruct it in every way they can, but we who have to render to God an account even of the omissions of this council do not have to look to them but [rather] to do always what is fitting without regard [for anyone]."[383] Perhaps Morone would have been more consoled if the pope had threatened to inflict some penalty on the cardinals who were throwing sand into the gears of the council.

The Roman cardinals succeeded in inducing many Italian bishops to speak against the proposed reforms. The cardinals had written them that not even the pope cared whether the reform followed in one way rather than another and that on the other hand it seemed to the ultramontane bishops to be too broad. The legates and Borromeo were said not to wish to busy themselves with another reform but to have left it to the council; hence, as the princes seized the opportunity to ask for more, it could easily follow, according to Morone, that if the reform did not pass in its present form but was broadened, they would have reason to complain and to seek to have it narrowed down. Seeing the difficulties on every side, Morone was doubtful, especially because he knew that he could not satisfy the Sacred College, although he said that he was not concerned about it

---

[382]Morone to Borromeo, Trent, September 1, 1563, Constant, *Légation*, pp. 247-248 (No. 79); with the date of September 5, Susta, IV, 227-228. Brus wrote to Archduke Ferdinand (a son of the emperor) that the Romans, especially the canonists, were strongly opposed to the reform; if they would do nothing else they would wish to tear the council apart with their machinations *(durch praktiken zertrennen)*; but the pope bade the imperial ambassadors to press the reform issue and to continue at it. [Trent,] September 5, 1563, Sickel, *Concil*, p. 601.

[383]Borromeo to Morone, Rome, September 11, 1563, Susta, IV, 250, and Constant, *Légation*, p. 248, n. 4.

as long as the reform succeeded.[384] In view of the opposition within
the council Morone feared that the next session (the twenty-fourth)
could not be held on the day fixed in the previous session, that is, on
September 16.

On September 12 and 13 Morone was still complaining to Borromeo that many cardinals had written to various bishops who were
their friends at the council, saying that if they voted for the proposed reform they would ruin the Court of Rome. Hence, these
bishops, partly because, perhaps, they disliked the reform, partly
because they feared a disruption or suspension of the council and
that the greater part of the reform would be made without that
touching the princes, and partly because of the persuasion coming
from Rome, at first refused to vote on the proposed articles;
then, after the legates had admonished them gently and had promised to release within two days the chapter pertaining to the princes
along with the other chapters that were prepared, the bishops began
to speak, but they proceeded so slowly that it was impossible to
hold the session on September 16 with even part of those articles.
Morone was so chagrined that he stated frankly to the cardinal
nephew that it was necessary to warn the cardinals in Rome not to
suborn the bishops, because by running away from reform, they
would prolong the council to the great detriment of the pope—not
only of his purse but also of his honor, because the princes thought
that the legates had plotted this course and thus would have their
ambassadors take a hard line and demand even worse things. "And
we legates," he lamented, "remain without the obedience of our own
[that is, the Italian bishops]."[385] If this sort of anarchy had been
allowed to continue, Morone's whole strategy would have failed.

In fact, the president of the council became so discouraged that he
asked the pope to recall him on the pretext that he could not endure
the harsh climate of Trent. The real motive of this request was prob-

---

[384]Visconti to Borromeo, Trent, September 6, 1563, Aymon, II, 326 & 328
(memoire to Letter LXXIII). Borromeo told the legates on September 15 that the
pope was extremely surprised to read that some in Rome had written to the fathers
of the council that neither the pope nor Borromeo liked the rigor of the reform, and
he was no less surprised to learn that this nonsense (queste ciancie) was believed in
the council after he had openly declared the sincerity and candor of his mind. Once
again Borromeo affirmed that the pope truly desired and willed that without any
human respect all the reforms be made which would be judged proper and fitting for
the service of God according to the exigencies of the times. Again too he assured the
legates that this was all idle talk and foolish illusions invented by those who did not
want the reform. Constant, Légation , p. 269, n. 2.

[385]Morone to Borromeo, Trent, September 12-13, 1563, Susta, IV, 241, and
Constant, Légation, pp. 258-261 (No. 84). Girolamo Gaddi, Bishop of Cortona and
Florentine ambassador to the council at this time, reported to the duke that several
cardinals at Rome had written to prelates who were friends of theirs in Trent, urging
them not to tolerate so severe a reform which would have to disfigure (deformare)
the Court of Rome and which could not be observed. Gaddi had heard that this had
come to the ears of the pope, who had rebuked Cardinal Farnese for it, and that
Morone had informed the pope "perhaps to excuse himself along with the other

ably his fear that through the reform of the Sacred College he was turning many of the influential cardinals, especially Alessandro Farnese, against himself and thus damaging his prospects in the next conclave; by hastening the closing of the council, he would, perhaps, also lose the good-will of Philip II. He found it difficult, moreover, to work with Simonetta, who defended the interests of the Curia and the College of Cardinals more energetically than Morone in regard to the reform of the system of benefices and judicial matters. The pope, however, did not accede to Morone's request and comforted him with the thought that the council would soon be over.[386]

Morone's protests against the Roman cardinals finally moved the pope to action. Borromeo replied that his uncle deeply regretted that his own and the legates' good intention was being slowed down by those who should least have been responsible. The pope, he said, would have to show his resentment to some of the cardinals, who

---

legates," alleging that if the session did not take place on September 16 it was because those cardinals had tampered with the prelates. From the same source Gaddi had learned that some cardinals in Rome had accused Morone of being more concerned, in these affairs of the council, to give satisfaction to the secular princes than to the pope and the Apostolic See. Gaddi admitted that he did not know whether that was true but asserted that he had it from a good source. He had even heard that the other legates took offense at the fact that the letters from the emperor were addressed to Morone alone and not to the legates in common and that the president of the council negotiated apart from them; they also disliked the fact that the nuncio Delfino wrote so often to Morone separately. One of the legates expressed this complaint covertly, and another had communicated it to some confidants from whom Gaddi learned it in confidence. Notwithstanding all this, the episcopal ambassador concluded, Morone managed everything skillfully and did and obtained what he wanted. Gaddi to Cosimo I, Trent, October 14, 1563, D'Addario, p. 404 (No. CCXLIX). No doubt Simonetta was the less discreet legate who resented Morone's self-reliant conduct of affairs, and probably Hosius was the other. They were not courageous or strong enough, however, to thwart the president's course of action; they could only grumble in secret.

Besides Alessandro Farnese, his brother Ranuccio, Ippolito d'Este, Rudolfo Pio Carpi, Giovanni Michele Saraceni, and Giovanni Battista Cicada were the Roman cardinals who incited their clients in Trent against Morone. Jedin, *Geschichte*, IV/2, 146. The leading *zelanti* who spoke in the council against the proposed reform were the Archbishop of Otranto, Pietro Antonio di Capua; the Latin Patriarch of Jerusalem, Antonio Elio; the Bishop of Capaccio, Paolo Emilio Verallo; the Bishop of Capodistria, Tommaso Stella, O.P.; and the Bishop of Orvieto, Sebastiano Vanzi. *Ibid.*, pp. 144-145 and 284-285, n. 4. Jedin comments that the predominant motive of this group was not concern about the pope's primatial power but dread of the "ruin of the Roman Curia." They feared that the system in which they had grown up and from which they lived was being threatened.

[386]Morone had orally commissioned Visconti, whom the legates were sending to Rome on conciliar business, to present this request to Pius. September 19,g 1563, Susta, IV, 263. Visconti reported to Morone on his audience (Rome, September 29, 1563, *ibid.*, pp. 567-568 /Beilage XXX/). In the conclave following the death of Pius IV, Morone was a prominent candidate for the tiara but was opposed by more than a third of the cardinals for various reasons, especially the fact that he had been tried by the Inquisition under Paul IV; he was supported by Simonetta. Pastor, XVII, 24-29.

should at least abstain in the future from carrying on intrigues with the prelates at Trent and leave their votes free so that the reform might be made in the way that would be shown to be best by the Holy Spirit.[387] A few days previously Borromeo had repudiated the rumors being spread that the pope intended to annul part of the reform. He confided to Morone: "I know well that Your Illustrious Lordship, who from long experience is familiar with Rome and the nature of the idle spirits and the wicked tongues of the court, will not be surprised, but His Holiness cannot but regret that the minds of those fathers remain unsettled because of such things, which in effect are nothing but pasquinades."[388] Paleotti recorded the story that in fact the pope rather severely inveighed against some of those cardinals in person.[389]

The chief legate had to contend with this opposition, nevertheless, until the next session. In the second half of October he was again assured by Borromeo that the pope had entrusted to him without reservation the reform of the cardinals and that he should procure a holy and worthy reform without regard for the letters of cardinals or of others.[390]

On the opposite side, the Cardinal of Lorraine recommended in September that a separate chapter be devoted to the cardinals, for it was of the greatest concern to the Church that there be good cardinals, especially because the pope was elected from their number; he thought it absurd that more care was required in choosing a judge for the Rota than a cardinal.[391] Many fathers of various na-

[387]Borromeo to the legates, Rome, September 25, 1563, Susta, IV, 292-293 (No. 66), and Constant, Légation, pp. 260-261, n. 8.
[388]Borromeo to Morone, Rome, September 22, 1563, Susta, IV, 276 (No. 63), and Constant, Légation, p. 269 (No. 88).
[389]"Paleotti Acta," September 28, 1563, CT, III, 730.
[390]Luigi Fedele (a chamberlain to Pius IV and agent of Morone) to Morone, Rome, October 23, 1563, Constant, Légation, pp. 345-346 (No. 113). Borromeo had ordered him to convey this message.
[391]In the general congregation of September 11, 1563, Acta, CT, IX, 795 (No. 278), and "Paleotti Acta," CT, III, 713. Besides Lorraine, the French bishops of Sens, Verdun, and Nîmes, the Spanish bishops of Granada, León, Almería, Lérida, and Barcelona, the Italian bishops of Zara, Fiesole, Chioggia, Acqui, and Pavia, the Archbishop of Prague, and the Bishop of Przemysl desired a separate chapter on the reform of the College of Cardinals; the Bishop of Gerona wished to include the papal election in the decree. Jedin, Geschichte, IV/2, 285, n. 5.
The Florentine ambassador to the council and bishop-elect of Cortona, Girolamo Gaddi, was told several weeks later by the Bishop of Parma, Alessandro Sforza, that he had been informed that the pope was resolved that a reform chapter pertaining to the cardinals should be passed in Trent and that the Cardinal of Lorraine had warmed him up to that idea; in that chapter the pope was said to wish that provision be made that in the future two brothers could not be cardinals. Sforza added that he supposed that Duke Cosimo would have sent an agent to Rome to make representations to the pope and dissuade him from that resolution. Gaddi to Cosimo I, Trent, October 28, 1563, D'Addario, p. 411 (No. CCLIV). Pius had created two of the duke's sons cardinals, though the first, Giovanni, had died before the second, Ferdinando, was named.

tionalities agreed with him.³⁹² When the general of the Jesuits spoke
to a numerous audience on the draft of the reform decree, however,
he said that there should be a separate chapter on the cardinals if
the pope really wished the council to treat this matter, but if he did
not order it Laínez would not advise it, because regardless of what
the council might ordain, the pope would do what he pleased, and
the conciliar decrees in this regard would do nothing but "uncover
our father's *verenda.*" In this speech, his last before the council,
Laínez harshly criticized Morone's reform project as being prolix,
verbose, obscure, varying too easily and without cause from what
had previously been decreed (even in the first two periods of the
Council of Trent), insupportable to human powers, and difficult, if
not impossible, to execute. He presented his position on the reform
of the cardinals in a somewhat more moderate way because he
understood that Morone had obtained the pope's support. The
general advanced a new idea when he asserted that even though the
council included the pope, it could not make a law that would bind a
future pope, *quia par in parem non habet imperium.* For this reason
he wanted to have the word *decernit* deleted from the decree and
replaced by others such as *declarat, rogat,* and *petit*; he did not obtain this change.³⁹³ His animadversions, nevertheless, did not
facilitate the work of the reformers on the deputation appointed to
revise the draft.

---

³⁹²For example, Martin Pérez de Ayala, Bishop of Segovia, requested that a
special chapter be composed regarding the cardinals, "with whom a strict reform
should begin, since principally on them depends the whole welfare and soundness of
the Church." In the general congregation of September 17, 1563, Acta, *CT*, IX, 827
(No. 289). Drasković requested a special chapter on the selection of cardinals,
"especially because the cardinals not only assist in governing the world but also are
the electors of the pope and out of their number the pope is chosen." In the general
congregation of September 23, *ibid.*, p. 851 (No. 298). The Bishop of Lérida, Antonio
Agustín, advised that the special chapter on cardinals should state of what kind of
life and doctrine they should be, that they should be free from all infamy and
especially from the stain of simony, that no brother or son of any cardinal or pope
should be chosen nor more than two from any one religious order, and that in the
creation of cardinals the offices which they held should not become vacant, as
usually happened, "since this seems to have a certain appearance of evil." In the
general congregation of September 24, *ibid.*, p. 854 (No. 301). On the same day the
Bishop of Nîmes, Bernardo del Bene, advocated "a serious reform of the Apostolic
See," without prejudice to its full authority; he especially sought a reform of the
Roman Curia, "because when the head aches, the other members feel pain." Del
Bene also desired some direction on papal elections and on matters pertaining to
cardinals. *Ibid.*, p. 858 (No. 303). The Bishop of Namur, Antoine Navet, O.P.,
requested a special decree on cardinals "that they may shine in age, morals, and
learning as they shine in attire." In the general congregation of September 27, *ibid.*,
p. 862 (No. 305).
³⁹³Cabanellas, *op. cit.*, pp. 112-114. In the last months of the council Laínez
considered it to be his duty to hinder as best he could the evil that he detected in
Morone's concession of some reforms (such as that of the cardinals) which touched
the head of the Church; his fear of such a policy of compromise led him to adopt a
negative attitude toward the conciliar decrees. Scaduto summarizes the general's

When the revised draft was submitted to the council a few weeks later, the *zelanti* again defended the interests of the Curia while others criticized the new text. In a scathing review of the articles the Bishop of Segovia, Martín Pérez de Ayala, rejected many of them as useless, fraught with abuses, and conducive to quarrels and disputes; he complained about the procedural question of choosing the deputation, for all nine Italians out of the eighteen members were unanimous, he charged, in opposing the principal points of this reform, such as the abolition of the plurality of benefices; finally, he pressingly begged the legates and the council to sympathize with the needs of the Church by seeing to it that "a serious and thorough reform in all ranks of the Church *in capite et in membris* and in the Curia be done in earnest and in general."[394] His anger at the watering down of the proposal may not have changed the minds of many fathers, but the address of the Archbishop of Braga, Bartholomaeus de Martyribus, undermined the position of the *zelanti*. The archbishop had accompanied the Cardinal of Lorraine to Rome, where he had presented Carlo Borromeo with a copy of his book for bishops, *Stimulus pastorum*, and had won the young cardinal's adherence to the ideas contained therein. Having returned to Trent, he reported in the general congregation of November 3 that in conversation with the pope he had been greatly excited (*inflammatus*) for the reform; he acknowledged that this business was not being hindered in any way by Pius or his nephew but that rather every obstruction depended on the council fathers. The effort of certain ones to maintain the flow of money to the Roman Curia, he said, was contrary to the intention of the pope, who had publicly asserted that for the sake of church reform he had lost 200,000 ducats *per annum* and was ready to lose more if it would promote the cause. The Portu-

---

address and recounts the reactions it provoked (*op. cit.*, pp. 240, 244). According to the secretary of the Society of Jesus, Laínez treated every rank of the clergy--pope, cardinals, bishops, chapters, curates, and others--in such a way as to make it clear that his zeal was directed against the abuses (not the persons) and was also mixed with charity and a desire to give each of those ranks its due; hence, Polanco asserted that Laínez had not exasperated any of them although he had touched on points of great importance regarding their temporal advantages and honors and other things that they clung to inordinately; Laínez had suggested means of reform which Polanco thought could not displease even those who were most concerned or, if such persons would not like to see them carried out, they at least could not deny that they were reasonable and appropriate. Polanco to Canisius and other superiors, Trent, October 3, 1563, Braunsberger, IV, 343-344 (No. 958). Calini, however, thought that Laínez had again manifested his ill-will against the bishops and his little respect for them. Calini to Cornaro, Trent, October 4, 1563, Marani, pp. 541-542. Jedin observes that in this speech Laínez attacked the reform proposal with arguments similar to those used by the *zelanti*; he believed that the council was slipping into conciliarism and regarded the draft as extremely dangerous for the supremacy of the papacy. *Geschichte*, IV/2, 148.

[394] In the general congregation of November 4, 1563, Acta, *CT*, IX, 928-929 (No. 330).

guese prelate then implored his colleagues to set aside their own interests and to devote themselves to the reform of the Church.[395]

After the Cardinal of Lorraine returned from Rome on November 5, he too entered into the discussion of the revised reform proposal. He began by commending the pope's diligence about everything pertaining to the council, especially a serious reform. He repeated what Pius had told him about members of his court who resisted reform for the sake of their own convenience. Guise said that the pope was content with all the decrees that had been made regarding the cardinals and had enjoined him to urge the fathers to make a serious reform of the cardinals. Hence, the French leader recommended that cardinals be examined just like bishops before their promotion, but he did not advocate a limitation on the number of cardinals, because this would not benefit the Church; on the other hand, he proposed that cardinals who were chosen to assist the pope not be bishops, but those who were appointed to govern the Church in various lands and afterwards to take part in a papal election be bishops.[396] Lorraine probably helped to undo the mischief of the Roman cardinals by convincing more of the Italian bishops at Trent of the pope's sincere desire for a reform of the Sacred College. Thus agreement on a moderate reform was finally attained.

On November 11 the long-deferred Twenty-Fourth Session was celebrated. In the decree on reform, Chapter I (entitled "Norms of Procedure in the Election of Bishops and Cardinals"), the following was laid down:

> . . . Each and all of the particulars relative to the life, age, learning and the other qualifications of those who are to be appointed bishops, which have been determined elsewhere by this council, the same it decrees are to be required in the election of the cardinals of the holy Roman Church, even though they be deacons, whom the most holy Roman pontiff shall, in so far as it can be conveniently done, choose from all the nations of Christendom according as he finds them competent. Finally, the same holy council, moved by so many very grave afflictions of the Church, cannot but call to mind that nothing is more necessary to the Church of God than that the holy Roman pontiff apply that solicitude which by the duty of his office he owes the universal Church in a very special way by associating with himself as cardinals the most select persons only, and appoint to each church most eminently upright and competent shepherds; and this the more so,

---

[395] Acta, CT, IX, 916-917 (No. 326). Cf. Jedin, Geschichte, IV/2, 153-154.
[396] In the general congregation of November 8, 1563, Acta, CT, IX, 950-951 (No. 337), and "Paleotti Acta," CT, III, 746.

because our Lord Jesus Christ will require at his hands the blood of the sheep of Christ that perish through the evil government of shepherds who are negligent and forgetful of their office.[397]

In Chapter XVII, moreover, the council, "desiring to restore discipline in the government of the churches, by the present decree, which it commands to be observed by all persons by whatever title distinguished, even though it be the dignity of the cardinalate, ordains that in the future one ecclesiastical benefice only shall be conferred on a person." These provisions were to apply not only to cathedral churches (residential episcopal sees) "but also to all other benefices, whether secular or regular, even those held in commendam." Those who were then holding several parochial churches, or one cathedral and one parochial church, were "strictly bound, all dispensations and unions for life notwithstanding," to retain only the see or the parish and to resign the other parishes within six months; otherwise the parishes and all the benefices which they held would be considered *ipso jure* vacant.[398] Finally, in Chapter XIX the council decreed that mandates concerning promotion and favors called expectancies (*exspectativae*) no longer be granted to anyone under any pretext and that no one be permitted to make use of those previously granted; the council likewise forbade mental reservations and any other favors whatsoever with regard to future vacancies, nor were indults respecting churches belonging to others, or monasteries, to be granted to anyone--"not even to cardinals of the holy Roman Church"--and those previously granted were to be considered abolished.[399] One could hardly say that the council was excessively severe in reforming the cardinals. In fact, Philip II, commenting on the draft of the reform articles that the legates had proposed for discussion, wrote to Luna that it contained some good things but it appeared that the council had done very little in the main matter affecting the Curia, for the provision of benefices was left as it had been, and those named to curacies could still appeal to Rome if the ordinary did not approve them in the prescribed examination.[400] The king did not suggest, however, any remedy for these defects.

Commenting on the session of November 11, Filippo Gherio, Bishop of Assisi and a confidant of Morone, wrote that since all the reforms just passed affected Rome and the court, they showed clearly that the pope sincerely wished the reform, even in his own house, and that the legates were proceeding along the same road at a good speed. He predicted that the council would show more

---

[397]Schroeder, p. 192; Latin text, p. 462.
[398]Schroeder, p. 207; Latin text, p. 476.
[399]Schroeder, pp. 210-211; Latin text, p. 479.
[400]Philip II to Luna, Monzón, November 15, 1563, *CDI,* CI (1891), 13-14.

respect for the princes when it would come to their reform than it did for the pope himself. The bishop was so impressed with these results that he added: "If Pius IV never gave the world another sample of his goodness, this action alone of the council and the decisions made in this session ought to be enough to canonize him." Gherio feared, however, that Morone would not be safe at Rome after the council, for he was being accused of having betrayed the honor of the Sacred College and the ease of the court and of being completely devoted to the princes, particularly to the King of Spain; with such slander they would make life unbearable for Morone in the Eternal City. On the other hand, perhaps the princes would also raise complaints, but it was enough for the cardinal, wrote Gherio, to have obeyed the pope, doing what little he could for the public good and satisfying God and his conscience.[401]

The council did not complete its reform of the cardinals until the very last session (the twenty-fifth). In the first chapter on reform it laid down rules for bishops, commanding "not only that bishops be content with modest furniture and a frugal table, but also that they take heed that in the rest of their manner of living and in their whole house" nothing should appear that would not manifest "simplicity, zeal for God, and a contempt for vanities." Above all, the council forbade them to attempt to enrich their relatives or domestics from the revenues of the Church, and it admonished them to lay aside completely all such human affection of the flesh toward brothers, nephews, and other relatives. Then it added:

> And what has been said of bishops is to be observed not only by all who hold ecclesiastical benefices, whether secular or regular, . . . but it decrees that it applies also to the cardinals of the holy Roman Church, for since the administration of the universal Church is supported by their advice to the most holy Roman pontiff, it can appear wicked if they do not shine in the splendor of the virtues and in the discipline of life, which should justly draw upon them the eyes of all.[402]

This was, indeed, a lofty exhortation, but it was least likely to be observed by those for whom it was most intended, and no machinery for its enforcement was provided. In Chapter VII, furthermore, access and regress to any ecclesiastical benefice of whatever kind were prohibited for the future, and those already granted were not to be suspended, extended, or transferred. The council added: "And this decree shall apply to all ecclesiastical

---

[401]Gherio to Don Juan Manrique, Marquis of Lara, Viceroy of Naples, Trent, November 14, 1563, Constant, *Légation*, pp. 573-574, 578 (Appendix, No. LXVI).

[402]December 3, 1563, Schroeder, p. 233; Latin text, p. 500.

benefices whatsoever and to all persons, even though distinguished with the dignity of the cardinalate."[403] This was the last of the abuses to be corrected as far as the cardinals were concerned.

Before this final session Morone had secured the consent of all but the Spanish ambassador and his adherents for the termination of the council. Earlier in the autumn Philip II had asked his uncle to use his influence to prevent a hasty conclusion, but the emperor declined, replying that several weeks before, at the earnest request of the pope, he had agreed not to hinder its closing and had directed his ambassadors at Trent to promote this object insofar as they could. Ferdinand explained to his nephew that many serious reasons had forced him to assume that position and he could not change it then without injury to his authority and reputation. With unconcealed disillusionment he confided to Philip that he had no reason to favor the continuation of the council whose procedure was such that it would have been much more proper, salutary, and advantageous if it had never been begun; in his opinion, the business of the council had been handled until then and was still being handled in such a way that even if it were prolonged for several more years, one could not hope that by means of it better or greater benefit could be derived than he saw from afar; instead of restoring the Catholic religion, he feared that the council would ruin it more and even destroy it completely.[404] Ferdinand did not mention that the sooner the council would be ended, the sooner he expected to obtain from the pope the chalice for the laity and marriage for the clergy, because he knew that Philip was firmly opposed to those concessions.

Hence, when Morone, executing the strict order of the pope, who had fallen gravely ill, proposed that the next session be advanced and the council be closed, all but fourteen of the fathers—Spaniards without exception—gave their consent. Thus, after passing the last decrees, the great assembly came to an end on December 4. Pius IV did not die, as had been feared, however, but rather he recovered his strength, and on December 30 he delivered an address to the College of Cardinals. After praising Ferdinand for having guarded the council and having kept it free and safe, he declared his determination to see to it that the system of discipline prescribed by the Tridentine decrees be brought into practice. If any persons had imbibed a bad opinion of him and thought that he would be the first to break through the bars (claustra) erected by the council, he would remove that error. Far from wishing to relax or take anything away from the council's legislation, he would correct and make up for its moderation. Hence, he ordered Cardinal Morone, who was so familiar with the council's actions, to take care that nothing contrary or alien to its decrees be done in the consistory or be at-

---

[403]Schroeder, p. 239; Latin text, p. 506.
[404]Ferdinand to Philip II, Posonia, November 9, 1563, *CDI*, CI, 3-4.

tempted privately through his ministers. He likewise assigned to Simonetta a share in scenting and seeing, with the assistance of the Datary, that nothing of that sort be asked of him, lest, being insufficiently noticed in the midst of his important occupations and therefore perhaps also granted, it might cause ill-will and give offense to those who did not know his intention or misinterpreted everything. He declared it to be his chief policy to add the papal authority to the Council of Trent so that its decrees would be ratified and enforced and not be violated for the sake of anyone.[405] On January 26, 1564, in response to the formal petition that Morone and Simonetta presented in consistory, Pius IV confirmed the decrees orally and promised to do so also in writing.[406]

Because of the resistance of certain cardinals, bishops, and curial officials the discussions regarding a bull of confirmation were protracted for five months. It was said that two-thirds of the Curia along with their dependents would have to leave Rome in order to obey the decree on residence. Not only prelates but all clerics and laymen who had a financial interest in maintaining the status quo were troubled. The "ruin of the Roman Curia," the specter of which had so often during the council been raised when reform decrees affecting the revenues of the curial offices and tribunals were proposed, now seemed to be imminent. The capital which was invested in the salable curial offices yielded a return out of these revenues; if the revenues decreased, the value of the offices would decline, and those who had bought them would lose much of their investment. Not only individual officeholders but also the much more numerous class of shareholders in the *societates officiorum*, who together with other interested persons had acquired shares in several offices, as well as the subscribers to the state loans *(monti)* which yielded a return from the revenues of the States of the Church, were threatened.[407] Undoubtedly with the encouragement and assistance of Cardinal Morone Pius ultimately overcame all such opposition; meanwhile, however, the publication of the bull was delayed until June 30, although it bore the date of January 26. In it the pope confirmed all the decrees of the council without exception or alteration,

[405]"Pii IV pont. max. . . .Oratio apud cardinalium collegium habita, *Vere haec dies*," Poggiani, III, 382-383 (No. LXIII).

[406]Raynaldus, 1564, No. 2, p. 457. In the final report which he delivered in this consistory Morone pointed out to his colleagues who were not altogether favorably disposed toward him that the reform of the cardinals had not been undertaken separately, as had been repeatedly demanded, but rather had been put on the same level *(in dozzina)* as the other reforms and, as it were, on the back *(in groppa)* of the bishops, and thus they avoided all the reefs that they encountered in this material which perhaps was not well understood by very many. Constant, *Légation*, p. 438 (No. 151).

[407]Jedin, *Geschichte*, IV/2, 230-231. On the delay see also Pastor, XVI, 8-9.

but he reserved to the Holy See the interpretation of their meaning and extent.[408]

One of those referred to by the pope on December 30 who did not expect him to observe the conciliar decrees was King Maximilian. He confided to the Venetian envoy that he had never considered the council worthy of that name; he regarded it rather as a gathering of men full of passions and their own self-interests. Laughing, he added that he now expected to see a promotion of thirty cardinals; he remarked also that the emperor had always made known his opinion about the appointment of unworthy cardinals, but his good intentions had little effect.[409]

Between the contentment of the pope and the disdain of the king one must seek a just evaluation of the council's reform decrees related to the College of Cardinals and the Roman Curia. Admittedly, this legislation was a compromise between the conceptions of the conservative-minded groups in Rome and the more far-reaching demands of the older reform groups in Italy and in other countries.[410] It refrained from directly attacking the organization of the Curia but intervened deeply in the competence and procedures of its offices and tribunals; it forbade or restricted certain practices which had previously fostered flagrant abuses, such as the accumulation of benefices and the regress; it rendered more difficult the appeals to the Roman tribunals which had interfered with the proper juridical order within the dioceses, and it turned over to the bishops certain powers of absolution, at least in the sphere of conscience, which until then had been reserved to the Penitentiary and the Roman Inquisition. Admittedly, as Hubert Jedin comments, it was content with short steps which could be taken in the quiet hope that a new spirit would enter into the Church and make longer steps possible. "What is usually called the 'Tridentine Reform' was at first only a chance, not a reality." It did not directly reform the College of Cardinals. The reform that was finally decreed did not by far satisfy all the demands that had been voiced, but it had the advantage of being realizable, although only if the pope would hold firm to it and not capitulate to the opposition of the Curia. "More was not

---

[408]*Benedictus Deus*, Schroeder, pp. 532-536; English translation, pp. 268-273.

[409]Leonardo Contarini to the Doge, Breslau, December 19, 1563, Turba, III, 249-251 (No. 124). The long-expected creation of new cardinals did not take place until March 12, 1565, when twenty-three were named--all Italians except one Frenchman; among these were several who had rendered important service during the council, namely, Commendone, Delfino (for whom the emperor had interceded), Paleotti, and Visconti. Pastor says "that on this occasion ecclesiastical interests were more taken into consideration than in the creations of 1561 and 1563" (XVI, 394).

[410]Hubert Jedin, *Tommaso Campeggio (1483-1564). Tridentinische Reform und kuriale Tradition* ("Katholisches Leben und Kämpfen im Zeitalter der Glaubensspaltung: Vereinsschriften der Gesellschaft zur Herausgabe des Corpus Catholicorum," 15 [Münster in Westfalen, 1958]), p. 76.

to be attained."[411] In any case, it was not, as Sarpi later contended, a deformation instead of a reform, for it was directed against many, if not all, of the abuses of the central administration of the Church and was designed to restore to resident bishops their proper authority over their dioceses. It was not an ideal solution but rather a practical accommodation to what was possible and feasible in those circumstances.

The execution of the Tridentine decrees was, of course, a task for the future, but one may ask what immediate effect the agitation for reform during the third period of the council produced in the Roman Curia. One reliable witness, Giovanni Francesco Commendone, described the Court of Rome shortly after the close of the council. This bishop and diplomat did not assert that the inveterate abuses had been corrected. Rome was still the city to which ambitious and avaricious people flocked to make their fortune. While the great prelates collected the revenues of the ecclesiastical benefices, they left the performance of the duties attached to those offices to unworthy and badly paid hirelings. The laity drew attention away from their own responsibility for the deterioration in ecclesiastical life by complaining loudly about the corruption of the Curia. The Curia, in fact, no longer had the free disposal of many benefices because they had become hereditary in certain powerful families that regarded them as their private property. Commendone recognized that it was easy to speak of the need for reform but difficult to find a way to effect it.[412] He did not extol the results of the reform work about which Pius IV had boasted during the council.

Toward the end of 1565, however, the Venetian ambassador, Giacomo Soranzo, who was recalled after nearly three years in that position, painted a much different picture. The Court of Rome, he said, was no longer what it had used to be either in the quality or in the number of the courtiers. He attributed this change principally to the poverty of the cardinals and the straitened circumstances of the pope but also to the fact that after the council the bishops were obliged to reside in their sees and the same was true of others who held benefices. Hence, a majority of the court had departed, and for the same reasons few wished to serve there and live at their own expense without hope of greater reward. The poverty of the cardinals he traced to two sources. One was the inability to confer on them important benefices as was the custom when England, Germany, and other countries were obedient to the Apostolic See, and the restric-

---

[411] Jedin, *Geschichte*, IV/2, 184-185, 245. Cf. *idem*, "Vorschläge und Entwürfe zur Kardinalsreform," *Kirche des Glaubens*, II, 146: The Tridentine reform of the cardinals was not a conclusion but only a passage; the ecclesiastical and political ideas that lay at the bottom of the many reform memorials and projects and individual enactments did not die at the end of the council but lived on and formed the College of Cardinals of the Counter-Reformation and the Baroque Age.

[412] "Discorso sopra la Corte di Roma," summary and excerpts in Pastor, XVI, 58-65.

tion to one bishopric for each cardinal when they used to have three or four besides other benefices. The other reason for their poverty was that their number had risen to seventy-five. Moreover, none of the princes gave them gifts or benefices any more, and the kings of Spain and France even forbade their subjects to be made cardinals. Soranzo believed that the reason for the division of the College of Cardinals into national factions had thus ceased. It was not only because of poverty, however, that life at the Court of Rome had become simple, but also because of the good example given by Cardinal Borromeo. The papal nephew, who controlled the bestowal of offices and favors, showed himself generous only to those who resembled him in his religious and withdrawn manner of life. Hence, the cardinals and others of the court, the Venetian reported, "have completely withdrawn, at least in public, from pleasures of all kinds; cardinals are no longer seen either in masks or on horseback or going for a ride through Rome in a coach with women, as was customary not long ago, but they hardly go [even] alone, all closed up in their coach. The banquets have entirely ceased, as have also the games, hunting parties, the liveries, and every other visible luxury," especially since no lay person of quality lived in the court any longer, as many relatives or dependents of the popes had been wont to do. "The priests all go about in habit," he added, "and thus the reform is clearly recognized in the appearance of men."[413] In spite of this improvement it was really only under Pius IV's successors, especially Pius V, that the reform of the Roman Curia was carried out with lasting effects.[414]

VIII. Conclusion

In order to be understood, the cries for the reform of the Church *in capite* must be separated into the individual calls that were mingled in the general clamor of the early 1560's. Some were demanding that the shocking abuses which had become common in conclaves be

---

[413]"Relazione di Roma di Giacomo Soranzo," 1565, Albèri, Vol. X (Series II, Tome IV [Florence, 1857]), pp. 136-138.

[414]J. B. Sägmüller commented that it was not such a serious failure that the reform of the Curia turned out to be milder than some rather unwisely desired, for Rome maintained her position as leader of the reform movement in the great resurgence of the Catholic Church resulting from the Council of Trent. *Die Papstwahlbullen und das staatliche Recht der Exklusive* (Tübingen, 1892), p. 181.

Like an echo from the past, Francisco de Córdoba, after nearly six years of the pontificate of Pius V, was still urging Philip II not to lose confidence in the remedy for the spreading heresy in Germany but to put greater efficacy in it, namely, that the pope should make a very severe reform, beginning with the cardinals and continuing with the rest of the clergy, for thus the heretics would not have any occasion to separate themselves from the Church and the pope. Salamanca, November 16, 1571, Döllinger, *Beiträge*, I, 656 (No. 209). The king had permitted him to return to Spain the preceding year.

prevented by changed arrangements and prescribed penalties. Others were asking that the appointment of men to the Sacred College be subjected to strict norms in order that the cardinals—the electors and advisers of the popes and in some cases future popes themselves—might not be too numerous, young, worldly, ignorant, and dependent on the secular princes. Some insisted, furthermore, that the cardinals and bishops in the Curia not hold residential sees and other benefices with the care of souls from which they were forced to be absent. Still others wished to alter certain financial and judicial practices of the Curia and its manner of granting dispensations, by which bishops were impeded in the administration of their dioceses and the lower clergy and laity were scandalized. It is obvious that these different kinds of reform were urgently needed; it remains to be determined, however, whether Ferdinand was justified in seeking them from the council and whether Pius IV was justified in prohibiting or limiting the council's activity in this area.

As far as the reform of the conclave is concerned, one cannot deny the danger that the council might have attempted to take the power of electing the pope away from the College of Cardinals, at least if Pius IV had died while the council was in session. It is unlikely, however, that, given the papal majority at Trent, it could have passed such a decree; if it had, it would indeed have opened the door to another great schism in the Western Church unless Pius approved the decree before dying. This danger was much smaller before the French prelates arrived at Trent and before the emperor permitted or directed his ambassadors to act in concert with those of other kings. Even during the first eleven months of the third period, nevertheless, Pius IV refused to let the council consider this matter in any way. He may have feared that once broached, the question would not have been settled before the French arrived, and he had reason to suspect that they would try to keep the papacy from remaining the exclusive possession of the Italians. But Pius provoked doubts about his sincerity by waiting so long to issue a bull, then by not letting the council even hear and approve it, and finally by not wishing the council to add sanctions against secular powers that would interfere in papal elections. He disregarded the fact that Catholics of all ranks and nations attached more weight to a conciliar decree than to a papal bull.

Secondly, Ferdinand had ample grounds to doubt that the creation of cardinals would ever be conformed to the needs of the Church unless it were regulated by the council. Pius IV, on the other hand, wished to maintain his freedom of choice in order that he might bestow the cardinalate for political or dynastic purposes. Eventually he was constrained by the overwhelming sentiment of the fathers at Trent and of the secular princes to let the council impose the same qualifications on candidates for this dignity as for the episcopate. While Ferdinand's position was vindicated in regard to the age, learning, and integrity required of future cardinals, his desire to limit their number to twenty-four or twenty-six would have frustrated his own purpose of reform, for it was practically impossible to deprive the existing cardinals of the purple and consequently not even good men could have been promoted for many years. Even many of the emperor's advisers recognized the impracticality of this demand.

Thirdly, that a cardinal or bishop holding an office in the Curia and obliged to live in Rome should not possess a see or other benefice requiring personal residence—much less a plurality of sees or benefices—was a reform that Ferdinand had no hope of obtaining from the pope and therefore sought from the council. Precisely because he could not persuade his assistants in the Curia to accept such a sacrifice willingly, Pius might have been expected to welcome the aid of the emperor and of other nationalities to impose it through the council. Yet while he let the council prohibit pluralism and enjoin residence, he retained the right to dispense the curialists from the obligation of residing in the one see or other benefice that they were permitted to keep. The result in this area, then, was only a partial reform.

Lastly, Pius admitted in practice the need, emphasized by the emperor, to reform the Curia's procedures, for he issued bulls for many individual offices in spite of the severe financial losses that he and his subordinates suffered in consequence. He did not admit, however, that Ferdinand and others were right in questioning the extent and permanency of such reforms as they naturally did in the light of past experience. Pius seemed incapable of comprehending that the credibility of a pope's word had been so greatly undermined that not even his most devoted sons, the Jesuits, were convinced by his issuing of bulls. Ferdinand, in turn, came to grasp that while the fathers at Trent could forbid certain evil pratices, such as regress, for the most part they lacked the detailed knowledge of the organization and operation of the Curia that would have been required for any particular reforms. He also understood the Holy See's need for financial support from the rest of the Church, and he was truly far-sighted in suggesting, although he dismissed the idea as infeasible, that a collection be taken up regularly in all Catholic countries to compensate the pope for the abolition of his previous income.

In all these matters those on the papal side did not wish the council to take any action that could be interpreted as an affirmation of conciliarism. They had received, of course, enough proofs and assurances of Ferdinand's orthodoxy and loyalty to be able to rest content that he would not induce the council to declare its superiority over the pope. They did not dispute the honesty of the emperor and his ministers and ambassadors when the latter denied that they wished the question of the relative superiority of pope and council even to be raised at Trent, and yet the pope and his supporters seemed to assume that conciliar decrees affecting his Curia would *ipso facto* imply the council's superiority over him.

It would seem, therefore, that Pius IV's and the Curia's opposition to the emperor's proposals was due not only to a distaste for reform but also to a theological conception of the primacy of the Roman pontiff which set the pope over against the council instead of placing him within it and at its head. Viewed in the latter way, the pope would not be subjected to the council's reform decrees regarding the conclave, the College of Cardinals, and the Curia but would himself decree these reforms with the advice and agreement of the council. It was some of the emperor's theologians, not the pope's, who expounded this ecclesiology which has now supplanted the theory of papal monarchy. On the other hand, if some of Ferdinand's proposals appear to have been prejudicial to the rights and prerogatives of the Holy See, they should be judged in the light of the theological uncertainty and moral crisis of that time, not in the light of the First Vatican Council's teaching on the primacy.

One may conclude, then, that the moderate conciliarists, such as Ferdinand and most of his counselors, were their own worst enemies. For what they really wanted was not a definitive settlement of the old controversy in favor of the council but rather the reform of the Church *in capite et in membris* through the only organ capable of effecting it in a fair, permanent, and credible way. Yet as long as the papalists could assert that discussion of the emperor's proposals in the council would awaken the sleeping monster of conciliarism, they could claim plausible grounds for resisting them. This excuse appeared more like a pretext, nevertheless, in the spring of 1562, when Ferdinand's *libellus* was presented to the legates. If the articles pertaining to reform *in capite* had been proposed to the council promptly, appropriate decrees might have been passed before the French conciliarists increased the risk half a year later. In that spring Pius could have nurtured a blossom that might have yielded a mature fruit by autumn.

Granted his traditional understanding of an emperor's functions within the Church, most of Ferdinand's actions during these years appear to be justifiable. That they were not more forceful may be attributable not only to the profound reverence for the Holy See that his faith inspired in him but also to his disadvantageous position, for he was simultaneously seeking so many favors from the pope: aid in the war against the Turks, permission for communion under both kinds for the laity and for the marriage of priests, and confirmation of the election of his son Maximilian as King of the Romans. Pius did not scruple at exploiting this relationship in order to hinder Ferdinand from laying disagreeable topics before the council and to secure his consent to its termination. On the other hand, Ferdinand did not use his demand for reform of the Sacred College and of the Curia as a lever to pry loose the concessions that he desired from Rome.

It would be wrong, of course, to overlook Ferdinand's faults. In the question of the reform of the princes his narrow-mindedness is evident. He lacked sympathy for Pius IV's sense of his duty to preserve intact and hand on to his successors the papal authority that he had received from his predecessors. Perhaps the emperor did not appreciate the difficulty that any pope would encounter in reforming recalcitrant cardinals and curialists without losing their loyalty. Ferdinand seems to have sought the reform of the Church in Rome, moreover, primarily for the sake of the strength and stability that this would confer on the Church in Germany and his hereditary lands, which were gravely threatened by heresy and irreligion; he was also aware of the benefits that religious pacification would bring to his civil government. Yet his concern for this part of Christendom did not contradict, but rather reinforced, his responsibilities for the universal Church. Though his motives were mixed, his goals were not selfish. Even if he did not realize his hopes to the full extent, he deserves much of the credit for the reform of the Church *in capite* that was decreed either by Pius IV alone or by the Council of Trent, for he applied the pressure that helped to make the pope feel the urgency of the situation and overcome the resistance of so many in the Court of Rome.

Abbreviations and Short References
Used in the Footnotes

Albèri: Eugenio Albèri (ed.), *Le Relazioni degli Ambasciatori Veneti al Senato durante il secolo decimosesto*

Aymon: *Lettres, anecdotes et memoires historiques du nonce Visconti, cardinal préconisé, & ministre secret de Pie IV. & de ses créatures, au Concile de Trente, dont plusieurs intrigues inouïes se trouvent dans ces rélations, mises au jour, en italien & en fraṅçois* (2 vols.; Amsterdam, 1719)

Baluze: *Stephani Baluzii Tutelensis Miscellanea novo ordine digesta et non paucis ineditis monumentis opportunisque animadversionibus aucta opera ac studio Joannis Dominici Mansi Lucensis* (4 vols.; Lucca, 1761-1764)

Birkner: Joachim Birkner, "Das Konzil von Trient und die Reform des Kardinalkollegiums unter Pius IV.," *Historisches Jahrbuch*, LII (1932), 340-355.

Braunsberger: *Beati Petri Canisii, Societatis Iesu, epistulae et acta,* collegit et adnotationibus illustravit Otto Braunsberger (8 vols.; Freiburg im Br., 1896-1923). Vol. II: 1556-1560 (1898); Vol. III: 1561-1562 (1901); Vol. IV: 1563-1565 (1905).

Brodrick: James Brodrick, S.J., *Saint Peter Canisius* (reprinted Chicago, 1962)

Bucholtz: Franz Bernhard von Bucholtz, *Geschichte der Regierung Ferdinand des Ersten* (9 vols.; Vienna, 1831-1838)

Bullarum: Bullarum, Diplomatum et Privilegiorum Sanctorum Romanorum Pontificum Taurinensis Editio. Tomus VII (a Pio IV ad Pium V) (Naples, 1882)

CDI: Colección de documentos inéditos para la historia de España (112 vols.; Madrid, 1842-1895)

COD: Conciliorum Oecumenicorum Decreta, edd. Giuseppe Alberigo, *et al.* (3d ed.; Bologna, 1973)

Constant, *Concession:* G. Constant, *Concession à l'Allemagne de la communion sous les deux espèces. Étude sur les débuts de la Réforme Catholique en Allemagne (1548-1621)* ("Bibliothèque des Écoles Françaises d'Athènes et de Rome," Fascicule 128 [2 vols.; Paris, 1923])

Constant, *Légation:* G. Constant, *La Légation du Cardinal Morone près l'Empereur et le Concile de Trente, avril-décembre 1563* ("Bibliothèque de l'École des Hautes Études, Sciences historiques et philosophiques," Fascicule 232 [Paris, 1922])

CSP: Calendar of State Papers, Foreign Series, of the Reign of Elizabeth, ed. Joseph Stevenson: *1559-1560, 1561-1562, 1563* (London, 1865, 1866, 1869)

CT: Concilium Tridentinum. Diariorum, actorum, epistularum, tractatuum nova collectio, ed. Societas Goerresiana (Freiburg im Breisgau)

Vols. II and III: *Concilii Tridentini Diariorum Pars Secunda* and *Pars Tertia,* collegit, edidit, illustravit Sebastianus Merkle (1911, 1931)

Vols. VIII and IX: *Concilii Tridentini Actorum Pars Quinta* and *Pars Sexta,* collegit, edidit, illustravit Stephanus Ehses (1919, 1926)

Vol. XIII: *Concilii Tridentini Tractatuum Pars Altera,* ex collectionibus Vincentii Schweitzer; auxit, edidit, illustravit Hubertus Jedin (1938)

D'Addario: Arnaldo d'Addario (ed.), "Il carteggio degli ambasciatori e degli informatori medicei da Trento nella terza fase del Concilio," *Archivio Storico Italiano,* CXXII (1964), 9-453.

Döllinger, *Beiträge:* Joh. Jos. Ign. v. Döllinger (ed.), *Beiträge zur politischen, kirchlichen und Cultur-Geschichte der sechs letzten Jahrhunderte,* Vol. I (Regensburg, 1862); Vol. III (Vienna, 1882)

Döllinger, *Ungedruckte:* J. v. Döllinger (ed.), *Ungedruckte Berichte und Tagebücher zur Geschichte des Concils von Trient* (2 vols.; Nördlingen, 1876)

Drei: Giovanni Drei (ed.), "La corrispondenza del card. Ercole Gonzaga, Presidente del Concilio di Trento (1562-1563)," *Archivio Storico per le provincie parmensi,* N.S., XVII (1917), 185-242; XVIII (1918), 30-143.

Dupuy: *Instructions et lettres des Rois tres-chrestiens, et de leurs ambassadeurs, et autres actes concernant le Concile de Trente, pris sur les originauz.* Quatrième Edition reueuë & augmentée d'un grand nombre d'actes & de lettres, tirez des Memoires de M.D. (Paris, 1654)

Eder: Gottfried Eder, *Die Reformvorschläge Kaiser Ferdinands I. auf dem Konzil von Trient* ("Reformationsgeschichtliche Studien und Texte," Heft 18 and 19]Münster i. W., 1911])

Grisar: Hartmann Grisar, S.J. (ed.), *Jacobi Lainez, secundi praepositi generalis Societatis Jesu, Disputationes Tridentinae* (° vols.; Innsbruck, 1886)

Helle: Philipp Helle, *Die Konferenzen Morones mit Kaiser Ferdinand I. (Mai 1563) und ihre Einwirkung auf den Gang des Trienter Konzils* (Inaugural-Dissertation zur Erlangung der Doktorwürde genehmigt von der hohen philosophischen Fakultät der Rheinischen Friedrich-Wilhelms-Universität zu Bonn [Bonn, 1911])

Jedin, *Geschichte,* IV/1 and IV/2: Hubert Jedin, *Geschichte des Konzils von Trient,* Band IV: *Dritte Tagungsperiode und Abschluss;* Erster Halbband: *Frankreich und der neue Anfang in Trient bis zum Tode der Legaten Gonzaga und Seripando;* Zweiter Halbband: *Uberwindung der Krise durch Morone, Schliessung und Bestätigung* (Freiburg, 1975)

Jedin, *Krisis:* Hubert Jedin (ed.), *Krisis und Wendepunkt des Trienter Konzils (1562/63). Die neuentdeckten Geheimberichte des Bischofs Gualterio von Viterbo an den heiligen Karl Borromäus* (Würzburg, 1941)

Jedin, *Seripando:* Hubert Jedin, *Papal Legate at the Council of Trent: Cardinal Seripando,* trans. Frederic C. Eckhoff (St. Louis and London, 1947)

336 REFORM AND AUTHORITY

Kassowitz: Theodor Bruno Kassowitz, *Die Reformvorschläge Kaiser Ferdinand' I. auf dem Konzil von Trient* (Inaugural-Dissertation verfasst und der Hohen Philosophischen Fakultät der Kgl. bayer. Julius-Maximilians-Universität Würzburg zur Erlangung der Doktorwürde vorgelegt [Würzburg, 1906])

Lainii Monumenta: Lainii Monumenta. Epistolae et Acta Patris Jacobi Lainii, secundi Praepositi Generalis Societatis Jesu (Madrid)
Vol. VI: *1561-1563* (1915)
Vol. VII: *1563-1564* (1916)
Vol. VIII: *1564-1565* (1917)

Le Plat: Judocus Le Plat (ed.), *Monumentorum ad Historiam Concilii Tridentini potissimum illustrandam spectantium amplissima collectio*, Vols. IV-VII (Louvain, 1784-1787)

Loewe: Hugo Loewe, *Die Stellung des Kaisers Ferdinand I. zum Trienter Konzil vom Oktober 1561 bis zum Mai 1562* (Inaugural-Dissertation zur Erlangung der Doktorwürde bei der hohen philosophischen Fakultät der Rheinischen Friederich-Wilhelms-Universität zu Bonn [Bonn, 1887])

Marani: Alberto Marani (ed.), *Muzio Calini. Lettere Conciliari (1561-1563)* (Brescia, 1963)

Meyenhofer: Werner Meyenhofer, "Frankreich, Kaiser Ferdinand I. und das Konzil von Trient 1562-63," *Annuarium Historiae Conciliorum*, 5 (1973), 152-197, 303-381

Pallavicini: [Pietro] Sforza Pallavicino, *Istoria del Concilio di Trento* (6 vols.; Milan, 1843-1844)

Pastor: Ludwig von Pastor, *The History of the Popes from the Close of the Middle Ages* (40 vols.; St. Louis, 1891-1953)

Poggiani: *Julii Pogiani Sunensis Epistolae et Orationes, olim collectae ab Antonio Maria Gratiano, nunc ab Hieronymo Lagomarsinio e Societate Jesu adnotationibus illustratae ac primum editae* (4 vols.; Rome, 1756-1762)

Raynaldus: Caesaris S.R.E. Card. Baronii, Od. Raynaldi et Jac. Laderchii *Annales Ecclesiastici* denuo et accurate excusi, Vol. XXXIV: *1557-1565* (Bar-le-Duc and Paris, 1879)

Rupert: Joannes H. Rupert, S.J., *De programmate Jacobi Lainii, secundi Praepositi Generalis Societatis Jesu, reformationem papatui per concilium generale imponere temptantis* (Excerpta ex dissertatione ad lauream in Facultate Historiae Ecclesiasticae Pontificiae Universitatis Gregorianae [Nijmegen, 1953])

Sarpi, ed. Gambarin: Fra Paolo Sarpi, *Istoria del Concilio Tridentino* (2 vols.; Florence, 1966) (Critical text of Giovanni Gambarin [Bari, 1935])

Sarpi, ed. Vivanti: Paolo Sarpi, *Istoria del Concilio Tridentino*, ed. Corrado Vivanti (2 vols.; Turin, 1974)

Schroeder: H. J. Schroeder, O.P. (ed. and trans.), *Canons and Decrees of the Council of Trent. Original Text with English Translation* (St. Louis and London, 1941)

Sickel, *Concil:* Th. R. von Sickel (ed.), *Zur Geschichte des Concils von Trient. Actenstücke aus österreichischen Archiven* (Vienna, 1870)

Sickel, "Libell": Th. R. von Sickel, "Das Reformations-Libell des Kaisers Ferdinand I. vom Jahre 1562 bis zur Absendung nach Trient," *Archiv für österreichische Geschichte*, XLV (1871), 1-96

Sickel, *Röm. Ber.:* Th. R. von Sickel, *Römische Berichte* (I and II) ("Sitzungsberichte der kaiserlichen Akademie der Wissenschaften in Wien, philosophisch-historische Classe," Vols. 133 [IX] and 135 [X] [Vienna, 1895])

Steinherz: S. Steinherz (ed.), *Nuntiaturberichte aus Deutschland nebst ergänzenden Actenstücken, zweite Abtheilung 1560-1572* (Vienna)

Vol. I: *Die Nuntien Hosius und Delfino, 1560-1561* (1897)

Vol. III: *Nuntius Delfino, 1562-1563* (1903)

Susta: Josef Susta (ed.), *Die römische Curie und das Concil von Trient unter Pius IV. Actenstücke zur Geschichte des Concils von Trient* (4 vols.; Vienna, 1904-1914)

Turba: Gustav Turba (ed.), *Venetianische Depeschen vom Kaiserhofe (Dispacci di Germania)* (3 vols.; Vienna, 1889-1895)